Contents

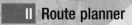

First published in 2003 by Philip's a division of Octopus Publishing Group Ltd 2–4 Heron Quays London E14 4JP

www.philips-maps.co.uk

Third edition 2005
First impression 2005

Cartography by Philip's
Copyright © 2005 Philip's

Ordnance Survey®

This product includes mapping data licensed from Ordnance Survey®, with the permission of the Controller of Her Majesty's Stationery Office. © Crown copyright 2005. All rights reserved. Licence number 100011710

Information for Tourist Attractions in England supplied by the British Tourist Authority / English Tourist Board.

Information for National Parks, Areas of Outstanding Natural Beauty, National Trails and Country Parks in Wales supplied by the Countryside Council for Wales. Information for National Parks, Areas of Outstanding Natural Beauty, National Trails and Country Parks in England supplied by the Countryside Agency. Data for Regional Parks, Long Distance Footpaths and Country Parks in Scotland provided by Scottish Natural Heritage.

Gaelic name forms used in the Western Isles provided by Comhairle nan Eilean.

Data for the National Nature Reserves in England provided by English Nature. Data for the National Nature Reserves in Wales provided by Countryside Council for Wales. Darparwyd data'n ymwneud â Gwarchodfeydd Natur Cenedlaethol Cymru gan Gyngor Cefn Gwlad Cymru.

Information on the location of National Nature Reserves in Scotland was provided by Scottish Natural Heritage.

Data for National Scenic Areas in Scotland provided by the Scottish Executive Office. Crown copyright material is reproduced with the permission of the Controller of HMSO and the Queen's Printer for Scotland. Licence number C02W0003960.

Printed in Great Britain by Scotprint

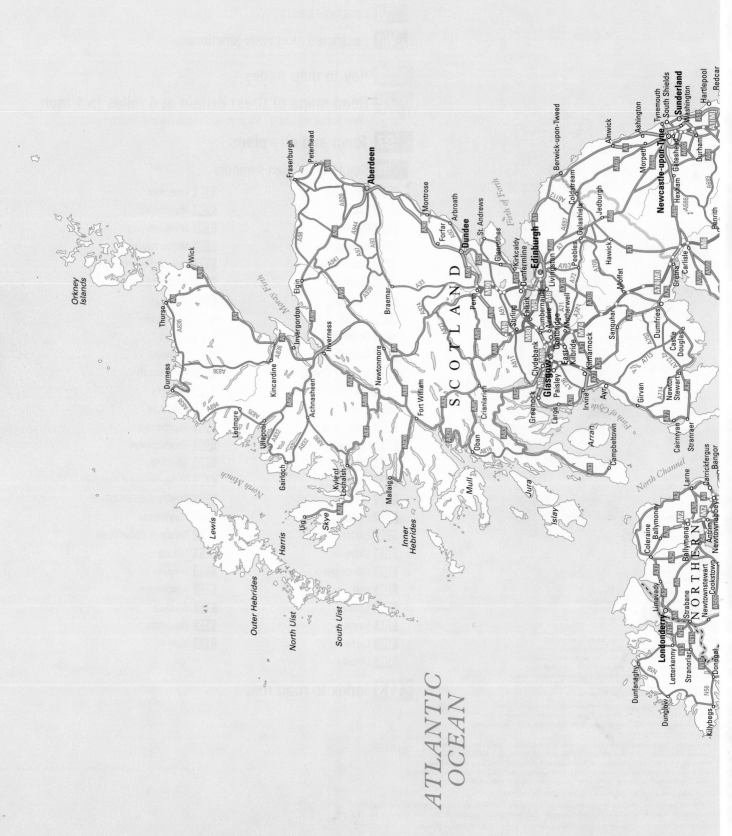

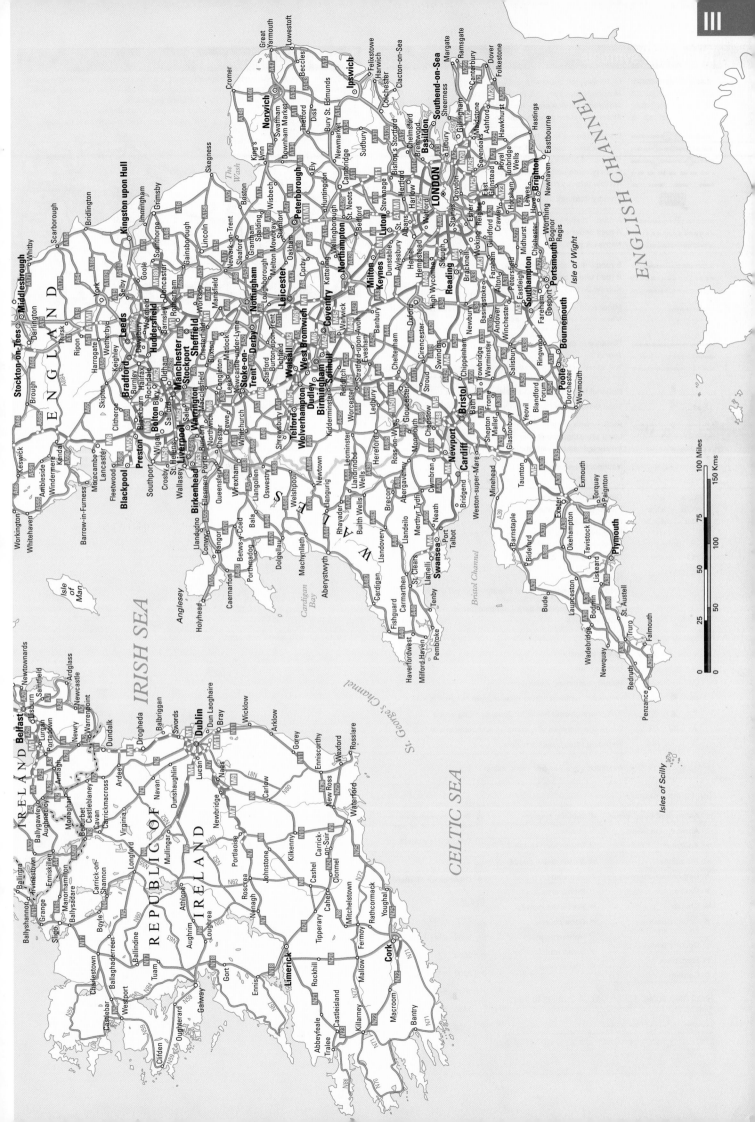

Road map symbols

M6 Motorway, toll motorway
Motorway junction – full, restricted access
Motorway service area – full, restricted access
Motorway under construction

A453 Primary route – dual, single carriageway
Service area, roundabout, multi-level junction
Numbered primary route junction – full, restricted access
Primary route under construction
Narrow primary route

Derby Primary destination

A34 A road – dual, single carriageway
A road under construction
Narrow A road

B2135 B road – dual, single carriageway
B road under construction
Narrow B road

Minor road – over 4 metres wide, under 4 metres wide
Minor road with restricted access

Distance in miles
Tunnel
TOLL Toll, steep gradient – arrow points downhill

National trail – England and Wales
Long distance footpath – Scotland

Railway with station
Level crossing, tunnel
Preserved railway with station

National boundary
County / unitary authority boundary

Car ferry, catamaran
Passenger ferry, catamaran
Hovercraft, freight ferry
Ferry destination, journey time – hrs : mins
CALAIS 1:15 Ferry Car ferry – river crossing
Principal airport, other airport

National park
Area of Outstanding Natural Beauty – England and Wales
National Scenic Area – Scotland
forest park / regional park / national forest
Woodland

Beach

Linear antiquity

Roman road

1066 Hillfort, battlefield – with date
795 Viewpoint, national nature reserve, spot height – in metres
Golf course, youth hostel, national sporting venue
Camp site, caravan site, camping and caravan site
P&R Shopping village, park and ride

29 Adjoining page number – road maps

Tourist information

✝ Abbey / cathedral / priory	Historic ship	🄸 Tourist information centre – open all year
Ancient monument	House	🄸 Tourist information centre – open seasonally
Aquarium	House and garden	
Art gallery	Motor racing circuit	Zoo
Bird collection/aviary	Museum	✦ Other place of interest
Castle	Picnic area	
Church	Preserved railway	
Country park – England and Wales	Race course	
Country park – Scotland	Roman antiquity	
Farm park	Safari park	
Garden	Theme park	

Relief

Feet	metres
3000	914
2600	792
2200	671
1800	549
1400	427
1000	305
0	0

Road map scale: 1: 265 320, 4·2 miles to 1 inch

0 1 2 3 4 5 6 7 8 9 miles
0 1 2 3 4 5 6 7 8 9 10 11 12 13 14 15km

Route-finding system

Town names printed in yellow on a green background are those used on Britain's signposts to indicate primary destinations. To find your route quickly and easily, simply follow the signs to the primary destination immediately beyond the place you require.
Below Driving from St Ives to Camborne, follow the signs to Redruth, the first primary destination beyond Camborne. These will indicate the most direct main route to the side turning for Camborne.

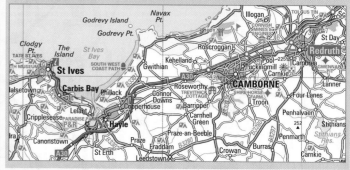

Distance table

London

How to use this table

Distances are shown in miles and, in *italics*, kilometres.
For example, the distance between Aberdeen and Bournemouth is 564 miles or *908* kilometres.

Going far?
Make time for a break every two hours.

THINK!
Tiredness Kills

517 / 832 Aberdeen

211 445 / 340 716 Aberystwyth

394 183 317 / 634 295 510 Ayr

352 182 311 134 / 567 293 501 216 Berwick-upon-Tweed

117 420 114 289 274 / 188 676 183 465 441 Birmingham

226 308 153 180 181 123 / 364 496 246 290 291 198 Blackpool

107 (564) 207 436 412 147 270 / 172 (908) 333 702 663 237 435 Bournemouth

482 59 405 143 148 385 281 524 / 776 95 652 230 238 620 452 843 Braemar

52 573 253 446 409 163 286 92 534 / 84 922 407 718 658 262 460 148 859 Brighton

122 493 125 370 362 81 204 82 477 147 / 196 793 201 595 583 130 328 132 768 237 Bristol

54 471 214 357 306 100 208 154 438 116 169 / 87 758 344 575 493 161 335 248 705 187 272 Cambridge

157 505 105 382 368 103 209 117 483 182 45 190 / 253 813 169 615 592 166 336 188 778 293 72 306 Cardiff

301 221 224 93 87 196 87 343 196 370 277 264 289 / 484 356 360 150 140 315 140 552 316 596 446 425 465 Carlisle

171 344 176 235 184 94 94 235 310 236 175 116 209 142 / 275 554 283 378 296 151 151 378 499 380 282 187 336 229 Doncaster

71 588 297 478 424 194 312 174 553 82 202 125 238 389 242 / 114 947 478 769 683 312 502 280 890 132 325 201 383 626 390 Dover

448 67 376 117 113 349 239 495 52 517 430 406 441 152 275 523 / 721 108 605 188 182 562 385 797 84 832 692 654 710 245 443 842 Dundee

390 125 320 73 57 292 183 439 91 456 373 345 385 96 219 462 56 / 628 201 515 117 92 470 295 707 146 734 600 555 620 154 352 744 90 Edinburgh

181 569 201 446 428 157 282 82 550 184 76 249 121 353 251 248 518 450 / 291 916 323 718 689 253 454 132 885 296 122 401 195 568 404 399 834 724 Exeter

260 504 56 373 371 170 209 222 493 291 154 270 112 297 247 331 460 399 230 / 418 811 90 600 597 274 336 357 794 468 248 435 180 478 398 533 740 642 370 Fishguard

510 149 430 133 190 392 296 539 125 575 486 479 485 206 357 596 127 144 560 486 / 821 240 692 214 306 631 476 867 201 926 782 771 781 332 575 959 204 232 901 782 Fort William

397 145 320 33 101 292 183 439 110 468 373 372 385 96 249 488 83 44 449 376 101 / 639 233 515 53 163 470 295 707 177 753 600 599 620 154 401 786 134 71 723 605 163 Glasgow

109 468 102 330 318 56 174 99 443 159 35 174 99 247 150 191 410 349 111 153 454 346 / 175 753 164 531 512 90 280 159 713 256 56 198 90 398 241 307 660 562 179 246 731 557 Gloucester

128 517 294 402 345 180 252 240 477 180 275 82 284 320 167 185 484 386 335 366 527 419 225 / 206 832 473 647 555 290 406 386 768 290 442 132 457 515 269 298 779 621 539 848 674 362 Great Yarmouth

76 535 281 425 372 167 275 187 540 128 217 67 246 336 194 128 413 279 337 543 432 196 82 / 122 861 452 684 599 269 443 301 811 206 349 108 396 541 312 201 755 665 449 542 874 695 316 132 Harwich

269 439 111 305 311 148 141 288 426 334 206 270 216 231 181 360 394 333 282 167 438 330 191 153 / 433 707 179 491 501 238 227 463 686 538 332 435 348 372 291 580 634 536 269 705 531 307 538 562 Holyhead

550 105 486 199 215 458 348 597 75 617 539 505 549 262 383 622 132 158 658 543 262 262 547 483 553 569 474 / 885 169 782 320 346 737 560 961 121 993 867 813 884 422 617 1001 212 254 995 872 106 267 811 890 916 763 Inverness

663 232 601 328 342 574 478 724 202 741 668 630 680 391 507 746 259 285 744 671 195 295 628 677 693 603 129 / 1067 373 967 528 550 924 769 1165 325 1193 1075 1014 1094 629 816 1201 417 475 1011 1090 314 475 1011 1090 1116 970 208 John o' Groats

184 364 223 251 185 134 127 264 327 245 233 139 244 158 47 256 295 234 309 244 158 207 196 231 394 518 / 296 586 359 404 298 216 204 425 526 394 375 224 393 254 76 412 475 377 497 451 594 409 272 333 316 372 634 834 Kingston upon Hull

586 189 499 212 263 471 372 618 159 651 552 555 564 275 432 671 186 216 628 567 79 179 528 602 611 514 84 189 445 / 943 304 803 341 423 758 599 1048 888 827 135 304 716 Kyle of Lochalsh

297 692 313 570 552 281 405 205 665 200 374 245 477 374 381 642 574 573 446 390 405 741 868 421 763 / 478 1114 504 917 888 452 652 330 1070 496 322 602 394 768 602 613 1033 924 198 568 1104 922 378 718 628 652 1193 1397 678 1228 Land's End

189 327 169 212 156 113 72 255 293 260 194 145 232 119 26 260 258 202 270 237 329 215 174 196 223 176 360 487 55 394 405 / 304 526 272 341 251 182 116 410 472 419 233 373 192 417 418 415 325 346 280 705 531 174 179 581 361 236 273 718 Leeds

97 414 153 299 252 39 140 158 389 166 120 68 154 206 74 185 349 296 196 209 462 314 85 140 147 190 461 588 102 500 320 95 / 156 666 246 481 406 63 225 254 626 267 193 109 248 332 119 298 562 476 315 336 679 505 137 225 237 306 742 947 164 805 515 153 Leicester

131 383 199 274 224 90 128 209 357 197 183 85 208 191 39 202 314 258 272 272 399 291 128 155 216 174 441 554 44 476 371 68 51 / 211 616 320 441 360 145 206 336 575 317 295 137 335 307 63 325 505 415 438 642 468 206 249 348 280 709 891 71 766 597 109 82 Lincoln

202 341 104 213 219 93 49 283 272 214 169 128 140 216 86 289 216 237 160 169 140 216 102 240 265 102 382 511 130 407 361 75 130 129 / 325 549 167 343 352 150 79 456 438 259 312 272 193 138 481 460 348 381 257 530 348 386 427 164 615 822 209 655 581 121 209 208 Liverpool

185 340 129 212 196 80 48 227 318 256 161 165 119 61 203 215 126 212 228 124 373 500 95 406 361 40 92 84 35 / 298 547 208 341 315 129 77 365 512 414 259 266 295 192 98 414 346 203 342 365 354 200 604 805 153 654 581 64 148 135 56 Manchester

286 235 257 149 64 207 129 347 201 352 299 241 335 57 114 358 166 110 364 329 253 148 266 281 308 272 268 395 132 318 498 92 187 159 168 132 / 460 378 414 240 103 333 208 558 323 567 481 388 523 92 183 576 267 177 586 529 407 238 428 452 496 438 431 636 212 512 802 148 301 256 270 212 Newcastle upon Tyne

114 496 276 382 328 166 232 214 457 175 252 62 262 289 147 174 422 366 308 343 504 385 204 20 73 311 529 654 149 582 421 176 119 105 220 185 264 / 183 798 444 615 528 267 373 344 735 282 406 100 422 465 237 280 589 496 552 811 620 328 32 117 501 852 1053 240 937 678 283 192 169 354 298 425 Norwich

122 383 164 274 221 50 111 183 353 193 145 81 134 277 69 330 289 262 289 354 646 472 298 73 157 209 / 196 633 264 441 356 80 179 295 568 311 233 134 277 312 69 330 528 422 356 354 646 472 177 246 241 298 692 896 145 771 555 113 40 56 158 118 253 209 Nottingham

499 178 412 94 180 384 285 530 141 565 465 468 468 188 346 585 117 123 584 481 49 92 441 515 524 427 117 244 346 128 665 307 419 387 308 307 233 492 390 / 803 286 663 151 290 618 459 853 227 910 748 753 768 303 557 942 188 198 884 774 79 148 710 829 843 687 188 393 557 206 1070 494 674 623 496 494 375 792 628 Oban

57 483 154 353 324 64 187 96 443 74 64 119 134 174 119 134 372 156 205 472 356 52 156 155 141 109 442 / 92 777 248 568 521 103 301 145 749 174 119 134 174 418 233 227 697 599 251 330 760 573 84 322 233 383 856 1056 309 885 441 270 117 221 277 232 418 233 175 744 Oxford

218 615 237 492 474 203 328 128 587 224 122 293 152 399 297 300 552 496 46 264 595 495 157 365 309 328 664 790 355 674 89 316 242 293 283 410 343 267 587 199 / 351 990 382 792 763 327 528 206 945 361 196 472 269 642 478 483 888 799 74 425 958 797 253 588 497 528 1069 1271 571 1085 143 509 389 472 455 660 552 430 945 320 Plymouth

70 562 222 430 401 141 264 52 597 144 162 268 121 397 287 327 553 460 49 272 540 453 135 336 255 313 554 700 191 597 124 232 229 560 387 200 191 545 77 / 113 901 357 692 645 227 425 84 881 77 156 232 195 560 327 404 893 721 192 356 867 729 217 501 411 261 320 409 380 542 333 307 380 542 124 283 Portsmouth

159 360 159 245 190 76 86 216 320 161 120 194 152 18 245 291 235 215 348 248 126 166 187 168 393 520 65 427 361 33 62 46 72 38 125 146 339 135 283 230 / 256 579 256 394 306 122 138 348 515 364 259 193 312 245 29 394 468 378 401 346 560 399 203 267 301 632 837 105 687 581 53 100 74 116 61 207 235 65 546 217 455 370 Sheffield

160 399 77 269 265 45 98 185 371 264 82 251 32 311 79 324 209 184 325 256 618 723 256 618 228 232 137 204 232 221 324 206 176 530 64 151 21 199 185 / 258 642 124 433 426 72 158 298 597 364 166 256 179 283 175 404 531 299 412 503 742 423 446 716 362 386 182 705 912 272 726 488 175 135 323 93 111 323 150 586 191 362 333 132 Shrewsbury

77 547 201 417 388 122 251 31 532 61 76 148 121 324 209 153 541 433 105 220 164 399 598 723 256 618 228 232 137 204 221 324 206 176 530 64 151 21 199 185 / 124 880 323 671 624 206 404 50 856 98 122 238 195 521 336 230 805 705 169 375 871 963 1164 412 995 367 373 283 853 103 243 34 320 298 Southampton

402 220 330 401 141 264 475 475 319 483 465 468 188 346 585 117 123 584 481 163 200 731 631 314 135 552 686 660 544 422 610 417 423 942 354 531 480 356 354 649 467 238 610 805 742 423 446 716 / 647 367 523 82 274 478 303 715 312 765 608 610 628 163 414 798 269 200 731 631 314 135 552 686 660 544 422 610 417 423 942 354 531 480 356 354 649 467 238 610 805 742 423 446 716 Stranraer

194 507 73 379 383 119 167 222 85 227 41 309 32 274 473 412 161 67 409 89 329 267 184 572 696 264 594 285 248 171 233 195 187 347 301 192 506 141 206 182 217 118 161 417 / 312 816 117 610 616 192 348 269 813 357 137 365 66 497 373 441 761 663 259 108 798 658 143 530 430 296 921 1120 420 956 459 399 285 375 314 301 559 485 309 815 227 332 293 349 190 259 671 Swansea

207 319 195 214 148 130 96 269 285 275 222 165 244 121 34 282 250 194 287 261 330 217 189 201 228 204 352 479 37 407 411 24 108 75 99 64 84 181 77 309 181 333 278 52 133 258 222 272 / 333 513 314 344 238 209 154 433 459 443 357 266 393 195 54 454 402 312 462 420 531 349 304 323 367 328 566 771 60 655 661 39 174 121 159 103 135 291 124 497 291 536 448 84 214 415 357 438 York

Restricted motorway junctions

M1	Northbound	Southbound
2	No exit	No access
4	No exit	No access
6a	No exit	No access
	Access from M25 only	Exit to M25 only
7	No exit	No access
	Access from M10 only	Exit to M10 only
17	No access	No exit
	Exit to M45 only	Access from M45 only
19	No exit to A14	No access from A14
21a	No access	No exit
23a	Exit to A42 only	
24a	No exit	No access
35a	No access	No exit
43	No exit to M621 northbound	
48	No exit to A1 southbound	

M2	Eastbound	Westbound
1	Access from A2 eastbound only	Exit to A2 westbound only

M3	Eastbound	Westbound
8	No exit	No access
10	No access	No exit
13	No access to M27 eastbound	
14	No exit	No access

M4	Eastbound	Westbound
1	Exit to A4 eastbound only	Access from A4 westbound only
2	Access to A4 eastbound only	Access to A4 westbound only
21	No exit	No access
23	No access	No exit
25	No exit	No access
25a	No exit	No access
29	No exit	No access
38		No access
39	No exit or access	No exit
41	No access	No exit
41a	No exit	No access
42		Exit to A483 only

M5	Northbound	Southbound
10	No exit	No access
11a	No access from A417 eastbound	No exit to A417 westbound

M6	Northbound	Southbound
4a	No exit	No access
	Access from M42 southbnd only	Exit to M42 only
5	No access	No exit
10a	No access	No exit
	Exit to M54 only	Access from M54 only
11a	No exit / access	No access / exit
	No access M6 TOLL	
20	No exit to M56 eastbound	No access from M56 westbound
24	No exit	No access
25	No access	No exit
30	No exit	No access
	Access from M61 northbound only	Exit to M61 southbound
31a	No access	No exit

M6 Toll	Northbound	Southbound
T1		No exit
T2	No exit / access	No access
T5	No exit	No access
T7	No access	No exit
T8	No access	No exit

M8	Eastbound	Westbound
8	No exit to M73 northbound	No access from M73 southbound
9	No access	No exit
13	No exit southbound	No access
14	No access	No exit
16	No exit	No access
17	No exit	No access
18		No exit
19	No exit to A814 eastbound	No access from A814 westbound
20	No exit	No access
21	No access	No exit
22	No exit	No access
	Access from M77 only	Exit to M77 only
23	No exit	No access
25	Exit to A739 northbound only	Exit to A739
	Access from A739 southbound only	northbound only
		Access from A739 southbound only
25a	No exit	No access
28	No exit	No access
28a	No exit	No access

M9	Eastbound	Westbound
1a	No exit	No access
2	No access	No exit
3	No exit	No access
6	No access	No exit
8	No exit	No access

M11	Northbound	Southbound
4	No exit	No access
5	No access	No exit
9	No access	No exit

13	No access	No exit
14	No exit to A428 westbound	No exit
		Access from A14 westbound only

M20	Eastbound	Westbound
2	No access	No exit
3	No exit	No access
	Access from M26 eastbound only	Exit to M26 westbound only
11a	No access	No exit

M23	Northbound	Southbound
7	No exit to A23 southbound	No access from A23 northbound
10a	No exit	No access

M25	Clockwise	Anticlockwise
5	No exit to M26 eastbound	No access from M26 westbound
19	No access	No exit
21	No exit to M1 southbound	No exit to M1 southbound
	Access from M1 southbound only	Access from M1 southbound only
31	No exit	No access

M27	Eastbound	Westbound
10	No exit	No access
12	No access	No exit

M40	Eastbound	Westbound
3	No exit	No access
7	No exit	No access
7a	No exit	No access
13	No exit	No access
14	No access	No exit
16	No access	No exit

M42	Northbound	Southbound
1	No exit	No access
7	No access	No exit
	Exit to M6 northbound only	Access from M6 northbound only
7a	No access	No exit
	Exit to M6 only	Access from M6 northbound only
8	No exit	Exit to M6 northbound
	Access from M6 southbound only	Access from M6 southbound only

M45	Eastbound	Westbound
M1 junc 17	Access to M1 southbound only	No access from M1 southbound
With A45 (Dunchurch)	No access	No exit

M49	Southbound	
18a	No exit to M5 northbound	

M53	Northbound	Southbound
11	Exit to M56 eastbound only	Exit to M56 eastbound only
	Access from M56 westbound only	Access from M56 westbound only

M56	Eastbound	Westbound
2	No exit	No access
4	No exit	No access
7		No access
8	No exit or access	No exit
9	No access from M6 northbound	No access to M6 southbound
15	No exit to M53	No access from M53 northbound

M57	Northbound	Southbound
3	No exit	No access
5	No exit	No access

M58	Eastbound	Westbound
1	No exit	No access

M60	Clockwise	Anticlockwise
2	No exit	No access
3	No exit to A34 northbound	No exit to A34 northbound
4	No access to M56	No exit to M56
5	No exit to A5103 southbound	No exit to A5103 northbound
7	No access	No exit (Exit to J8 only)
14	No exit to A580	No access from A580
16	No exit	No access
20	No access	No exit
22		No access
25	No access	
26		No exit or access
27	No exit	No access

M61	Northbound	Southbound
2	No access from A580 eastbound	No exit to A580 westbound
3	No access from A580 eastbound	No exit to A580 westbound
	No access from A666 southbound	
M6 junc 30	No exit to M6 southbound	No access from M6 northbound

M62	Eastbound	Westbound
23	No access	No exit

M65	Eastbound	Westbound
9	No access	No exit
11	No exit	No access

M66	Northbound	Southbound
1	No access	No exit

M67	Eastbound	Westbnd
1a	No access	No exit
2	No exit	No access

M69	Northbound	Southbound
2	No exit	No access

M73	Northbound	Southbound
2	No access from M8	No exit to M8
	or A89 eastbound	or A89 westbound
	No exit to A89	No access from A89
3	Exit to A80 northbound only	Access from A80 southbound only

M74	Northbound	Southbound
2	No access	No exit
3	No exit	No access
7	No exit	No access
9	No exit or access	No access
10		No access
11	No exit	No access
12	No access	No exit

M77	Northbound	Southbound
4	No exit	No access
M8 junc 22	Exit to M8 eastbound only	Access from M8 westbound only

M80	Northbound	Southbound
3	No access	No exit
5	No access from M876	No exit to M876

M90	Northbound	Southbound
2a	No access	No exit
7	No exit	No access
8	No exit	No access
10	No access from A912	No exit to A912

M180	Northbound	Southbound
1	No access	No exit

M621	Eastbound	Westbound
4	No exit or access	
5	No exit	No access
6	No access	No exit

M876	Northbound	Southbound
2	No access	No exit

A1(M)	Northbound	Southbound
2	No access	No exit
3		No access
5	No exit	No access
44	No exit, access from M1 only	Exit to M1 only
57	No access	No exit
65	No access	No exit

A3(M)	Northbound	Southbound
1		No access
4	No access	No exit

A38(M)	Northbound	Southbound
With Victoria Road (Park Circus) Birmingham	No exit	No access

A48(M)	Northbound	Southbound
M4 Junc 29	Exit to M4 eastbound only	Access from M4 westbound only
29a	Access from A48 eastbound only	Exit to A48 westbound only

A57(M)	Eastbound	Westbound
With A5103	No access	No exit
With A34	No access	No exit

A58(M)	Southbound	
With Park Lane and Westgate, Leeds	No access	

A64(M)	Eastbound	Westbound
With A58 Clay Pit Lane, Leeds	No access	No exit
With Regent Street, Leeds	No access	No access

A74(M)	Northbound	Southbound
18	No access	No exit
22	No access	No exit

A167(M)	Northbound	Southbound
With Camden St, Newcastle	No exit	No exit or access

A194(M)	Northbound	Southbound
A1(M) junc 65 Gateshead Western Bypass	Access from A1(M) northbound only	Exit to A1(M) southbound only

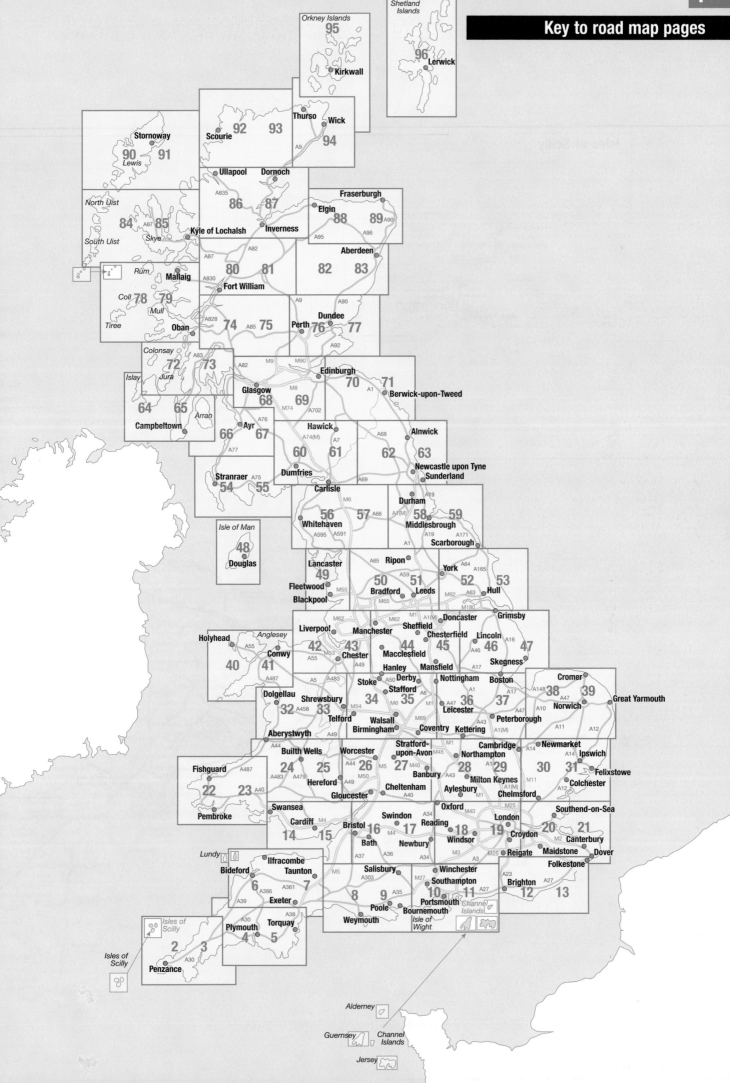

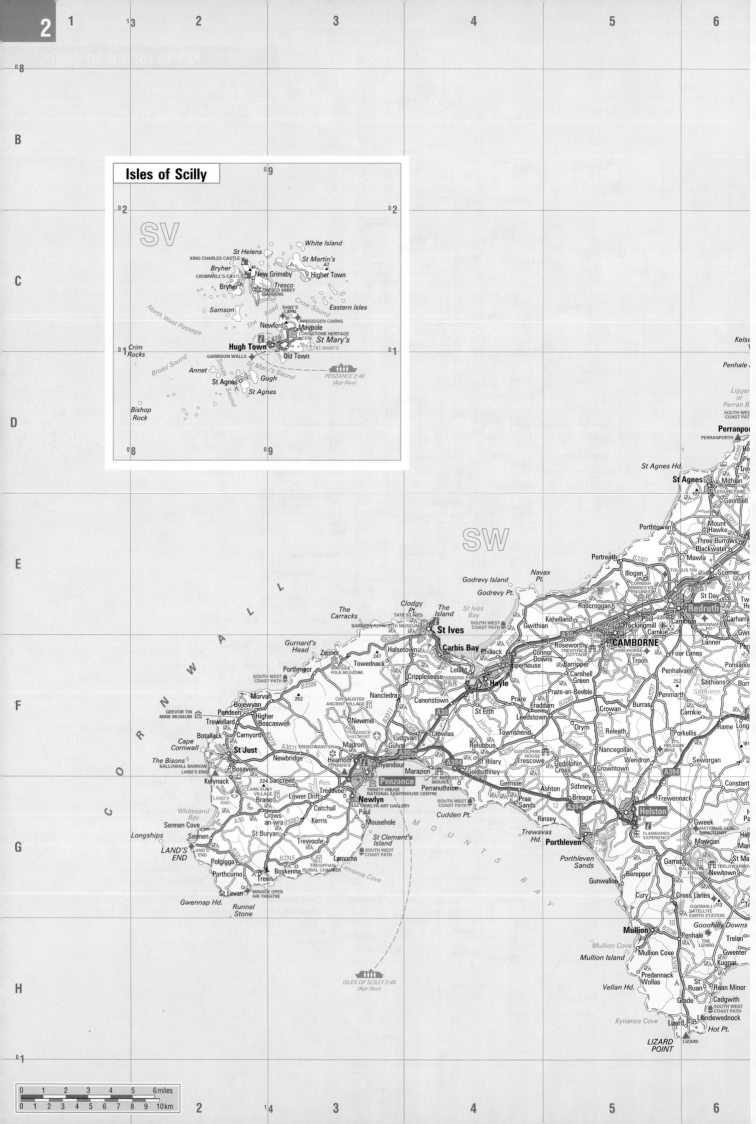

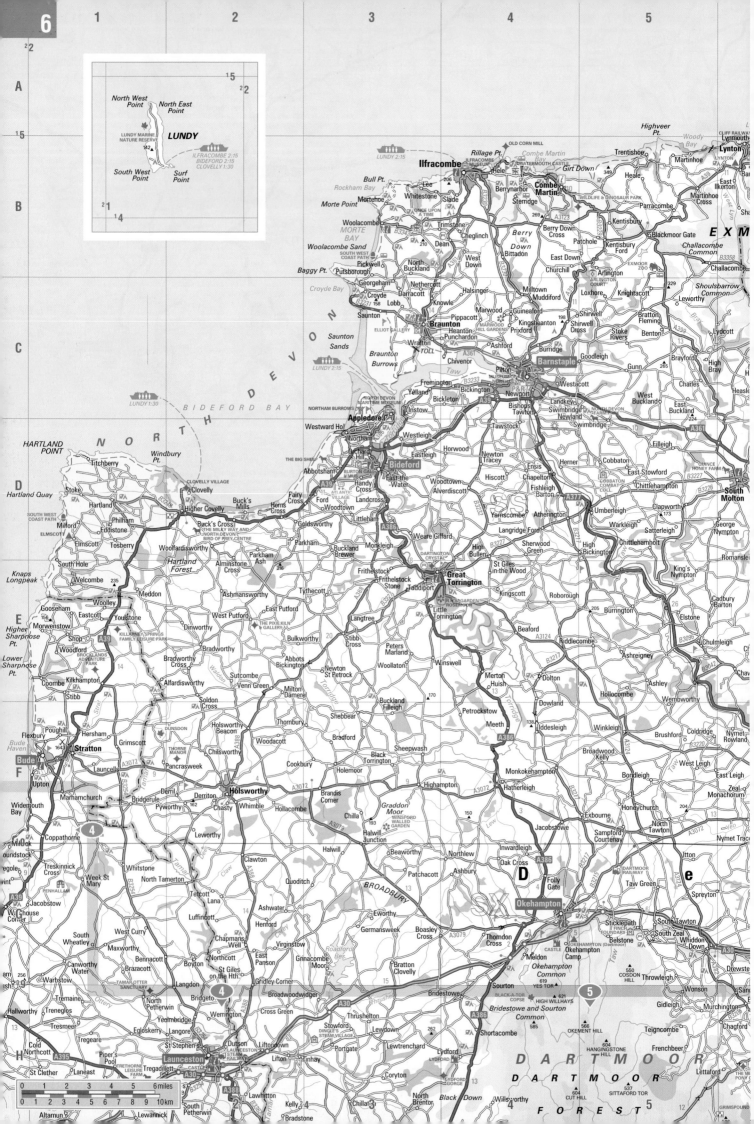

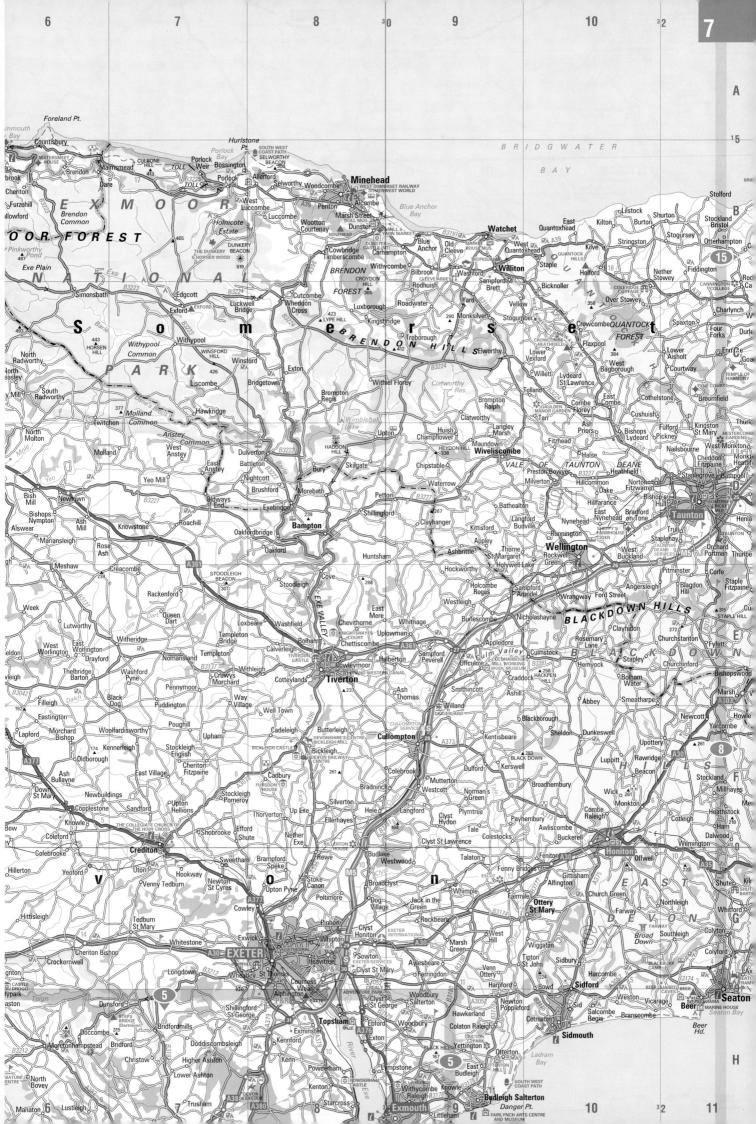

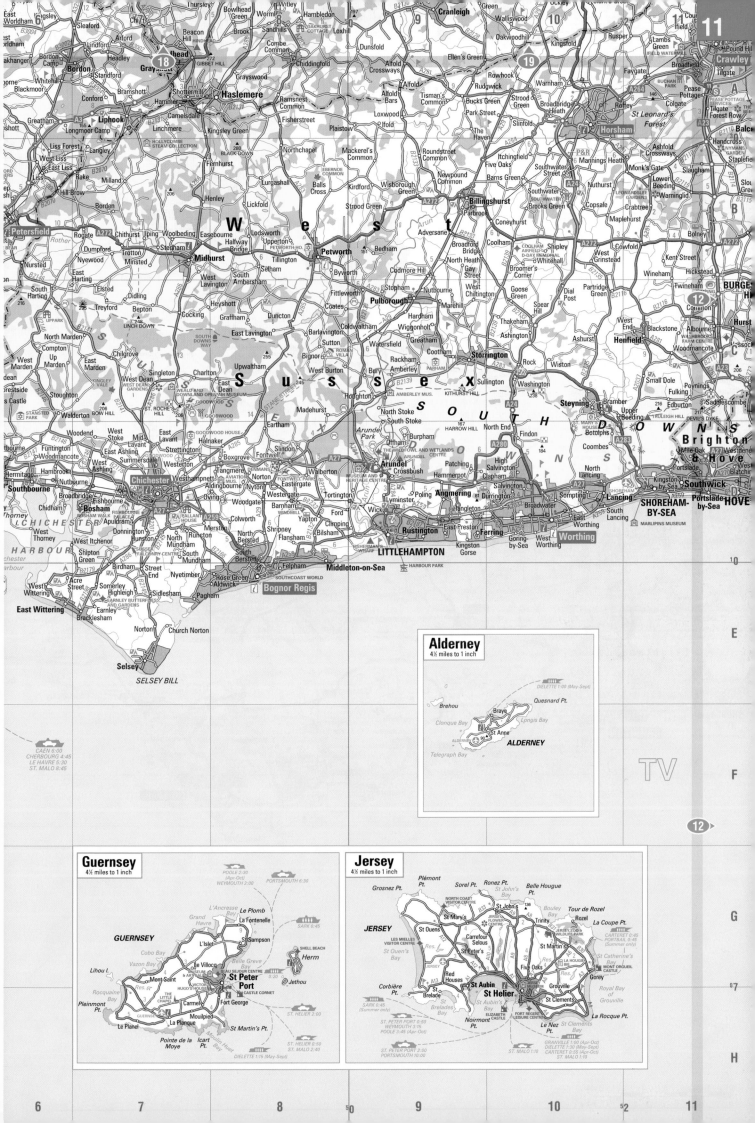

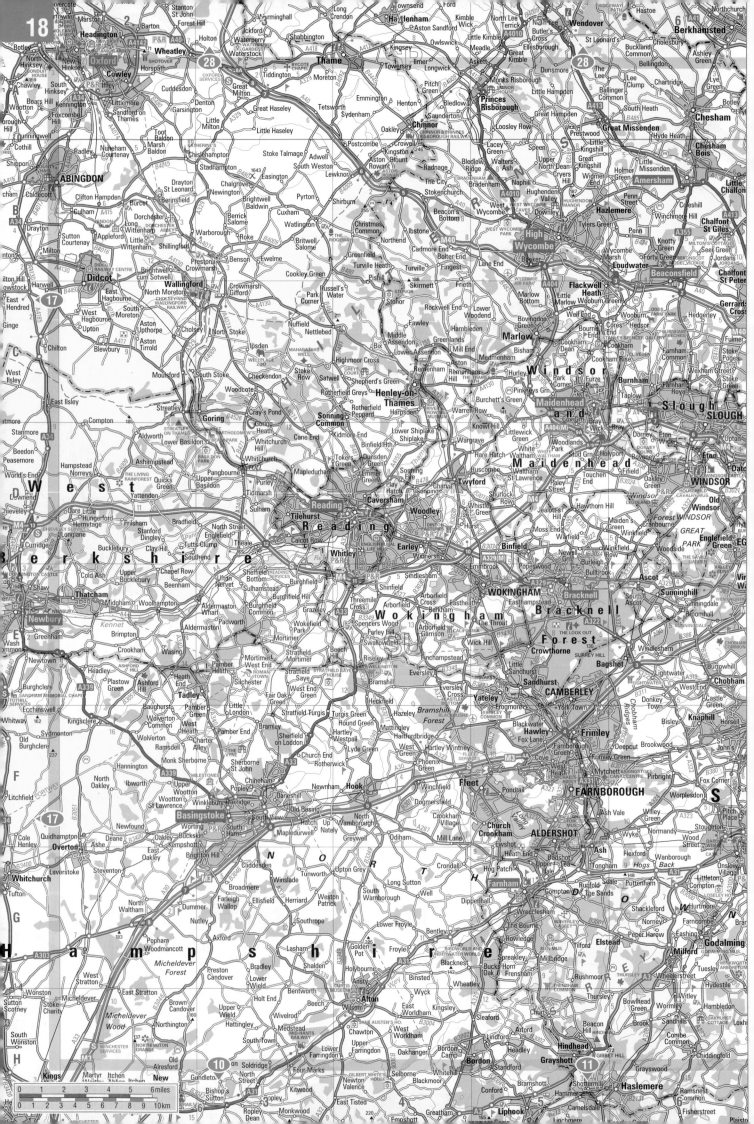

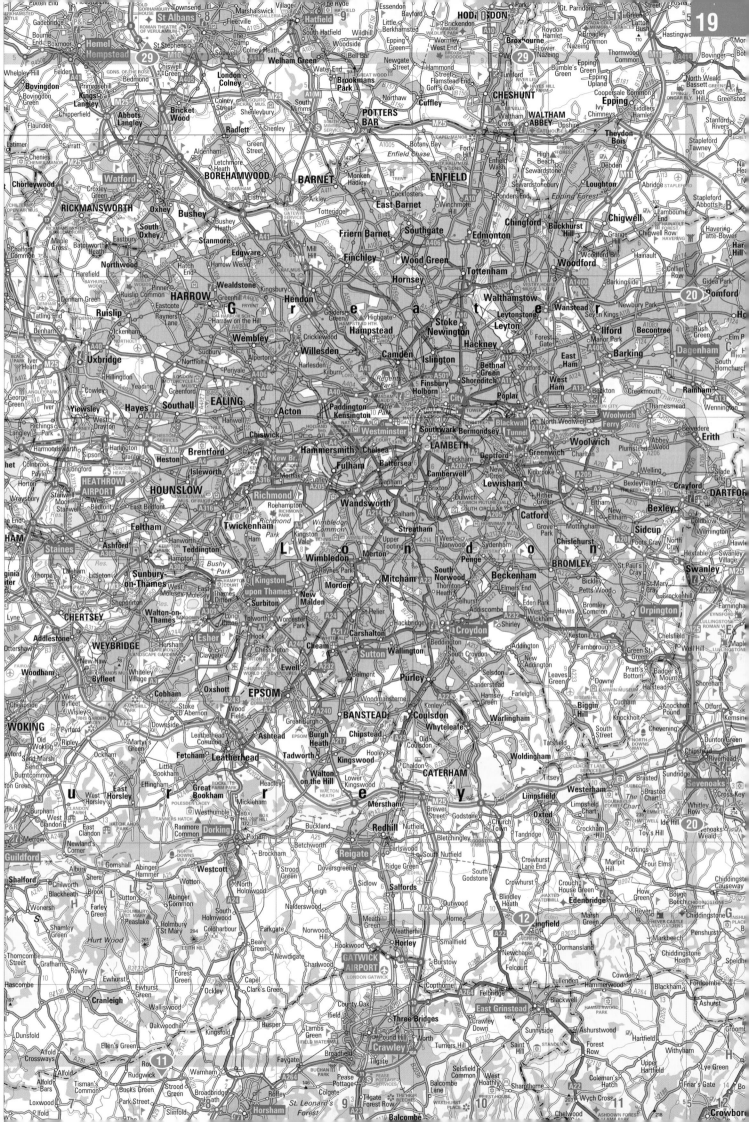

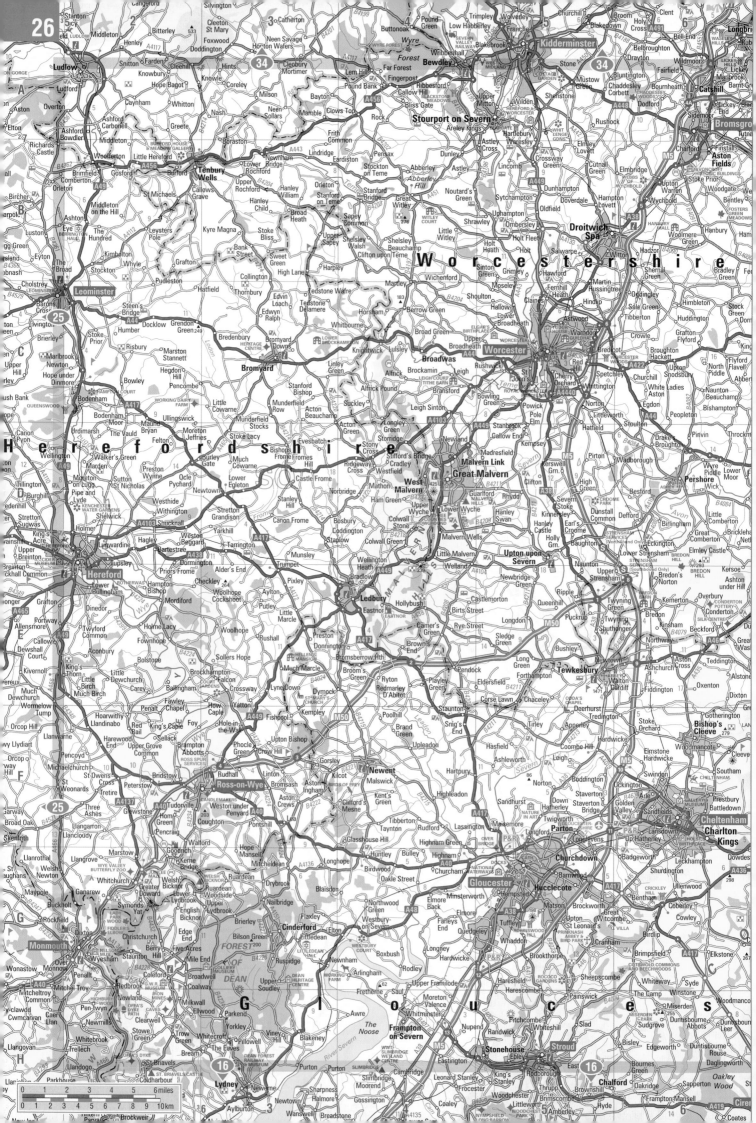

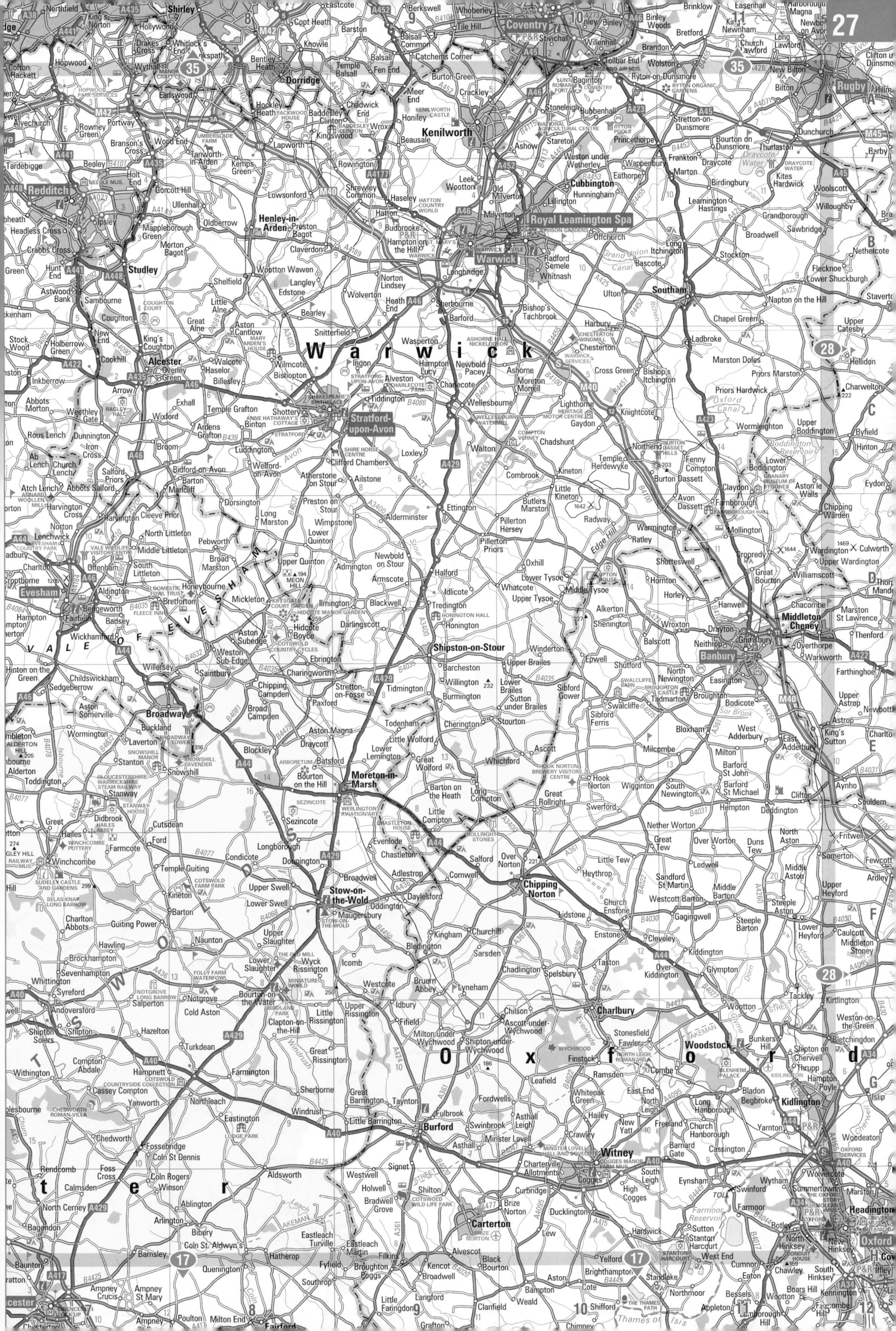
Warwick
Oxford
Coventry
Kenilworth
Royal Leamington Spa
Warwick
Rugby
Redditch
Studley
Alcester
Henley-in-Arden
Dorridge
Shirley
Stratford-upon-Avon
Evesham
Cubbington
Southam
Kineton
Shipston-on-Stour
Banbury
Middleton Cheney
Broadway
Moreton-in-Marsh
Stow-on-the-Wold
Chipping Norton
Charlbury
Woodstock
Kidlington
Witney
Burford
Carterton
Headington
Winchcombe
Northleach
Fairford
Chipping Campden
VALE OF EVESHAM
Edge Hill
Oxford Canal
Grand Union Canal
Thames or Isis
Draycote Water
Farmoor Reservoir
Boddington Reservoir
Windrush
Evenlode
Cherwell
Leach
Coln
Stour
Avon
35
28
17
A46
A44
A429
A3400
A40
A423
A45
A361
A34
A422
A435
A448
A441
A4177
A452
A424
A436
A417
M40
M42
M45

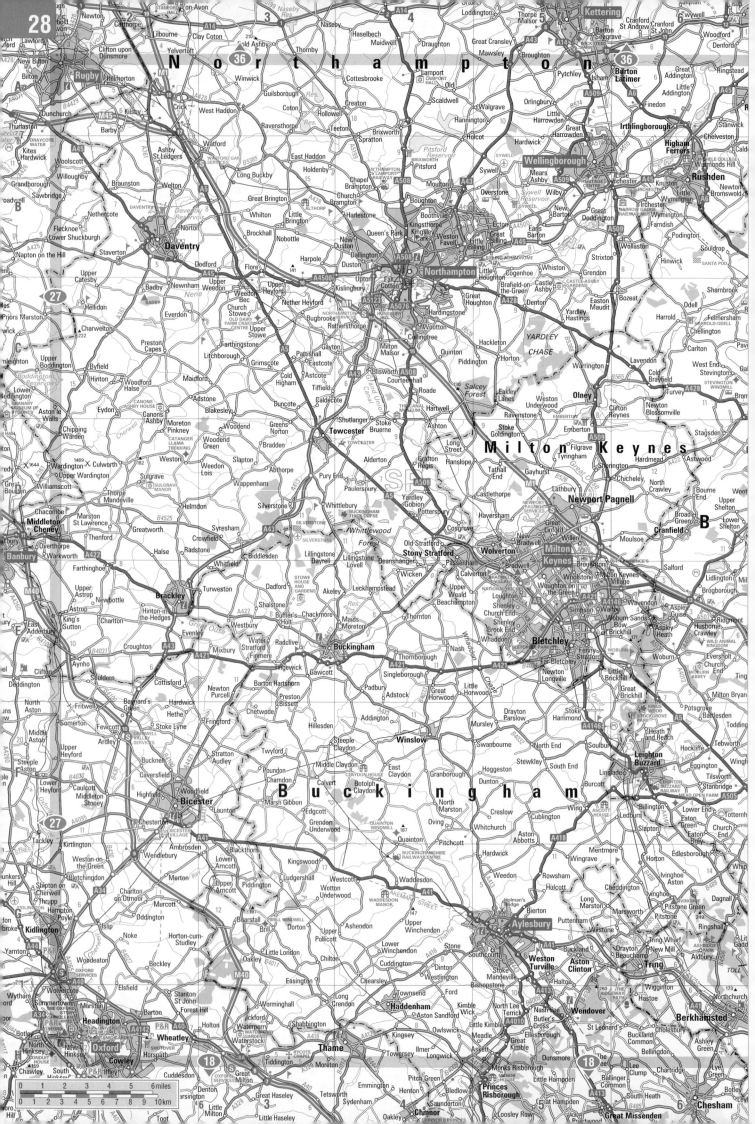

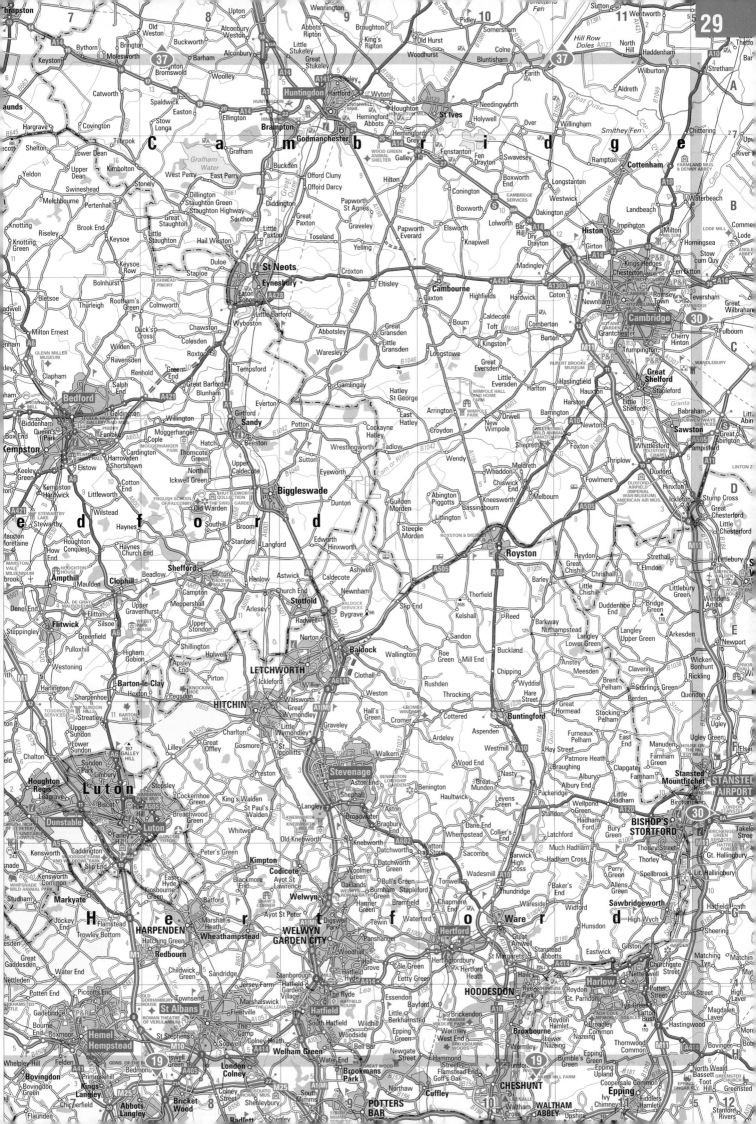

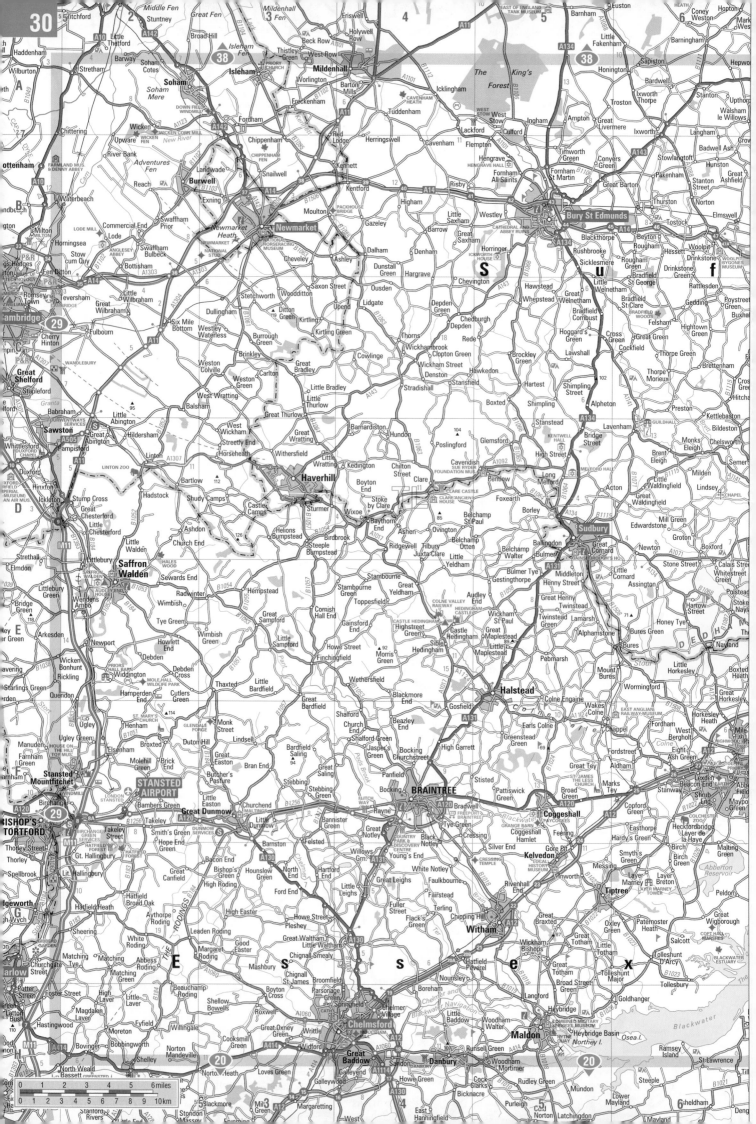

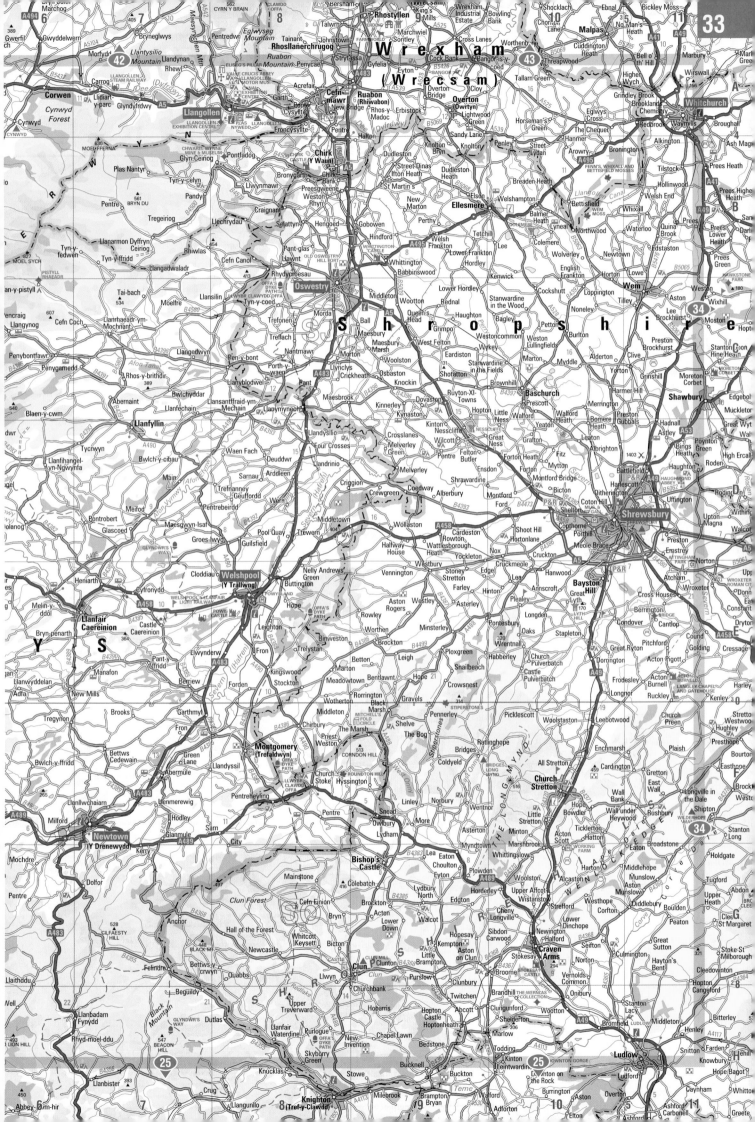

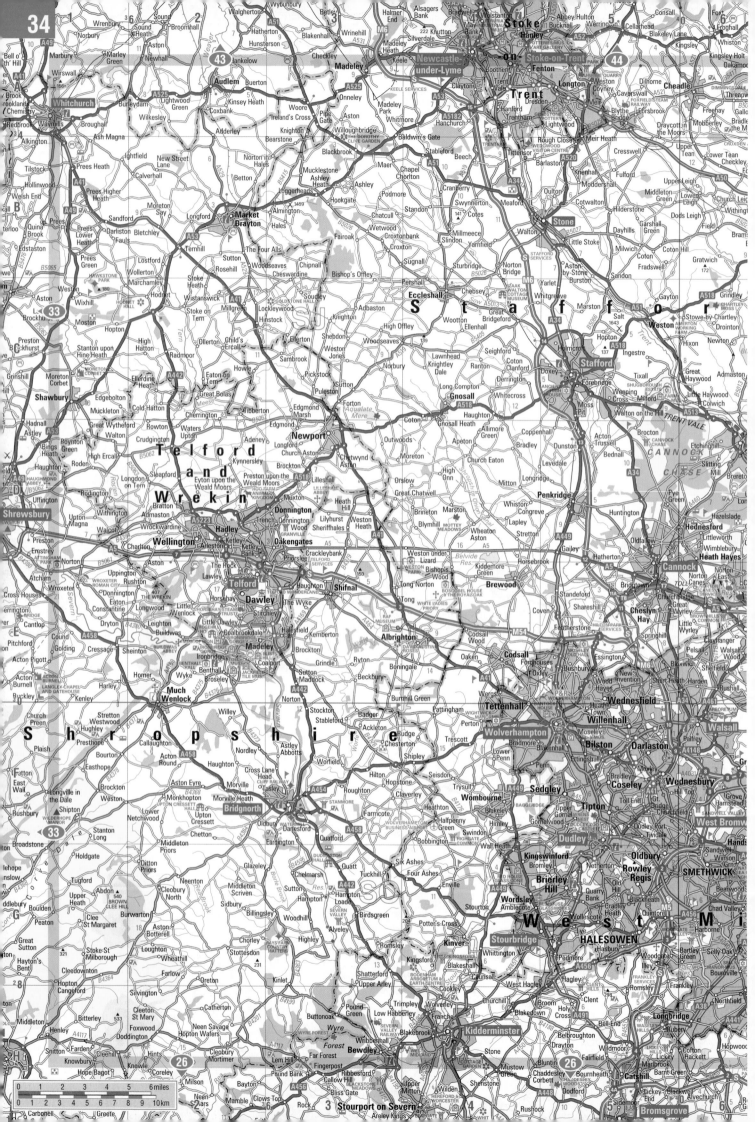

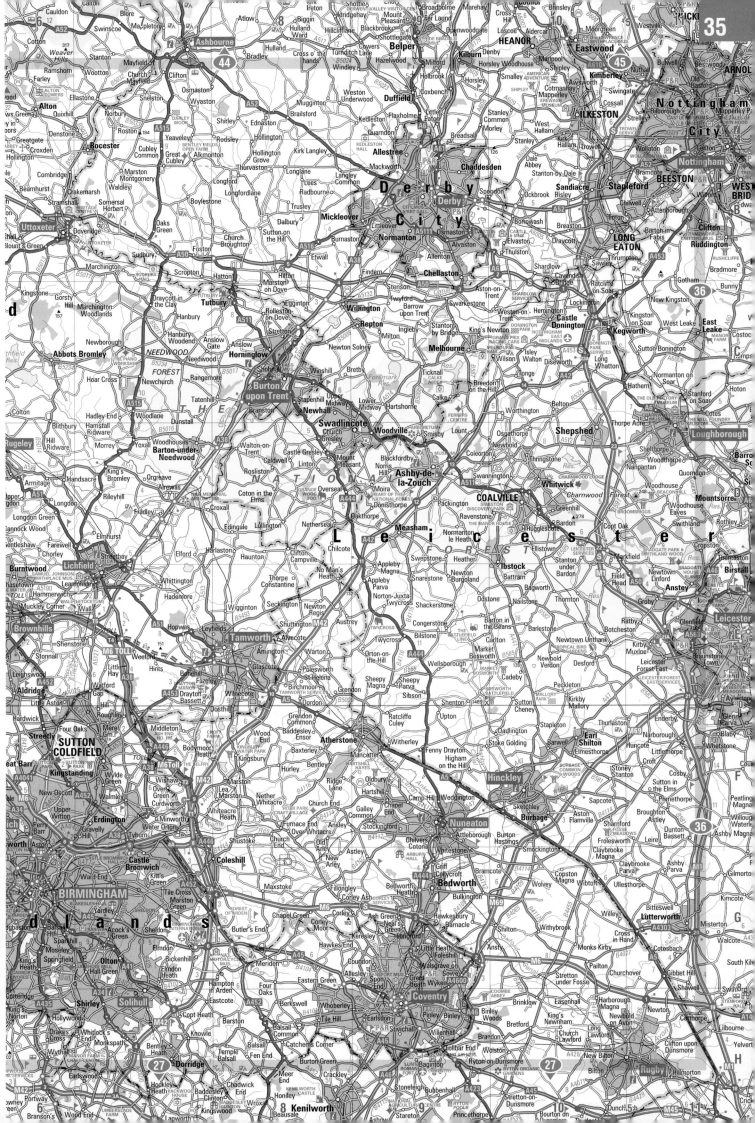

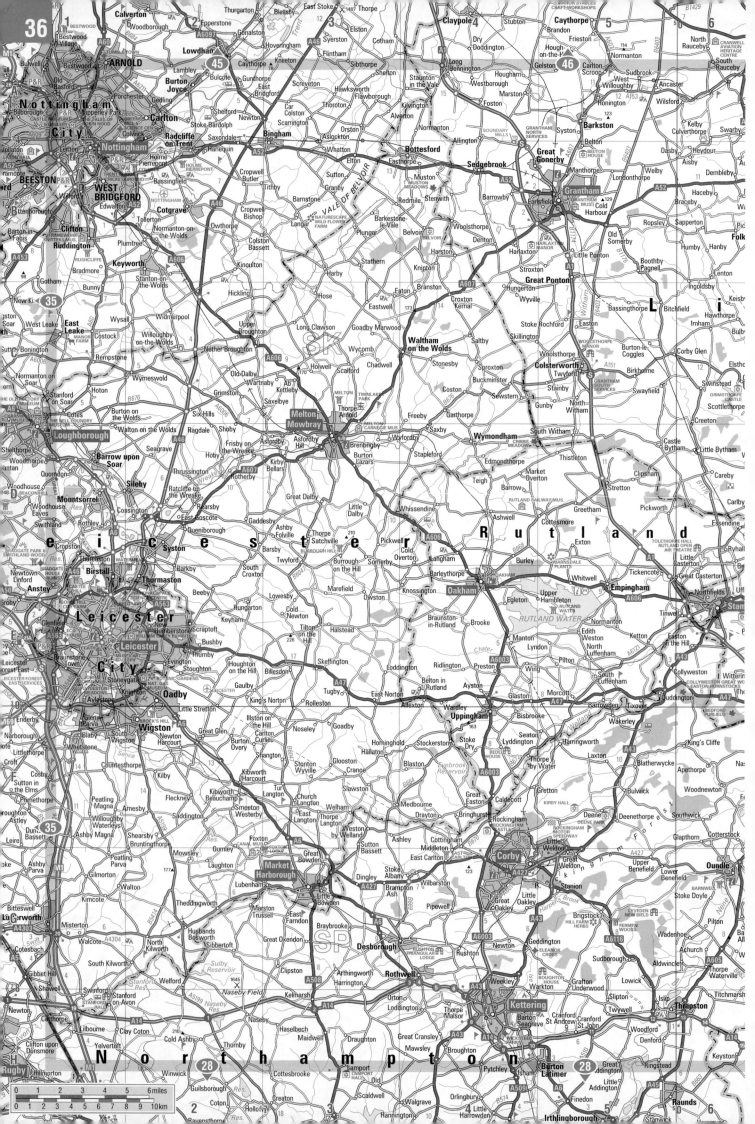

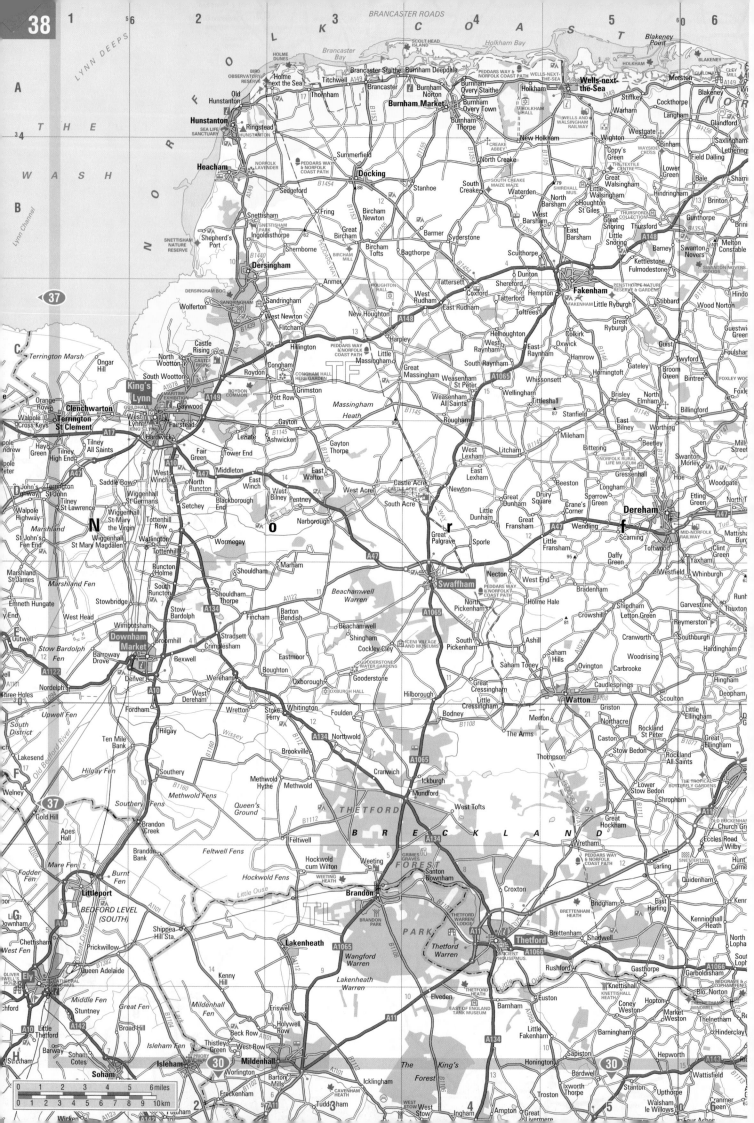

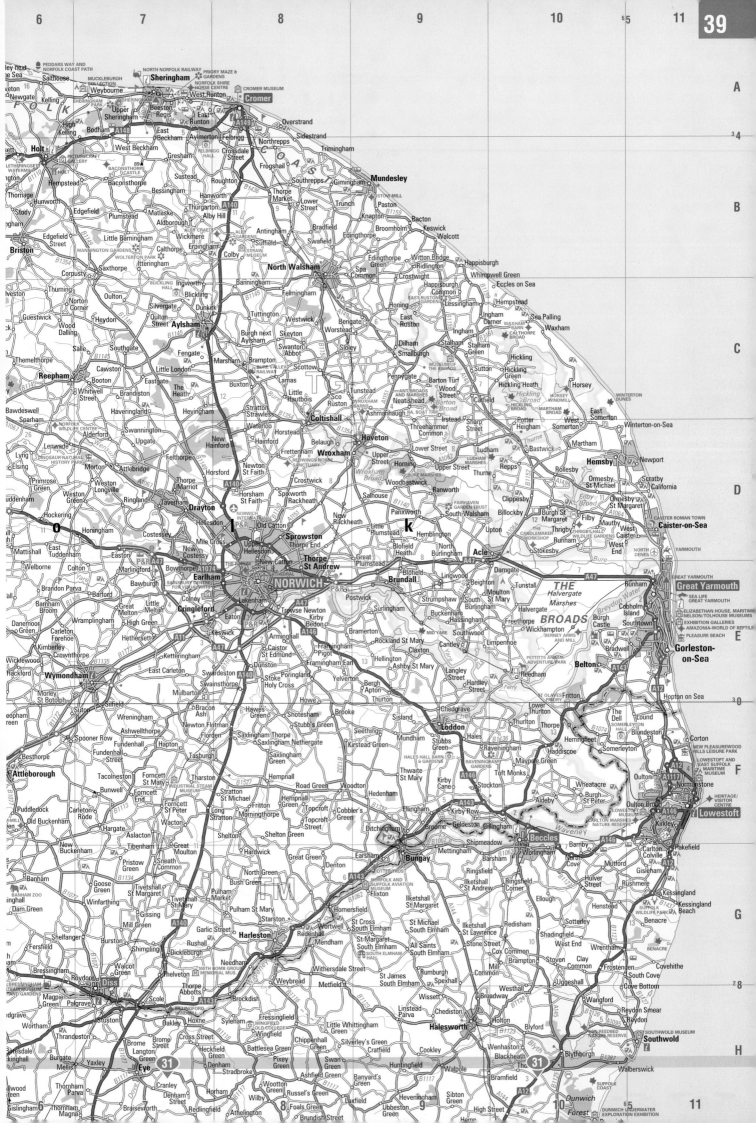

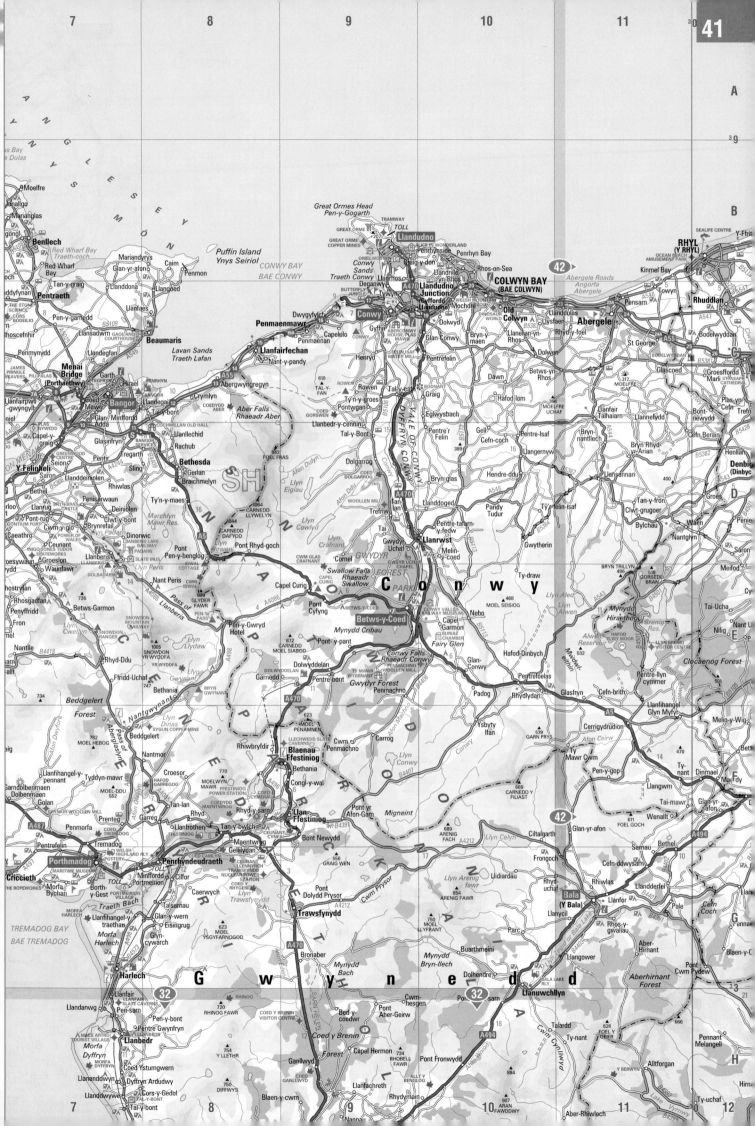

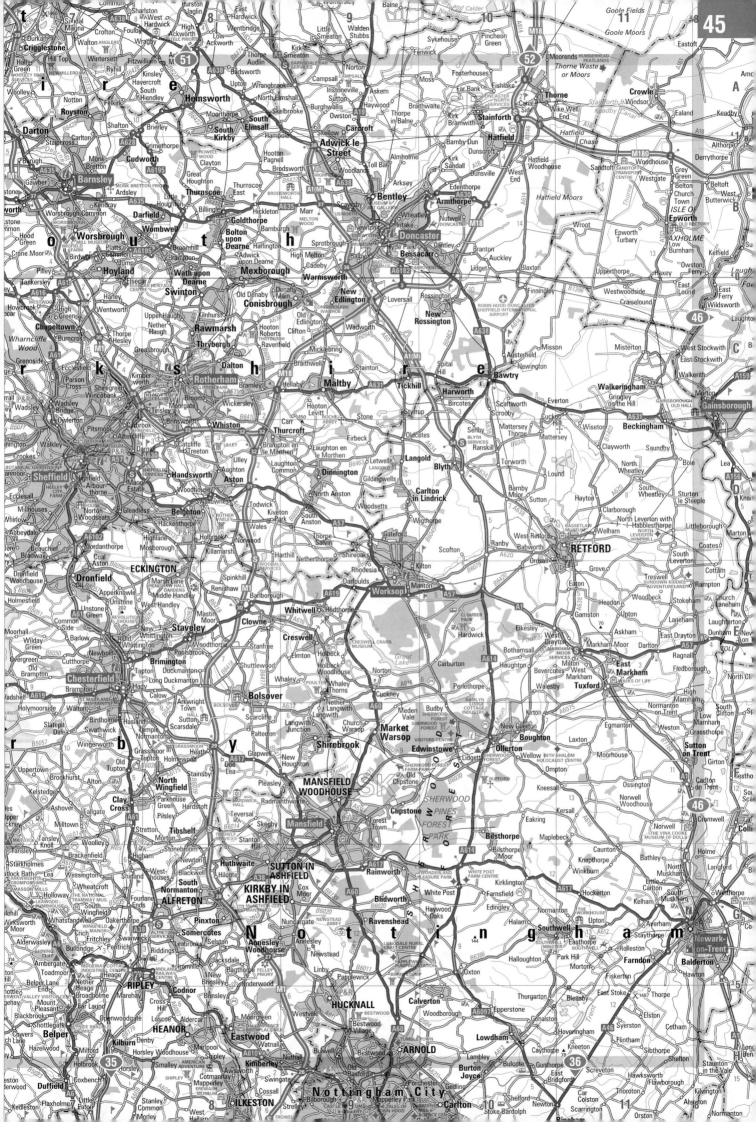

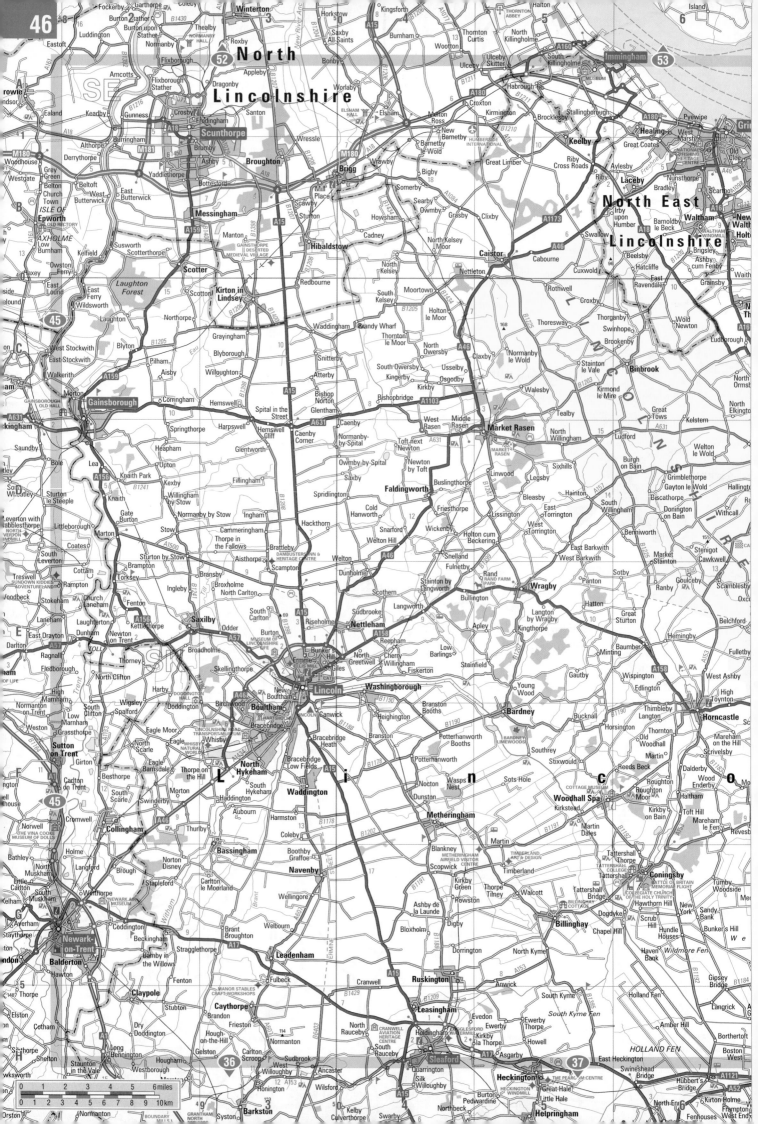

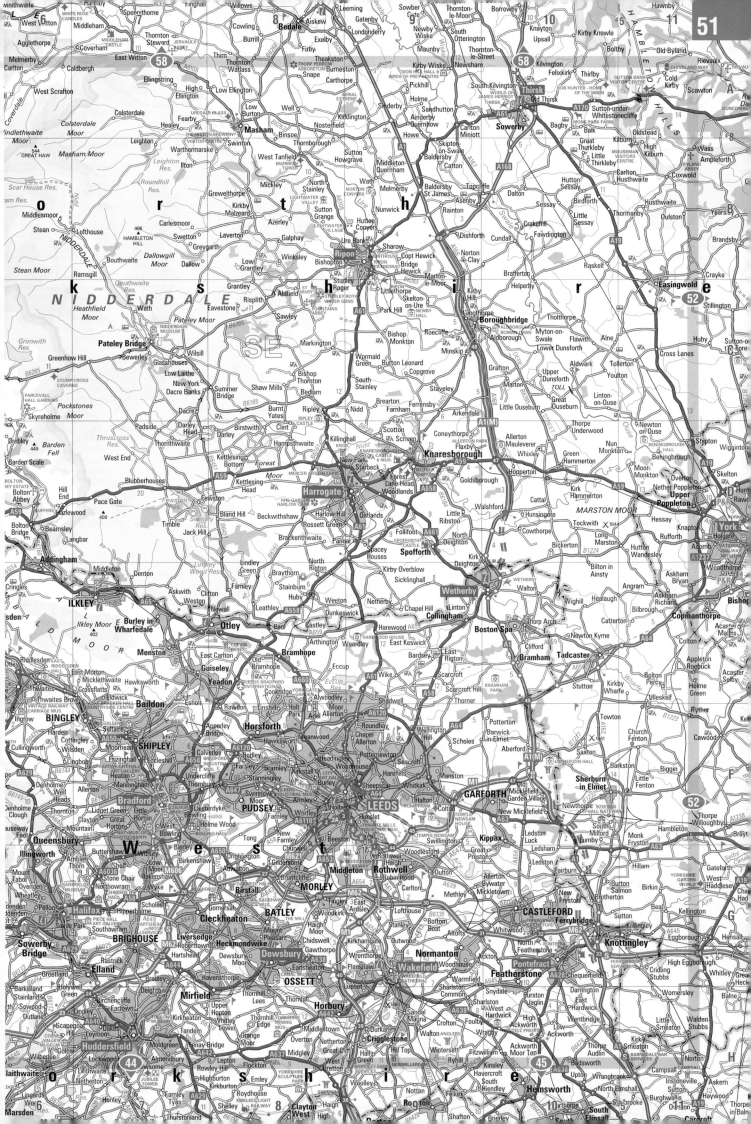

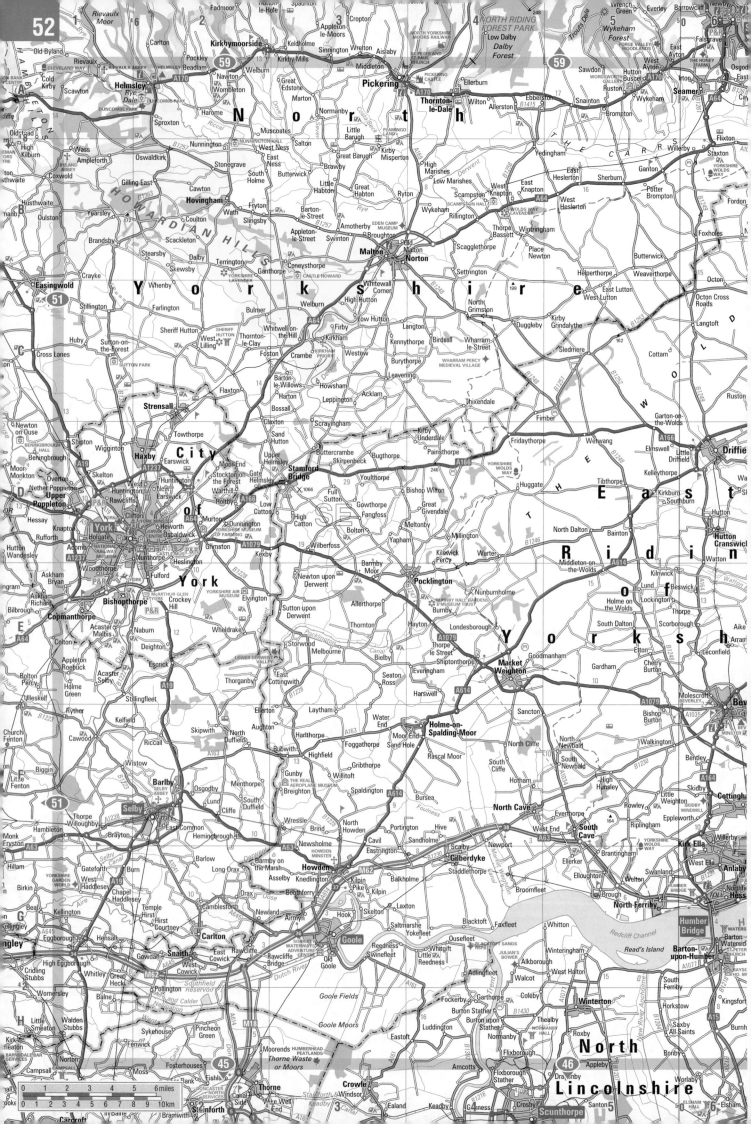

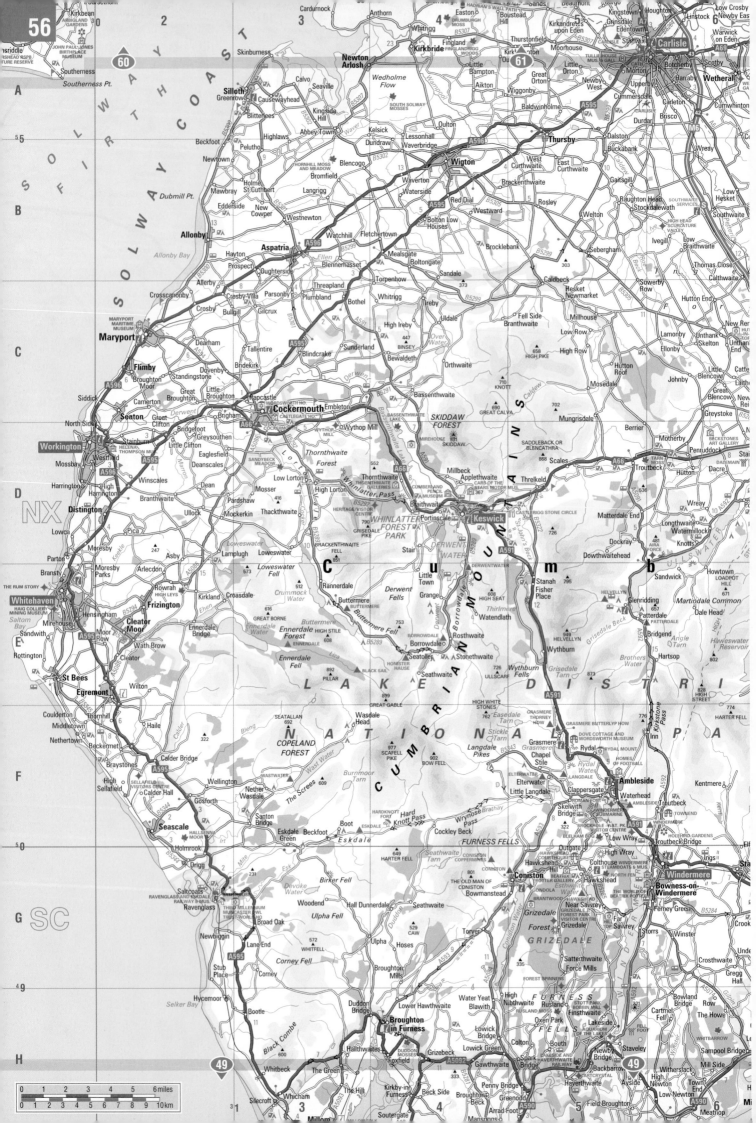

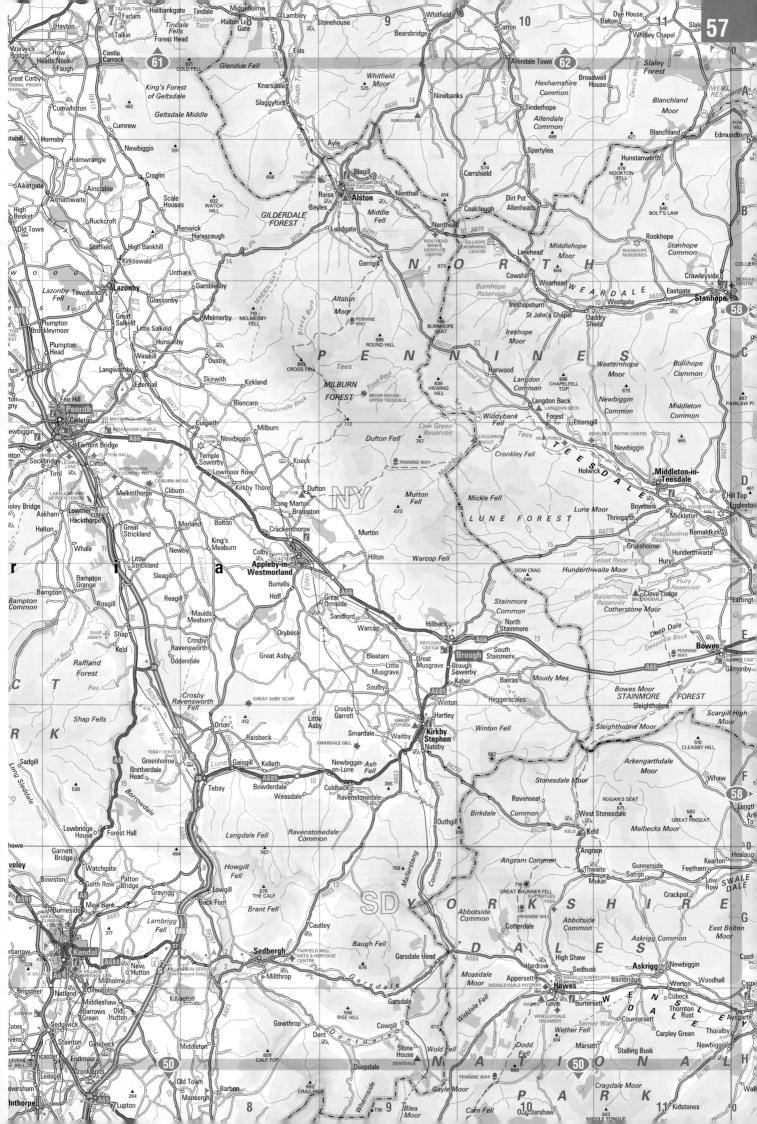

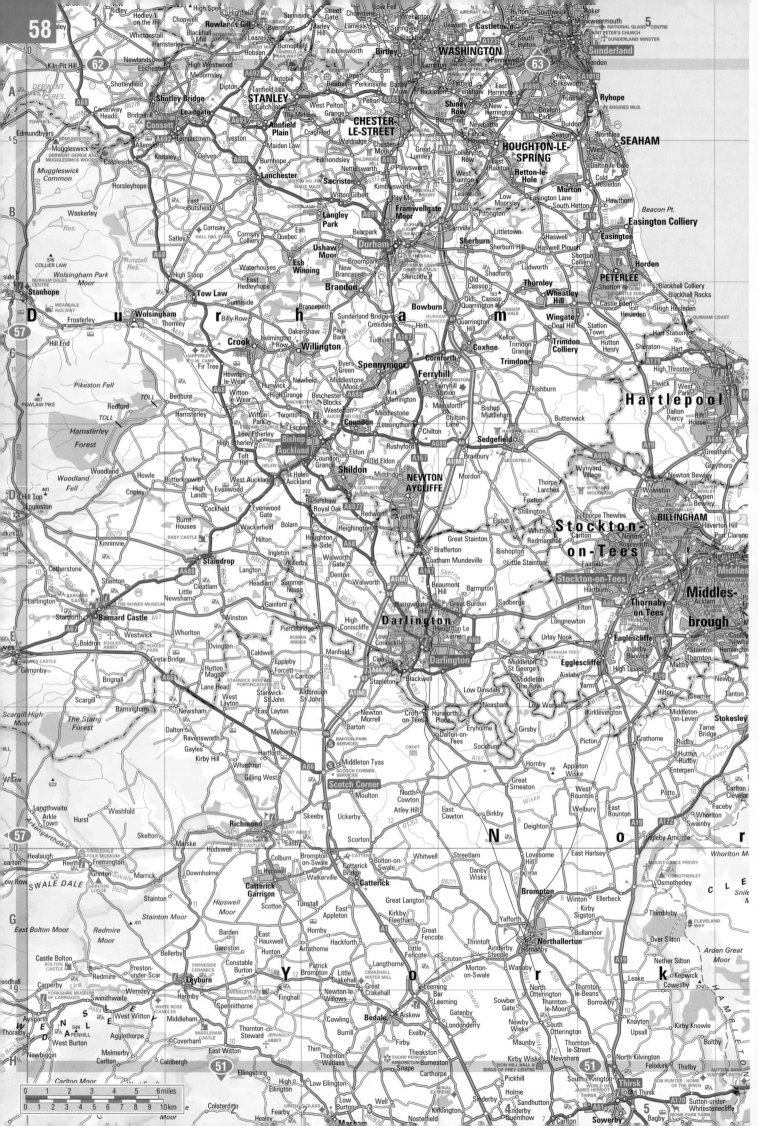

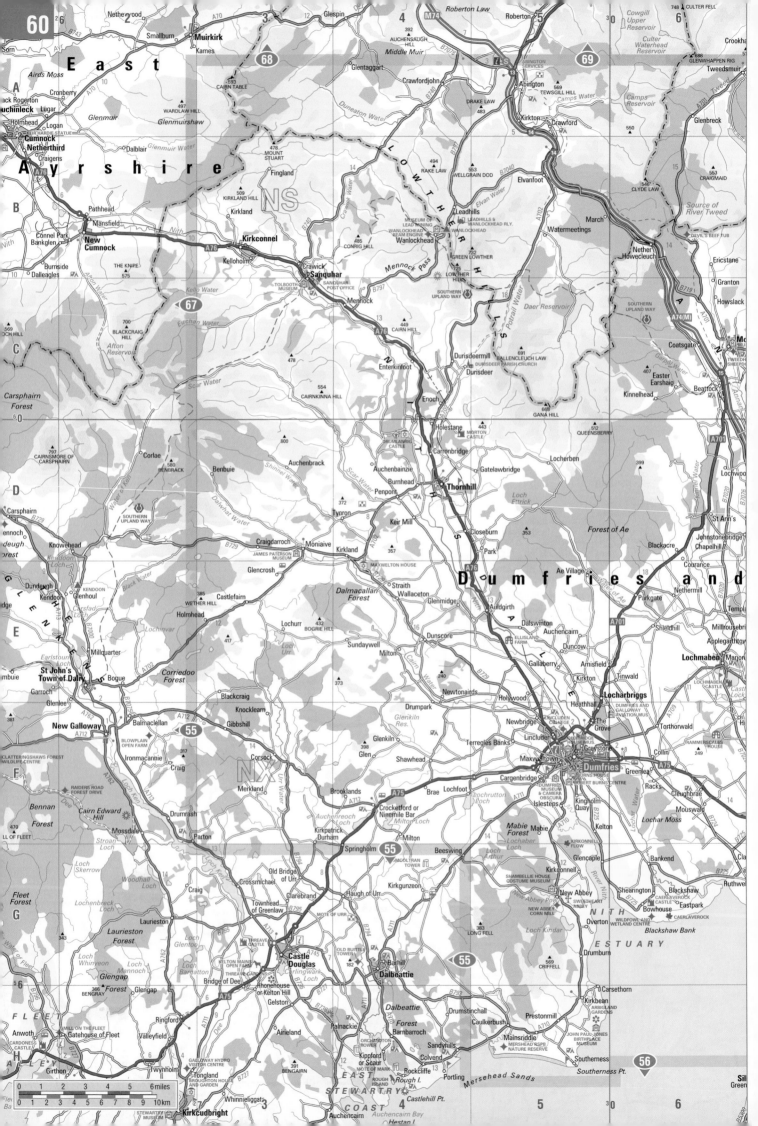

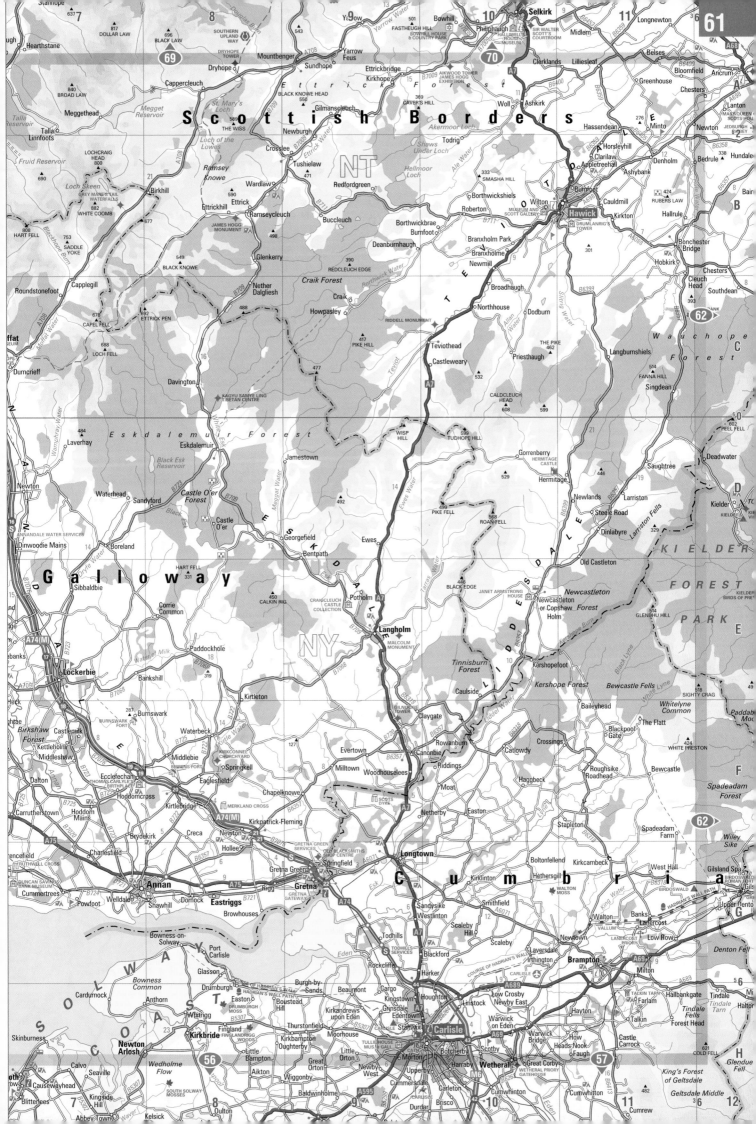

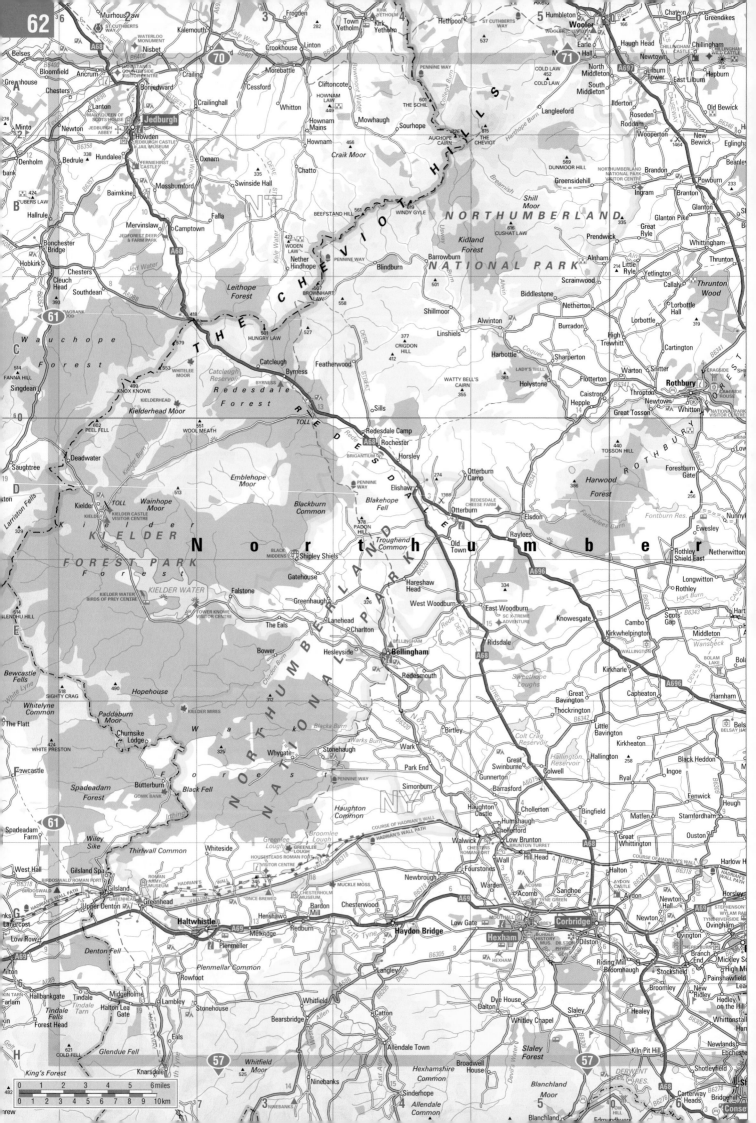

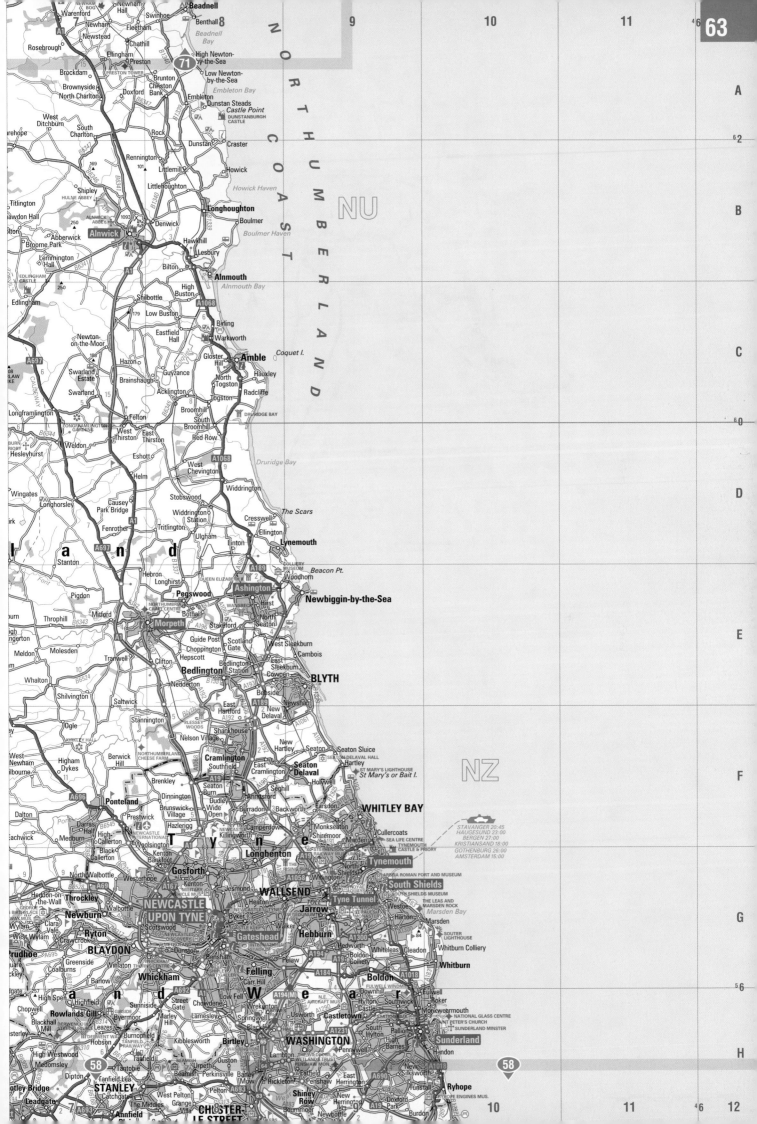

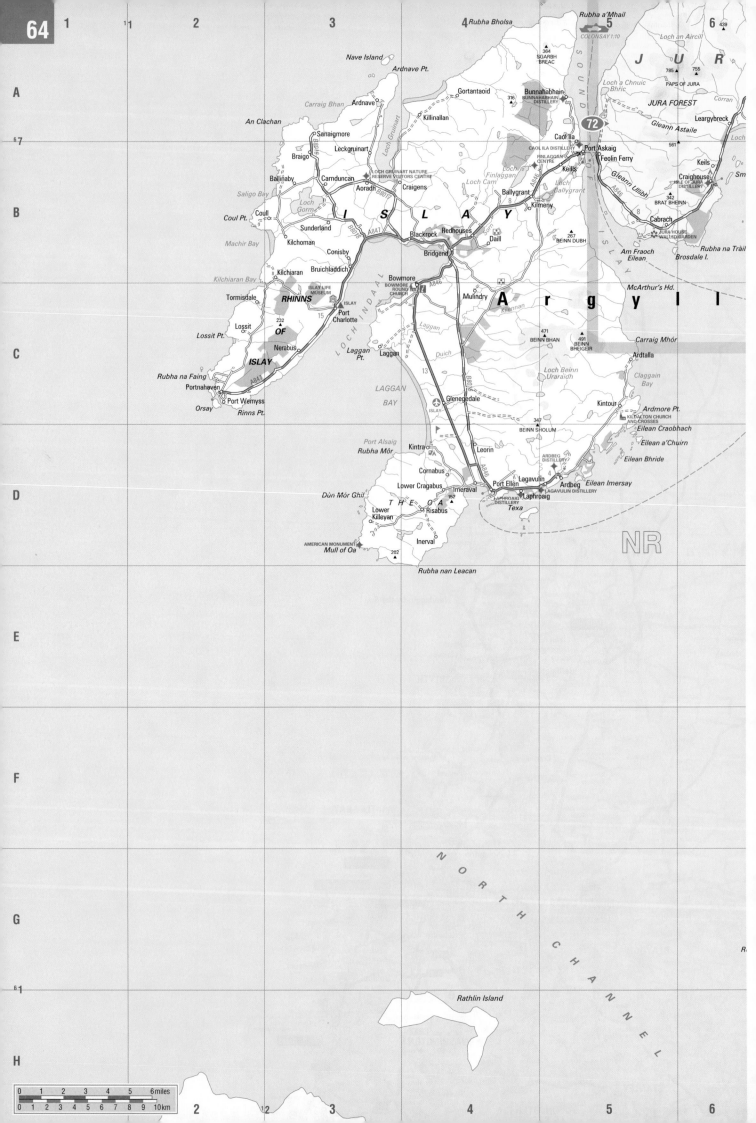

1   1   2   3   4 Rubha Bholsa   Rubha a'Mhail   5   6 439

COLONSAY 1:10

Loch an Aircill

J U R

Nave Island

364
SGARBH
BREAC

785   755
PAPS OF JURA

Loch a Chnuic
Bhric

JURA FOREST

A

Ardnave Pt.

Gortantaoid

Bunnahabhain
BUNNAHABHAIN
DISTILLERY

316

Corran

Leargybreck

Carraig Bhan

Ardnave

Killinallan

Gleann Astaile

561

An Clachan

7

Caol Ila

Keils

Sanaigmore

Leckgruinart

CAOL ILA DISTILLERY

Port Askaig

Feolin Ferry

Craighouse

Braigo

FINLAGGAN
CENTRE

Keills

ISLE OF JURA
DISTILLERY

Loch Gruinart

Loch
Finlaggan

Gleann Ullibh

342
BRAT BHEINN

Ballinaby

Carnduncan

LOCH GRUINART NATURE
RESERVE VISITORS CENTRE

Loch Cam

Ballygrant

B

Aoradh

Craigens

Ballygrant

Kilmeny

JURA HOUSE
WALLED GARDEN

Cabrach

Saligo Bay

I S L A Y

Blackrock

Redhouses

267
BEINN DUBH

Am Fraoch
Eilean

Rubha na Tràill

Coul Pt.

Coull

Loch
Gorm

Daill

Brosdale I.

Machir Bay

Sunderland

Bridgend

Kilchoman

Conisby

Bowmore

C

Bruichladdich

BOWMORE
ROUND CHURCH

Mulindry

A r g y l l

McArthur's Hd.

Kilchiaran Bay

Kilchiaran

ISLAY LIFE
MUSEUM

Carraig Mhór

Tormisdale

RHINNS

ISLAY

Kilennan

471
BEINN BHAN

Ardtalla

Lossit

Lossit Pt.

232

Port
Charlotte

15

Laggan
Pt.

Laggan

Duich

491
BEINN
BHEIGEIR

Loch Beinn
Uraraidh

Claggain
Bay

Nerabus

OF

13

ISLAY

Rubha na Faing

LAGGAN

Kintour

Ardmore Pt.

Portnahaven

Port Wemyss

BAY

Glenegedale

KILDALTON CHURCH
AND CROSSES

Orsay

Rinns Pt.

ISLAY

Eilean Craobhach

D

Port Alsaig
Rubha Mòr

Kintra

Leorin

347
BEINN SHOLUM

ARDBEG
DISTILLERY

Eilean a'Chuirn

Dùn Mòr Ghil

Cornabus

Imeraval

Port Ellen

Lagavulin

Eilean Bhride

THE OA

152

Lower Cragabus

LAGAVULIN DISTILLERY

Eilean Imersay

Lower
Killeyan

Risabus

Texa

Ardbeg

Laphroaig

LAPHROAIG
DISTILLERY

Inerval

NR

AMERICAN MONUMENT
Mull of Oa

202

Rubha nan Leacan

E

F

N O R T H

G

C H A N N E L

1

Rathlin Island

H

2   2   3   4   5   6

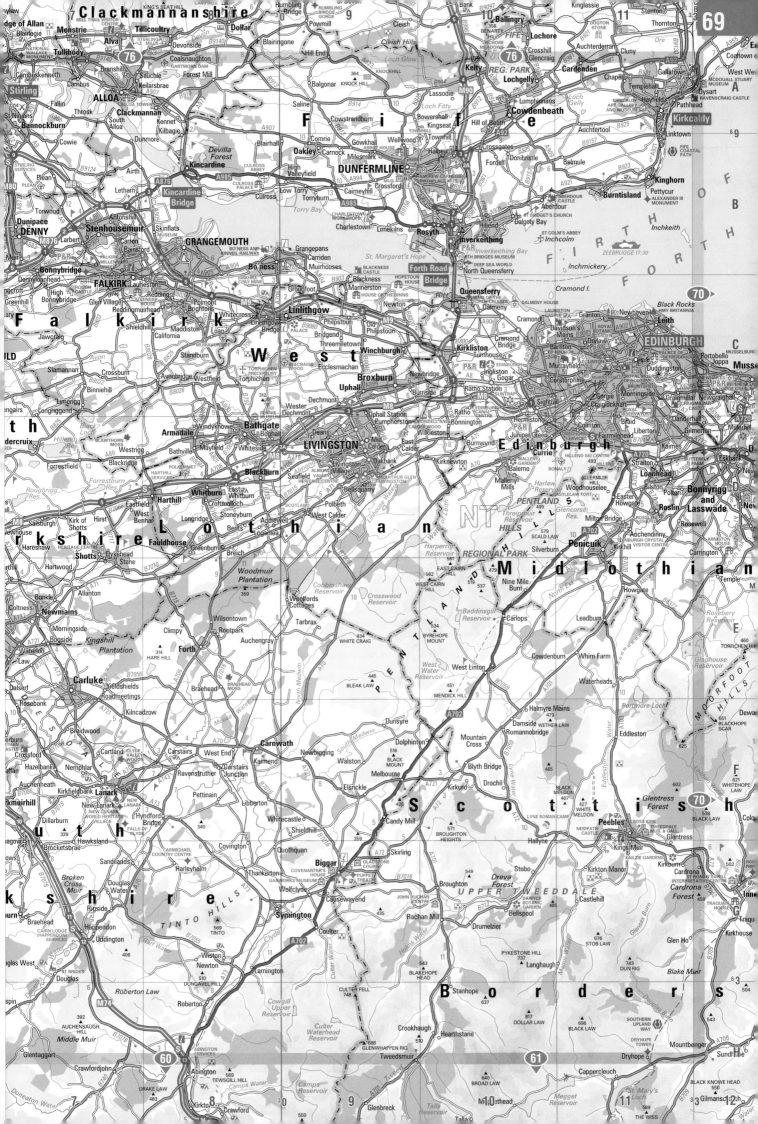

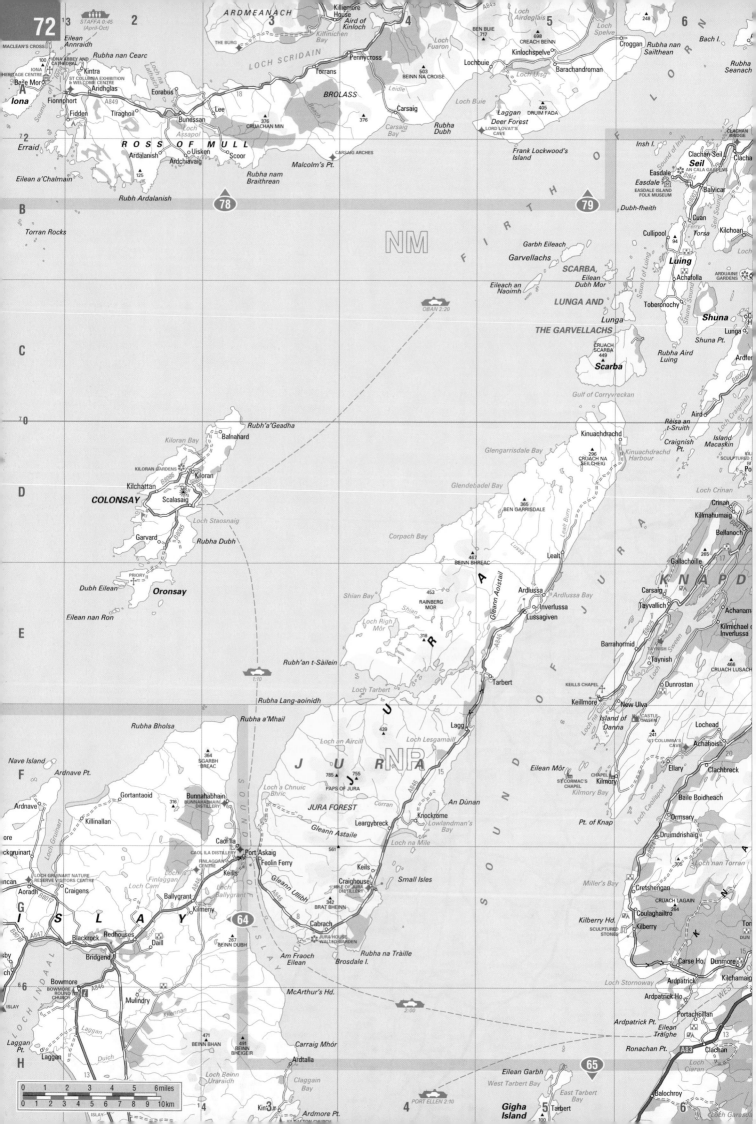

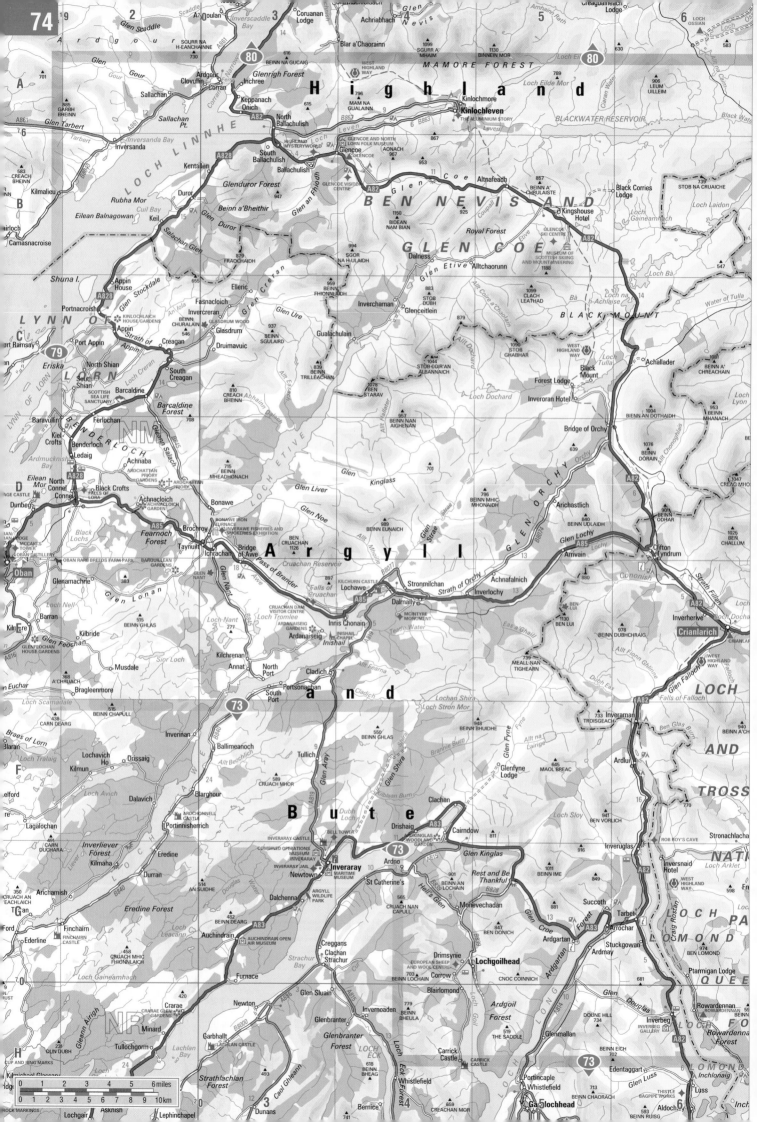

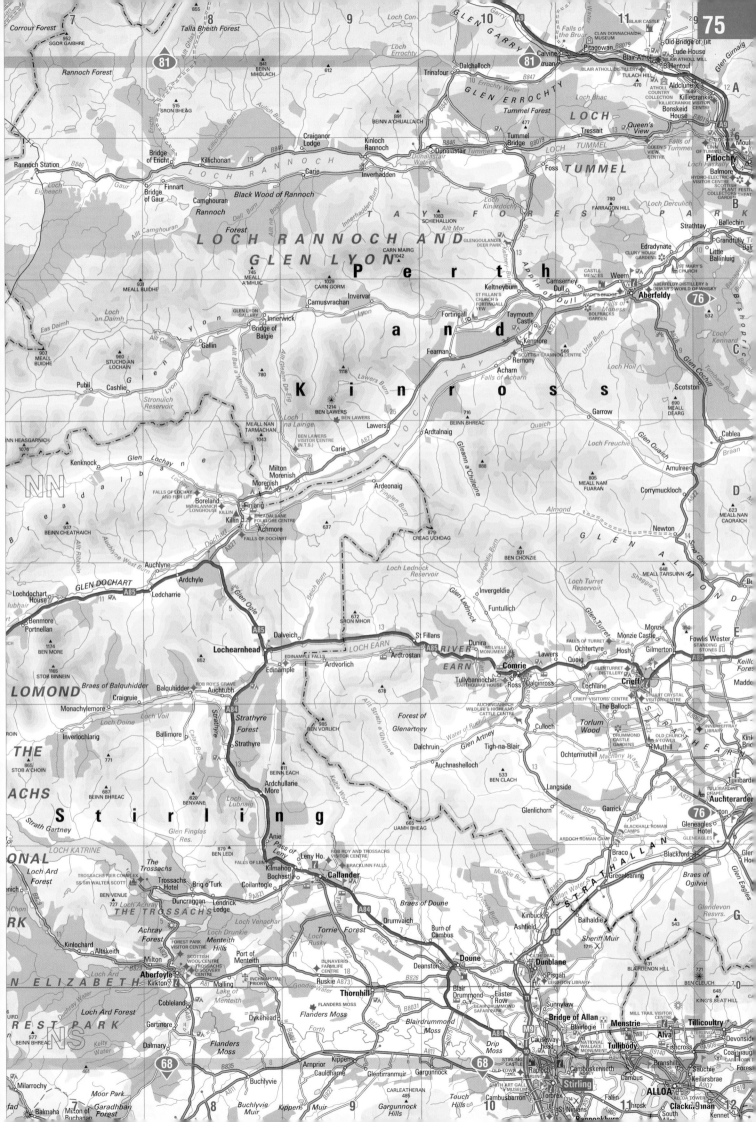

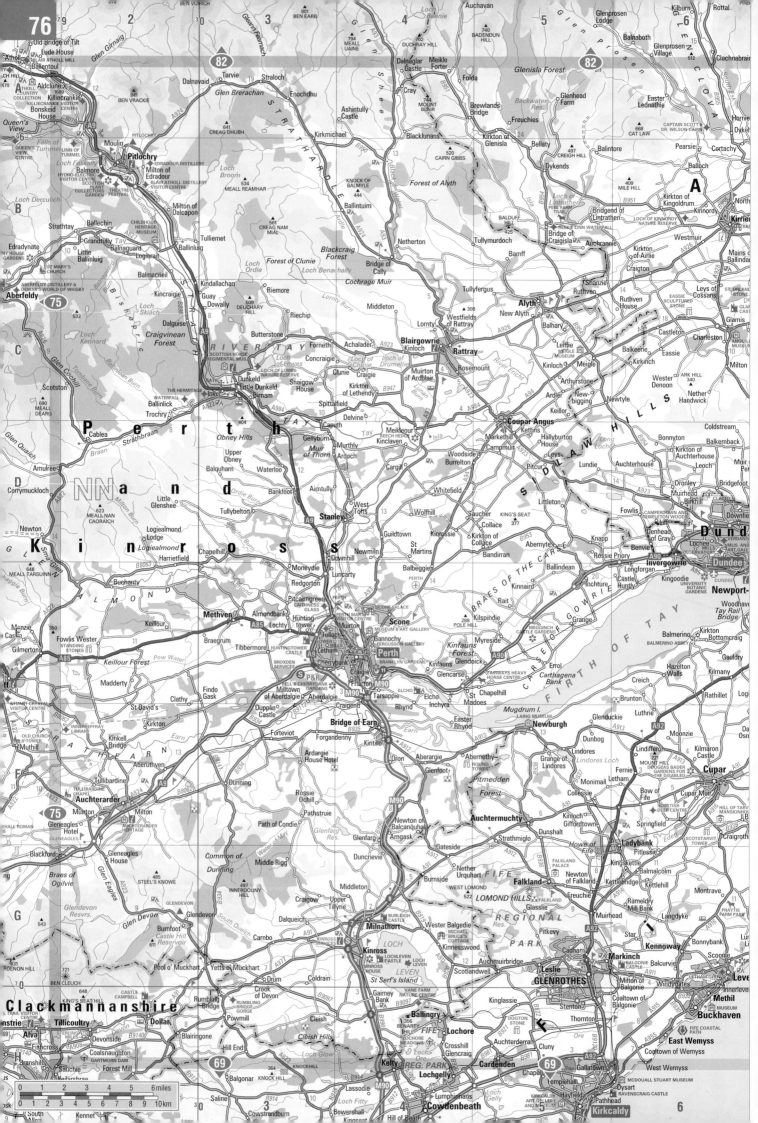

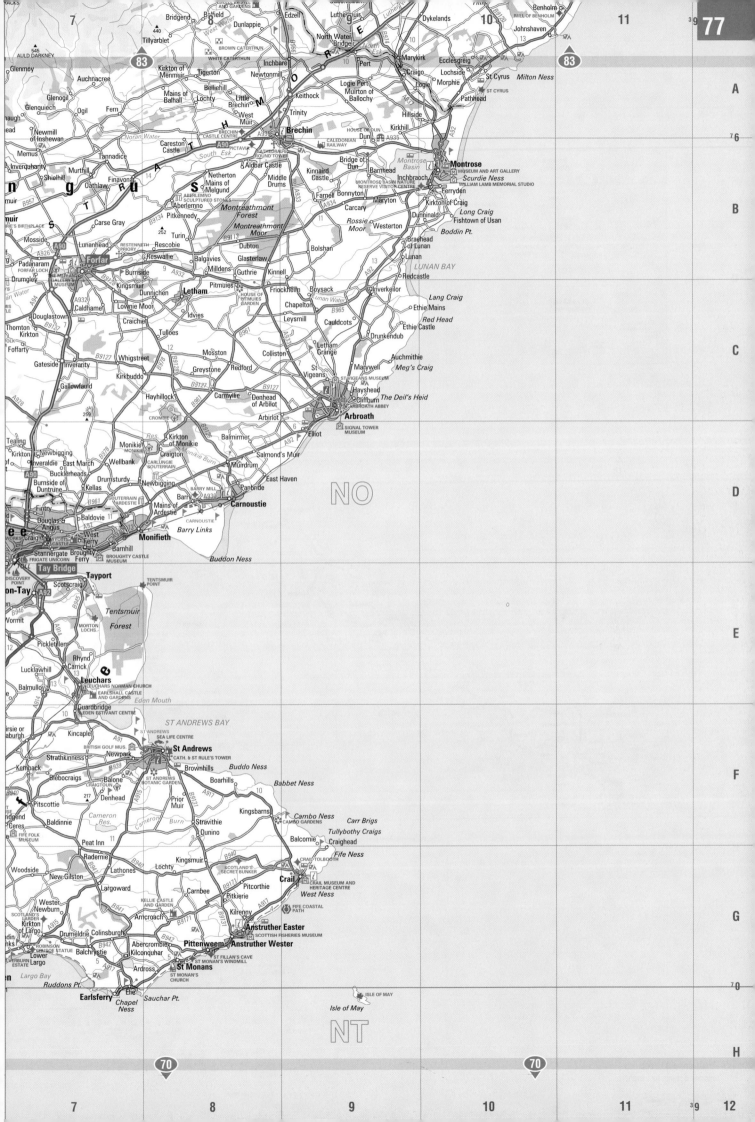

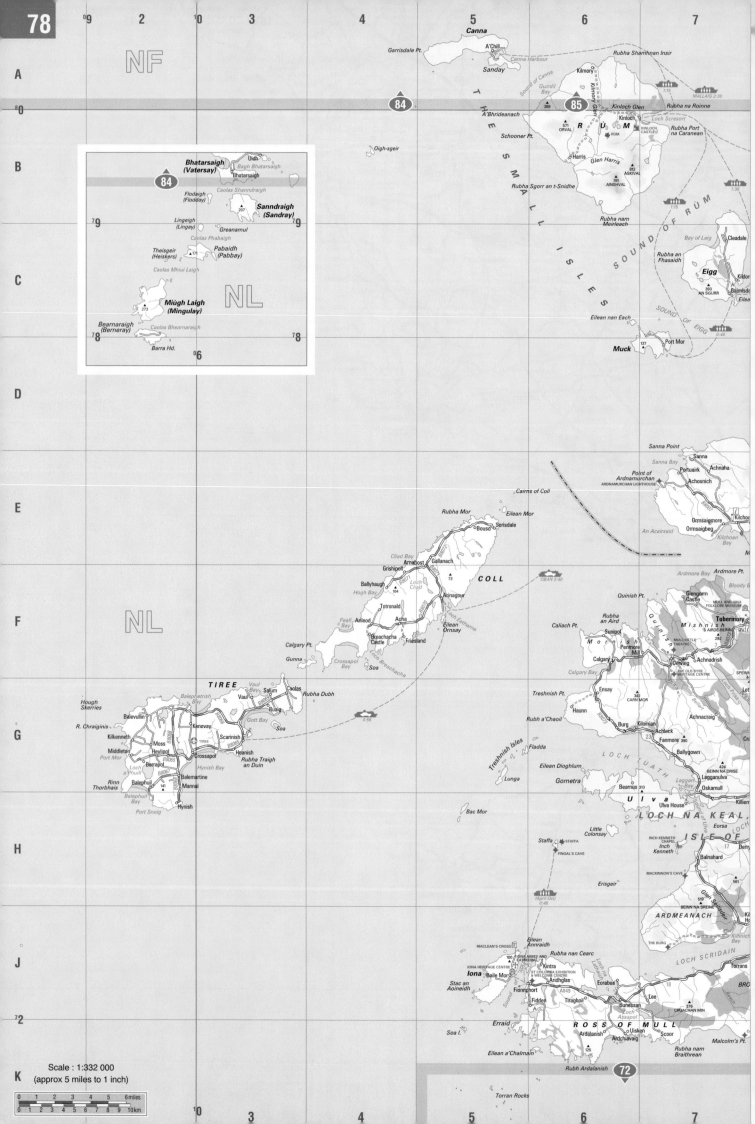

Scale : 1:332 000
(approx 5 miles to 1 inch)

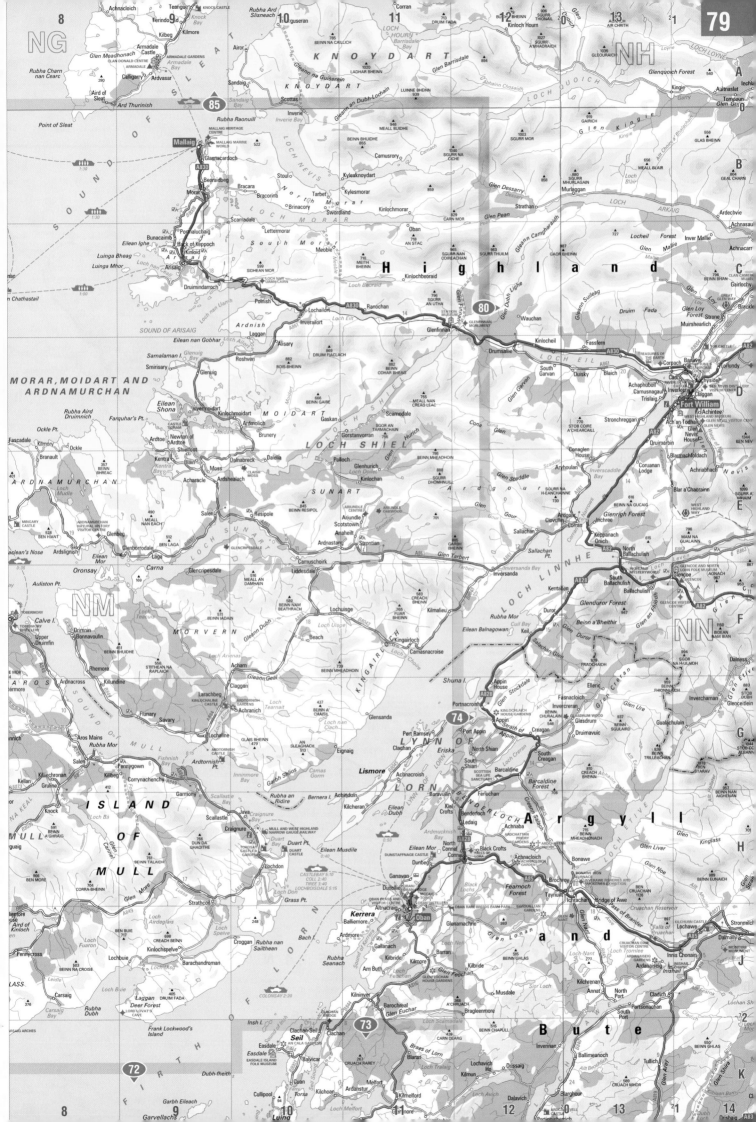

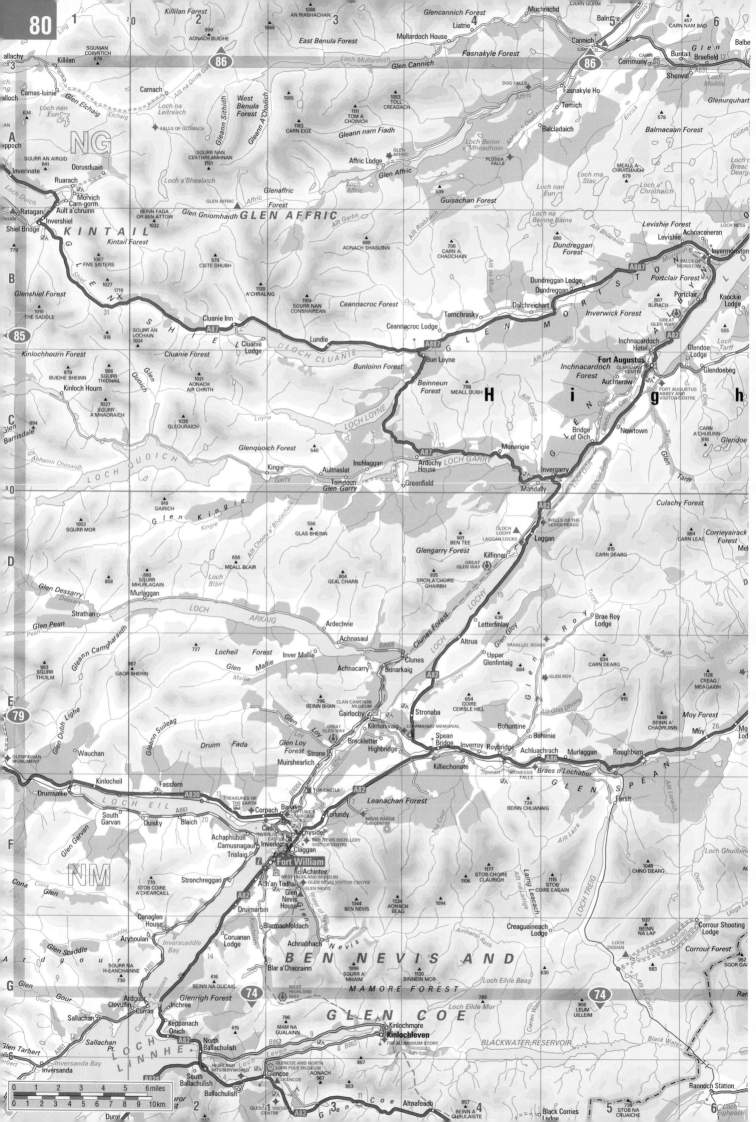

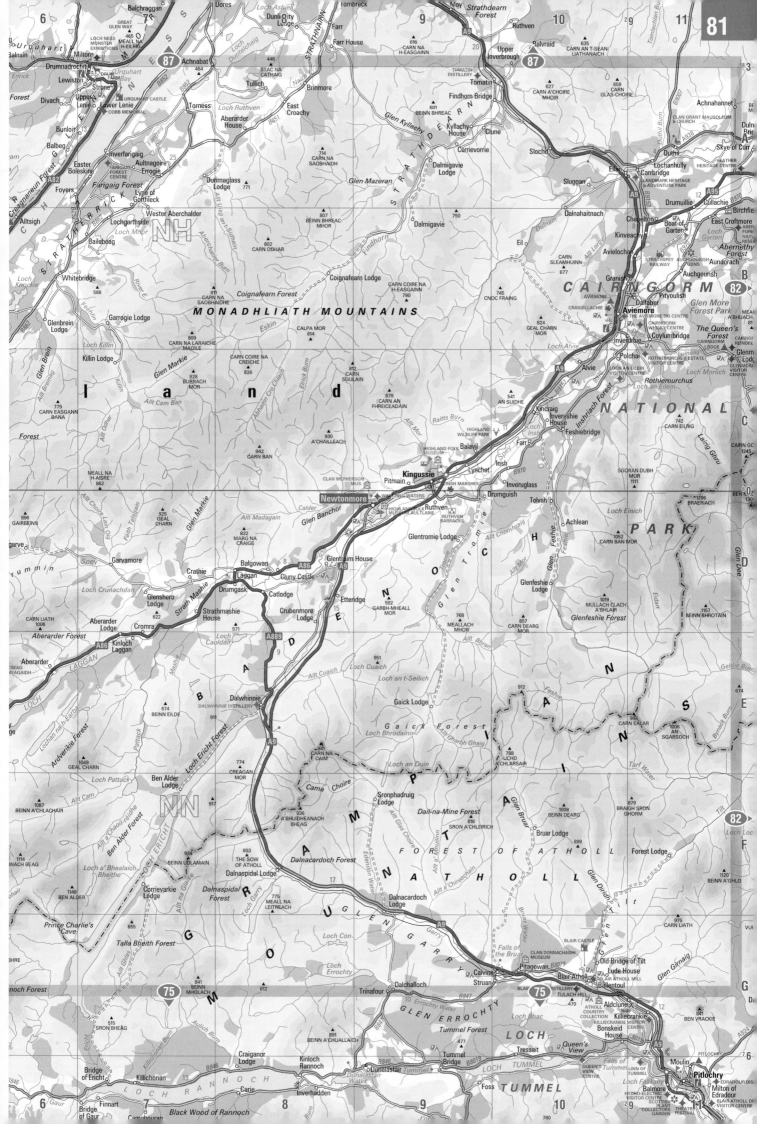

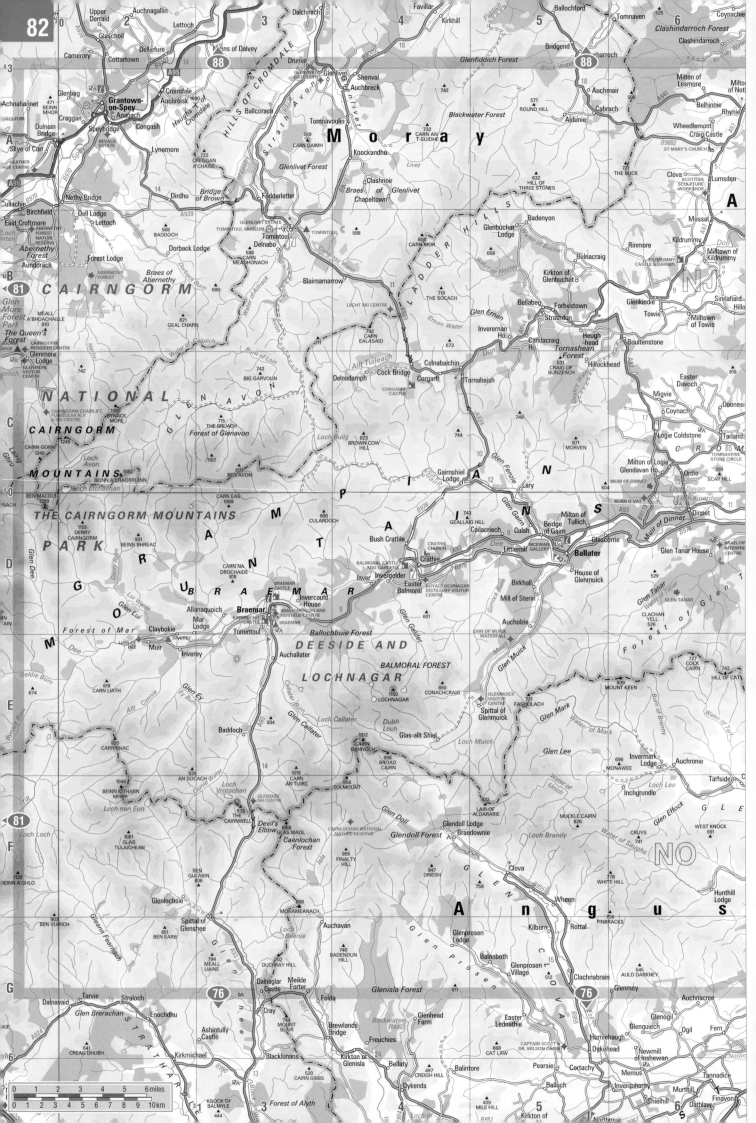

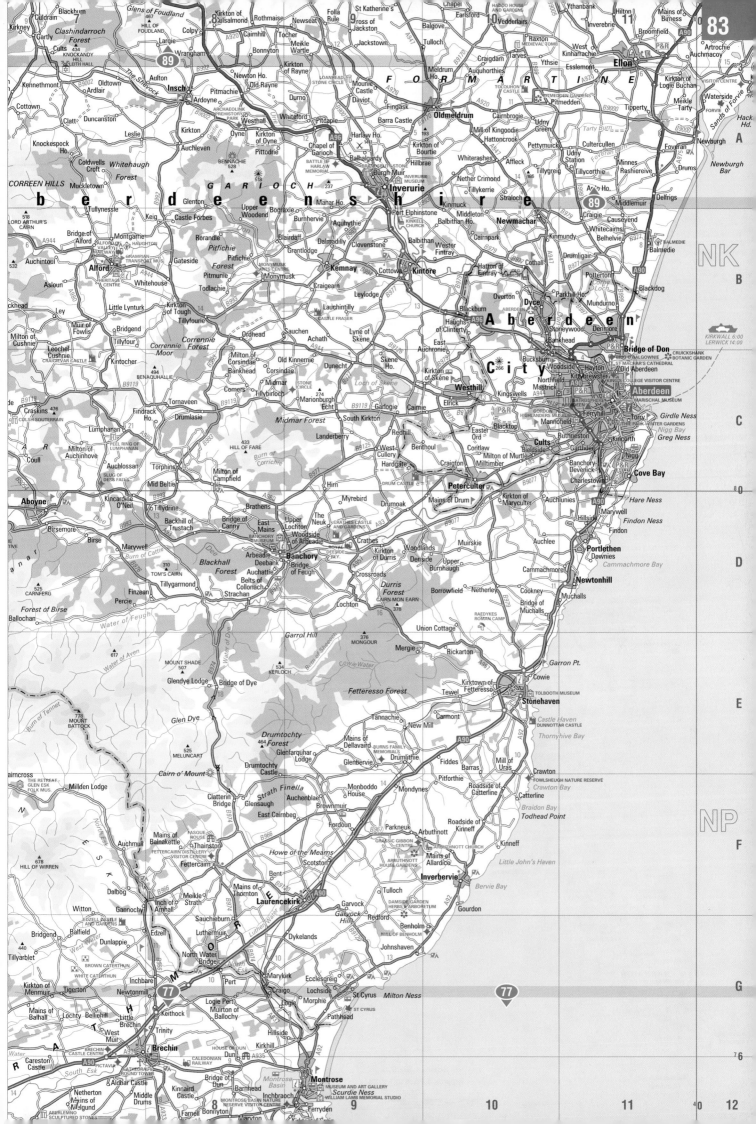

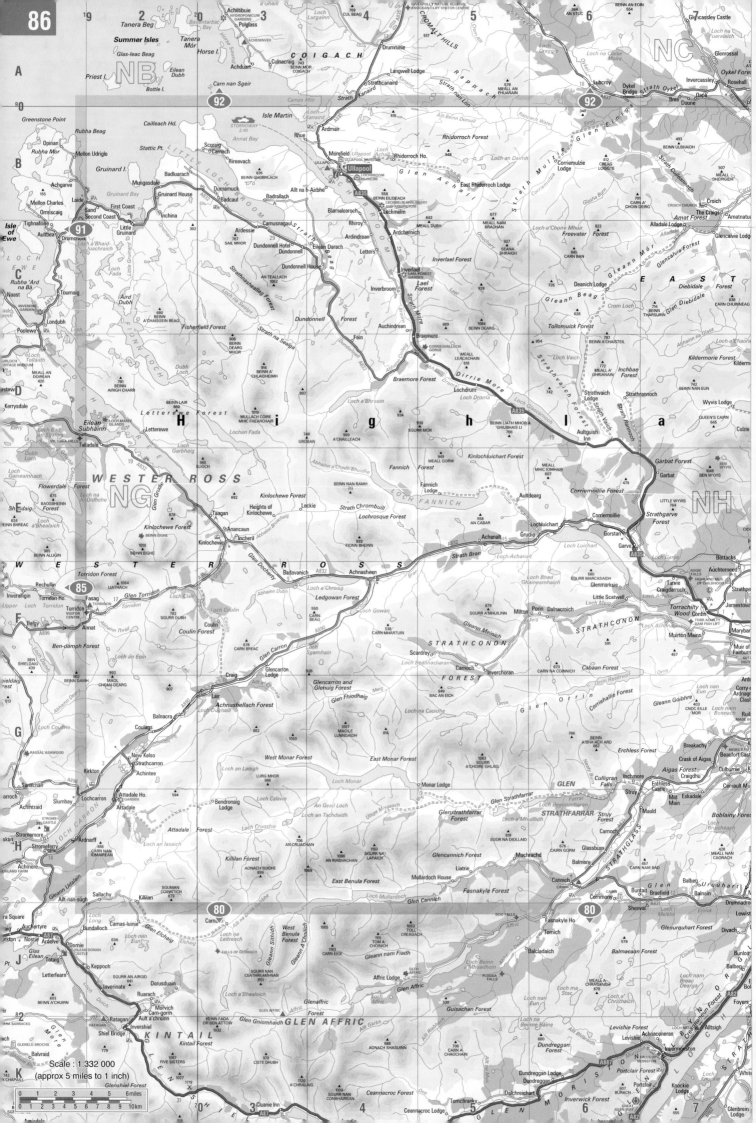

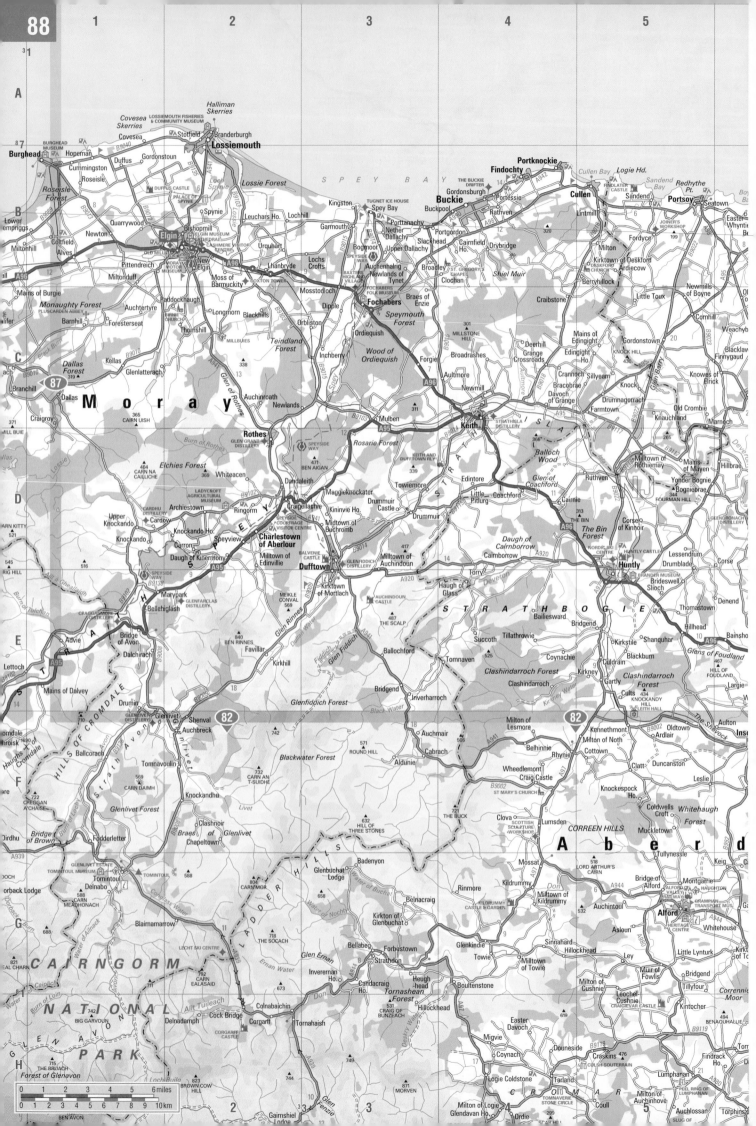

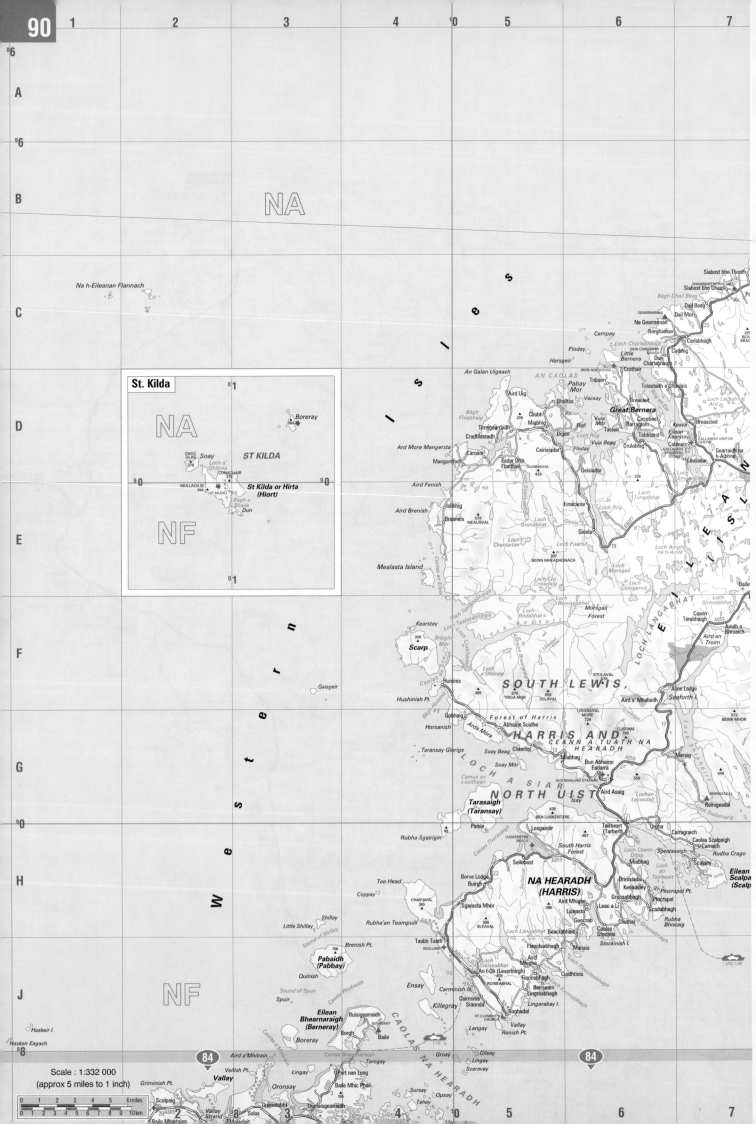

St. Kilda

NA

NF

ST KILDA

Boreray

CNOC GLAS
Soay
Loch a' Ghlinne
CONACHAIR
MULLACH BI
ST KILDA
St Kilda or Hirta (Hiort)
Bàgh a Bhaile
Dun

NA

W e s t e r n

I s l e s

Na h-Eileanan Flannach

Siabost bho Thuath
Siabost bho Dheas
SHAWBOST NORSE MILL
Bàgh Dhail Beag
Dail Beag
GEARRANNAN
Na Gearrannan
Dail Mor
Borghastan
Carlabhagh
Loch Chàrlabhaigh
DUN CARLOWAY BROCH
Little Bernera
Crothair
Cirbhig
BEINN BRAG
261

Campay
Floday
Harsgeir
AN CAOLAS
IRON AGE HOUSE
Pabay Mor
Tobson
Breacleit
Great Bernera
Loch Lacasaidh Ard

An Galan Uigeach
Aird Uig
Cliobh
Miabhig
Riof
Bhaltos
Vacsay
Uig
Barraglom
Circebost
Vuia Mor
Tacleit
Keava
Eilean Kearstay
Tobhtarol
Linsiadar
Breascleit
Calanais
CALLANISH VISITOR CENTRE
CALLANISH STANDING STONES
Gearraidh na h-Aibhne

Ard More Mangersta
Timsgearraidh
Cradhlastadh
Càrnais
Eadar Dha Fhadhail
Loch Ròg
Vuia Beag
Crulabhig
Floday
Cairisiadar
Geisiadar
256

Aird Fenish
Mangurstadh
Islibhig
SUAINAVAL
429
Einacleite
Loch Ròg
Loch Tungabhat
Loch Smuaiseabh

Aird Brenish
Brunnais
574
MEALISVAL
Loch Grunabhat
Giosla
Giosla
B8011
19
Loch Fuaroil

Mealasta Island
Loch Chaolartan
BEINN MHEADHONACH
397
Loch Morsgail
Loch Airigh na h-Airde
Baile

Loch Cro Croisaig
Loch Bòdabhat
Morsgail Forest
Loch Coingerod
Loch Strandabhat
A859
Ceann Tàrabhaigh
Airidh an Bhruaich
A859
Aird an Troim

Kearstay
Bràighe Mor
Loch Tealasabhaigh
Loch Tarbhabhaigh
Loch Beiniseabhat
308
Loch a'Ghlinne
Scarp
Huisinis
Bàgh Huisinis
489
STULAVAL
679
TIRGA MOR
ULLAVAL
Aird a'Mhulaidh
Aline Lodge
Seaforth I.
S O U T H   L E W I S
572
BEINN MHOR

Hushinish Pt.
Gobhaig
Horsanish
Arda Mora
Forest of Harris
Abhainn Suidhe
UISGNAVAL MORE
729
CLISHAM
799
A859
449

Gaisgeir

Taransay Glorigs
Soay Beag
Cliasmol
13
H A R R I S   A N D
CEANN A TUATH NA HEARADH
Maraig
Loch Seaforth
559
REINIGEADAL

Miabhag
Bun Abhainn Eadarra
OLD WHALING STATION
L O C H   A   S I A R
Camus an t-suithean
Aird Asaig
Isay
3
Lochan Lacasdail
REINIGEADAL

Tarasaigh (Taransay)
N O R T H   U I S T
BEN LUSKENTYRE
436
Loch Trollamarig

Rubha Sgeirigin
99
Paible
Losgaintir
467
Tairbeart (Tarbert)
Urgha
Carragraich
Caolas Scalpaigh
Carnach
Rudha Crago

LUSKENTYRE BEACH
South Harris Forest
Loch Ceann Dibig
Miabhag
Loch an Tairbeart
Spestasaigh
Scalpay

Seilebost
A859
Drinisiadar
Plocropol Pt.
Eilean Scalpa (Scalp)

Toe Head
Borve Lodge
Buirgh
23
N A   H E A R A D H   (H A R R I S)
Aird Mhighe
Kennacley
Greosabhagh
Leac a Li
Plocrapol
Scadabhagh

Coppay
CHAIPAVAL
365
Sgarasta Mhor
Liceasto
386
Geocrab
Caolas Stochnis
Rubha Bhocaig

Little Shillay
Shillay
Rubha'an Teampuill
398
BLEAVAL
Loch Langabhat
Beacrabhaic
Stockinish I.

Sound of Shillay
Brenish Pt.
Taobh Tuath
SEALLAMM
Fleodabhagh
Manais

196
Pabaidh (Pabbay)
Quinish
Loch Steiseabhat
Aird Mhighe
Bolrseam
Cuidhtinis
UIG 1:46

Sound of Spuir
Spuir
Ensay
An t-Ob (Leverburgh)
459
ROINEABHAL
Fionnsbhagh

NF
Eilean Bhearnaraigh (Berneray)
Ruisigearraidh
Carminish Is.
Cairminis
Srannda
Killegray
ST CLEMENT'S CHURCH
Roghadal
Lingarabay I.

Haskeir I.
Borgh
BERNERAY
Baile
Langay
Valllay
Renish Pt.

Haskeir Eagach

Aird a'Mhòrain
Torogay
Gilsay
Groay
Lingay
Scaravay

Griminish Pt.
Veilish Pt.
Lingay
Port nan Long
Opsay
Sursay
Tahay

Scale : 1:332 000
(approx 5 miles to 1 inch)

Scolpaig
Valllay Strand
Oronsay
Greinetobht
Baile Mhic Phail
Solas
Malaclit

0 1 2 3 4 5 6 miles
0 1 2 3 4 5 6 7 8 9 10km

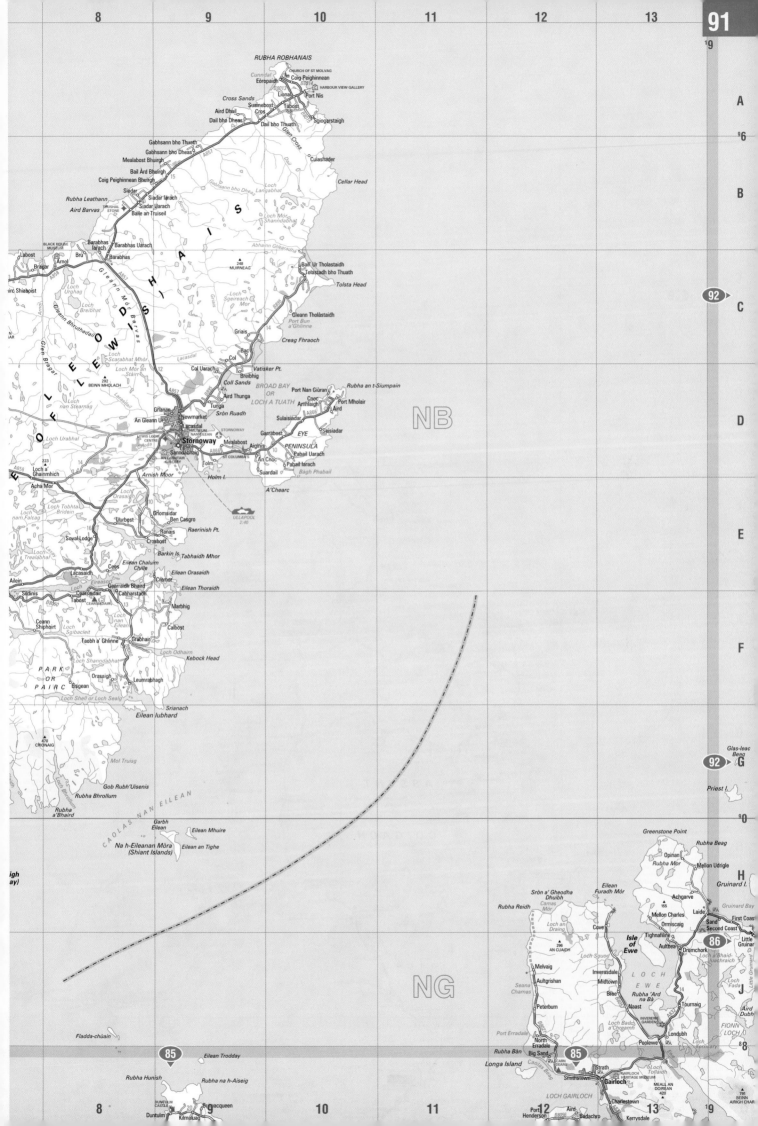

RUBHA ROBHANAIS
CHURCH OF ST MOLVAG
Cunndal
Eòropaidh
Coig Peighinnean
Lional
Port Nis
HARBOUR VIEW GALLERY
Cross Sands
Suainebost
Tabost
Aird Dhail
Cros
Sgiogarstaigh
Dail bho Dheas
Dail bho Thuath

Gabhsann bho Thuath
Gabhsann bho Dheas
A857
Glen Cross
Mealabost Bhuirgh
Cuiashader
Bail Àrd Bhuirgh
Coig Peighinnean Bhuirgh
Cellar Head
Siadar
15
Rubha Leathann
Siadar Ìarach
TRUSHAL STONE
Siadar Uarach
Aird Barvas
Baile an Truiseil
Loch Mòr Shanndabhat

L E W I S

Barabhas Ìarach
Abhainn Ghearadha
BLACK HOUSE MUSEUM
Barabhas Uarach
Labost
Brù
Barabhas
Bail Ur Tholastaidh
248
MUIRNEAG
Tolastadh bho Thuath
Bragar
Arnol
A858
Loch Sgeireach Mòr
Tolsta Head
Loch Urghag
Loch Breibhat
Port Bun a'Ghlinne
Gleann Tholàstaidh
Airc Shiaboist
Loch Scarabhat Mhòr
Loch Mòr an Stàirr
Griais
14
Creag Fhraoch
Loch nan Stearnag
292
BEINN MHOLACH
Lacasdal
Griais
12
Bac
Gleann Bhruthadail
Col
Col Uarach
Vatisker Pt.
Breibhig
Glen Bragar
A857
B895
Coll Sands
Rubha an t-Siumpain
Loch a' Ghainmhich
Loch Urabhal
Grianan
Aird Thunga
BROAD BAY OR LOCH A TUATH
Port Nan Giùran
223
Newmarket
Tunga
Cnoc
Amhlaigh
Port Mholair
An Gleann Ur
Sròn Ruadh
A866
Aird
Acha Mòr
14
Sulaisiadar
Seisiadar
Lacasaidh
A859
LEWIS LOOM CENTRE
STORNOWAY
MUSEUM NAN EILEAN
Garrabost
EYE
Arnish Moor
Sanndabhaig
Mealabost
Aiglinis
PENINSULA
Loch Tobhta Bridein
Griomsidar
Ben Casgro
Tolm
Pabail Uarach
Loch Orasaigh
St COLUMBA'S
An Cnoc
Pabail Ìarach
Llurbost
ST COLUMBA'S
Suardail
Bàgh Phabail
16
Ranais
Holm I.
A'Chearc
Soval Lodge
Crosbost
ULLAPOOL 2:40
Barkin Is. Tabhaidh Mhor
Eilean Chalum Chille
Ailein
Cees
Eilean Orasaidh
Sildinis
Gearraidh Bhaird
Crìomor
Cabharstadh
Eilean Thoraidh
Tabost
13
CEARSIADAIR
Marbhig
Ceann Shiphairt
Loch nan Eilean
Calbost
Loch Sgibacleit
Taobh a' Ghlinne
Grabhair
Loch Shanndabhat
Kebock Head
Loch Odhairn
P A R K
Leumrabhagh
O R
Orasaigh
P A I R C
Eisgean
Loch Shell or Loch Sealg
Srianach
Eilean Iubhard

470
CRIONAIG
Mol Truisg
Caolas Nan Eilean
Gob Rubh'Uisenis
Rubha Bhrollum
Garbh Eilean
Rubha a'Bhaird
Eilean Mhuire
Na h-Eileanan Mòra (Shiant Islands)
Eilean an Tighe

igh ay)

Greenstone Point
Rubha Beag
Opinan
Rubha Mòr
Mellon Udrigle
Gruinard I.
Sròn a' Gheodha Dhuibh
Eilean Furadh Mòr
Achgarve
155
Rubha Reidh
Camas Mòr
Mellon Charles
Gruinard Bay
Loch an Draing
Cove
Ormiscaig
Laide
Sand
First Coast
Isle of Ewe
Tighnafiline
Second Coast
Loch a'Bhaid-luachraich
Melvaig
Aultbea
Drumchork
Inverasdale
Midtown
L O C H
Aultgrishan
Brae
E W E
Seana Chamas
Naast
Rubha 'Ard na Bà
Tournaig
FIONN LOCH
Peterburn
INVEREWE GARDENS
14
Port Erradale
Loch Badan a'Chreamh
Aird Dubh
North Erradale
Londubh
Loch Fada
Rubha Bàn
Big Sand
Poolewe
Loch Kernsary

Eilean Trodday
Fladda-chùain
GAIRLOCH HERITAGE MUSEUM
Strath
Rubha Hunish
Smithstown
Gairloch
Rubha na h-Aiseig
Longa Island
Loch Tollaidh
DUNTULM CASTLE
MEALL AN DOIREAN
420
Bigmacqueen
LOCH GAIRLOCH
791
BEINN AIRIGH CHAR
Duntulm
Kilmaluag
Port Henderson
Aird
Charlestown
Badachro
Kerrysdale

NB

NG

92

92

86

Glas-leac Beag

Priest I.

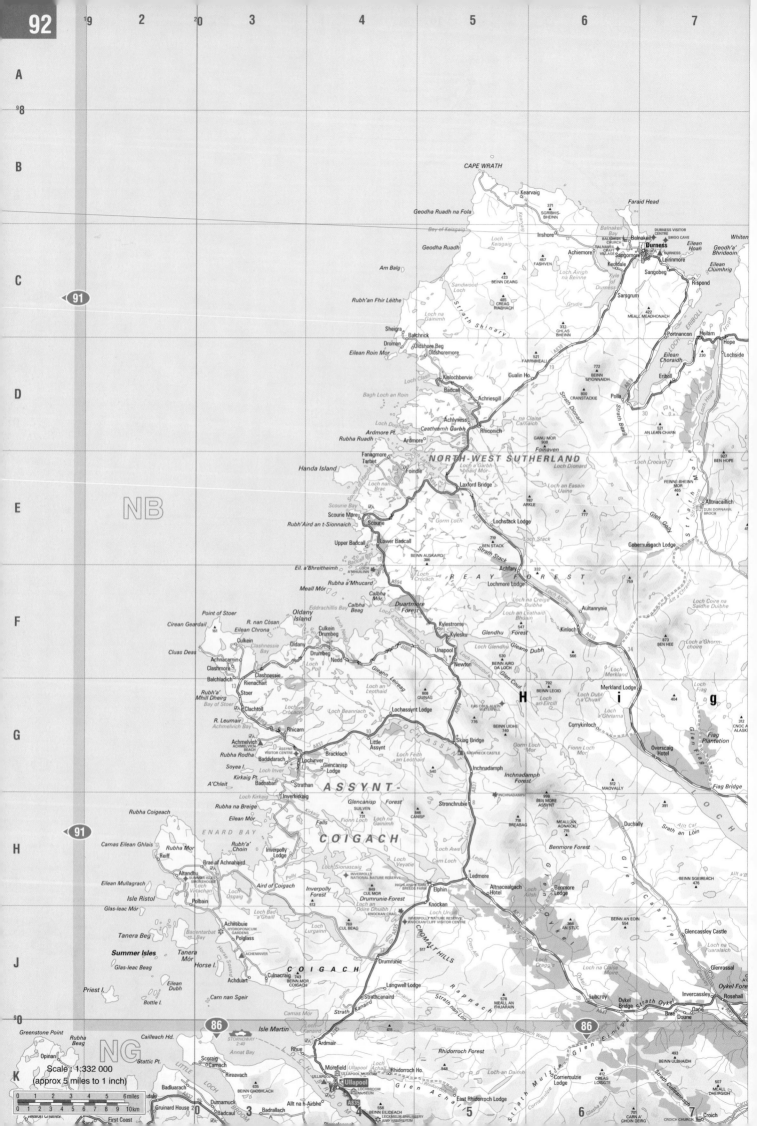

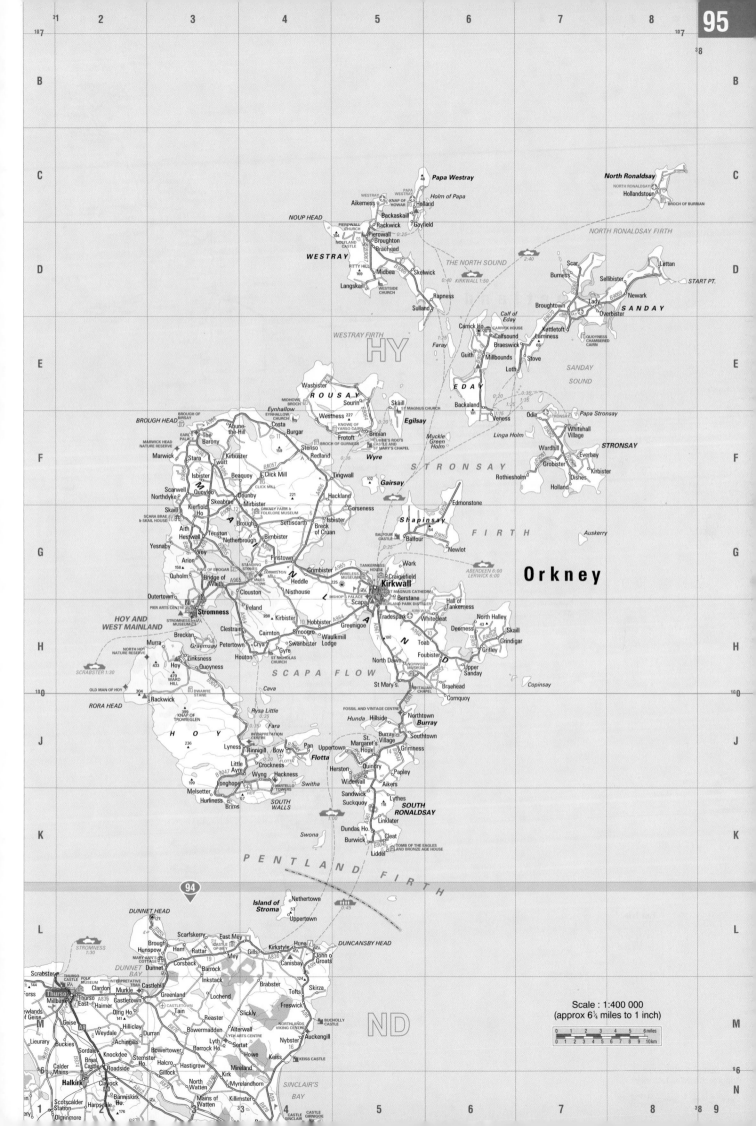

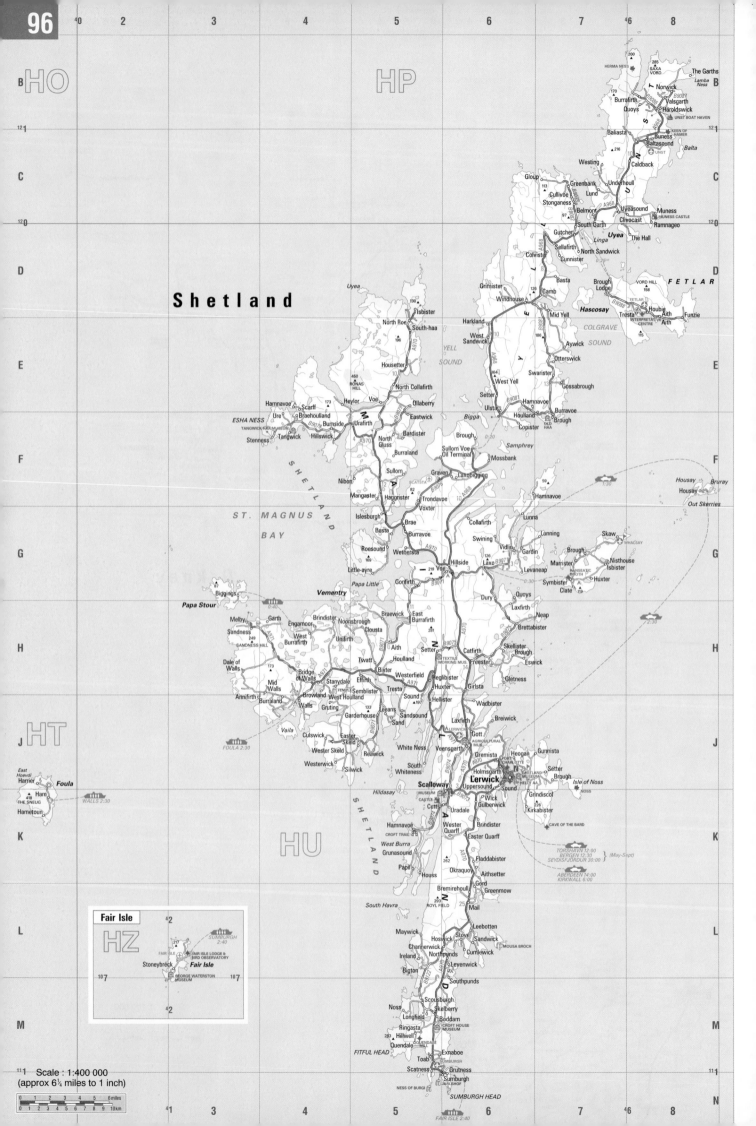

Key to Town Plan Symbols

Symbol	Description	Symbol	Description
	Motorway		Shopping Streets
	Primary Route Dual/Single		Railway
	Main Road Dual/Single	City Hall	Tramway with Station
	Secondary Road Dual/Single		Railway/Bus Station
	Minor Through Road/One Way Street		Shopping Precinct/Retail Park
	Pedestrian Roads		Park

✝	Abbey/Cathedral		Railway Station
	Ancient Monument		Roman Antiquity
	Aquarium		Safari Park
G	Art Gallery		Shopmobility
	Bird Garden		Theatre
	Building of Public Interest	i	Tourist Information Centre (open all year)
	Castle	i	Tourist Information Centre (open summer only)
	Church of interest		Zoo
	Cinema	Bank West St	Underground/Metro Station
	Garden		
	Historic Ship	H	Hospital
	House	P	Parking
	House & Garden		Police
	Museum	PO	Post Office
	Preserved Railway	▲	Youth Hostel

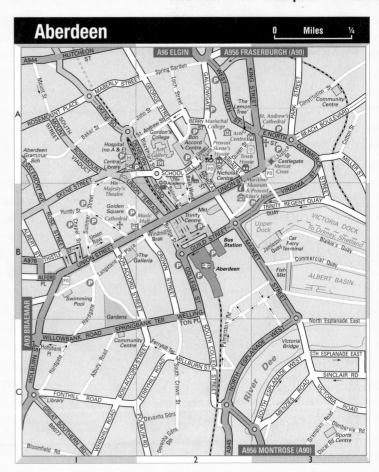

Aberdeen

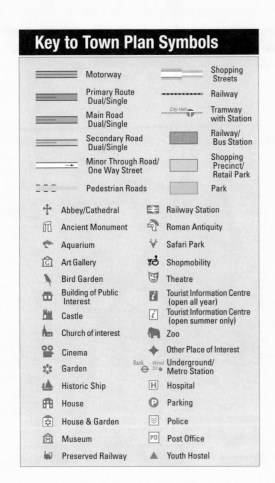

Bath

Blackpool

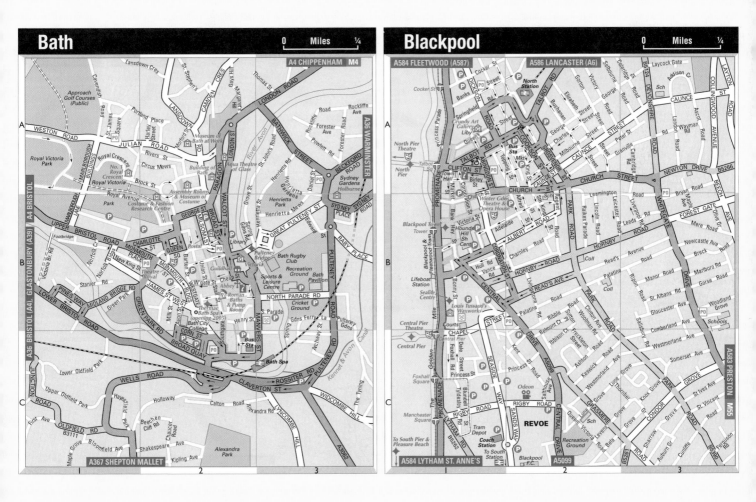

Birmingham

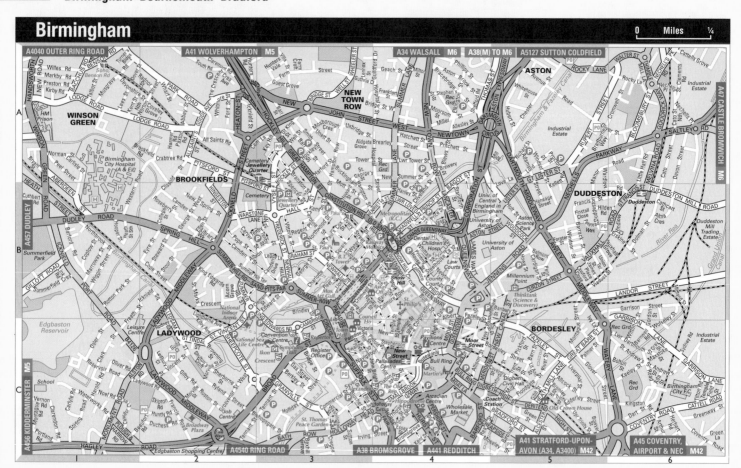

Bournemouth

Bradford

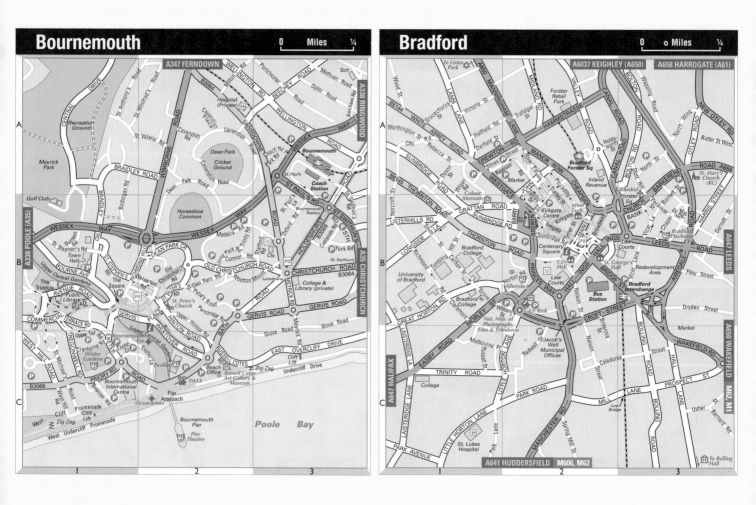

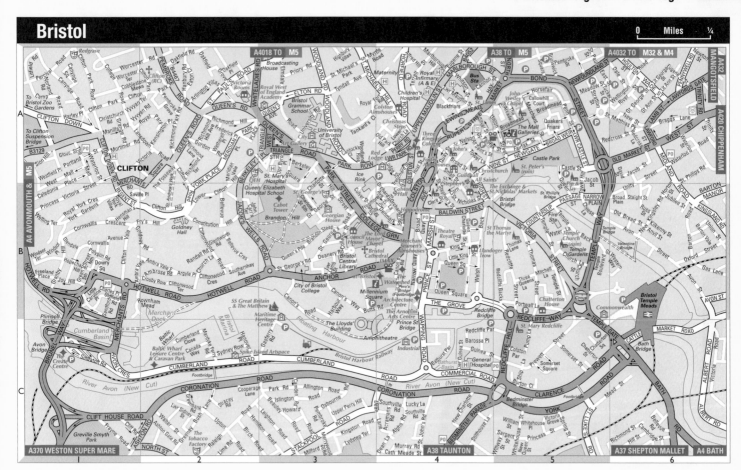

Bristol

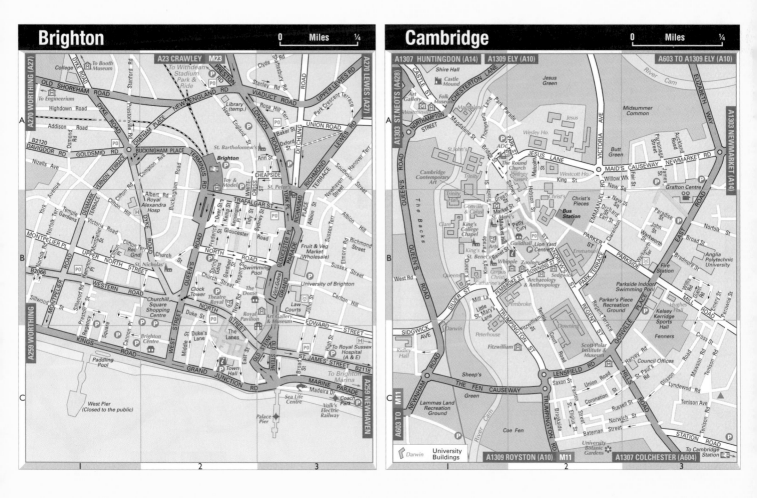

Brighton

Cambridge

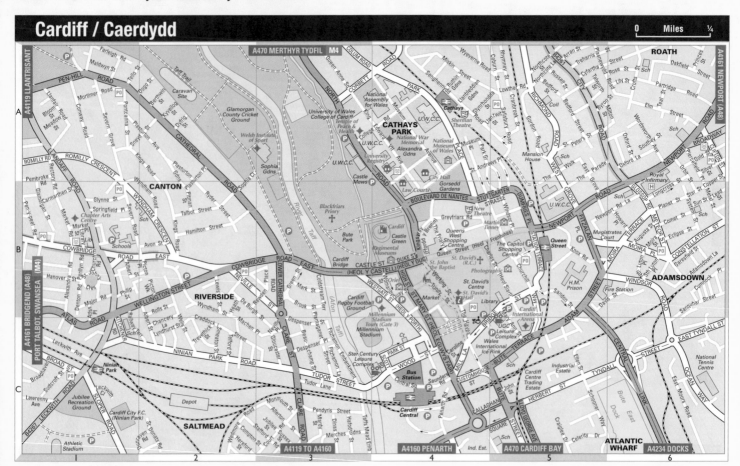

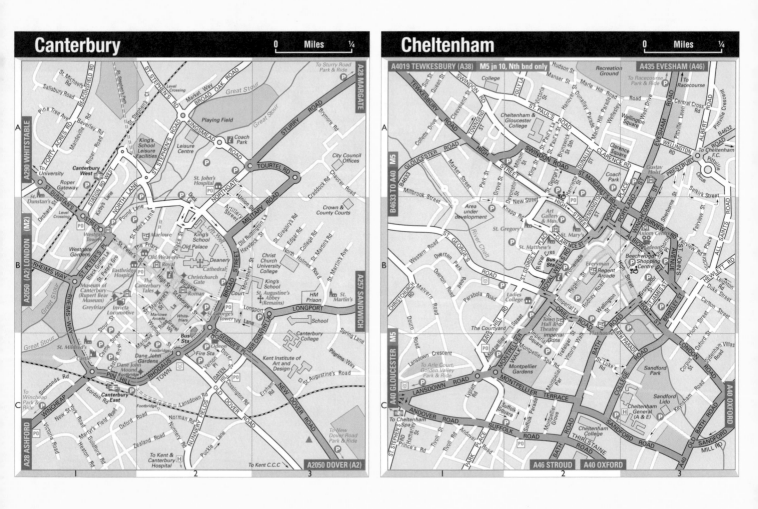

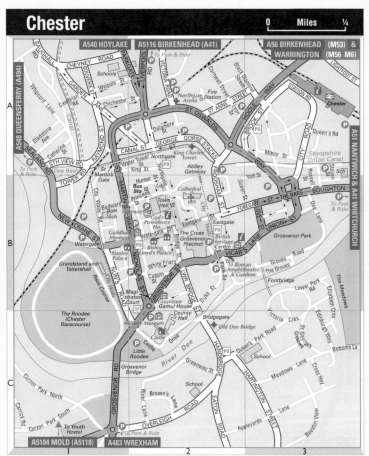

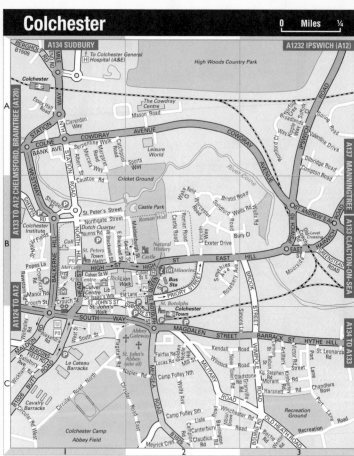

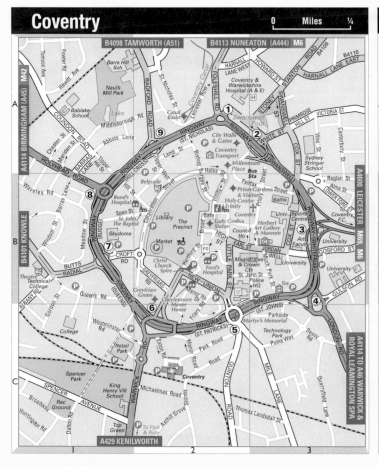

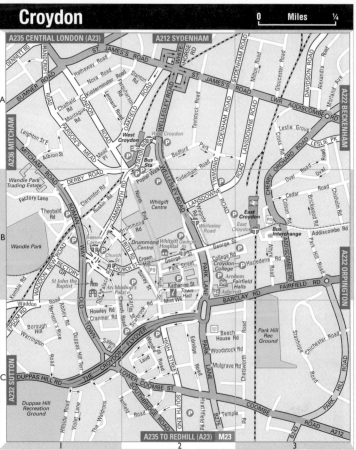

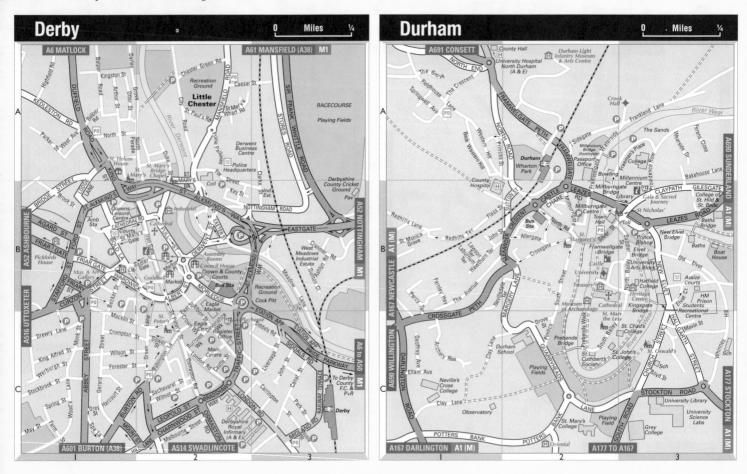

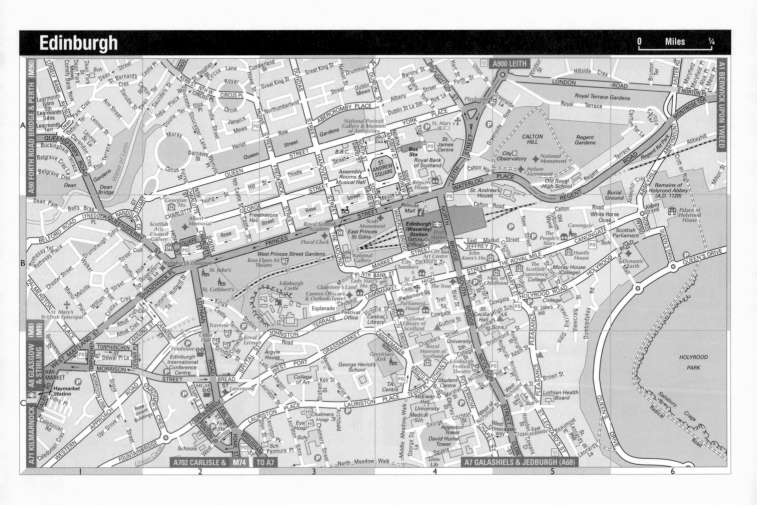

Exeter

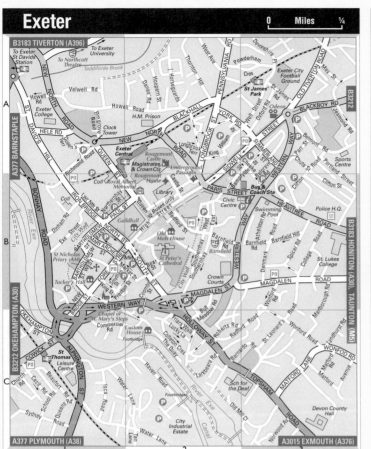

Gloucester

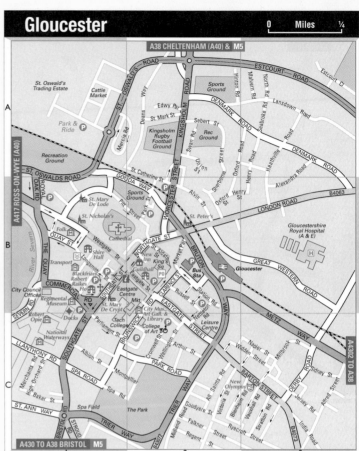

Glasgow

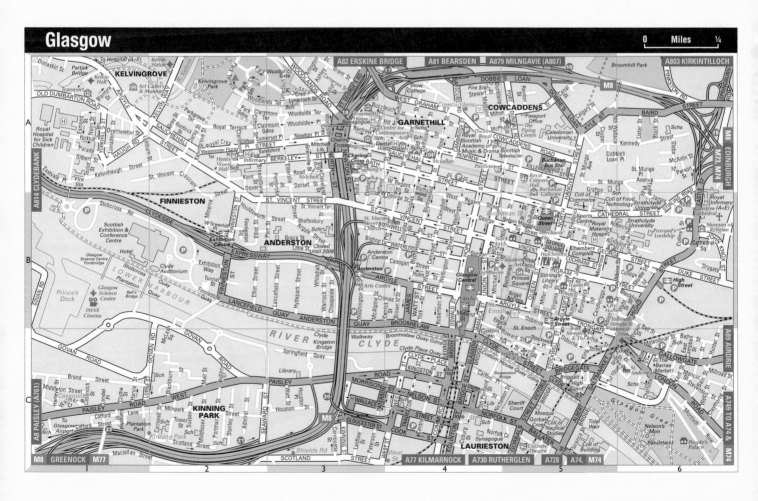

Hull

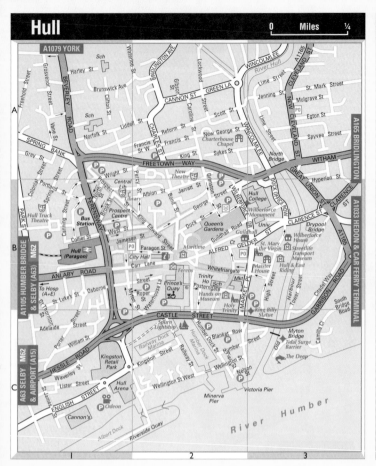

Ipswich

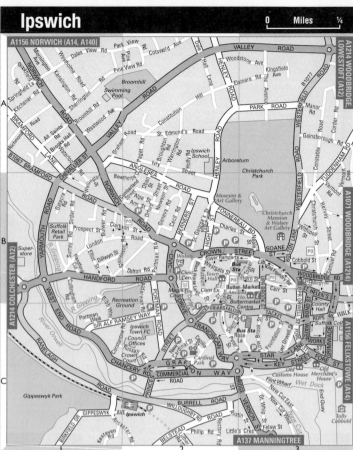

Leeds

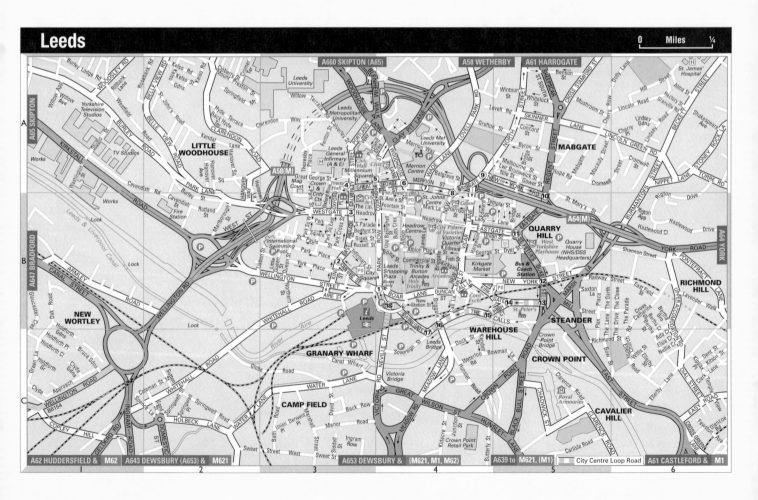

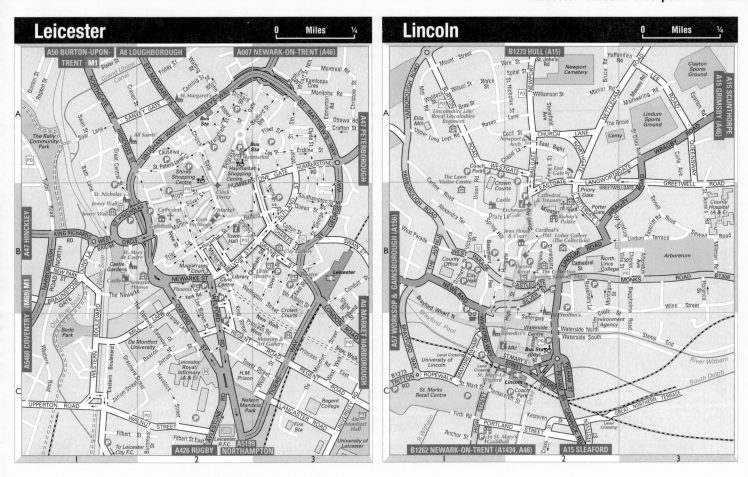

Leicester

A50 BURTON-UPON-TRENT M1 | A6 LOUGHBOROUGH | A607 NEWARK-ON-TRENT (A46)

A47 PETERBOROUGH

A47 HINCKLEY

A5460 COVENTRY (M69) M1

A6 MARKET HARBOROUGH

A426 RUGBY | A5199 NORTHAMPTON

Lincoln

B1273 HULL (A15)

A15 SCUNTHORPE A15 GRIMSBY (A46)

A57 WORKSOP & GAINSBOROUGH (A156)

B1262 NEWARK-ON-TRENT (A1434, A46) | A15 SLEAFORD

Liverpool

A5036 TO A565 | A565 SOUTHPORT | A5038 KIRKDALE | A59 PRESTON | M57 & M58 & KINGSWAY TUNNEL | A580 TO A59 | A5049 WEST DERBY

A57 WARRINGTON

A5047 TO M62 & MANCHESTER

RIVER MERSEY

A5036 TO A562 | A561 GARSTON | A5038 TO A561

Manchester

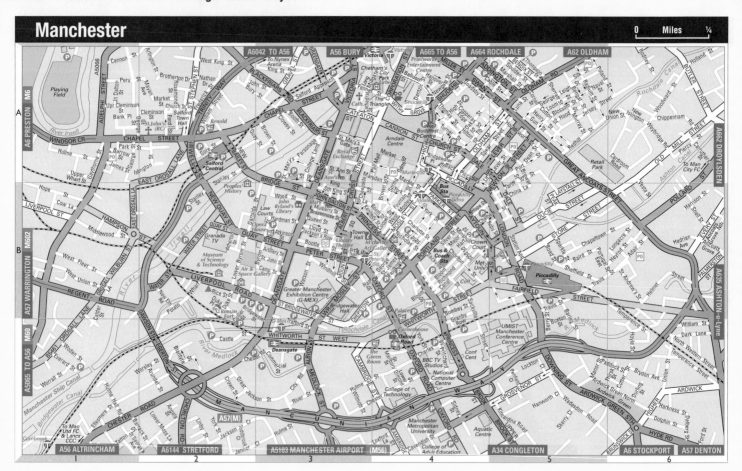

Middlesbrough

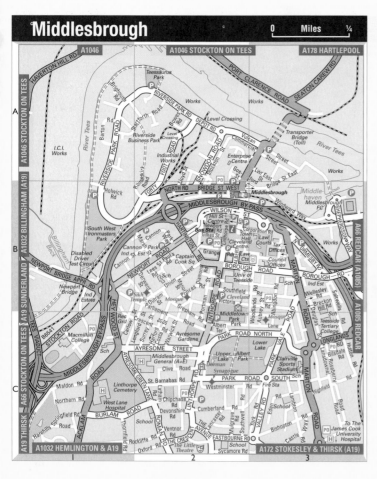

Milton Keynes

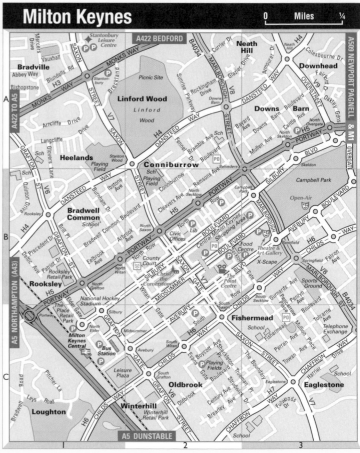

Newcastle upon Tyne

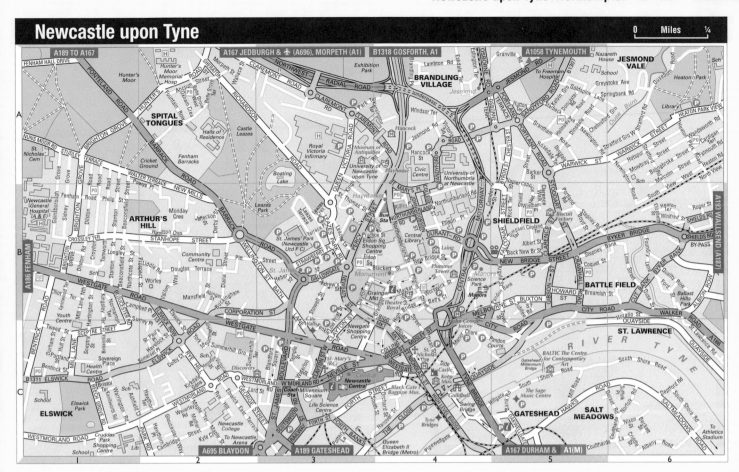

Northampton

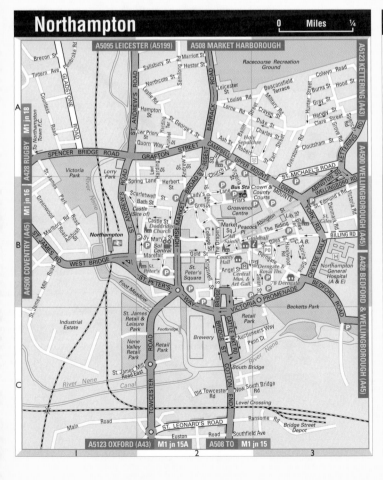

Norwich

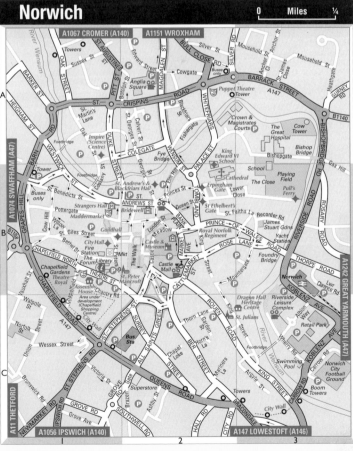

Nottingham

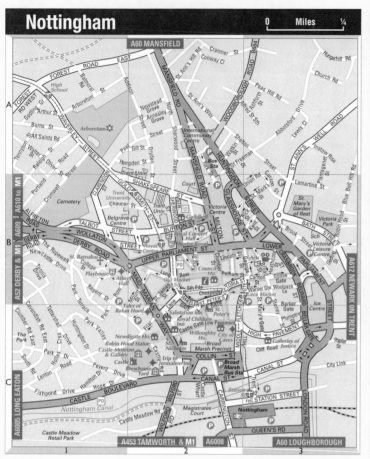

Oxford

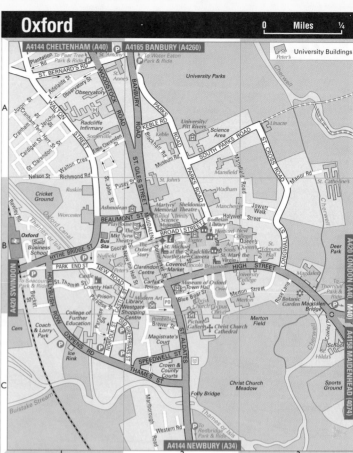

Plymouth

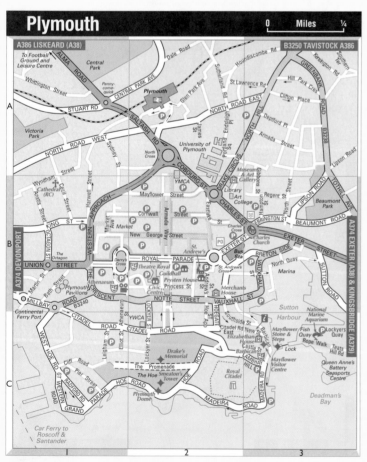

Portsmouth

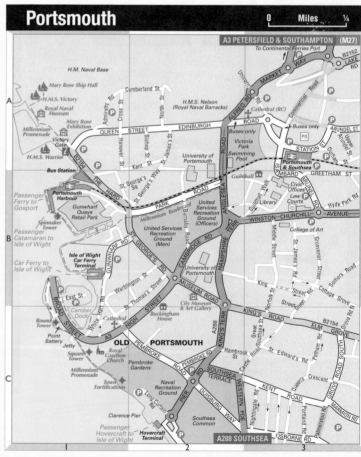

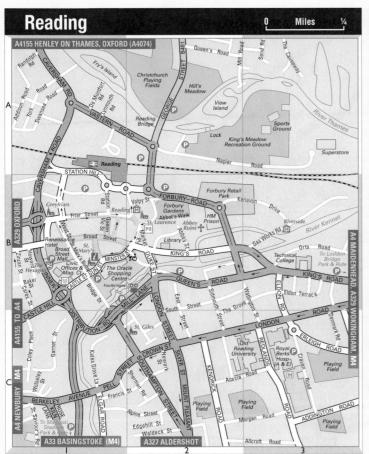

Reading

0 — Miles — ¼

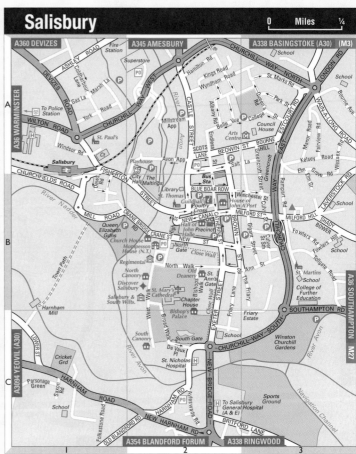

Salisbury

0 — Miles — ¼

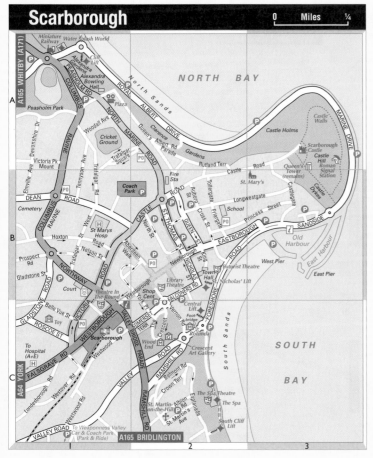

Scarborough

0 — Miles — ¼

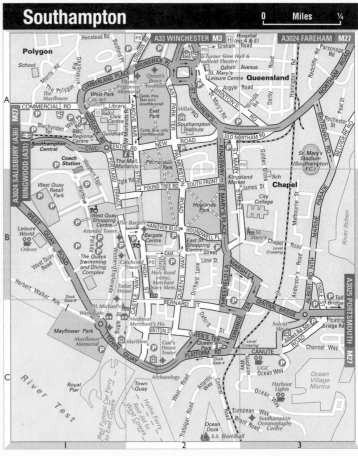

Southampton

0 — Miles — ¼

Sheffield

0   Miles   ¼

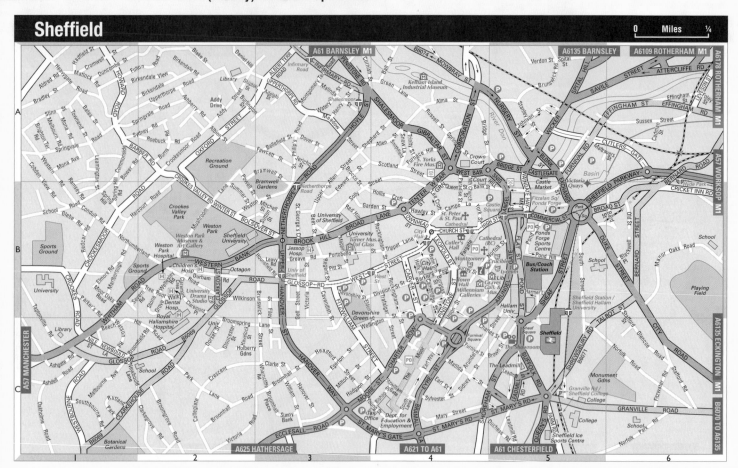

Stoke-on-Trent (Hanley)

0   Miles   ¼

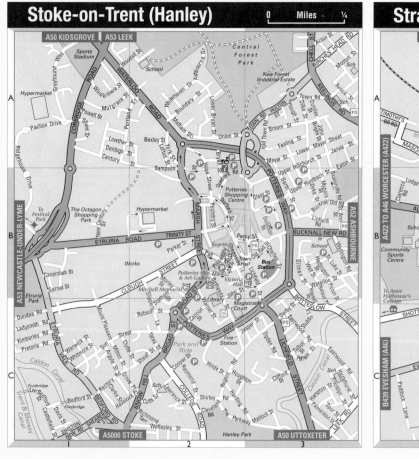

Stratford-upon-Avon

0   Miles   ¼

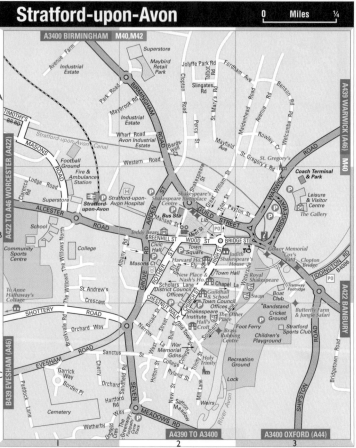

Sunderland

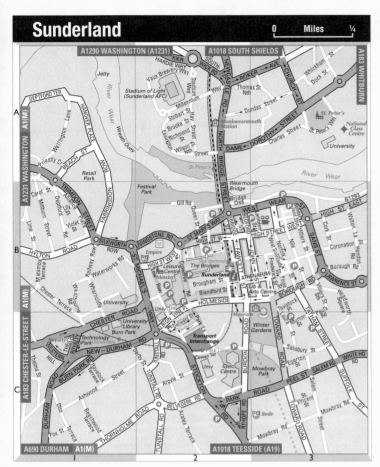

Swansea / Abertawe

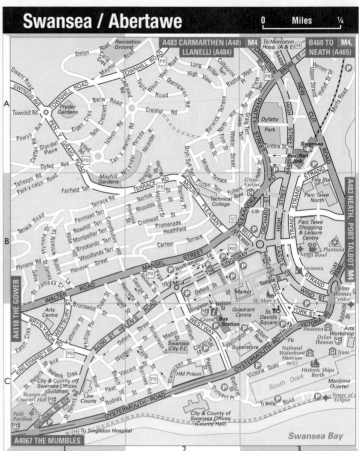

Telford

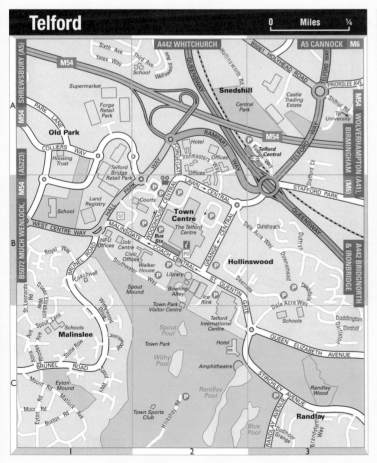

Torquay

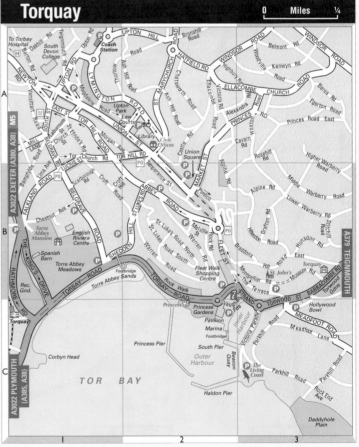

Winchester

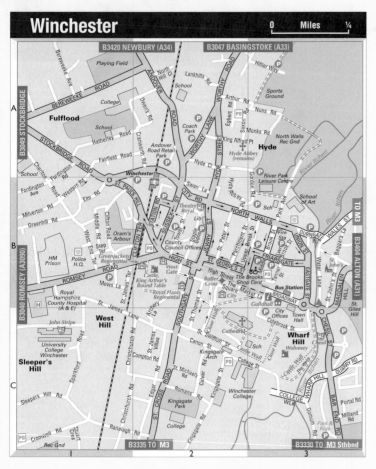

Windsor

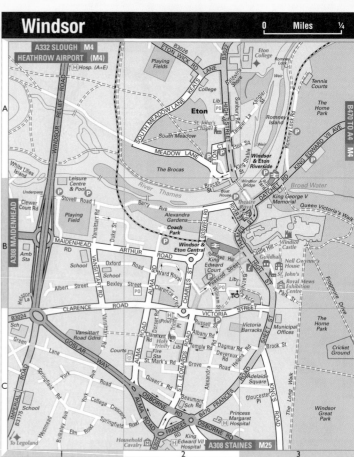

Worcester

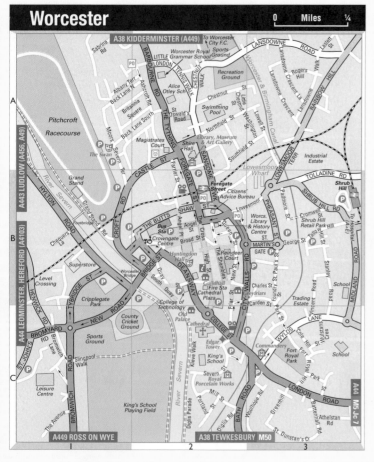

York

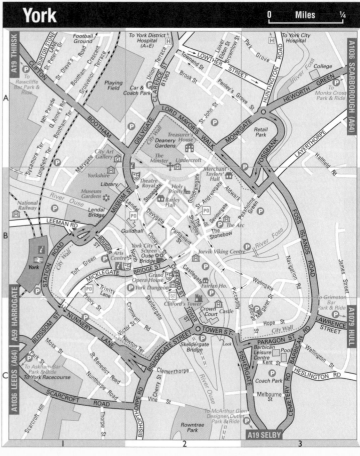

How to use the index

Example: Westcott *Devon* 7 F9
- grid square
- page number
- county or unitary authority

Abbreviations

Aberd C	Aberdeen City
Aberds	Aberdeenshire
Angl	Isle of Anglesey
Arg/Bute	Argyll & Bute
Bath/NE Som'set	Bath & North East Somerset
Beds	Bedfordshire
Bl Gwent	Blaenau Gwent
Blackb'n	Blackburn with Darwen
Blackp'l	Blackpool
Bournem'th	Bournemouth
Brackn'l	Bracknell Forest
Bridg	Bridgend
Brighton/Hove	City of Brighton and Hove
Bristol	City and County of Bristol
Bucks	Buckinghamshire
C/Edinb	City of Edinburgh
C/Glasg	Glasgow City
C/York	City of York
Caerph	Caerphilly
Cambs	Cambridgeshire
Card	Cardiff
Carms	Carmarthenshire
Ceredig'n	Ceredigion
Ches	Cheshire
Clack	Clackmannanshire
Cornw'l	Cornwall
Cumb	Cumbria
D'lington	Darlington
Denbs	Denbighshire
Derby	Derbyshire
Derby C	Derby City
Dumf/Gal	Dumfries & Galloway
Dundee C	Dundee City
E Ayrs	East Ayrshire
E Dunb	East Dunbartonshire
E Loth	East Lothian
E Renf	East Renfrewshire
ER Yorks	East Riding of Yorkshire
E Sussex	East Sussex
Falk	Falkirk
Flints	Flintshire
Glos	Gloucestershire
Gtr Man	Greater Manchester
Gwyn	Gwynedd
H'land	Highland
Hants	Hampshire
Hartlep'l	Hartlepool
Heref'd	Herefordshire
Herts	Hertfordshire
I/Man	Isle of Man
I/Scilly	Isles of Scilly
I/Wight	Isle of Wight
Invercl	Inverclyde
Kingston/Hull	Kingston upon Hull
Lancs	Lancashire
Leics	Leicestershire
Leics C	Leicester City
Lincs	Lincolnshire
London	Greater London
M/Keynes	Milton Keynes
Mersey	Merseyside
Merth Tyd	Merthyr Tydfil
Middlesbro	Middlesbrough
Midloth	Midlothian
Monmouths	Monmouthshire
N Ayrs	North Ayrshire
N Lanarks	North Lanarkshire
N Lincs	North Lincolnshire
N Som'set	North Somerset
N Yorks	North Yorkshire
NE Lincs	North East Lincolnshire
Neath P Talb	Neath Port Talbot
Newp	City and County of Newport
Northants	Northamptonshire
Northum	Northumberland
Nott'ham	City of Nottingham
Notts	Nottinghamshire
Oxon	Oxfordshire
Pembs	Pembrokeshire
Perth/Kinr	Perth and Kinross
Peterbro	Peterborough
Plym'th	Plymouth
Portsm'th	Portsmouth
Redcar/Clevel'd	Redcar and Cleveland
Renf	Renfrewshire
Rh Cyn Taff	Rhondda Cynon Taff
Rutl'd	Rutland
S'thampton	Southampton
S Ayrs	South Ayrshire
S Gloucs	South Gloucestershire
S Lanarks	South Lanarkshire
S Yorks	South Yorkshire
Scot Borders	Scottish Borders
Shetl'd	Shetland
Shrops	Shropshire
Som'set	Somerset
Southend	Southend-on-Sea
Staffs	Staffordshire
Stirl	Stirling
Stockton	Stockton on Tees
Stoke	Stoke-on-Trent
Swan	Swansea
Telford	Telford and Wrekin
Thurr'k	Thurrock
Torf	Torfaen
Tyne/Wear	Tyne and Wear
V/Glam	Vale of Glamorgan
W Berks	West Berkshire
W Dunb	West Dunbartonshire
W Isles	Western Isles
W Loth	West Lothian
W Midlands	West Midlands
W Sussex	West Sussex
W Yorks	West Yorkshire
Warwick	Warwickshire
Wilts	Wiltshire
Windsor	Windsor and Maidenhead
Worcs	Worcestershire
Wrex	Wrexham

A

Ab Kettleby *Leics*	36	C3
Ab Lench *Worcs*	27	C7
Abbas Combe *Som'set*	8	B6
Abberley *Worcs*	26	B4
Abberton *Essex*	31	G7
Abberton *Worcs*	26	C6
Abberwick *Northum*	63	B7
Abbess Roding *Essex*	30	G2
Abbey *Devon*	7	E10
Abbey-cwm-hir *Powys*	25	A7
Abbey Dore *Heref'd*	25	E10
Abbey Field *Essex*	30	F6
Abbey Hulton *Stoke*	44	H3
Abbey St Bathans *Scot Borders*	70	D6
Abbey Village *Lancs*	50	G2
Abbey Wood *London*	19	D11
Abbeydale *S Yorks*	45	D7
Abbeystead *Lancs*	50	D1
Abbeytown *Cumb*	56	A3
Abbots Bickington *Devon*	6	E2
Abbots Bromley *Staffs*	35	C6
Abbots Langley *Herts*	19	A7
Abbots Leigh *N Som'set*	15	D11
Abbots Morton *Worcs*	27	C7
Abbots Ripton *Cambs*	37	H8
Abbots Salford *Warwick*	27	C7
Abbotsbury *Dorset*	8	F4
Abbotsham *Devon*	6	D3
Abbotskerswell *Devon*	5	E9
Abbotsley *Cambs*	29	C9
Abbotswood *Hants*	10	B2
Abbotts Ann *Hants*	17	G10
Abcott *Shrops*	33	H9
Abdon *Shrops*	34	G1
Aber *Ceredig'n*	23	B9
Aber-Arad *Carms*	23	C8
Aber-banc *Ceredig'n*	23	B8
Aber Cowarch *Gwyn*	32	D4
Aber-Giâr *Carms*	23	B10
Aber-gwynfi *Neath P Talb*	14	B4
Aber-Hirnant *Gwyn*	32	B5
Aber-nant *Rh Cyn Taff*	14	A6
Aber-Rhiwlech *Gwyn*	32	C5
Aber-Village *Powys*	25	F8
Aberaeron *Ceredig'n*	24	B1
Aberaman *Rh Cyn Taff*	14	A6
Aberangell *Gwyn*	32	D4
Aberarder *H'land*	81	E6
Aberarder House *H'land*	81	A8
Aberarder Lodge *H'land*	81	E7
Aberargie *Perth/Kinr*	76	F4
Aberarth *Ceredig'n*	24	B1
Aberavon *Neath P Talb*	14	B3
Aberbeeg *Bl Gwent*	15	A8
Abercanaid *Merth Tyd*	14	A6
Abercarn *Caerph*	15	B8
Abercastle *Pembs*	22	C3
Abercegir *Powys*	32	E4
Aberchirder *Aberds*	88	C6
Abercraf *Powys*	24	G5
Abercrombie *Fife*	77	G8
Abercych *Pembs*	23	B7
Abercynafon *Powys*	25	G7
Abercynon *Rh Cyn Taff*	14	B6
Aberdalgie *Perth/Kinr*	76	E3
Aberdâr = Aberdare *Rh Cyn Taff*	14	A5
Aberdare = Aberdâr *Rh Cyn Taff*	14	A5
Aberdaron *Gwyn*	40	H3
Aberdaugleddau = Milford Haven *Pembs*	22	F4
Aberdeen *Aberd C*	83	C11
Aberdesach *Gwyn*	40	E6
Aberdour *Fife*	69	B10
Aberdovey *Gwyn*	32	F2
Aberdulais *Neath P Talb*	14	A3
Aberedw *Powys*	25	D7
Abereiddy *Pembs*	22	C2
Abererch *Gwyn*	40	G5
Aberfan *Merth Tyd*	14	A6
Aberfeldy *Perth/Kinr*	75	C11
Aberffraw *Angl*	40	D5
Aberffrwd *Ceredig'n*	32	H2
Aberford *W Yorks*	51	F10
Aberfoyle *Stirl*	75	G8
Abergavenny = Y Fenni *Monmouths*	25	G9
Abergele *Conwy*	42	E2
Abergorlech *Carms*	23	C10
Abergwaun = Fishguard *Pembs*	22	C4
Abergwesyn *Powys*	24	C5
Abergwili *Carms*	23	D9
Abergwynant *Gwyn*	32	D2
Abergwyngregyn *Gwyn*	41	C8
Abergynolwyn *Gwyn*	32	E2
Aberhonddu = Brecon *Powys*	25	F7
Aberhosan *Powys*	32	F4
Aberkenfig *Bridg*	14	C4
Aberlady *E Loth*	70	B3
Aberlemno *Angus*	77	B8
Aberllefenni *Gwyn*	32	E3
Abermagwr *Ceredig'n*	24	A3
Abermaw = Barmouth *Gwyn*	32	D2
Abermeurig *Ceredig'n*	23	A10
Abermule *Powys*	33	F7
Abernaint *Powys*	33	C7
Abernant *Carms*	23	D8
Abernethy *Perth/Kinr*	76	F4
Abernyte *Perth/Kinr*	76	D5
Aberpennar = Mountain Ash *Rh Cyn Taff*	14	B6
Aberporth *Ceredig'n*	23	A7
Abersoch *Gwyn*	40	H5
Abersychan *Torf*	15	A8
Abertawe = Swansea *Swan*	14	B2
Aberteifi = Cardigan *Ceredig'n*	22	B6
Aberthin *V/Glam*	14	D6
Abertillery = Abertyleri *Bl Gwent*	15	A8
Abertridwr *Caerph*	15	C7
Abertridwr *Powys*	32	D6
Abertyleri = Abertillery *Bl Gwent*	15	A8
Abertysswg *Caerph*	25	H8
Aberuthven *Perth/Kinr*	76	F2
Aberyscir *Powys*	24	F6
Aberystwyth *Ceredig'n*	32	G1
Abhainn Suidhe *W Isles*	90	G5
Abingdon *Oxon*	17	B11
Abinger Common *Surrey*	19	G8
Abinger Hammer *Surrey*	19	G7
Abington *S Lanarks*	60	A5
Abington Piggotts *Cambs*	29	D10
Ablington *Glos*	27	H8
Ablington *Wilts*	17	G8
Abney *Derby*	44	E5
Aboyne *Aberds*	83	D7
Abram *Gtr Man*	43	B9
Abriachan *H'land*	87	H8
Abridge *Essex*	19	B11
Abronhill *N Lanarks*	68	C6
Abson *S Gloucs*	16	D4
Abthorpe *Northants*	28	D3
Abune-the-Hill *Orkney*	95	F3
Aby *Lincs*	47	E8
Acaster Malbis *C/York*	52	E1
Acaster Selby *N Yorks*	52	E1
Accrington *Lancs*	50	G3
Acha *Arg/Bute*	78	F4
Acha Mor *W Isles*	91	E8
Achabraid *Arg/Bute*	73	E7
Achachork *H'land*	85	D9
Achafolla *Arg/Bute*	72	B6
Achagary *H'land*	93	D10
Achahoish *Arg/Bute*	72	F6
Achalader *Perth/Kinr*	76	C4
Achallader *Arg/Bute*	74	C6
Ach'an Todhair *H'land*	80	F2
Achanalt *H'land*	86	E5
Achanamara *Arg/Bute*	72	E6
Achandunie *H'land*	87	D9
Achany *H'land*	93	J8
Achaphubuil *H'land*	80	F2
Acharacle *H'land*	79	E9
Acharn *H'land*	79	F10
Acharn *Perth/Kinr*	75	C10
Acharole *H'land*	94	E4
Achath *Aberds*	83	B9
Achavanich *H'land*	94	F3
Achavraat *H'land*	87	G12
Achddu *Carms*	23	F9
Achduart *H'land*	92	J3
Achentoul *H'land*	93	F11
Achfary *H'land*	92	F5
Achgarve *H'land*	91	H13
Achiemore *H'land*	92	C6
Achiemore *H'land*	93	D11
A'Chill *H'land*	84	H7
Achiltibuie *H'land*	92	J3
Achina *H'land*	93	C10
Achinduich *H'land*	93	J8
Achinduin *Arg/Bute*	79	H11
Achingills *H'land*	94	D3
Achintee *H'land*	80	F3
Achintee *H'land*	86	G2
Achintraid *H'land*	85	E13
Achlean *H'land*	81	D10
Achleck *Arg/Bute*	78	G7
Achluachrach *H'land*	80	E4
Achlyness *H'land*	92	D5
Achmelvich *H'land*	92	G3
Achmore *H'land*	85	E13
Achmore *Stirl*	75	D8
Achnaba *Arg/Bute*	74	D2
Achnaba *Arg/Bute*	73	E8
Achnabat *H'land*	87	H8
Achnacarnin *H'land*	92	F3
Achnacarry *H'land*	80	E3
Achnacloich *Arg/Bute*	74	D2
Achnacloich *H'land*	85	H10
Achnaconeran *H'land*	80	B6
Achnacraig *Arg/Bute*	78	G7
Achnacroish *Arg/Bute*	79	G11
Achnadrish *Arg/Bute*	78	F7
Achnafalnich *Arg/Bute*	74	E5
Achnagarron *H'land*	87	E9
Achnaha *H'land*	78	E7
Achnahanat *H'land*	87	B8
Achnahannet *H'land*	82	A1
Achnairn *H'land*	93	H8
Achnaluachrach *H'land*	93	J9
Achnasaul *H'land*	80	E3
Achnasheen *H'land*	86	F4
Achosnich *H'land*	78	E7
Achranich *H'land*	79	G10
Achreamie *H'land*	93	C13
Achriabhach *H'land*	80	G3
Achriesgill *H'land*	92	D5
Achrimsdale *H'land*	93	J12
Achtoty *H'land*	93	C9
Achurch *Northants*	36	G6
Achuvoldrach *H'land*	93	D8
Achvaich *H'land*	87	B10
Achvarasdal *H'land*	93	C12
Ackergill *H'land*	94	E5
Acklam *Middlesbro'*	58	E5
Acklam *N Yorks*	52	C3
Ackleton *Shrops*	34	F3
Acklington *Northum*	63	C8
Ackton *W Yorks*	51	G10
Ackworth Moor Top *W Yorks*	51	H10
Acle *Norfolk*	39	D10
Acock's Green *W Midlands*	35	G7
Acol *Kent*	21	E10
Acomb *Northum*	62	G5
Acomb *C/York*	52	D1
Aconbury *Heref'd*	26	E2
Acre *Lancs*	50	G3
Acre Street *W Sussex*	11	E6
Acrefair *Wrex*	33	A8
Acton *Ches*	43	G9
Acton *Dorset*	9	G8
Acton *London*	19	C9
Acton *Shrops*	33	G9
Acton *Suffolk*	30	D5
Acton *Wrex*	42	G6
Acton Beauchamp *Heref'd*	26	C3
Acton Bridge *Ches*	43	E8
Acton Burnell *Shrops*	33	E11
Acton Green *Heref'd*	26	C3
Acton Pigott *Shrops*	33	E11
Acton Round *Shrops*	34	F2
Acton Scott *Shrops*	33	G10
Acton Trussell *Staffs*	34	D5
Acton Turville *S Gloucs*	16	C5
Adbaston *Staffs*	34	C3
Adber *Dorset*	8	B4
Adderley *Shrops*	34	A2
Adderstone *Northum*	71	G10
Addiewell *W Loth*	69	D8
Addingham *W Yorks*	51	E6
Addington *Bucks*	28	F4
Addington *London*	19	E10
Addington *Kent*	20	F3
Addinston *Scot Borders*	70	E4
Addiscombe *London*	19	E10
Addlestone *Surrey*	19	E7
Addlethorpe *Lincs*	47	F9
Adel *W Yorks*	51	F8
Adeney *Telford*	34	D3
Adfa *Powys*	33	E6
Adforton *Heref'd*	25	A11
Adisham *Kent*	21	F9
Adlestrop *Glos*	27	F9
Adlingfleet *ER Yorks*	52	G4
Adlington *Lancs*	43	A9
Admaston *Staffs*	34	C6
Admaston *Telford*	34	D2
Admington *Warwick*	27	D9
Adstock *Bucks*	28	E4
Adstone *Northants*	28	C2
Adversane *W Sussex*	11	B9
Advie *H'land*	88	E1
Adwalton *W Yorks*	51	G8
Adwell *Oxon*	18	B3
Adwick le Street *S Yorks*	45	B9
Adwick upon Dearne *S Yorks*	45	B8
Adziel *Aberds*	89	C9
Ae Village *Dumf/Gal*	60	E5
Affleck *Aberds*	89	F8
Affpuddle *Dorset*	9	E7
Affric Lodge *H'land*	80	A3
Afon-wen *Flints*	42	E4
Afton *I/Wight*	10	F2
Agglethorpe *N Yorks*	58	H1
Agneash *I/Man*	48	D4
Aigburth *Mersey*	43	D6
Aiginis *W Isles*	91	D9
Aike *ER Yorks*	52	E6
Aikerness *Orkney*	95	C5
Aikers *Orkney*	95	J5
Aiketgate *Cumb*	57	B6
Aikton *Cumb*	56	A4
Ailey *Heref'd*	25	D10
Ailstone *Warwick*	27	C9
Ailsworth *Peterbro*	37	F7
Ainderby Quernhow *N Yorks*	51	A9
Ainderby Steeple *N Yorks*	58	G4
Aingers Green *Essex*	31	F8
Ainsdale *Mersey*	42	A6
Ainsdale-on-Sea *Mersey*	42	A6
Ainstable *Cumb*	57	B7
Ainsworth *Gtr Man*	43	A10
Ainthorpe *N Yorks*	59	F8
Aintree *Mersey*	43	C6
Aird *Arg/Bute*	72	C6
Aird *Dumf/Gal*	54	C3
Aird *H'land*	85	A12
Aird *W Isles*	91	D10
Aird a Mhachair *W Isles*	84	D2
Aird a'Mhulaidh *W Isles*	90	F6
Aird Asaig *W Isles*	90	G6
Aird Dhail *W Isles*	91	A9
Aird Mhidhinis *W Isles*	84	H2
Aird Mhighe *W Isles*	90	H6
Aird Mhighe *W Isles*	90	J5
Aird Mhor *W Isles*	84	H2
Aird of Sleat *H'land*	85	H10
Aird Thunga *W Isles*	91	D9
Aird Uig *W Isles*	90	D5
Airdens *H'land*	87	B9
Airdrie *N Lanarks*	68	D6
Airdtorrisdale *H'land*	93	C9
Airidh a Bhruaich *W Isles*	90	F7
Airieland *Dumf/Gal*	55	D10
Airmyn *ER Yorks*	52	G3
Airntully *Perth/Kinr*	76	D3
Airor *H'land*	85	H12
Airth *Falk*	69	B7
Airton *N Yorks*	50	D5
Airyhassen *Dumf/Gal*	54	E6
Aisby *Lincs*	46	C2
Aisby *Lincs*	36	B6
Aisgernis *W Isles*	84	F2
Aiskew *N Yorks*	58	H3
Aislaby *N Yorks*	59	H8
Aislaby *N Yorks*	59	F9
Aislaby *Stockton*	58	E5
Aisthorpe *Lincs*	46	D3
Aith *Orkney*	95	G3
Aith *Shetl'd*	96	H5
Aith *Shetl'd*	96	D8
Aithsetter *Shetl'd*	96	K6
Aitkenhead *S Ayrs*	66	F6
Aitnoch *H'land*	87	H12
Akeld *Northum*	71	H8
Akeley *Bucks*	28	E4
Akenham *Suffolk*	31	D8
Albaston *Cornw'l*	4	D5
Alberbury *Shrops*	33	D9
Albourne *W Sussex*	12	E1
Albrighton *Shrops*	33	D10
Albrighton *Shrops*	34	E4
Alburgh *Norfolk*	39	G8
Albury *Herts*	29	F11
Albury *Surrey*	19	G7
Albury End *Herts*	29	F11
Alby Hill *Norfolk*	39	B7
Alcaig *H'land*	87	F8
Alcaston *Shrops*	33	G10
Alcester *Warwick*	27	C7
Alciston *E Sussex*	12	F4
Alcombe *Som'set*	7	B8
Alcombe *Wilts*	16	E5
Alconbury *Cambs*	37	H7
Alconbury Weston *Cambs*	37	H7
Aldbar Castle *Angus*	77	B8
Aldborough *Norfolk*	39	B7
Aldborough *N Yorks*	51	C10
Aldbourne *Wilts*	17	D9
Aldbrough *ER Yorks*	53	F8
Aldbrough St John *N Yorks*	58	E3
Aldbury *Herts*	28	G6
Aldcliffe *Lancs*	49	C4
Aldclune *Perth/Kinr*	76	A2
Aldeburgh *Suffolk*	31	C11
Aldeby *Norfolk*	39	F10
Aldenham *Herts*	19	B8
Alderbury *Wilts*	9	B10
Aldercar *Derby*	45	H8
Alderford *Norfolk*	39	D7
Alderholt *Dorset*	9	C10
Alderley *Glos*	16	B4
Alderley Edge *Ches*	44	E2
Aldermaston *W Berks*	18	E2
Aldermaston Wharf *W Berks*	18	E3
Alderminster *Warwick*	27	D9
Alder's End *Heref'd*	26	D3
Aldersey Green *Ches*	43	G7
Aldershot *Hants*	18	F5
Alderton *Glos*	27	E7
Alderton *Northants*	28	D4
Alderton *Shrops*	33	C10
Alderton *Suffolk*	31	D10
Alderton *Wilts*	16	C5
Alderwasley *Derby*	45	G7
Aldfield *N Yorks*	51	C8
Aldford *Ches*	43	G7
Aldham *Essex*	30	F6
Aldham *Suffolk*	31	D7
Aldie *H'land*	87	C10
Aldingbourne *W Sussex*	11	D8
Aldingham *Cumb*	49	B2
Aldington *Kent*	13	C9
Aldington *Worcs*	27	D7
Aldington Frith *Kent*	13	C9
Aldochlay *Arg/Bute*	68	A2
Aldreth *Cambs*	29	A11
Aldridge *W Midlands*	35	E6
Aldringham *Suffolk*	31	B11
Aldsworth *Glos*	27	G8
Aldunie *Moray*	82	A5
Aldwark *Derby*	44	G6
Aldwark *N Yorks*	51	C10
Aldwick *W Sussex*	11	E8
Aldwincle *Northants*	36	G6
Aldworth *W Berks*	18	D2
Alexandria *W Dunb*	68	C2
Alfardisworthy *Devon*	6	E1
Alfington *Devon*	7	G10
Alfold *Surrey*	11	A9
Alfold Bars *W Sussex*	11	A9
Alfold Crossways *Surrey*	19	H7
Alford *Aberds*	83	B7
Alford *Lincs*	47	E8
Alford *Som'set*	8	A5
Alfreton *Derby*	45	G8
Alfrick *Worcs*	26	C4
Alfrick Pound *Worcs*	26	C4
Alfriston *E Sussex*	12	F4
Algaltraig *Arg/Bute*	73	F9
Algarkirk *Lincs*	37	B8
Alhampton *Som'set*	8	A5
Aline Lodge *W Isles*	90	F6
Alisary *H'land*	79	D10
Alkborough *N Lincs*	52	G4
Alkerton *Oxon*	27	D10
Alkham *Kent*	21	G9
Alkington *Shrops*	33	B11
Alkmonton *Derby*	35	B7
All Cannings *Wilts*	17	E7
All Saints South Elmham *Suffolk*	39	G9
All Stretton *Shrops*	33	F10
Alladale Lodge *H'land*	86	C7
Allaleigh *Devon*	5	F9
Allanaquoich *Aberds*	82	D3
Allangrange Mains *H'land*	87	F9
Allanton *Scot Borders*	71	E7
Allanton *N Lanarks*	69	E7
Allathasdal *W Isles*	84	H1
Allendale Town *Northum*	62	H4
Allenheads *Northum*	57	B10
Allens Green *Herts*	29	G11
Allensford *Durham*	58	A1
Allensmore *Heref'd*	25	E11
Allenton *Derby C*	35	B9
Aller *Som'set*	8	B3
Allerby *Cumb*	56	C2
Allerford *Som'set*	7	B8
Allerston *N Yorks*	52	A4
Allerthorpe *ER Yorks*	52	E3
Allerton *Mersey*	43	D7
Allerton *W Yorks*	51	F7
Allerton Bywater *W Yorks*	51	G10
Allerton Mauleverer *N Yorks*	51	D10
Allesley *W Midlands*	35	G9
Allestree *Derby C*	35	B9
Allet *Cornw'l*	3	E6
Allexton *Leics*	36	E4
Allgreave *Ches*	44	F3
Allhallows *Medway*	20	D5
Allhallows-on-Sea *Medway*	20	D5
Alligin Shuas *H'land*	85	C13
Allimore Green *Staffs*	34	D4
Allington *Lincs*	36	A4
Allington *Wilts*	17	H9
Allington *Wilts*	17	E7
Allithwaite *Cumb*	49	B3
Alloa *Clack*	69	A7
Allonby *Cumb*	56	B2
Alloway *S Ayrs*	66	E6
Allt *Carms*	23	F10
Allt na h-Airbhe *H'land*	86	B4
Allt-nan-sùgh *H'land*	85	F14
Alltchaorunn *H'land*	74	B4
Alltforgan *Powys*	32	C5
Alltmawr *Powys*	25	D7
Alltnacaillich *H'land*	92	E7
Alltsigh *H'land*	81	B6
Alltwalis *Carms*	23	C9
Alltwen *Neath P Talb*	14	A3
Alltyblaca *Ceredig'n*	23	B10
Allwood Green *Suffolk*	31	A7
Almeley *Heref'd*	25	C10
Almer *Dorset*	9	E8
Almholme *S Yorks*	45	B9
Almington *Staffs*	34	B3
Alminstone Cross *Devon*	6	D2
Almondbank *Perth/Kinr*	76	E3
Almondbury *W Yorks*	51	H7
Almondsbury *S Gloucs*	16	C3
Alne *N Yorks*	51	C10
Alness *H'land*	87	E9
Alnham *Northum*	62	B5
Alnmouth *Northum*	63	B8
Alnwick *Northum*	63	B7
Alperton *London*	19	C8
Alphamstone *Essex*	30	E5
Alpheton *Suffolk*	30	C5
Alphington *Devon*	7	G8
Alport *Derby*	44	F6
Alpraham *Ches*	43	G8
Alresford *Essex*	31	F7
Alrewas *Staffs*	35	D7
Alsager *Ches*	43	G10
Alsagers Bank *Staffs*	44	H2
Alsop en le Dale *Derby*	44	G5
Alston *Cumb*	57	B9
Alston *Devon*	8	D2
Alstone *Glos*	26	E6
Alstonefield *Staffs*	44	G5
Alswear *Devon*	7	D6
Altandhu *H'land*	92	H2
Altanduin *H'land*	93	G11
Altarnun *Cornw'l*	4	C3
Altass *H'land*	92	J7
Alterwall *H'land*	94	D4
Altham *Lancs*	50	F3
Althorne *Essex*	20	B6
Althorpe *N Lincs*	46	B2
Alticry *Dumf/Gal*	54	D5
Altnabreac Station *H'land*	93	E13
Altnacealgach Hotel *H'land*	92	H5
Altnacraig *Arg/Bute*	79	J11
Altnafeadh *H'land*	74	B5
Altnaharra *H'land*	93	F8
Altofts *W Yorks*	51	G9
Alton *Derby*	45	F7
Alton *Hants*	18	H4
Alton *Staffs*	35	A6
Alton Pancras *Dorset*	8	D6
Alton Priors *Wilts*	17	E8
Altrincham *Gtr Man*	43	D10
Altrua *H'land*	80	E4
Altskeith *Stirl*	75	G7
Altyre Ho. *Moray*	87	F13
Alva *Clack*	75	H11
Alvanley *Ches*	43	E7
Alvaston *Derby C*	35	B9
Alvechurch *Worcs*	27	A7
Alvecote *Warwick*	35	E8
Alvediston *Wilts*	9	B8
Alveley *Shrops*	34	G3
Alverdiscott *Devon*	6	D4
Alverstoke *Hants*	10	E5
Alverstone *I/Wight*	10	F4
Alverton *Notts*	36	A3
Alves *Moray*	88	B1
Alvescot *Oxon*	17	A9
Alveston *S Gloucs*	16	C3
Alveston *Warwick*	27	C9
Alvie *H'land*	81	C10
Alvingham *Lincs*	47	C7
Alvington *Glos*	16	A3
Alwalton *Cambs*	37	F7
Alweston *Dorset*	8	C5
Alwinton *Northum*	62	C5
Alwoodley *W Yorks*	51	E8
Alyth *Perth/Kinr*	76	C5
Am Baile *W Isles*	84	G2
Am Buth *Arg/Bute*	79	J11
Amatnatua *H'land*	86	B7
Amber Hill *Lincs*	46	H6
Ambergate *Derby*	45	G7
Amberley *Glos*	16	A5
Amberley *W Sussex*	11	C9
Amble *Northum*	63	C8
Amblecote *W Midlands*	34	G4
Ambler Thorn *W Yorks*	51	G6
Ambleside *Cumb*	56	F5
Ambleston *Pembs*	22	D5
Ambrosden *Oxon*	28	G3
Amcotts *N Lincs*	46	A2
Amersham *Bucks*	18	B6
Amesbury *Wilts*	17	G8
Amington *Staffs*	35	E8
Amisfield *Dumf/Gal*	60	E5
Amlwch *Angl*	40	A6
Amlwch Port *Angl*	40	A6
Ammanford = Rhydaman *Carms*	24	G3
Amod *Arg/Bute*	65	E8
Amotherby *N Yorks*	52	B3
Ampfield *Hants*	10	B3
Ampleforth *N Yorks*	52	B1
Ampney Crucis *Glos*	17	A7
Ampney St Mary *Glos*	17	A7
Ampney St Peter *Glos*	17	A7
Amport *Hants*	17	G9
Ampthill *Beds*	29	E7
Ampton *Suffolk*	30	A5
Amroth *Pembs*	22	F6
Amulree *Perth/Kinr*	75	D11
An Caol *H'land*	85	C11
An Cnoc *W Isles*	91	D9
An Gleann Ur *W Isles*	91	D9
An t-Ob = Leverburgh *W Isles*	90	J5
Anagach *H'land*	82	A2
Anaheilt *H'land*	79	E11
Anancaun *H'land*	86	E3
Ancaster *Lincs*	36	A5
Anchor *Shrops*	33	G7
Anchorsholme *Blackp'l*	49	E3
Ancroft *Northum*	71	F8
Ancrum *Scot Borders*	62	A2
Anderby *Lincs*	47	E9
Anderson *Dorset*	9	E7
Anderton *Ches*	43	E9
Andover *Hants*	17	G10
Andover Down *Hants*	17	G10
Andoversford *Glos*	27	G7
Andreas *I/Man*	48	C4
Anfield *Mersey*	43	C6
Angersleigh *Som'set*	7	E10
Angle *Pembs*	22	F3
Angmering *W Sussex*	11	D9
Angram *N Yorks*	51	E11
Angram *N Yorks*	57	G10
Anie *Stirl*	75	F8
Ankerville *H'land*	87	D11
Anlaby *ER Yorks*	52	G6
Anmer *Norfolk*	38	C3
Anna Valley *Hants*	17	G10
Annan *Dumf/Gal*	61	G7
Annat *Arg/Bute*	74	E3
Annat *H'land*	85	C13
Annbank *S Ayrs*	67	D7
Annesley *Notts*	45	G9
Annesley Woodhouse *Notts*	45	G8
Annfield Plain *Durham*	58	A2
Annifirth *Shetl'd*	96	J3
Annitsford *Tyne/Wear*	63	F8
Annscroft *Shrops*	33	E10
Ansdell *Lancs*	49	G3
Ansford *Som'set*	8	A5
Ansley *Warwick*	35	F8
Anslow *Staffs*	35	C8
Anslow Gate *Staffs*	35	C7
Anstey *Herts*	29	E11
Anstey *Leics*	35	E11
Anstruther Easter *Fife*	77	G8
Anstruther Wester *Fife*	77	G8
Ansty *Hants*	18	G4
Ansty *Warwick*	35	G9
Ansty *Wilts*	9	B8
Ansty *W Sussex*	12	D1
Anthill Common *Hants*	10	C5
Anthorn *Cumb*	61	H7
Antingham *Norfolk*	39	B8
Anton's Gowt *Lincs*	46	H6
Antonshill *Falk*	69	B7
Antony *Cornw'l*	4	F4
Anwick *Lincs*	46	G5
Anwoth *Dumf/Gal*	55	D8
Aoradh *Arg/Bute*	64	B3
Apes Hall *Cambs*	38	F1
Apethorpe *Northants*	36	F6
Apeton *Staffs*	34	D4
Apley *Lincs*	46	E5
Apperknowle *Derby*	45	E7
Apperley *Glos*	26	F5
Apperley Bridge *W Yorks*	51	F7
Appersett *N Yorks*	57	G10
Appin *Arg/Bute*	74	C2
Appin House *Arg/Bute*	74	C2
Appleby *N Lincs*	46	A3
Appleby-in-Westmorland *Cumb*	57	D8
Appleby Magna *Leics*	35	E9
Appleby Parva *Leics*	35	E9
Applecross *H'land*	85	D12
Applecross Ho. *H'land*	85	D12
Appledore *Devon*	6	C3
Appledore *Devon*	7	E9
Appledore *Kent*	13	D8
Appledore Heath *Kent*	13	C8
Appleford *Oxon*	18	B2
Applegarthtown *Dumf/Gal*	61	E7
Appleshaw *Hants*	17	G10
Applethwaite *Cumb*	56	D4
Appleton *Halton*	43	D8
Appleton *Oxon*	17	A11
Appleton-le-Moors *N Yorks*	59	H8
Appleton-le-Street *N Yorks*	52	B3
Appleton Roebuck *N Yorks*	52	E1
Appleton Thorn *Warrington*	43	D9
Appleton Wiske *N Yorks*	58	F4
Appletreehall *Scot Borders*	61	B11
Appletreewick *N Yorks*	51	C6
Appley *Som'set*	7	D9
Appley Bridge *Lancs*	43	B8
Apse Heath *I/Wight*	10	F4
Apsley End *Beds*	29	E8
Apuldram *W Sussex*	11	D7
Aquhythie *Aberds*	83	B9
Arabella *H'land*	87	D11
Arbeadie *Aberds*	83	D8
Arberth = Narberth *Pembs*	22	E6
Arbirlot *Angus*	77	C9
Arboll *H'land*	87	C11
Arborfield *Wokingham*	18	E4
Arborfield Cross *Wokingham*	18	E4
Arborfield Garrison *Wokingham*	18	E4
Arbour-thorne *S Yorks*	45	D7
Arbroath *Angus*	77	C9
Arbuthnott *Aberds*	83	F9
Archiestown *Moray*	88	D2
Arclid *Ches*	43	F10
Ard-dhubh *H'land*	85	D12
Ardachu *H'land*	93	J9
Ardalanish *Arg/Bute*	78	K6
Ardanaiseig *Arg/Bute*	74	E3
Ardaneaskan *H'land*	85	E13
Ardanstur *Arg/Bute*	73	B7
Ardargie House Hotel *Perth/Kinr*	76	F3
Ardarroch *H'land*	85	E13
Ardbeg *Arg/Bute*	64	D5
Ardbeg *Arg/Bute*	73	E10
Ardcharnich *H'land*	86	C4
Ardchiavaig *Arg/Bute*	78	K6
Ardchullarie More *Stirl*	75	F8
Ardchyle *Stirl*	75	E8
Arddleen *Powys*	33	D8
Ardechvie *H'land*	80	D3
Ardeley *Herts*	29	F10
Ardelve *H'land*	85	F13
Arden *Arg/Bute*	68	B2
Ardens Grafton *Warwick*	27	C8
Ardentinny *Arg/Bute*	73	E10
Ardentraive *Arg/Bute*	73	F9
Ardeonaig *Stirl*	75	D9
Ardersier *H'land*	87	F10
Ardessie *H'land*	86	C3
Ardfern *Arg/Bute*	73	C7
Ardgartan *Arg/Bute*	74	G5
Ardgay *H'land*	87	B8
Ardgour *H'land*	74	A3
Ardheslaig *H'land*	85	C12
Ardiecow *Moray*	88	B5
Ardindrean *H'land*	86	C4
Ardingly *W Sussex*	12	D2
Ardington *Oxon*	17	C11
Ardlair *Aberds*	83	A7
Ardlamont Ho. *Arg/Bute*	73	G8
Ardleigh *Essex*	31	F7
Ardler *Perth/Kinr*	76	C5
Ardley *Oxon*	28	F2
Ardlui *Arg/Bute*	74	F6
Ardlussa *Arg/Bute*	72	E5
Ardmair *H'land*	86	B4
Ardmay *Arg/Bute*	74	G5
Ardminish *Arg/Bute*	65	D7
Ardmolich *H'land*	79	D10
Ardmore *Arg/Bute*	79	J10
Ardmore *H'land*	92	D5
Ardmore *H'land*	87	C10
Ardnacross *Arg/Bute*	79	G8
Ardnadam *Arg/Bute*	73	F10
Ardnagrask *H'land*	87	G8
Ardnarff *H'land*	85	E13
Ardnastang *H'land*	79	E11
Ardnave *Arg/Bute*	64	A3
Ardno *Arg/Bute*	73	C10
Ardo *Aberds*	89	E8
Ardo Ho. *Aberds*	89	F9
Ardoch *Perth/Kinr*	76	D3
Ardochy House *H'land*	80	C4
Ardoyne *Aberds*	83	A8
Ardpatrick *Arg/Bute*	72	G6
Ardpatrick Ho. *Arg/Bute*	72	H6
Ardpeaton *Arg/Bute*	73	E11
Ardrishaig *Arg/Bute*	73	E7
Ardross *Fife*	77	G8
Ardross *H'land*	87	D9
Ardross Castle *H'land*	87	D9
Ardrossan *N Ayrs*	66	B5
Ardshealach *H'land*	79	E9
Ardsley *S Yorks*	45	B7
Ardslignish *H'land*	79	E8
Ardtalla *Arg/Bute*	64	C5
Ardtalnaig *Perth/Kinr*	75	D10
Ardtoe *H'land*	79	D9
Ardtrostan *Perth/Kinr*	75	E9
Arduaine *Arg/Bute*	72	B6
Ardullie *H'land*	87	E8
Ardvasar *H'land*	85	H11
Ardvorlich *Perth/Kinr*	75	E9
Ardwell *Dumf/Gal*	54	E4
Ardwell Mains *Dumf/Gal*	54	E4
Ardwick *Gtr Man*	44	C2
Areley Kings *Worcs*	26	A5
Arford *Hants*	18	H5
Argoed *Caerph*	15	B7
Argoed Mill *Powys*	24	B6
Arichamish *Arg/Bute*	73	C8
Arichastlich *Arg/Bute*	74	D5
Aridhglas *Arg/Bute*	78	J6
Arileod *Arg/Bute*	78	F4
Arinacrinachd *H'land*	85	C12
Arinagour *Arg/Bute*	78	F5
Arion *Orkney*	95	G3
Arisaig *H'land*	79	C9
Ariundle *H'land*	79	E11
Arkendale *N Yorks*	51	C9
Arkesden *Essex*	29	E11
Arkholme *Lancs*	50	B1
Arkle Town *N Yorks*	58	F1
Arkley *London*	19	B9
Arksey *S Yorks*	45	B9
Arkwright Town *Derby*	45	E8
Arle *Glos*	26	F6
Arlecdon *Cumb*	56	E2
Arlesey *Beds*	29	E8
Arleston *Telford*	34	D2
Arley *Ches*	43	D9
Arlingham *Glos*	26	G4
Arlington *Devon*	6	B5
Arlington *E Sussex*	12	F4
Arlington *Glos*	27	H8
Armadale *H'land*	93	C10
Armadale *W Loth*	69	D8
Armadale Castle *H'land*	85	H11
Armathwaite *Cumb*	57	B7
Arminghall *Norfolk*	39	E8
Armitage *Staffs*	35	D6
Armley *W Yorks*	51	F8
Armscote *Warwick*	27	D9
Armthorpe *S Yorks*	45	B10
Arnabost *Arg/Bute*	78	F5
Arncliffe *N Yorks*	50	B5
Arncroach *Fife*	77	G8
Arne *Dorset*	9	F8
Arnesby *Leics*	36	F2
Arngask *Perth/Kinr*	76	F4
Arnisdale *H'land*	85	G13
Arnish *H'land*	85	D10
Arniston Engine *Midloth*	70	D2
Arnol *W Isles*	91	C8
Arnold *ER Yorks*	53	E7
Arnold *Notts*	45	H9
Arnprior *Stirl*	68	A5
Arnside *Cumb*	49	B4
Aros Mains *Arg/Bute*	79	G8
Arowry *Wrex*	33	B10
Arpafeelie *H'land*	87	F9
Arrad Foot *Cumb*	49	A3
Arram *ER Yorks*	52	E6
Arrathorne *N Yorks*	58	G3
Arreton *I/Wight*	10	F4
Arrington *Cambs*	29	C10
Arrivain *Arg/Bute*	74	D5
Arrochar *Arg/Bute*	74	G5
Arrow *Warwick*	27	C7
Arthington *W Yorks*	51	E8
Arthingworth *Northants*	36	G3
Arthog *Gwyn*	32	D2
Arthrath *Aberds*	89	E9
Arthurstone *Perth/Kinr*	76	C5
Artrochie *Aberds*	89	E10
Arundel *W Sussex*	11	D9
Aryhoulan *H'land*	80	G2
Asby *Cumb*	56	D2
Ascog *Arg/Bute*	73	G10
Ascot *Windsor*	18	E6
Ascott *Warwick*	27	E10
Ascott-under-Wychwood *Oxon*	27	G10
Asenby *N Yorks*	51	B9
Asfordby *Leics*	36	D3
Asfordby Hill *Leics*	36	D3
Asgarby *Lincs*	46	H5

Asgarby Lincs 47 F7
Ash Kent 20 E2
Ash Kent 21 F9
Ash Som'set 8 B3
Ash Surrey 18 F5
Ash Bullayne Devon 7 F6
Ash Green Warwick 35 G9
Ash Magna Shrops 34 B1
Ash Mill Devon 7 D6
Ash Priors Som'set 7 D10
Ash Street Suffolk 31 D7
Ash Thomas Devon 7 E9
Ash Vale Surrey 18 F5
Ashampstead W Berks 18 D2
Ashbocking Suffolk 31 C8
Ashbourne Derby 44 H5
Ashbrittle Som'set 7 D9
Ashburton Devon 5 E8
Ashbury Devon 6 G4
Ashbury Oxon 17 C9
Ashby N Lincs 46 B3
Ashby by Partney Lincs 47 F8
Ashby cum Fenby NE Lincs 46 B6
Ashby de la Launde Lincs 46 G4
Ashby-de-la-Zouch Leics 35 D9
Ashby Folville Leics 36 D3
Ashby Magna Leics 36 F1
Ashby Parva Leics 35 G11
Ashby Puerorum Lincs 47 E7
Ashby St Ledgers Northants 28 B2
Ashby St Mary Norfolk 39 E9
Ashchurch Glos 26 E6
Ashcombe Devon 5 D10
Ashcott Som'set 15 H10
Ashdon Essex 30 D2
Ashe Hants 18 G2
Asheldham Essex 20 A6
Ashen Essex 30 D4
Ashendon Bucks 28 G4
Ashfield Carms 24 F3
Ashfield Stirl 75 G10
Ashfield Suffolk 31 B9
Ashfield Green Suffolk 31 A9
Ashfold Crossways W Sussex 11 B11
Ashford Devon 6 C4
Ashford Hants 9 C10
Ashford Kent 13 B9
Ashford Surrey 19 D7
Ashford Bowdler Shrops 26 A2
Ashford Carbonell Shrops 26 A2
Ashford Hill Hants 18 E2
Ashford in the Water Derby 44 F5
Ashgill S Lanarks 68 F6
Ashill Devon 7 E9
Ashill Norfolk 38 E4
Ashill Som'set 8 C2
Ashingdon Essex 20 B5
Ashington Northum 63 E8
Ashington Som'set 8 B4
Ashington W Sussex 11 C10
Ashintully Castle Perth/Kinr 76 A4
Ashkirk Scot Borders 61 A10
Ashlett Hants 10 D3
Ashleworth Glos 26 F5
Ashley Cambs 30 B3
Ashley Ches 43 D10
Ashley Devon 6 E5
Ashley Dorset 9 D10
Ashley Glos 16 B6
Ashley Hants 10 E1
Ashley Hants 10 A2
Ashley Northants 36 F3
Ashley Staffs 34 B3
Ashley Green Bucks 28 H6
Ashley Heath Dorset 9 D10
Ashley Heath Staffs 34 B3
Ashmanhaugh Norfolk 39 C9
Ashmansworth Hants 17 F11
Ashmansworthy Devon 6 E2
Ashmore Dorset 9 C8
Ashorne Warwick 27 C10
Ashover Derby 45 F7
Ashow Warwick 27 A10
Ashprington Devon 5 F9
Ashreigney Devon 6 E5
Ashtead Surrey 19 F8
Ashton Ches 43 F8
Ashton Cornw'l 2 G5
Ashton Hants 10 C4
Ashton Heref'd 26 B2
Ashton Inverci 73 F11
Ashton Northants 28 D4
Ashton Northants 37 G6
Ashton Common Wilts 16 F5
Ashton-In-Makerfield Gtr Man 43 C8
Ashton Keynes Wilts 17 B7
Ashton under Hill Worcs 26 E6
Ashton-under-Lyne Gtr Man 44 C3
Ashton upon Mersey Gtr Man 43 C10
Ashurst Hants 10 C2
Ashurst Kent 12 C4
Ashurst W Sussex 11 C10
Ashurstwood W Sussex 12 C3
Ashwater Devon 6 G3
Ashwell Herts 29 E9
Ashwell Rutl'd 36 D4
Ashwell Som'set 8 C2
Ashwellthorpe Norfolk 39 F7
Ashwick Som'set 16 G3
Ashwicken Norfolk 38 D3
Ashybank Scot Borders 61 B11
Askam in Furness Cumb 49 B2
Askern S Yorks 45 A9
Askerswell Dorset 8 E4
Askett Bucks 28 H5
Askham Cumb 57 D7
Askham Notts 45 E11
Askham Bryan C/York 52 E1
Askham Richard C/York 51 E11
Asknish Arg/Bute 73 D8
Askrigg N Yorks 57 G11
Askwith N Yorks 51 E7
Aslackby Lincs 37 B6
Aslacton Norfolk 39 F7
Aslockton Notts 36 B3
Asloun Aberds 83 B7
Aspatria Cumb 56 B3
Aspenden Herts 29 F10
Asperton Lincs 37 B8
Aspley Guise Beds 28 E6
Aspley Heath Beds 28 E6
Aspull Gtr Man 43 B9
Asselby ER Yorks 52 G3
Asserby Lincs 47 E8
Assington Suffolk 30 E6
Assynt Ho. H'land 87 E8
Astbury Ches 44 F2
Astcote Northants 28 C3
Asterley Shrops 33 E9
Asterton Shrops 33 F9
Asthall Oxon 27 G9
Asthall Leigh Oxon 27 G10
Astley Shrops 33 D11
Astley Warwick 35 G9
Astley Worcs 26 B4
Astley Abbotts Shrops 34 F3
Astley Bridge Gtr Man 43 A10
Astley Cross Worcs 26 B5
Astley Green Gtr Man 43 C10
Aston Ches 43 H9
Aston Ches 43 E8
Aston Derby 44 D5
Aston Heref'd 25 A11
Aston Herts 29 F9
Aston Oxon 17 A10
Aston Shrops 33 C11
Aston Staffs 34 A3
Aston S Yorks 45 D8
Aston Telford 34 E2
Aston W Midlands 35 G6
Aston Wokingham 18 C4
Aston Abbotts Bucks 28 F5
Aston Botterell Shrops 34 G2
Aston-by-Stone Staffs 34 B5
Aston Cantlow Warwick 27 C8
Aston Clinton Bucks 28 G5
Aston Crews Heref'd 26 F3
Aston Cross Glos 26 E6
Aston End Herts 29 F9
Aston Eyre Shrops 34 F2
Aston Fields Worcs 26 B6
Aston Flamville Leics 35 F10
Aston Ingham Heref'd 26 F3
Aston juxta Mondrum Ches 43 G9
Aston le Walls Northants 27 C11
Aston Magna Glos 27 E8
Aston Munslow Shrops 33 G11
Aston on Clun Shrops 33 G9
Aston-on-Trent Derby 35 C10
Aston Rogers Shrops 33 E9
Aston Rowant Oxon 18 B4
Aston Sandford Bucks 28 H4
Aston Somerville Worcs 27 E7
Aston Subedge Glos 27 D8
Aston Tirrold Oxon 18 C2
Aston Upthorpe Oxon 18 C2
Astrop Northants 28 E2
Astwick Beds 29 E9
Astwood M/Keynes 28 D6
Astwood Worcs 26 C5
Astwood Bank Worcs 27 B7
Aswarby Lincs 37 B6
Aswardby Lincs 47 E7
Atch Lench Worcs 27 C7
Atcham Shrops 33 E11
Athelhampton Dorset 9 E6
Athelington Suffolk 31 A9
Athelney Som'set 8 B2
Athelstaneford E Loth 70 C4
Atherington Devon 6 D4
Atherstone Warwick 35 F9
Atherstone on Stour Warwick 27 C9
Atherton Gtr Man 43 B9
Atley Hill N Yorks 58 F3
Atlow Derby 44 H6
Attadale H'land 86 H2
Attadale Ho. H'land 86 H2
Attenborough Notts 35 B11
Atterby Lincs 46 C3
Attercliffe S Yorks 45 D7
Attleborough Norfolk 38 F6
Attleborough Warwick 35 F9
Attlebridge Norfolk 39 D7
Atwick ER Yorks 53 D7
Atworth Wilts 16 E5
Aubourn Lincs 46 F3
Auchagallon N Ayrs 66 C1
Auchallater Aberds 82 E3
Aucharnie Aberds 89 D6
Auchattie Aberds 83 D8
Auchavan Angus 82 G3
Auchbreck Moray 82 A4
Auchenback E Renf 68 E4
Auchenbainzie Dumf/Gal 60 D4
Auchenblae Aberds 83 F9
Auchenbrack Dumf/Gal 60 D3
Auchenbreck Arg/Bute 73 E9
Auchencairn Dumf/Gal 55 D10
Auchencairn Dumf/Gal 60 E5
Auchencairn N Ayrs 66 D3
Auchencrosh S Ayrs 54 B4
Auchencrow Scot Borders 71 D7
Auchendinny Midloth 69 D11
Auchengray S Lanarks 69 E8
Auchenhalrig Moray 88 B3
Auchenheath S Lanarks 69 F7
Auchenlochan Arg/Bute 73 F8
Auchenmalg Dumf/Gal 54 D5
Auchensoul S Ayrs 66 G5
Auchentiber N Ayrs 67 B6
Auchertyre H'land 85 F13
Auchgourish H'land 81 B11
Auchincarroch W Dunb 68 B3
Auchindrain Arg/Bute 73 C9
Auchindrean H'land 86 C4
Auchininna Aberds 89 D6
Auchinleck E Ayrs 67 D8
Auchinloch N Lanarks 68 C5
Auchinroath Moray 88 C2
Auchintoul Aberds 83 B7
Auchiries Aberds 89 E10
Auchlee Aberds 83 D10
Auchleven Aberds 83 A8
Auchlochan S Lanarks 69 G7
Auchlossan Aberds 83 C7
Auchlunies Aberds 83 D10
Auchlyne Stirl 75 E8
Auchmacoy Aberds 89 E9
Auchmair Moray 82 A5
Auchmantle Dumf/Gal 54 C4
Auchmillan E Ayrs 67 D8
Auchmithie Angus 77 C9
Auchmuirbridge Fife 76 G5
Auchmull Angus 83 F7
Auchnacree Angus 77 A7
Auchnagallin H'land 87 H13
Auchnagatt Aberds 89 D9
Auchnaha Arg/Bute 73 E8
Auchnashelloch Perth/Kinr 75 F10
Aucholzie Aberds 82 D5
Auchrannie Angus 76 B5
Auchroisk H'land 82 A2
Auchronie Angus 82 E6
Auchterarder Perth/Kinr 76 F2
Auchteraw H'land 80 C5
Auchterderran Fife 76 H5
Auchterhouse Angus 76 D6
Auchtermuchty Fife 76 F5
Auchterneed H'land 86 F7
Auchtertool Fife 69 A11
Auchtertyre Moray 88 C1
Auchtubh Stirl 75 E8
Auckengill H'land 94 D5
Auckley S Yorks 45 B10
Audenshaw Gtr Man 44 C3
Audlem Ches 34 A2
Audley Staffs 43 G10
Audley End Essex 30 E5
Auds Aberds 89 B6
Aughton ER Yorks 52 F3
Aughton Lancs 43 B6
Aughton Lancs 50 C1
Aughton S Yorks 45 D8
Aughton Wilts 17 F9
Aughton Park Lancs 43 B7
Auldearn H'land 87 F12
Aulden Heref'd 25 C11
Auldgirth Dumf/Gal 60 E5
Auldhame E Loth 70 B4
Auldhouse S Lanarks 68 E5
Ault a'chruinn H'land 80 A1
Aultanrynie H'land 92 F6
Aultbea H'land 91 J13
Aultdearg H'land 86 E5
Aultgrishan H'land 91 J12
Aultguish Inn H'land 86 D6
Aultibea H'land 93 G13
Aultiphurst H'land 93 C11
Aultmore Moray 88 C4
Aultnagoire H'land 81 A7
Aultnamain Inn H'land 87 C9
Aultnaslat H'land 80 C3
Aulton Aberds 83 A8
Aundorach H'land 82 B1
Aunsby Lincs 36 B6
Auquhorthies Aberds 89 F8
Aust S Glos 16 C2
Austendike Lincs 37 C8
Austerfield S Yorks 45 C10
Austrey Warwick 35 E8
Austwick N Yorks 50 C3
Authorpe Lincs 47 D8
Authorpe Row Lincs 47 E9
Avebury Wilts 17 E8
Aveley Thurr'k 20 C2
Avening Glos 16 B5
Averham Notts 45 G11
Aveton Gifford Devon 5 G8
Avielochan H'land 81 B11
Aviemore H'land 81 B10
Avington Hants 10 A4
Avington W Berks 17 E10
Avoch H'land 87 F10
Avon Hants 9 E10
Avon Dassett Warwick 27 D11
Avonbridge Falk 69 C8
Avonmouth Bristol 15 D11
Avonwick Devon 5 F8
Awbridge Hants 10 B2
Awhirk Dumf/Gal 54 D3
Awkley S Glouc 16 C2
Awliscombe Devon 7 F10
Awre Glos 26 H4
Awsworth Notts 35 A10
Axbridge Som'set 15 F10
Axford Hants 18 G3
Axford Wilts 17 D9
Axminster Devon 8 E1
Axmouth Devon 8 E1
Axton Flints 42 D4
Aycliff Kent 21 G10
Aycliffe Durham 58 D3
Aydon Northum 62 G6
Aylburton Glos 16 A3
Ayle Northum 57 B9
Aylesbeare Devon 7 G9
Aylesbury Bucks 28 G5
Aylesby NE Lincs 46 B6
Aylesford Kent 20 F4
Aylesham Kent 21 F9
Aylestone Leics C 36 E1
Aylmerton Norfolk 39 B7
Aylsham Norfolk 39 C7
Aylton Heref'd 26 E3
Aymestrey Heref'd 25 B11
Aynho Northants 28 E2
Ayot St Lawrence Herts 29 G8
Ayot St Peter Herts 29 G9
Ayr S Ayrs 66 D6
Aysgarth N Yorks 58 H1
Ayside Cumb 49 A3
Ayston Rutl'd 36 E4
Aythorpe Roding Essex 30 G2
Ayton Scot Borders 71 D8
Aywick Shetl'd 96 E7
Azerley N Yorks 51 B8

B

Babbacombe Torbay 5 E10
Babbinswood Shrops 33 B9
Babcary Som'set 8 B4
Babel Carms 24 E5
Babell Flints 42 E4
Babraham Cambs 30 C2
Babworth Notts 45 D10
Bac W Isles 91 C9
Bachau Angl 40 B6
Back of Keppoch H'land 79 C9
Back Rogerton E Ayrs 67 D8
Backaland Orkney 95 E6
Backaskaill Orkney 95 C5
Backbarrow Cumb 49 A3
Backe Carms 23 E7
Backfolds Aberds 89 C10
Backford Ches 43 E7
Backford Cross Ches 43 E6
Backhill Aberds 89 E7
Backhill Aberds 89 E10
Backhill of Clackriach Aberds 89 D9
Backhill of Fortree Aberds 89 D9
Backhill of Trustach Aberds 83 D8
Backies H'land 93 J11
Backlass H'land 94 E4
Backwell N Som'set 15 E10
Backworth Tyne/Wear 63 F9
Bacon End Essex 30 G3
Baconsthorpe Norfolk 39 B7
Bacton Heref'd 25 E10
Bacton Norfolk 39 B9
Bacton Suffolk 31 B7
Bacton Green Suffolk 31 B7
Bacup Lancs 50 G4
Badachro H'land 85 A12
Badanloch Lodge H'land 93 F10
Badavanich H'land 86 F4
Badbury Swindon 17 C8
Badby Northants 28 C2
Badcall H'land 92 D5
Badcaul H'land 86 B3
Baddeley Green Stoke 44 G3
Baddesley Clinton Warwick 27 A9
Baddesley Ensor Warwick 35 F8
Baddidarach H'land 92 G3
Baddoch Aberds 82 E3
Baddock H'land 87 F10
Badenscoth Aberds 89 E7
Badenyon Aberds 82 B5
Badger Shrops 34 F3
Badger's Mount Kent 19 E11
Badgeworth Glos 26 G6
Badgworth Som'set 15 F9
Badicaul H'land 85 F12
Badingham Suffolk 31 B10
Badlesmere Kent 21 F7
Badlipster H'land 94 F4
Badluarach H'land 86 B2
Badminton S Glos 16 C5
Badnaban H'land 92 G3
Badninish H'land 87 B10
Badrallach H'land 86 B3
Badsey Worcs 27 D7
Badshot Lea Surrey 18 G5
Badsworth W Yorks 45 A8
Badwell Ash Suffolk 30 B6
Bae Colwyn = Colwyn Bay Conwy 41 C10
Bag Enderby Lincs 47 E7
Bagby N Yorks 51 A10
Bagendon Glos 27 H7
Bagh a Chaisteil = Castlebay W Isles 84 J1
Bagh Mor W Isles 84 C3
Bagh Shiarabhagh W Isles 84 H2
Baghasdal W Isles 84 G2
Bagillt Flints 42 E5
Baginton Warwick 27 A10
Baglan Neath P Talb 14 B3
Bagley Shrops 33 C10
Bagnall Staffs 44 G3
Bagnor W Berks 17 E11
Bagshot Surrey 18 E6
Bagshot Wilts 17 E10
Bagthorpe Norfolk 38 B3
Bagthorpe Notts 45 G8
Bagworth Leics 35 E10
Bagwy Llydiart Heref'd 25 F11
Bail Ard Bhuirgh W Isles 91 B9
Bail Uachdraich W Isles 84 B3
Baildon W Yorks 51 F7
Baile W Isles 90 J4
Baile a Mhanaich W Isles 84 C2
Baile Ailein W Isles 91 E7
Baile an Truiseil W Isles 91 B8
Baile Boidheach Arg/Bute 72 F6
Baile Glas W Isles 84 C3
Baile Mhartainn W Isles 84 A2
Baile Mhic Phail W Isles 84 A3
Baile Mor Arg/Bute 78 J5
Baile Mor W Isles 84 B2
Baile na Creige W Isles 84 H1
Baile nan Cailleach W Isles 84 C2
Baile Raghaill W Isles 84 A2
Baileyhead Cumb 61 F11
Bailiesward Aberds 88 E4
Baillieston C/Glasg 68 D5
Bail'lochdrach W Isles 84 C3
Bail'Ur Tholastaidh W Isles 91 C10
Bainbridge N Yorks 57 G11
Bainsford Falk 69 B7
Bainshole Aberds 88 E6
Bainton ER Yorks 52 D5
Bainton Peterbro 37 E6
Bairnkine Scot Borders 62 B2
Baker Street Thurr'k 20 C3
Baker's End Herts 29 G10
Bakewell Derby 44 F6
Bala = Y Bala Gwyn 32 B5
Balachuirn H'land 85 D10
Balavil H'land 81 C9
Balbeg H'land 86 H7
Balbeg H'land 81 A6
Balbeggie Perth/Kinr 76 E4
Balbithan Aberds 83 B9
Balbithan Ho. Aberds 83 B10
Balblair H'land 87 E10
Balblair H'land 87 B8
Balby S Yorks 45 B9
Balchladich H'land 92 F3
Balchraggan H'land 87 H8
Balchraggan H'land 87 G8
Balchrick H'land 92 D4
Balchrystie Fife 77 G7
Balcladaich H'land 80 A4
Balcombe W Sussex 12 C2
Balcombe Lane W Sussex 12 C2
Balcomie Fife 77 F9
Balcurvie Fife 76 G6
Baldersby N Yorks 51 B9
Baldersby St James N Yorks 51 B9
Balderstone Lancs 50 F2
Balderton Ches 42 F6
Balderton Notts 46 G2
Baldhu Cornw'l 3 E6
Baldinnie Fife 77 F7
Baldock Herts 29 E9
Baldovie Dundee C 77 D7
Baldrine I/Man 48 D4
Baldslow E Sussex 13 E6
Baldwin I/Man 48 D3
Baldwinholme Cumb 56 A5
Baldwin's Gate Staffs 34 A3
Bale Norfolk 38 B6
Balearn Aberds 89 C10
Balemartine Arg/Bute 78 G2
Balephuil Arg/Bute 78 G2
Balerno C/Edinb 69 D10
Balevullin Arg/Bute 78 G2
Balfield Angus 83 G7
Balfour Orkney 95 G5
Balfron Stirl 68 B4
Balfron Station Stirl 68 B4
Balgaveny Aberds 89 D6
Balgavies Angus 77 B8
Balgonar Fife 69 A9
Balgove Aberds 89 E8
Balgowan H'land 81 D8
Balgown H'land 85 B8
Balgrochan E Dunb 68 C5
Balgy H'land 85 C13
Balhaldie Stirl 75 G11
Balhalgardy Aberds 83 A9
Balham London 19 D9
Balhary Perth/Kinr 76 C5
Baliasta Shetl'd 96 C8
Baligill H'land 93 C11
Balintore Angus 76 B5
Balintore H'land 87 D11
Balintraid H'land 87 D10
Balk N Yorks 51 A10
Balkeerie Angus 76 C6
Balkemback Angus 76 D6
Balkholme ER Yorks 52 G3
Balkissock S Ayrs 54 A4
Ball Shrops 33 C9
Ball Haye Green Staffs 44 G3
Ball Hill Hants 17 E11
Ballabeg I/Man 48 E2
Ballacannel I/Man 48 D4
Ballachulish H'land 74 B3
Ballajora I/Man 48 C4
Ballaleigh I/Man 48 D3
Ballamodha I/Man 48 E2
Ballantrae S Ayrs 54 A3
Ballaquine I/Man 48 D4
Ballards Gore Essex 20 B6
Ballasalla I/Man 48 C3
Ballasalla I/Man 48 E2
Ballater Aberds 82 D5
Ballaugh I/Man 48 C3
Ballaveare I/Man 48 E3
Ballcorach Moray 82 A3
Ballechin Perth/Kinr 76 B2
Balleigh H'land 87 C10
Ballencrieff E Loth 70 C3
Ballentoul Perth/Kinr 81 G10
Ballidon Derby 44 G6
Balliemore Arg/Bute 73 E9
Balliemore Arg/Bute 79 J11
Ballikinrain Stirl 68 B4
Ballimeanoch Arg/Bute 73 B9
Ballimore Arg/Bute 73 E8
Ballimore Stirl 75 F8
Ballinaby Arg/Bute 64 B3
Ballindean Perth/Kinr 76 E5
Ballingdon Suffolk 30 D5
Ballinger Common Bucks 18 A6
Ballingham Heref'd 26 E2
Ballingry Fife 76 H4
Ballinlick Perth/Kinr 76 C2
Ballinluig Perth/Kinr 76 B2
Ballintuim Perth/Kinr 76 B4
Balloch Angus 76 B6
Balloch H'land 87 G10
Balloch N Lanarks 68 C6
Balloch W Dunb 68 B2
Ballochan Aberds 83 D7
Ballochford Moray 88 E3
Ballochmorrie S Ayrs 54 A5
Balls Cross W Sussex 11 B8
Balls Green Essex 31 F7
Ballygown Arg/Bute 78 G7
Ballygrant Arg/Bute 64 B4
Ballyhaugh Arg/Bute 78 F4
Balmacara H'land 85 F13
Balmacara Square H'land 85 F13
Balmaclellan Dumf/Gal 55 B9
Balmacneil Perth/Kinr 76 B2
Balmacqueen H'land 85 A9
Balmae Dumf/Gal 55 E9
Balmaha Stirl 68 A3
Balmalcolm Fife 76 G6
Balmeanach H'land 85 D10
Balmedie Aberds 83 B11
Balmer Heath Shrops 33 B10
Balmerino Fife 76 E6
Balmerlawn Hants 10 D2
Balmichael N Ayrs 66 C2
Balmirmer Angus 77 D8
Balmore H'land 85 D7
Balmore H'land 86 H6
Balmore H'land 87 G11
Balmore Perth/Kinr 76 B2
Balmule Fife 69 B11
Balmullo Fife 77 E7
Balmungie H'land 87 F10
Balnaboth Angus 82 G5
Balnabruaich H'land 87 E10
Balnabruich H'land 94 H3
Balnacoil H'land 93 H11
Balnacra H'land 86 G2
Balnafoich H'land 87 H9
Balnagall H'land 87 C11
Balnaguard Perth/Kinr 76 B2
Balnahard Arg/Bute 72 D3
Balnahard Arg/Bute 78 H7
Balnain H'land 86 H7
Balnakeil H'land 92 C6
Balnaknock H'land 85 B9
Balnapaling H'land 87 E10
Balne N Yorks 52 H1
Balochroy Arg/Bute 65 C8
Balone Fife 77 F7
Balornock C/Glasg 68 D5
Balquharn Perth/Kinr 76 D3
Balquhidder Stirl 75 E8
Balsall W Midlands 35 H8
Balsall Common W Midlands 35 H8
Balsall Heath W Midlands 35 G6
Balscott Oxon 27 D10
Balsham Cambs 30 C2
Baltasound Shetl'd 96 C8
Balterley Staffs 43 G10
Baltersan Dumf/Gal 55 C7
Balthangie Aberds 89 C8
Baltonsborough Som'set 8 A4
Balvaird H'land 87 F8
Balvicar Arg/Bute 72 B6
Balvraid H'land 85 G13
Balvraid H'land 87 H11
Bamber Bridge Lancs 50 G1
Bambers Green Essex 30 F2
Bamburgh Northum 71 G10
Bamff Perth/Kinr 76 B5
Bamford Derby 44 D6
Bamford Gtr Man 44 A2
Bampton Cumb 57 E7
Bampton Devon 7 D8
Bampton Oxon 17 A10
Bampton Grange Cumb 57 E7
Banavie H'land 80 F3
Banbury Oxon 27 D11
Bancffosfelen Carms 23 E9
Banchory Aberds 83 D8
Banchory-Devenick Aberds 83 C11
Bancycapel Carms 23 E9
Bancyfelin Carms 23 E8
Bancyffordd Carms 23 C9
Bandirran Perth/Kinr 76 D5
Banff Aberds 89 B6
Bangor Gwyn 41 C7
Bangor-is-y-coed Wrex 43 H6
Banham Norfolk 39 G6
Bank Hants 10 D1
Bank Newton N Yorks 50 D5
Bank Street Worcs 26 B3
Bankend Dumf/Gal 60 G6
Bankfoot Perth/Kinr 76 D3
Bankglen E Ayrs 67 E9
Bankhead Aberd C 83 B10
Bankhead Aberds 83 C8
Banknock Falk 68 C6
Banks Cumb 61 G11
Banks Lancs 49 G3
Bankshill Dumf/Gal 61 E7
Banningham Norfolk 39 C8
Banniskirk Ho. H'land 94 E3
Bannister Green Essex 30 F3
Bannockburn Stirl 69 A7
Banstead Surrey 19 F9
Bantham Devon 5 G7
Banton N Lanarks 68 C6
Banwell N Som'set 15 F9
Banyard's Green Suffolk 31 A9
Bapchild Kent 20 E6
Bar Hill Cambs 29 B10
Barabhas W Isles 91 C8
Barabhas Iarach W Isles 91 C8
Barabhas Uarach W Isles 91 B8
Barachandroman Arg/Bute 79 J9
Barassie S Ayrs 66 C6
Baravullin Arg/Bute 79 H11
Barbaraville H'land 87 D10
Barber Booth Derby 44 D5
Barbieston S Ayrs 67 E7
Barbon Cumb 50 A2
Barbridge Ches 43 G9
Barbrook Devon 6 B6
Barby Northants 28 A2
Barcaldine Arg/Bute 74 C2
Barcheston Warwick 27 E9
Barcombe E Sussex 12 E3
Barcombe Cross E Sussex 12 E3
Barden N Yorks 58 G2
Barden Scale N Yorks 51 D6
Bardennoch Dumf/Gal 67 G8
Bardfield Saling Essex 30 F3
Bardister Shetl'd 96 F5
Bardney Lincs 46 F5
Bardon Leics 35 D10
Bardon Mill Northum 62 G3
Bardowie E Dunb 68 C4
Bardrainney Inverci 68 C2
Bardsea Cumb 49 B3
Bardsey W Yorks 51 E9
Bardwell Suffolk 30 A6
Bare Lancs 49 C4
Barfad Arg/Bute 73 G7
Barford Norfolk 39 E7
Barford Warwick 27 B9
Barford St John Oxon 27 E11
Barford St Martin Wilts 9 A9
Barford St Michael Oxon 27 E11
Barfreston Kent 21 F9
Bargod = Bargoed Caerph 15 B7
Bargoed = Bargod Caerph 15 B7
Bargrennan Dumf/Gal 54 B6
Barham Cambs 37 H7
Barham Kent 21 F9
Barham Suffolk 31 C8
Barharrow Dumf/Gal 55 D9
Barhill Dumf/Gal 55 C11
Barholm Lincs 37 D6
Barkby Leics 36 E2
Barkestone-le-Vale Leics 36 B3
Barkham Wokingham 18 E4
Barking London 19 C11
Barking Suffolk 31 C7
Barking Tye Suffolk 31 C7
Barkingside London 19 C11
Barkisland W Yorks 51 H6
Barkston Lincs 36 A5
Barkston N Yorks 51 F10
Barkway Herts 29 E10
Barlaston Staffs 34 B4
Barlavington W Sussex 11 C8
Barlborough Derby 45 E8
Barlby N Yorks 52 F2
Barlestone Leics 35 E10
Barley Herts 29 E10
Barley Lancs 50 E4
Barley Mow Tyne/Wear 58 A3
Barleythorpe Rutl'd 36 E4
Barling Essex 20 C6
Barlow Derby 45 E7
Barlow N Yorks 52 G2
Barlow Tyne/Wear 63 G7
Barmby Moor ER Yorks 52 E3
Barmby on the Marsh ER Yorks 52 G2
Barmer Norfolk 38 B4
Barmoor Castle Northum 71 G8
Barmoor Lane End Northum 71 G9
Barmouth = Abermaw Gwyn 32 D2
Barmpton D'lington 58 E4
Barmston ER Yorks 53 D7
Barnack Peterbro 37 E6
Barnacle Warwick 35 G9
Barnard Castle Durham 58 E1
Barnard Gate Oxon 27 G11
Barnardiston Suffolk 30 D4
Barnbarroch Dumf/Gal 55 D11
Barnburgh S Yorks 45 B8
Barnby Suffolk 39 G10
Barnby Dun S Yorks 45 B10
Barnby in the Willows Notts 46 G2
Barnby Moor Notts 45 D10
Barnes Street Kent 20 G3
Barnet London 19 B9
Barnetby le Wold N Lincs 46 B4
Barney Norfolk 38 B5
Barnham Suffolk 38 H4
Barnham W Sussex 11 D8
Barnham Broom Norfolk 39 E6
Barnhead Angus 77 B9
Barnhill Ches 43 G7
Barnhill Dundee C 77 D7
Barnhill Moray 88 C1
Barnhills Dumf/Gal 54 B2
Barningham Durham 58 E1
Barningham Suffolk 38 H5
Barnoldby le Beck NE Lincs 46 B6
Barnoldswick Lancs 50 E4
Barns Green W Sussex 11 B10
Barnsley Glos 27 H7
Barnsley S Yorks 45 B7
Barnstaple Devon 6 C4
Barnston Essex 30 G3
Barnston Mersey 42 D5
Barnstone Notts 36 B3
Barnt Green Worcs 27 A7
Barnton Ches 43 E9
Barnton C/Edinb 69 C10
Barnwell All Saints Northants 36 G6
Barnwell St Andrew Northants 36 G6
Barnwood Glos 26 G5
Barochreal Arg/Bute 79 J11
Barons Cross Heref'd 25 C11
Barr S Ayrs 66 G5
Barra Castle Aberds 83 A9
Barrachan Dumf/Gal 54 E6
Barrack Aberds 89 D8
Barraglom W Isles 90 D6
Barrahormid Arg/Bute 72 E6
Barran Arg/Bute 79 J11
Barrapol Arg/Bute 78 G2
Barras Aberds 83 E10
Barras Cumb 57 E10
Barrasford Northum 62 F5
Barravullin Arg/Bute 73 C7
Barregarrow I/Man 48 D3
Barrhead E Renf 68 E3
Barrhill S Ayrs 54 A5
Barrington Cambs 29 D10
Barrington Som'set 8 C2
Barripper Cornw'l 2 F5
Barrmill N Ayrs 67 A6
Barrock H'land 94 C4
Barrock Ho. H'land 94 D4
Barrow Lancs 50 F3
Barrow Rutl'd 36 D4
Barrow Suffolk 30 B4
Barrow Green Kent 20 E6
Barrow Gurney N Som'set 15 E11
Barrow Haven N Lincs 53 G6
Barrow-in-Furness Cumb 49 C2
Barrow Island Cumb 49 C1
Barrow Nook Lancs 43 B7
Barrow Street Wilts 9 A7
Barrow upon Humber N Lincs 53 G6
Barrow upon Soar Leics 36 D1
Barrow upon Trent Derby 35 C9
Barroway Drove Norfolk 38 E2
Barrowburn Northum 62 B4
Barrowby Lincs 36 B4
Barrowcliff N Yorks 59 H11
Barrowden Rutl'd 36 E5
Barrowford Lancs 50 F4
Barrows Green Ches 43 G9
Barrows Green Cumb 57 H7
Barrow's Green Mersey 43 D8
Barry Angus 77 D8
Barry = Y Barri V/Glam 15 E7
Barry Island V/Glam 15 E7
Barsby Leics 36 D2
Barsham Suffolk 39 G9
Barston W Midlands 35 H8
Bartestree Heref'd 26 D2
Barthol Chapel Aberds 89 E8
Barthomley Ches 43 G10
Bartley Hants 10 C2
Bartley Green W Midlands 34 G6
Bartlow Cambs 30 D2
Barton Cambs 29 C11
Barton Ches 43 G7
Barton Glos 27 F8
Barton Lancs 42 B6
Barton Lancs 49 F5
Barton N Yorks 58 F3
Barton Oxon 28 H2
Barton Torbay 5 E10
Barton Warwick 27 C8
Barton Bendish Norfolk 38 E3
Barton Hartshorn Bucks 28 E3
Barton in Fabis Notts 35 B11
Barton in the Beans Leics 35 E9
Barton-le-Clay Beds 29 E7
Barton-le-Street N Yorks 52 B3
Barton-le-Willows N Yorks 52 C3
Barton Mills Suffolk 30 A4
Barton on Sea Hants 9 E11
Barton on the Heath Warwick 27 E9
Barton St David Som'set 8 A4
Barton Seagrave Northants 36 H4
Barton Stacey Hants 17 G11
Barton Turf Norfolk 39 C9
Barton-under-Needwood Staffs 35 D7
Barton-upon-Humber N Lincs 52 G6
Barton Waterside N Lincs 52 G6
Barugh S Yorks 45 B7
Barway Cambs 37 H11
Barwell Leics 35 F10
Barwick Herts 29 G10
Barwick Som'set 8 C4
Barwick in Elmet W Yorks 51 F9
Baschurch Shrops 33 C10
Bascote Warwick 27 B11
Basford Green Staffs 44 G3
Bashall Eaves Lancs 50 E2
Bashley Hants 9 E11
Basildon Essex 20 C4
Basingstoke Hants 18 F3
Baslow Derby 44 E6
Bason Bridge Som'set 15 G9
Bassaleg Newp 15 C8
Bassenthwaite Cumb 56 C4
Bassett S'thampton 10 C3
Bassingbourn Cambs 29 D10
Bassingfield Notts 36 B2
Bassingham Lincs 46 F3
Bassingthorpe Lincs 36 C5
Basta Shetl'd 96 D7
Baston Lincs 37 D7
Bastwick Norfolk 39 D10
Baswick Steer ER Yorks 53 E6
Batchworth Heath Herts 19 B7
Batcombe Dorset 8 D5
Batcombe Som'set 16 H3
Bate Heath Ches 43 E9
Batford Herts 29 G8
Bath Bath/NE Som'set 16 E4
Bathampton Bath/NE Som'set 16 E4
Bathealton Som'set 7 D9
Batheaston Bath/NE Som'set 16 E4
Bathford Bath/NE Som'set 16 E4
Bathgate W Loth 69 D8
Bathley Notts 45 G11
Bathpool Cornw'l 4 D3
Bathpool Som'set 8 B1
Bathville W Loth 69 D8
Batley W Yorks 51 G8
Batsford Glos 27 E8
Battersby N Yorks 59 F6
Battersea London 19 D9
Battisborough Cross Devon 5 G6
Battisford Suffolk 31 C7
Battisford Tye Suffolk 31 C7
Battle E Sussex 12 E6
Battle Powys 25 E7
Battledown Glos 26 F6
Battlefield Shrops 33 D11
Battlesbridge Essex 20 B4
Battlesden Beds 28 F6
Battlesea Green Suffolk 39 H8
Battleton Som'set 7 D8
Battram Leics 35 E10
Battramsley Hants 10 E2
Baughton Worcs 26 D5
Baughurst Hants 18 F2
Baulking Oxon 17 B10
Baumber Lincs 46 E6
Baunton Glos 17 A7
Baverstock Wilts 9 A9
Bawburgh Norfolk 39 E7
Bawdeswell Norfolk 38 C6
Bawdrip Som'set 15 H9
Bawdsey Suffolk 31 D10
Bawtry S Yorks 45 C10
Baxenden Lancs 50 G3
Baxterley Warwick 35 F8
Baybridge Hants 10 B4
Baycliff Cumb 49 B2
Baydon Wilts 17 D9
Bayford Herts 29 H10
Bayford Som'set 8 B6
Bayles Cumb 57 B9
Baylham Suffolk 31 C8
Baynard's Green Oxon 28 F2
Bayston Hill Shrops 33 E10
Baythorn End Essex 30 D4
Bayton Worcs 26 A3
Beach H'land 79 F10
Beachampton Bucks 28 E4
Beachamwell Norfolk 38 E3
Beachans Moray 87 G13
Beacharr Arg/Bute 65 D7
Beachborough Kent 21 H8
Beachley Glos 16 B2
Beacon Devon 7 F10
Beacon End Essex 30 F6
Beacon Hill Surrey 18 H5
Beacon's Bottom Bucks 18 B4
Beaconsfield Bucks 18 C6
Beacrabhaic W Isles 90 H6
Beadlam N Yorks 52 A2
Beadlow Beds 29 E8
Beadnell Northum 71 H11
Beaford Devon 6 E4
Beal Northum 71 F9
Beal N Yorks 51 G11
Beamhurst Staffs 35 B6
Beaminster Dorset 8 D3
Beamish Durham 58 A3
Beamsley N Yorks 51 D6
Bean Kent 20 D2
Beanacre Wilts 16 E6
Beanley Northum 62 B6
Beaquoy Orkney 95 F4
Bear Cross Bournem'th 9 E9
Beardwood Blackb'n 50 G2
Beare Green Surrey 19 G8
Bearley Warwick 27 B8
Bearnus Arg/Bute 78 G6
Bearpark Durham 58 B3
Bearsbridge Northum 62 H3
Bearsden E Dunb 68 C4
Bearsted Kent 20 F4
Bearstone Shrops 34 B3
Bearwood Heref'd 25 C10
Bearwood Poole 9 E9
Bearwood W Midlands 34 G6
Beattock Dumf/Gal 60 C6
Beauchamp Roding Essex 30 G2
Beauchief S Yorks 45 D7
Beaufort Bl Gwent 25 G8
Beaufort Castle H'land 87 G8
Beaulieu Hants 10 D2
Beauly H'land 87 G8
Beaumaris Angl 41 C8
Beaumont Cumb 61 H9
Beaumont Essex 31 F8
Beaumont Hill D'lington 58 E3
Beausale Warwick 27 A9
Beauworth Hants 10 B4
Beaworthy Devon 6 G3
Beazley End Essex 30 F4
Bebington Mersey 42 D6
Bebside Northum 63 E8
Beccles Suffolk 39 F10
Becconsall Lancs 49 G4
Beck Foot Cumb 57 G8
Beck Hole N Yorks 59 F9
Beck Row Suffolk 38 H2
Beck Side Cumb 49 A2
Beckbury Shrops 34 E3
Beckenham London 19 E10
Beckermet Cumb 56 F2
Beckfoot Cumb 56 F3
Beckfoot Cumb 56 B2
Beckford Worcs 26 E6
Beckhampton Wilts 17 E7
Beckingham Lincs 46 G2
Beckingham Notts 45 D11
Beckington Som'set 16 F5
Beckley E Sussex 13 D7
Beckley Hants 9 E11
Beckley Oxon 28 G2
Beckton London 19 C11
Beckwithshaw N Yorks 51 D8
Becontree London 19 C11
Bed-y-coedwr Gwyn 32 C3
Bedale N Yorks 58 H3
Bedburn Durham 58 C2
Bedchester Dorset 9 C7
Beddau Rh Cyn Taff 14 C6
Beddgelert Gwyn 41 F7
Beddingham E Sussex 12 F3
Beddington London 19 E10
Bedfield Suffolk 31 B9
Bedford Beds 29 C7
Bedham W Sussex 11 B9
Bedhampton Hants 10 D6
Bedingfield Suffolk 31 B8
Bedlam N Yorks 51 C8
Bedlington Northum 63 E8
Bedlington Station Northum 63 E8
Bedlinog Merth Tyd 14 A6
Bedminster Bristol 16 D2
Bedmond Herts 19 A7
Bednall Staffs 34 D5
Bedrule Scot Borders 62 B2
Bedstone Shrops 33 H9
Bedwas Caerph 15 C7
Bedworth Warwick 35 G9
Bedworth Little Heath Warwick 35 G9
Beeby Leics 36 E2
Beech Hants 18 H3
Beech Staffs 34 B4
Beech Hill Gtr Man 43 B8
Beech Hill W Berks 18 E3
Beechingstoke Wilts 17 F7
Beedon W Berks 17 D11
Beeford ER Yorks 53 D7
Beeley Derby 44 F6
Beelsby NE Lincs 46 B6
Beenham W Berks 18 E2
Beeny Cornw'l 4 B2
Beer Devon 7 H11
Beer Hackett Dorset 8 C4
Beercrocombe Som'set 8 B2
Beesands Devon 5 G9
Beesby Lincs 47 D8
Beeson Devon 5 G9
Beeston Beds 29 D8
Beeston Ches 43 G8
Beeston Norfolk 38 D5
Beeston Notts 35 B11
Beeston W Yorks 51 F8
Beeston Regis Norfolk 39 A7
Beeswing Dumf/Gal 55 C11
Beetham Cumb 49 B4
Beetley Norfolk 38 D5
Begbroke Oxon 27 G11
Begelly Pembs 22 F6
Beggar's Bush Powys 25 B9
Beguildy Powys 33 H7
Beighton Norfolk 39 E9
Beighton S Yorks 45 D8
Beighton Hill Derby 44 G6
Beith N Ayrs 66 A6
Bekesbourne Kent 21 F8
Belaugh Norfolk 39 D8
Belbroughton Worcs 34 H5
Belchamp Otten Essex 30 D5
Belchamp St Paul Essex 30 D4
Belchamp Walter Essex 30 D5
Belchford Lincs 46 E6
Belford Northum 71 G10
Belhaven E Loth 70 C5
Belhelvie Aberds 83 B11
Belhinnie Aberds 82 A6
Bell Bar Herts 29 H9
Bell Busk N Yorks 50 D5
Bell End Worcs 34 H5
Bell o'th'Hill Ches 43 H8
Bellabeg Aberds 82 B5
Bellamore S Ayrs 66 H5
Bellanoch Arg/Bute 72 D6
Bellaty Angus 76 B5
Belleau Lincs 47 E8
Belleheiglash Moray 88 E1
Bellerby N Yorks 58 G2
Bellever Devon 5 D7
Belliehill Angus 77 A8
Bellingdon Bucks 28 H6
Bellingham Northum 62 E4
Belloch Arg/Bute 65 E7
Bellochantuy Arg/Bute 65 E7
Bells Yew Green E Sussex 12 C5
Bellsbank E Ayrs 67 F7
Bellshill N Lanarks 68 D6
Bellshill Northum 71 G10
Bellspool Scot Borders 69 G10
Bellsquarry W Loth 69 D9
Belmaduthy H'land 87 F9
Belmesthorpe Rutl'd 36 D6
Belmont Blackb'n 50 H2
Belmont London 19 E9
Belmont S Ayrs 66 D6
Belmont Shetl'd 96 C7
Belnacraig Aberds 82 B5
Belowda Cornw'l 3 C8
Belper Derby 45 H7
Belper Lane End Derby 45 H7
Belsay Northum 63 F7

Caldwell Derby 35 D8
Caldwell N Yorks 58 E2
Caldy Mersey 42 D5
Caledrhydiau Ceredig'n 23 A9
Calfsound Orkney 95 E6
Calgary Arg/Bute 78 F6
Califer Moray 87 F13
California Falk 69 C8
California Norfolk 39 D11
Calke Derby 35 C9
Callakille H'land 85 C11
Callaly Northum 62 C6
Callander Stirl 75 G9
Callaughton Shrops 34 F2
Callestick Cornw'l 3 D6
Calligarry H'land 85 H11
Callington Cornw'l 4 E4
Callow Heref'd 25 E11
Callow End Worcs 26 D5
Callow Hill Wilts 17 C7
Callow Hill Worcs 26 A4
Callows Grave Worcs 26 B2
Calmore Hants 10 C2
Calmsden Glos 27 H7
Calne Wilts 17 D7
Calow Derby 45 E8
Calshot Hants 10 D3
Calstock Cornw'l 4 E5
Calstone Wellington Wilts 17 E7
Calthorpe Norfolk 39 B7
Calthwaite Cumb 56 B6
Calton N Yorks 50 D5
Calton Staffs 44 G5
Calveley Ches 43 G8
Calver Derby 44 E6
Calver Hill Heref'd 25 D10
Calverhall Shrops 34 B2
Calverleigh Devon 7 E8
Calverley W Yorks 51 F8
Calvert Bucks 28 F3
Calverton M/Keynes 28 E4
Calverton Notts 45 H10
Calvine Perth/Kinr 81 G10
Calvo Cumb 56 A3
Cam Glos 16 B4
Camas-luinie H'land 80 A1
Camasnacroise H'land 79 F11
Camastianavaig H'land 85 E10
Camasunary H'land 85 G10
Camault Muir H'land 87 G8
Camb Shetl'd 96 D7
Camber E Sussex 13 E8
Camberley Surrey 18 E5
Camberwell London 19 D10
Camblesforth N Yorks 52 G2
Cambo Northum 62 E6
Cambois Northum 63 E9
Camborne Cornw'l 2 E5
Cambourne Cambs 29 C10
Cambridge Cambs 29 C11
Cambridge Glos 16 A4
Cambridge Town Southend 20 C6
Cambus Clack 69 A7
Cambusavie Farm H'land 87 B10
Cambusbarron Stirl 68 A6
Cambuskenneth Stirl 69 A7
Cambuslang S Lanarks 68 D5
Cambusmore Lodge H'land 87 B10
Camden London 19 C9
Camelford Cornw'l 4 C2
Camelsdale W Sussex 11 A7
Camerory H'land 87 H13
Camer's Green Worcs 26 E4
Camerton Bath/NE Som'set 16 F3
Camerton Cumb 56 C2
Camerton ER Yorks 53 G8
Camghouran Perth/Kinr 75 B8
Cammachmore Aberds 83 D11
Cammeringham Lincs 46 D3
Camore H'land 87 B10
Camp Hill Warwick 35 F9
Campbeltown Arg/Bute 65 F8
Camperdown Tyne/Wear 63 F8
Campmuir Perth/Kinr 76 D5
Campsall S Yorks 45 A9
Campsey Ash Suffolk 31 C10
Campton Beds 29 E8
Camptown Scot Borders 62 B2
Camrose Pembs 22 D4
Camserney Perth/Kinr 75 C11
Camster H'land 94 F4
Camuschoirk H'land 79 E10
Camuscross H'land 85 G11
Camusnagaul H'land 80 F2
Camusnagaul H'land 86 C3
Camusrory H'land 79 B11
Camusteel H'land 85 D12
Camusterrach H'land 85 D12
Camusvrachan Perth/Kinr 75 C9
Canada Hants 10 C1
Canadia E Sussex 12 E6
Canal Side S Yorks 45 A10
Candacraig Ho. Aberds 82 B5
Candlesby Lincs 47 F8
Candy Mill S Lanarks 69 F9
Cane End Oxon 18 D3
Canewdon Essex 20 B5
Canford Bottom Dorset 9 D9
Canford Cliffs Poole 9 F9
Canford Magna Poole 9 E9
Canham's Green Suffolk 31 B7
Canholes Derby 44 E4
Canisbay H'land 94 C5
Cann Dorset 9 B7
Cann Common Dorset 9 B7
Cannard's Grave Som'set 16 G3
Cannich H'land 86 H6
Cannington Som'set 15 H8
Cannock Staffs 34 E5
Cannock Wood Staffs 34 D6
Canon Bridge Heref'd 25 D11
Canon Frome Heref'd 26 D3
Canon Pyon Heref'd 25 D11
Canonbie Dumf/Gal 61 F9
Canons Ashby Northants 28 C2
Canonstown Cornw'l 2 F4
Canterbury Kent 21 F8
Cantley Norfolk 39 E9
Cantley S Yorks 45 B10
Cantlop Shrops 33 E11
Canton Card 15 D7
Cantraybruich H'land 87 G10
Cantraydoune H'land 87 G10
Cantraywood H'land 87 G10
Cantsfield Lancs 50 B2
Canvey Island Essex 20 C4
Canwick Lincs 46 F3
Canworthy Water Cornw'l 4 B3
Caol H'land 80 F3
Caol Ila Arg/Bute 64 A5
Caolas Arg/Bute 78 G3
Caolas Scalpaigh W Isles 90 H7
Caolas Stocinis W Isles 90 H6
Capel Surrey 19 G8
Capel Bangor Ceredig'n 32 G2
Capel Betws Lleucu Ceredig'n 24 C3
Capel Carmel Gwyn 40 H3
Capel Coch Angl 40 B6
Capel Curig Conwy 41 E9
Capel Cynon Ceredig'n 23 B8
Capel Dewi Ceredig'n 23 B9
Capel Dewi Ceredig'n 32 G2
Capel Dewi Carms 23 D9
Capel Garmon Conwy 41 E10
Capel-gwyn Angl 40 C5
Capel Gwyn Carms 23 D9
Capel Gwynfe Carms 24 F4
Capel Hendre Carms 23 E10
Capel Hermon Gwyn 32 C3
Capel Isaac Carms 23 D10
Capel Iwan Carms 23 C7
Capel le Ferne Kent 21 H9
Capel Llanilltern Card 14 C6
Capel Mawr Angl 40 C6
Capel St Andrew Suffolk 31 D10
Capel St Mary Suffolk 31 E7
Capel Seion Ceredig'n 32 H2
Capel Tygwydd Ceredig'n 23 B7
Capel Uchaf Gwyn 40 F6
Capel-y-graig Gwyn 41 D7
Capelulo Conwy 41 C9
Capenhurst Ches 42 E6
Capernwray Lancs 49 B5
Capheaton Northum 62 E6
Cappercleuch Scot Borders 61 A8
Capplegill Dumf/Gal 61 C7
Capton Devon 5 F9
Caputh Perth/Kinr 76 D3
Car Colston Notts 36 A3
Carbis Bay Cornw'l 2 F4
Carbost H'land 85 E8
Carbost H'land 85 D9
Carbrook S Yorks 45 D7
Carbrooke Norfolk 38 E5
Carburton Notts 45 E10
Carcant Scot Borders 70 E2
Carcary Angus 77 B9
Carclaze Cornw'l 3 D9
Carcroft S Yorks 45 A9
Cardenden Fife 69 A11
Cardeston Shrops 33 D9
Cardiff = Caerdydd Card 15 D7
Cardigan = Aberteifi Ceredig'n 22 B6
Cardington Beds 29 D7
Cardington Shrops 33 F11
Cardinham Cornw'l 4 E2
Cardonald C/Glasg 68 D4
Cardow Moray 88 D1
Cardrona Scot Borders 70 G2
Cardross Arg/Bute 68 C2
Cardurnock Cumb 61 H7
Careby Lincs 36 D6
Careston Angus 77 B8
Carew Pembs 22 F5
Carew Cheriton Pembs 22 F5
Carew Newton Pembs 22 F5
Carey Heref'd 26 E2
Carfrae E Loth 70 D4
Cargenbridge Dumf/Gal 60 F5
Cargill Perth/Kinr 76 D4
Cargo Cumb 61 H9
Cargreen Cornw'l 4 E5
Carham Northum 71 G7
Carhampton Som'set 7 B9
Carharrack Cornw'l 2 E6
Carie Perth/Kinr 75 D9
Carie Perth/Kinr 75 B9
Carines Cornw'l 3 D6
Carisbrooke I/Wight 10 F3
Cark Cumb 49 B3
Carlabhagh W Isles 90 C7
Carland Cross Cornw'l 3 D7
Carlby Lincs 37 D6
Carlecotes S Yorks 44 B5
Carlesmoor N Yorks 51 B7
Carleton Cumb 57 D7
Carleton Cumb 56 A6
Carleton Lancs 49 F3
Carleton N Yorks 50 E5
Carleton Forehoe Norfolk 39 E6
Carleton Rode Norfolk 39 F7
Carlin How Redcar/Clevel'd 59 E8
Carlingcott Bath/NE Som'set 16 F3
Carlisle Cumb 61 H10
Carlops Scot Borders 69 E10
Carlton Beds 28 C6
Carlton Cambs 30 C3
Carlton Leics 35 E9
Carlton Notts 36 A2
Carlton N Yorks 52 G2
Carlton N Yorks 59 H7
Carlton N Yorks 51 A6
Carlton N Yorks 58 E2
Carlton Stockton 58 D4
Carlton Suffolk 31 B10
Carlton S Yorks 45 A7
Carlton W Yorks 51 G9
Carlton Colville Suffolk 39 G11
Carlton Curlieu Leics 36 F2
Carlton Husthwaite N Yorks 51 B10
Carlton in Cleveland N Yorks 58 F6
Carlton in Lindrick Notts 45 D9
Carlton le Moorland Lincs 46 G3
Carlton Miniott N Yorks 51 A9
Carlton on Trent Notts 45 F11
Carlton Scroop Lincs 36 A5
Carluke S Lanarks 69 E7
Carmarthen = Caerfyrddin Carms 23 D9
Carmel Angl 40 B5
Carmel Carms 23 E10
Carmel Flints 42 E4
Carmel Guernsey 11
Carmel Gwyn 40 E6
Carmont Aberds 83 E10
Carmunnock C/Glasg 68 E5
Carmyle C/Glasg 68 D5
Carmyllie Angus 77 C8
Carn-gorm H'land 80 A1
Carnaby ER Yorks 53 C7
Carnach H'land 86 B3
Carnach H'land 80 A2
Carnach W Isles 90 H7
Carnachy H'land 93 D10
Càrnais W Isles 90 D5
Carnbee Fife 77 G8
Carnbo Perth/Kinr 76 G3
Carnbrea Cornw'l 2 E5
Carnduff S Lanarks 68 F5
Carnduncan Arg/Bute 64 B3
Carne Cornw'l 3 F8
Carnforth Lancs 49 B4
Carnhedryn Pembs 22 D3
Carnhell Green Cornw'l 2 F5
Carnkie Cornw'l 2 F6
Carnkie Cornw'l 2 F5
Carno Powys 32 F5
Carnoch H'land 86 H6
Carnoch H'land 86 F5
Carnock Fife 69 B9
Carnon Downs Cornw'l 3 E6
Carnousie Aberds 89 C6
Carnoustie Angus 77 D8
Carnwath S Lanarks 69 F8
Carnyorth Cornw'l 2 F2
Carperby N Yorks 58 H1
Carpley Green N Yorks 57 H11
Carr S Yorks 45 C9
Carr Hill Tyne/Wear 63 G8
Carradale Arg/Bute 65 E9
Carragraich W Isles 90 H6
Carrbridge H'land 81 A11
Carrefour Selous Jersey 11
Carreg-wen Pembs 23 B7
Carreglefn Angl 40 B5
Carrick Arg/Bute 73 E8
Carrick Fife 77 E7
Carrick Castle Arg/Bute 73 D10
Carrick Ho. Orkney 95 E6
Carriden Falk 69 B9
Carrington Gtr Man 43 C10
Carrington Lincs 47 G7
Carrington Midloth 70 D2
Carrog Conwy 41 F9
Carrog Denbs 33 A7
Carron Falk 69 B7
Carron Moray 88 D2
Carron Bridge N Lanarks 68 B6
Carronbridge Dumf/Gal 60 D4
Carrshield Northum 57 B10
Carrutherstown Dumf/Gal 61 F7
Carrville Durham 58 B4
Carsaig Arg/Bute 79 J8
Carsaig Arg/Bute 72 E6
Carscreugh Dumf/Gal 54 D5
Carse Gray Angus 77 B7
Carse Ho. Arg/Bute 72 G6
Carsegowan Dumf/Gal 55 D7
Carseriggan Dumf/Gal 54 C6
Carsethorn Dumf/Gal 60 H5
Carshalton London 19 E9
Carsington Derby 44 G6
Carskiey Arg/Bute 65 H7
Carsluith Dumf/Gal 55 D7
Carsphairn Dumf/Gal 67 G8
Carstairs S Lanarks 69 F8
Carstairs Junction S Lanarks 69 F8
Carswell Marsh Oxon 17 B10
Carter's Clay Hants 10 B2
Carterton Oxon 27 H9
Carterway Heads Northum 58 A1
Carthew Cornw'l 3 D9
Carthorpe N Yorks 51 A9
Cartington Northum 62 C6
Cartland S Lanarks 69 F7
Cartmel Cumb 49 B3
Cartmel Fell Cumb 56 H6
Carway Carms 23 F9
Cary Fitzpaine Som'set 8 B4
Cas-gwent = Chepstow Monmouths 15 B11
Cascob Powys 25 B9
Cashlie Perth/Kinr 75 C7
Cashmoor Dorset 9 C8
Casnewydd = Newport Newp 15 C9
Cassey Compton Glos 27 G7
Cassington Oxon 27 G11
Cassop Durham 58 C4
Castell Denbs 42 F4
Castell-Howell Ceredig'n 23 B9
Castell-Nedd = Neath Neath P Talb 14 B3
Castell Newydd Emlyn = Newcastle Emlyn Carms 23 B8
Castell-y-bwch Torf 15 B8
Castellau Rh Cyn Taff 14 C6
Casterton Cumb 50 B2
Castle Acre Norfolk 38 D4
Castle Ashby Northants 28 C5
Castle Bolton N Yorks 58 G1
Castle Bromwich W Midlands 35 G7
Castle Bytham Lincs 36 D5
Castle Caereinion Powys 33 E7
Castle Camps Cambs 30 D3
Castle Carrock Cumb 61 H11
Castle Cary Som'set 8 A5
Castle Combe Wilts 16 D5
Castle Donington Leics 35 C10
Castle Douglas Dumf/Gal 55 C10
Castle Eaton Swindon 17 B8
Castle Eden Durham 58 C5
Castle Forbes Aberds 83 B8
Castle Frome Heref'd 26 D3
Castle Green Surrey 18 E6
Castle Gresley Derby 35 D8
Castle Heaton Northum 71 F8
Castle Hedingham Essex 30 E4
Castle Hill Kent 12 B5
Castle Huntly Perth/Kinr 76 E6
Castle Kennedy Dumf/Gal 54 D4
Castle O'er Dumf/Gal 61 D8
Castle Pulverbatch Shrops 33 E10
Castle Rising Norfolk 38 C2
Castle Stuart H'land 87 G10
Castlebay = Bagh a Chaisteil W Isles 84 J1
Castlebythe Pembs 22 D5
Castlecary N Lanarks 68 C6
Castlecraig H'land 87 E11
Castlefairn Dumf/Gal 60 E3
Castleford W Yorks 51 G10
Castlehill Scot Borders 69 G11
Castlehill H'land 94 D3
Castlehill W Dunb 68 C2
Castlemaddy Dumf/Gal 67 H8
Castlemartin Pembs 22 G4
Castlemilk Dumf/Gal 61 F7
Castlemilk C/Glasg 68 E5
Castlemorris Pembs 22 C4
Castlemorton Worcs 26 E4
Castleside Durham 58 B1
Castlethorpe M/Keynes 28 D5
Castleton Angus 76 C6
Castleton Arg/Bute 73 E7
Castleton Derby 44 D5
Castleton Gtr Man 44 A2
Castleton Newp 15 C8
Castleton N Yorks 59 F7
Castletown Ches 43 G7
Castletown H'land 94 D3
Castletown H'land 87 G10
Castletown I/Man 48 F2
Castletown Tyne/Wear 63 H9
Castleweary Scot Borders 61 C10
Castley N Yorks 51 E8
Caston Norfolk 38 F5
Castor Peterbro 37 F7
Catacol N Ayrs 66 B2
Catbrain S Glocs 16 C2
Catbrook Monmouths 15 A11
Catchall Cornw'l 2 G3
Catchems Corner W Midlands 35 H8
Catchgate Durham 58 A2
Catcleugh Northum 62 C3
Catcliffe S Yorks 45 D8
Catcott Som'set 15 H9
Caterham Surrey 19 F10
Catfield Norfolk 39 C9
Catfirth Shetl'd 96 H6
Catford London 19 D10
Catforth Lancs 49 F4
Cathays Card 15 D7
Cathcart C/Glasg 68 D4
Cathedine Powys 25 F8
Catherington Hants 10 C5
Catherton Shrops 34 H2
Catlodge H'land 81 D8
Catlowdy Cumb 61 F10
Catmore W Berks 17 C11
Caton Lancs 49 C5
Caton Green Lancs 49 C5
Catrine E Ayrs 67 D8
Cat's Ash Newp 15 B9
Catsfield E Sussex 12 E6
Catshill Worcs 26 A6
Cattal N Yorks 51 D10
Cattawade Suffolk 31 E8
Catterall Lancs 49 E4
Catterick N Yorks 58 G3
Catterick Bridge N Yorks 58 G3
Catterick Garrison N Yorks 58 G2
Catterlen Cumb 57 C6
Catterline Aberds 83 F10
Catterton N Yorks 51 E11
Catthorpe Leics 35 H11
Cattistock Dorset 8 E4
Catton Northum 62 H4
Catton N Yorks 51 B9
Catwick ER Yorks 53 E7
Catworth Cambs 29 A7
Caudlesprings Norfolk 38 E5
Caulcott Oxon 28 F2
Cauldcots Angus 77 C9
Cauldhame Stirl 68 A5
Cauldmill Scot Borders 61 B11
Cauldon Staffs 44 H4
Caulkerbush Dumf/Gal 60 H5
Caulside Dumf/Gal 61 E10
Caunsall Worcs 34 G4
Caunton Notts 45 G11
Causeway End Dumf/Gal 55 C7
Causeway Foot W Yorks 51 F6
Causeway-head Stirl 75 H10
Causewayend S Lanarks 69 G9
Causewayhead Cumb 56 A3
Causey Park Bridge Northum 63 D7
Causeyend Aberds 83 B11
Cautley Cumb 57 G8
Cavendish Suffolk 30 D5
Cavendish Bridge Leics 35 C10
Cavenham Suffolk 30 B4
Caversfield Oxon 28 F2
Caversham Reading 18 D4
Caverswall Staffs 34 A5
Cavil ER Yorks 52 F3
Cawdor H'land 87 F11
Cawkwell Lincs 46 E6
Cawood N Yorks 52 F1
Cawsand Cornw'l 4 F5
Cawston Norfolk 39 C7
Cawthorne S Yorks 44 B6
Cawthorpe Lincs 37 C6
Cawton N Yorks 52 B2
Caxton Cambs 29 C10
Caynham Shrops 26 A2
Caythorpe Lincs 46 H3
Caythorpe Notts 45 H10
Cayton N Yorks 53 A6
Ceann a Bhaigh W Isles 84 B2
Ceann a Deas Loch Baghasdail W Isles 84 G2
Ceann Shiphoirt W Isles 91 F7
Ceann Tarabhaigh W Isles 90 F7
Ceannacroc Lodge H'land 80 B4
Cearsiadair W Isles 91 E8
Cefn Berain Conwy 42 F2
Cefn-brith Conwy 42 G2
Cefn Canol Powys 33 B8
Cefn-coch Conwy 41 D10
Cefn Coch Powys 33 C7
Cefn-coed-y-cymmer Merth Tyd 25 H7
Cefn Cribbwr Bridg 14 C4
Cefn Cross Bridg 14 C4
Cefn-ddwysarn Gwyn 32 B5
Cefn Einion Shrops 33 G8
Cefn-gorwydd Powys 24 D6
Cefn-mawr Wrex 33 A8
Cefn-y-bedd Flints 42 G6
Cefn-y-pant Carms 22 D6
Cefneithin Carms 23 E10
Cei-bach Ceredig'n 23 A9
Ceinewydd = New Quay Ceredig'n 23 A8
Ceint Angl 40 C6
Cellan Ceredig'n 24 D3
Cellarhead Staffs 44 H3
Cemaes Angl 40 A5
Cemmaes Powys 32 E4
Cemmaes Road Powys 32 E4
Cenarth Carms 23 B7
Cenin Gwyn 40 F6
Central Inverci 73 F11
Ceos W Isles 91 E8
Ceres Fife 77 F7
Cerne Abbas Dorset 8 D5
Cerney Wick Glos 17 B7
Cerrigceinwen Angl 40 C6
Cerrigydrudion Conwy 42 H2
Cessford Scot Borders 62 A3
Ceunant Gwyn 41 D7
Chaceley Glos 26 E5
Chacewater Cornw'l 3 E6
Chackmore Bucks 28 E3
Chacombe Northants 27 D11
Chad Valley W Midlands 34 G6
Chadderton Gtr Man 44 B3
Chadderton Fold Gtr Man 44 B2
Chaddesden Derby C 35 B9
Chaddesley Corbett Worcs 26 A5
Chaddleworth W Berks 17 D11
Chadlington Oxon 27 F10
Chadshunt Warwick 27 C10
Chadwell Leics 36 C3
Chadwell St Mary Thurr'k 20 D3
Chadwick End W Midlands 27 A9
Chadwick Green Mersey 43 C8
Chaffcombe Som'set 8 C2
Chagford Devon 5 C8
Chailey E Sussex 12 D2
Chain Bridge Lincs 37 A9
Chainbridge Cambs 37 E10
Chainhurst Kent 20 G4
Chalbury Dorset 9 D9
Chalbury Common Dorset 9 D9
Chaldon Surrey 19 F10
Chaldon Herring or Dorset 9 F6
Chale I/Wight 10 G3
Chale Green I/Wight 10 G3
Chalfont Common Bucks 19 B7
Chalfont St Giles Bucks 18 B6
Chalfont St Peter Bucks 19 B7
Chalford Glos 16 A5
Chalgrove Oxon 18 B3
Chalk Kent 20 D3
Challacombe Devon 6 B5
Challoch Dumf/Gal 54 C6
Challock Kent 21 F7
Chalton Beds 29 F7
Chalton Hants 10 C6
Chalvington E Sussex 12 F4
Chancery Ceredig'n 32 H1
Chandler's Ford Hants 10 B3
Channel Tunnel Kent 21 H8
Channerwick Shetl'd 96 L6
Chantry Som'set 16 G4
Chantry Suffolk 31 D8
Chapel Fife 69 A11
Chapel Allerton Som'set 15 F10
Chapel Allerton W Yorks 51 F9
Chapel Amble Cornw'l 3 B8
Chapel Brampton Northants 28 B4
Chapel Chorlton Staffs 34 B4
Chapel-en-le-Frith Derby 44 D4
Chapel End Warwick 35 F9
Chapel Green Warwick 35 G8
Chapel Green Warwick 27 B11
Chapel Haddlesey N Yorks 52 G1
Chapel Head Cambs 37 G9
Chapel Hill Aberds 89 E10
Chapel Hill Lincs 46 G6
Chapel Hill Monmouths 15 B11
Chapel Hill N Yorks 51 E9
Chapel Lawn Shrops 33 H9
Chapel-le-Dale N Yorks 50 B3
Chapel Milton Derby 44 D4
Chapel of Garioch Aberds 83 A9
Chapel Row W Berks 18 E2
Chapel St Leonards Lincs 47 E9
Chapel Stile Cumb 56 F5
Chapelgate Lincs 37 C10
Chapelhall N Lanarks 68 D6
Chapelhill Dumf/Gal 60 D6
Chapelhill H'land 87 D11
Chapelhill N Ayrs 66 B5
Chapelhill Perth/Kinr 76 E5
Chapelhill Perth/Kinr 76 D3
Chapelknowe Dumf/Gal 61 F9
Chapelton Angus 77 C9
Chapelton Devon 6 D4
Chapelton H'land 81 B11
Chapelton S Lanarks 68 F5
Chapeltown Blackb'n 50 H3
Chapeltown Moray 82 A4
Chapeltown S Yorks 45 C7
Chapmans Well Devon 6 G2
Chapmanslade Wilts 16 G5
Chapmore End Herts 29 G10
Chappel Essex 30 F5
Chard Som'set 8 D2
Chardstock Devon 8 D2
Charfield S Glocs 16 B4
Charford Worcs 26 B6
Charing Kent 20 G6
Charing Cross Dorset 9 C10
Charing Heath Kent 20 G6
Charingworth Glos 27 E9
Charlbury Oxon 27 G10
Charlcombe Bath/NE Som'set 16 E4
Charlecote Warwick 27 C9
Charles Devon 6 C5
Charles Tye Suffolk 31 C7
Charlesfield Dumf/Gal 61 G7
Charleston Angus 76 C6
Charleston Renf 68 D3
Charlestown Aberd C 83 C11
Charlestown Cornw'l 3 D9
Charlestown Derby 44 C4
Charlestown Dorset 8 G5
Charlestown Fife 69 B9
Charlestown Gtr Man 44 B2
Charlestown H'land 87 G9
Charlestown H'land 85 A13
Charlestown W Yorks 50 G5
Charlestown of Aberlour Moray 88 D2
Charlesworth Derby 44 C4
Charleton Devon 5 G8
Charlton London 19 D11
Charlton Hants 17 G10
Charlton Herts 29 F8
Charlton Northants 28 E2
Charlton Northum 62 E4
Charlton Som'set 16 F3
Charlton Telford 34 D1
Charlton Wilts 9 B8
Charlton Wilts 17 F8
Charlton Wilts 16 C6
Charlton Worcs 27 D7
Charlton W Sussex 11 C7
Charlton Abbots Glos 27 F7
Charlton Adam Som'set 8 B4
Charlton-All-Saints Wilts 9 B10
Charlton Down Dorset 8 E5
Charlton Horethorne Som'set 8 B5
Charlton Kings Glos 26 F6
Charlton Mackerell Som'set 8 B4
Charlton Marshall Dorset 9 D7
Charlton Musgrove Som'set 8 B6
Charlton on Otmoor Oxon 28 G2
Charltons Redcar/Clevel'd 59 E7
Charlwood Surrey 19 G9
Charlynch Som'set 7 C11
Charminster Dorset 8 E5
Charmouth Dorset 8 E2
Charndon Bucks 28 F3
Charney Bassett Oxon 17 B10
Charnock Richard Lancs 50 H1
Charsfield Suffolk 31 C9
Chart Corner Kent 20 F4
Chart Sutton Kent 20 G5
Charter Alley Hants 18 F2
Charterhouse Som'set 15 F10
Charterville Allotments Oxon 27 G10
Chartham Kent 21 F8
Chartham Hatch Kent 21 F8
Chartridge Bucks 18 A6
Charvil Wokingham 18 D4
Charwelton Northants 28 C2
Chasetown Staffs 34 E6
Chastleton Oxon 27 F9
Chasty Devon 6 F2
Chatburn Lancs 50 E3
Chatcull Staffs 34 B3
Chatham Medway 20 E4
Chathill Northum 71 H10
Chattenden Medway 20 D4
Chatteris Cambs 37 G9
Chattisham Suffolk 31 D7
Chatto Scot Borders 62 B3
Chatton Northum 71 H9
Chawleigh Devon 6 E6
Chawley Oxon 17 A11
Chawston Beds 29 C8
Chawton Hants 18 H4
Cheadle Gtr Man 44 D2
Cheadle Staffs 34 A6
Cheadle Heath Gtr Man 44 D2
Cheadle Hulme Gtr Man 44 D2
Cheam London 19 E9
Cheapside Surrey 19 F7
Chearsley Bucks 28 G4
Chebsey Staffs 34 C4
Checkendon Oxon 18 C3
Checkley Ches 43 H10
Checkley Heref'd 26 E2
Checkley Staffs 34 B6
Chedburgh Suffolk 30 C4
Cheddar Som'set 15 F10
Cheddington Bucks 28 G6
Cheddleton Staffs 44 G3
Cheddon Fitzpaine Som'set 8 B1
Chedglow Wilts 16 B6
Chedgrave Norfolk 39 F9
Chedington Dorset 8 D3
Chediston Suffolk 39 H9
Chedworth Glos 27 G7
Chedzoy Som'set 15 H9
Cheeklaw Scot Borders 70 E6
Cheeseman's Green Kent 13 C9
Cheglinch Devon 6 B4
Cheldon Devon 7 E6
Chelford Ches 44 E2
Chell Heath Stoke 44 G2
Chellaston Derby C 35 B9
Chellington Beds 28 C6
Chelmarsh Shrops 34 G3
Chelmer Village Essex 30 H4
Chelmondiston Suffolk 31 E9
Chelmorton Derby 44 F5
Chelmsford Essex 30 H4
Chelsea London 19 D9
Chelsfield London 19 E11
Chelsworth Suffolk 30 D6
Cheltenham Glos 26 F6
Chelveston Northants 28 B6
Chelvey N Som'set 15 E10
Chelwood Bath/NE Som'set 16 E3
Chelwood Common E Sussex 12 D3
Chelwood Gate E Sussex 12 D3
Chelworth Wilts 16 B6
Chelworth Green Wilts 17 B7
Chemistry Shrops 33 A11
Chenies Bucks 19 B7
Cheny Longville Shrops 33 G10
Chepstow = Cas-gwent Monmouths 15 B11
Chequerfield W Yorks 51 G10
Cherhill Wilts 17 D7
Cherington Glos 16 B6
Cherington Warwick 27 E9
Cheriton Devon 7 B6
Cheriton Hants 10 B4
Cheriton Kent 21 H8
Cheriton Swan 23 G9
Cheriton Bishop Devon 7 G6
Cheriton Fitzpaine Devon 7 F7
Cheriton or Stackpole Elidor Pembs 22 G4
Cherrington Telford 34 C2
Cherry Burton ER Yorks 52 E5
Cherry Hinton Cambs 29 C11
Cherry Orchard Worcs 26 C5
Cherry Willingham Lincs 46 E4
Cherrybank Perth/Kinr 76 E4
Chertsey Surrey 19 E7
Cheselbourne Dorset 9 E6
Chesham Bucks 18 A6
Chesham Bois Bucks 18 B6
Cheshunt Herts 19 A10
Cheslyn Hay Staffs 34 E5
Chessington London 19 E8
Chester Ches 43 F7
Chester-Le-Street Durham 58 A3
Chester Moor Durham 58 B3
Chesterblade Som'set 16 G3
Chesterfield Derby 45 E7
Chesters Scot Borders 62 B2
Chesters Scot Borders 62 A2
Chesterton Cambs 37 F7
Chesterton Cambs 29 B11
Chesterton Glos 17 A7
Chesterton Oxon 28 F2
Chesterton Shrops 34 F3
Chesterton Staffs 44 H2
Chesterton Warwick 27 C10
Chesterwood Northum 62 G4
Chestfield Kent 21 E8
Cheston Devon 5 F7
Cheswardine Shrops 34 C3
Cheswick Northum 71 F9
Chetnole Dorset 8 D5
Chettiscombe Devon 7 E8
Chettisham Cambs 37 G11
Chettle Dorset 9 C8
Chetton Shrops 34 F2
Chetwode Bucks 28 F3
Chetwynd Aston Telford 34 D3
Cheveley Cambs 30 B3
Chevening Kent 19 F11
Chevington Suffolk 30 C4
Chevithorne Devon 7 E8
Chew Magna Bath/NE Som'set 16 E2
Chew Stoke Bath/NE Som'set 16 E2
Chewton Keynsham Bath/NE Som'set 16 E3
Chewton Mendip Som'set 16 F2
Chicheley M/Keynes 28 D6
Chichester W Sussex 11 D7
Chickerell Dorset 8 F5
Chicklade Wilts 9 A8
Chicksgrove Wilts 9 A8
Chidden Hants 10 C5
Chiddingfold Surrey 18 H6
Chiddingly E Sussex 12 E4
Chiddingstone Kent 19 G11
Chiddingstone Causeway Kent 20 G2
Chiddingstone Hoath Kent 12 B3
Chideock Dorset 8 E3
Chidham W Sussex 11 D6
Chidswell W Yorks 51 G8
Chieveley W Berks 17 D11
Chignall St James Essex 30 H3
Chignall Smealy Essex 30 G3
Chigwell Essex 19 B11
Chigwell Row Essex 19 B11
Chilbolton Hants 17 H10
Chilcomb Hants 10 B4
Chilcombe Dorset 8 E4
Chilcompton Som'set 16 F3
Chilcote Leics 35 D8
Child Okeford Dorset 9 C7
Childer Thornton Ches 42 E6
Childrey Oxon 17 C10
Child's Ercall Shrops 34 C2
Childswickham Worcs 27 E7
Childwall Mersey 43 D7
Childwick Green Herts 29 G8
Chilfrome Dorset 8 E4
Chilgrove W Sussex 11 C7
Chilham Kent 21 F7
Chilhampton Wilts 9 A9
Chilla Devon 6 F3
Chillaton Devon 4 C5
Chillenden Kent 21 F9
Chillerton I/Wight 10 F3
Chillesford Suffolk 31 C10
Chillingham Northum 71 H9
Chillington Devon 5 G8
Chillington Som'set 8 C2
Chilmark Wilts 9 A8
Chilson Oxon 27 G10
Chilsworthy Cornw'l 4 D5
Chilsworthy Devon 6 F2
Chilthorne Domer Som'set 8 C4
Chiltington E Sussex 12 E2
Chilton Bucks 28 G3
Chilton Durham 58 D3
Chilton Oxon 17 C11
Chilton Cantelo Som'set 8 B4
Chilton Foliat Wilts 17 D10
Chilton Lane Durham 58 C4
Chilton Polden Som'set 15 H9
Chilton Street Suffolk 30 D4
Chilton Trinity Som'set 15 H8
Chilvers Coton Warwick 35 F9
Chilwell Notts 35 B11
Chilworth Hants 10 C3
Chilworth Surrey 19 G7
Chimney Oxon 17 A10
Chineham Hants 18 F3
Chingford London 19 B10
Chinley Derby 44 D4
Chinley Head Derby 44 D4
Chinnor Oxon 18 A4
Chipnall Shrops 34 B3
Chippenhall Green Suffolk 39 H8
Chippenham Cambs 30 B3
Chippenham Wilts 16 D6
Chipperfield Herts 19 A7
Chipping Herts 29 E10
Chipping Lancs 50 E2
Chipping Campden Glos 27 E8
Chipping Hill Essex 30 G5
Chipping Norton Oxon 27 F10
Chipping Ongar Essex 20 A2
Chipping Sodbury S Glocs 16 C4
Chipping Warden Northants 27 D11
Chipstable Som'set 7 D9
Chipstead Kent 19 F11
Chipstead Surrey 19 F9
Chirbury Shrops 33 F8
Chirk = Y Waun Wrex 33 B8
Chirk Bank Shrops 33 B8
Chirmorrie S Ayrs 54 B5
Chirnside Scot Borders 71 E7
Chirnsidebridge Scot Borders 71 E7
Chirton Wilts 17 F7
Chisbury Wilts 17 E9
Chiselborough Som'set 8 C3
Chiseldon Swindon 17 D8
Chiserley W Yorks 50 G6
Chislehampton Oxon 18 B2
Chislehurst London 19 D11
Chislet Kent 21 E9
Chiswell Green Herts 19 A8
Chiswick London 19 D9
Chiswick End Cambs 29 D10
Chisworth Derby 44 C3
Chithurst W Sussex 11 B7
Chittering Cambs 29 A11
Chitterne Wilts 16 G6
Chittlehamholt Devon 6 D5
Chittlehampton Devon 6 D5
Chittoe Wilts 16 E6
Chivenor Devon 6 C4
Chobham Surrey 18 E6
Choicelee Scot Borders 70 E6
Cholderton Wilts 17 G9
Cholesbury Bucks 28 H6
Chollerford Northum 62 F5
Chollerton Northum 62 F5
Cholmondeston Ches 43 F9
Cholsey Oxon 18 C2
Cholstrey Heref'd 25 C11
Chop Gate N Yorks 59 G6
Choppington Northum 63 E8
Chopwell Tyne/Wear 63 H7
Chorley Ches 43 G8
Chorley Lancs 50 H1
Chorley Shrops 34 G2
Chorley Staffs 35 D6
Chorleywood Herts 19 B7
Chorlton cum Hardy Gtr Man 44 C2
Chorlton Lane Ches 43 H7
Choulton Shrops 33 G9
Chowdene Tyne/Wear 63 H8
Chowley Ches 43 G7
Chrishall Essex 29 E11
Christchurch Cambs 37 F10
Christchurch Dorset 9 E10
Christchurch Glos 26 G2
Christchurch Newp 15 C9
Christian Malford Wilts 16 D6
Christleton Ches 43 F7
Christmas Common Oxon 18 B4
Christon N Som'set 15 F9
Christon Bank Northum 63 A8
Christow Devon 5 C9
Chryston N Lanarks 68 C5
Chudleigh Devon 5 D9
Chudleigh Knighton Devon 5 D9
Chulmleigh Devon 6 E5
Chunal Derby 44 C4
Church Lancs 50 G3
Church Aston Telford 34 D3
Church Brampton Northants 28 B4
Church Broughton Derby 35 B8
Church Crookham Hants 18 F5
Church Eaton Staffs 34 D4
Church End Beds 28 F6
Church End Beds 28 E3
Church End Beds 28 E6
Church End Cambs 37 E9
Church End Cambs 37 G8
Church End ER Yorks 53 D6
Church End Essex 30 D2
Church End Essex 30 F4
Church End Hants 18 F3
Church End Lincs 37 B8
Church End Warwick 35 F8
Church End Warwick 35 F8
Church End Wilts 17 D7
Church Enstone Oxon 27 F10
Church Fenton N Yorks 51 F11
Church Green Devon 7 G10
Church Green Norfolk 39 F6
Church Gresley Derby 35 D8
Church Hanborough Oxon 27 G11
Church Hill Ches 43 F9
Church Houses N Yorks 59 G7
Church Knowle Dorset 9 F8
Church Laneham Notts 46 E2
Church Langton Leics 36 F3
Church Lawford Warwick 35 H10
Church Lawton Ches 44 G2
Church Leigh Staffs 34 B6
Church Lench Worcs 27 C7
Church Mayfield Staffs 35 A7
Church Minshull Ches 43 F9
Church Norton W Sussex 11 E7
Church Preen Shrops 33 F11
Church Pulverbatch Shrops 33 E10
Church Stoke Powys 33 F8
Church Stowe Northants 28 C3
Church Street Kent 20 D4
Church Stretton Shrops 33 F10
Church Town N Lincs 45 B11
Church Town Surrey 19 F10
Church Village Rh Cyn Taff 14 C6
Church Warsop Notts 45 F9
Churcham Glos 26 G4
Churchbank Shrops 33 H8
Churchbridge Staffs 34 E5
Churchdown Glos 26 G5
Churchend Essex 30 F3
Churchend Essex 21 B7
Churchend S Glocs 16 B4
Churchfield W Midlands 34 F6
Churchgate Street Essex 29 G11
Churchill Devon 6 B4
Churchill Devon 8 D2
Churchill N Som'set 15 F10
Churchill Oxon 27 F9
Churchill Worcs 34 H4
Churchill Worcs 26 C6
Churchinford Som'set 7 E11
Churchover Warwick 35 G11
Churchstanton Som'set 7 E10
Churchstow Devon 5 G8
Churchtown Derby 44 F6
Churchtown I/Man 48 C4
Churchtown Lancs 49 E4
Churchtown Mersey 49 H3
Churnsike Lodge Northum 62 F2
Churston Ferrers Torbay 5 F10
Churt Surrey 18 H5
Churton Ches 43 G7
Churwell W Yorks 51 G8
Chute Standen Wilts 17 F10
Chwilog Gwyn 40 G6
Chyandour Cornw'l 2 F3
Cilan Uchaf Gwyn 40 H4
Cilcain Flints 42 F4
Cilcennin Ceredig'n 24 B2
Cilfor Gwyn 41 G8
Cilfrew Neath P Talb 14 A3
Cilfynydd Rh Cyn Taff 14 B6
Cilgerran Pembs 22 B6
Cilgwyn Carms 24 F4
Cilgwyn Gwyn 40 E6
Cilgwyn Pembs 22 C5
Ciliau Aeron Ceredig'n 23 A9
Cill Donnain W Isles 84 F2
Cille Bhrighde W Isles 84 G2
Cille Pheadair W Isles 84 G2
Cilmery Powys 25 C7
Cilsan Carms 23 D10
Ciltalgarth Gwyn 41 F10
Cilwendeg Pembs 23 C7
Cilybebyll Neath P Talb 14 A3
Cilycwm Carms 24 E4
Cimla Neath P Talb 14 B3
Cinderford Glos 26 G3
Cippyn Pembs 22 B6
Circebost W Isles 90 D6
Cirencester Glos 17 A7
Ciribhig W Isles 90 C6
City London 19 C10
City Powys 33 G8
City Dulas Angl 40 B6
Clachaig Arg/Bute 73 E10
Clachan Arg/Bute 72 H6
Clachan Arg/Bute 72 B6
Clachan Arg/Bute 79 G11
Clachan Arg/Bute 74 F4
Clachan H'land 85 E10
Clachan W Isles 84 D2
Clachan na Luib W Isles 84 B3
Clachan of Campsie E Dunb 68 C5
Clachan of Glendaruel Arg/Bute 73 E8
Clachan-Seil Arg/Bute 72 B6
Clachan Strachur Arg/Bute 73 C9
Clachaneasy Dumf/Gal 54 B6
Clachanmore Dumf/Gal 54 E3
Clachbreck Arg/Bute 72 F6
Clachnabrain Angus 82 G5
Clachtoll H'land 92 G3
Clackmannan Clack 69 A8
Clacton-on-Sea Essex 31 G8
Cladach Chireboist W Isles 84 B2
Claddach-knockline W Isles 84 B2
Cladich Arg/Bute 74 E3
Claggan H'land 79 G9
Claggan H'land 80 F3
Claigan H'land 84 C7
Claines Worcs 26 C5
Clandown Bath/NE Som'set 16 F3
Clanfield Hants 10 C5
Clanfield Oxon 17 A9
Clanville Hants 17 G10
Claonaig Arg/Bute 73 H7
Claonel H'land 93 J8
Clap Hill Kent 13 C9
Clapgate Dorset 9 D9
Clapgate Herts 29 F11
Clapham Beds 29 C7
Clapham London 19 D9
Clapham N Yorks 50 C3
Clapham W Sussex 11 D9
Clappers Scot Borders 71 E8
Clappersgate Cumb 56 F5
Clapton Som'set 8 D3
Clapton-in-Gordano N Som'set 15 D10
Clapton-on-the-Hill Glos 27 G8
Clapworthy Devon 6 D5
Clara Vale Tyne/Wear 63 G7
Clarach Ceredig'n 32 G2
Clarbeston Pembs 22 D5
Clarbeston Road Pembs 22 D5
Clarborough Notts 45 D11
Clardon H'land 94 D3
Clare Suffolk 30 D4
Clarebrand Dumf/Gal 55 C10
Clarencefield Dumf/Gal 60 G6
Clarilaw Scot Borders 61 B11
Clark's Green Surrey 19 H8
Clarkston E Renf 68 E4
Clashandorran H'land 87 G8
Clashcoig H'land 87 B9
Clashindarroch Aberds 88 E4
Clashmore H'land 92 F3
Clashmore H'land 87 C10
Clashnessie H'land 92 F3
Clashnoir Moray 82 A4
Clate Shetl'd 96 G7
Clathy Perth/Kinr 76 F2
Clatt Aberds 83 A7
Clatter Powys 32 F5
Clatterford I/Wight 10 F3
Clatterin Bridge Aberds 83 F8
Clatworthy Som'set 7 C9
Claughton Lancs 49 E5
Claughton Lancs 50 C1
Claughton Mersey 42 D6
Claverdon Warwick 27 B8
Claverham N Som'set 15 E10
Clavering Essex 29 E11
Claverley Shrops 34 F3
Claverton Bath/NE Som'set 16 E4
Clawdd-newydd Denbs 42 G3
Clawthorpe Cumb 49 B5
Clawton Devon 6 G2
Claxby Lincs 46 C5
Claxby Lincs 47 E8
Claxton Norfolk 39 E9
Claxton N Yorks 52 C2
Clay Common Suffolk 39 G10
Clay Coton Northants 36 H1
Clay Cross Derby 45 F7
Clay Hill W Berks 18 D2
Clay Lake Lincs 37 C8

Claybokie Aberds 82 D2
Claybrooke Magna Leics 35 G10
Claybrooke Parva Leics 35 G10
Claydon Oxon 27 C11
Claydon Suffolk 31 C8
Claygate Dumf/Gal 61 F9
Claygate Kent 12 B6
Claygate Surrey 19 E8
Claygate Cross Kent 20 F3
Clayhanger Devon 7 D9
Clayhanger W Midlands 34 E6
Clayhidon Devon 7 E10
Clayhill E Sussex 13 D7
Clayhill Hants 10 D2
Clayock H'land 94 E3
Claypole Lincs 46 H2
Clayton Staffs 34 A4
Clayton S Yorks 45 B8
Clayton W Sussex 12 E1
Clayton W Yorks 51 F7
Clayton Green Lancs 50 G1
Clayton-le-Moors Lancs 50 F3
Clayton-le-Woods Lancs 50 G1
Clayton West W Yorks 44 A6
Clayworth Notts 45 D11
Cleadale H'land 78 C7
Cleadon Tyne/Wear 63 G9
Clearbrook Devon 4 E6
Clearwell Glos 26 H2
Cleasby N Yorks 58 E3
Cleat Orkney 95 K5
Cleatlam Durham 58 E2
Cleator Cumb 56 E2
Cleator Moor Cumb 56 E2
Clebrig H'land 93 F8
Cleckheaton W Yorks 51 G7
Clee St Margaret Shrops 34 G1
Cleedownton Shrops 34 G1
Cleehill Shrops 34 H1
Cleethorpes NE Lincs 47 B7
Cleeton St Mary Shrops 34 H2
Cleeve N Som'set 15 E10
Cleeve Hill Glos 26 F6
Cleeve Prior Worcs 27 D7
Clegyrnant Powys 32 E5
Clehonger Heref'd 25 E11
Cleish Perth/Kinr 76 H3
Cleland N Lanarks 69 E7
Clench Common Wilts 17 E8
Clenchwarton Norfolk 38 C1
Clent Worcs 34 H5
Cleobury Mortimer Shrops 34 H2
Cleobury North Shrops 34 G2
Cleongart Arg/Bute 65 E7
Clephanton H'land 87 F11
Clerklands Scot Borders 61 A11
Clestrain Orkney 95 H4
Cleuch Head Scot Borders 61 B11
Cleughbrae Dumf/Gal 60 F6
Clevancy Wilts 17 D7
Clevedon N Som'set 15 D10
Cleveley Oxon 27 F10
Cleveleys Lancs 49 E3
Cleverton Wilts 16 C6
Clevis Bridg 14 D4
Clewer Som'set 15 F10
Cley next the Sea Norfolk 38 A6
Cliaid W Isles 84 H1
Cliasmol W Isles 90 G5
Cliburn Cumb 57 D8
Click Mill Orkney 95 F4
Cliddesden Hants 18 F3
Cliff End E Sussex 13 E7
Cliffburn Angus 77 C9
Cliffe Medway 20 D4
Cliffe N Yorks 52 F2
Cliffe Woods Medway 20 D4
Clifford Heref'd 25 D9
Clifford W Yorks 51 E10
Clifford Chambers Warwick 27 C8
Clifford's Mesne Glos 26 F4
Cliffsend Kent 21 E10
Clifton Beds 29 E8
Clifton Bristol 16 D2
Clifton Cumb 57 D7
Clifton Derby 35 A7
Clifton Lancs 49 F4
Clifton Nott'ham 36 B1
Clifton Northum 63 E8
Clifton N Yorks 51 E7
Clifton Oxon 27 E11
Clifton Stirl 74 D6
Clifton S Yorks 45 C9
Clifton Worcs 26 D5
Clifton C/York 52 D1
Clifton Campville Staffs 35 D8
Clifton Green Gtr Man 43 B10
Clifton Hampden Oxon 18 B2
Clifton Reynes M/Keynes 28 C6
Clifton upon Dunsmore Warwick 35 H11
Clifton upon Teme Worcs 26 B4
Cliftoncote Scot Borders 62 A4
Cliftonville Kent 21 D10
Climaen gwyn Neath P Talb 24 H4
Climping W Sussex 11 D9
Climpy S Lanarks 69 E8
Clink Som'set 16 G4
Clint N Yorks 51 D8
Clint Green Norfolk 38 D6
Clintmains Scot Borders 70 G5
Cliobh W Isles 90 D5
Clippesby Norfolk 39 D10
Clipsham Rutl'd 36 D5
Clipston Northants 36 G3
Clipstone Notts 45 F9
Clitheroe Lancs 50 E3
Cliuthar W Isles 90 H6
Clive Shrops 33 C11
Clivocast Shetl'd 96 C8
Clixby Lincs 46 B5
Clocaenog Denbs 42 G3
Clochan Moray 88 B4
Clock Face Mersey 43 C8
Clockmill Scot Borders 70 E6
Cloddiau Powys 33 E8
Clodock Heref'd 25 F10
Clola Aberds 89 D10
Clophill Beds 29 E7
Clopton Northants 37 G6
Clopton Suffolk 31 C9
Clopton Corner Suffolk 31 C9
Clopton Green Suffolk 30 C4
Close Clark I/Man 48 E2
Closeburn Dumf/Gal 60 D4
Closworth Som'set 8 C4
Clothall Herts 29 E9
Clotton Ches 43 F8
Clough Foot W Yorks 50 G5
Cloughton N Yorks 59 G11
Cloughton Newlands N Yorks 59 G11
Clousta Shetl'd 96 H5
Clouston Orkney 95 G3
Clova Aberds 82 A6
Clova Angus 82 F5
Clove Lodge Durham 57 E11
Clovelly Devon 6 D2
Clovenfords Scot Borders 70 G3
Clovenstone Aberds 83 B9
Clovullin H'land 74 A3
Clow Bridge Lancs 50 G4
Clowne Derby 45 E8
Clows Top Worcs 26 A4
Cloy Wrex 33 A9
Cluanie Inn H'land 80 B2
Cluanie Lodge H'land 80 B2
Clun Shrops 33 G9
Clunbury Shrops 33 G9
Clunderwen Carms 22 E6
Clune H'land 81 A9
Clunes H'land 80 E4
Clungunford Shrops 33 H9
Clunie Aberds 89 C6
Clunie Perth/Kinr 76 C4
Clunton Shrops 33 G9
Cluny Fife 76 H5
Cluny Castle H'land 81 D8
Clutton Bath/NE Som'set 16 F3
Clutton Ches 43 G7
Clwt-grugoer Conwy 42 F2
Clwt-y-bont Gwyn 41 D7
Clydach Monmouths 25 G9
Clydach Swan 14 A2
Clydach Vale Rh Cyn Taff 14 B5
Clydebank W Dunb 68 C3
Clydey Pembs 23 C7
Clyffe Pypard Wilts 17 D7
Clynder Arg/Bute 73 E11
Clyne Neath P Talb 14 A4
Clynelish H'land 93 J11
Clynnog-fawr Gwyn 40 E6
Clyro Powys 25 D9
Clyst Honiton Devon 7 G8
Clyst Hydon Devon 7 F9
Clyst St George Devon 5 C10
Clyst St Lawrence Devon 7 F9
Clyst St Mary Devon 7 G8
Cnoc Amhlaigh W Isles 91 D10
Cnwch-coch Ceredig'n 32 H2
Coachford Aberds 88 D4
Coad's Green Cornw'l 4 D3
Coal Aston Derby 45 E7
Coalbrookdale Telford 34 E2
Coalbrookvale Bl Gwent 25 H8
Coalburn S Lanarks 69 G7
Coalburns Tyne/Wear 63 G7
Coalcleugh Northum 57 B10
Coaley Glos 16 A4
Coalhall E Ayrs 67 E7
Coalhill Essex 20 B4
Coalpit Heath S Gloucs 16 C3
Coalport Telford 34 E2
Coalsnaughton Clack 76 H2
Coaltown of Balgonie Fife 76 H5
Coaltown of Wemyss Fife 76 H6
Coalville Leics 35 D10
Coalway Glos 26 G2
Coat Som'set 8 B3
Coatbridge N Lanarks 68 D6
Coatdyke N Lanarks 68 D6
Coate Swindon 17 C8
Coate Wilts 17 E7
Coates Cambs 37 F9
Coates Glos 16 A6
Coates Lancs 50 E4
Coates Notts 46 D2
Coates W Sussex 11 C8
Coatham Redcar/Clevel'd 59 D6
Coatham Mundeville D'lington 58 D3
Coatsgate Dumf/Gal 60 C6
Cobbaton Devon 6 D5
Cobbler's Green Norfolk 39 F8
Coberley Glos 26 G6
Cobham Kent 20 E3
Cobham Surrey 19 E8
Cobholm Island Norfolk 39 E11
Cobleland Stirl 75 H8
Cobnash Heref'd 25 B11
Coburty Aberds 89 B9
Cock Bank Wrex 42 H6
Cock Bridge Aberds 82 C4
Cock Clarks Essex 20 A5
Cockayne N Yorks 59 G7
Cockayne Hatley Cambs 29 D9
Cockburnspath Scot Borders 70 C6
Cockenzie and Port Seton E Loth 70 C3
Cockerham Lancs 49 D4
Cockermouth Cumb 56 C3
Cockernhoe Green Herts 29 F8
Cockfield Durham 58 D2
Cockfield Suffolk 30 C6
Cockfosters London 19 B9
Cocking W Sussex 11 C7
Cockington Torbay 5 E9
Cocklake Som'set 15 G10
Cockley Beck Cumb 56 F4
Cockley Cley Norfolk 38 E3
Cockshutt Shrops 33 C10
Cockthorpe Norfolk 38 A5
Cockwood Devon 5 C10
Cockyard Heref'd 25 E11
Codda Cornw'l 4 D2
Coddenham Suffolk 31 C8
Coddington Ches 43 G7
Coddington Heref'd 26 D4
Coddington Notts 46 G2
Codford St Mary Wilts 16 H6
Codford St Peter Wilts 16 H6
Codicote Herts 29 G9
Codmore Hill W Sussex 11 B9
Codnor Derby 45 H8
Codrington S Gloucs 16 D4
Codsall Staffs 34 E4
Codsall Wood Staffs 34 E4
Coed Duon = Blackwood Caerph 15 B7
Coed Mawr Gwyn 41 C7
Coed Morgan Monmouths 25 G10
Coed-Talon Flints 42 G5
Coed-y-bryn Ceredig'n 23 B8
Coed-y-paen Monmouths 15 B9
Coed-yr-ynys Powys 25 F8
Coed Ystumgwern Gwyn 32 C1
Coedely Rh Cyn Taff 14 C6
Coedkernew Newp 15 C8
Coedpoeth Wrex 42 G5
Coedway Powys 33 D9
Coelbren Powys 24 G5
Coffinswell Devon 5 E9
Cofton Hackett Worcs 34 H6
Cogan V/Glam 15 D7
Cogenhoe Northants 28 B5
Cogges Oxon 27 H10
Coggeshall Essex 30 F5
Coggeshall Hamlet Essex 30 F5
Coggins Mill E Sussex 12 D4
Coig Peighinnean W Isles 91 A10
Coig Peighinnean Bhuirgh W Isles 91 B9
Coignafearn Lodge H'land 81 B8
Coilacriech Aberds 82 D5
Coilantogle Stirl 75 G8
Coilleag W Isles 84 G2
Coillore H'land 85 E8
Coity Bridg 14 C5
Col W Isles 91 C9
Col Uarach W Isles 91 D9
Colaboll H'land 93 H8
Colan Cornw'l 3 C7
Colaton Raleigh Devon 7 H9
Colbost H'land 84 D7
Colburn N Yorks 58 G2
Colby Cumb 57 D8
Colby I/Man 48 E2
Colby Norfolk 39 B8
Colchester Essex 31 F7
Colcot V/Glam 15 E7
Cold Ash W Berks 18 E2
Cold Ashby Northants 36 H2
Cold Ashton S Gloucs 16 D4
Cold Aston Glos 27 G8
Cold Blow Pembs 22 E6
Cold Brayfield M/Keynes 28 C6
Cold Hanworth Lincs 46 D4
Cold Harbour Lincs 36 B5
Cold Hatton Telford 34 C2
Cold Hesledon Durham 58 B5
Cold Higham Northants 28 C3
Cold Kirby N Yorks 51 A11
Cold Newton Leics 36 E3
Cold Northcott Cornw'l 4 C3
Cold Norton Essex 20 A5
Cold Overton Leics 36 D4
Coldbackie H'land 93 C9
Coldbeck Cumb 57 F9
Coldblow London 20 D2
Coldean Brighton/Hove 12 F2
Coldeast Devon 5 D9
Colden W Yorks 50 G5
Colden Common Hants 10 B3
Coldfair Green Suffolk 31 B11
Coldham Cambs 37 E10
Coldharbour Glos 16 A2
Coldharbour Kent 20 F2
Coldharbour Surrey 19 G8
Coldingham Scot Borders 71 D8
Coldrain Perth/Kinr 76 G3
Coldred Kent 21 G9
Coldridge Devon 6 F5
Coldstream Angus 76 D6
Coldstream Scot Borders 71 G7
Coldwaltham W Sussex 11 C9
Coldwells Aberds 89 D11
Coldwells Croft Aberds 83 A7
Coldyeld Shrops 33 F9
Cole Som'set 8 A5
Cole Green Herts 29 G9
Cole Henley Hants 17 F11
Colebatch Shrops 33 G9
Colebrook Devon 7 F9
Colebrooke Devon 7 G6
Coleby Lincs 46 F3
Coleby N Lincs 52 H4
Coleford Devon 7 F6
Coleford Glos 26 G2
Coleford Som'set 16 G3
Colehill Dorset 9 D9
Coleman's Hatch E Sussex 12 C3
Colemere Shrops 33 B10
Colemore Hants 10 A6
Coleorton Leics 35 D10
Colerne Wilts 16 D5
Cole's Green Suffolk 31 B9
Coles Green Suffolk 31 D7
Colesbourne Glos 26 G6
Colesden Beds 29 C8
Coleshill Bucks 18 B6
Coleshill Oxon 17 B9
Coleshill Warwick 35 G8
Colestocks Devon 7 F9
Colgate W Sussex 11 A11
Colgrain Arg/Bute 68 B2
Colinsburgh Fife 77 G7
Colinton C/Edinb 69 D11
Colintraive Arg/Bute 73 F9
Colkirk Norfolk 38 C5
Collace Perth/Kinr 76 D5
Collafirth Shetl'd 96 G6
Collaton St Mary Torbay 5 F9
College Milton S Lanarks 68 E5
Collessie Fife 76 F5
Collier Row London 20 B2
Collier Street Kent 20 G4
Collier's End Herts 29 F10
Collier's Green Kent 13 C6
Colliery Row Tyne/Wear 58 B4
Collieston Aberds 89 F10
Collin Dumf/Gal 60 F6
Collingbourne Ducis Wilts 17 F9
Collingbourne Kingston Wilts 17 F9
Collingham Notts 46 F2
Collingham W Yorks 51 E9
Collington Heref'd 26 B3
Collingtree Northants 28 C4
Collins Green Warrington 43 C8
Colliston Angus 77 C9
Collycroft Warwick 35 G9
Collynie Aberds 89 E8
Collyweston Northants 36 E5
Colmonell S Ayrs 66 H4
Colmworth Beds 29 C8
Coln Rogers Glos 27 H7
Coln St Aldwyn's Glos 27 H8
Coln St Dennis Glos 27 G7
Colnabaichin Aberds 82 C4
Colnbrook Slough 19 D7
Colne Cambs 37 H9
Colne Lancs 50 E4
Colne Edge Lancs 50 E4
Colne Engaine Essex 30 E5
Colney Norfolk 39 E7
Colney Heath Herts 29 H9
Colney Street Herts 19 A8
Colpy Aberds 89 E6
Colquhar Scot Borders 70 F2
Colsterdale N Yorks 51 A7
Colsterworth Lincs 36 C5
Colston Bassett Notts 36 B2
Coltfield Moray 87 E14
Colthouse Cumb 56 G5
Coltishall Norfolk 39 D8
Coltness N Lanarks 69 E7
Colton Cumb 56 H5
Colton Norfolk 39 E7
Colton N Yorks 51 E11
Colton Staffs 35 C6
Colton W Yorks 51 F9
Colva Powys 25 C9
Colvend Dumf/Gal 55 D11
Colvister Shetl'd 96 D7
Colwall Green Heref'd 26 D4
Colwall Stone Heref'd 26 D4
Colwell Northum 62 F5
Colwich Staffs 34 C6
Colwick Notts 36 A2
Colwinston V/Glam 14 D5
Colworth W Sussex 11 D8
Colwyn Bay = Bae Colwyn Conwy 41 C10
Colyford Devon 8 E1
Colyton Devon 8 E1
Combe Heref'd 25 B10
Combe Oxon 27 G11
Combe W Berks 17 E10
Combe Common Surrey 18 H6
Combe Down Bath/NE Som'set 16 E4
Combe Florey Som'set 7 C10
Combe Hay Bath/NE Som'set 16 F4
Combe Martin Devon 6 B4
Combe Moor Heref'd 25 B10
Combe Raleigh Devon 7 F10
Combe St Nicholas Som'set 8 C2
Combeinteignhead Devon 5 D10
Comberbach Ches 43 E9
Comberton Cambs 29 C10
Comberton Heref'd 25 B11
Combpyne Devon 8 E1
Combridge Staffs 35 B6
Combrook Warwick 27 C10
Combs Derby 44 E4
Combs Suffolk 31 C7
Combs Ford Suffolk 31 C7
Combwich Som'set 15 G8
Comers Aberds 83 C8
Comins Coch Ceredig'n 32 G2
Commercial End Cambs 30 B2
Commins Capel Betws Ceredig'n 24 C3
Commins Coch Powys 32 E4
Common Edge Blackp'l 49 F3
Common Side Derby 45 E7
Commondale N Yorks 59 E7
Commonmoor Cornw'l 4 E3
Commonside Ches 43 E8
Compstall Gtr Man 44 C3
Compton Devon 5 E9
Compton Hants 10 B3
Compton Surrey 18 G5
Compton Surrey 18 G6
Compton W Berks 18 D2
Compton Wilts 17 F8
Compton W Sussex 11 C6
Compton Abbas Dorset 9 C7
Compton Abdale Glos 27 G7
Compton Bassett Wilts 17 D7
Compton Beauchamp Oxon 17 C9
Compton Bishop Som'set 15 F9
Compton Chamberlayne Wilts 9 B9
Compton Dando Bath/NE Som'set 16 E3
Compton Dundon Som'set 8 A3
Compton Martin Bath/NE Som'set 15 F11
Compton Pauncefoot Som'set 8 B5
Compton Valence Dorset 8 E4
Comrie Fife 69 B9
Comrie Perth/Kinr 75 E10
Conaglen House H'land 80 G2
Conchra Arg/Bute 73 E9
Concraigie Perth/Kinr 76 C4
Conder Green Lancs 49 D4
Conderton Worcs 26 E6
Condicote Glos 27 F8
Condorrat N Lanarks 68 C6
Condover Shrops 33 E10
Coney Weston Suffolk 38 H5
Coneyhurst W Sussex 11 B10
Coneysthorpe N Yorks 52 B3
Coneythorpe N Yorks 51 D9
Conford Hants 11 A7
Congash H'land 82 A2
Congdon's Shop Cornw'l 4 D3
Congerstone Leics 35 E9
Congham Norfolk 38 C3
Congl-y-wal Gwyn 41 F9
Congleton Ches 44 F2
Congresbury N Som'set 15 E10
Congreve Staffs 34 D5
Conicavel Moray 87 F12
Coningsby Lincs 46 G6
Conington Cambs 37 G7
Conington Cambs 29 B10
Conisbrough S Yorks 45 C9
Conisby Arg/Bute 64 B3
Conisholme Lincs 47 C8
Coniston Cumb 56 G5
Coniston ER Yorks 53 F7
Coniston Cold N Yorks 50 D5
Conistone N Yorks 50 C5
Connah's Quay Flints 42 F5
Connel Arg/Bute 74 D2
Connel Park E Ayrs 67 E9
Connor Downs Cornw'l 2 F4
Conon Bridge H'land 87 F8
Conon House H'land 87 F8
Cononley N Yorks 50 E5
Conordan H'land 85 E10
Consall Staffs 44 H3
Consett Durham 58 A2
Constable Burton N Yorks 58 G2
Constantine Cornw'l 2 G6
Constantine Bay Cornw'l 3 B7
Contin H'land 86 F7
Contlaw Aberd C 83 C10
Conwy Conwy 41 C9
Conyer Kent 20 E6
Conyers Green Suffolk 30 B5
Cooden E Sussex 12 F6
Cooil I/Man 48 E3
Cookbury Devon 6 F3
Cookham Windsor 18 C5
Cookham Dean Windsor 18 C5
Cookham Rise Windsor 18 C5
Cookhill Worcs 27 C7
Cookley Suffolk 39 H9
Cookley Worcs 34 G4
Cookley Green Oxon 18 B3
Cookney Aberds 83 D10
Cookridge W Yorks 51 E8
Cooksbridge E Sussex 12 E3
Cooksmill Green Essex 30 H3
Coolham W Sussex 11 B10
Cooling Medway 20 D4
Coombe Cornw'l 6 E1
Coombe Cornw'l 3 D8
Coombe Hants 10 B5
Coombe Wilts 17 F8
Coombe Bissett Wilts 9 B10
Coombe Hill Glos 26 F5
Coombe Keynes Dorset 9 F7
Coombes W Sussex 11 D10
Coopersale Common Essex 19 A11
Cootham W Sussex 11 C9
Copdock Suffolk 31 D8
Copford Green Essex 30 F6
Copgrove N Yorks 51 C9
Copister Shetl'd 96 F6
Cople Beds 29 D8
Copley Durham 58 D1
Coplow Dale Derby 44 E5
Copmanthorpe C/York 52 E1
Coppathorne Cornw'l 4 A3
Coppenhall Staffs 34 D5
Coppenhall Moss Ches 43 G10
Copperhouse Cornw'l 2 F4
Coppingford Cambs 37 G7
Copplestone Devon 7 F6
Coppull Lancs 43 A8
Coppull Moor Lancs 43 A8
Copsale W Sussex 11 B10
Copster Green Lancs 50 F2
Copston Magna Warwick 35 G10
Copt Heath W Midlands 35 H7
Copt Hewick N Yorks 51 B9
Copt Oak Leics 35 D10
Copthorne Shrops 33 D10
Copthorne W Sussex 12 C2
Copy's Green Norfolk 38 B5
Copythorne Hants 10 C2
Corbets Tey London 20 C2
Corbridge Northum 62 G5
Corby Northants 36 G4
Corby Glen Lincs 36 C5
Cordon N Ayrs 66 C3
Coreley Shrops 26 A3
Cores End Bucks 18 C6
Corfe Som'set 7 E11
Corfe Castle Dorset 9 F8
Corfe Mullen Dorset 9 E8
Corfton Shrops 33 G10
Corgarff Aberds 82 C4
Corhampton Hants 10 B5
Corlae Dumf/Gal 67 G9
Corley Warwick 35 G9
Corley Ash Warwick 35 G8
Corley Moor Warwick 35 G8
Cornaa I/Man 48 D4
Cornabus Arg/Bute 64 D4
Cornel Conwy 41 D9
Corner Row Lancs 49 F4
Corney Cumb 56 G3
Cornforth Durham 58 C4
Cornhill Aberds 88 C5
Cornhill-on-Tweed Northum 71 G7
Cornholme W Yorks 50 G5
Cornish Hall End Essex 30 E3
Cornquoy Orkney 95 J6
Cornsay Durham 58 B2
Cornsay Colliery Durham 58 B2
Corntown H'land 87 F8
Corntown V/Glam 14 D5
Cornwell Oxon 27 F9
Cornwood Devon 5 F7
Cornworthy Devon 5 F9
Corpach H'land 80 F2
Corpusty Norfolk 39 B7
Corran H'land 74 A3
Corran H'land 85 H13
Corranbuie Arg/Bute 73 G7
Corrany I/Man 48 D4
Corrie N Ayrs 66 B3
Corrie Common Dumf/Gal 61 E8
Corriecravie N Ayrs 66 D2
Corriemoillie H'land 86 E6
Corriemulzie Lodge H'land 86 B6
Corrievarkie Lodge Perth/Kinr 81 F7
Corrievorrie H'land 81 A9
Corrimony H'land 86 H6
Corringham Lincs 46 C2
Corringham Thurr'k 20 C4
Corris Gwyn 32 E3
Corris Uchaf Gwyn 32 E3
Corrour Shooting Lodge H'land 80 G6
Corrow Arg/Bute 74 G4
Corry H'land 85 F11
Corry of Ardnagrask H'land 87 G8
Corrykinloch H'land 92 G6
Corrymuckloch Perth/Kinr 75 D11
Corrynachenchy Arg/Bute 79 G9
Cors-y-Gedol Gwyn 32 C1
Corsback H'land 94 C4
Corscombe Dorset 8 D4
Corse Aberds 88 D6
Corse Lawn Worcs 26 E5
Corse of Kinnoir Aberds 88 D5
Corsewall Dumf/Gal 54 C3
Corsham Wilts 16 D5
Corsindae Aberds 83 C8
Corsley Wilts 16 G5
Corsley Heath Wilts 16 G5
Corsock Dumf/Gal 60 F3
Corston Bath/NE Som'set 16 E3
Corston Wilts 16 C6
Corstorphine C/Edinb 69 C10
Cortachy Angus 76 B6
Corton Suffolk 39 F11
Corton Wilts 16 G6
Corton Denham Som'set 8 B5
Coruanan Lodge H'land 80 G2
Corunna W Isles 84 B3
Corwen Denbs 33 A6
Coryton Devon 4 C5
Coryton Thurr'k 20 C4
Cosby Leics 35 F11
Coseley W Midlands 34 F5
Cosgrove Northants 28 D4
Cosham Portsm'th 10 D5
Cosheston Pembs 22 F5
Cossall Notts 35 A10
Cossington Leics 36 D2
Cossington Som'set 15 G9
Costa Orkney 95 F4
Costessey Norfolk 39 D7
Costock Notts 36 C1
Coston Leics 36 C4
Cote Oxon 17 A10
Cotebrook Ches 43 F8
Cotehill Cumb 56 A6
Cotes Cumb 57 H6
Cotes Leics 36 C1
Cotes Staffs 34 B4
Cotesbach Leics 35 G11
Cotgrave Notts 36 B2
Cothall Aberds 83 B10
Cotham Notts 45 H11
Cothelstone Som'set 7 C10
Cotherstone Durham 58 E1
Cothill Oxon 17 B11
Cotleigh Devon 7 F11
Cotmanhay Derby 35 A10
Cotmaton Devon 7 H10
Coton Cambs 29 C11
Coton Northants 28 A3
Coton Staffs 34 C4
Coton Staffs 34 B5
Coton Clanford Staffs 34 C4
Coton Hill Shrops 33 D10
Coton Hill Staffs 34 B5
Coton in the Elms Derby 35 D8
Cott Devon 5 E8
Cottam ER Yorks 52 C5
Cottam Lancs 49 F5
Cottam Notts 46 E2
Cottartown H'land 87 H13
Cottenham Cambs 29 B11
Cotterdale N Yorks 57 G10
Cottered Herts 29 F10
Cotteridge W Midlands 34 H6
Cotterstock Northants 36 F6
Cottesbrooke Northants 28 A4
Cottesmore Rutl'd 36 D5
Cotteylands Devon 7 E8
Cottingham ER Yorks 52 F6
Cottingham Northants 36 F4
Cottingley W Yorks 51 F7
Cottisford Oxon 28 E2
Cotton Staffs 44 H4
Cotton Suffolk 31 B7
Cotton End Beds 29 D7
Cottown Aberds 83 A7
Cottown Aberds 83 B9
Cottown Aberds 89 D8
Cotwalton Staffs 34 B5
Couch's Mill Cornw'l 4 F2
Coughton Heref'd 26 F2
Coughton Warwick 27 B7
Coulaghailtro Arg/Bute 72 G6
Coulags H'land 86 G2
Coulby Newham Middlesbro' 58 E6
Coulderton Cumb 56 F1
Coulin H'land 86 F3
Coull Aberds 83 C7
Coull Arg/Bute 64 B3
Coulport Arg/Bute 73 E11
Coulsdon London 19 F9
Coulston Wilts 16 F6
Coulter S Lanarks 69 G9
Coulton N Yorks 52 B2
Cound Shrops 34 E1
Coundon Durham 58 D3
Coundon W Midlands 35 G9
Coundon Grange Durham 58 D3
Countersett N Yorks 57 H11
Countess Wilts 17 G8
Countess Wear Devon 5 C10
Countesthorpe Leics 36 F1
Countisbury Devon 7 B6
County Oak W Sussex 12 C1
Coup Green Lancs 50 G1
Coupar Angus Perth/Kinr 76 C5
Coupland Northum 71 G8
Cour Arg/Bute 65 D9
Courance Dumf/Gal 60 D6
Court-at-Street Kent 13 C9
Court Henry Carms 23 D10
Courteenhall Northants 28 C4
Courtsend Essex 21 B7
Courtway Som'set 7 C11
Cousland Midloth 70 D2
Cousley Wood E Sussex 12 C5
Cove Arg/Bute 73 E11
Cove Scot Borders 70 C6
Cove Devon 7 E8
Cove Hants 18 F5
Cove H'land 91 H13
Cove Bay Aberd C 83 C11
Cove Bottom Suffolk 39 H10
Covehithe Suffolk 39 G11
Coven Staffs 34 E5
Coveney Cambs 37 G10
Covenham St Bartholomew Lincs 47 C7
Covenham St Mary Lincs 47 C7
Coventry W Midlands 35 H9
Coverack Cornw'l 3 H6
Coverham N Yorks 58 H1
Covesea Moray 88 A1
Covington Cambs 29 A7
Covington S Lanarks 69 G8
Cow Ark Lancs 50 E2
Cowan Bridge Lancs 50 B2
Cowbeech E Sussex 12 E5
Cowbit Lincs 37 D8
Cowbridge Lincs 47 H7
Cowbridge Som'set 7 B8
Cowbridge = Y Bont-Faen V/Glam 14 D5
Cowdale Derby 44 E4
Cowden Kent 12 B3
Cowdenbeath Fife 69 A10
Cowdenburn Scot Borders 69 E11
Cowers Lane Derby 45 H7
Cowes I/Wight 10 E3
Cowesby N Yorks 58 H5
Cowfold W Sussex 11 B11
Cowgill Cumb 57 H9
Cowie Aberds 83 E10
Cowie Stirl 69 B7
Cowley Devon 7 G8
Cowley Glos 26 G6
Cowley London 19 C7
Cowley Oxon 18 A2
Cowleymoor Devon 7 E8
Cowling Lancs 50 H1
Cowling N Yorks 50 E5
Cowling N Yorks 58 H3
Cowlinge Suffolk 30 C4
Cowpe Lancs 50 G4
Cowpen Northum 63 E8
Cowpen Bewley Stockton 58 D5
Cowplain Hants 10 C5
Cowshill Durham 57 B10
Cowstrandburn Fife 69 A9
Cowthorpe N Yorks 51 D10
Cox Common Suffolk 39 G9
Cox Green Windsor 18 D5
Cox Moor Notts 45 G9
Coxbank Ches 34 A2
Coxbench Derby 35 A9
Coxford Norfolk 38 C4
Coxford S'hampton 10 C2
Coxheath Kent 20 F4
Coxhoe Durham 58 C4
Coxley Som'set 15 G11
Coxwold N Yorks 51 B11
Coychurch Bridg 14 D5
Coylton S Ayrs 67 D7
Coylumbridge H'land 81 B11
Coynach Aberds 82 C6
Coynachie Aberds 88 E4
Coytrahen Bridg 14 C4
Crabadon Devon 5 F8
Crabbs Cross Worcs 27 B7
Crabtree W Sussex 11 B11
Crackenthorpe Cumb 57 D8
Crackington Haven Cornw'l 4 B2
Crackley Warwick 27 A9
Crackleybank Shrops 34 D3
Crackpot N Yorks 57 G11
Cracoe N Yorks 50 C5
Craddock Devon 7 E9
Cradhlastadh W Isles 90 D5
Cradley Heref'd 26 D4
Cradley Heath W Midlands 34 G5
Crafthole Cornw'l 4 F4
Cragg Vale W Yorks 50 G6
Craggan H'land 82 A2
Craggie H'land 93 H11
Craggie H'land 87 H10
Craghead Durham 58 A3
Crai Powys 24 F5
Craibstone Moray 88 C4
Craichie Angus 77 C8
Craig Dumf/Gal 55 B9
Craig Dumf/Gal 55 C9
Craig H'land 86 G3
Craig Castle Aberds 82 A6
Craig-cefn-parc Swan 14 A2
Craig Penllyn V/Glam 14 D5
Craig-y-don Conwy 41 B9
Craig-y-nos Powys 24 G5
Craiganor Lodge Perth/Kinr 75 B9
Craigdam Aberds 89 E8
Craigdarroch Dumf/Gal 60 D3
Craigdarroch H'land 86 F7
Craigdhu H'land 86 G7
Craigearn Aberds 83 B9
Craigellachie Moray 88 D2
Craigencross Dumf/Gal 54 C3
Craigend Perth/Kinr 76 E4
Craigend Stirl 68 B6
Craigendive Arg/Bute 73 E9
Craigendoran Arg/Bute 68 B2
Craigends Renf 68 D3
Craigens Arg/Bute 64 B3
Craigens E Ayrs 67 E8
Craighat Stirl 68 B3
Craighead Fife 77 G9
Craighlaw Mains Dumf/Gal 54 C6
Craighouse Arg/Bute 72 G4
Craigie Aberds 83 B11
Craigie Dundee C 77 D7
Craigie Perth/Kinr 76 E4
Craigie Perth/Kinr 76 C4
Craigie S Ayrs 67 C7
Craigiefield Orkney 95 G5
Craigielaw E Loth 70 C3
Craiglockhart C/Edinb 69 C11
Craigmalloch E Ayrs 67 G7
Craigmaud Aberds 89 C8
Craigmillar C/Edinb 69 C11
Craigmore Arg/Bute 73 G10
Craignant Shrops 33 B8
Craigneuk N Lanarks 68 E6
Craigneuk N Lanarks 68 D6
Craignure Arg/Bute 79 H10
Craigo Angus 77 A9
Craigow Perth/Kinr 76 G3
Craigrothie Fife 76 F6
Craigroy Moray 87 F14
Craigruie Stirl 75 E7
Craigston Castle Aberds 89 C7
Craigton Aberd C 83 C10
Craigton Angus 76 B6
Craigton Angus 77 D8
Craigton H'land 87 B9
Craigtown H'land 93 D11
Craik Scot Borders 61 C9
Crail Fife 77 G9
Crailing Scot Borders 62 A2
Crailinghall Scot Borders 62 A2
Craiselound N Lincs 45 C11
Crakehill N Yorks 51 B10
Crakemarsh Staffs 35 B6
Crambe N Yorks 52 C3
Cramlington Northum 63 F8
Cramond C/Edinb 69 C10
Cramond Bridge C/Edinb 69 C10
Cranage Ches 43 F10
Cranberry Staffs 34 B4
Cranborne Dorset 9 C9
Cranbourne Brackn'l 18 D6
Cranbrook Kent 13 C6
Cranbrook Common Kent 13 C6
Crane Moor S Yorks 45 B7
Crane's Corner Norfolk 38 D5
Cranfield Beds 28 D6
Cranford London 19 D8
Cranford St Andrew Northants 36 H5
Cranford St John Northants 36 H5
Cranham Glos 26 G5
Cranham London 20 C2
Crank Mersey 43 C8
Crank Wood Gtr Man 43 B9
Cranleigh Surrey 19 H7
Cranley Suffolk 31 A8
Cranmer Green Suffolk 31 A7
Cranmore I/Wight 10 F2
Cranna Aberds 89 C6
Crannich Arg/Bute 79 G8
Crannoch Moray 88 C4
Cranoe Leics 36 F3
Cransford Suffolk 31 B10
Cranshaws Scot Borders 70 D5
Cranstal I/Man 48 B4
Crantock Cornw'l 3 C6
Cranwell Lincs 46 H4
Cranwich Norfolk 38 F3
Cranworth Norfolk 38 E5
Craobh Haven Arg/Bute 72 C6
Crapstone Devon 4 E6
Crarae Arg/Bute 73 D8
Crask Inn H'land 93 G8
Crask of Aigas H'land 86 G7
Craskins Aberds 83 C7
Craster Northum 63 B8
Craswall Heref'd 25 E9
Cratfield Suffolk 39 H9
Crathes Aberds 83 D9
Crathie Aberds 82 D4
Crathie H'land 81 D7
Crathorne N Yorks 58 F5
Craven Arms Shrops 33 G10
Crawcrook Tyne/Wear 63 G7
Crawford Lancs 43 B7
Crawford S Lanarks 60 A5
Crawfordjohn S Lanarks 60 A4
Crawick Dumf/Gal 60 B3
Crawley Hants 10 A3
Crawley Oxon 27 G10
Crawley W Sussex 12 C1
Crawley Down W Sussex 12 C2
Crawleyside Durham 57 B11
Crawshawbooth Lancs 50 G4
Crawton Aberds 83 F10
Cray N Yorks 50 B5
Cray Perth/Kinr 76 A4
Crayford London 20 D2
Crayke N Yorks 52 B1
Crays Hill Essex 20 B4
Cray's Pond Oxon 18 C3
Creacombe Devon 7 E7
Creag Ghoraidh W Isles 84 D2
Creagan Arg/Bute 74 C2
Creaguaineach Lodge H'land 80 G5
Creaksea Essex 20 B6
Creaton Northants 28 A4
Creca Dumf/Gal 61 F8
Credenhill Heref'd 25 D11
Crediton Devon 7 F7
Creebridge Dumf/Gal 55 C7
Creech Heathfield Som'set 8 B1
Creech St Michael Som'set 8 B1
Creed Cornw'l 3 E8
Creekmouth London 19 C11
Creeting Bottoms Suffolk 31 C8
Creeting St Mary Suffolk 31 C7
Creeton Lincs 36 C6
Creetown Dumf/Gal 55 D7
Creg-ny-Baa I/Man 48 D3
Creggans Arg/Bute 73 C9
Cregneash I/Man 48 F1
Cregrina Powys 25 C8
Creich Fife 76 E6
Creigiau Card 14 C6
Cremyll Cornw'l 4 F5
Creslow Bucks 28 F5
Cressage Shrops 34 E1
Cressbrook Derby 44 E5
Cresselly Pembs 22 F5
Cressing Essex 30 F4
Cresswell Northum 63 D8
Cresswell Staffs 34 B5
Cresswell Quay Pembs 22 F5
Creswell Derby 45 E9
Cretingham Suffolk 31 B9
Cretshengan Arg/Bute 72 G6
Crewe Ches 43 G7
Crewe Ches 43 G10
Crewgreen Powys 33 D9
Crewkerne Som'set 8 D3
Crianlarich Stirl 74 E6
Cribyn Ceredig'n 23 A10
Criccieth Gwyn 40 G6
Crich Derby 45 G7
Crichie Aberds 89 D9
Crichton Midloth 70 D2
Crick Monmouths 15 B10
Crick Northants 28 A2
Crickadarn Powys 25 D7
Cricket Malherbie Som'set 8 C2
Cricket St Thomas Som'set 8 D2
Crickheath Shrops 33 C8
Crickhowell Powys 25 G9
Cricklade Wilts 17 B8
Cricklewood London 19 C9
Cridling Stubbs N Yorks 51 G11
Crieff Perth/Kinr 75 E11
Criggion Powys 33 D8
Crigglestone W Yorks 51 H8
Crimond Aberds 89 C10
Crimonmogate Aberds 89 C10
Crimplesham Norfolk 38 E2
Crinan Arg/Bute 72 D6
Cringleford Norfolk 39 E7
Cringles W Yorks 50 E6
Crinow Pembs 22 E6
Cripplesease Cornw'l 2 F4
Cripplestyle Dorset 9 C9
Cripp's Corner E Sussex 13 D6
Croasdale Cumb 56 E2
Crock Street Som'set 8 C2
Crockenhill Kent 20 E2
Crockernwell Devon 7 G6
Crockerton Wilts 16 G5
Crocketford or Ninemile Bar Dumf/Gal 60 F4
Crockey Hill C/York 52 E2
Crockham Hill Kent 19 F11
Crockleford Heath Essex 31 F7
Crockness Orkney 95 J4
Croes-goch Pembs 22 C3
Croes-lan Ceredig'n 23 B8
Croes-y-mwyalch Torf 15 B9
Croeserw Neath P Talb 14 B4
Croesor Gwyn 41 F8
Croesyceiliog Carms 23 E9
Croesyceiliog Torf 15 B9
Croesywaun Gwyn 41 E7
Croft Leics 35 F11
Croft Lincs 47 F9
Croft Pembs 22 B6
Croft Warrington 43 C9
Croft-on-Tees N Yorks 58 F3
Croftamie Stirl 68 B3
Croftmalloch W Loth 69 D8
Crofton Wilts 17 E9
Crofton W Yorks 51 H9
Crofts of Benachielt H'land 94 G3
Crofts of Haddo Aberds 89 E8
Crofts of Inverthernie Aberds 89 D7
Crofts of Meikle Ardo Aberds 89 D8
Crofty Swan 23 G10
Croggan Arg/Bute 79 J10
Croglin Cumb 57 B7
Croich H'land 86 B7
Crois Dughaill W Isles 84 F2
Cromarty H'land 87 E10
Cromblet Aberds 89 E7
Cromdale H'land 82 A2
Cromer Herts 29 F9
Cromer Norfolk 39 A8
Cromford Derby 44 G6
Cromhall S Gloucs 16 B3
Cromhall Common S Gloucs 16 C3
Cromor W Isles 91 E9
Cromra H'land 81 D7
Cromwell Notts 45 F11
Cronberry E Ayrs 67 D9
Crondall Hants 18 G4
Cronk-y-Voddy I/Man 48 D3
Cronton Mersey 43 D7
Crook Cumb 56 G6
Crook Durham 58 C2
Crook of Devon Perth/Kinr 76 G3
Crookedholm E Ayrs 67 C7
Crookes S Yorks 45 D7
Crookham Northum 71 G8
Crookham W Berks 18 E2
Crookham Village Hants 18 F4
Crookhaugh Scot Borders 69 H10
Crookhouse Scot Borders 70 H6
Crooklands Cumb 49 A5
Cropredy Oxon 27 D11
Cropston Leics 36 D1
Cropthorne Worcs 26 D6
Cropton N Yorks 59 H8
Cropwell Bishop Notts 36 B2
Cropwell Butler Notts 36 B2
Cros W Isles 91 A10
Crosbost W Isles 91 E8
Crosby Cumb 56 C2
Crosby I/Man 48 E3
Crosby N Lincs 46 A2
Crosby Garrett Cumb 57 F9
Crosby Ravensworth Cumb 57 E8
Crosby Villa Cumb 56 C2
Croscombe Som'set 16 G2
Cross Som'set 15 F10
Cross Ash Monmouths 25 G11
Cross-at-Hand Kent 20 G4
Cross Green Devon 4 C4
Cross Green Suffolk 30 C6
Cross Green Suffolk 30 C5
Cross Green Warwick 27 C10
Cross Hands Carms 23 E10
Cross-hands Carms 22 D6
Cross Hands Pembs 22 E5
Cross Hill Derby 45 H8
Cross Houses Shrops 33 E11
Cross in Hand E Sussex 12 D4
Cross in Hand Leics 35 G11
Cross Inn Ceredig'n 24 B2
Cross Inn Ceredig'n 23 A8
Cross Inn Rh Cyn Taff 14 C6
Cross Keys Kent 20 F2
Cross Lane Head Shrops 34 F3
Cross Lanes Cornw'l 2 G5
Cross Lanes N Yorks 51 C11
Cross Lanes Wrex 43 H6
Cross Oak Powys 25 F8
Cross o' Jackston Aberds 89 E7
Cross o'th'hands Derby 44 H6
Cross Street Suffolk 39 H7
Crossaig Arg/Bute 65 C9
Crossal H'land 85 E9
Crossapol Arg/Bute 78 G2
Crossburn Falk 69 C7
Crossbush W Sussex 11 D9
Crosscanonby Cumb 56 C2
Crossdale Street Norfolk 39 B8
Crossens Mersey 49 H3
Crossflatts W Yorks 51 E7
Crossford Fife 69 B9
Crossford S Lanarks 69 F7
Crossgate Lincs 37 C8
Crossgatehall E Loth 70 D2
Crossgates Fife 69 B10
Crossgates Powys 25 B7
Crossgill Lancs 50 C1

Crosshill *E Ayrs* 67 D7
Crosshill *Fife* 76 H4
Crosshill *S Ayrs* 66 F6
Crosshouse *E Ayrs* 67 C6
Crossings *Cumb* 61 F11
Crosskeys *Caerph* 15 B8
Crosskirk *H'land* 93 B13
Crosslanes *Shrops* 33 D9
Crosslee *Scot Borders* 61 B9
Crosslee *Renf* 68 D3
Crossmichael *Dumf/Gal* 55 C10
Crossmoor *Lancs* 49 F4
Crossroads *Aberds* 83 D9
Crossroads *E Ayrs* 67 C7
Crossway *Heref'd* 26 E3
Crossway *Monmouths* 25 G11
Crossway *Powys* 25 C7
Crossway Green *Worcs* 26 B5
Crossways *Dorset* 9 F6
Crosswell *Pembs* 22 C6
Crosswood *Ceredig'n* 24 A3
Crosthwaite *Cumb* 56 G6
Croston *Lancs* 49 H4
Crostwick *Norfolk* 39 D8
Crostwight *Norfolk* 39 C9
Crothair *W Isles* 90 D6
Crouch *Kent* 20 F3
Crouch Hill *Dorset* 8 C6
Crouch House Green *Kent* 19 G11
Croucheston *Wilts* 9 B9
Croughton *Northants* 28 E2
Crovie *Aberds* 89 B8
Crow Edge *S Yorks* 44 B5
Crow Hill *Heref'd* 26 F3
Crowan *Cornw'l* 2 F5
Crowborough *E Sussex* 12 C4
Crowcombe *Som'set* 7 C10
Crowdecote *Derby* 44 F5
Crowden *Derby* 44 C4
Crowell *Oxon* 18 B4
Crowfield *Northants* 28 D3
Crowfield *Suffolk* 31 C8
Crowhurst *E Sussex* 13 E6
Crowhurst *Surrey* 19 G10
Crowhurst Lane End *Surrey* 19 G10
Crowland *Lincs* 37 D8
Crowlas *Cornw'l* 2 F4
Crowle *N Lincs* 45 A11
Crowle *Worcs* 26 C6
Crowmarsh Gifford *Oxon* 18 C3
Crown Corner *Suffolk* 31 A9
Crownhill *Plym'th* 4 F5
Crownland *Suffolk* 31 B7
Crownthorpe *Norfolk* 39 E6
Crowntown *Cornw'l* 2 F5
Crows-an-wra *Cornw'l* 2 G2
Crowshill *Norfolk* 38 E5
Crowsnest *Shrops* 33 E9
Crowthorne *Brackn'l* 18 E5
Crowton *Ches* 43 E8
Croxall *Staffs* 35 D7
Croxby *Lincs* 46 C5
Croxdale *Durham* 58 C3
Croxden *Staffs* 35 B6
Croxley Green *Herts* 19 B7
Croxton *Cambs* 29 B9
Croxton *N Lincs* 46 A4
Croxton *Norfolk* 38 G4
Croxton *Staffs* 34 B3
Croxton Kerrial *Leics* 36 C4
Croxtonbank *Staffs* 34 B3
Croy *H'land* 87 G10
Croy *N Lanarks* 68 C6
Croyde *Devon* 6 C3
Croydon *Cambs* 29 D10
Croydon *London* 19 E10
Crubenmore Lodge *H'land* 81 D8
Cruckmeole *Shrops* 33 E10
Cruckton *Shrops* 33 D10
Cruden Bay *Aberds* 89 E10
Crudgington *Telford* 34 D2
Crudwell *Wilts* 16 B6
Crug *Powys* 25 A8
Crugmeer *Cornw'l* 3 B8
Crugybar *Carms* 24 E3
Crulabhig *W Isles* 90 D6
Crumlin = Crymlyn *Caerph* 15 B8
Crumpsall *Gtr Man* 44 B2
Crundale *Kent* 21 G7
Crundale *Pembs* 22 E4
Cruwys Morchard *Devon* 7 E7
Crux Easton *Hants* 17 F11
Crwbin *Carms* 23 E9
Crya *Orkney* 95 H4
Cryers Hill *Bucks* 18 B5
Crymlyn *Gwyn* 41 C8
Crymlyn = Crumlin *Caerph* 15 B8
Crymych *Pembs* 22 C6
Crynant *Neath P Talb* 14 A3
Crynfryn *Ceredig'n* 24 B2
Cuaig *H'land* 85 C12
Cuan *Arg/Bute* 72 B6
Cubbington *Warwick* 27 B10
Cubeck *N Yorks* 57 H11
Cubert *Cornw'l* 3 D6
Cubley *S Yorks* 44 B6
Cubley Common *Derby* 35 B7
Cublington *Bucks* 28 F5
Cublington *Heref'd* 25 E11
Cuckfield *W Sussex* 12 D2
Cucklington *Som'set* 9 B6
Cuckney *Notts* 45 E9
Cuckoo Hill *Notts* 45 C11
Cuddesdon *Oxon* 18 A3
Cuddington *Bucks* 28 G4
Cuddington *Ches* 43 E9
Cuddington Heath *Ches* 43 H7
Cuddy Hill *Lancs* 49 F4
Cudham *London* 19 F11
Cudliptown *Devon* 4 D6
Cudworth *Som'set* 8 C2
Cudworth *S Yorks* 45 B7
Cuffley *Herts* 19 A10
Cuiashader *W Isles* 91 B10
Cuidhir *W Isles* 84 H1
Cuidhtinis *W Isles* 90 J5
Culbo *H'land* 87 E9
Culbokie *H'land* 87 F9
Culburnie *H'land* 86 G7
Culcabock *H'land* 87 G9
Culcairn *H'land* 87 E9
Culcharry *H'land* 87 F11
Culcheth *Warrington* 43 C9
Culdrain *Aberds* 88 E5
Culduie *H'land* 85 D12
Culford *Suffolk* 30 A5
Culgaith *Cumb* 57 D8
Culham *Oxon* 18 B2
Culkein *H'land* 92 F3
Culkein Drumbeg *H'land* 92 F4
Culkerton *Glos* 16 B6
Cullachie *H'land* 81 A11
Cullen *Moray* 88 B5
Cullercoats *Tyne/Wear* 63 F9
Cullicudden *H'land* 87 E9
Cullingworth *W Yorks* 51 F6
Cullipool *Arg/Bute* 72 B6
Cullivoe *Shetl'd* 96 C7
Culloch *Perth/Kinr* 75 F10
Culloden *H'land* 87 G10
Cullompton *Devon* 7 F9
Culmaily *H'land* 87 B11
Culmazie *Dumf/Gal* 54 D6
Culmington *Shrops* 33 G10
Culmstock *Devon* 7 E10
Culnacraig *H'land* 92 J3
Culnaknock *H'land* 85 B10
Culpho *Suffolk* 31 D9
Culrain *H'land* 87 B8
Culross *Fife* 69 B8
Culroy *S Ayrs* 66 E6
Culsh *Aberds* 89 D8
Culsh *Aberds* 82 D5
Culshabbin *Dumf/Gal* 54 D6
Culswick *Shetl'd* 96 J4
Cultercullen *Aberds* 89 F9
Cults *Aberd C* 83 C10
Cults *Aberds* 88 E5
Cults *Dumf/Gal* 55 E7
Culverstone Green *Kent* 20 E3
Culverthorpe *Lincs* 36 A6
Culworth *Northants* 28 D2
Culzie Lodge *H'land* 87 D8
Cumbernauld *N Lanarks* 68 C6
Cumbernauld Village *N Lanarks* 68 C6
Cumberworth *Lincs* 47 E9
Cuminestown *Aberds* 89 C8
Cumlewick *Shetl'd* 96 L6
Cummersdale *Cumb* 56 A5
Cummertrees *Dumf/Gal* 61 G7
Cummingston *Moray* 88 B1
Cumnock *E Ayrs* 67 D8
Cumnor *Oxon* 17 A11
Cumrew *Cumb* 57 A7
Cumwhinton *Cumb* 56 A6
Cumwhitton *Cumb* 57 A7
Cundall *N Yorks* 51 B10
Cunninghamhead *N Ayrs* 67 B6
Cunnister *Shetl'd* 96 D7
Cupar *Fife* 76 F6
Cupar Muir *Fife* 76 F6
Cupernham *Hants* 10 B2
Curbar *Derby* 44 E6
Curbridge *Hants* 10 C4
Curbridge *Oxon* 27 H10
Curdridge *Hants* 10 C4
Curdworth *Warwick* 35 F7
Curland *Som'set* 8 C1
Curlew Green *Suffolk* 31 B10
Currarie *S Ayrs* 66 G4
Curridge *W Berks* 17 D11
Currie *C/Edinb* 69 D10
Curry Mallet *Som'set* 8 B2
Curry Rivel *Som'set* 8 B2
Curtisden Green *Kent* 12 B6
Curtisknowle *Devon* 5 F8
Cury *Cornw'l* 2 G5
Cushnie *Aberds* 89 B7
Cushuish *Som'set* 7 C10
Cusop *Heref'd* 25 D9
Cutcloy *Dumf/Gal* 55 F7
Cutcombe *Som'set* 7 C8
Cutgate *Gtr Man* 44 A2
Cutiau *Gwyn* 32 D2
Cutlers Green *Essex* 30 E2
Cutnall Green *Worcs* 26 B5
Cutsdean *Glos* 27 E7
Cutthorpe *Derby* 45 E7
Cutts *Shetl'd* 96 K6
Cuxham *Oxon* 18 B3
Cuxton *Medway* 20 E4
Cuxwold *Lincs* 46 B5
Cwm *Bl Gwent* 25 H8
Cwm *Denbs* 42 E3
Cwm *Swan* 14 B2
Cwm-byr *Carms* 24 E3
Cwm-Cewydd *Gwyn* 32 D4
Cwm-cou *Ceredig'n* 23 B7
Cwm-Dulais *Swan* 14 A2
Cwm-felin-fach *Caerph* 15 B7
Cwm Ffrwd-oer *Torf* 15 A8
Cwm-hesgen *Gwyn* 32 C3
Cwm-hwnt *Rh Cyn Taff* 24 H6
Cwm Irfon *Powys* 24 D5
Cwm-Llinau *Powys* 32 E4
Cwm-mawr *Carms* 23 E10
Cwm-parc *Rh Cyn Taff* 14 B5
Cwm Penmachno *Conwy* 41 F9
Cwm-y-glo *Carms* 23 E10
Cwm-y-glo *Gwyn* 41 D7
Cwmafan *Neath P Talb* 14 B3
Cwmaman *Rh Cyn Taff* 14 B6
Cwmann *Carms* 23 B10
Cwmavon *Torf* 25 H9
Cwmbach *Carms* 23 D7
Cwmbach *Carms* 23 F9
Cwmbach *Powys* 25 C7
Cwmbach *Powys* 25 E8
Cwmbâch *Rh Cyn Taff* 14 A6
Cwmbelan *Powys* 32 G5
Cwmbran = Cwmbrân *Torf* 15 B8
Cwmbrân = Cwmbran *Torf* 15 B8
Cwmbrwyno *Ceredig'n* 32 G3
Cwmcarn *Caerph* 15 B8
Cwmcarvan *Monmouths* 25 H11
Cwmcych *Pembs* 23 C7
Cwmdare *Rh Cyn Taff* 14 A5
Cwmderwen *Powys* 32 E5
Cwmdu *Carms* 24 E3
Cwmdu *Powys* 25 F8
Cwmdu *Swan* 14 B2
Cwmduad *Carms* 23 C8
Cwmdwr *Carms* 24 E4
Cwmfelin *Bridg* 14 C4
Cwmfelin *Merth Tyd* 14 A6
Cwmfelin Boeth *Carms* 22 E6
Cwmfelin Mynach *Carms* 23 D7
Cwmffrwd *Carms* 23 E9
Cwmgiedd *Powys* 24 G4
Cwmgors *Neath P Talb* 24 G4
Cwmgwili *Carms* 23 E10
Cwmgwrach *Neath P Talb* 14 A4
Cwmhiraeth *Carms* 23 C8
Cwmifor *Carms* 24 F3
Cwmisfael *Carms* 23 E9
Cwmllynfell *Neath P Talb* 24 G4
Cwmorgan *Carms* 23 C7
Cwmpengraig *Carms* 23 C8
Cwmrhos *Powys* 25 F8
Cwmsychpant *Ceredig'n* 23 B9
Cwmtillery *Bl Gwent* 25 H9
Cwmwysg *Powys* 24 F5
Cwmyoy *Monmouths* 25 F9
Cwmystwyth *Ceredig'n* 24 A4
Cwrt *Gwyn* 32 E2
Cwrt-newydd *Ceredig'n* 23 B9
Cwrt-y-cadno *Carms* 24 D3
Cwrt-y-gollen *Powys* 25 G9
Cydweli = Kidwelly *Carms* 23 F9
Cyffordd Llandudno = Llandudno Junction *Conwy* 41 C9
Cyffylliog *Denbs* 42 G3
Cyfronydd *Powys* 33 E7
Cymer *Neath P Talb* 14 B4
Cyncoed *Card* 15 C7
Cynghordy *Carms* 24 D5
Cynheidre *Carms* 23 F9
Cynwyd *Denbs* 33 A6
Cynwyl Elfed *Carms* 23 D8
Cywarch *Gwyn* 32 D4

D

Dacre *Cumb* 56 D6
Dacre *N Yorks* 51 C7
Dacre Banks *N Yorks* 51 C7
Daddry Shield *Durham* 57 C10
Dadford *Bucks* 28 E3
Dadlington *Leics* 35 F10
Dafarn Faig *Gwyn* 40 F6
Dafen *Carms* 23 F10
Daffy Green *Norfolk* 38 E5
Dagenham *London* 19 C11
Daglingworth *Glos* 26 H6
Dagnall *Bucks* 28 G6
Dail Beag *W Isles* 90 C7
Dail bho Dheas *W Isles* 91 A9
Dail bho Thuath *W Isles* 91 A9
Dail Mor *W Isles* 90 C7
Daill *Arg/Bute* 64 B4
Dailly *S Ayrs* 66 F5
Dairsie or Osnaburgh *Fife* 77 F7
Daisy Hill *Gtr Man* 43 B9
Dalabrog *W Isles* 84 F2
Dalavich *Arg/Bute* 73 B8
Dalbeattie *Dumf/Gal* 55 C11
Dalblair *E Ayrs* 67 E9
Dalbog *Angus* 83 F7
Dalbury *Derby* 35 B8
Dalby *I/Man* 48 E2
Dalby *N Yorks* 52 B2
Dalchalloch *Perth/Kinr* 75 A10
Dalchalm *H'land* 93 J12
Dalchenna *Arg/Bute* 73 C9
Dalchirach *Moray* 88 E1
Dalchork *H'land* 93 H8
Dalchreichart *H'land* 80 B4
Dalchruin *Perth/Kinr* 75 F10
Dalderby *Lincs* 46 F6
Dale *Pembs* 22 F3
Dale Abbey *Derby* 35 B10
Dale Head *Cumb* 56 E6
Dale of Walls *Shetl'd* 96 H3
Dalelia *H'land* 79 E10
Daless *H'land* 87 H11
Dalfaber *H'land* 81 B11
Dalgarven *N Ayrs* 66 B5
Dalgety Bay *Fife* 69 B10
Dalginross *Perth/Kinr* 75 E10
Dalguise *Perth/Kinr* 76 C2
Dalhalvaig *H'land* 93 D11
Dalham *Suffolk* 30 B4
Dalinlongart *Arg/Bute* 73 E10
Dalkeith *Midloth* 70 D2
Dallam *Warrington* 43 C8
Dallas *Moray* 87 F14
Dalleagles *E Ayrs* 67 E8
Dallinghoo *Suffolk* 31 C9
Dallington *E Sussex* 12 E5
Dallington *Northants* 28 B4
Dallow *N Yorks* 51 B7
Dalmadilly *Aberds* 83 B9
Dalmally *Arg/Bute* 74 E4
Dalmarnock *C/Glasg* 68 D5
Dalmary *Stirl* 75 H8
Dalmellington *E Ayrs* 67 F7
Dalmeny *C/Edinb* 69 C10
Dalmigavie *H'land* 81 B9
Dalmigavie Lodge *H'land* 81 A9
Dalmore *H'land* 87 E9
Dalmuir *W Dunb* 68 C3
Dalnabreck *H'land* 79 E9
Dalnacardoch Lodge *Perth/Kinr* 81 F9
Dalnacroich *H'land* 86 F6
Dalnaglar Castle *Perth/Kinr* 76 A4
Dalnahaitnach *H'land* 81 A10
Dalnaspidal Lodge *Perth/Kinr* 81 F8
Dalnavaid *Perth/Kinr* 76 A3
Dalnavie *H'land* 87 D9
Dalnawillan Lodge *H'land* 93 E13
Dalness *H'land* 74 B4
Dalnessie *H'land* 93 H9
Dalqueich *Perth/Kinr* 76 G3
Dalreavoch *H'land* 93 J10
Dalry *N Ayrs* 66 B5
Dalrymple *E Ayrs* 67 E6
Dalserf *S Lanarks* 69 E7
Dalston *Cumb* 56 A5
Dalswinton *Dumf/Gal* 60 E5
Dalton *Dumf/Gal* 61 F7
Dalton *Lancs* 43 B7
Dalton *Northum* 62 H5
Dalton *Northum* 63 F7
Dalton *N Yorks* 51 B10
Dalton *N Yorks* 58 F2
Dalton *S Yorks* 45 C8
Dalton-in-Furness *Cumb* 49 B2
Dalton-le-Dale *Durham* 58 B5
Dalton-on-Tees *N Yorks* 58 F3
Dalton Piercy *Hartlep'l* 58 C5
Dalveich *Stirl* 75 E9
Dalvina Lodge *H'land* 93 E9
Dalwhinnie *H'land* 81 E8
Dalwood *Devon* 8 D1
Dalwyne *S Ayrs* 66 G6
Dam Green *Norfolk* 39 G6
Dam Side *Lancs* 49 E4
Damerham *Hants* 9 C10
Damgate *Norfolk* 39 E10
Damnaglaur *Dumf/Gal* 54 F4
Damside *Scot Borders* 69 F10
Danbury *Essex* 30 H4
Danby *N Yorks* 59 F8
Danby Wiske *N Yorks* 58 G4
Dandaleith *Moray* 88 D2
Danderhall *Midloth* 70 D2
Dane End *Herts* 29 F10
Danebridge *Ches* 44 F3
Danehill *E Sussex* 12 D3
Danemoor Green *Norfolk* 39 E6
Danesford *Shrops* 34 F3
Daneshill *Hants* 18 F3
Dangerous Corner *Lancs* 43 A8
Danskine *E Loth* 70 D4
Darcy Lever *Gtr Man* 43 B10
Darenth *Kent* 20 D2
Daresbury *Halton* 43 D8
Darfield *S Yorks* 45 B8
Darfoulds *Notts* 45 E9
Dargate *Kent* 21 E7
Darite *Cornw'l* 4 E3
Darlaston *W Midlands* 34 F5
Darley *N Yorks* 51 D8
Darley Bridge *Derby* 44 F6
Darley Head *N Yorks* 51 D7
Darlingscott *Warwick* 27 D9
Darlington *D'lington* 58 E3
Darliston *Shrops* 34 B1
Darlton *Notts* 45 E11
Darnall *S Yorks* 45 D7
Darnick *Scot Borders* 70 G4
Darowen *Powys* 32 E4
Darra *Aberds* 89 D7
Darracott *Devon* 6 C3
Darras Hall *Northum* 63 F7
Darrington *W Yorks* 51 G10
Darsham *Suffolk* 31 B11
Dartford *Kent* 20 D2
Dartford Crossing *Kent* 20 D2
Dartington *Devon* 5 E8
Dartmeet *Devon* 5 D7
Dartmouth *Devon* 5 F9
Darton *S Yorks* 45 B7
Darvel *E Ayrs* 68 G4
Darwell Hole *E Sussex* 12 E5
Darwen *Blackb'n* 50 G2
Datchet *Windsor* 18 D6
Datchworth *Herts* 29 G9
Datchworth Green *Herts* 29 G9
Daubhill *Gtr Man* 43 B10
Daugh of Kinermony *Moray* 88 D2
Dauntsey *Wilts* 16 C6
Dava *Moray* 87 H13
Davenham *Ches* 43 E9
Davenport Green *Ches* 44 E2
Daventry *Northants* 28 B2
David's Well *Powys* 33 H6
Davidson's Mains *C/Edinb* 69 C11
Davidstow *Cornw'l* 4 C2
Davington *Dumf/Gal* 61 C8
Daviot *Aberds* 83 A9
Daviot *H'land* 87 H10
Davoch of Grange *Moray* 88 C4
Davyhulme *Gtr Man* 43 C10
Dawley *Telford* 34 E2
Dawlish *Devon* 5 D10
Dawlish Warren *Devon* 5 D10
Dawn *Conwy* 41 C10
Daws Heath *Essex* 20 C5
Daw's House *Cornw'l* 4 C4
Dawsmere *Lincs* 37 B10
Dayhills *Staffs* 34 B5
Daylesford *Glos* 27 F9
Ddôl-Cownwy *Powys* 32 D6
Ddrydwy *Angl* 40 C5
Deadwater *Northum* 62 D2
Deaf Hill *Durham* 58 C4
Deal *Kent* 21 F10
Deal Hall *Essex* 21 B7
Dean *Cumb* 56 D2
Dean *Devon* 5 E8
Dean *Devon* 6 B4
Dean *Dorset* 9 C8
Dean *Hants* 10 C4
Dean *Som'set* 16 G3
Dean Prior *Devon* 5 E8
Dean Row *Ches* 44 D2
Deanburnhaugh *Scot Borders* 61 B9
Deane *Gtr Man* 43 B9
Deane *Hants* 18 F2
Deanich Lodge *H'land* 86 C6
Deanland *Dorset* 9 C8
Deans *W Loth* 69 D9
Deanscales *Cumb* 56 D2
Deanshanger *Northants* 28 E4
Deanston *Stirl* 75 G10
Dearham *Cumb* 56 C2
Debach *Suffolk* 31 C9
Debden *Essex* 30 E2
Debden *Essex* 19 B11
Debden Cross *Essex* 30 E2
Debenham *Suffolk* 31 B8
Dechmont *W Loth* 69 C9
Deddington *Oxon* 27 E11
Dedham *Essex* 31 E7
Dedham Heath *Essex* 31 E7
Deebank *Aberds* 83 D8
Deene *Northants* 36 F5
Deenethorpe *Northants* 36 F5
Deepcar *S Yorks* 44 C6
Deepcut *Surrey* 18 F6
Deepdale *Cumb* 50 A3
Deeping Gate *Lincs* 37 E7
Deeping St James *Lincs* 37 E7
Deeping St Nicholas *Lincs* 37 D8
Deerhill *Moray* 88 C4
Deerhurst *Glos* 26 F5
Deerness *Orkney* 95 H6
Defford *Worcs* 26 D6
Defynnog *Powys* 24 F6
Deganwy *Conwy* 41 C9
Deighton *N Yorks* 58 F4
Deighton *W Yorks* 51 H7
Deighton *C/York* 52 E2
Deiniolen *Gwyn* 41 D7
Delabole *Cornw'l* 4 C1
Delamere *Ches* 43 F8
Delfrigs *Aberds* 89 F9
Dell Lodge *H'land* 82 B2
Delliefure *H'land* 87 H13
Delnabo *Moray* 82 B3
Delnadamph *Aberds* 82 C4
Delph *Gtr Man* 44 B3
Delves *Durham* 58 B2
Delvine *Perth/Kinr* 76 C4
Dembleby *Lincs* 36 B6
Denaby Main *S Yorks* 45 C8
Denbigh = Dinbych *Denbs* 42 F3
Denbury *Devon* 5 E9
Denby *Derby* 45 H7
Denby Dale *W Yorks* 44 B6
Denchworth *Oxon* 17 B10
Dendron *Cumb* 49 B2
Denel End *Beds* 29 E7
Denend *Aberds* 88 E6
Denford *Northants* 36 H5
Dengie *Essex* 20 A6
Denham *Bucks* 19 C7
Denham *Suffolk* 30 B4
Denham *Suffolk* 31 A8
Denham Green *Bucks* 19 C7
Denham Street *Suffolk* 31 A8
Denhead *Aberds* 89 C9
Denhead *Fife* 77 F7
Denhead of Arbilot *Angus* 77 C8
Denhead of Gray *Dundee C* 76 D6
Denholm *Scot Borders* 61 B11
Denholme *W Yorks* 51 F6
Denholme Clough *W Yorks* 51 F6
Denio *Gwyn* 40 G5
Denmead *Hants* 10 C5
Denmore *Aberd C* 83 B11
Denmoss *Aberds* 89 D6
Dennington *Suffolk* 31 B9
Denny *Falk* 69 B7
Denny Lodge *Hants* 10 D2
Dennyloanhead *Falk* 69 B7
Denshaw *Gtr Man* 44 A3
Denside *Aberds* 83 D10
Densole *Kent* 21 G9
Denston *Suffolk* 30 C4
Denstone *Staffs* 35 A7
Dent *Cumb* 57 H9
Denton *Cambs* 37 G7
Denton *D'lington* 58 E3
Denton *E Sussex* 12 F3
Denton *Gtr Man* 44 C3
Denton *Kent* 21 G9
Denton *Lincs* 36 B4
Denton *Norfolk* 39 G8
Denton *Northants* 28 C5
Denton *N Yorks* 51 E7
Denton *Oxon* 18 A2
Denton's Green *Mersey* 43 C7
Denver *Norfolk* 38 E2
Denwick *Northum* 63 B8
Deopham *Norfolk* 39 E6
Deopham Green *Norfolk* 38 F6
Depden *Suffolk* 30 C4
Depden Green *Suffolk* 30 C4
Deptford *London* 19 D10
Deptford *Wilts* 17 H7
Derby *Derby C* 35 B9
Derbyhaven *I/Man* 48 F2
Dereham *Norfolk* 38 D5
Deri *Caerph* 15 A7
Derril *Devon* 6 F2
Derringstone *Kent* 21 G9
Derrington *Staffs* 34 C4
Derriton *Devon* 6 F2
Derry Hill *Wilts* 16 D6
Derryguaig *Arg/Bute* 78 H7
Derrythorpe *N Lincs* 46 B2
Dersingham *Norfolk* 38 B2
Dervaig *Arg/Bute* 78 F7
Derwen *Denbs* 42 G3
Derwenlas *Powys* 32 F3
Desborough *Northants* 36 G4
Desford *Leics* 35 E10
Detchant *Northum* 71 G9
Detling *Kent* 20 F4
Deuddwr *Powys* 33 D8
Devauden *Monmouths* 15 B10
Devil's Bridge *Ceredig'n* 32 H3
Devizes *Wilts* 17 E7
Devol *Invercl* 68 C2
Devonport *Plym'th* 4 F5
Devonside *Clack* 76 H2
Devoran *Cornw'l* 3 F6
Dewar *Scot Borders* 70 F2
Dewlish *Dorset* 9 E6
Dewsbury *W Yorks* 51 G8
Dewsbury Moor *W Yorks* 51 G8
Dewshall Court *Heref'd* 25 E11
Dhoon *I/Man* 48 D4
Dhoor *I/Man* 48 C4
Dhowin *I/Man* 48 B4
Dial Post *W Sussex* 11 C10
Dibden *Hants* 10 D3
Dibden Purlieu *Hants* 10 D3
Dickleburgh *Norfolk* 39 G7
Didbrook *Glos* 27 E7
Didcot *Oxon* 18 C2
Diddington *Cambs* 29 B8
Diddlebury *Shrops* 33 G11
Didley *Heref'd* 25 E11
Didling *W Sussex* 11 C7
Didmarton *Glos* 16 C5
Didsbury *Gtr Man* 44 C2
Didworthy *Devon* 5 E7
Digby *Lincs* 46 G4
Digg *H'land* 85 B9
Diggle *Gtr Man* 44 B4
Digmoor *Lancs* 43 B7
Digswell Park *Herts* 29 G9
Dihewid *Ceredig'n* 23 A9
Dilham *Norfolk* 39 C9
Dilhorne *Staffs* 34 A5
Dillarburn *S Lanarks* 69 F7
Dillington *Cambs* 29 B8
Dilston *Northum* 62 G5
Dilton Marsh *Wilts* 16 G5
Dilwyn *Heref'd* 25 C11
Dinas *Carms* 23 C7
Dinas *Gwyn* 40 G4
Dinas Cross *Pembs* 22 C5
Dinas Dinlle *Gwyn* 40 E6
Dinas-Mawddwy *Gwyn* 32 D4
Dinas Powys *V/Glam* 15 D7
Dinbych = Denbigh *Denbs* 42 F3
Dinbych-y-Pysgod = Tenby *Pembs* 22 F6
Dinder *Som'set* 16 G2
Dinedor *Heref'd* 26 E2
Dingestow *Monmouths* 25 G11
Dingle *Mersey* 42 D6
Dingleden *Kent* 13 C7
Dingley *Northants* 36 G3
Dingwall *H'land* 87 F8
Dinlabyre *Scot Borders* 61 D11
Dinmael *Conwy* 32 A6
Dinnet *Aberds* 82 D6
Dinnington *Som'set* 8 C3
Dinnington *S Yorks* 45 D9
Dinnington *Tyne/Wear* 63 F8
Dinorwic *Gwyn* 41 D7
Dinton *Bucks* 28 G4
Dinton *Wilts* 9 A9
Dinwoodie Mains *Dumf/Gal* 61 D7
Dinworthy *Devon* 6 E2
Dippen *N Ayrs* 66 D3
Dippenhall *Surrey* 18 G5
Dipple *Moray* 88 C3
Dipple *S Ayrs* 66 F5
Diptford *Devon* 5 F8
Dipton *Durham* 58 A2
Dirdhu *H'land* 82 A2
Dirleton *E Loth* 70 B4
Dirt Pot *Northum* 57 B10
Discoed *Powys* 25 B9
Diseworth *Leics* 35 C10
Dishes *Orkney* 95 F7
Dishforth *N Yorks* 51 B9
Disley *Ches* 44 D3
Diss *Norfolk* 39 H7
Disserth *Powys* 25 C7
Distington *Cumb* 56 D2
Ditchampton *Wilts* 9 A9
Ditcheat *Som'set* 16 H3
Ditchingham *Norfolk* 39 F9
Ditchling *E Sussex* 12 E2
Ditherington *Shrops* 33 D11
Dittisham *Devon* 5 F9
Ditton *Halton* 43 D7
Ditton *Kent* 20 F4
Ditton Green *Cambs* 30 C3
Ditton Priors *Shrops* 34 G2
Divach *H'land* 81 A6
Divlyn *Carms* 24 E4
Dixton *Glos* 26 E6
Dixton *Monmouths* 26 G2
Dobcross *Gtr Man* 44 B3
Dobwalls *Cornw'l* 4 E3
Doc Penfro = Pembroke Dock *Pembs* 22 F4
Doccombe *Devon* 5 C8
Dochfour Ho. *H'land* 87 H9
Dochgarroch *H'land* 87 G9
Docking *Norfolk* 38 B3
Docklow *Heref'd* 26 C2
Dockray *Cumb* 56 D5
Dockroyd *W Yorks* 50 F6
Dodburn *Scot Borders* 61 C10
Doddinghurst *Essex* 20 B2
Doddington *Cambs* 37 F9
Doddington *Kent* 20 F6
Doddington *Lincs* 46 E3
Doddington *Northum* 71 G8
Doddington *Shrops* 34 H2
Doddiscombsleigh *Devon* 5 C9
Dodford *Northants* 28 B3
Dodford *Worcs* 26 A6
Dodington *S Gloucs* 16 C4
Dodleston *Ches* 42 F6
Dods Leigh *Staffs* 34 B6
Dodworth *S Yorks* 45 B7
Doe Green *Warrington* 43 D8
Doe Lea *Derby* 45 F8
Dog Village *Devon* 7 G8
Dogdyke *Lincs* 46 G6
Dogmersfield *Hants* 18 F4
Dogridge *Wilts* 17 C7
Dogsthorpe *Peterbro* 37 E7
Dol-fôr *Powys* 32 E4
Dôl-y-Bont *Ceredig'n* 32 G2
Dol-y-cannau *Powys* 25 D9
Dolanog *Powys* 33 D6
Dolau *Powys* 25 B8
Dolau *Rh Cyn Taff* 14 C5
Dolbenmaen *Gwyn* 41 F7
Dolfach *Powys* 32 E5
Dolfor *Powys* 33 G7
Dolgarrog *Conwy* 41 D9
Dolgellau *Gwyn* 32 D3
Dolgran *Carms* 23 C9
Dolhendre *Gwyn* 41 G10
Doll *H'land* 93 J11
Dollar *Clack* 76 H2
Dolley Green *Powys* 25 B9
Dollwen *Ceredig'n* 32 G2
Dolphin *Flints* 42 E4
Dolphinholme *Lancs* 49 D5
Dolphinton *S Lanarks* 69 F10
Dolton *Devon* 6 E4
Dolwen *Conwy* 41 C10
Dolwen *Powys* 32 E5
Dolwyd *Conwy* 41 C10
Dolwyddelan *Conwy* 41 E9
Dolyhir *Powys* 25 C9
Doncaster *S Yorks* 45 B9
Dones Green *Ches* 43 E9
Donhead St Andrew *Wilts* 9 B8
Donhead St Mary *Wilts* 9 B8
Donibristle *Fife* 69 B10
Donington *Lincs* 37 B8
Donington on Bain *Lincs* 46 D6
Donington South Ing *Lincs* 37 B8
Donisthorpe *Leics* 35 D9
Donkey Town *Surrey* 18 E6
Donnington *Glos* 27 F8
Donnington *Heref'd* 26 E4
Donnington *Shrops* 34 E1
Donnington *Telford* 34 D3
Donnington *W Berks* 17 E11
Donnington *W Sussex* 11 D7
Donnington Wood *Telford* 34 D3
Donyatt *Som'set* 8 C2
Doonfoot *S Ayrs* 66 E6
Dorback Lodge *H'land* 82 B2
Dorchester *Dorset* 8 E5
Dorchester *Oxon* 18 B2
Dordon *Warwick* 35 E8
Dore *S Yorks* 45 D7
Dores *H'land* 87 H8
Dorking *Surrey* 19 G8
Dormansland *Surrey* 12 B3
Dormanstown *Redcar/Clevel'd* 59 D6
Dormington *Heref'd* 26 D2
Dormston *Worcs* 26 C6
Dornal *S Ayrs* 54 B5
Dorney *Bucks* 18 D6
Dornie *H'land* 85 F13
Dornoch *H'land* 87 C10
Dornock *Dumf/Gal* 61 G8
Dorrery *H'land* 94 E2
Dorridge *W Midlands* 35 H7
Dorrington *Lincs* 46 G4
Dorrington *Shrops* 33 E10
Dorsington *Warwick* 27 D8
Dorstone *Heref'd* 25 D10
Dorton *Bucks* 28 G3
Dorusduain *H'land* 80 A1
Dosthill *Staffs* 35 F8
Dottery *Dorset* 8 E3
Doublebois *Cornw'l* 4 E2
Dougarie *N Ayrs* 66 C1
Doughton *Glos* 16 B5
Douglas *I/Man* 48 E3
Douglas *S Lanarks* 69 G7
Douglas & Angus *Dundee C* 77 D7
Douglas Water *S Lanarks* 69 G7
Douglas West *S Lanarks* 69 G7
Douglastown *Angus* 77 C7
Doulting *Som'set* 16 G3
Dounby *Orkney* 95 F3
Doune *H'land* 92 J7
Doune *Stirl* 75 G10
Doune Park *Aberds* 89 B7
Douneside *Aberds* 82 C6
Dounie *H'land* 87 B8
Dounreay *H'land* 93 C12
Dousland *Devon* 4 E6
Dovaston *Shrops* 33 C9
Dove Holes *Derby* 44 E4
Dovenby *Cumb* 56 C2
Dover *Kent* 21 G10
Dovercourt *Essex* 31 E9
Doverdale *Worcs* 26 B5
Doveridge *Derby* 35 B7
Doversgreen *Surrey* 19 G9
Dowally *Perth/Kinr* 76 C3
Dowbridge *Lancs* 49 F4
Dowdeswell *Glos* 26 G6
Dowlais *Merth Tyd* 25 H7
Dowland *Devon* 6 E4
Dowlish Wake *Som'set* 8 C2
Down Ampney *Glos* 17 B8
Down Hatherley *Glos* 26 F5
Down St Mary *Devon* 7 F6
Down Thomas *Devon* 4 F6
Downcraig Ferry *N Ayrs* 73 H10
Downderry *Cornw'l* 4 F4
Downe *London* 19 E11
Downend *I/Wight* 10 F4
Downend *S Gloucs* 16 D3
Downend *W Berks* 17 D11
Downfield *Dundee C* 76 D6
Downgate *Cornw'l* 4 D4
Downham *Essex* 20 B4
Downham *Lancs* 50 E3
Downham *Northum* 71 G7
Downham Market *Norfolk* 38 E2
Downhead *Som'set* 16 G3
Downhill *Perth/Kinr* 76 D3
Downhill *Tyne/Wear* 63 H9
Downholland Cross *Lancs* 42 B6
Downholme *N Yorks* 58 G2
Downies *Aberds* 83 D11
Downley *Bucks* 18 B5
Downside *Som'set* 16 G3
Downside *Surrey* 19 F8
Downton *Hants* 10 E1
Downton *Wilts* 9 B10
Downton on the Rock *Heref'd* 25 A11
Dowsby *Lincs* 37 C7
Dowsdale *Lincs* 37 D8
Dowthwaitehead *Cumb* 56 D5
Doxey *Staffs* 34 C5
Doxford *Northum* 63 A7
Doxford Park *Tyne/Wear* 58 A4
Doynton *S Gloucs* 16 D4
Draffan *S Lanarks* 68 F6
Dragonby *N Lincs* 46 A3
Drakeland Corner *Devon* 5 F6
Drakemyre *N Ayrs* 66 A5
Drake's Broughton *Worcs* 26 D6
Drakes Cross *Worcs* 35 H6
Drakewalls *Cornw'l* 4 D5
Draughton *Northants* 36 H3
Draughton *N Yorks* 50 D6
Drax *N Yorks* 52 G2
Draycote *Warwick* 27 A11
Draycott *Derby* 35 B10
Draycott *Glos* 27 E8
Draycott *Som'set* 15 F10
Draycott in the Clay *Staffs* 35 C7
Draycott in the Moors *Staffs* 34 A5
Drayford *Devon* 7 E6
Drayton *Leics* 36 F4
Drayton *Lincs* 37 B8
Drayton *Norfolk* 39 D7
Drayton *Oxon* 27 D11
Drayton *Oxon* 17 B11
Drayton *Portsm'th* 10 D5
Drayton *Som'set* 8 B3
Drayton *Worcs* 34 H5
Drayton Bassett *Staffs* 35 E7
Drayton Beauchamp *Bucks* 28 G6
Drayton Parslow *Bucks* 28 F5
Drayton St Leonard *Oxon* 18 B2
Dre-fach *Ceredig'n* 23 B10
Dre-fach *Carms* 24 G3
Drebley *N Yorks* 51 D6
Dreemskerry *I/Man* 48 C4
Dreenhill *Pembs* 22 E4
Drefach *Carms* 23 C8
Drefach *Carms* 23 E10
Drefelin *Carms* 23 C8
Dreghorn *N Ayrs* 67 C6
Drellingore *Kent* 21 G9
Drem *E Loth* 70 C4
Dresden *Stoke* 34 A5
Dreumasdal *W Isles* 84 E2
Drewsteignton *Devon* 7 G6
Driby *Lincs* 47 E7
Driffield *ER Yorks* 52 D6
Driffield *Glos* 17 B7
Drigg *Cumb* 56 G2
Drighlington *W Yorks* 51 G8
Drimnin *H'land* 79 F8
Drimpton *Dorset* 8 D3
Drimsynie *Arg/Bute* 74 G4
Drinisiadar *W Isles* 90 H6
Drinkstone *Suffolk* 30 B6
Drinkstone Green *Suffolk* 30 B6
Drishaig *Arg/Bute* 74 F4
Drissaig *Arg/Bute* 73 B8
Drochil *Scot Borders* 69 F10
Drointon *Staffs* 34 C6
Droitwich Spa *Worcs* 26 B5
Droman *H'land* 92 D4
Dron *Perth/Kinr* 76 F4
Dronfield *Derby* 45 E7
Dronfield Woodhouse *Derby* 45 E7
Drongan *E Ayrs* 67 E7
Dronley *Angus* 76 D6
Droxford *Hants* 10 C5
Droylsden *Gtr Man* 44 C3
Druid *Denbs* 32 A6
Druidston *Pembs* 22 E3
Druimarbin *H'land* 80 F2
Druimavuic *Arg/Bute* 74 C3
Druimdrishaig *Arg/Bute* 72 F6
Druimindarroch *H'land* 79 C9
Druimyeon More *Arg/Bute* 65 C7
Drum *Arg/Bute* 73 F8
Drum *Perth/Kinr* 76 G3
Drumbeg *H'land* 92 F4
Drumblade *Aberds* 88 D5
Drumblair *Aberds* 89 D6
Drumbuie *Dumf/Gal* 55 A8
Drumbuie *H'land* 85 E12
Drumburgh *Cumb* 61 H8
Drumburn *Dumf/Gal* 60 G5
Drumchapel *C/Glasg* 68 C4
Drumchardine *H'land* 87 G8
Drumchork *H'land* 91 J13
Drumclog *S Lanarks* 68 G5
Drumderfit *H'land* 87 F9
Drumeldrie *Fife* 77 G7
Drumelzier *Scot Borders* 69 G10
Drumfearn *H'land* 85 G11
Drumgask *H'land* 81 D8
Drumgley *Angus* 77 B7
Drumguish *H'land* 81 D9
Drumin *Moray* 88 E1
Drumlasie *Aberds* 83 C8
Drumlemble *Arg/Bute* 65 G7
Drumligair *Aberds* 83 B11
Drumlithie *Aberds* 83 E9
Drummoddie *Dumf/Gal* 54 E6
Drummond *H'land* 87 E9
Drummore *Dumf/Gal* 54 F4
Drummuir *Moray* 88 D3
Drummuir Castle *Moray* 88 D3
Drumnadrochit *H'land* 81 A7
Drumnagorrach *Moray* 88 C5
Drumoak *Aberds* 83 D9
Drumpark *Dumf/Gal* 60 E4
Drumphail *Dumf/Gal* 54 C5
Drumrash *Dumf/Gal* 55 B9
Drumrunie *H'land* 92 J4
Drums *Aberds* 89 F9
Drumsallie *H'land* 80 F1
Drumstinchall *Dumf/Gal* 55 D11
Drumsturdy *Angus* 77 D7
Drumtochty Castle *Aberds* 83 F8
Drumtroddan *Dumf/Gal* 54 E6
Drumuie *H'land* 85 D9
Drumuillie *H'land* 81 A11
Drumvaich *Stirl* 75 G9
Drumwhindle *Aberds* 89 E9
Drunkendub *Angus* 77 C9
Drury *Flints* 42 F5
Drury Square *Norfolk* 38 D5
Dry Doddington *Lincs* 46 H2
Dry Drayton *Cambs* 29 B10
Drybeck *Cumb* 57 E8
Drybridge *Moray* 88 B4
Drybridge *N Ayrs* 67 C6
Drybrook *Glos* 26 G3
Dryburgh *Scot Borders* 70 G4
Dryhope *Scot Borders* 61 A8
Drylaw *C/Edinb* 69 C11
Drym *Cornw'l* 2 F5
Drymen *Stirl* 68 B3
Drymuir *Aberds* 89 D9
Drynoch *H'land* 85 E9
Dryslwyn *Carms* 23 D10
Dryton *Shrops* 34 E1
Dubford *Aberds* 89 B8
Dubton *Angus* 77 B8
Duchally *H'land* 92 H6
Duchlage *Arg/Bute* 68 B2
Duck Corner *Suffolk* 31 D10
Duckington *Ches* 43 G7
Ducklington *Oxon* 27 H10
Duckmanton *Derby* 45 E8
Duck's Cross *Beds* 29 C8
Duddenhoe End *Essex* 29 E11
Duddingston *C/Edinb* 69 C11
Duddington *Northants* 36 E5
Duddleswell *E Sussex* 12 D3
Duddo *Northum* 71 F8
Duddon *Ches* 43 F8
Duddon Bridge *Cumb* 56 H4
Dudleston *Shrops* 33 B9
Dudleston Heath *Shrops* 33 B9
Dudley *Tyne/Wear* 63 F8
Dudley *W Midlands* 34 F5
Dudley Port *W Midlands* 34 F5
Duffield *Derby* 35 A9
Duffryn *Newp* 15 C8
Duffryn *Neath P Talb* 14 B4
Dufftown *Moray* 88 E3
Duffus *Moray* 88 B1
Dufton *Cumb* 57 D8
Duggleby *N Yorks* 52 C4
Duirinish *H'land* 85 E12
Duisdalemore *H'land* 85 G12
Duisky *H'land* 80 F2
Dukestown *Bl Gwent* 25 G8
Dukinfield *Gtr Man* 44 C3
Dulas *Angl* 40 B6
Dulcote *Som'set* 16 G2
Dulford *Devon* 7 F9
Dull *Perth/Kinr* 75 C11
Dullatur *N Lanarks* 68 C6
Dullingham *Cambs* 30 C3
Dulnain Bridge *H'land* 82 A1
Duloe *Beds* 29 B8
Duloe *Cornw'l* 4 F3
Dulsie *H'land* 87 G12
Dulverton *Som'set* 7 D8
Dulwich *London* 19 D10
Dumbarton *W Dunb* 68 C2
Dumbleton *Glos* 27 E7
Dumcrieff *Dumf/Gal* 61 C7
Dumfries *Dumf/Gal* 60 F5
Dumgoyne *Stirl* 68 B4
Dummer *Hants* 18 G2
Dumpford *W Sussex* 11 B7
Dumpton *Kent* 21 E10
Dun *Angus* 77 B9
Dun Charlabhaigh *W Isles* 90 C6
Dunain Ho. *H'land* 87 G9
Dunalastair *Perth/Kinr* 75 B10
Dunan *H'land* 85 F10
Dunans *Arg/Bute* 73 D9
Dunball *Som'set* 15 G9
Dunbar *E Loth* 70 C5
Dunbeath *H'land* 94 H3
Dunbeg *Arg/Bute* 79 H11
Dunblane *Stirl* 75 G10
Dunbog *Fife* 76 F5
Duncanston *Aberds* 83 A7
Duncanston *H'land* 87 F8
Dunchurch *Warwick* 27 A11
Duncote *Northants* 28 C3
Duncow *Dumf/Gal* 60 E5
Duncraggan *Stirl* 75 G8
Duncrievie *Perth/Kinr* 76 G4
Duncton *W Sussex* 11 C8
Dundas Ho. *Orkney* 95 K5
Dundee *Dundee C* 77 D7
Dundeugh *Dumf/Gal* 67 H8
Dundon *Som'set* 8 A3
Dundonald *S Ayrs* 67 C6
Dundonnell *H'land* 86 C3
Dundonnell Hotel *H'land* 86 C3
Dundonnell House *H'land* 86 C4
Dundraw *Cumb* 56 B4
Dundreggan *H'land* 80 B5
Dundreggan Lodge *H'land* 80 B5
Dundrennan *Dumf/Gal* 55 E10
Dundry *N Som'set* 16 E2
Dunecht *Aberds* 83 C9
Dunfermline *Fife* 69 B9
Dunfield *Glos* 17 B8
Dunford Bridge *S Yorks* 44 B5
Dungworth *S Yorks* 44 D6
Dunham *Notts* 46 E2
Dunham-on-the-Hill *Ches* 43 E7
Dunham Town *Gtr Man* 43 D10
Dunhampton *Worcs* 26 B5
Dunholme *Lincs* 46 E4
Dunino *Fife* 77 F8
Dunipace *Falk* 69 B7
Dunira *Perth/Kinr* 75 E10
Dunkeld *Perth/Kinr* 76 C3
Dunkerton *Bath/NE Som'set* 16 F4
Dunkeswell *Devon* 7 F10
Dunkeswick *N Yorks* 51 E9
Dunkirk *Kent* 21 F7
Dunkirk *Norfolk* 39 C8
Dunk's Green *Kent* 20 F3
Dunlappie *Angus* 83 G7
Dunley *Hants* 17 F11
Dunley *Worcs* 26 B4
Dunlichity Lodge *H'land* 87 H9
Dunlop *E Ayrs* 67 B7
Dunmaglass Lodge *H'land* 81 A7
Dunmore *Arg/Bute* 72 G6
Dunmore *Falk* 69 B7
Dunnet *H'land* 94 C4
Dunnichen *Angus* 77 C8
Dunninald *Angus* 77 B10
Dunning *Perth/Kinr* 76 F3
Dunnington *ER Yorks* 53 D7
Dunnington *Warwick* 27 C7
Dunnington *C/York* 52 D2
Dunnockshaw *Lancs* 50 G4
Dunollie *Arg/Bute* 79 H11
Dunoon *Arg/Bute* 73 F10
Dunragit *Dumf/Gal* 54 D4
Dunrostan *Arg/Bute* 72 E6
Duns *Scot Borders* 70 E6
Duns Tew *Oxon* 27 F11
Dunsby *Lincs* 37 C7
Dunscore *Dumf/Gal* 60 E4
Dunscroft *S Yorks* 45 B10
Dunsdale *Redcar/Clevel'd* 59 E7
Dunsden Green *Oxon* 18 D4
Dunsfold *Surrey* 19 H7
Dunsford *Devon* 5 C9
Dunshalt *Fife* 76 F5
Dunshillock *Aberds* 89 D9
Dunskey Ho. *Dumf/Gal* 54 D3
Dunsley *N Yorks* 59 E9
Dunsmore *Bucks* 28 H5
Dunsop Bridge *Lancs* 50 D2
Dunstable *Beds* 29 F7
Dunstall *Staffs* 35 C7
Dunstall Common *Worcs* 26 D5
Dunstall Green *Suffolk* 30 B4
Dunstan *Northum* 63 B8
Dunstan Steads *Northum* 63 A8
Dunster *Som'set* 7 B8
Dunston *Lincs* 46 F4
Dunston *Norfolk* 39 E8
Dunston *Staffs* 34 D5
Dunston *Tyne/Wear* 63 G8
Dunsville *S Yorks* 45 B10
Dunswell *ER Yorks* 53 F6
Dunsyre *S Lanarks* 69 F9
Dunterton *Devon* 4 D4
Duntisbourne Abbots *Glos* 26 H6
Duntisbourne Leer *Glos* 26 H6
Duntisbourne Rouse *Glos* 26 H6
Duntish *Dorset* 8 D5
Duntocher *W Dunb* 68 C3
Dunton *Beds* 29 D9
Dunton *Bucks* 28 F5
Dunton *Norfolk* 38 B4
Dunton Bassett *Leics* 35 F11
Dunton Green *Kent* 20 F2

Dunton Wayletts Essex 20 B3
Duntulm H'land 85 A9
Dunure S Ayrs 66 E5
Dunvant Swan 23 G10
Dunvegan H'land 84 D7
Dunwich Suffolk 31 A11
Dunwood Staffs 44 G3
Dupplin Castle Perth/Kinr 76 F3
Durdar Cumb 56 A6
Durgates E Sussex 12 C5
Durham Durham 58 B3
Durisdeer Dumf/Gal 60 C4
Durisdeermill Dumf/Gal 60 C4
Durkar W Yorks 51 H9
Durleigh Som'set 15 H8
Durley Hants 10 C4
Durley Wilts 17 E9
Durnamuck H'land 86 B3
Durness H'land 92 C7
Durno Aberds 83 A9
Duror H'land 74 B2
Durran Arg/Bute 73 C8
Durran H'land 94 D3
Durrington Wilts 17 G8
Durrington W Sussex 11 D10
Dursley Glos 16 B4
Durston Som'set 8 B1
Durweston Dorset 9 D7
Dury Shetl'd 96 G6
Duston Northants 28 B4
Duthil H'land 81 A11
Dutlas Powys 33 H8
Duton Hill Essex 30 F3
Dutson Cornw'l 4 C4
Dutton Ches 43 E8
Duxford Cambs 29 D11
Duxford Oxon 17 B10
Dwygyfylchi Conwy 41 C9
Dwyran Angl 40 D6
Dyce Aberd C 83 B10
Dye House Northum 62 H5
Dyffryn Bridg 14 B4
Dyffryn Carms 23 D8
Dyffryn Pembs 22 C4
Dyffryn Ardudwy Gwyn 32 C1
Dyffryn Castell Ceredig'n 32 G3
Dyffryn Ceidrych Carms 24 F4
Dyffryn Cellwen
Neath P Talb 24 H5
Dyke Lincs 37 C7
Dyke Moray 87 F12
Dykehead Angus 76 A6
Dykehead N Lanarks 69 E7
Dykehead Stirl 75 H8
Dykelands Aberds 83 G9
Dykends Angus 76 B5
Dykeside Aberds 89 D7
Dykesmains N Ayrs 66 B5
Dylife Powys 32 F4
Dymchurch Kent 13 D9
Dymock Glos 26 E4
Dyrham S Gloucs 16 D4
Dysart Fife 70 A2
Dyserth Denbs 42 E3

E

Eachwick Northum 63 F7
Eadar Dha Fhadhail W Isles 90 D5
Eagland Hill Lancs 49 E4
Eagle Lincs 46 F2
Eagle Barnsdale Lincs 46 F2
Eagle Moor Lincs 46 F2
Eaglescliffe Stockton 58 E5
Eaglesfield Cumb 56 D2
Eaglesfield Dumf/Gal 61 F8
Eaglesham E Renf 68 E4
Eaglethorpe Northants 37 F6
Eairy I/Man 48 E2
Eakley Lanes M/Keynes 28 C5
Eakring Notts 45 F10
Ealand N Lincs 45 A11
Ealing London 19 C8
Eals Northum 62 H2
Eamont Bridge Cumb 57 D7
Earby Lancs 50 E5
Earcroft Blackb'n 50 G2
Eardington Shrops 34 F3
Eardisland Heref'd 25 C11
Eardisley Heref'd 25 D10
Eardiston Shrops 33 C9
Eardiston Worcs 26 B3
Earith Cambs 29 A10
Earl Shilton Leics 35 F10
Earl Soham Suffolk 31 B9
Earl Sterndale Derby 44 F4
Earl Stonham Suffolk 31 C8
Earle Northum 71 H8
Earley Wokingham 18 D4
Earlham Norfolk 39 E8
Earlish H'land 85 B8
Earls Barton Northants 28 B5
Earls Colne Essex 30 F5
Earl's Croome Worcs 26 D5
Earl's Green Suffolk 31 B7
Earlsdon W Midlands 35 H9
Earlsferry Fife 77 H7
Earlsfield Lincs 36 B5
Earlsford Aberds 89 E8
Earlsheaton W Yorks 51 G8
Earlsmill Moray 87 F12
Earlston Scot Borders 70 G4
Earlston E Ayrs 67 C7
Earlswood Monmouths 15 B10
Earlswood Surrey 19 G9
Earlswood Warwick 27 A8
Earnley W Sussex 11 E7
Earsairidh W Isles 84 J2
Earsdon Tyne/Wear 63 F9
Earsham Norfolk 39 G9
Earswick C/York 52 D2
Eartham W Sussex 11 D8
Easby N Yorks 59 F6
Easby N Yorks 58 F2
Easdale Arg/Bute 72 B6
Easebourne W Sussex 11 B7
Easenhall Warwick 35 H10
Eashing Surrey 18 G6
Easington Bucks 28 G3
Easington Durham 58 B5
Easington ER Yorks 53 H9
Easington Northum 71 G10
Easington Oxon 27 E11
Easington Oxon 18 B3
Easington Redcar/Clevel'd 59 E8
Easington Colliery Durham 58 B5
Easington Lane Tyne/Wear 58 B4
Easingwold N Yorks 51 C11
Easole Street Kent 21 F9
Eassie Angus 76 C6
East Aberthaw V/Glam 14 E6
East Adderbury Oxon 27 E11
East Allington Devon 5 G8
East Anstey Devon 7 D7
East Appleton N Yorks 58 G3
East Ardsley W Yorks 51 G9
East Ashling W Sussex 11 D7
East Auchronie Aberds 83 C10
East Ayton N Yorks 59 H10
East Bank Bl Gwent 25 H9
East Barkwith Lincs 46 D5
East Barming Kent 20 F4
East Barnby N Yorks 59 E9
East Barnet London 19 B9
East Barns E Loth 70 C6
East Barsham Norfolk 38 B5
East Beckham Norfolk 39 B7
East Bedfont London 19 D7
East Bergholt Suffolk 31 E7
East Bilney Norfolk 38 D5
East Blatchington E Sussex 12 F3
East Boldre Hants 10 D2
East Brent Som'set 15 F9
East Bridgford Notts 36 A2
East Buckland Devon 6 C5
East Budleigh Devon 7 H9
East Burrafirth Shetl'd 96 H5
East Burton Dorset 9 F7
East Butsfield Durham 58 B2
East Butterwick N Lincs 46 B2
East Cairnbeg Aberds 83 F9
East Calder W Loth 69 D9
East Carleton Norfolk 39 E7
East Carlton Northants 36 G4
East Carlton W Yorks 51 E8
East Chaldon Dorset 9 F6
East Challow Oxon 17 C10
East Chiltington E Sussex 12 E2
East Chinnock Som'set 8 C3
East Chisenbury Wilts 17 F8
East Clandon Surrey 19 F7
East Claydon Bucks 28 F4
East Clyne H'land 93 J12
East Coker Som'set 8 C4
East Combe Som'set 7 C10
East Common N Yorks 52 F2
East Compton Som'set 16 G3
East Cottingwith ER Yorks 52 E3
East Cowes I/Wight 10 E4
East Cowick ER Yorks 52 G2
East Cowton N Yorks 58 F4
East Cramlington Northum 63 F8
East Cranmore Som'set 16 G3
East Creech Dorset 9 F8
East Croachy H'land 81 A8
East Croftmore H'land 81 B11
East Curthwaite Cumb 56 B5
East Dean E Sussex 12 G4
East Dean Hants 10 B1
East Dean W Sussex 11 C8
East Down Devon 6 B5
East Drayton Notts 45 E11
East Ella Kingston/Hull 53 G6
East End Dorset 9 E8
East End ER Yorks 53 G8
East End Hants 10 E2
East End Hants 10 B5
East End Hants 17 E11
East End Hants 29 F11
East End Kent 13 C7
East End N Som'set 15 D10
East End Oxon 27 G10
East Farleigh Kent 20 F4
East Farndon Northants 36 G3
East Ferry Lincs 46 C2
East Fortune E Loth 70 C4
East Garston W Berks 17 D10
East Ginge Oxon 17 C11
East Goscote Leics 36 D2
East Grafton Wilts 17 E9
East Grimstead Wilts 9 B11
East Grinstead W Sussex 12 C2
East Guldeford E Sussex 13 D8
East Haddon Northants 28 B3
East Hagbourne Oxon 18 C2
East Halton N Lincs 53 H7
East Ham London 19 C11
East Hanney Oxon 17 B11
East Hanningfield Essex 20 A4
East Hardwick W Yorks 51 H10
East Harling Norfolk 38 G5
East Harlsey N Yorks 58 G5
East Harnham Wilts 9 B10
East Harptree
Bath/NE Som'set 16 F2
East Hartford Northum 63 F8
East Harting W Sussex 11 C6
East Hatley Cambs 29 C9
East Hauxwell N Yorks 58 G2
East Haven Angus 77 D8
East Heckington Lincs 37 A7
East Hedleyhope Durham 58 B2
East Hendred Oxon 17 C11
East Herrington Tyne/Wear 58 A4
East Heslerton N Yorks 52 B5
East Hoathly E Sussex 12 E4
East Horrington Som'set 16 G2
East Horsley Surrey 19 F7
East Horton Northum 71 G9
East Huntspill Som'set 15 G9
East Hyde Beds 29 G8
East Ilkerton Devon 6 B6
East Ilsley W Berks 17 C11
East Keal Lincs 47 F7
East Kennett Wilts 17 E8
East Keswick W Yorks 51 E9
East Kilbride S Lanarks 68 E5
East Kirkby Lincs 47 F7
East Knapton N Yorks 52 B4
East Knighton Dorset 9 F7
East Knoyle Wilts 9 A7
East Kyloe Northum 71 G9
East Lambrook Som'set 8 C3
East Lamington H'land 87 D10
East Langdon Kent 21 G10
East Langton Leics 36 F3
East Langwell H'land 93 J10
East Lavant W Sussex 11 D7
East Lavington W Sussex 11 C8
East Layton N Yorks 58 F2
East Leake Notts 36 C1
East Learmouth Northum 71 G7
East Leigh Devon 6 F5
East Lexham Norfolk 38 D4
East Lilburn Northum 62 A6
East Linton E Loth 70 C4
East Liss Hants 11 B6
East Looe Cornw'l 4 F3
East Lound N Lincs 45 C11
East Lulworth Dorset 9 F7
East Lutton N Yorks 52 C5
East Lydford Som'set 8 A4
East Mains Aberds 83 D8
East Malling Kent 20 F4
East March Angus 77 D7
East Marden W Sussex 11 C7
East Markham Notts 45 E11
East Marton N Yorks 50 D5
East Meon Hants 10 B5
East Mere Devon 7 E8
East Mersea Essex 31 G7
East Mey H'land 94 C5
East Molesey Surrey 19 E8
East Morden Dorset 9 E8
East Morton W Yorks 51 E6
East Ness N Yorks 52 B2
East Newton ER Yorks 53 F8
East Norton Leics 36 E3
East Nynehead Som'set 7 D10
East Oakley Hants 18 F2
East Ogwell Devon 5 D9
East Orchard Dorset 9 C7
East Ord Northum 71 E8
East Panson Devon 6 G2
East Peckham Kent 20 G3
East Pennard Som'set 16 H2
East Perry Cambs 29 B8
East Portlemouth Devon 5 H8
East Prawle Devon 5 H8
East Preston W Sussex 11 D9
East Putford Devon 6 E2
East Quantoxhead Som'set 7 B10
East Rainton Tyne/Wear 58 B4
East Ravendale NE Lincs 46 C6
East Raynham Norfolk 38 C4
East Rhidorroch Lodge
H'land 86 B5
East Rigton W Yorks 51 E9
East Rounton N Yorks 58 F5
East Row N Yorks 59 E9
East Rudham Norfolk 38 C4
East Runton Norfolk 39 A7
East Ruston Norfolk 39 C9
East Saltoun E Loth 70 D3
East Sleekburn Northum 63 E8
East Somerton Norfolk 39 D10
East Stockwith Lincs 45 C11
East Stoke Dorset 9 F7
East Stoke Notts 45 H11
East Stour Dorset 9 B7
East Stourmouth Kent 21 E9
East Stowford Devon 6 D5
East Stratton Hants 18 H2
East Studdal Kent 21 G10
East Suisnish H'land 85 E10
East Taphouse Cornw'l 4 E2
East-the-Water Devon 6 D3
East Thirston Northum 63 D7
East Tilbury Thurr'k 20 D3
East Tisted Hants 10 A6
East Torrington Lincs 46 D5
East Tuddenham Norfolk 39 D6
East Tytherley Hants 10 B1
East Tytherton Wilts 16 D6
East Village Devon 7 F7
East Wall Shrops 33 F11
East Walton Norfolk 38 D3
East Wellow Hants 10 B2
East Wemyss Fife 76 H6
East Whitburn W Loth 69 D8
East Williamston Pembs 22 F5
East Winch Norfolk 38 D2
East Winterslow Wilts 9 A11
East Wittering W Sussex 11 E6
East Witton N Yorks 58 H2
East Woodburn Northum 62 E5
East Woodhay Hants 17 E11
East Worldham Hants 18 H4
East Worlington Devon 7 E6
East Worthing W Sussex 11 D10
Eastbourne E Sussex 12 G5
Eastbridge Suffolk 31 B11
Eastburn W Yorks 50 E6
Eastbury Herts 19 B7
Eastbury W Berks 17 D10
Eastby N Yorks 50 D6
Eastchurch Kent 20 D6
Eastcombe Glos 16 A5
Eastcote London 19 C8
Eastcote Northants 28 C3
Eastcote W Midlands 35 H7
Eastcott Cornw'l 6 E1
Eastcott Wilts 17 F7
Eastcourt Wilts 16 B6
Eastcourt Wilts 17 E9
Easter Ardross H'land 87 D9
Easter Balmoral Aberds 82 D4
Easter Boleskine H'land 81 A7
Easter Compton S Gloucs 16 C2
Easter Cringate Stirl 68 B6
Easter Davoch Aberds 82 C6
Easter Earshaig Dumf/Gal 60 C6
Easter Fearn H'land 87 C9
Easter Galcantray H'land 87 G11
Easter Howgate Midloth 69 D11
Easter Howlaws
Scot Borders 70 F6
Easter Kinkell H'land 87 F8
Easter Lednathie Angus 76 A6
Easter Milton H'land 87 F12
Easter Moniack H'land 87 G8
Easter Ord Aberds 83 C10
Easter Quarff Shetl'd 96 K6
Easter Rhynd Perth/Kinr 76 F4
Easter Row Stirl 75 H10
Easter Silverford Aberds 89 B7
Easter Skeld Shetl'd 96 J5
Easter Whyntie Aberds 88 B6
Eastergate W Sussex 11 D8
Easterhouse C/Glasg 68 D5
Eastern Green W Midlands 35 G8
Easterton Wilts 17 F7
Eastertown Som'set 15 F9
Eastertown of
Auchleuchries Aberds 89 E10
Eastfield N Lanarks 69 D7
Eastfield N Yorks 52 A6
Eastfield Hall Northum 63 C8
Eastgate Durham 57 C11
Eastgate Norfolk 39 C7
Eastham Mersey 42 D6
Eastham Ferry Mersey 42 D6
Easthampstead Brackn'l 18 E5
Eastheath Wokingham 18 E5
Easthope Shrops 34 F1
Easthorpe Essex 30 F6
Easthorpe Leics 36 B4
Easthorpe Notts 45 G11
Easthouses Midloth 70 D2
Eastington Devon 7 F6
Eastington Glos 26 H4
Eastington Glos 27 G8
Eastleach Martin Glos 27 H9
Eastleach Turville Glos 27 H8
Eastleigh Devon 6 D3
Eastleigh Hants 10 C3
Eastling Kent 20 F6
Eastmoor Derby 45 E7
Eastmoor Norfolk 38 E3
Eastney Portsm'th 10 E5
Eastnor Heref'd 26 E4
Eastoft N Lincs 52 H4
Eastoke Hants 10 E6
Easton Cambs 29 A8
Easton Cumb 61 H8
Easton Cumb 61 F10
Easton Devon 5 C8
Easton Dorset 8 G5
Easton Hants 10 A4
Easton Lincs 36 C5
Easton Norfolk 39 D7
Easton Som'set 15 G11
Easton Suffolk 31 C9
Easton Wilts 16 D5
Easton Grey Wilts 16 C5
Easton-in-Gordano
N Som'set 15 D11
Easton Maudit Northants 28 C5
Easton on the Hill
Northants 36 E6
Easton Royal Wilts 17 E9
Eastpark Dumf/Gal 61 G6
Eastrea Cambs 37 F8
Eastriggs Dumf/Gal 61 G8
Eastrington ER Yorks 52 G3
Eastry Kent 21 F10
Eastville Bristol 16 D3
Eastville Lincs 47 G8
Eastwell Leics 36 C3
Eastwick Herts 29 G11
Eastwick Shetl'd 96 F5
Eastwood Notts 45 H8
Eastwood Southend 20 C5
Eastwood W Yorks 50 G5
Eathorpe Warwick 27 B10
Eaton Ches 43 F8
Eaton Ches 44 F2
Eaton Leics 36 C3
Eaton Norfolk 39 E8
Eaton Notts 45 E11
Eaton Oxon 27 H11
Eaton Shrops 33 G9
Eaton Shrops 33 G11
Eaton Bishop Heref'd 25 E11
Eaton Bray Beds 28 F6
Eaton Constantine Shrops 34 E1
Eaton Green Beds 28 F6
Eaton Hastings Oxon 17 B9
Eaton on Tern Shrops 34 C2
Eaton Socon Cambs 29 C8
Eavestone N Yorks 51 C8
Ebberston N Yorks 52 A4
Ebbesbourne Wake Wilts 9 B8
Ebbw Vale = Glyn Ebwy
Bl Gwent 25 H8
Ebchester Durham 63 H7
Ebford Devon 5 C10
Ebley Glos 26 H5
Ebnal Ches 43 H7
Ebrington Glos 27 D8
Ecchinswell Hants 17 F11
Ecclaw Scot Borders 70 D6
Ecclefechan Dumf/Gal 61 F7
Eccles Scot Borders 70 F6
Eccles Gtr Man 43 C10
Eccles Kent 20 E4
Eccles on Sea Norfolk 39 C10
Eccles Road Norfolk 38 F6
Ecclesall S Yorks 45 D7
Ecclesfield S Yorks 45 C7
Ecclesgreig Aberds 83 G9
Eccleshall Staffs 34 C4
Eccleshill W Yorks 51 F7
Ecclesmachan W Loth 69 C9
Eccleston Ches 43 F7
Eccleston Lancs 49 H5
Eccleston Mersey 43 C7
Eccleston Park Mersey 43 C7
Eccup W Yorks 51 E8
Echt Aberds 83 C9
Eckford Scot Borders 70 H6
Eckington Derby 45 E8
Eckington Worcs 26 D6
Ecton Northants 28 B5
Edale Derby 44 D5
Edburton W Sussex 11 C11
Edderside Cumb 56 B2
Edderton H'land 87 C10
Eddistone Devon 6 D1
Eddleston Scot Borders 69 F11
Eden Park London 19 E10
Edenbridge Kent 19 G11
Edenfield Lancs 50 H3
Edenhall Cumb 57 C7
Edenham Lincs 37 C6
Edensor Derby 44 F6
Edentaggart Arg/Bute 68 A2
Edenthorpe S Yorks 45 B10
Edentown Cumb 61 H9
Ederline Arg/Bute 73 C7
Edern Gwyn 40 G4
Edgarley Som'set 15 H11
Edgbaston W Midlands 35 G6
Edgcott Bucks 28 F3
Edgcott Som'set 7 C7
Edge Shrops 33 E9
Edge End Glos 26 G2
Edge Green Ches 43 G7
Edge Hill Mersey 42 D6
Edgebolton Shrops 34 C1
Edgefield Norfolk 39 B6
Edgefield Street Norfolk 39 B6
Edgeside Lancs 50 G4
Edgeworth Glos 26 H6
Edgmond Telford 34 D3
Edgmond Marsh Telford 34 C3
Edgton Shrops 33 G9
Edgware London 19 B8
Edgworth Blackb'n 50 H3
Edinample Stirl 75 E8
Edinbane H'land 85 C8
Edinburgh C/Edinb 69 C11
Edingale Staffs 35 D8
Edingight Ho. Moray 88 C5
Edingley Notts 45 G10
Edingthorpe Norfolk 39 B9
Edingthorpe Green Norfolk 39 B9
Edington Som'set 15 H9
Edington Wilts 16 F6
Edintore Moray 88 D4
Edith Weston Rutl'd 36 E5
Edithmead Som'set 15 G9
Edlesborough Bucks 28 G6
Edlingham Northum 63 C7
Edlington Lincs 46 E6
Edmondsham Dorset 9 C9
Edmondsley Durham 58 B3
Edmondthorpe Leics 36 D4
Edmonstone Orkney 95 F6
Edmonton London 19 B10
Edmundbyers Durham 58 A1
Ednam Scot Borders 70 G6
Ednaston Derby 35 A8
Edradynate Perth/Kinr 75 B11
Edrom Scot Borders 71 E7
Edstaston Shrops 33 B11
Edstone Warwick 27 B8
Edvin Loach Heref'd 26 C3
Edwalton Notts 36 B1
Edwardstone Suffolk 30 D6
Edwinsford Carms 24 E3
Edwinstowe Notts 45 F10
Edworth Beds 29 D9
Edwyn Ralph Heref'd 26 C3
Edzell Angus 83 G7
Efail Isaf Rh Cyn Taff 14 C6
Efailnewydd Gwyn 40 G5
Efailwen Carms 22 D6
Efenechtyd Denbs 42 G4
Effingham Surrey 19 F8
Effirth Shetl'd 96 H5
Efford Devon 7 F7
Egdon Worcs 26 C6
Egerton Gtr Man 43 A10
Egerton Kent 20 G6
Egerton Forstal Kent 20 G5
Eggborough N Yorks 52 G1
Eggbuckland Plym'th 4 F6
Eggington Beds 28 F6
Egginton Derby 35 C8
Egglescliffe Stockton 58 E5
Eggleston Durham 57 D11
Egham Surrey 19 D7
Egleton Rutl'd 36 E4
Eglingham Northum 63 B7
Egloshayle Cornw'l 3 B8
Egloskerry Cornw'l 4 C3
Eglwys-Brewis V/Glam 14 E6
Eglwys Cross Wrex 33 A10
Eglwys Fach Ceredig'n 32 F2
Eglwysbach Conwy 41 C10
Eglwyswen Pembs 22 C6
Eglwyswrw Pembs 22 C6
Egmanton Notts 45 F11
Egremont Cumb 56 E2
Egremont Mersey 42 C6
Egton N Yorks 59 F9
Egton Bridge N Yorks 59 F9
Eight Ash Green Essex 30 F6
Eignaig H'land 79 G10
Eil H'land 81 B10
Eilanreach H'land 85 G13
Eilean Darach H'land 86 C4
Eileanach Lodge H'land 87 E8
Einacleite W Isles 90 E6
Eisgean W Isles 91 F8
Eisingrug Gwyn 41 G8
Elan Village Powys 24 B6
Elberton S Gloucs 16 C3
Elburton Plym'th 4 F6
Elcho Perth/Kinr 76 E4
Elcombe Swindon 17 C8
Eldernell Cambs 37 F9
Eldersfield Worcs 26 E5
Elderslie Renf 68 D3
Eldon Durham 58 D3
Eldrick S Ayrs 54 A5
Eldroth N Yorks 50 C3
Eldwick W Yorks 51 E7
Elfhowe Cumb 56 G6
Elford Northum 71 G10
Elford Staffs 35 D7
Elgin Moray 88 B2
Elgol H'land 85 G10
Elham Kent 21 G8
Elie Fife 77 G7
Elim Angl 40 B5
Eling Hants 10 C2
Elishader H'land 85 B10
Elishaw Northum 62 D4
Elkesley Notts 45 E10
Elkstone Glos 26 G6
Ellan H'land 81 A10
Elland W Yorks 51 G7
Ellary Arg/Bute 72 F6
Ellastone Staffs 35 A7
Ellemford Scot Borders 70 D6
Ellenbrook I/Man 48 E3
Ellenhall Staffs 34 C4
Ellen's Green Surrey 19 H7
Ellerbeck N Yorks 58 G5
Ellerburn N Yorks 52 A4
Ellerby N Yorks 59 E8
Ellerdine Heath Telford 34 C2
Ellerhayes Devon 7 F8
Elleric Arg/Bute 74 C3
Ellerker ER Yorks 52 G5
Ellerton ER Yorks 52 F3
Ellerton Shrops 34 C3
Ellesborough Bucks 28 H5
Ellesmere Shrops 33 B10
Ellesmere Port Ches 43 E7
Ellingham Norfolk 39 F9
Ellingham Northum 71 H10
Ellingstring N Yorks 51 A7
Ellington Cambs 29 A8
Ellington Northum 63 D8
Elliot Angus 77 D9
Ellisfield Hants 18 G3
Ellistown Leics 35 D10
Ellon Aberds 89 E9
Ellonby Cumb 56 C6
Ellough Suffolk 39 G10
Elloughton ER Yorks 52 G5
Ellwood Glos 26 H2
Elm Cambs 37 E10
Elm Hill Dorset 9 B7
Elm Park London 20 C2
Elmbridge Worcs 26 B6
Elmdon Essex 29 E11
Elmdon W Midlands 35 G7
Elmdon Heath W Midlands 35 G7
Elmers End London 19 E10
Elmesthorpe Leics 35 F10
Elmfield I/Wight 10 E5
Elmhurst Staffs 35 D7
Elmley Castle Worcs 26 D6
Elmley Lovett Worcs 26 B5
Elmore Glos 26 G4
Elmore Back Glos 26 G4
Elmscott Devon 6 D1
Elmsett Suffolk 31 D7
Elmstead Market Essex 31 F7
Elmsted Kent 13 B10
Elmstone Kent 21 E9
Elmstone Hardwicke Glos 26 F6
Elmswell ER Yorks 52 D5
Elmswell Suffolk 30 B6
Elmton Derby 45 E9
Elphin H'land 92 H5
Elphinstone E Loth 70 C2
Elrick Aberds 83 C10
Elrig Dumf/Gal 54 E6
Elsdon Northum 62 D5
Elsecar S Yorks 45 C7
Elsenham Essex 30 F2
Elsfield Oxon 28 G2
Elsham N Lincs 46 A4
Elsing Norfolk 39 D6
Elslack N Yorks 50 E5
Elson Shrops 33 B9
Elsrickle S Lanarks 69 F9
Elstead Surrey 18 G6
Elsted W Sussex 11 C7
Elsthorpe Lincs 37 C6
Elstob Durham 58 D4
Elston Notts 45 H11
Elston Wilts 17 G7
Elstone Devon 6 E5
Elstow Beds 29 D7
Elstree Herts 19 B8
Elstronwick ER Yorks 53 F8
Elswick Lancs 49 F4
Elsworth Cambs 29 B10
Elterwater Cumb 56 F5
Eltham London 19 D11
Eltisley Cambs 29 C9
Elton Cambs 37 F6
Elton Ches 43 E7
Elton Derby 44 F6
Elton Glos 26 G4
Elton Heref'd 25 A11
Elton Notts 36 B3
Elton Stockton 58 E5
Elton Green Ches 43 E7
Elvanfoot S Lanarks 60 B5
Elvaston Derby 35 B10
Elveden Suffolk 38 H4
Elvingston E Loth 70 C3
Elvington Kent 21 F9
Elvington C/York 52 E2
Elwick Hartlep'l 58 C5
Elwick Northum 71 G10
Elworth Ches 43 F10
Elworthy Som'set 7 C9
Ely Cambs 37 G11
Ely Card 15 D7
Emberton M/Keynes 28 D5
Embleton Cumb 56 C3
Embleton Northum 63 A8
Embo H'land 87 B11
Embo Street H'land 87 B11
Emborough Som'set 16 F3
Embsay N Yorks 50 D6
Emery Down Hants 10 D1
Emley W Yorks 44 A6
Emmbrook Wokingham 18 E4
Emmer Green Reading 18 D4
Emmington Oxon 18 A4
Emneth Norfolk 37 E10
Emneth Hungate Norfolk 37 E11
Empingham Rutl'd 36 E5
Empshott Hants 11 A6
Emstrey Shrops 33 D11
Emsworth Hants 10 D6
Enborne W Berks 17 E11
Enchmarsh Shrops 33 F11
Enderby Leics 35 F11
Endmoor Cumb 49 A5
Endon Staffs 44 G3
Endon Bank Staffs 44 G3
Enfield London 19 B10
Enfield Wash London 19 B10
Enford Wilts 17 F8
Engamoor Shetl'd 96 H4
Engine Common S Gloucs 16 C3
Englefield W Berks 18 D3
Englefield Green Surrey 18 D6
Englesea-brook Ches 43 G10
English Bicknor Glos 26 G2
English Frankton Shrops 33 C10
Englishcombe
Bath/NE Som'set 16 E4
Enham-Alamein Hants 17 G10
Enmore Som'set 8 A1
Ennerdale Bridge Cumb 56 E2
Enoch Dumf/Gal 60 C4
Enochdhu Perth/Kinr 76 A3
Ensay Arg/Bute 78 G6
Ensbury Bournem'th 9 E9
Ensdon Shrops 33 D10
Ensis Devon 6 D4
Enstone Oxon 27 F10
Enterkinfoot Dumf/Gal 60 C4
Enterpen N Yorks 58 F5
Enville Staffs 34 G4
Eolaigearraidh W Isles 84 H2
Eorabus Arg/Bute 78 J6
Eòropaidh W Isles 91 A10
Epperstone Notts 45 H10
Epping Essex 19 A11
Epping Green Essex 29 H11
Epping Green Herts 29 H9
Epping Upland Essex 19 A11
Eppleby N Yorks 58 E2
Eppleworth ER Yorks 52 F6
Epsom Surrey 19 E9
Epwell Oxon 27 D10
Epworth N Lincs 45 B11
Epworth Turbary N Lincs 45 B11
Erbistock Wrex 33 A9
Erbusaig H'land 85 F12
Erchless Castle H'land 86 G7
Erdington W Midlands 35 F7
Eredine Arg/Bute 73 C8
Eriboll H'land 92 D7
Ericstane Dumf/Gal 60 B6
Eridge Green E Sussex 12 C4
Erines Arg/Bute 73 F7
Eriswell Suffolk 38 H3
Erith London 20 D2
Erlestoke Wilts 16 F6
Ermine Lincs 46 E3
Ermington Devon 5 F7
Erpingham Norfolk 39 B7
Errogie H'land 81 A7
Errol Perth/Kinr 76 E5
Erskine Renf 68 C3
Erskine Bridge Renf 68 C3
Ervie Dumf/Gal 54 C3
Erwarton Suffolk 31 E9
Erwood Powys 25 D7
Eryholme N Yorks 58 F4
Eryrys Denbs 42 G5
Escomb Durham 58 D2
Escrick N Yorks 52 E2
Esgairdawe Carms 24 D3
Esgairgeiliog Powys 32 E3
Esh Durham 58 B2
Esh Winning Durham 58 B2
Esher Surrey 19 E8
Esholt W Yorks 51 E7
Eshott Northum 63 D8
Eshton N Yorks 50 D5
Esk Valley N Yorks 59 F9
Eskadale H'land 86 H7
Eskbank Midloth 70 D2
Eskdale Green Cumb 56 F3
Eskdalemuir Dumf/Gal 61 D8
Eske ER Yorks 53 E6
Eskham Lincs 47 C7
Esprick Lancs 49 F4
Essendine Rutl'd 36 D6
Essendon Herts 29 H9
Essich H'land 87 H9
Essington Staffs 34 E5
Esslemont Aberds 89 F9
Eston Redcar/Clevel'd 59 E6
Eswick Shetl'd 96 H6
Etal Northum 71 G8
Etchilhampton Wilts 17 E7
Etchingham E Sussex 12 D6
Etchinghill Kent 21 H8
Etchinghill Staffs 34 D6
Ethie Castle Angus 77 C9
Ethie Mains Angus 77 C9
Etling Green Norfolk 38 D6
Eton Windsor 18 D6
Eton Wick Windsor 18 D6
Etteridge H'land 81 D8
Ettersgill Durham 57 D10
Ettingshall W Midlands 34 F5
Ettington Warwick 27 D9
Etton ER Yorks 52 E5
Etton Peterbro 37 E7
Ettrick Scot Borders 61 B8
Ettrickbridge Scot Borders 61 A9
Ettrickhill Scot Borders 61 B8
Etwall Derby 35 B8
Euston Suffolk 38 H4
Euximoor Drove Cambs 37 F10
Euxton Lancs 50 H1
Evanstown Bridg 14 C5
Evanton H'land 87 E9
Evedon Lincs 46 H4
Evelix H'land 87 B10
Evenjobb Powys 25 B9
Evenley Northants 28 E2
Evenlode Glos 27 F9
Evenwood Durham 58 D2
Evenwood Gate Durham 58 D2
Everbay Orkney 95 F7
Evercreech Som'set 16 H3
Everdon Northants 28 C2
Everingham ER Yorks 52 E4
Everleigh Wilts 17 F9
Everley N Yorks 59 H10
Eversholt Beds 28 E6
Evershot Dorset 8 D4
Eversley Hants 18 E4
Eversley Cross Hants 18 E4
Everthorpe ER Yorks 52 F5
Everton Beds 29 C9
Everton Hants 10 E1
Everton Mersey 42 C6
Everton Notts 45 C10
Evertown Dumf/Gal 61 F9
Evesbatch Heref'd 26 D3
Evesham Worcs 27 D7
Evington Leics C 36 E2
Ewden Village S Yorks 44 C6
Ewell Surrey 19 E9
Ewell Minnis Kent 21 G9
Ewelme Oxon 18 B3
Ewen Glos 17 B7
Ewenny V/Glam 14 D5
Ewerby Lincs 46 H5
Ewerby Thorpe Lincs 46 H5
Ewes Dumf/Gal 61 D9
Ewesley Northum 62 D6
Ewhurst Surrey 19 G7
Ewhurst Green E Sussex 13 D6
Ewhurst Green Surrey 19 H7
Ewloe Flints 42 F6
Ewloe Green Flints 42 F5
Ewood Blackb'n 50 G2
Eworthy Devon 6 G3
Ewshot Hants 18 G5
Ewyas Harold Heref'd 25 F10
Exbourne Devon 6 F5
Exbury Hants 10 E3
Exebridge Som'set 7 D8
Exelby N Yorks 58 H3
Exeter Devon 7 G8
Exford Som'set 7 C7
Exhall Warwick 27 C8
Exley Head W Yorks 50 F6
Exminster Devon 5 C10
Exmouth Devon 5 C11
Exnaboe Shetl'd 96 M5
Exning Suffolk 30 B3
Exton Devon 5 C10
Exton Hants 10 B5
Exton Rutl'd 36 D5
Exton Som'set 7 C8
Exwick Devon 7 G8
Eyam Derby 44 E6
Eydon Northants 28 C2
Eye Heref'd 25 B11
Eye Peterbro 37 E8
Eye Suffolk 31 A8
Eye Green Peterbro 37 E8
Eyemouth Scot Borders 71 D8
Eyeworth Beds 29 D9
Eyhorne Street Kent 20 F5
Eyke Suffolk 31 C10
Eynesbury Cambs 29 C8
Eynort H'land 85 F8
Eynsford Kent 20 E2
Eynsham Oxon 27 H11
Eype Dorset 8 E3
Eyre H'land 85 C9
Eyre H'land 85 E10
Eythorne Kent 21 G9
Eyton Heref'd 25 B11
Eyton Shrops 33 G9
Eyton Wrex 33 A9
Eyton upon the Weald
Moors Telford 34 D2

F

Faccombe Hants 17 F10
Faceby N Yorks 58 F5
Facit Lancs 50 H4
Faddiley Ches 43 G8
Fadmoor N Yorks 59 H7
Faerdre Swan 14 A2
Failford S Ayrs 67 D7
Failsworth Gtr Man 44 B2
Fain H'land 86 D4
Fair Green Norfolk 38 D2
Fair Hill Cumb 57 C7
Fair Oak Hants 10 C3
Fair Oak Green Hants 18 E3
Fairbourne Gwyn 32 D2
Fairburn N Yorks 51 G10
Fairfield Derby 44 E4
Fairfield Stockton 58 E5
Fairfield Worcs 27 D7
Fairfield Worcs 34 H5
Fairford Glos 17 A8
Fairhaven Lancs 49 G3
Fairlie N Ayrs 73 H11
Fairlight E Sussex 13 E7
Fairlight Cove E Sussex 13 E7
Fairmile Devon 7 G9
Fairmilehead C/Edinb 69 D11
Fairoak Staffs 34 B3
Fairseat Kent 20 E3
Fairstead Essex 30 G4
Fairstead Norfolk 38 D2
Fairwarp E Sussex 12 D3
Fairy Cottage I/Man 48 D4
Fairy Cross Devon 6 D3
Fakenham Norfolk 38 C5
Fakenham Magna Suffolk 38 H5
Fala Midloth 70 D3
Fala Dam Midloth 70 D3
Falahill Scot Borders 70 E2
Falcon Heref'd 26 E3
Faldingworth Lincs 46 D4
Falfield S Gloucs 16 B3
Falkenham Suffolk 31 E9
Falkirk Falk 69 C7
Falkland Fife 76 G5
Falla Scot Borders 62 B3
Fallgate Derby 45 F7
Fallin Stirl 69 A7
Fallowfield Gtr Man 44 C2
Fallsidehill Scot Borders 70 F5
Falmer E Sussex 12 F2
Falmouth Cornw'l 3 F7
Falsgrave N Yorks 59 H11
Falstone Northum 62 E3
Fanagmore H'land 92 E4
Fangdale Beck N Yorks 59 G6
Fangfoss ER Yorks 52 D3
Fankerton Falk 68 B6
Fanmore Arg/Bute 78 G7
Fannich Lodge H'land 86 E5
Fans Scot Borders 70 F5
Far Bank S Yorks 45 A10
Far Bletchley M/Keynes 28 E5
Far Cotton Northants 28 C4
Far Forest Worcs 26 A4
Far Laund Derby 45 H7
Far Sawrey Cumb 56 G5
Farcet Cambs 37 F8
Farden Shrops 34 H1
Fareham Hants 10 D4
Farewell Staffs 35 D6
Farforth Lincs 47 E7
Faringdon Oxon 17 B9
Farington Lancs 49 G5
Farlam Cumb 61 H11
Farlary H'land 93 J10
Farleigh N Som'set 15 E10
Farleigh Surrey 19 E10
Farleigh Hungerford
Som'set 16 F5
Farleigh Wallop Hants 18 G3
Farlesthorpe Lincs 47 E8
Farleton Cumb 49 A5
Farleton Lancs 50 C1
Farley Shrops 33 E9
Farley Staffs 35 A6
Farley Wilts 9 B11
Farley Green Surrey 19 G7
Farley Hill Luton 29 F7
Farley Hill Wokingham 18 E4
Farleys End Glos 26 G4
Farlington N Yorks 52 C2
Farlow Shrops 34 G2
Farmborough
Bath/NE Som'set 16 E3
Farmcote Glos 27 F7
Farmcote Shrops 34 F3
Farmington Glos 27 G8
Farmoor Oxon 27 H11
Farmtown Moray 88 C5
Farnborough London 19 E11
Farnborough Hants 18 F5
Farnborough Warwick 27 D11
Farnborough W Berks 17 C11
Farnborough Green Hants 18 F5
Farncombe Surrey 18 G6
Farndish Beds 28 B6
Farndon Ches 43 G7
Farndon Notts 45 G11
Farnell Angus 77 B9
Farnham Dorset 9 C8
Farnham Essex 29 F11
Farnham N Yorks 51 C9
Farnham Suffolk 31 B10
Farnham Surrey 18 G5
Farnham Common Bucks 18 C6
Farnham Green Essex 29 F11
Farnham Royal Bucks 18 C6
Farnhill N Yorks 50 E6
Farningham Kent 20 E2
Farnley N Yorks 51 E8
Farnley W Yorks 51 F8
Farnley Tyas W Yorks 44 A5
Farnsfield Notts 45 G10
Farnworth Gtr Man 43 B10
Farnworth Halton 43 D8
Farr H'land 87 H9
Farr H'land 81 C10
Farr H'land 93 C10
Farr House H'land 87 H9
Farringdon Devon 7 G9
Farrington Gurney
Bath/NE Som'set 16 F3
Farsley W Yorks 51 F8
Farthinghoe Northants 28 E2
Farthingloe Kent 21 G9
Farthingstone Northants 28 C3
Fartown W Yorks 51 H7
Farway Devon 7 G10
Fasag H'land 85 C13
Fascadale H'land 79 D8
Faslane Port Arg/Bute 73 E11
Fasnacloich Arg/Bute 74 C3
Fasnakyle Ho. H'land 80 A5
Fassfern H'land 80 F2
Fatfield Tyne/Wear 58 A4
Fattahead Aberds 89 C6
Faugh Cumb 57 A7
Fauldhouse W Loth 69 D8
Faulkbourne Essex 30 G4
Faulkland Som'set 16 F4
Fauls Shrops 34 B1
Faversham Kent 21 E7
Favillar Moray 88 E2
Fawdington N Yorks 51 B10
Fawfieldhead Staffs 44 F4
Fawkham Green Kent 20 E2
Fawler Oxon 27 G10
Fawley Bucks 18 C4
Fawley Hants 10 D3
Fawley W Berks 17 C10
Fawley Chapel Heref'd 26 F2
Faxfleet ER Yorks 52 G4
Faygate W Sussex 11 A11
Fazakerley Mersey 43 C6
Fazeley Staffs 35 E8
Fearby N Yorks 51 A7
Fearn H'land 87 D11
Fearn Lodge H'land 87 C9
Fearn Station H'land 87 D11
Fearnan Perth/Kinr 75 C10
Fearnbeg H'land 85 C12
Fearnhead Warrington 43 C9
Fearnmore H'land 85 B12
Featherstone Staffs 34 E5
Featherstone W Yorks 51 G10
Featherwood Northum 62 C4
Feckenham Worcs 27 B7
Feering Essex 30 F5
Feetham N Yorks 57 G11
Feizor N Yorks 50 C3
Felbridge Surrey 12 C2
Felbrigg Norfolk 39 B8
Felcourt Surrey 12 B2
Felden Herts 19 A7
Felin-Crai Powys 24 F5
Felindre Ceredig'n 23 A10
Felindre Carms 23 D10
Felindre Carms 24 E3
Felindre Carms 24 F4
Felindre Carms 23 C8
Felindre Powys 33 G7
Felindre Swan 14 A2
Felindre Farchog Pembs 22 C6
Felinfach Ceredig'n 23 A10
Felinfach Powys 25 E7
Felinfoel Carms 23 F10
Felingwm isaf Carms 23 D10
Felingwm uchaf Carms 23 D10
Felinwynt Ceredig'n 23 A7
Felixkirk N Yorks 51 A10
Felixstowe Suffolk 31 E9
Felixstowe Ferry Suffolk 31 E10
Felkington Northum 71 F8
Felkirk W Yorks 45 A7
Fell Side Cumb 56 C5
Felling Tyne/Wear 63 G8
Felmersham Beds 28 C6
Felmingham Norfolk 39 C8
Felpham W Sussex 11 E8
Felsham Suffolk 30 C6
Felsted Essex 30 F3
Feltham London 19 D8
Felthorpe Norfolk 39 D7
Felton Heref'd 26 D2
Felton Northum 63 C7
Felton N Som'set 15 E11
Felton Butler Shrops 33 D9
Feltwell Norfolk 38 F3
Fen Ditton Cambs 29 B11
Fen Drayton Cambs 29 B10
Fen End W Midlands 35 H8
Fen Side Lincs 47 G7

Godolphin Cross Cornw'l 2 F5
Godre'r-graig Neath P Talb 24 H4
Godshill Hants 9 C10
Godshill I/Wight 10 F4
Godstone Surrey 19 F10
Godwinscroft Hants 9 E10
Goetre Monmouths 25 H10
Goferydd Angl 40 B4
Goff's Oak Herts 19 A10
Gogar C/Edinb 69 C10
Goginan Ceredig'n 32 G2
Golan Gwyn 41 F7
Golant Cornw'l 4 F2
Golberdon Cornw'l 4 D4
Golborne Gtr Man 43 C9
Golcar W Yorks 51 H7
Gold Hill Norfolk 37 F11
Goldcliff Newp 15 C9
Golden Cross E Sussex 12 E4
Golden Green Kent 20 G3
Golden Grove Carms 23 E10
Golden Hill Hants 10 E1
Golden Pot Hants 18 G4
Golden Valley Glos 26 F6
Goldenhill Stoke 44 G2
Golders Green London 19 C9
Goldhanger Essex 30 H6
Golding Shrops 33 E11
Goldington Beds 29 C7
Goldsborough N Yorks 51 D9
Goldsborough N Yorks 59 E9
Goldsithney Cornw'l 2 F4
Goldsworthy Devon 6 D2
Goldthorpe S Yorks 45 B8
Gollanfield H'land 87 F11
Golspie H'land 93 J11
Golval H'land 93 C11
Gomeldon Wilts 17 H8
Gomersal W Yorks 51 G8
Gomshall Surrey 19 G7
Gonalston Notts 45 H10
Gonfirth Shetl'd 96 G5
Good Easter Essex 30 G3
Gooderstone Norfolk 38 E3
Goodleigh Devon 6 C5
Goodmanham ER Yorks 52 E4
Goodnestone Kent 21 F7
Goodnestone Kent 21 F9
Goodrich Heref'd 26 G2
Goodrington Torbay 5 F9
Goodshaw Lancs 50 G4
Goodwick = Wdig Pembs 22 C4
Goodworth Clatford Hants 17 G10
Goole ER Yorks 52 G3
Goonbell Cornw'l 2 E6
Goonhavern Cornw'l 3 D6
Goose Eye W Yorks 50 E6
Goose Green Gtr Man 43 B8
Goose Green Norfolk 39 G7
Goose Green W Sussex 11 C10
Gooseham Cornw'l 6 E1
Goosey Oxon 17 B10
Goosnargh Lancs 50 F1
Goostrey Ches 43 E10
Gorcott Hill Warwick 27 B7
Gord Shetl'd 96 L6
Gordon Scot Borders 70 F5
Gordonbush H'land 93 J11
Gordonstoun Moray 88 B4
Gordonstoun Moray 88 B1
Gordonstown Aberds 88 C5
Gordonstown Aberds 89 E7
Gore Kent 21 F10
Gore Cross Wilts 17 F7
Gore Pit Essex 30 G5
Gorebridge Midloth 70 D2
Gorefield Cambs 37 D10
Gorey Jersey 11
Gorgie C/Edinb 69 C11
Goring Oxon 18 C3
Goring-by-Sea W Sussex 11 D10
Goring Heath Oxon 18 D3
Gorleston-on-Sea Norfolk 39 E11
Gornalwood W Midlands 34 F5
Gorrachie Aberds 89 C7
Gorran Churchtown Cornw'l 3 E8
Gorran Haven Cornw'l 3 E9
Gorrenberry Scot Borders 61 D10
Gors Ceredig'n 32 H2
Gorse Hill Swindon 17 C8
Gorsedd Flints 42 E4
Gorseinon Swan 23 G10
Gorseness Orkney 95 G5
Gorsgoch Ceredig'n 23 A9
Gorslas Carms 23 E10
Gorsley Glos 26 F3
Gorstan H'land 86 E6
Gorstanvorran H'land 79 D11
Gorsteyhill Staffs 43 G10
Gorsty Hill Staffs 35 C7
Gortantaoid Arg/Bute 64 A4
Gorton Gtr Man 44 C2
Gosbeck Suffolk 31 C8
Gosberton Lincs 37 B8
Gosberton Clough Lincs 37 C7
Gosfield Essex 30 F4
Gosford Heref'd 26 B2
Gosforth Cumb 56 F2
Gosforth Tyne/Wear 63 G8
Gosmore Herts 29 F8
Gosport Hants 10 E5
Gossabrough Shetl'd 96 E7
Gossington Glos 16 A4
Goswick Northum 71 F9
Gotham Notts 35 B11
Gotherington Glos 26 F6
Gott Shetl'd 96 J6
Goudhurst Kent 12 C6
Goulceby Lincs 46 E6
Gourdas Aberds 89 D7
Gourdon Aberds 83 F10
Gourock Inverc'l 73 F11
Govan C/Glasg 68 D4
Govanhill C/Glasg 68 D4
Goveton Devon 5 G8
Govilon Monmouths 25 G9
Gowanhill Aberds 89 B10
Gowdall ER Yorks 52 G2
Gowerton Swan 23 G10
Gowkhall Fife 69 B9
Gowthorpe ER Yorks 52 D3
Goxhill ER Yorks 53 E7
Goxhill N Lincs 53 G7
Goxhill Haven N Lincs 53 G7
Goybre Neath P Talb 14 C3
Grabhair W Isles 91 F8
Graby Lincs 37 C6
Grade Cornw'l 2 H6
Graffham W Sussex 11 C8
Grafham Cambs 29 B8
Grafham Surrey 19 G7
Grafton Heref'd 25 E11
Grafton N Yorks 51 C10
Grafton Oxon 17 A9
Grafton Shrops 33 D10
Grafton Worcs 26 B2
Grafton Flyford Worcs 26 C6
Grafton Regis Northants 28 D4
Grafton Underwood Northants 36 G5
Grafty Green Kent 20 G5
Graianrhyd Denbs 42 G5
Graig Conwy 41 C10
Graig Denbs 42 E3
Graig-fechan Denbs 42 G4
Grain Medway 20 D5
Grainsby Lincs 46 C6
Grainthorpe Lincs 47 C7
Grampound Cornw'l 3 E8
Grampound Road Cornw'l 3 D8
Gramsdal W Isles 84 C3
Granborough Bucks 28 F4
Granby Notts 36 B3
Grandborough Warwick 27 B11
Grandtully Perth/Kinr 76 B2
Grange Cumb 56 E4
Grange E Ayrs 67 C7
Grange Medway 20 E4
Grange Mersey 42 D5
Grange Perth/Kinr 76 E5
Grange Crossroads Moray 88 C4
Grange Hall Moray 87 E13
Grange Hill Essex 19 B11
Grange Moor W Yorks 51 H8
Grange of Lindores Fife 76 F5
Grange-over-Sands Cumb 49 B4
Grange Villa Durham 58 A3
Grangemill Derby 44 G6
Grangemouth Falk 69 B8
Grangepans Falk 69 B9
Grangetown Card 15 D7
Grangetown Redcar/Clevel'd 59 D6
Granish H'land 81 B11
Gransmoor ER Yorks 53 D7
Granston Pembs 22 C3
Grantchester Cambs 29 C11
Grantham Lincs 36 B5
Grantley N Yorks 51 C8
Grantlodge Aberds 83 B9
Granton Dumf/Gal 60 C6
Granton C/Edinb 69 C11
Grantown-on-Spey H'land 82 A2
Grantshouse Scot Borders 71 D7
Grappenhall Warrington 43 D9
Grasby Lincs 46 B4
Grasmere Cumb 56 F5
Grasscroft Gtr Man 44 B3
Grassendale Mersey 43 D6
Grassholme Durham 57 D11
Grassington N Yorks 50 C6
Grassmoor Derby 45 F8
Grassthorpe Notts 45 F11
Grateley Hants 17 G9
Gratwich Staffs 34 B6
Graveley Cambs 29 B9
Graveley Herts 29 F9
Gravelly Hill W Midlands 35 F7
Gravels Shrops 33 E9
Graven Shetl'd 96 F6
Graveney Kent 21 E7
Gravesend Kent 20 D3
Grayingham Lincs 46 C3
Grayrigg Cumb 57 G7
Grays Thurr'k 20 D3
Grayshott Hants 18 H5
Grayswood Surrey 11 A8
Graythorp Hartlep'l 58 D6
Grazeley Wokingham 18 E3
Greasbrough S Yorks 45 C8
Greasby Mersey 42 D5
Great Abington Cambs 30 D2
Great Addington Northants 28 A6
Great Alne Warwick 27 C8
Great Altcar Lancs 42 B6
Great Amwell Herts 29 G10
Great Asby Cumb 57 E8
Great Ashfield Suffolk 30 B6
Great Ayton N Yorks 59 E6
Great Baddow Essex 20 A4
Great Bardfield Essex 30 E3
Great Barford Beds 29 C8
Great Barr W Midlands 34 F6
Great Barrington Glos 27 G9
Great Barrow Ches 43 F7
Great Barton Suffolk 30 B5
Great Barugh N Yorks 52 B3
Great Bavington Northum 62 E5
Great Bealings Suffolk 31 D9
Great Bedwyn Wilts 17 E9
Great Bentley Essex 31 F8
Great Billing Northants 28 B5
Great Bircham Norfolk 38 B3
Great Blakenham Suffolk 31 C8
Great Blencow Cumb 56 C6
Great Bolas Telford 34 C2
Great Bookham Surrey 19 F8
Great Bourton Oxon 27 D11
Great Bowden Leics 36 G3
Great Bradley Suffolk 30 C3
Great Braxted Essex 30 G5
Great Bricett Suffolk 31 C7
Great Brickhill Bucks 28 E6
Great Bridge W Midlands 34 F5
Great Bridgeford Staffs 34 C4
Great Brington Northants 28 B3
Great Bromley Essex 31 F7
Great Broughton Cumb 56 C2
Great Broughton N Yorks 59 F6
Great Budworth Ches 43 E9
Great Burdon D'lington 58 E4
Great Burgh Surrey 19 F9
Great Burstead Essex 20 B3
Great Busby N Yorks 58 F6
Great Canfield Essex 30 G2
Great Carlton Lincs 47 D8
Great Casterton Rutl'd 36 E6
Great Chart Kent 13 B8
Great Chatwell Staffs 34 D3
Great Chesterford Essex 30 D2
Great Cheverell Wilts 16 F6
Great Chishill Cambs 29 E11
Great Clacton Essex 31 G8
Great Cliff W Yorks 51 H9
Great Clifton Cumb 56 D2
Great Coates NE Lincs 46 B6
Great Comberton Worcs 26 D6
Great Corby Cumb 57 A6
Great Cornard Suffolk 30 D5
Great Cowden ER Yorks 53 E8
Great Coxwell Oxon 17 B9
Great Crakehall N Yorks 58 G3
Great Cransley Northants 36 H4
Great Cressingham Norfolk 38 E4
Great Crosby Mersey 42 C6
Great Cubley Derby 35 B7
Great Dalby Leics 36 D3
Great Doddington Northants 28 B5
Great Dunham Norfolk 38 D4
Great Dunmow Essex 30 F3
Great Durnford Wilts 17 H8
Great Easton Essex 30 F3
Great Easton Leics 36 F4
Great Eccleston Lancs 49 E4
Great Edstone N Yorks 52 A3
Great Ellingham Norfolk 38 F6
Great Elm Som'set 16 G4
Great Eversden Cambs 29 C10
Great Fencote N Yorks 58 G3
Great Finborough Suffolk 31 C7
Great Fransham Norfolk 38 D4
Great Gaddesden Herts 29 G7
Great Gidding Cambs 37 G7
Great Givendale ER Yorks 52 D4
Great Glemham Suffolk 31 B10
Great Glen Leics 36 F2
Great Gonerby Lincs 36 B4
Great Gransden Cambs 29 C9
Great Green Norfolk 39 G8
Great Green Suffolk 30 C6
Great Habton N Yorks 52 B3
Great Hale Lincs 37 A7
Great Hallingbury Essex 30 G2
Great Hampden Bucks 18 A5
Great Harrowden Northants 28 A5
Great Harwood Lancs 50 F3
Great Haseley Oxon 18 A3
Great Hatfield ER Yorks 53 E7
Great Haywood Staffs 34 C6
Great Heath W Midlands 35 G9
Great Heck N Yorks 52 G1
Great Henny Essex 30 E5
Great Hinton Wilts 16 F6
Great Hockham Norfolk 38 F5
Great Holland Essex 31 G9
Great Horkesley Essex 30 E6
Great Hormead Herts 29 F10
Great Horton W Yorks 51 F7
Great Horwood Bucks 28 E4
Great Houghton Northants 28 C4
Great Houghton S Yorks 45 B8
Great Hucklow Derby 44 E5
Great Kelk ER Yorks 53 D7
Great Kimble Bucks 28 H5
Great Kingshill Bucks 18 B5
Great Langton N Yorks 58 G3
Great Leighs Essex 30 G4
Great Lever Gtr Man 43 B10
Great Limber Lincs 46 B5
Great Linford M/Keynes 28 D5
Great Livermere Suffolk 30 A5
Great Longstone Derby 44 E6
Great Lumley Durham 58 B3
Great Lyth Shrops 33 E10
Great Malvern Worcs 26 D4
Great Maplestead Essex 30 E5
Great Marton Blackp'l 49 F3
Great Massingham Norfolk 38 C3
Great Melton Norfolk 39 E7
Great Milton Oxon 18 A3
Great Missenden Bucks 18 A5
Great Mitton Lancs 50 F3
Great Mongeham Kent 21 F10
Great Moulton Norfolk 39 F7
Great Munden Herts 29 F10
Great Musgrave Cumb 57 E9
Great Ness Shrops 33 D9
Great Notley Essex 30 F4
Great Oakley Essex 31 F8
Great Oakley Northants 36 G4
Great Offley Herts 29 F8
Great Ormside Cumb 57 E9
Great Orton Cumb 56 A5
Great Ouseburn N Yorks 51 C10
Great Oxendon Northants 36 G3
Great Oxney Green Essex 30 H3
Great Palgrave Norfolk 38 D4
Great Parndon Essex 29 H11
Great Paxton Cambs 29 B9
Great Plumpton Lancs 49 F3
Great Plumstead Norfolk 39 D9
Great Ponton Lincs 36 B5
Great Preston W Yorks 51 G10
Great Raveley Cambs 37 G8
Great Rissington Glos 27 G8
Great Rollright Oxon 27 E10
Great Ryburgh Norfolk 38 C5
Great Ryle Northum 62 B6
Great Ryton Shrops 33 E10
Great Saling Essex 30 F4
Great Salkeld Cumb 57 C7
Great Sampford Essex 30 E3
Great Sankey Warrington 43 D8
Great Saxham Suffolk 30 B4
Great Shefford W Berks 17 D10
Great Shelford Cambs 29 C11
Great Smeaton N Yorks 58 F4
Great Snoring Norfolk 38 B5
Great Somerford Wilts 16 C6
Great Stainton D'lington 58 D4
Great Stambridge Essex 20 B5
Great Staughton Cambs 29 B8
Great Steeping Lincs 47 F8
Great Stonar Kent 21 F10
Great Strickland Cumb 57 D7
Great Stukeley Cambs 29 A9
Great Sturton Lincs 46 E6
Great Sutton Ches 43 E6
Great Sutton Shrops 33 G11
Great Swinburne Northum 62 F5
Great Tew Oxon 27 F10
Great Tey Essex 30 F5
Great Thurkleby N Yorks 51 B10
Great Thurlow Suffolk 30 C3
Great Torrington Devon 6 E3
Great Tosson Northum 62 C6
Great Totham Essex 30 G5
Great Totham Essex 30 G5
Great Tows Lincs 46 C6
Great Urswick Cumb 49 B2
Great Wakering Essex 20 C6
Great Waldingfield Suffolk 30 D6
Great Walsingham Norfolk 38 B5
Great Waltham Essex 30 G3
Great Warley Essex 20 B2
Great Washbourne Glos 26 E6
Great Weldon Northants 36 G5
Great Welnetham Suffolk 30 C5
Great Wenham Suffolk 31 E7
Great Whittington Northum 62 F6
Great Wigborough Essex 30 G6
Great Wilbraham Cambs 30 C2
Great Wishford Wilts 17 H7
Great Witcombe Glos 26 G6
Great Witley Worcs 26 B4
Great Wolford Warwick 27 E9
Great Wratting Suffolk 30 D3
Great Wymondley Herts 29 F9
Great Wyrley Staffs 34 E5
Great Wytheford Shrops 34 D1
Great Yarmouth Norfolk 39 E11
Great Yeldham Essex 30 E4
Greater Doward Heref'd 26 G2
Greatford Lincs 37 D6
Greatgate Staffs 35 A6
Greatham Hants 11 A6
Greatham Hartlep'l 58 D5
Greatham W Sussex 11 C9
Greatstone on Sea Kent 13 D9
Greatworth Northants 28 D2
Greave Lancs 50 G4
Greeba I/Man 48 D3
Green Denbs 42 F3
Green End Beds 29 C8
Green Hammerton N Yorks 51 D10
Green Lane Powys 33 F7
Green Ore Som'set 16 F2
Green St Green London 19 E11
Green Street Herts 19 B8
Greenbank Shetl'd 96 C7
Greenburn W Loth 69 D8
Greendikes Northum 71 H9
Greenfield Beds 29 E7
Greenfield Flints 42 E4
Greenfield Gtr Man 44 B3
Greenfield H'land 80 C4
Greenfield Oxon 18 B4
Greenford London 19 C8
Greengairs N Lanarks 68 C6
Greenham W Berks 17 E11
Greenhaugh Northum 62 E3
Greenhead Northum 62 G2
Greenhill Falk 69 C7
Greenhill London 19 C8
Greenhill Kent 21 E8
Greenhill Leics 35 D10
Greenhills N Ayrs 67 A6
Greenhithe Kent 20 D2
Greenholm E Ayrs 67 C8
Greenholme Cumb 57 F7
Greenhouse Scot Borders 61 A11
Greenhow Hill N Yorks 51 C7
Greenigoe Orkney 95 H5
Greenland H'land 94 D4
Greenlands Bucks 18 C4
Greenlaw Aberds 89 C6
Greenlaw Scot Borders 70 F6
Greenlea Dumf/Gal 60 F6
Greenloaning Perth/Kinr 75 G11
Greenmount Gtr Man 43 A10
Greenmow Shetl'd 96 L6
Greenock Inverc'l 73 F11
Greenock West Inverc'l 73 F11
Greenodd Cumb 49 A3
Greenrow Cumb 56 A3
Greens Norton Northants 28 D3
Greenside Tyne/Wear 63 G7
Greensidehill Northum 62 B5
Greenstead Green Essex 30 F5
Greensted Essex 20 A2
Greenway Pembs 22 C5
Greenwich London 19 D10
Greet Glos 27 E7
Greete Shrops 26 A2
Greetham Lincs 47 E7
Greetham Rutl'd 36 D5
Greetland W Yorks 51 G6
Gregg Hall Cumb 56 G6
Gregson Lane Lancs 50 G1
Greinetobht W Isles 84 A3
Greinton Som'set 15 H10
Gremista Shetl'd 96 J6
Grenaby I/Man 48 E2
Grendon Northants 28 B5
Grendon Warwick 35 E8
Grendon Common Warwick 35 F8
Grendon Green Heref'd 26 C2
Grendon Underwood Bucks 28 F3
Grenofen Devon 4 D5
Grenoside S Yorks 45 C7
Greosabhagh W Isles 90 H6
Gresford Wrex 42 G6
Gresham Norfolk 39 B7
Greshornish H'land 85 C8
Gressenhall Norfolk 38 D5
Gressingham Lancs 50 C1
Gresty Green Ches 43 G10
Greta Bridge Durham 58 E1
Gretna Dumf/Gal 61 G9
Gretna Green Dumf/Gal 61 G9
Gretton Glos 27 E7
Gretton Northants 36 F4
Gretton Shrops 33 F11
Grewelthorpe N Yorks 51 B8
Grey Green N Lincs 45 B11
Greygarth N Yorks 51 B7
Greynor Carms 23 F10
Greysouthen Cumb 56 D2
Greystoke Cumb 56 C6
Greystone Angus 77 C8
Greystone Dumf/Gal 60 F5
Greywell Hants 18 F4
Griais W Isles 91 C9
Grianan W Isles 91 D9
Gribthorpe ER Yorks 52 F3
Gridley Corner Devon 6 G2
Griff Warwick 35 G9
Griffithstown Torf 15 B8
Grimbister Orkney 95 G4
Grimblethorpe Lincs 46 D6
Grimeford Village Lancs 43 A9
Grimethorpe S Yorks 45 B8
Griminis W Isles 84 C2
Grimister Shetl'd 96 D6
Grimley Worcs 26 B5
Grimness Orkney 95 J5
Grimoldby Lincs 47 D7
Grimpo Shrops 33 C9
Grimsargh Lancs 50 F1
Grimsbury Oxon 27 D11
Grimsby NE Lincs 46 A6
Grimscote Northants 28 C3
Grimscott Cornw'l 6 F1
Grimsthorpe Lincs 36 C6
Grimston ER Yorks 53 F8
Grimston Leics 36 C2
Grimston Norfolk 38 C2
Grimston C/York 52 D2
Grimstone Dorset 8 E5
Grinacombe Moor Devon 6 G3
Grindale ER Yorks 53 B7
Grindigar Orkney 95 H6
Grindiscol Shetl'd 96 K6
Grindle Shrops 34 E3
Grindleford Derby 44 E6
Grindleton Lancs 50 E3
Grindley Staffs 34 C6
Grindley Brook Shrops 33 A11
Grindlow Derby 44 E5
Grindon Northum 71 F8
Grindon Staffs 44 G4
Grindonmoor Gate Staffs 44 G4
Gringley on the Hill Notts 45 C11
Grinsdale Cumb 61 H9
Grinshill Shrops 33 C11
Grinton N Yorks 58 G1
Griomsidar W Isles 91 E8
Grishipoll Arg/Bute 78 F4
Grisling Common E Sussex 12 D3
Gristhorpe N Yorks 53 A6
Griston Norfolk 38 F5
Gritley Orkney 95 H6
Grittenham Wilts 17 C7
Grittleton Wilts 16 C5
Grizebeck Cumb 49 A2
Grizedale Cumb 56 G5
Grobister Orkney 95 F7
Groby Leics 35 E11
Groes Conwy 42 F3
Groes Neath P Talb 14 C3
Groes-faen Rh Cyn Taff 14 C6
Groes-lwyd Powys 33 D8
Groesffordd Marli Denbs 42 E3
Groeslon Gwyn 41 D7
Groeslon Gwyn 40 E6
Grogport Arg/Bute 65 D9
Gromford Suffolk 31 C10
Gronant Flints 42 D3
Groombridge E Sussex 12 C4
Grosmont Monmouths 25 F11
Grosmont N Yorks 59 F9
Groton Suffolk 30 D6
Grougfoot Falk 69 C9
Grouville Jersey 11
Grove Dorset 8 G6
Grove Kent 21 E9
Grove Notts 45 E11
Grove Oxon 17 B11
Grove Park London 19 D11
Grove Vale W Midlands 34 F6
Grovesend Swan 23 F10
Grudie H'land 86 E6
Gruids H'land 93 J8
Gruinard House H'land 86 B2
Grula H'land 85 F8
Gruline Arg/Bute 79 G8
Grunasound Shetl'd 96 K5
Grundisburgh Suffolk 31 C9
Grunsagill Lancs 50 D3
Gruting Shetl'd 96 J4
Grutness Shetl'd 96 N6
Gualachulain H'land 74 C4
Gualin Ho. H'land 92 D6
Guardbridge Fife 77 F7
Guarlford Worcs 26 D5
Guay Perth/Kinr 76 C3
Guestling Green E Sussex 13 E7
Guestling Thorn E Sussex 13 E7
Guestwick Norfolk 39 C6
Guestwick Green Norfolk 39 C6
Guide Blackb'n 50 G3
Guide Post Northum 63 E8
Guilden Morden Cambs 29 D9
Guilden Sutton Ches 43 F7
Guildford Surrey 18 G6
Guildtown Perth/Kinr 76 D4
Guilsborough Northants 28 A3
Guilsfield Powys 33 D8
Guilton Kent 21 F9
Guineaford Devon 6 C4
Guisborough Redcar/Clevel'd 59 E7
Guiseley W Yorks 51 E7
Guist Norfolk 38 C5
Guith Orkney 95 E6
Guiting Power Glos 27 F7
Gulberwick Shetl'd 96 K6
Gullane E Loth 70 B3
Gulval Cornw'l 2 F3
Gulworthy Devon 4 D5
Gumfreston Pembs 22 F6
Gumley Leics 36 F2
Gummow's Shop Cornw'l 3 D7
Gun Hill E Sussex 12 E4
Gunby ER Yorks 52 F3
Gunby Lincs 36 C5
Gundleton Hants 10 A5
Gunn Devon 6 C5
Gunnerside N Yorks 57 G11
Gunnerton Northum 62 F5
Gunness N Lincs 46 A2
Gunnislake Cornw'l 4 D5
Gunnista Shetl'd 96 J7
Gunthorpe Norfolk 38 B6
Gunthorpe Notts 36 A2
Gunthorpe Peterbro 37 E7
Gunville I/Wight 10 F3
Gunwalloe Cornw'l 2 G5
Gurnard I/Wight 10 E3
Gurnett Ches 44 E3
Gurney Slade Som'set 16 G3
Gurnos Powys 24 H4
Gussage All Saints Dorset 9 C9
Gussage St Michael Dorset 9 C8
Guston Kent 21 G10
Gutcher Shetl'd 96 D7
Guthrie Angus 77 B8
Guyhirn Cambs 37 E9
Guyhirn Gull Cambs 37 E9
Guy's Head Lincs 37 C10
Guy's Marsh Dorset 9 B7
Guyzance Northum 63 C8
Gwaenysgor Flints 42 D3
Gwalchmai Angl 40 C5
Gwaun-Cae-Gurwen Neath P Talb 24 G4
Gwaun-Leision Neath P Talb 24 G4
Gwbert Ceredig'n 22 B6
Gweek Cornw'l 2 G6
Gwehelog Monmouths 15 A9
Gwenddwr Powys 25 D7
Gwennap Cornw'l 2 F6
Gwenter Cornw'l 2 H6
Gwernaffield Flints 42 F5
Gwernesney Monmouths 15 A10
Gwernogle Carms 23 C10
Gwernymynydd Flints 42 F5
Gwersyllt Wrex 42 G6
Gwespyr Flints 42 D4
Gwithian Cornw'l 2 E4
Gwredog Angl 40 B6
Gwyddelwern Denbs 42 H3
Gwyddgrug Carms 23 C9
Gwydyr Uchaf Conwy 41 D9
Gwynfryn Wrex 42 G5
Gwystre Powys 25 B7
Gwytherin Conwy 41 D10
Gyfelia Wrex 42 H6
Gyffin Conwy 41 C9
Gyre Orkney 95 H4
Gym-goch Gwyn 40 F6

H

Habberley Shrops 33 E9
Habergham Lancs 50 F4
Habrough NE Lincs 46 A5
Haceby Lincs 36 B6
Hacheston Suffolk 31 C10
Hackbridge London 19 E9
Hackenthorpe S Yorks 45 D8
Hackford Norfolk 39 E6
Hackforth N Yorks 58 G3
Hackland Orkney 95 F4
Hackleton Northants 28 C5
Hackness N Yorks 59 G10
Hackness Orkney 95 J4
Hackney London 19 C10
Hackthorn Lincs 46 D3
Hackthorpe Cumb 57 D7
Haconby Lincs 37 C7
Hacton London 20 C2
Hadden Scot Borders 70 G6
Haddenham Bucks 28 H4
Haddenham Cambs 37 H10
Haddington E Loth 70 C4
Haddington Lincs 46 F3
Haddiscoe Norfolk 39 F10
Haddon Cambs 37 F7
Haddon Ches 44 F3
Hade Edge W Yorks 44 B5
Hademore Staffs 35 E7
Hadfield Derby 44 C4
Hadham Cross Herts 29 G11
Hadham Ford Herts 29 F11
Hadleigh Essex 20 C5
Hadleigh Suffolk 31 D7
Hadley Telford 34 D2
Hadley End Staffs 35 C7
Hadlow Kent 20 G3
Hadlow Down E Sussex 12 D4
Hadnall Shrops 33 D11
Hadstock Essex 30 D2
Hady Derby 45 E7
Hadzor Worcs 26 B6
Haffenden Quarter Kent 13 B7
Hafod-Dinbych Conwy 41 E10
Hafod-Iom Conwy 41 C10
Haggate Lancs 50 F4
Haggbeck Cumb 61 F10
Haggerston Northum 71 F9
Haggrister Shetl'd 96 F5
Hagley Heref'd 26 D2
Hagley Worcs 34 G5
Hagworthingham Lincs 47 F7
Haigh Gtr Man 43 B9
Haigh S Yorks 44 A6
Haigh Moor W Yorks 51 G8
Haighton Green Lancs 50 F1
Hail Weston Cambs 29 B8
Haile Cumb 56 F2
Hailes Glos 27 E7
Hailey Herts 29 G10
Hailey Oxon 27 G10
Hailsham E Sussex 12 F4
Haimer H'land 94 D3
Hainault London 19 B11
Hainford Norfolk 39 D8
Hainton Lincs 46 D5
Hairmyres S Lanarks 68 E5
Haisthorpe ER Yorks 53 C7
Hakin Pembs 22 F3
Halam Notts 45 G10
Halbeath Fife 69 B10
Halberton Devon 7 E9
Halcro H'land 94 D4
Hale Gtr Man 43 D10
Hale Halton 43 D7
Hale Hants 9 C10
Hale Bank Halton 43 D7
Hale Street Kent 20 G3
Halebarns Gtr Man 43 D10
Hales Norfolk 39 F9
Hales Staffs 34 B3
Hales Place Kent 21 F8
Halesfield Telford 34 E3
Halesgate Lincs 37 C9
Halesowen W Midlands 34 G5
Halesworth Suffolk 39 H9
Halewood Mersey 43 D7
Halford Shrops 33 G10
Halford Warwick 27 D9
Halfpenny Furze Carms 23 E7
Halfpenny Green Staffs 34 F4
Halfway Carms 24 E3
Halfway Carms 24 E5
Halfway W Berks 17 E11
Halfway Bridge W Sussex 11 B8
Halfway House Shrops 33 D9
Halfway Houses Kent 20 D6
Halifax W Yorks 51 G6
Halket E Ayrs 67 A7
Halkirk H'land 94 E3
Halkyn Flints 42 E5
Hall Dunnerdale Cumb 56 G4
Hall Green W Midlands 35 G7
Hall Green W Yorks 51 H9
Hall Grove Herts 29 G9
Hall of Tankerness Orkney 95 H6
Hall of the Forest Shrops 33 G8
Halland E Sussex 12 E3
Hallaton Leics 36 F3
Hallatrow Bath/NE Som'set 16 F3
Hallbankgate Cumb 61 H11
Hallen S Glouc 15 C11
Halliburton Scot Borders 70 F5
Hallin H'land 84 C7
Halling Medway 20 E4
Hallington Lincs 47 D7
Hallington Northum 62 F5
Halliwell Gtr Man 43 A10
Halloughton Notts 45 G10
Hallow Worcs 26 C5
Hallrule Scot Borders 61 B11
Halls E Loth 70 C5
Hall's Green Herts 29 F9
Hallsands Devon 5 H9
Hallthwaites Cumb 56 H3
Hallworthy Cornw'l 4 C2
Hallyburton House Perth/Kinr 76 D5
Hallyne Scot Borders 69 F10
Halmer End Staffs 43 H10
Halmore Glos 16 A3
Halmyre Mains Scot Borders 69 F10
Halnaker W Sussex 11 D8
Halsall Lancs 42 A6
Halse Northants 28 D2
Halse Som'set 7 D10
Halsetown Cornw'l 2 F4
Halsham ER Yorks 53 G8
Halsinger Devon 6 C4
Halstead Essex 30 E5
Halstead Kent 19 E11
Halstead Leics 36 E3
Halstock Dorset 8 D4
Haltham Lincs 46 F6
Haltoft End Lincs 47 H7
Halton Bucks 28 G5
Halton Halton 43 D8
Halton Lancs 49 C5
Halton Northum 62 G5
Halton W Yorks 51 F9
Halton Wrex 33 B9
Halton East N Yorks 50 D6
Halton Gill N Yorks 50 B4
Halton Holegate Lincs 47 F8
Halton Lea Gate Northum 62 H2
Halton West N Yorks 50 D4
Haltwhistle Northum 62 G3
Halvergate Norfolk 39 E10
Halwell Devon 5 F8
Halwill Devon 6 G3
Halwill Junction Devon 6 F3
Ham Devon 7 F11
Ham Glos 16 B3
Ham London 19 D8
Ham H'land 94 C4
Ham Kent 21 F10
Ham Shetl'd 96 K1
Ham Wilts 17 E10
Ham Common Dorset 9 B7
Ham Green Heref'd 26 D4
Ham Green Kent 13 D7
Ham Green Kent 20 E5
Ham Green N Som'set 15 D11
Ham Green Worcs 27 B7
Ham Street Som'set 8 A4
Hamble-le-Rice Hants 10 D3
Hambleden Bucks 18 C4
Hambledon Hants 10 C5
Hambledon Surrey 18 H6
Hambleton Lancs 49 E3
Hambleton N Yorks 52 F1
Hambridge Som'set 8 B2
Hambrook S Glouc 16 D3
Hambrook W Sussex 11 D6
Hameringham Lincs 47 F7
Hamerton Cambs 37 H7
Hametoun Shetl'd 96 K1
Hamilton S Lanarks 68 E6
Hammer W Sussex 11 A7
Hammerpot W Sussex 11 D9
Hammersmith London 19 D9
Hammerwich Staffs 35 E6
Hammerwood E Sussex 12 C3
Hammond Street Herts 19 A10
Hammoon Dorset 9 C7
Hamnavoe Shetl'd 96 E4
Hamnavoe Shetl'd 96 K5
Hamnavoe Shetl'd 96 E6
Hamnavoe Shetl'd 96 F6
Hampden Park E Sussex 12 F5
Hamperden End Essex 30 E2
Hampnett Glos 27 G7
Hampole S Yorks 45 A9
Hampreston Dorset 9 E9
Hampstead London 19 C9
Hampstead Norreys W Berks 18 D2
Hampsthwaite N Yorks 51 D8
Hampton London 19 E8
Hampton Shrops 34 G3
Hampton Worcs 27 D7
Hampton Bishop Heref'd 26 E2
Hampton Heath Ches 43 H7
Hampton in Arden W Midlands 35 G8
Hampton Loade Shrops 34 G3
Hampton Lovett Worcs 26 B5
Hampton Lucy Warwick 27 C9
Hampton on the Hill Warwick 27 B9
Hampton Poyle Oxon 28 G2
Hamrow Norfolk 38 C5
Hamsey E Sussex 12 E3
Hamsey Green Surrey 19 F10
Hamstall Ridware Staffs 35 D7
Hamstead I/Wight 10 E3
Hamstead W Midlands 34 F6
Hamstead Marshall W Berks 17 E11
Hamsterley Durham 58 C2
Hamsterley Durham 63 H7
Hamstreet Kent 13 C9
Hamworthy Poole 9 E8
Hanbury Staffs 35 C7
Hanbury Worcs 26 B6
Hanbury Woodend Staffs 35 C7
Hanby Lincs 36 B6
Hanchurch Staffs 34 A4
Handbridge Ches 43 F7
Handcross W Sussex 12 D1
Handforth Ches 44 D2
Handley Ches 43 G7
Handsacre Staffs 35 D6
Handsworth S Yorks 45 D8
Handsworth W Midlands 34 F6
Handy Cross Devon 6 D3
Hanford Stoke 34 A4
Hanging Langford Wilts 17 H7
Hangleton W Sussex 11 D9
Hanham S Glouc 16 D3
Hankelow Ches 43 H9
Hankerton Wilts 16 B6
Hankham E Sussex 12 F5
Hanley Stoke 44 H2
Hanley Castle Worcs 26 D5
Hanley Child Worcs 26 B3
Hanley Swan Worcs 26 D5
Hanley William Worcs 26 B3
Hanlith N Yorks 50 C5
Hanmer Wrex 33 B10
Hannah Lincs 47 E9
Hannington Hants 18 F2
Hannington Northants 28 A5
Hannington Swindon 17 B8
Hannington Wick Swindon 17 B8
Hansel Village S Ayrs 67 C6
Hanslope M/Keynes 28 D5
Hanthorpe Lincs 37 C6
Hanwell London 19 C8
Hanwell Oxon 27 D11
Hanwood Shrops 33 E10
Hanworth London 19 D8
Hanworth Norfolk 39 B7
Happendon S Lanarks 69 G7
Happisburgh Norfolk 39 B9
Happisburgh Common Norfolk 39 C9
Hapsford Ches 43 E7
Hapton Lancs 50 F3
Hapton Norfolk 39 F7
Harberton Devon 5 F8
Harbertonford Devon 5 F8
Harbledown Kent 21 F8
Harborne W Midlands 34 G6
Harborough Magna Warwick 35 H10
Harbottle Northum 62 C5
Harbury Warwick 27 C10
Harby Leics 36 B3
Harby Notts 46 E2
Harcombe Devon 7 G10
Harden W Midlands 34 E6
Harden W Yorks 51 F6
Hardenhuish Wilts 16 D6
Hardgate Aberds 83 C9
Hardham W Sussex 11 C9
Hardingham Norfolk 38 E6
Hardingstone Northants 28 C4
Hardington Som'set 16 F4
Hardington Mandeville Som'set 8 C4
Hardington Marsh Som'set 8 D4
Hardley Hants 10 D3
Hardley Street Norfolk 39 E9
Hardmead M/Keynes 28 D6
Hardrow N Yorks 57 G10
Hardstoft Derby 45 F8
Hardway Hants 10 D5
Hardway Som'set 8 A6
Hardwick Bucks 28 G5
Hardwick Cambs 29 C10
Hardwick Norfolk 38 D2
Hardwick Norfolk 39 G8
Hardwick Notts 45 E10
Hardwick Northants 28 B5
Hardwick Oxon 27 H10
Hardwick Oxon 28 F2
Hardwick W Midlands 35 F6
Hardwicke Glos 26 G4
Hardwicke Glos 26 F6
Hardwicke Heref'd 25 D9
Hardy's Green Essex 30 F6
Hare Green Essex 31 F7
Hare Hatch Wokingham 18 D5
Hare Street Herts 29 F10
Hareby Lincs 47 F7
Hareden Lancs 50 D2
Harefield London 19 B7
Harehills W Yorks 51 F9
Harehope Northum 62 A6
Haresceugh Cumb 57 B8
Harescombe Glos 26 G5
Haresfield Glos 26 G5
Hareshaw N Lanarks 69 D7
Hareshaw Head Northum 62 E4
Harewood W Yorks 51 E9
Harewood End Heref'd 26 F2
Harford Carms 24 D3
Harford Devon 5 F7
Hargate Norfolk 39 F7
Hargatewall Derby 44 E5
Hargrave Ches 43 F7
Hargrave Northants 29 A7
Hargrave Suffolk 30 C4
Harker Cumb 61 G9
Harkland Shetl'd 96 E6
Harkstead Suffolk 31 E8
Harlaston Staffs 35 D8
Harlaw Ho. Aberds 83 A9
Harlaxton Lincs 36 B4
Harle Syke Lancs 50 F4
Harlech Gwyn 41 G7
Harlequin Notts 36 B2
Harlescott Shrops 33 D11
Harlesden London 19 C9
Harleston Devon 5 G8
Harleston Norfolk 39 G8
Harleston Suffolk 31 C7
Harlestone Northants 28 B4
Harley Shrops 34 E1
Harley S Yorks 45 C7
Harleyholm S Lanarks 69 G8
Harlington Beds 29 E7
Harlington London 19 D7
Harlington S Yorks 45 B8
Harlosh H'land 85 D7
Harlow Essex 29 G11
Harlow Hill Northum 62 G6
Harlow Hill N Yorks 51 D8
Harlthorpe ER Yorks 52 F3
Harlton Cambs 29 C10
Harman's Cross Dorset 9 F8
Harmby N Yorks 58 H2
Harmer Green Herts 29 G9
Harmer Hill Shrops 33 C10
Harmondsworth London 19 D7
Harmston Lincs 46 F3
Harnham Northum 62 F6
Harnhill Glos 17 A7
Harold Hill London 20 B2
Harold Wood London 20 B2
Haroldston West Pembs 22 E3
Haroldswick Shetl'd 96 B8
Harome N Yorks 52 A2
Harpenden Herts 29 G8
Harpford Devon 7 G9
Harpham ER Yorks 53 C6
Harpley Norfolk 38 C3
Harpley Worcs 26 B3
Harpole Northants 28 B3
Harpsdale H'land 94 E3
Harpsden Oxon 18 C4
Harpswell Lincs 46 D3
Harpur Hill Derby 44 E4
Harpurhey Gtr Man 44 B2
Harraby Cumb 56 A6
Harrapool H'land 85 F11
Harrier Shetl'd 96 J1
Harrietfield Perth/Kinr 76 E2
Harrietsham Kent 20 F5
Harrington Cumb 56 D1
Harrington Lincs 47 E7
Harrington Northants 36 G3
Harringworth Northants 36 F5
Harris H'land 78 B6
Harrogate N Yorks 51 D9
Harrold Beds 28 C6
Harrow London 19 C8
Harrow on the Hill London 19 C8
Harrow Street Suffolk 30 E6
Harrow Weald London 19 B8
Harrowbarrow Cornw'l 4 E4
Harrowden Beds 29 D7
Harrowgate Hill D'lington 58 E3
Harston Cambs 29 C11
Harston Leics 36 B4
Harswell ER Yorks 52 E4
Hart Hartlep'l 58 C5
Hart Common Gtr Man 43 B9
Hart Hill Luton 29 F8
Hart Station Hartlep'l 58 C5
Hartburn Northum 62 E6
Hartburn Stockton 58 E5
Hartest Suffolk 30 C5
Hartfield E Sussex 12 C3
Hartford Cambs 29 A9
Hartford Ches 43 E9
Hartford End Essex 30 G3
Hartfordbridge Hants 18 F4
Hartforth N Yorks 58 F2
Harthill Ches 43 G8
Harthill N Lanarks 69 D8
Harthill S Yorks 45 D8
Hartington Derby 44 F5
Hartland Devon 6 D1
Hartlebury Worcs 26 A5
Hartlepool Hartlep'l 58 C6
Hartley Cumb 57 F9
Hartley Kent 20 E3
Hartley Kent 13 C6
Hartley Northum 63 F9
Hartley Westpall Hants 18 F3
Hartley Wintney Hants 18 F4
Hartlip Kent 20 E5
Hartoft End N Yorks 59 G8
Harton N Yorks 52 C3
Harton Shrops 33 G10
Harton Tyne/Wear 63 G9
Hartpury Glos 26 F4
Hartshead W Yorks 51 G7
Hartshill Warwick 35 F9
Hartshorne Derby 35 C9
Hartsop Cumb 56 E6
Hartwell Northants 28 C4
Hartwood N Lanarks 69 E7
Harvieston Stirl 68 B4
Harvington Worcs 27 D7
Harvington Cross Worcs 27 D7
Harwell Oxon 17 C11
Harwich Essex 31 E9
Harwood Durham 57 C10
Harwood Gtr Man 43 A10
Harwood Dale N Yorks 59 G10
Harworth Notts 45 C10
Hasbury W Midlands 34 G5
Hascombe Surrey 18 G6
Haselbech Northants 36 H3
Haselbury Plucknett Som'set 8 C3
Haseley Warwick 27 B9
Haselor Warwick 27 C8
Hasfield Glos 26 F5
Hasguard Pembs 22 F3
Haskayne Lancs 42 B6
Hasketon Suffolk 31 C9
Hasland Derby 45 F7
Haslemere Surrey 11 A8
Haslingden Lancs 50 G3
Haslingfield Cambs 29 C11
Haslington Ches 43 G10
Hassall Ches 43 G10
Hassall Green Ches 43 G10
Hassell Street Kent 21 G7
Hassendean Scot Borders 61 A11
Hassingham Norfolk 39 E9
Hassocks W Sussex 12 E1
Hassop Derby 44 E6
Hastigrow H'land 94 D4
Hastingleigh Kent 13 B9
Hastings E Sussex 13 F7

Place	County	Page	Ref
Hastingwood	*Essex*	29	H11
Hastoe	*Herts*	28	H6
Haswell	*Durham*	58	B4
Haswell Plough	*Durham*	58	B4
Hatch	*Beds*	29	D8
Hatch	*Hants*	18	F3
Hatch	*Wilts*	9	B8
Hatch Beauchamp	*Som'set*	8	B8
Hatch End	*London*	19	B8
Hatch Green	*Som'set*	8	C2
Hatchet Gate	*Hants*	10	D2
Hatching Green	*Herts*	29	G8
Hatchmere	*Ches*	43	E8
Hatcliffe	*NE Lincs*	46	B6
Hatfield	*Heref'd*	26	C2
Hatfield	*Herts*	29	H9
Hatfield	*S Yorks*	45	B10
Hatfield	*Worcs*	26	C5
Hatfield Broad Oak	*Essex*	30	G2
Hatfield Garden Village	*Herts*	29	H9
Hatfield Heath	*Essex*	30	G2
Hatfield Hyde	*Herts*	29	G9
Hatfield Peverel	*Essex*	30	G4
Hatfield Woodhouse	*S Yorks*	45	B10
Hatford	*Oxon*	17	B10
Hatherden	*Hants*	17	F10
Hatherleigh	*Devon*	6	F4
Hathern	*Leics*	35	C10
Hathersage	*Derby*	44	D6
Hathershaw	*Gtr Man*	44	B3
Hatherton	*Ches*	43	H9
Hatherton	*Staffs*	34	D5
Hatley St George	*Cambs*	29	C9
Hatt	*Cornw'l*	4	E4
Hattingley	*Hants*	18	H3
Hatton	*Aberds*	89	E10
Hatton	*Derby*	35	C8
Hatton	*Lincs*	46	E5
Hatton	*Shrops*	33	F10
Hatton	*Warwick*	27	B9
Hatton	*Warrington*	43	D8
Hatton Castle	*Aberds*	89	D7
Hatton Heath	*Ches*	43	F7
Hatton of Fintray	*Aberds*	83	B10
Hattoncrook	*Aberds*	89	F8
Haugh	*E Ayrs*	67	D7
Haugh	*Gtr Man*	44	A3
Haugh	*Lincs*	47	E8
Haugh Head	*Northum*	71	H9
Haugh of Glass	*Moray*	88	E4
Haugh of Urr	*Dumf/Gal*	55	C11
Haugham	*Lincs*	47	D7
Haughley	*Suffolk*	31	B7
Haughley Green	*Suffolk*	31	B7
Haughs of Clinterty	*Aberd C*	83	B10
Haughton	*Notts*	45	E10
Haughton	*Shrops*	34	F2
Haughton	*Shrops*	33	C9
Haughton	*Shrops*	34	E3
Haughton	*Shrops*	34	C3
Haughton	*Staffs*	34	C4
Haughton Castle	*Northum*	62	F5
Haughton Green	*Gtr Man*	44	C3
Haughton Le Skerne	*D'lington*	58	E4
Haughton Moss	*Ches*	43	G8
Haultwick	*Herts*	29	F10
Haunn	*Arg/Bute*	78	G6
Haunn	*W Isles*	84	G2
Haunton	*Staffs*	35	D8
Hauxley	*Northum*	63	D8
Hauxton	*Cambs*	29	C11
Havant	*Hants*	10	D6
Haven	*Heref'd*	25	C11
Haven Bank	*Lincs*	46	G6
Haven Side	*ER Yorks*	53	G7
Havenstreet	*I/Wight*	10	E4
Havercroft	*W Yorks*	45	A7
Haverfordwest = Hwlffordd	*Pembs*	22	E4
Haverhill	*Suffolk*	30	D3
Haverigg	*Cumb*	49	B1
Havering-atte-Bower	*London*	20	B2
Haveringland	*Norfolk*	39	C7
Haversham	*M/Keynes*	28	D5
Haverthwaite	*Cumb*	49	A3
Haverton Hill	*Stockton*	58	D5
Hawarden = Penarlâg	*Flints*	42	F6
Hawcoat	*Cumb*	49	B2
Hawen	*Ceredig'n*	23	B8
Hawes	*N Yorks*	57	H10
Hawes Side	*Blackp'l*	49	F3
Hawes Green	*Norfolk*	39	F8
Hawford	*Worcs*	26	B5
Hawick	*Scot Borders*	61	B11
Hawk Green	*Gtr Man*	44	D3
Hawkchurch	*Devon*	8	D2
Hawkedon	*Suffolk*	30	C4
Hawkenbury	*Kent*	13	B7
Hawkenbury	*Kent*	20	G3
Hawkeridge	*Wilts*	16	F5
Hawkerland	*Devon*	7	H9
Hawkes End	*W Midlands*	35	G9
Hawkesbury	*S Gloucs*	16	C4
Hawkesbury	*Warwick*	35	G9
Hawkesbury Upton	*S Gloucs*	16	C4
Hawkhill	*Northum*	63	B8
Hawkhurst	*Kent*	13	C6
Hawkinge	*Kent*	21	H9
Hawkley	*Hants*	10	B6
Hawkridge	*Som'set*	7	C7
Hawkshead	*Cumb*	56	G5
Hawkshead Hill	*Cumb*	56	G5
Hawksland	*S Lanarks*	69	G7
Hawkswick	*N Yorks*	50	B5
Hawksworth	*Notts*	36	A3
Hawksworth	*W Yorks*	51	E7
Hawksworth	*W Yorks*	51	F8
Hawkwell	*Essex*	20	B5
Hawley	*Hants*	18	F5
Hawley	*Kent*	20	D2
Hawling	*Glos*	27	F7
Hawnby	*N Yorks*	59	H6
Haworth	*W Yorks*	50	F6
Hawstead	*Suffolk*	30	C5
Hawthorn	*Durham*	58	B5
Hawthorn	*Rh Cyn Taff*	15	C7
Hawthorn	*Wilts*	16	E5
Hawthorn Hill	*Brack'l*	18	E5
Hawthorn Hill	*Lincs*	46	G6
Hawthorpe	*Lincs*	36	C6
Hawton	*Notts*	45	G11
Haxby	*C/York*	52	D2
Haxey	*N Lincs*	45	B11
Hay Green	*Norfolk*	38	D1
Hay-on-Wye = Y Gelli Gandryll	*Powys*	25	D9
Hay Street	*Herts*	29	F10
Haydock	*Mersey*	43	C8
Haydon	*Dorset*	8	C5
Haydon Bridge	*Northum*	62	G4
Haydon Wick	*Swindon*	17	C8
Haye	*Cornw'l*	4	E4
Hayes	*London*	19	E11
Hayes	*London*	19	D9
Hayfield	*Derby*	44	D4
Hayhill	*E Ayrs*	67	E7
Hayhillock	*Angus*	77	C8
Haylands	*I/Wight*	10	E4
Hayle	*Cornw'l*	2	F4
Haynes	*Beds*	29	D7
Haynes Church End	*Beds*	29	D7
Hayscastle	*Pembs*	22	D3
Hayscastle Cross	*Pembs*	22	D3
Hayshead	*Angus*	77	C9
Hayton	*Aberd C*	83	C11
Hayton	*Cumb*	56	B3
Hayton	*Cumb*	61	H11
Hayton	*ER Yorks*	52	E4
Hayton	*Notts*	45	D11
Hayton's Bent	*Shrops*	33	G11
Haytor Vale	*Devon*	5	D8
Haywards Heath	*W Sussex*	12	E2
Haywood	*S Yorks*	45	A9
Haywood Oaks	*Notts*	45	G10
Hazel Grove	*Gtr Man*	44	D3
Hazel Street	*Kent*	12	C5
Hazelbank	*S Lanarks*	69	F7
Hazelbury Bryan	*Dorset*	8	D6
Hazeley	*Hants*	18	F4
Hazelhurst	*Gtr Man*	44	B3
Hazelslade	*Staffs*	34	D6
Hazelton	*Glos*	27	G7
Hazelton Walls	*Fife*	76	E6
Hazelwood	*Derby*	45	H7
Hazlemere	*Bucks*	18	B5
Hazlerigg	*Tyne/Wear*	63	F8
Hazlewood	*N Yorks*	51	D6
Hazon	*Northum*	63	C7
Heacham	*Norfolk*	38	B2
Head of Muir	*Falk*	69	B7
Headbourne Worthy	*Hants*	10	A3
Headbrook	*Heref'd*	25	C10
Headcorn	*Kent*	13	B7
Headingley	*W Yorks*	51	F8
Headington	*Oxon*	28	H2
Headlam	*Durham*	58	E2
Headless Cross	*Worcs*	27	B7
Headley	*Hants*	18	E2
Headley	*Hants*	18	H5
Headley	*Surrey*	19	F9
Headon	*Notts*	45	E11
Heads	*S Lanarks*	68	F6
Heads Nook	*Cumb*	61	H10
Heage	*Derby*	45	G7
Healaugh	*N Yorks*	51	E10
Healaugh	*N Yorks*	58	G1
Heald Green	*Gtr Man*	44	D2
Heale	*Devon*	6	B5
Heale	*Som'set*	16	G3
Healey	*Gtr Man*	50	H4
Healey	*Northum*	62	H6
Healey	*N Yorks*	51	A7
Healing	*NE Lincs*	46	A6
Heamoor	*Cornw'l*	2	F3
Heanish	*Arg/Bute*	78	G3
Heanor	*Derby*	45	H8
Heanton Punchardon	*Devon*	6	C4
Heapham	*Lincs*	46	D2
Hearthstane	*Scot Borders*	69	H10
Heasley Mill	*Devon*	7	C6
Heast	*H'land*	85	G11
Heath	*Card'f*	15	D7
Heath	*Derby*	45	F8
Heath and Reach	*Beds*	28	F6
Heath End	*Hants*	18	E2
Heath End	*Surrey*	18	G5
Heath End	*Warwick*	27	B9
Heath Hayes	*Staffs*	34	D6
Heath Hill	*Shrops*	34	D3
Heath House	*Som'set*	15	G10
Heath Town	*W Midlands*	34	F5
Heathcote	*Derby*	44	F5
Heather	*Leics*	35	D9
Heatherfield	*H'land*	85	D9
Heathfield	*E Sussex*	12	D4
Heathfield	*Som'set*	7	D10
Heathhall	*Dumf/Gal*	60	F5
Heathrow Airport	*London*	19	D7
Heathstock	*Devon*	8	D1
Heathton	*Shrops*	34	F4
Heatley	*Warrington*	43	D10
Heaton	*Lancs*	49	C4
Heaton	*Staffs*	44	F3
Heaton	*Tyne/Wear*	63	G8
Heaton	*W Yorks*	51	F7
Heaton Moor	*Gtr Man*	44	C2
Heaverham	*Kent*	20	F2
Heaviley	*Gtr Man*	44	D3
Heavitree	*Devon*	7	G8
Hebburn	*Tyne/Wear*	63	G9
Hebden	*N Yorks*	50	C6
Hebden Bridge	*W Yorks*	50	G5
Hebron	*Angl*	40	B6
Hebron	*Carms*	22	D6
Hebron	*Northum*	63	E7
Heck	*Dumf/Gal*	60	E6
Heckfield	*Hants*	18	E4
Heckfield Green	*Suffolk*	39	H7
Heckfordbridge	*Essex*	30	F6
Heckington	*Lincs*	37	A7
Heckmondwike	*W Yorks*	51	G8
Heddington	*Wilts*	16	E6
Heddle	*Orkney*	95	G4
Heddon-on-the-Wall	*Northum*	63	G7
Hedenham	*Norfolk*	39	F9
Hedge End	*Hants*	10	C3
Hedgerley	*Bucks*	18	C6
Hedging	*Som'set*	8	B2
Hedley on the Hill	*Northum*	62	H6
Hednesford	*Staffs*	34	D6
Hedon	*ER Yorks*	53	G7
Hedsor	*Bucks*	18	C6
Hedworth	*Tyne/Wear*	63	G9
Hegdon Hill	*Heref'd*	26	C2
Heggerscales	*Cumb*	57	E10
Heglibister	*Shetl'd*	96	H5
Heighington	*D'lington*	58	D3
Heighington	*Lincs*	46	F4
Heights of Brae	*H'land*	87	E8
Heights of Kinlochewe	*H'land*	86	E3
Heilam	*H'land*	92	C7
Heiton	*Scot Borders*	70	G6
Hele	*Devon*	6	B4
Hele	*Devon*	7	F8
Helensburgh	*Arg/Bute*	73	E11
Helford	*Cornw'l*	3	G6
Helford Passage	*Cornw'l*	3	G6
Helhoughton	*Norfolk*	38	C4
Helions Bumpstead	*Essex*	30	D3
Hellaby	*S Yorks*	45	C9
Helland	*Cornw'l*	4	D1
Hellesdon	*Norfolk*	39	D8
Hellidon	*Northants*	28	C2
Hellifield	*N Yorks*	50	D3
Hellingly	*E Sussex*	12	E4
Hellington	*Norfolk*	39	E9
Hellister	*Shetl'd*	96	J5
Helm	*Northum*	63	D7
Helmdon	*Northants*	28	D2
Helmingham	*Suffolk*	31	C8
Helmington Row	*Durham*	58	C2
Helmsdale	*H'land*	93	H13
Helmshore	*Lancs*	50	G3
Helmsley	*N Yorks*	59	H6
Helperby	*N Yorks*	51	C10
Helperthorpe	*N Yorks*	52	B5
Helpringham	*Lincs*	37	A7
Helpston	*Peterbro*	37	E7
Helsby	*Ches*	43	E7
Helsey	*Lincs*	47	E9
Helston	*Cornw'l*	3	G5
Helstone	*Cornw'l*	4	C1
Helton	*Cumb*	57	D7
Helwith Bridge	*N Yorks*	50	C4
Hemblington	*Norfolk*	39	D9
Hemel Hempstead	*Herts*	29	H7
Hemingbrough	*N Yorks*	52	G2
Hemingby	*Lincs*	46	E6
Hemingford Abbots	*Cambs*	29	A9
Hemingford Grey	*Cambs*	29	A9
Hemingstone	*Suffolk*	31	C8
Hemington	*Leics*	35	C10
Hemington	*Northants*	37	G6
Hemington	*Som'set*	16	F4
Hemley	*Suffolk*	31	D9
Hemlington	*Middlesbro*	58	E6
Hemp Green	*Suffolk*	31	B10
Hempholme	*ER Yorks*	53	D6
Hempnall	*Norfolk*	39	F8
Hempnall Green	*Norfolk*	39	F8
Hempriggs House	*H'land*	94	F5
Hempstead	*Essex*	30	E3
Hempstead	*Medway*	20	E4
Hempstead	*Norfolk*	39	B9
Hempstead	*Norfolk*	39	D7
Hempsted	*Glos*	26	G5
Hempton	*Norfolk*	38	C5
Hempton	*Oxon*	27	E11
Hemsby	*Norfolk*	39	D10
Hemswell	*Lincs*	46	C3
Hemswell Cliff	*Lincs*	46	C3
Hemsworth	*W Yorks*	45	A8
Hemyock	*Devon*	7	E10
Hen-feddau fawr	*Pembs*	23	C7
Henbury	*Bristol*	16	D2
Henbury	*Ches*	44	E2
Hendon	*London*	19	C9
Hendon	*Tyne/Wear*	63	H10
Hendre	*Flints*	42	F4
Hendre-ddu	*Conwy*	41	D10
Hendreforgan	*Rh Cyn Taff*	14	C5
Hendy	*Carms*	23	F10
Heneglwys	*Angl*	40	C6
Henfield	*W Sussex*	11	C11
Henford	*Devon*	6	G2
Henghurst	*Kent*	13	C8
Hengoed	*Caerph*	15	B7
Hengoed	*Powys*	25	C9
Hengoed	*Shrops*	33	B8
Hengrave	*Suffolk*	30	B5
Henham	*Essex*	30	F2
Heniarth	*Powys*	33	E7
Henlade	*Som'set*	8	B1
Henley	*Shrops*	33	H11
Henley	*Som'set*	8	A3
Henley	*Suffolk*	31	C8
Henley	*W Sussex*	11	B7
Henley-in-Arden	*Warwick*	27	B8
Henley-on-Thames	*Oxon*	18	C4
Henley's Down	*E Sussex*	12	E6
Henllan	*Ceredig'n*	23	B8
Henllan	*Denbs*	42	F3
Henllan Amgoed	*Carms*	22	D6
Henllys	*Torf*	15	B8
Henlow	*Beds*	29	E8
Hennock	*Devon*	5	C9
Henny Street	*Essex*	30	E5
Henryd	*Conwy*	41	C9
Henry's Moat	*Pembs*	22	D5
Hensall	*N Yorks*	52	G1
Henshaw	*Northum*	62	G3
Hensingham	*Cumb*	56	E1
Henstead	*Suffolk*	39	G10
Henstridge	*Som'set*	8	B6
Henstridge Ash	*Som'set*	8	B6
Henstridge Marsh	*Som'set*	8	B6
Henton	*Oxon*	18	A4
Henton	*Som'set*	15	G10
Henwood	*Cornw'l*	4	D3
Heogan	*Shetl'd*	96	J6
Heol-las	*Swan*	14	B2
Heol-y-Cyw	*Bridg*	14	C5
Hepburn	*Northum*	62	A6
Hepple	*Northum*	62	C5
Hepscott	*Northum*	63	E8
Heptonstall	*W Yorks*	50	G5
Hepworth	*Suffolk*	30	A6
Hepworth	*W Yorks*	44	B5
Herbrandston	*Pembs*	22	F3
Hereford	*Heref'd*	26	D2
Heriot	*Scot Borders*	70	E2
Hermiston	*C/Edinb*	69	C10
Hermitage	*Scot Borders*	61	D11
Hermitage	*Dorset*	8	D5
Hermitage	*W Berks*	18	D2
Hermitage	*W Sussex*	11	D6
Hermon	*Angl*	40	D5
Hermon	*Carms*	23	C8
Hermon	*Carms*	24	F3
Hermon	*Pembs*	23	C7
Herne	*Kent*	21	E8
Herne Bay	*Kent*	21	E8
Herner	*Devon*	6	D4
Hernhill	*Kent*	21	E7
Herodsfoot	*Cornw'l*	4	E3
Herongate	*Essex*	20	B3
Heronsford	*S Ayrs*	54	A4
Herriard	*Hants*	18	G3
Herringfleet	*Suffolk*	39	F10
Herringswell	*Suffolk*	30	A4
Hersden	*Kent*	21	E9
Hersham	*Cornw'l*	6	F1
Hersham	*Surrey*	19	E8
Herstmonceux	*E Sussex*	12	E5
Herston	*Orkney*	95	J5
Hertford	*Herts*	29	G10
Hertford Heath	*Herts*	29	G10
Hertingfordbury	*Herts*	29	G10
Hesket Newmarket	*Cumb*	56	C5
Hesketh Bank	*Lancs*	49	G4
Hesketh Lane	*Lancs*	50	E2
Heskin Green	*Lancs*	49	H5
Hesleden	*Durham*	58	C5
Hesleyside	*Northum*	62	E4
Heslington	*C/York*	52	D2
Hessay	*C/York*	51	D11
Hessenford	*Cornw'l*	4	F4
Hessett	*Suffolk*	30	B6
Hessle	*ER Yorks*	52	G6
Hest Bank	*Lancs*	49	C4
Heston	*London*	19	D8
Hestwall	*Orkney*	95	G3
Heswall	*Mersey*	42	D5
Hethe	*Oxon*	28	F2
Hethersett	*Norfolk*	39	E7
Hethersgill	*Cumb*	61	G10
Hethpool	*Northum*	71	H7
Hett	*Durham*	58	C3
Hetton	*N Yorks*	50	D5
Hetton-le-Hole	*Tyne/Wear*	58	B4
Hetton Steads	*Northum*	71	G9
Heugh	*Northum*	62	F6
Heugh-head	*Aberds*	82	B5
Heveningham	*Suffolk*	31	A10
Hever	*Kent*	12	B3
Heversham	*Cumb*	49	A4
Hevingham	*Norfolk*	39	C7
Hewas Water	*Cornw'l*	3	E8
Hewelsfield	*Glos*	16	A2
Hewish	*N Som'set*	15	E10
Hewish	*Som'set*	8	D3
Heworth	*C/York*	52	D2
Hexham	*Northum*	62	G5
Hextable	*Kent*	20	D2
Hexton	*Herts*	29	E8
Hexworthy	*Devon*	5	D7
Hey	*Lancs*	50	E4
Heybridge	*Essex*	20	A5
Heybridge	*Essex*	30	H5
Heybridge Basin	*Essex*	30	H5
Heybrook Bay	*Devon*	4	G6
Heydon	*Cambs*	29	D11
Heydon	*Norfolk*	39	C7
Heydour	*Lincs*	36	B6
Heylipol	*Arg/Bute*	78	G2
Heylor	*Shetl'd*	96	E4
Heysham	*Lancs*	49	C4
Heyshott	*W Sussex*	11	C7
Heyside	*Gtr Man*	44	B3
Heytesbury	*Wilts*	16	G6
Heythrop	*Oxon*	27	F10
Heywood	*Gtr Man*	44	A2
Heywood	*Wilts*	16	F5
Hibaldstow	*N Lincs*	46	B3
Hickleton	*S Yorks*	45	B8
Hickling	*Norfolk*	39	C10
Hickling	*Notts*	36	C2
Hickling Green	*Norfolk*	39	C10
Hickling Heath	*Norfolk*	39	C10
Hickstead	*W Sussex*	12	D1
Hidcote Boyce	*Glos*	27	D8
High Ackworth	*W Yorks*	51	H10
High Angerton	*Northum*	62	E6
High Bankhill	*Cumb*	57	B7
High Beach	*Essex*	19	B11
High Bentham	*N Yorks*	50	C2
High Bickington	*Devon*	6	D5
High Birkwith	*N Yorks*	50	B4
High Blantyre	*S Lanarks*	68	E5
High Bonnybridge	*Falk*	69	C7
High Bradfield	*S Yorks*	44	C6
High Bray	*Devon*	6	C5
High Brooms	*Kent*	12	B4
High Bullen	*Devon*	6	D4
High Buston	*Northum*	63	C8
High Callerton	*Northum*	63	F7
High Catton	*ER Yorks*	52	D3
High Cogges	*Oxon*	27	H10
High Coniscliffe	*D'lington*	58	E3
High Cross	*Hants*	10	B6
High Cross	*Herts*	29	G10
High Easter	*Essex*	30	G3
High Eggborough	*N Yorks*	51	G11
High Ellington	*N Yorks*	51	A7
High Ercall	*Telford*	34	D1
High Etherley	*Durham*	58	D2
High Garrett	*Essex*	30	F4
High Grange	*Durham*	58	C2
High Green	*Norfolk*	39	E7
High Green	*S Yorks*	45	C7
High Green	*Worcs*	26	D5
High Halden	*Kent*	13	C7
High Halstow	*Medway*	20	D4
High Ham	*Som'set*	8	A3
High Harrington	*Cumb*	56	D2
High Hatton	*Shrops*	34	C2
High Hawsker	*N Yorks*	59	F10
High Hesket	*Cumb*	57	B6
High Hesleden	*Durham*	58	C5
High Hoyland	*S Yorks*	44	A6
High Hunsley	*ER Yorks*	52	F5
High Hurstwood	*E Sussex*	12	D3
High Hutton	*N Yorks*	52	C3
High Ireby	*Cumb*	56	C4
High Kelling	*Norfolk*	39	A7
High Kilburn	*N Yorks*	51	B11
High Lands	*Durham*	58	D2
High Lane	*Gtr Man*	44	D3
High Lane	*Heref'd*	26	B3
High Laver	*Essex*	30	H2
High Legh	*Ches*	43	D10
High Leven	*Stockton*	58	E5
High Littleton	*Bath/NE Som'set*	16	F3
High Lorton	*Cumb*	56	D3
High Marishes	*N Yorks*	52	B4
High Marnham	*Notts*	46	E2
High Melton	*S Yorks*	45	B9
High Mickley	*Northum*	62	G6
High Mindork	*Dumf/Gal*	54	D6
High Newton	*Cumb*	49	A4
High Newton-by-the-Sea	*Northum*	71	H11
High Nibthwaite	*Cumb*	56	H4
High Offley	*Staffs*	34	C3
High Ongar	*Essex*	20	A2
High Onn	*Staffs*	34	D4
High Roding	*Essex*	30	G3
High Row	*Cumb*	56	D5
High Salvington	*W Sussex*	11	D10
High Shaw	*N Yorks*	57	G10
High Spen	*Tyne/Wear*	63	H7
High Stoop	*Durham*	58	B2
High Street	*Cornw'l*	3	D8
High Street	*Kent*	12	C6
High Street	*Suffolk*	31	C11
High Street	*Suffolk*	31	A11
High Street	*Suffolk*	30	C5
High Street Green	*Suffolk*	31	C7
High Throston	*Hartlep'l*	58	C5
High Toynton	*Lincs*	46	F6
High Trewhitt	*Northum*	62	C6
High Valleyfield	*Fife*	69	B9
High Westwood	*Durham*	63	H7
High Wray	*Cumb*	56	G5
High Wych	*Herts*	29	G11
High Wycombe	*Bucks*	18	B5
Higham	*Derby*	45	G7
Higham	*Kent*	20	D4
Higham	*Lancs*	50	F4
Higham	*Suffolk*	31	E7
Higham	*Suffolk*	30	B4
Higham Dykes	*Northum*	63	F7
Higham Ferrers	*Northants*	28	B6
Higham Gobion	*Beds*	29	E8
Higham on the Hill	*Leics*	35	F9
Higham Wood	*Kent*	20	G2
Highampton	*Devon*	6	F3
Highbridge	*H'land*	80	E3
Highbridge	*Som'set*	15	G9
Highbrook	*W Sussex*	12	C2
Highburton	*W Yorks*	44	A5
Highbury	*Som'set*	16	G3
Highclere	*Hants*	17	E11
Highcliffe	*Dorset*	9	E11
Higher Ansty	*Dorset*	9	D6
Higher Ashton	*Devon*	5	C9
Higher Ballam	*Lancs*	49	F3
Higher Bartle	*Lancs*	49	F5
Higher Boscaswell	*Cornw'l*	2	F2
Higher Burwardsley	*Ches*	43	G8
Higher End	*Gtr Man*	43	B8
Higher Kinnerton	*Flints*	42	G6
Higher Penwortham	*Lancs*	49	G5
Higher Town	*I/Scilly*	2	C3
Higher Walreddon	*Devon*	4	D5
Higher Walton	*Lancs*	50	G1
Higher Walton	*Warrington*	43	D8
Higher Wheelton	*Lancs*	50	G2
Higher Whitley	*Ches*	43	D9
Higher Wincham	*Ches*	43	E9
Higher Wych	*Ches*	33	A10
Highfield	*ER Yorks*	52	F3
Highfield	*Gtr Man*	43	B10
Highfield	*N Ayrs*	66	A6
Highfield	*Oxon*	28	F2
Highfield	*S Yorks*	45	D7
Highfield	*Tyne/Wear*	63	H7
Highfields	*Cambs*	29	C10
Highfields	*Northum*	71	E8
Highgate	*London*	19	C9
Highlane	*Ches*	44	F2
Highlane	*Derby*	45	D8
Highlaws	*Cumb*	56	B3
Highleadon	*Glos*	26	F4
Highleigh	*W Sussex*	11	E7
Highley	*Shrops*	34	G3
Highmoor Cross	*Oxon*	18	C4
Highmoor Hill	*Monmouths*	15	C10
Highnam	*Glos*	26	G4
Highnam Green	*Glos*	26	F4
Highsted	*Kent*	20	E6
Highstreet Green	*Essex*	30	E4
Hightae	*Dumf/Gal*	60	F6
Hightown	*Ches*	44	F2
Hightown	*Mersey*	42	B6
Hightown Green	*Suffolk*	30	C6
Highway	*Wilts*	17	D7
Highweek	*Devon*	5	D9
Highworth	*Swindon*	17	B9
Hilborough	*Norfolk*	38	E4
Hilcote	*Derby*	45	G8
Hilcott	*Wilts*	17	F8
Hilden Park	*Kent*	20	G2
Hildenborough	*Kent*	20	G2
Hildersham	*Cambs*	30	C2
Hilderstone	*Staffs*	34	B5
Hilderthorpe	*ER Yorks*	53	C7
Hilfield	*Dorset*	8	D5
Hilgay	*Norfolk*	38	F2
Hill	*Pembs*	22	F6
Hill	*S Gloucs*	16	B3
Hill	*W Midlands*	35	F7
Hill Brow	*W Sussex*	11	B6
Hill Dale	*Lancs*	43	A8
Hill Dyke	*Lincs*	47	H7
Hill End	*Durham*	58	C1
Hill End	*Fife*	76	H3
Hill End	*N Yorks*	51	D6
Hill Head	*Hants*	10	D4
Hill Head	*Northum*	62	G5
Hill of Beath	*Fife*	69	A10
Hill of Fearn	*H'land*	87	D11
Hill of Mountblairy	*Aberds*	89	C6
Hill Ridware	*Staffs*	35	D6
Hill Top	*Durham*	58	D1
Hill Top	*Hants*	10	D3
Hill Top	*W Midlands*	34	F5
Hill Top	*W Yorks*	51	H9
Hill View	*Dorset*	9	E8
Hillam	*N Yorks*	51	G11
Hillbeck	*Cumb*	57	E9
Hillborough	*Kent*	21	E9
Hillbrae	*Aberds*	89	D7
Hillbrae	*Aberds*	89	E8
Hillbutts	*Dorset*	9	D8
Hillclifflane	*Derby*	45	H7
Hillcommon	*Som'set*	7	D10
Hilldyke	*Lincs*	47	H7
Hillend	*Fife*	69	B10
Hillerton	*Devon*	6	G6
Hillesden	*Bucks*	28	F3
Hillesley	*Glos*	16	B4
Hillfarance	*Som'set*	7	D10
Hillhead	*Aberds*	88	E5
Hillhead	*Devon*	5	F9
Hillhead	*S Ayrs*	67	E7
Hillhead of Auchentumb	*Aberds*	89	D9
Hillhead of Cocklaw	*Aberds*	89	D10
Hillhouse	*Scot Borders*	70	E4
Hilliclay	*H'land*	94	D3
Hillingdon	*London*	19	C7
Hillington	*C/Glasg*	68	D4
Hillington	*Norfolk*	38	C3
Hillmorton	*Warwick*	28	A2
Hillockhead	*Aberds*	82	B6
Hillockhead	*Aberds*	82	C5
Hillside	*Aberds*	83	D11
Hillside	*Angus*	77	A10
Hillside	*Mersey*	42	A6
Hillside	*Orkney*	95	J5
Hillside	*Shetl'd*	96	G6
Hillswick	*Shetl'd*	96	F4
Hillway	*I/Wight*	10	F5
Hillwell	*Shetl'd*	96	M5
Hilmarton	*Wilts*	17	D7
Hilperton	*Wilts*	16	F5
Hilsea	*Portsm'th*	10	D5
Hilston	*ER Yorks*	53	F8
Hilton	*Aberds*	89	E9
Hilton	*Cambs*	29	B9
Hilton	*Cumb*	57	D9
Hilton	*Derby*	35	B8
Hilton	*Dorset*	9	D6
Hilton	*Durham*	58	D2
Hilton	*H'land*	87	C10
Hilton	*Shrops*	34	F3
Hilton	*Stockton*	58	E5
Hilton of Cadboll	*H'land*	87	D11
Himbleton	*Worcs*	26	C6
Himley	*Staffs*	34	F4
Hincaster	*Cumb*	49	A5
Hinckley	*Leics*	35	F10
Hinderclay	*Suffolk*	38	H6
Hinderton	*Ches*	42	E6
Hinderwell	*N Yorks*	59	E8
Hindford	*Shrops*	33	B9
Hindhead	*Surrey*	18	H5
Hindley	*Gtr Man*	43	B9
Hindley Green	*Gtr Man*	43	B9
Hindlip	*Worcs*	26	C5
Hindolveston	*Norfolk*	38	C6
Hindon	*Wilts*	9	A8
Hindringham	*Norfolk*	38	B5
Hingham	*Norfolk*	38	E6
Hinstock	*Shrops*	34	C2
Hintlesham	*Suffolk*	31	D7
Hinton	*Hants*	9	E11
Hinton	*Heref'd*	25	E10
Hinton	*Northants*	28	C2
Hinton	*Shrops*	33	E10
Hinton	*S Gloucs*	16	D4
Hinton Ampner	*Hants*	10	B4
Hinton Blewett	*Bath/NE Som'set*	16	F2
Hinton Charterhouse	*Bath/NE Som'set*	16	F4
Hinton-in-the-Hedges	*Northants*	28	E2
Hinton Martell	*Dorset*	9	D9
Hinton on the Green	*Worcs*	27	D7
Hinton Parva	*Swindon*	17	C9
Hinton St George	*Som'set*	8	C3
Hinton St Mary	*Dorset*	9	C6
Hinton Waldrist	*Oxon*	17	B10
Hints	*Shrops*	26	A3
Hints	*Staffs*	35	E7
Hinwick	*Beds*	28	B6
Hinxhill	*Kent*	13	B9
Hinxton	*Cambs*	29	D11
Hinxworth	*Herts*	29	D9
Hipperholme	*W Yorks*	51	G7
Hipswell	*N Yorks*	58	G2
Hirael	*Gwyn*	41	C7
Hiraeth	*Carms*	22	D6
Hirn	*Aberds*	83	C9
Hirnant	*Powys*	33	C6
Hirst	*N Lanarks*	69	D7
Hirst	*Northum*	63	E8
Hirst Courtney	*N Yorks*	52	G2
Hirwaen	*Denbs*	42	F4
Hirwaun	*Rh Cyn Taff*	14	A5
Hiscott	*Devon*	6	D4
Histon	*Cambs*	29	B11
Hitcham	*Suffolk*	30	C6
Hitchin	*Herts*	29	F8
Hither Green	*London*	19	D10
Hittisleigh	*Devon*	7	G6
Hive	*ER Yorks*	52	F4
Hixon	*Staffs*	34	C6
Hoaden	*Kent*	21	F9
Hoaldalbert	*Monmouths*	25	F10
Hoar Cross	*Staffs*	35	C7
Hoarwithy	*Heref'd*	26	F2
Hoath	*Kent*	21	E9
Hobarris	*Shrops*	33	H9
Hobbister	*Orkney*	95	H4
Hobkirk	*Scot Borders*	61	B11
Hobson	*Durham*	63	H7
Hoby	*Leics*	36	D2
Hockering	*Norfolk*	39	D6
Hockerton	*Notts*	45	G11
Hockley	*Essex*	20	B5
Hockley Heath	*W Midlands*	27	A8
Hockliffe	*Beds*	28	F6
Hockwold cum Wilton	*Norfolk*	38	G3
Hockworthy	*Devon*	7	E9
Hoddesdon	*Herts*	29	H10
Hoddlesden	*Blackb'n*	50	G3
Hoddomcross	*Dumf/Gal*	61	F7
Hodgeston	*Pembs*	22	G5
Hodley	*Powys*	33	F7
Hodnet	*Shrops*	34	C2
Hodthorpe	*Derby*	45	E9
Hoe	*Hants*	10	C4
Hoe	*Norfolk*	38	D6
Hoe Gate	*Hants*	10	C5
Hoff	*Cumb*	57	D8
Hog Patch	*Surrey*	18	G5
Hoggard's Green	*Suffolk*	30	C5
Hoggeston	*Bucks*	28	F5
Hogha Gearraidh	*W Isles*	84	A2
Hoghton	*Lancs*	50	G2
Hognaston	*Derby*	44	G6
Hogsthorpe	*Lincs*	47	E9
Holbeach	*Lincs*	37	C9
Holbeach Bank	*Lincs*	37	C9
Holbeach Clough	*Lincs*	37	C9
Holbeach Drove	*Lincs*	37	D9
Holbeach Hurn	*Lincs*	37	C9
Holbeach St Johns	*Lincs*	37	D9
Holbeach St Marks	*Lincs*	37	B9
Holbeach St Matthew	*Lincs*	37	B10
Holbeck	*Notts*	45	E9
Holbeck	*W Yorks*	51	F8
Holbeck Woodhouse	*Notts*	45	E9
Holberrow Green	*Worcs*	27	C7
Holbeton	*Devon*	5	F7
Holborn	*London*	19	C10
Holbrook	*Derby*	45	H7
Holbrook	*S Yorks*	45	D8
Holbrook	*Suffolk*	31	E8
Holburn	*Northum*	71	G9
Holbury	*Hants*	10	D3
Holcombe	*Devon*	5	D10
Holcombe	*Som'set*	16	G3
Holcombe Rogus	*Devon*	7	E9
Holcot	*Northants*	28	B4
Holden	*Lancs*	50	E3
Holdenby	*Northants*	28	B3
Holdenhurst	*Bourn'm'th*	9	E10
Holdgate	*Shrops*	34	G1
Holdich	*Dorset*	8	D3
Hole-in-the-Wall	*Heref'd*	26	F3
Holefield	*Scot Borders*	71	G7
Holehouses	*Ches*	43	E10
Holemoor	*Devon*	6	F3
Holestane	*Dumf/Gal*	60	D4
Holford	*Som'set*	7	B10
Holgate	*C/York*	52	D1
Holker	*Cumb*	49	B3
Holkham	*Norfolk*	38	A4
Hollacombe	*Devon*	6	F2
Holland	*Orkney*	95	C5
Holland	*Orkney*	95	F7
Holland Fen	*Lincs*	46	H6
Holland-on-Sea	*Essex*	31	G9
Hollandstoun	*Orkney*	95	C8
Hollee	*Dumf/Gal*	61	G8
Hollesley	*Suffolk*	31	D10
Hollicombe	*Torbay*	5	E9
Hollingbourne	*Kent*	20	F5
Hollington	*Derby*	35	B8
Hollington	*E Sussex*	13	E6
Hollington	*Staffs*	35	B6
Hollington Grove	*Derby*	35	B8
Hollingworth	*Gtr Man*	44	C4
Hollins	*Gtr Man*	44	B2
Hollins Green	*Warrington*	43	C9
Hollins Lane	*Lancs*	49	D4
Hollinsclough	*Staffs*	44	F4
Hollinwood	*Gtr Man*	44	B3
Hollinwood	*Shrops*	33	B11
Hollocombe	*Devon*	6	E5
Holloway	*Derby*	45	G7
Hollowell	*Northants*	28	A3
Holly End	*Norfolk*	37	E10
Holly Green	*Worcs*	26	D5
Hollybush	*Caerph*	15	A7
Hollybush	*E Ayrs*	67	E6
Hollybush	*Worcs*	26	E4
Hollym	*ER Yorks*	53	G9
Hollywood	*Worcs*	35	H6
Holmbridge	*W Yorks*	44	B5
Holmbury St Mary	*Surrey*	19	G8
Holmbush	*Cornw'l*	3	D9
Holmcroft	*Staffs*	34	C5
Holme	*Cambs*	37	G7
Holme	*Cumb*	49	B5
Holme	*N Yorks*	51	A9
Holme	*Notts*	46	G2
Holme	*W Yorks*	44	B5
Holme Chapel	*Lancs*	50	G4
Holme Green	*N Yorks*	52	E1
Holme Hale	*Norfolk*	38	E4
Holme Lacy	*Heref'd*	26	E2
Holme Marsh	*Heref'd*	25	C10
Holme next the Sea	*Norfolk*	38	A3
Holme-on-Spalding-Moor	*ER Yorks*	52	F4
Holme on the Wolds	*ER Yorks*	52	E5
Holme Pierrepont	*Notts*	36	B2
Holme St Cuthbert	*Cumb*	56	B3
Holme Wood	*W Yorks*	51	F7
Holmer	*Heref'd*	26	D2
Holmer Green	*Bucks*	18	B6
Holmes Chapel	*Ches*	43	F10
Holmesfield	*Derby*	45	E7
Holmeswood	*Lancs*	49	H4
Holmewood	*Derby*	45	F8
Holmfirth	*W Yorks*	44	B5
Holmhead	*E Ayrs*	67	D8
Holmhead	*Dumf/Gal*	60	D3
Holmisdale	*H'land*	84	D6
Holmpton	*ER Yorks*	53	G9
Holmrook	*Cumb*	56	G2
Holmsgarth	*Shetl'd*	96	J6
Holmwrangle	*Cumb*	57	B7
Holne	*Devon*	5	E8
Holnest	*Dorset*	8	D5
Holsworthy	*Devon*	6	F2
Holsworthy Beacon	*Devon*	6	F2
Holt	*Dorset*	9	D9
Holt	*Norfolk*	39	B6
Holt	*Wilts*	16	E5
Holt	*Worcs*	26	B5
Holt	*Wrex*	43	G7
Holt End	*Hants*	18	H3
Holt End	*Worcs*	27	B7
Holt Fleet	*Worcs*	26	B5
Holt Heath	*Worcs*	26	B5
Holt Park	*W Yorks*	51	E8
Holtby	*C/York*	52	D2
Holton	*Oxon*	28	H3
Holton	*Som'set*	8	B5
Holton	*Suffolk*	39	H9
Holton cum Beckering	*Lincs*	46	D5
Holton Heath	*Dorset*	9	E8
Holton le Clay	*Lincs*	46	B6
Holton le Moor	*Lincs*	46	C4
Holton St Mary	*Suffolk*	31	E7
Holwell	*Dorset*	8	C6
Holwell	*Herts*	29	E8
Holwell	*Leics*	36	C3
Holwell	*Oxon*	27	H9
Holwick	*Durham*	57	D11
Holworth	*Dorset*	9	F6
Holy Cross	*Worcs*	34	H5
Holy Island	*Northum*	71	F10
Holybourne	*Hants*	18	G4
Holyhead = Caergybi	*Angl*	40	B4
Holymoorside	*Derby*	45	F7
Holyport	*Windsor*	18	D5
Holystone	*Northum*	62	C5
Holytown	*N Lanarks*	68	D6
Holywell	*Cambs*	29	A10
Holywell	*Cornw'l*	3	D6
Holywell	*E Sussex*	12	G4
Holywell = Treffynnon	*Flints*	42	E4
Holywell	*Northum*	63	F9
Holywell Green	*W Yorks*	51	H6
Holywell Lake	*Som'set*	7	D10
Holywell Row	*Suffolk*	38	H3
Holywood	*Dumf/Gal*	60	E5
Homer	*Shrops*	34	E2
Homersfield	*Suffolk*	39	G8
Homington	*Wilts*	9	B10
Honey Hill	*Kent*	21	E8
Honey Street	*Wilts*	17	E8
Honey Tye	*Suffolk*	30	E6
Honeyborough	*Pembs*	22	F4
Honeybourne	*Worcs*	27	D8
Honeychurch	*Devon*	6	F5
Honiley	*Warwick*	27	A9
Honing	*Norfolk*	39	C9
Honingham	*Norfolk*	39	D7
Honington	*Lincs*	36	A5
Honington	*Suffolk*	30	A6
Honington	*Warwick*	27	D9
Honiton	*Devon*	7	F10
Honley	*W Yorks*	44	A5
Hoo	*Medway*	20	D4
Hoo Green	*Ches*	43	D10
Hood Green	*S Yorks*	45	B7
Hooe	*E Sussex*	12	F5
Hooe	*Plym'th*	4	F6
Hooe Common	*E Sussex*	12	E5
Hook	*ER Yorks*	52	G3
Hook	*Hants*	18	F4
Hook	*Hants*	10	D5
Hook	*London*	19	E8
Hook	*Pembs*	22	E4
Hook	*Wilts*	17	C7
Hook Green	*Kent*	12	C5
Hook Green	*Kent*	20	E3
Hook Norton	*Oxon*	27	E10
Hooke	*Dorset*	8	E4
Hookgate	*Staffs*	34	B3
Hookway	*Devon*	7	G7
Hookwood	*Surrey*	12	B1
Hoole	*Ches*	43	F7
Hooley	*Surrey*	19	F9
Hooton	*Ches*	42	E6
Hooton Levitt	*S Yorks*	45	C9
Hooton Pagnell	*S Yorks*	45	B8
Hooton Roberts	*S Yorks*	45	C8
Hop Pole	*Lincs*	37	D7
Hope	*Derby*	44	D5
Hope	*Devon*	5	H7
Hope	*H'land*	92	C7
Hope	*Powys*	33	E8
Hope	*Shrops*	33	E9
Hope	*Staffs*	44	G5
Hope = Yr Hôb	*Flints*	42	G6
Hope Bagot	*Shrops*	26	A2
Hope Bowdler	*Shrops*	33	F10
Hope End Green	*Essex*	30	F2
Hope Green	*Ches*	44	D3
Hope Mansell	*Heref'd*	26	G3
Hope under Dinmore	*Heref'd*	26	C2
Hopeman	*Moray*	88	B1
Hope's Green	*Essex*	20	C4
Hopesay	*Shrops*	33	G9
Hopley's Green	*Heref'd*	25	C10
Hopperton	*N Yorks*	51	D10
Hopstone	*Shrops*	34	F3
Hopton	*Shrops*	33	C9
Hopton	*Shrops*	34	C5
Hopton	*Staffs*	34	C5
Hopton	*Suffolk*	38	H5
Hopton Castle	*Shrops*	33	H9
Hopton on Sea	*Norfolk*	39	E11
Hopton Wafers	*Shrops*	34	H2
Hoptonheath	*Shrops*	33	H9
Hopwas	*Staffs*	35	E7
Hopwood	*Gtr Man*	44	B2
Hopwood	*Worcs*	34	H6
Horam	*E Sussex*	12	E4
Horbling	*Lincs*	37	B7
Horbury	*W Yorks*	51	H8
Horcott	*Glos*	17	A8
Horden	*Durham*	58	B5
Horderley	*Shrops*	33	G9
Hordle	*Hants*	10	E1
Hordley	*Shrops*	33	C9
Horeb	*Ceredig'n*	23	B8
Horeb	*Carms*	23	C9
Horeb	*Carms*	23	D10
Horfield	*Bristol*	16	D3
Horham	*Suffolk*	31	A9
Horkesley Heath	*Essex*	30	F6
Horkstow	*N Lincs*	52	H5
Horley	*Oxon*	27	D11
Horley	*Surrey*	12	B1
Hornblotton Green	*Som'set*	8	A4
Hornby	*Lancs*	50	C1
Hornby	*N Yorks*	58	G4
Hornby	*N Yorks*	58	F4
Horncastle	*Lincs*	46	F6
Hornchurch	*London*	20	C2
Horncliffe	*Northum*	71	F8
Horndean	*Scot Borders*	71	F7
Horndean	*Hants*	10	C6
Horndon	*Devon*	4	D6
Horndon on the Hill	*Thurr'k*	20	C3
Horne	*Surrey*	12	B2
Horniehaugh	*Angus*	77	A7
Horning	*Norfolk*	39	D9
Horninghold	*Leics*	36	F4
Horninglow	*Staffs*	35	C8
Horningsea	*Cambs*	29	B11
Horningsham	*Wilts*	16	G5
Horningtoft	*Norfolk*	38	C5
Horns Corner	*Kent*	12	D6
Horns Cross	*Devon*	6	D2
Horns Cross	*E Sussex*	13	D7
Hornsby	*Cumb*	57	A7
Hornsea	*ER Yorks*	53	E8
Hornsea Bridge	*ER Yorks*	53	E8
Hornsey	*London*	19	C10
Hornton	*Oxon*	27	D10
Horrabridge	*Devon*	4	D6
Horringer	*Suffolk*	30	B5
Horringford	*I/Wight*	10	F4
Horse Bridge	*Staffs*	44	G3
Horsebridge	*Devon*	4	D5
Horsebridge	*Hants*	10	A2
Horsebrook	*Staffs*	34	D4
Horsehay	*Telford*	34	E2
Horseheath	*Cambs*	30	D3
Horsehouse	*N Yorks*	50	A6
Horsell	*Surrey*	18	F6
Horseman's Green	*Wrex*	33	A10
Horseway	*Cambs*	37	G10
Horsey	*Norfolk*	39	C10
Horsey	*Som'set*	8	A2
Horsford	*Norfolk*	39	D7
Horsforth	*W Yorks*	51	F8
Horsham	*Worcs*	26	C4
Horsham	*W Sussex*	11	A10
Horsham St Faith	*Norfolk*	39	D8
Horsington	*Lincs*	46	F5
Horsington	*Som'set*	8	B6
Horsley	*Derby*	45	H7
Horsley	*Glos*	16	B5
Horsley	*Northum*	62	C4
Horsley	*Northum*	63	G6
Horsley Cross	*Essex*	31	F8
Horsley Woodhouse	*Derby*	45	H7
Horsleycross Street	*Essex*	31	F8
Horsleyhope	*Durham*	58	B1
Horsmonden	*Kent*	12	B5
Horspath	*Oxon*	28	H2
Horstead	*Norfolk*	39	D8
Horsted Keynes	*W Sussex*	12	D2
Horton	*Bucks*	28	G6
Horton	*Lancs*	50	D4
Horton	*Northants*	28	C5
Horton	*Shrops*	33	C10
Horton	*S Gloucs*	16	C4
Horton	*Som'set*	8	C2
Horton	*Staffs*	44	G3
Horton	*Swan*	23	H9
Horton	*Wilts*	17	E7
Horton	*Windsor*	19	D7
Horton-cum-Studley	*Oxon*	28	G2
Horton Green	*Ches*	43	H7
Horton Heath	*Hants*	10	C3
Horton-in-Ribblesdale	*N Yorks*	50	B4
Horton Kirby	*Kent*	20	E2
Hortonlane	*Shrops*	33	D10
Horwich	*Gtr Man*	43	A9
Horwich End	*Derby*	44	D4
Horwood	*Devon*	6	D4
Hose	*Leics*	36	C3
Hoselaw	*Scot Borders*	71	G7
Hoses	*Cumb*	56	G4
Hosh	*Perth/Kinr*	75	E11
Hosta	*W Isles*	84	A2
Hoswick	*Shetl'd*	96	L6
Hotham	*ER Yorks*	52	F4
Hothfield	*Kent*	13	B8
Hoton	*Leics*	36	C1
Houbie	*Shetl'd*	96	D8
Houdston	*S Ayrs*	66	G4
Hough	*Ches*	43	G10
Hough	*Ches*	44	E2
Hough Green	*Halton*	43	D7
Hough-on-the-Hill	*Lincs*	46	H3
Houghton	*Cambs*	29	A9
Houghton	*Cumb*	61	H10
Houghton	*Hants*	10	A2
Houghton	*Pembs*	22	F4
Houghton	*W Sussex*	11	C9
Houghton Conquest	*Beds*	29	D7
Houghton Green	*E Sussex*	13	D8
Houghton Green	*Warrington*	43	C9
Houghton-le-Side	*D'lington*	58	D3
Houghton-le-Spring	*Tyne/Wear*	58	B4
Houghton on the Hill	*Leics*	36	E2
Houghton Regis	*Beds*	29	F7
Houghton St Giles	*Norfolk*	38	B5
Houlland	*Shetl'd*	96	H5
Houlland	*Shetl'd*	96	F6
Houlsyke	*N Yorks*	59	F8
Hound	*Hants*	10	D3
Hound Green	*Hants*	18	F4
Houndslow	*Scot Borders*	70	F5
Houndwood	*Scot Borders*	71	D7
Hounslow	*London*	19	D8
Hounslow Green	*Essex*	30	G3
Housay	*Shetl'd*	96	F8
House of Daviot	*H'land*	87	G10
House of Glenmuick	*Aberds*	82	D5
Housetter	*Shetl'd*	96	E5
Houss	*Shetl'd*	96	K5
Houston	*Renf*	68	D3
Houstry	*H'land*	94	G3
Houton	*Orkney*	95	H4
Hove	*Brighton/Hove*	12	F1
Hoveringham	*Notts*	45	H11
Hoveton	*Norfolk*	39	D9
Hovingham	*N Yorks*	52	B2
How	*Cumb*	61	H11
How Caple	*Heref'd*	26	E3
How End	*Beds*	29	D7

How Green Kent 19 G11
Howbrook S Yorks 45 C7
Howden Scot Borders 62 A2
Howden ER Yorks 52 G3
Howden-le-Wear Durham 58 C2
Howe H'land 94 D5
Howe Norfolk 39 E8
Howe N Yorks 51 A9
Howe Bridge Gtr Man 43 B9
Howe Green Essex 20 A4
Howe of Teuchar Aberds 89 D7
Howe Street Essex 30 G3
Howe Street Essex 30 E3
Howell Lincs 46 H5
Howey Powys 25 C7
Howgate Midloth 69 E11
Howick Northum 63 B8
Howle Durham 58 D1
Howle Telford 34 C2
Howlett End Essex 30 E2
Howley Som'set 8 D1
Hownam Scot Borders 62 B3
Hownam Mains
Scot Borders 62 A3
Howpasley Scot Borders 61 C9
Howsham N Lincs 46 B4
Howsham N Yorks 52 C2
Howslack Dumf/Gal 60 C6
Howtel Northum 71 G7
Howton Heref'd 25 F11
Howtown Cumb 56 E6
Howwood Renf 68 D2
Hoxne Suffolk 39 H7
Hoy Orkney 95 H3
Hoylake Mersey 42 D5
Hoyland S Yorks 45 B7
Hoylandswaine S Yorks 44 B6
Hubberholme N Yorks 50 B5
Hubbert's Bridge Lincs 37 A9
Huby N Yorks 51 E8
Huby N Yorks 52 C1
Hucclecote Glos 26 G5
Hucking Kent 20 F5
Hucknall Notts 45 H9
Huddersfield W Yorks 51 H7
Huddington Worcs 26 C6
Hudswell N Yorks 58 F2
Huggate ER Yorks 52 D4
Hugglescote Leics 35 D10
Hugh Town I/Scilly 2 C3
Hughenden Valley Bucks 18 B5
Hughley Shrops 34 F1
Huish Devon 6 E4
Huish Wilts 17 E8
Huish Champflower
Som'set 7 D9
Huish Episcopi Som'set 8 B3
Huisinis W Isles 90 F4
Hulcott Bucks 28 G5
Hulland Derby 44 H6
Hulland Ward Derby 44 H6
Hullavington Wilts 16 C5
Hullbridge Essex 20 B5
Hulme Gtr Man 44 C2
Hulme End Staffs 44 G5
Hulme Walfield Ches 44 F2
Hulver Street Suffolk 39 G10
Hulverstone I/Wight 10 F2
Humber Heref'd 26 C2
Humber Bridge ER Yorks 52 G6
Humberston NE Lincs 47 B7
Humbie E Loth 70 D3
Humbleton ER Yorks 53 F8
Humbleton Northum 71 H8
Humby Lincs 36 B6
Hume Scot Borders 70 F6
Humshaugh Northum 62 F5
Huna H'land 94 C5
Huncoat Lancs 50 F3
Huncote Leics 35 F11
Hundalee Scot Borders 62 B2
Hunderthwaite Durham 57 D11
Hundle Houses Lincs 46 G6
Hundleby Lincs 47 F7
Hundleton Pembs 22 F4
Hundon Suffolk 30 D4
Hundred Acres Hants 10 C4
Hundred End Lancs 49 G4
Hundred House Powys 25 C8
Hungarton Leics 36 E2
Hungerford Hants 9 C10
Hungerford W Berks 17 E10
Hungerford Newtown
W Berks 17 D10
Hungerton Lincs 36 C4
Hungladder H'land 85 A8
Hunmanby N Yorks 53 B6
Hunmanby Moor N Yorks 53 B7
Hunningham Warwick 27 B10
Hunny Hill I/Wight 10 F3
Hunsdon Herts 29 G11
Hunsingore N Yorks 51 D10
Hunslet W Yorks 51 F9
Hunsonby Cumb 57 C7
Hunspow H'land 94 C4
Hunstanton Norfolk 38 A2
Hunstanworth Durham 57 B11
Hunsterson Ches 43 H9
Hunston Suffolk 30 B6
Hunston W Sussex 11 D7
Hunstrete Bath/NE Som'set 16 E3
Hunt End Worcs 27 B7
Hunter's Quay Arg/Bute 73 F10
Hunthill Lodge Angus 82 F6
Huntingdon Cambs 29 A9
Huntingfield Suffolk 31 A10
Huntingford Dorset 9 A7
Huntington E Loth 70 C3
Huntington Heref'd 25 C9
Huntington Staffs 34 D5
Huntington C/York 52 D2
Huntley Glos 26 G4
Huntly Aberds 88 E5
Huntlywood Scot Borders 70 F5
Hunton Kent 20 G4
Hunton N Yorks 58 G2
Hunt's Corner Norfolk 39 G6
Hunt's Cross Mersey 43 D7
Huntsham Devon 7 D9
Huntspill Som'set 15 G9
Huntworth Som'set 8 A2
Hunwick Durham 58 C2
Hunworth Norfolk 39 B6
Hurdsfield Ches 44 E3
Hurley Warwick 35 F8
Hurley Windsor 18 C5
Hurlford E Ayrs 67 C7
Hurliness Orkney 95 K3
Hurn Dorset 9 E10
Hurn's End Lincs 47 H8
Hursley Hants 10 B3
Hurst N Yorks 58 F1
Hurst Som'set 8 C3
Hurst Wokingham 18 D4
Hurst Green E Sussex 12 D6
Hurst Green Lancs 50 F2
Hurst Wickham W Sussex 12 E1
Hurstbourne Priors Hants 17 G11
Hurstbourne Tarrant Hants 17 F10
Hurstpierpoint W Sussex 12 E1
Hurstway Common Heref'd 25 D9
Hurstwood Lancs 50 F4
Hurtmore Surrey 18 G6
Hurworth Place D'lington 58 F3
Hury Durham 57 E11
Husabost H'land 84 C7
Husbands Bosworth Leics 36 G2
Husborne Crawley Beds 28 E6
Husthwaite N Yorks 51 B11
Hutchwns Bridg 14 D4
Huthwaite Notts 45 G8
Huttoft Lincs 47 E9
Hutton Scot Borders 71 E8
Hutton Cumb 56 D6
Hutton ER Yorks 52 D6
Hutton Essex 20 B3
Hutton Lancs 49 G4
Hutton N Som'set 15 F9
Hutton Buscel N Yorks 52 A5
Hutton Conyers N Yorks 51 B9
Hutton Cranswick ER Yorks 52 D6
Hutton End Cumb 56 C6
Hutton Gate
Redcar/Clevel'd 59 E6
Hutton Henry Durham 58 C5
Hutton-le-Hole N Yorks 59 G8
Hutton Magna Durham 58 E2
Hutton Roof Cumb 56 C5
Hutton Roof Cumb 50 B1
Hutton Rudby N Yorks 58 F5
Hutton Sessay N Yorks 51 B10
Hutton Village
Redcar/Clevel'd 59 E6
Hutton Wandesley N Yorks 51 D11
Huxley Ches 43 F8
Huxter Shetl'd 96 H5
Huxter Shetl'd 96 G7
Huxton Scot Borders 71 D7
Huyton Mersey 43 C7
Hwlffordd = Haverfordwest
Pembs 22 E4
Hycemoor Cumb 56 H2
Hyde Glos 16 A5
Hyde Gtr Man 44 C3
Hyde Hants 9 C10
Hyde Heath Bucks 18 A6
Hyde Park S Yorks 45 B9
Hydestile Surrey 18 G6
Hylton Castle Tyne/Wear 63 H9
Hyndford Bridge S Lanarks 69 F8
Hynish Arg/Bute 78 H2
Hyssington Powys 33 F9
Hythe Hants 10 D3
Hythe Kent 21 H8
Hythe End Windsor 19 D7
Hythie Aberds 89 C10

I

Ibberton Dorset 9 D6
Ible Derby 44 G6
Ibsley Hants 9 D10
Ibstock Leics 35 D10
Ibstone Bucks 18 B4
Ibthorpe Hants 17 F10
Ibworth Hants 18 F2
Ichrachan Arg/Bute 74 D3
Ickburgh Norfolk 38 F4
Ickenham London 19 C7
Ickford Bucks 28 H3
Ickham Kent 21 F9
Ickleford Herts 29 E8
Icklesham E Sussex 13 E7
Ickleton Cambs 29 D11
Icklingham Suffolk 30 A4
Ickwell Green Beds 29 D8
Icomb Glos 27 F9
Idbury Oxon 27 G9
Iddesleigh Devon 6 F4
Ide Devon 7 G7
Ide Hill Kent 19 F11
Ideford Devon 5 D9
Iden E Sussex 13 D8
Iden Green Kent 13 C7
Iden Green Kent 12 C6
Idle W Yorks 51 F7
Idlicote Warwick 27 D9
Idmiston Wilts 17 H8
Idole Carms 23 E9
Idridgehay Derby 44 H6
Idrigill H'land 85 B8
Idstone Oxon 17 C9
Idvies Angus 77 C8
Iffley Oxon 18 A2
Ifield W Sussex 19 H9
Ifold W Sussex 11 A9
Iford E Sussex 12 F3
Ifton Heath Shrops 33 B9
Ightfield Shrops 34 B1
Ightham Kent 20 F2
Iken Suffolk 31 C11
Ilam Staffs 44 G5
Ilchester Som'set 8 B4
Ilderton Northum 62 A6
Ilford London 19 C11
Ilfracombe Devon 6 B4
Ilkeston Derby 35 A10
Ilketshall St Andrew Suffolk 39 G9
Ilketshall St Lawrence
Suffolk 39 G9
Ilketshall St Margaret
Suffolk 39 G9
Ilkley W Yorks 51 E7
Illey W Midlands 34 G5
Illingworth W Yorks 51 G6
Illogan Cornw'l 2 E5
Illston on the Hill Leics 36 F3
Ilmer Bucks 28 H4
Ilmington Warwick 27 D9
Ilminster Som'set 8 C2
Ilsington Devon 5 D8
Ilston Swan 23 G10
Ilton N Yorks 51 B7
Ilton Som'set 8 C2
Imachar N Ayrs 66 B1
Imeraval Arg/Bute 64 D4
Immingham NE Lincs 46 A5
Impington Cambs 29 B11
Ince Ches 43 E7
Ince Blundell Mersey 42 B6
Ince in Makerfield Gtr Man 43 B8
Inch of Arnhall Aberds 83 F8
Inchbare Angus 83 G8
Inchberry Moray 88 C3
Inchbraoch Angus 77 B10
Incheril H'land 86 E3
Inchgrundle Angus 82 F6
Inchina H'land 86 B2
Inchinnan Renf 68 D3
Inchkinloch H'land 93 E8
Inchlaggan H'land 80 C3
Inchlumpie H'land 87 D8
Inchmore H'land 86 G6
Inchnacardoch Hotel
H'land 80 B5
Inchnadamph H'land 92 G5
Inchree H'land 74 A3
Inchture Perth/Kinr 76 E5
Inchyra Perth/Kinr 76 E4
Indian Queens Cornw'l 3 D8
Inerval Arg/Bute 64 D4
Ingatestone Essex 20 B3
Ingbirchworth S Yorks 44 B6
Ingestre Staffs 34 C5
Ingham Lincs 46 D3
Ingham Norfolk 39 C9
Ingham Suffolk 30 A5
Ingham Corner Norfolk 39 C9
Ingleborough Norfolk 37 D10
Ingleby Derby 35 C9
Ingleby Lincs 46 E2
Ingleby Arncliffe N Yorks 58 F5
Ingleby Barwick Stockton 58 E5
Ingleby Greenhow N Yorks 59 F6
Inglemire Kingston/Hull 53 F6
Inglesbatch
Bath/NE Som'set 16 E4
Inglesham Swindon 17 B9
Ingleton Durham 58 D2
Ingleton N Yorks 50 B2
Inglewhite Lancs 49 F5
Ingliston C/Edinb 69 C10
Ingoe Northum 62 F6
Ingol Lancs 49 F5
Ingoldisthorpe Norfolk 38 B2
Ingoldmells Lincs 47 F9
Ingoldsby Lincs 36 B6
Ingon Warwick 27 C9
Ingram Northum 62 B6
Ingrave Essex 20 B3
Ingrow W Yorks 51 F6
Ings Cumb 56 G6
Ingst S Gloucs 16 C2
Ingworth Norfolk 39 C7
Inham's End Cambs 37 F8
Inkberrow Worcs 27 C7
Inkpen W Berks 17 E10
Inkstack H'land 94 C4
Inn Cumb 56 F6
Innellan Arg/Bute 73 F10
Innerleithen Scot Borders 70 G2
Innerleven Fife 76 G6
Innermessan Dumf/Gal 54 C3
Innerwick E Loth 70 C6
Innerwick Perth/Kinr 75 C8
Innis Chonain Arg/Bute 74 E4
Insch Aberds 83 A8
Insh H'land 81 C10
Inshore H'land 92 C6
Inskip Lancs 49 F4
Instoneville S Yorks 45 A9
Instow Devon 6 C3
Intake S Yorks 45 B9
Inver Aberds 82 D4
Inver H'land 87 C11
Inver Perth/Kinr 76 C3
Inver Mallie H'land 80 E3
Inverailort H'land 79 C10
Inveraldie Angus 77 D7
Inverallighin H'land 85 C13
Inverallochy Aberds 89 B10
Inveran H'land 87 B8
Inveraray Arg/Bute 73 C9
Inverarish H'land 85 E10
Inverarity Angus 77 C7
Inverarnan Stirl 74 F6
Inverasdale H'land 91 J13
Inverbeg Arg/Bute 74 H6
Inverbervie Aberds 83 F10
Inverboyndie Aberds 89 B6
Inverbroom H'land 86 C4
Invercassley H'land 92 J7
Invercauld House Aberds 82 D3
Inverchaolain Arg/Bute 73 F9
Invercharnan H'land 74 C4
Inverchoran H'land 86 F5
Invercreran Arg/Bute 74 C3
Inverdruie H'land 81 B11
Inverebrie Aberds 89 E9
Invereck Arg/Bute 73 E10
Inveremman Ho. Aberds 82 B5
Invereshie House H'land 81 C10
Inveresk E Loth 70 C2
Inverey Aberds 82 E2
Inverfarigaig H'land 81 A7
Invergarry H'land 80 C5
Invergelder Aberds 82 D4
Invergeldie Perth/Kinr 75 E10
Invergordon H'land 87 E10
Invergowrie Perth/Kinr 76 D6
Inverguseran H'land 85 H12
Inverhadden Perth/Kinr 75 B9
Inverharroch Moray 88 E3
Inverherive Stirl 74 E6
Inverie H'land 79 B10
Inverinan Arg/Bute 73 B8
Inverinate H'land 85 F14
Inverkeilor Angus 77 C9
Inverkeithing Fife 69 B10
Inverkeithny Aberds 89 D6
Inverkip Inverc'l 73 F11
Inverkirkaig H'land 92 H3
Inverlael H'land 86 C4
Inverlochlarig Stirl 75 F7
Inverlochy Arg/Bute 74 E4
Inverlochy H'land 80 F3
Inverlussa Arg/Bute 72 E5
Invermark Lodge Angus 82 E6
Invermoidart H'land 79 D9
Invermoriston H'land 80 B6
Invernaver H'land 93 C10
Inverneill Arg/Bute 73 E7
Inverness H'land 87 G9
Invernettie Aberds 89 D11
Invernoaden Arg/Bute 73 D10
Inveroran Hotel Arg/Bute 74 C5
Inverpolly Lodge H'land 92 H3
Inverquharity Angus 77 B7
Inverquhomery Aberds 89 D10
Inverroy H'land 80 E4
Inversanda H'land 74 B2
Invershiel H'land 80 B1
Invershin H'land 87 B8
Inversnaid Hotel Stirl 74 G6
Inverugie Aberds 89 D11
Inveruglas Arg/Bute 74 G6
Inveruglass H'land 81 C10
Inverurie Aberds 83 A9
Invervar Perth/Kinr 75 C9
Inverythan Aberds 89 D7
Inwardleigh Devon 6 G4
Inworth Essex 30 G5
Iochdar W Isles 84 D2
Iping W Sussex 11 B7
Ipplepen Devon 5 E9
Ipsden Oxon 18 C3
Ipsley Worcs 27 B7
Ipstones Staffs 44 G4
Ipswich Suffolk 31 D8
Irby Mersey 42 D5
Irby in the Marsh Lincs 47 F8
Irby upon Humber NE Lincs 46 B5
Irchester Northants 28 B6
Ireby Cumb 56 C4
Ireby Lancs 50 B2
Ireland Orkney 95 H4
Ireland Shetl'd 96 L5
Ireland's Cross Shrops 34 A3
Ireleth Cumb 49 B2
Ireshopeburn Durham 57 C10
Irlam Gtr Man 43 C10
Irnham Lincs 36 C6
Iron Acton S Gloucs 16 C3
Iron Cross Warwick 27 C7
Ironbridge Telford 34 E2
Ironmacannie Dumf/Gal 55 B9
Ironside Aberds 89 C8
Ironville Derby 45 G8
Irstead Norfolk 39 C9
Irthington Cumb 61 G10
Irthlingborough Northants 28 A6
Irton N Yorks 52 A6
Irvine N Ayrs 66 C6
Isauld H'land 93 C12
Isbister Orkney 95 F3
Isbister Orkney 95 G4
Isbister Shetl'd 96 D5
Isbister Shetl'd 96 G7
Isfield E Sussex 12 E3
Isham Northants 28 A5
Isle Abbotts Som'set 8 B2
Isle Brewers Som'set 8 B2
Isle of Whithorn Dumf/Gal 54 F6
Isleham Cambs 30 A3
Isleornsay H'land 85 G12
Islesburgh Shetl'd 96 G5
Islesteps Dumf/Gal 60 F5
Isleworth London 19 D8
Isley Walton Leics 35 C10
Islibhig W Isles 90 E4
Islington London 19 C10
Islip Northants 36 H5
Islip Oxon 28 G2
Istead Rise Kent 20 E3
Isycoed Wrex 43 G7
Itchen Soton 10 C3
Itchen Abbas Hants 10 A4
Itchen Stoke Hants 10 A4
Itchingfield W Sussex 11 B10
Itchington S Gloucs 16 C3
Itteringham Norfolk 39 B7
Itton Devon 6 G5
Itton Common Monmouths 15 B10
Ivegill Cumb 56 B6
Iver Bucks 19 C7
Iver Heath Bucks 19 C7
Iveston Durham 58 A2
Ivinghoe Bucks 28 G6
Ivinghoe Aston Bucks 28 G6
Ivington Heref'd 25 C11
Ivington Green Heref'd 25 C11
Ivy Chimneys Essex 19 A11
Ivy Cross Dorset 9 B7
Ivy Hatch Kent 20 F2
Ivybridge Devon 5 F7
Ivychurch Kent 13 D9
Iwade Kent 20 E6
Iwerne Courtney or Shroton
Dorset 9 C7
Iwerne Minster Dorset 9 C7
Ixworth Suffolk 30 A6
Ixworth Thorpe Suffolk 30 A6

J

Jack Hill N Yorks 51 D8
Jack in the Green Devon 7 G9
Jacksdale Notts 45 G8
Jackstown Aberds 89 E7
Jacobstow Cornw'l 4 B2
Jacobstowe Devon 6 F4
Jameston Pembs 22 G5
Jamestown Dumf/Gal 61 D9
Jamestown H'land 86 F7
Jamestown W Dunb 68 B2
Jarrow Tyne/Wear 63 G9
Jarvis Brook E Sussex 12 D4
Jasper's Green Essex 30 F4
Java Arg/Bute 79 H10
Jawcraig Falk 69 C7
Jaywick Essex 31 G8
Jealott's Hill Brackn'l 18 D5
Jedburgh Scot Borders 62 A2
Jeffreyston Pembs 22 F5
Jellyhill E Dunb 68 C5
Jemimaville H'land 87 E10
Jersey Farm Herts 29 H8
Jesmond Tyne/Wear 63 G8
Jevington E Sussex 12 F4
Jockey End Herts 29 G7
John o'Groats H'land 94 C5
Johnby Cumb 56 C6
John's Cross E Sussex 12 D6
Johnshaven Aberds 83 G9
Johnston Pembs 22 E4
Johnstone Renf 68 D3
Johnstonebridge Dumf/Gal 60 D6
Johnstown Carms 23 E9
Johnstown Wrex 42 H6
Joppa C/Edinb 70 C2
Joppa S Ayrs 67 E7
Jordans Bucks 18 B6
Jordanthorpe S Yorks 45 D7
Jump S Yorks 45 B7
Jumpers Green Dorset 9 E10
Juniper Green C/Edinb 69 D10
Jurby East I/Man 48 C3
Jurby West I/Man 48 C3

K

Kaber Cumb 57 E9
Kaimend S Lanarks 69 F8
Kaimes C/Edinb 69 D11
Kalemouth Scot Borders 70 H6
Kames Arg/Bute 73 F8
Kames Arg/Bute 73 B7
Kames E Ayrs 68 H5
Kea Cornw'l 3 E7
Keadby N Lincs 46 A2
Keal Cotes Lincs 47 F7
Kearsley Gtr Man 43 B10
Kearstwick Cumb 50 A2
Kearton N Yorks 57 G11
Kearvaig H'land 92 B5
Keasden N Yorks 50 C3
Keckwick Halton 43 D8
Keddington Lincs 47 D7
Kedington Suffolk 30 D4
Kedleston Derby 35 A9
Keelby Lincs 46 A5
Keele Staffs 44 H2
Keeley Green Beds 29 D7
Keeston Pembs 22 E4
Keevil Wilts 16 F6
Kegworth Leics 35 C10
Kehelland Cornw'l 2 E5
Keig Aberds 83 B8
Keighley W Yorks 51 E6
Keil H'land 74 B2
Keilarsbrae Clack 69 A7
Keilhill Aberds 89 C7
Keillmore Arg/Bute 72 E5
Keillor Perth/Kinr 76 C5
Keillour Perth/Kinr 76 E2
Keills Arg/Bute 64 B5
Keils Arg/Bute 72 G4
Keinton Mandeville
Som'set 8 A4
Keir Mill Dumf/Gal 60 D4
Keisby Lincs 36 C6
Keiss H'land 94 D5
Keith Moray 88 C4
Keith Inch Aberds 89 D11
Keithock Angus 77 A9
Kelbrook Lancs 50 E5
Kelby Lincs 36 A6
Keld Cumb 57 E7
Keld N Yorks 57 F10
Keldholme N Yorks 59 H8
Kelfield N Lincs 46 B2
Kelfield N Yorks 52 F1
Kelham Notts 45 G11
Kellan Arg/Bute 79 G8
Kellas Angus 77 D7
Kellas Moray 88 C1
Kellaton Devon 5 H9
Kelleth Cumb 57 F8
Kelleythorpe ER Yorks 52 D5
Kelling Norfolk 39 A6
Kellingley N Yorks 51 G11
Kellington N Yorks 52 G1
Kelloe Durham 58 C4
Kelloholm Dumf/Gal 60 B3
Kelly Devon 4 C4
Kelly Bray Cornw'l 4 D4
Kelmarsh Northants 36 H3
Kelmscot Oxon 17 B9
Kelsale Suffolk 31 B10
Kelsall Ches 43 F8
Kelsall Hill Ches 43 F8
Kelshall Herts 29 E10
Kelsick Cumb 56 A3
Kelso Scot Borders 70 G6
Kelstedge Derby 45 F7
Kelstern Lincs 46 C6
Kelston Bath/NE Som'set 16 E4
Keltneyburn Perth/Kinr 75 C10
Kelton Dumf/Gal 60 F5
Kelty Fife 69 A10
Kelvedon Essex 30 G5
Kelvedon Hatch Essex 20 B2
Kelvin S Lanarks 68 E5
Kelvinside C/Glasg 68 D4
Kelynack Cornw'l 2 F2
Kemback Fife 77 F7
Kemberton Shrops 34 E3
Kemble Glos 16 B6
Kemerton Worcs 26 E6
Kemeys Commander
Monmouths 15 A9
Kemnay Aberds 83 B9
Kemp Town Brighton/Hove 12 F2
Kempley Glos 26 F3
Kemps Green Warwick 27 A8
Kempsey Worcs 26 D5
Kempsford Glos 17 B8
Kempshott Hants 18 F3
Kempston Beds 29 D7
Kempston Hardwick Beds 29 D7
Kempton Shrops 33 G9
Kemsing Kent 20 F2
Kemsley Kent 20 E6
Kenardington Kent 13 C8
Kenchester Heref'd 25 D11
Kencot Oxon 17 A9
Kendal Cumb 57 G7
Kendoon Dumf/Gal 67 H9
Kendray S Yorks 45 B7
Kenfig Bridg 14 C4
Kenfig Hill Bridg 14 C4
Kenilworth Warwick 27 A9
Kenknock Stirl 75 D7
Kenley London 19 F10
Kenley Shrops 34 E1
Kenmore H'land 85 C12
Kenmore Perth/Kinr 75 C10
Kenn Devon 5 C10
Kenn N Som'set 15 E10
Kennacley W Isles 90 H6
Kennacraig Arg/Bute 73 G7
Kennerleigh Devon 7 F7
Kennet Clack 69 A8
Kennethmont Aberds 83 A7
Kennett Cambs 30 B3
Kennford Devon 5 C10
Kenninghall Norfolk 38 G6
Kenninghall Heath Norfolk 38 G6
Kennington Kent 13 B9
Kennington Oxon 18 A2
Kennoway Fife 76 G6
Kenny Hill Suffolk 38 H2
Kennythorpe N Yorks 52 C3
Kenovay Arg/Bute 78 G2
Kensaleyre H'land 85 C9
Kensington London 19 D9
Kensworth Beds 29 G7
Kensworth Common Beds 29 G7
Kent Street E Sussex 13 E6
Kent Street Kent 20 F3
Kent Street W Sussex 11 B11
Kentallen H'land 74 B3
Kentchurch Heref'd 25 F11
Kentford Suffolk 30 B4
Kentisbeare Devon 7 F9
Kentisbury Devon 6 B5
Kentisbury Ford Devon 6 B5
Kentmere Cumb 56 F6
Kenton Devon 5 C10
Kenton Suffolk 31 B8
Kenton Tyne/Wear 63 G8
Kenton Bankfoot
Tyne/Wear 63 G8
Kentra H'land 79 E9
Kents Bank Cumb 49 B3
Kent's Green Glos 26 F4
Kent's Oak Hants 10 B2
Kenwick Shrops 33 B10
Kenwyn Cornw'l 3 E7
Keoldale H'land 92 C6
Keppanach H'land 74 A3
Keppoch H'land 85 F14
Keprigan Arg/Bute 65 G7
Kepwick N Yorks 58 G5
Kerchesters Scot Borders 70 G6
Keresley W Midlands 35 G9
Kernborough Devon 5 G8
Kerne Bridge Heref'd 26 G2
Kerris Cornw'l 2 G3
Kerry Powys 33 G7
Kerrycroy Arg/Bute 73 G10
Kerry's Gate Heref'd 25 E10
Kerrysdale H'land 85 A13
Kersall Notts 45 F11
Kersey Suffolk 31 D7
Kershopefoot Cumb 61 E10
Kersoe Worcs 26 E6
Kerswell Devon 7 F9
Kerswell Green Worcs 26 D5
Kesgrave Suffolk 31 D9
Kessingland Suffolk 39 G11
Kessingland Beach Suffolk 39 G11
Kessington E Dunb 68 C4
Kestle Cornw'l 3 E8
Kestle Mill Cornw'l 3 D7
Keston London 19 E11
Keswick Cumb 56 D4
Keswick Norfolk 39 E8
Keswick Norfolk 39 B9
Ketley Telford 34 D2
Ketley Bank Telford 34 D2
Ketsby Lincs 47 E7
Kettering Northants 36 H4
Ketteringham Norfolk 39 E7
Kettins Perth/Kinr 76 D5
Kettlebaston Suffolk 30 C6
Kettlebridge Fife 76 G6
Kettleburgh Suffolk 31 B9
Kettlehill Fife 76 G6
Kettleholm Dumf/Gal 61 F7
Kettleness N Yorks 59 E9
Kettleshume Ches 44 E3
Kettlesing Bottom N Yorks 51 D8
Kettlesing Head N Yorks 51 D8
Kettlestone Norfolk 38 B5
Kettlethorpe Lincs 46 E2
Kettletoft Orkney 95 E7
Kettlewell N Yorks 50 B5
Ketton Rutl'd 36 E5
Kew London 19 D8
Kew Bridge London 19 D8
Kewstoke N Som'set 15 E9
Kexbrough S Yorks 45 B7
Kexby Lincs 46 D2
Kexby C/York 52 D3
Key Green Ches 44 F2
Keyham Leics 36 E2
Keyhaven Hants 10 E2
Keyingham ER Yorks 53 G8
Keymer W Sussex 12 E2
Keynsham
Bath/NE Som'set 16 E3
Keysoe Beds 29 B7
Keysoe Row Beds 29 B7
Keyston Cambs 36 H6
Keyworth Notts 36 B2
Kibblesworth Tyne/Wear 63 H8
Kibworth Beauchamp Leics 36 F2
Kibworth Harcourt Leics 36 F2
Kidbrooke London 19 D11
Kiddemore Green Staffs 34 E4
Kidderminster Worcs 34 H4
Kiddington Oxon 27 F11
Kidlington Oxon 27 G11
Kidmore End Oxon 18 D3
Kidsgrove Staffs 44 G2
Kidstones N Yorks 50 A5
Kidwelly = Cydweli Carms 23 F9
Kiel Crofts Arg/Bute 74 D2
Kielder Northum 62 D2
Kierfiold Ho. Orkney 95 G3
Kilbagie Clack 69 B8
Kilbarchan Renf 68 D3
Kilbeg H'land 85 H11
Kilberry Arg/Bute 72 G6
Kilbirnie N Ayrs 66 A6
Kilbride Arg/Bute 74 E2
Kilbride Arg/Bute 74 E2
Kilbride H'land 85 F10
Kilburn Angus 82 G5
Kilburn Derby 45 H7
Kilburn London 19 C9
Kilburn N Yorks 51 B11
Kilby Leics 36 F2
Kilchamaig Arg/Bute 73 G7
Kilchattan Arg/Bute 72 D2
Kilchattan Bay Arg/Bute 66 A4
Kilchenzie Arg/Bute 65 F7
Kilcheran Arg/Bute 79 H11
Kilchiaran Arg/Bute 64 B3
Kilchoan Arg/Bute 72 B6
Kilchoan H'land 78 E7
Kilchoman Arg/Bute 64 B3
Kilchrenan Arg/Bute 74 E3
Kilconquhar Fife 77 G7
Kilcot Glos 26 F3
Kilcoy H'land 87 F8
Kilcreggan Arg/Bute 73 E11
Kildale N Yorks 59 F7
Kildalloig Arg/Bute 65 G8
Kildary H'land 87 D10
Kildermorie Lodge H'land 87 D8
Kildonan N Ayrs 66 D3
Kildonan Lodge H'land 93 G12
Kildonnan H'land 78 C7
Kildrummy Aberds 82 B6
Kildwick N Yorks 50 E6
Kilfinan Arg/Bute 73 F8
Kilfinnan H'land 80 D4
Kilgetty Pembs 22 F6
Kilgwrrwg Common
Monmouths 15 B10
Kilham ER Yorks 53 C6
Kilham Northum 71 G7
Kilkenneth Arg/Bute 78 G2
Kilkerran Arg/Bute 65 G8
Kilkhampton Cornw'l 6 E1
Killamarsh Derby 45 D8
Killay Swan 14 B2
Killbeg Arg/Bute 79 G9
Killean Arg/Bute 65 D7
Killearn Stirl 68 B4
Killen H'land 87 F9
Killerby D'lington 58 E2
Killichonan Perth/Kinr 75 B8
Killiechonate H'land 80 E4
Killiechronan Arg/Bute 79 G8
Killiecrankie Perth/Kinr 76 A2
Killiemor Arg/Bute 78 H7
Killiemore House Arg/Bute 78 J7
Killilan H'land 86 H2
Killimster H'land 94 E5
Killin Stirl 75 D8
Killin Lodge H'land 81 C7
Killinallan Arg/Bute 64 A4
Killinghall N Yorks 51 D8
Killington Cumb 57 H8
Killingworth Tyne/Wear 63 F8
Killmahumaig Arg/Bute 72 D6
Killochyett Scot Borders 70 F3
Killocraw Arg/Bute 65 E7
Killundine H'land 79 G8
Kilmacolm Inverc'l 68 D2
Kilmaha Arg/Bute 73 C8
Kilmahog Stirl 75 G9
Kilmalieu H'land 79 F11
Kilmaluag H'land 85 A9
Kilmany Fife 76 E6
Kilmarie H'land 85 G10
Kilmarnock E Ayrs 67 C7
Kilmaron Castle Fife 76 F6
Kilmartin Arg/Bute 73 D7
Kilmaurs E Ayrs 67 B7
Kilmelford Arg/Bute 73 B7
Kilmeny Arg/Bute 64 B4
Kilmersdon Som'set 16 F3
Kilmeston Hants 10 B4
Kilmichael Arg/Bute 65 F7
Kilmichael Glassary
Arg/Bute 73 D7
Kilmichael of Inverlussa
Arg/Bute 72 E6
Kilmington Devon 8 E1
Kilmington Wilts 16 H4
Kilmonivaig H'land 80 E3
Kilmorack H'land 86 G7
Kilmore Arg/Bute 79 J11
Kilmore H'land 85 H11
Kilmory Arg/Bute 72 F6
Kilmory H'land 79 D8
Kilmory H'land 85 H8
Kilmory N Ayrs 66 D2
Kilmuir H'land 84 D7
Kilmuir H'land 87 G9
Kilmuir H'land 87 D10
Kilmuir H'land 85 A8
Kilmun Arg/Bute 73 E10
Kilmun Arg/Bute 73 B8
Kiln Pit Hill Northum 58 A1
Kilncadzow S Lanarks 69 F7
Kilndown Kent 12 C6
Kilnhurst S Yorks 45 C8
Kilninian Arg/Bute 78 G6
Kilninver Arg/Bute 79 J11
Kilnsea ER Yorks 53 H10
Kilnsey N Yorks 50 C5
Kilnwick ER Yorks 52 E5
Kilnwick Percy ER Yorks 52 D4
Kiloran Arg/Bute 72 D2
Kilpatrick N Ayrs 66 D2
Kilpeck Heref'd 25 E11
Kilphedir H'land 93 H12
Kilpin ER Yorks 52 G3
Kilpin Pike ER Yorks 52 G3
Kilrenny Fife 77 G8
Kilsby Northants 28 A2
Kilspindie Perth/Kinr 76 E5
Kilsyth N Lanarks 68 C6
Kiltarlity H'land 87 G8
Kilton Notts 45 E9
Kilton Som'set 7 B10
Kilton Thorpe
Redcar/Clevel'd 59 E7
Kilvaxter H'land 85 B8
Kilve Som'set 7 B10
Kilvington Notts 36 A3
Kilwinning N Ayrs 66 B6
Kimber worth S Yorks 45 C8
Kimberley Norfolk 39 E6
Kimberley Notts 35 A11
Kimble Wick Bucks 28 H5
Kimblesworth Durham 58 B3
Kimbolton Cambs 29 B7
Kimbolton Heref'd 26 B2
Kimcote Leics 36 G1
Kimmeridge Dorset 9 G8
Kimmerston Northum 71 G8
Kimpton Hants 17 G9
Kimpton Herts 29 G8
Kinbrace H'land 93 F11
Kinbuck Stirl 75 G10
Kincaple Fife 77 F7
Kincardine Fife 69 B8
Kincardine H'land 87 C9
Kincardine Bridge Fife 69 B8
Kincardine O'Neil Aberds 83 D7
Kinclaven Perth/Kinr 76 D4
Kincorth Aberd C 83 C11
Kincorth Ho. Moray 87 E13
Kincraig H'land 81 C10
Kincraigie Perth/Kinr 76 C2
Kindallachan Perth/Kinr 76 C2
Kineton Glos 27 F7
Kineton Warwick 27 C10
Kinfauns Perth/Kinr 76 E4
King Edward Aberds 89 C7
King Sterndale Derby 44 E4
Kingairloch H'land 79 F11
Kingarth Arg/Bute 73 H9
Kingcoed Monmouths 25 H11
Kingerby Lincs 46 C4
Kingham Oxon 27 F9
Kingholm Quay Dumf/Gal 60 F5
Kinghorn Fife 69 B11
Kingie H'land 80 C3
Kinglassie Fife 76 H5
Kingoodie Perth/Kinr 76 E6
King's Acre Heref'd 25 D11
King's Bromley Staffs 35 D7
King's Caple Heref'd 26 F2
King's Cliffe Northants 36 F6
King's Coughton Warwick 27 C7
King's Heath W Midlands 35 G6
Kings Hedges Cambs 29 B11
Kings Langley Herts 19 A7
King's Lynn Norfolk 38 C2
King's Meaburn Cumb 57 D8
King's Mills Wrex 42 H6
Kings Muir Scot Borders 69 G11
King's Newnham Warwick 35 H10
King's Newton Derby 35 C9
King's Norton Leics 36 E2
King's Norton W Midlands 35 H6
King's Nympton Devon 6 E5
King's Pyon Heref'd 25 C11
King's Ripton Cambs 37 H8
King's Somborne Hants 10 A2
King's Stag Dorset 8 C6
King's Stanley Glos 16 A5
King's Sutton Northants 27 E11
King's Thorn Heref'd 26 E2
King's Walden Herts 29 F8
Kings Worthy Hants 10 A3
Kingsand Cornw'l 4 F5
Kingsbarns Fife 77 F8
Kingsbridge Devon 5 G8
Kingsbridge Som'set 7 C8
Kingsburgh H'land 85 C8
Kingsbury London 19 C9
Kingsbury Warwick 35 F8
Kingsbury Episcopi
Som'set 8 B3
Kingsclere Hants 18 F2
Kingscote Glos 16 B5
Kingscott Devon 6 E4
Kingscross N Ayrs 66 D3
Kingsdon Som'set 8 B4
Kingsdown Kent 21 G10
Kingseat Fife 69 A10
Kingsey Bucks 28 H4
Kingsfold W Sussex 19 H8
Kingsford E Ayrs 67 B7
Kingsford Worcs 34 G4
Kingsforth N Lincs 52 H6
Kingsgate Kent 21 D10
Kingsheanton Devon 6 C4
Kingshouse Hotel H'land 74 B5
Kingside Hill Cumb 56 A3
Kingskerswell Devon 5 E9
Kingskettle Fife 76 G6
Kingsland Angl 40 B4
Kingsland Heref'd 25 B11
Kingsley Ches 43 E8
Kingsley Hants 18 H4
Kingsley Staffs 44 H4
Kingsley Green W Sussex 11 A7
Kingsley Holt Staffs 44 H4
Kingsley Park Northants 28 B4
Kingsmuir Angus 77 C7
Kingsmuir Fife 77 G8
Kingsnorth Kent 13 C9
Kingstanding W Midlands 35 F6
Kingsteignton Devon 5 D9
Kingsthorpe Northants 28 B4
Kingston Cambs 29 C10
Kingston Devon 5 G7
Kingston Dorset 9 D6
Kingston Dorset 9 G8
Kingston E Loth 70 B4
Kingston Hants 9 D10
Kingston I/Wight 10 F3
Kingston Kent 21 F8
Kingston Moray 88 B3
Kingston Bagpuize Oxon 17 B11
Kingston Blount Oxon 18 B4
Kingston by Sea W Sussex 11 D11
Kingston Deverill Wilts 16 H5
Kingston Gorse W Sussex 11 D9
Kingston Lisle Oxon 17 C10
Kingston Maurward Dorset 8 E6
Kingston near Lewes
E Sussex 12 F2
Kingston on Soar Notts 35 C11
Kingston Russell Dorset 8 E4
Kingston St Mary Som'set 7 D11
Kingston Seymour
N Som'set 15 E10
Kingston Upon Hull
Kingston/Hull 53 G6
Kingston upon Thames
London 19 E8
Kingston Vale London 19 D9
Kingstone Heref'd 25 E11
Kingstone Som'set 8 C2
Kingstone Staffs 35 C6
Kingstown Cumb 61 H9
Kingswear Devon 5 F9
Kingswells Aberd C 83 C10
Kingswinford W Midlands 34 G4
Kingswood Bucks 28 G3
Kingswood Glos 16 B4
Kingswood Heref'd 25 C9
Kingswood Kent 20 F5
Kingswood Powys 33 E8
Kingswood S Gloucs 16 D3
Kingswood Surrey 19 F9
Kingswood Warwick 27 A8
Kingthorpe Lincs 46 E5
Kington Heref'd 25 C9
Kington Worcs 26 C6
Kington Langley Wilts 16 D6
Kington Magna Dorset 9 B6
Kington St Michael Wilts 16 D6
Kingussie H'land 81 C9
Kingweston Som'set 8 A4
Kininvie Ho. Moray 88 D3
Kinkell Bridge Perth/Kinr 76 F2
Kinknockie Aberds 89 D10
Kinlet Shrops 34 G3
Kinloch Fife 76 F5
Kinloch H'land 78 B6
Kinloch H'land 92 F6
Kinloch H'land 85 G11
Kinloch Perth/Kinr 76 C4
Kinloch Perth/Kinr 76 C5
Kinloch Hourn H'land 80 C1
Kinloch Laggan H'land 81 E7
Kinloch Lodge H'land 93 D8
Kinloch Rannoch Perth/Kinr 75 B9
Kinlochan H'land 79 E11
Kinlochard Stirl 75 G7
Kinlochbeoraid H'land 79 C11
Kinlochbervie H'land 92 D5
Kinlocheil H'land 80 F1
Kinlochewe H'land 86 E3
Kinlochleven H'land 74 A4
Kinlochmoidart H'land 79 D10
Kinlochmorar H'land 79 B11
Kinlochmore H'land 74 A4
Kinlochspelve Arg/Bute 79 J9
Kinloid H'land 79 C9
Kinloss Moray 87 E13
Kinmel Bay Conwy 42 D2
Kinmuck Aberds 83 B10
Kinmundy Aberds 83 B10
Kinnadie Aberds 89 D9
Kinnaird Perth/Kinr 76 E5
Kinnaird Castle Angus 77 B9
Kinneff Aberds 83 F10
Kinnelhead Dumf/Gal 60 C6
Kinnell Angus 77 B9
Kinnerley Shrops 33 C9
Kinnersley Heref'd 25 D10
Kinnersley Worcs 26 D5
Kinnerton Powys 25 B9
Kinnesswood Perth/Kinr 76 G4
Kinninvie Durham 58 D1
Kinnordy Angus 76 B6
Kinoulton Notts 36 B2
Kinross Perth/Kinr 76 G4
Kinrossie Perth/Kinr 76 D4
Kinsbourne Green Herts 29 G8
Kinsey Heath Ches 34 A2
Kinsham Heref'd 25 B10
Kinsham Worcs 26 E6
Kinsley W Yorks 45 A8
Kinson Bournem'th 9 E9
Kintbury W Berks 17 E10
Kintessack Moray 87 E12
Kintillo Perth/Kinr 76 F4
Kintocher Aberds 83 C7
Kinton Heref'd 25 A11
Kinton Shrops 33 D9
Kintore Aberds 83 B9
Kintour Arg/Bute 64 C5
Kintra Arg/Bute 78 J6
Kintra Arg/Bute 64 D4
Kintraw Arg/Bute 73 C7
Kinuachdrachd Arg/Bute 72 D6
Kinveachy H'land 81 B11
Kinver Staffs 34 G4
Kippax W Yorks 51 F10
Kippen Stirl 68 A5
Kippford or Scaur
Dumf/Gal 55 D11
Kirbister Orkney 95 H4
Kirbister Orkney 95 F7
Kirbuster Orkney 95 F3
Kirby Bedon Norfolk 39 E8
Kirby Bellars Leics 36 D3
Kirby Cane Norfolk 39 F9
Kirby Cross Essex 31 F9
Kirby Grindalythe N Yorks 52 C5
Kirby Hill N Yorks 58 F2
Kirby Hill N Yorks 51 C9
Kirby Knowle N Yorks 58 H5
Kirby-le-Soken Essex 31 F9
Kirby Misperton N Yorks 52 B3
Kirby Muxloe Leics 35 E11
Kirby Overblow N Yorks 51 E9
Kirby Row Norfolk 39 F9
Kirby Sigston N Yorks 58 G5
Kirby Underdale ER Yorks 52 D4
Kirby Wiske N Yorks 51 A9
Kirdford W Sussex 11 B9
Kirk H'land 94 E4
Kirk Bramwith S Yorks 45 A10
Kirk Deighton N Yorks 51 D9
Kirk Ella ER Yorks 52 G6
Kirk Hallam Derby 35 A10
Kirk Hammerton N Yorks 51 D10
Kirk Ireton Derby 44 G6
Kirk Langley Derby 35 B8
Kirk Merrington Durham 58 C3
Kirk Michael I/Man 48 C3
Kirk of Shotts N Lanarks 69 D7
Kirk Sandall S Yorks 45 B10
Kirk Smeaton N Yorks 51 H11
Kirk Yetholm Scot Borders 71 H7
Kirkabister Shetl'd 96 K6

Kirkandrews Dumf/Gal 55 E9
Kirkandrews upon Eden Cumb 61 H9
Kirkbampton Cumb 61 H9
Kirkbean Dumf/Gal 60 H5
Kirkbride Cumb 61 H8
Kirkbuddo Angus 77 C8
Kirkburn Scot Borders 69 G11
Kirkburn ER Yorks 52 D5
Kirkburton W Yorks 44 A5
Kirkby Lincs 46 C4
Kirkby Mersey 43 C7
Kirkby N Yorks 59 F6
Kirkby Fleetham N Yorks 58 G3
Kirkby Green Lincs 46 G4
Kirkby In Ashfield Notts 45 G9
Kirkby-in-Furness Cumb 49 A2
Kirkby la Thorpe Lincs 46 H5
Kirkby Lonsdale Cumb 50 B2
Kirkby Malham N Yorks 50 C4
Kirkby Mallory Leics 35 E10
Kirkby Malzeard N Yorks 51 B8
Kirkby Mills N Yorks 59 H8
Kirkby on Bain Lincs 46 F6
Kirkby Stephen Cumb 57 F9
Kirkby Thore Cumb 57 D8
Kirkby Underwood Lincs 37 C6
Kirkby Wharfe N Yorks 51 E11
Kirkbymoorside N Yorks 59 H7
Kirkcaldy Fife 69 A11
Kirkcambeck Cumb 61 G11
Kirkcarswell Dumf/Gal 55 E10
Kirkcolm Dumf/Gal 54 C3
Kirkconnel Dumf/Gal 60 B3
Kirkconnell Dumf/Gal 60 G5
Kirkcowan Dumf/Gal 54 C6
Kirkcudbright Dumf/Gal 55 D9
Kirkdale Mersey 42 C6
Kirkfieldbank S Lanarks 69 F7
Kirkgunzeon Dumf/Gal 55 C11
Kirkham Lancs 49 F4
Kirkham N Yorks 52 C3
Kirkhamgate W Yorks 51 G8
Kirkharle Northum 62 E6
Kirkheaton Northum 62 F6
Kirkheaton W Yorks 51 H7
Kirkhill Angus 77 A9
Kirkhill H'land 87 G8
Kirkhill Midloth 69 D11
Kirkhill Moray 88 E2
Kirkhope Scot Borders 61 A9
Kirkhouse Scot Borders 70 G2
Kirkiboll H'land 93 D8
Kirkibost H'land 85 G10
Kirkinch Angus 76 C6
Kirkinner Dumf/Gal 55 D7
Kirkintilloch E Dunb 68 C5
Kirkland Cumb 56 E2
Kirkland Cumb 57 C8
Kirkland Dumf/Gal 60 D4
Kirkland Dumf/Gal 60 B3
Kirkleatham Redcar/Clevel'd 59 D6
Kirklevington Stockton 58 F5
Kirkley Suffolk 39 F11
Kirklington Notts 45 G10
Kirklington N Yorks 51 A9
Kirklinton Cumb 61 G10
Kirkliston C/Edinb 69 C10
Kirkmaiden Dumf/Gal 54 F4
Kirkmichael Perth/Kinr 76 B3
Kirkmichael S Ayrs 66 F6
Kirkmuirhill S Lanarks 68 F6
Kirknewton Northum 71 G8
Kirknewton W Loth 69 D10
Kirkney Aberds 88 E5
Kirkoswald Cumb 57 B7
Kirkoswald S Ayrs 66 F5
Kirkpatrick Durham Dumf/Gal 60 F3
Kirkpatrick-Fleming Dumf/Gal 61 F8
Kirksanton Cumb 49 A1
Kirkstall W Yorks 51 F8
Kirkstead Lincs 46 F5
Kirkstile Aberds 88 E5
Kirkstyle H'land 94 C5
Kirkton Aberds 83 A8
Kirkton Aberds 89 D6
Kirkton Angus 77 C7
Kirkton Angus 77 D7
Kirkton Scot Borders 61 B11
Kirkton Dumf/Gal 60 E5
Kirkton Fife 76 E6
Kirkton H'land 85 F13
Kirkton H'land 86 G2
Kirkton H'land 87 B10
Kirkton H'land 87 F10
Kirkton Perth/Kinr 76 F2
Kirkton S Lanarks 60 A5
Kirkton Stirl 75 G8
Kirkton Manor Scot Borders 69 G11
Kirkton of Airlie Angus 76 B6
Kirkton of Auchterhouse Angus 76 D6
Kirkton of Auchterless Aberds 89 D7
Kirkton of Barevan H'land 87 G11
Kirkton of Bourtie Aberds 89 F8
Kirkton of Collace Perth/Kinr 76 D4
Kirkton of Craig Angus 77 B10
Kirkton of Culsalmond Aberds 89 E6
Kirkton of Durris Aberds 83 D9
Kirkton of Glenbuchat Aberds 82 B5
Kirkton of Glenisla Angus 76 A5
Kirkton of Kingoldrum Angus 76 B6
Kirkton of Largo Fife 77 G7
Kirkton of Lethendy Perth/Kinr 76 C4
Kirkton of Logie Buchan Aberds 89 F9
Kirkton of Maryculter Aberds 83 D10
Kirkton of Menmuir Angus 77 A8
Kirkton of Monikie Angus 77 D8
Kirkton of Oyne Aberds 83 A8
Kirkton of Rayne Aberds 83 A8
Kirkton of Skene Aberds 83 C10
Kirkton of Tough Aberds 83 B8
Kirktonhill Scot Borders 70 E3
Kirktown Aberds 89 C10
Kirktown of Alvah Aberds 89 B6
Kirktown of Deskford Moray 88 B5
Kirktown of Fetteresso Aberds 83 E10
Kirktown of Mortlach Moray 88 E3
Kirktown of Slains Aberds 89 F10
Kirkurd Scot Borders 69 F10
Kirkwall Orkney 95 G5
Kirkwhelpington Northum 62 E5
Kirmington N Lincs 46 A5
Kirmond le Mire Lincs 46 C5
Kirn Arg/Bute 73 F10
Kirriemuir Angus 76 B6
Kirstead Green Norfolk 39 F8
Kirtlebridge Dumf/Gal 61 F8
Kirtleton Dumf/Gal 61 E8
Kirtling Cambs 30 C3
Kirtling Green Cambs 30 C3
Kirtlington Oxon 27 G11
Kirtomy H'land 93 C10
Kirton Lincs 37 B9
Kirton Notts 45 F10
Kirton Suffolk 31 E9
Kirton End Lincs 37 A8
Kirton Holme Lincs 37 A8
Kirton in Lindsey N Lincs 46 C3
Kislingbury Northants 28 C3
Kites Hardwick Warwick 27 B11
Kittisford Som'set 7 D9
Kittle Swan 23 H10
Kitt's Green W Midlands 35 G7
Kitt's Moss Gtr Man 44 D2
Kittybrewster Aberd C 83 C11
Kitwood Hants 10 A5
Kivernoll Heref'd 25 E11
Kiveton Park S Yorks 45 D8
Knaith Lincs 46 D2
Knaith Park Lincs 46 D2
Knap Corner Dorset 9 B7
Knaphill Surrey 18 F6
Knapp Perth/Kinr 76 D5
Knapp Som'set 8 B2
Knapthorpe Notts 45 G11
Knapton Norfolk 39 B9
Knapton C/York 52 D1
Knapton Green Heref'd 25 C11
Knapwell Cambs 29 B10
Knaresborough N Yorks 51 D9
Knarsdale Northum 57 A8
Knauchland Moray 88 C5
Knaven Aberds 89 D8
Knayton N Yorks 58 H5
Knebworth Herts 29 F9
Knedlington ER Yorks 52 G3
Kneesall Notts 45 F11
Kneesworth Cambs 29 D10
Kneeton Notts 45 H11
Knelston Swan 23 H9
Knenhall Staffs 34 B5
Knettishall Suffolk 38 G5
Knightacott Devon 6 C5
Knightcote Warwick 27 C10
Knightley Dale Staffs 34 C4
Knighton Devon 4 G6
Knighton Leics C 36 E1
Knighton Staffs 34 C3
Knighton Staffs 34 A3
Knighton = Tref-y-Clawdd Powys 25 A9
Knightswood C/Glasg 68 D4
Knightwick Worcs 26 C4
Knill Heref'd 25 B9
Knipton Leics 36 B4
Knitsley Durham 58 B2
Kniveton Derby 44 G6
Knock Arg/Bute 79 H8
Knock Cumb 57 D8
Knock Moray 88 C5
Knockally H'land 94 H3
Knockan H'land 92 H5
Knockandhu Moray 82 A4
Knockando Moray 88 D1
Knockando Ho. Moray 88 D2
Knockbain H'land 87 F9
Knockbreck H'land 84 B7
Knockbrex Dumf/Gal 55 E8
Knockdee H'land 94 D3
Knockdolian S Ayrs 66 H4
Knockenkelly N Ayrs 66 D3
Knockentiber E Ayrs 67 C6
Knockespock Ho. Aberds 83 A7
Knockfarrel H'land 87 F8
Knockglass Dumf/Gal 54 D3
Knockholt Kent 19 F11
Knockholt Pound Kent 19 F11
Knockie Lodge H'land 80 B6
Knockin Shrops 33 C9
Knockinlaw E Ayrs 67 C7
Knocklearn Dumf/Gal 60 F3
Knocknaha Arg/Bute 65 G7
Knocknain Dumf/Gal 54 C2
Knockrome Arg/Bute 72 F4
Knocksharry I/Man 48 D2
Knodishall Suffolk 31 B11
Knolls Green Ches 44 E2
Knolton Wrex 33 B9
Knolton Bryn Wrex 33 B9
Knook Wilts 16 G6
Knossington Leics 36 E4
Knott End-on-Sea Lancs 49 E3
Knotting Beds 29 B7
Knotting Green Beds 29 B7
Knottingley W Yorks 51 G11
Knotts Cumb 56 D6
Knotts Lancs 50 D3
Knotty Ash Mersey 43 C7
Knotty Green Bucks 18 B6
Knowbury Shrops 26 A2
Knowe Dumf/Gal 54 B6
Knowehead Dumf/Gal 67 G9
Knowes of Elrick Aberds 88 C6
Knowesgate Northum 62 E5
Knoweton N Lanarks 68 E6
Knowhead Aberds 89 C9
Knowl Hill Windsor 18 D5
Knowle Bristol 16 D3
Knowle Devon 7 F6
Knowle Devon 7 H9
Knowle Devon 6 C3
Knowle Shrops 26 A2
Knowle W Midlands 35 H7
Knowle Green Lancs 50 F2
Knowle Park W Yorks 51 E6
Knowlton Dorset 9 C9
Knowlton Kent 21 F9
Knowsley Mersey 43 C7
Knowstone Devon 7 D7
Knox Bridge Kent 13 B6
Knucklas Powys 25 A9
Knuston Northants 28 B6
Knutsford Ches 43 E10
Knutton Staffs 44 H2
Knypersley Staffs 44 G2
Kuggar Cornw'l 2 H6
Kyle of Lochalsh H'land 85 F12
Kyleakin H'land 85 F12
Kylerhea H'land 85 F12
Kylesknoydart H'land 79 B11
Kylesku H'land 92 F5
Kylesmorar H'land 79 B11
Kylestrome H'land 92 F5
Kyllachy House H'land 81 A9
Kynaston Shrops 33 C9
Kynnersley Telford 34 D2
Kyre Magna Worcs 26 B3

L

La Fontenelle Guernsey 11
La Planque Guernsey 11
Labost W Isles 91 C7
Lacasaidh W Isles 91 E8
Lacasdal W Isles 91 D9
Laceby NE Lincs 46 B6
Lacey Green Bucks 18 B5
Lach Dennis Ches 43 E10
Lackford Suffolk 30 A4
Lacock Wilts 16 E6
Ladbroke Warwick 27 C11
Laddingford Kent 20 G3
Lade Bank Lincs 47 G7
Ladock Cornw'l 3 D7
Lady Orkney 95 D7
Ladybank Fife 76 F6
Ladykirk Scot Borders 71 F7
Ladysford Aberds 89 B9
Laga H'land 79 E9
Lagalochan Arg/Bute 73 B7
Lagavulin Arg/Bute 64 D5
Lagg Arg/Bute 72 F4
Lagg N Ayrs 66 D2
Laggan Arg/Bute 64 C3
Laggan H'land 80 D4
Laggan H'land 81 D8
Laggan H'land 79 D10
Laggan S Ayrs 54 A5
Lagganulva Arg/Bute 78 G7
Laide H'land 91 H13
Laigh Fenwick E Ayrs 67 B7
Laigh Glengall S Ayrs 66 E6
Laighmuir E Ayrs 67 B7
Laindon Essex 20 C3
Lair H'land 86 G3
Lairg H'land 93 J8
Lairg Lodge H'land 93 J8
Lairg Muir H'land 93 J8
Lairgmore H'land 87 H8
Laisterdyke W Yorks 51 F7
Laithes Cumb 56 C6
Lake I/Wight 10 F4
Lake Wilts 17 H8
Lakenham Norfolk 39 E8
Lakenheath Suffolk 38 G3
Lakesend Norfolk 37 F11
Lakeside Cumb 56 H5
Laleham Surrey 19 E7
Laleston Bridg 14 D4
Lamarsh Essex 30 E5
Lamas Norfolk 39 C8
Lambden Scot Borders 70 F6
Lamberhurst Kent 12 C5
Lamberhurst Quarter Kent 12 C5
Lamberton Scot Borders 71 E8
Lambeth London 19 D10
Lambhill C/Glasg 68 D4
Lambley Notts 45 H10
Lambley Northum 62 H2
Lamborough Hill Oxon 17 A11
Lambourn W Berks 17 D10
Lambourne End Essex 19 B11
Lambs Green W Sussex 19 H9
Lambston Pembs 22 E4
Lambton Tyne/Wear 58 A3
Lamerton Devon 4 D5
Lamesley Tyne/Wear 63 H8
Laminess Orkney 95 E7
Lamington H'land 87 D10
Lamington S Lanarks 69 G8
Lamlash N Ayrs 66 C3
Lamloch Dumf/Gal 67 G8
Lamonby Cumb 56 C6
Lamorna Cornw'l 2 G3
Lamorran Cornw'l 3 E7
Lampardbrook Suffolk 31 B9
Lampeter = Llandebr Pont Steffan Ceredig'n 23 B10
Lampeter Velfrey Pembs 22 E6
Lamphey Pembs 22 F5
Lamplugh Cumb 56 D2
Lamport Northants 28 A4
Lamyatt Som'set 16 H3
Lana Devon 6 G2
Lanark S Lanarks 69 F7
Lancaster Lancs 49 C4
Lanchester Durham 58 B2
Lancing W Sussex 11 D10
Landbeach Cambs 29 B11
Landcross Devon 6 D3
Landerberry Aberds 83 C9
Landford Wilts 10 C1
Landford Manor Wilts 10 B1
Landimore Swan 23 G9
Landkey Devon 6 C4
Landore Swan 14 B2
Landrake Cornw'l 4 E4
Landscove Devon 5 E8
Landshipping Pembs 22 E5
Landshipping Quay Pembs 22 E5
Landulph Cornw'l 4 E5
Landwade Suffolk 30 B3
Lane Cornw'l 3 C7
Lane End Bucks 18 B5
Lane End Cumb 56 G3
Lane End Dorset 9 E7
Lane End Hants 10 B4
Lane End I/Wight 10 F5
Lane End Lancs 50 E4
Lane Ends Lancs 50 F3
Lane Ends Lancs 50 D3
Lane Ends N Yorks 50 E5
Lane Head Derby 44 E5
Lane Head Durham 58 E2
Lane Head Gtr Man 43 C9
Lane Head W Yorks 44 B5
Lane Side Lancs 50 G3
Laneast Cornw'l 4 C3
Laneham Notts 46 E2
Lanehead Durham 57 B10
Lanehead Northum 62 E3
Lanercost Cumb 61 G11
Laneshaw Bridge Lancs 50 E5
Lanfach Caerph 15 B8
Langar Notts 36 B3
Langbank Renf 68 C2
Langbar N Yorks 51 D6
Langburnshiels Scot Borders 61 C11
Langcliffe N Yorks 50 C4
Langdale H'land 93 E9
Langdale End N Yorks 59 G10
Langdon Cornw'l 4 C4
Langdon Beck Durham 57 C10
Langdon Hills Essex 20 C3
Langdyke Fife 76 G6
Langenhoe Essex 31 G7
Langford Beds 29 D8
Langford Devon 7 F9
Langford Essex 30 H5
Langford Notts 46 G2
Langford Oxon 17 A9
Langford Budville Som'set 7 D10
Langham Essex 31 E7
Langham Norfolk 38 A6
Langham Rutl'd 36 D4
Langham Suffolk 30 B6
Langhaugh Scot Borders 69 G11
Langho Lancs 50 F3
Langholm Dumf/Gal 61 E9
Langleeford Northum 62 A5
Langley Ches 44 E3
Langley Hants 10 D3
Langley Herts 29 F9
Langley Kent 20 F5
Langley Northum 62 G4
Langley Slough 19 D7
Langley Warwick 27 B8
Langley W Sussex 11 B7
Langley Burrell Wilts 16 D6
Langley Common Derby 35 B8
Langley Heath Kent 20 F5
Langley Lower Green Essex 29 E11
Langley Marsh Som'set 7 D9
Langley Park Durham 58 B3
Langley Street Norfolk 39 E9
Langley Upper Green Essex 29 E11
Langney E Sussex 12 F5
Langold Notts 45 D9
Langore Cornw'l 4 C4
Langport Som'set 8 B3
Langrick Lincs 46 H6
Langridge Bath/NE Som'set 16 E4
Langridge Ford Devon 6 D4
Langrigg Cumb 56 B3
Langrish Hants 10 B6
Langsett S Yorks 44 B6
Langshaw Scot Borders 70 G4
Langside Perth/Kinr 75 F10
Langskaill Orkney 95 D5
Langstone Hants 10 D6
Langstone Newp 15 B9
Langthorne N Yorks 58 G3
Langthorpe N Yorks 51 C9
Langthwaite N Yorks 58 F1
Langtoft ER Yorks 52 C6
Langtoft Lincs 37 D7
Langton Durham 58 E2
Langton Lincs 46 F6
Langton Lincs 47 E7
Langton N Yorks 52 C3
Langton by Wragby Lincs 46 E5
Langton Green Kent 12 C4
Langton Green Suffolk 31 A8
Langton Herring Dorset 8 F5
Langton Matravers Dorset 9 G9
Langtree Devon 6 E3
Langwathby Cumb 57 C7
Langwell Ho. H'land 94 H3
Langwell Lodge H'land 92 J4
Langwith Derby 45 F9
Langwith Junction Derby 45 F9
Langworth Lincs 46 E4
Lanivet Cornw'l 3 C9
Lanlivery Cornw'l 4 F1
Lanner Cornw'l 2 F6
Lanreath Cornw'l 4 F2
Lansallos Cornw'l 4 F2
Lansdown Glos 26 F6
Lanteglos Highway Cornw'l 4 F2
Lanton Scot Borders 62 A2
Lanton Northum 71 G8
Lapford Devon 7 F6
Laphroaig Arg/Bute 64 D4
Lapley Staffs 34 D4
Lapworth Warwick 27 A8
Larachbeg H'land 79 G9
Larbert Falk 69 B7
Larden Green Ches 43 G8
Largie Aberds 88 E6
Largiemore Arg/Bute 73 E8
Largoward Fife 77 G7
Largs N Ayrs 73 H11
Largybeg N Ayrs 66 D3
Largymore N Ayrs 66 D3
Larkfield Invercl 73 F11
Larkhall S Lanarks 68 E6
Larkhill Wilts 17 G8
Larling Norfolk 38 G5
Larriston Scot Borders 61 D11
Lartington Durham 58 E1
Lary Aberds 82 C5
Lasham Hants 18 G3
Lashenden Kent 13 B7
Lassington Glos 26 F4
Lassodie Fife 69 A10
Lastingham N Yorks 59 G8
Latcham Som'set 15 G10
Latchford Herts 29 F10
Latchford Warrington 43 D9
Latchingdon Essex 20 A5
Latchley Cornw'l 4 D5
Lately Common Warrington 43 C9
Lathbury M/Keynes 28 D5
Latheron H'land 94 G3
Latheronwheel H'land 94 G3
Latheronwheel Ho. H'land 94 G3
Lathones Fife 77 G7
Latimer Bucks 19 B7
Latteridge S Gloucs 16 C3
Lattiford Som'set 8 B5
Latton Wilts 17 B7
Latton Bush Essex 29 H11
Lauchintilly Aberds 83 B9
Lauder Scot Borders 70 F4
Laugharne Carms 23 E8
Laughterton Lincs 46 E2
Laughton E Sussex 12 E4
Laughton Leics 36 G2
Laughton Lincs 37 B6
Laughton Lincs 46 C2
Laughton Common S Yorks 45 D9
Laughton en le Morthen S Yorks 45 D9
Launcells Cornw'l 6 F1
Launceston Cornw'l 4 C4
Launton Oxon 28 F3
Laurencekirk Aberds 83 F9
Laurieston Dumf/Gal 55 C9
Laurieston Falk 69 C8
Lavendon M/Keynes 28 C6
Lavenham Suffolk 30 D6
Laverhay Dumf/Gal 61 D7
Laversdale Cumb 61 G10
Laverstock Wilts 9 A10
Laverstoke Hants 17 G11
Laverton Glos 27 E7
Laverton N Yorks 51 B8
Laverton Som'set 16 F4
Lavister Wrex 42 G6
Law S Lanarks 69 E7
Lawers Perth/Kinr 75 D9
Lawers Perth/Kinr 75 E10
Lawford Essex 31 E7
Lawhitton Cornw'l 4 C4
Lawkland N Yorks 50 C3
Lawley Telford 34 E2
Lawnhead Staffs 34 C4
Lawrenny Pembs 22 F5
Lawshall Suffolk 30 C5
Lawton Heref'd 25 C11
Laxey I/Man 48 D4
Laxfield Suffolk 31 A9
Laxfirth Shetl'd 96 J6
Laxfirth Shetl'd 96 H6
Laxford Bridge H'land 92 E5
Laxo Shetl'd 96 G6
Laxobigging Shetl'd 96 F6
Laxton ER Yorks 52 G3
Laxton Notts 45 F11
Laxton Northants 36 F5
Laycock W Yorks 50 E6
Layer Breton Essex 30 G6
Layer de la Haye Essex 30 G6
Layer Marney Essex 30 G6
Layham Suffolk 31 D7
Laylands Green W Berks 17 E10
Laytham ER Yorks 52 F3
Layton Blackp'l 49 F3
Lazenby Redcar/Clevel'd 59 D6
Lazonby Cumb 57 C7
Le Planel Guernsey 11
Le Villocq Guernsey 11
Lea Derby 45 G7
Lea Heref'd 26 F3
Lea Lincs 46 D2
Lea Shrops 33 G9
Lea Shrops 33 E10
Lea Wilts 16 C6
Lea Marston Warwick 35 F8
Lea Town Lancs 49 F4
Leabrooks Derby 45 G8
Leac a Li W Isles 90 H6
Leachkin H'land 87 G9
Leadburn Midloth 69 E11
Leaden Roding Essex 30 G2
Leadenham Lincs 46 G3
Leadgate Cumb 57 B9
Leadgate Durham 58 A2
Leadgate Northum 63 H7
Leadhills S Lanarks 60 B4
Leafield Oxon 27 G10
Leagrave Luton 29 F7
Leake N Yorks 58 G5
Leake Commonside Lincs 47 G7
Lealholm N Yorks 59 F8
Lealt Arg/Bute 72 D5
Lealt H'land 85 B10
Leamington Hastings Warwick 27 B11
Leamonsley Staffs 35 E7
Leamside Durham 58 B4
Leanaig H'land 87 F8
Leargybreck Arg/Bute 72 F4
Leasgill Cumb 49 A4
Leasingham Lincs 46 H4
Leasingthorne Durham 58 D3
Leasowe Mersey 42 C5
Leatherhead Surrey 19 F8
Leatherhead Common Surrey 19 F8
Leathley N Yorks 51 E8
Leaton Shrops 33 D10
Leaveland Kent 21 F7
Leavening N Yorks 52 C3
Leaves Green London 19 E11
Leazes Durham 63 H7
Lebberston N Yorks 53 A6
Lechlade-on-Thames Glos 17 B9
Leck Lancs 50 B2
Leckford Hants 17 H10
Leckfurin H'land 93 D10
Leckgruinart Arg/Bute 64 B3
Leckhampstead Bucks 28 E4
Leckhampstead W Berks 17 D11
Leckhampstead Thicket W Berks 17 D11
Leckhampton Glos 26 G6
Leckie H'land 86 E3
Leckmelm H'land 86 B4
Leckwith V/Glam 15 D7
Leconfield ER Yorks 52 E6
Ledaig Arg/Bute 74 D2
Ledburn Bucks 28 F6
Ledbury Heref'd 26 E4
Ledcharrie Stirl 75 E8
Ledgemoor Heref'd 25 C11
Ledicot Heref'd 25 B11
Ledmore H'land 92 H5
Lednagullin H'land 93 C10
Ledsham Ches 42 E6
Ledsham W Yorks 51 G10
Ledston W Yorks 51 G10
Ledston Luck W Yorks 51 F10
Ledwell Oxon 27 F11
Lee Arg/Bute 78 J7
Lee Devon 6 B3
Lee Hants 10 C2
Lee Lancs 50 D1
Lee Shrops 33 B10
Lee Brockhurst Shrops 33 C11
Lee Clump Bucks 18 A6
Lee Mill Devon 5 F7
Lee Moor Devon 5 E6
Lee-on-the-Solent Hants 10 D4
Leeans Shetl'd 96 J5
Leebotten Shetl'd 96 L6
Leebotwood Shrops 33 F10
Leece Cumb 49 C2
Leechpool Pembs 22 E4
Leeds Kent 20 F5
Leeds W Yorks 51 F8
Leedstown Cornw'l 2 F5
Leek Staffs 44 G3
Leek Wootton Warwick 27 B9
Leekbrook Staffs 44 G3
Leeming N Yorks 58 H3
Leeming Bar N Yorks 58 G3
Lees Derby 35 B8
Lees Gtr Man 44 B3
Lees W Yorks 50 F6
Leeswood Flints 42 F5
Legbourne Lincs 47 D7
Legerwood Scot Borders 70 F4
Legsby Lincs 46 D5
Leicester Leics C 36 E1
Leicester Forest East Leics 35 E11
Leigh Dorset 8 D5
Leigh Glos 26 F5
Leigh Gtr Man 43 B9
Leigh Kent 20 G2
Leigh Shrops 33 E9
Leigh Surrey 19 G9
Leigh Wilts 17 B7
Leigh Worcs 26 C4
Leigh Beck Essex 20 C5
Leigh Common Som'set 8 B6
Leigh Delamere Wilts 16 D5
Leigh Green Kent 13 C8
Leigh on Sea Southend 20 C5
Leigh Park Hants 10 D6
Leigh Sinton Worcs 26 C4
Leigh upon Mendip Som'set 16 G3
Leigh Woods N Som'set 16 D2
Leighswood W Midlands 35 E6
Leighterton Glos 16 B5
Leighton N Yorks 51 B7
Leighton Powys 33 E8
Leighton Shrops 34 E2
Leighton Som'set 16 G4
Leighton Bromswold Cambs 37 H7
Leighton Buzzard Beds 28 F6
Leinthall Earls Heref'd 25 B11
Leinthall Starkes Heref'd 25 B11
Leintwardine Heref'd 25 A11
Leire Leics 35 F11
Leirinmore H'land 92 C7
Leiston Suffolk 31 B11
Leitfie Perth/Kinr 76 C5
Leith C/Edinb 69 C11
Leitholm Scot Borders 70 F6
Lelant Cornw'l 2 F4
Lelley ER Yorks 53 F8
Lem Hill Worcs 26 A4
Lemmington Hall Northum 63 B7
Lempitlaw Scot Borders 70 G6
Lenchwick Worcs 27 D7
Lendalfoot S Ayrs 66 H4
Lendrick Lodge Stirl 75 G8
Lenham Kent 20 F5
Lenham Heath Kent 20 G6
Lennel Scot Borders 71 F7
Lennoxtown E Dunb 68 C5
Lenton Lincs 36 B6
Lenton Nott'ham 36 B1
Lentran H'land 87 G8
Lenwade Norfolk 39 D6
Leny Ho. Stirl 75 G9
Lenzie E Dunb 68 C5
Leoch Angus 76 D6
Leochel-Cushnie Aberds 83 B7
Leominster Heref'd 25 C11
Leonard Stanley Glos 16 A5
Leorin Arg/Bute 64 D4
Lepe Hants 10 E3
Lephin H'land 84 D6
Lephinchapel Arg/Bute 73 D8
Lephinmore Arg/Bute 73 D8
Leppington N Yorks 52 C3
Lepton W Yorks 51 H8
Lerryn Cornw'l 4 F2
Lerwick Shetl'd 96 J6
Lesbury Northum 63 B8
Leslie Aberds 83 A7
Leslie Fife 76 G5
Lesmahagow S Lanarks 69 G7
Lesnewth Cornw'l 4 B2
Lessendrum Aberds 88 D5
Lessingham Norfolk 39 C9
Lessonhall Cumb 56 A4
Leswalt Dumf/Gal 54 C3
Letchmore Heath Herts 19 B8
Letchworth Herts 29 E9
Letcombe Bassett Oxon 17 C10
Letcombe Regis Oxon 17 C10
Letham Angus 77 C8
Letham Falk 69 B7
Letham Fife 76 F6
Letham Perth/Kinr 76 E3
Letham Grange Angus 77 C9
Lethenty Aberds 89 D8
Letheringham Suffolk 31 C9
Letheringsett Norfolk 39 B6
Lettaford Devon 5 C8
Lettan Orkney 95 D8
Letterewe H'land 86 D2
Letterfearn H'land 85 F13
Letterfinlay H'land 80 D4
Lettermorar H'land 79 C10
Lettermore Arg/Bute 78 G7
Letters H'land 86 C4
Letterston Pembs 22 D4
Lettoch H'land 82 B2
Lettoch H'land 87 H13
Letton Heref'd 25 D10
Letton Heref'd 25 A10
Letton Green Norfolk 38 E5
Letty Green Herts 29 G9
Letwell S Yorks 45 D9
Leuchars Fife 77 E7
Leuchars Ho. Moray 88 B2
Leumrabhagh W Isles 91 F8
Levan Invercl 73 F11
Levaneap Shetl'd 96 G6
Levedale Staffs 34 D4
Leven ER Yorks 53 E7
Leven Fife 76 G6
Levencorroch N Ayrs 66 D3
Levens Cumb 57 H6
Levens Green Herts 29 F10
Levenshulme Gtr Man 44 C2
Levenwick Shetl'd 96 L6
Leverburgh = An t-Ob W Isles 90 J5
Leverington Cambs 37 D10
Leverton Lincs 47 H8
Leverton Highgate Lincs 47 H8
Leverton Lucasgate Lincs 47 H8
Leverton Outgate Lincs 47 H8
Levington Suffolk 31 E9
Levisham N Yorks 59 G9
Levishie H'land 80 B6
Lew Oxon 27 H10
Lewannick Cornw'l 4 C3
Lewdown Devon 4 C5
Lewes E Sussex 12 E3
Leweston Pembs 22 D4
Lewisham London 19 D10
Lewiston H'land 81 A7
Lewistown Bridg 14 C5
Lewknor Oxon 18 B4
Leworthy Devon 6 F2
Leworthy Devon 6 C5
Lewtrenchard Devon 4 C5
Lexden Essex 30 F6
Ley Aberds 83 B7
Ley Cornw'l 4 E2
Leybourne Kent 20 F3
Leyburn N Yorks 58 G2
Leyfields Staffs 35 E8
Leyhill Bucks 18 A6
Leyland Lancs 49 G5
Leylodge Aberds 83 B9
Leymoor W Yorks 51 H7
Leys Aberds 89 C10
Leys Perth/Kinr 76 D5
Leys Castle H'land 87 G9
Leys of Cossans Angus 76 C6
Leysdown-on-Sea Kent 21 D7
Leysmill Angus 77 C9
Leysters Pole Heref'd 26 B2
Leyton London 19 C10
Leytonstone London 19 C10
Lezant Cornw'l 4 D4
Leziate Norfolk 38 D2
Lhanbryde Moray 88 B2
Liatrie H'land 86 H5
Libanus Powys 24 F6
Libberton S Lanarks 69 F8
Liberton C/Edinb 69 D11
Liceasto W Isles 90 H6
Lichfield Staffs 35 E7
Lickey Worcs 34 H5
Lickey End Worcs 26 A6
Lickfold W Sussex 11 B8
Liddel Orkney 95 K5
Liddesdale H'land 79 F10
Liddington Swindon 17 C9
Lidgate Suffolk 30 C4
Lidget S Yorks 45 B10
Lidget Green W Yorks 51 F7
Lidgett Notts 45 F10
Lidlington Beds 28 E6
Lidstone Oxon 27 F10
Lieurary H'land 94 D2
Liff Angus 76 D6
Lifton Devon 4 C4
Liftondown Devon 4 C4
Lighthorne Warwick 27 C10
Lightwater Surrey 18 E6
Lightwood Stoke 34 A5
Lightwood Green Ches 34 A2
Lightwood Green Wrex 33 A9
Lilbourne Northants 36 H1
Lilburn Tower Northum 62 A6
Lilleshall Telford 34 D3
Lilley Herts 29 F8
Lilley W Berks 17 D11
Lilliesleaf Scot Borders 61 A11
Lillingstone Dayrell Bucks 28 E4
Lillingstone Lovell Bucks 28 D4
Lillington Dorset 8 C5
Lillington Warwick 27 B10
Lilliput Poole 9 E9
Lilstock Som'set 7 B10
Lilyhurst Shrops 34 D3
Limbury Luton 29 F7
Limebrook Heref'd 25 B10
Limefield Gtr Man 44 A2
Limekilnburn S Lanarks 68 E6
Limekilns Fife 69 B9
Limerigg Falk 69 C7
Limerstone I/Wight 10 F3
Limington Som'set 8 B4
Limpenhoe Norfolk 39 E9
Limpley Stoke Wilts 16 E4
Limpsfield Surrey 19 F11
Limpsfield Chart Surrey 19 F11
Linby Notts 45 G9
Linchmere W Sussex 11 A7
Lincluden Dumf/Gal 60 F5
Lincoln Lincs 46 E3
Lincomb Worcs 26 B5
Lincombe Devon 5 F8
Lindal in Furness Cumb 49 B2
Lindale Cumb 49 A4
Lindean Scot Borders 70 G3
Lindfield W Sussex 12 D2
Lindford Hants 18 H5
Lindifferon Fife 76 F6
Lindley W Yorks 51 H7
Lindley Green N Yorks 51 E8
Lindores Fife 76 F5
Lindridge Worcs 26 B3
Lindsell Essex 30 F3
Lindsey Suffolk 30 D6
Linford Hants 9 D10
Linford Thurr'k 20 D3
Lingague I/Man 48 E2
Lingards Wood W Yorks 44 A4
Lingbob W Yorks 51 F6
Lingdale Redcar/Clevel'd 59 E7
Lingen Heref'd 25 B10
Lingfield Surrey 12 B2
Lingreabhagh W Isles 90 J5
Lingwood Norfolk 39 E9
Linicro H'land 85 B8
Linkenholt Hants 17 F10
Linkhill Kent 13 D7
Linkinhorne Cornw'l 4 D4
Linklater Orkney 95 K5
Linksness Orkney 95 H3
Linktown Fife 69 A11
Linley Shrops 33 F9
Linley Green Heref'd 26 C3
Linlithgow W Loth 69 C9
Linlithgow Bridge W Loth 69 C8
Linshiels Northum 62 C4
Linsiadar W Isles 90 D7
Linsidemore H'land 87 B8
Linslade Beds 28 F6
Linstead Parva Suffolk 39 H9
Linstock Cumb 61 H10
Linthwaite W Yorks 44 A5
Lintlaw Scot Borders 71 E7
Lintmill Moray 88 B5
Linton Scot Borders 70 H6
Linton Cambs 30 D2
Linton Derby 35 D8
Linton Heref'd 26 F3
Linton Kent 20 G4
Linton Northum 63 D8
Linton N Yorks 50 C5
Linton W Yorks 51 E9
Linton-on-Ouse N Yorks 51 C10
Linwood Hants 9 D10
Linwood Lincs 46 D5
Linwood Renf 68 D3
Lionacleit W Isles 84 D2
Lional W Isles 91 A10
Liphook Hants 11 A7
Liscard Mersey 42 C6
Liscombe Som'set 7 C7
Liskeard Cornw'l 4 E3
L'Islet Guernsey 11
Liss Hants 11 B6
Liss Forest Hants 11 B6
Lissett ER Yorks 53 D7
Lissington Lincs 46 D5
Lisvane Card 15 C7
Liswerry Newp 15 C9
Litcham Norfolk 38 D4
Litchborough Northants 28 C3
Litchfield Hants 17 F11
Litherland Mersey 42 C6
Litlington Cambs 29 D10
Litlington E Sussex 12 F4
Little Abington Cambs 30 D2
Little Addington Northants 28 A6
Little Alne Warwick 27 B8
Little Altcar Mersey 42 B6
Little Asby Cumb 57 F8
Little Assynt H'land 92 G4
Little Aston Staffs 35 E6
Little Atherfield I/Wight 10 F3
Little Ayre Orkney 95 J4
Little-ayre Shetl'd 96 G5
Little Ayton N Yorks 59 E6
Little Baddow Essex 30 H4
Little Badminton S Gloucs 16 C5
Little Ballinluig Perth/Kinr 76 B2
Little Bampton Cumb 61 H8
Little Bardfield Essex 30 E3
Little Barford Beds 29 C8
Little Barningham Norfolk 39 B7
Little Barrington Glos 27 G9
Little Barrow Ches 43 E7
Little Barugh N Yorks 52 B3
Little Bavington Northum 62 F5
Little Bealings Suffolk 31 D9
Little Bedwyn Wilts 17 E9
Little Bentley Essex 31 F8
Little Berkhamsted Herts 29 H9
Little Billing Northants 28 B5
Little Birch Heref'd 26 E2
Little Blakenham Suffolk 31 D8
Little Blencow Cumb 56 C6
Little Bollington Ches 43 D10
Little Bookham Surrey 19 F8
Little Bowden Leics 36 G3
Little Bradley Suffolk 30 C3
Little Brampton Shrops 33 G9
Little Brechin Angus 77 A8
Little Brickhill M/Keynes 28 E6
Little Brington Northants 28 B3
Little Bromley Essex 31 F7
Little Broughton Cumb 56 C2
Little Budworth Ches 43 F8
Little Burstead Essex 20 B3
Little Bytham Lincs 36 D6
Little Carlton Lincs 47 D7
Little Carlton Notts 45 G11
Little Casterton Rutl'd 36 E6
Little Cawthorpe Lincs 47 D7
Little Chalfont Bucks 18 B6
Little Chart Kent 20 G6
Little Chesterford Essex 30 D2
Little Cheverell Wilts 16 F6
Little Chishill Cambs 29 E11
Little Clacton Essex 31 G8
Little Clifton Cumb 56 D2
Little Colp Aberds 89 D7
Little Comberton Worcs 26 D6
Little Common E Sussex 12 F6
Little Compton Warwick 27 E9
Little Cornard Suffolk 30 E5
Little Cowarne Heref'd 26 C3
Little Coxwell Oxon 17 B9
Little Crakehall N Yorks 58 G3
Little Cressingham Norfolk 38 E4
Little Crosby Mersey 42 B6
Little Dalby Leics 36 D3
Little Dawley Telford 34 E2
Little Dens Aberds 89 D10
Little Dewchurch Heref'd 26 E2
Little Downham Cambs 37 G11
Little Driffield ER Yorks 52 D6
Little Dunham Norfolk 38 D4
Little Dunkeld Perth/Kinr 76 C3
Little Dunmow Essex 30 F3
Little Easton Essex 30 F3
Little Eaton Derby 35 A9
Little Eccleston Lancs 49 E4
Little Ellingham Norfolk 38 F6
Little End Essex 20 A2
Little Eversden Cambs 29 C10
Little Fakenham Suffolk 38 H5
Little Faringdon Oxon 17 A9
Little Fencote N Yorks 58 G3
Little Fenton N Yorks 51 F11
Little Finborough Suffolk 31 C7
Little Fransham Norfolk 38 D5
Little Gaddesden Herts 28 G6
Little Gidding Cambs 37 G7
Little Glemham Suffolk 31 C10
Little Glenshee Perth/Kinr 76 D2
Little Gransden Cambs 29 C9
Little Green Som'set 16 G4
Little Grimsby Lincs 47 C7
Little Gruinard H'land 86 C2
Little Habton N Yorks 52 B3
Little Hadham Herts 29 F11
Little Hale Lincs 37 A7
Little Hallingbury Essex 29 G11
Little Hampden Bucks 18 A5
Little Harrowden Northants 28 A5
Little Haseley Oxon 18 A3
Little Hatfield ER Yorks 53 E7
Little Hautbois Norfolk 39 C8
Little Haven Pembs 22 E3
Little Hay Staffs 35 E7
Little Hayfield Derby 44 D4
Little Haywood Staffs 34 C6
Little Heath W Midlands 35 G9
Little Hereford Heref'd 26 B2
Little Horkesley Essex 30 E6
Little Horsted E Sussex 12 E3
Little Horton W Yorks 51 F7
Little Horwood Bucks 28 E4
Little Houghton Northants 28 C5
Little Houghton S Yorks 45 B8
Little Hucklow Derby 44 E5
Little Hulton Gtr Man 43 B10
Little Humber ER Yorks 53 G7
Little Hungerford W Berks 18 D2
Little Irchester Northants 28 B6
Little Kimble Bucks 28 H5
Little Kineton Warwick 27 C10
Little Kingshill Bucks 18 B5
Little Langdale Cumb 56 F5
Little Langford Wilts 17 H7
Little Laver Essex 30 H2
Little Leigh Ches 43 E9
Little Leighs Essex 30 G4
Little Lever Gtr Man 43 B10
Little London Bucks 28 G3
Little London E Sussex 12 E4
Little London Hants 17 G10
Little London Hants 18 F3
Little London Lincs 37 C8
Little London Lincs 37 C10
Little London Norfolk 39 C7
Little London Powys 32 G6
Little Longstone Derby 44 E5
Little Lynturk Aberds 83 B7
Little Malvern Worcs 26 D4
Little Maplestead Essex 30 E5
Little Marcle Heref'd 26 E3
Little Marlow Bucks 18 C5
Little Marsden Lancs 50 F4
Little Massingham Norfolk 38 C3
Little Melton Norfolk 39 E7
Little Mill Monmouths 15 A9
Little Milton Oxon 18 A3
Little Missenden Bucks 18 B6
Little Musgrave Cumb 57 E9
Little Ness Shrops 33 D10
Little Neston Ches 42 E5
Little Newcastle Pembs 22 D4
Little Newsham Durham 58 E2
Little Oakley Essex 31 F9
Little Oakley Northants 36 G4
Little Orton Cumb 61 H9
Little Ouseburn N Yorks 51 C10
Little Paxton Cambs 29 B8
Little Petherick Cornw'l 3 B8
Little Pitlurg Moray 88 D4
Little Plumpton Lancs 49 F3
Little Plumstead Norfolk 39 D9
Little Ponton Lincs 36 B5
Little Raveley Cambs 37 H8
Little Reedness ER Yorks 52 G4
Little Ribston N Yorks 51 D9
Little Rissington Glos 27 G8
Little Ryburgh Norfolk 38 C5
Little Ryle Northum 62 B6
Little Salkeld Cumb 57 C7
Little Sampford Essex 30 E3
Little Sandhurst Brackn'l 18 E5
Little Saxham Suffolk 30 B4
Little Scatwell H'land 86 F6
Little Sessay N Yorks 51 B10
Little Shelford Cambs 29 C11
Little Singleton Lancs 49 F3
Little Skillymarno Aberds 89 C9
Little Smeaton N Yorks 51 H11
Little Snoring Norfolk 38 B5
Little Sodbury S Gloucs 16 C4
Little Somborne Hants 10 A2
Little Somerford Wilts 16 C6
Little Stainforth N Yorks 50 C4
Little Stainton D'lington 58 D4
Little Stanney Ches 43 E7
Little Staughton Beds 29 B8
Little Steeping Lincs 47 F8
Little Stoke Staffs 34 B5
Little Stonham Suffolk 31 B8
Little Stretton Leics 36 E2
Little Stretton Shrops 33 F10
Little Strickland Cumb 57 E7
Little Stukeley Cambs 37 H8
Little Sutton Ches 42 E6
Little Tew Oxon 27 F10
Little Thetford Cambs 37 H11
Little Thirkleby N Yorks 51 B10
Little Thurlow Suffolk 30 C3
Little Thurrock Thurr'k 20 D3
Little Torboll H'land 87 B10
Little Torrington Devon 6 E3

Morton Lincs 37 C6
Morton Lincs 46 C2
Morton Lincs 46 F2
Morton Norfolk 39 D7
Morton Notts 45 G11
Morton Shrops 33 C8
Morton S Gloucs 16 B3
Morton Bagot Warwick 27 B8
Morton-on-Swale N Yorks 58 G4
Morvah Cornw'l 2 F3
Morval Cornw'l 4 F3
Morvich H'land 80 A1
Morvich H'land 93 J10
Morville Shrops 34 F2
Morville Heath Shrops 34 F2
Morwenstow Cornw'l 6 E1
Mosborough S Yorks 45 D8
Moscow E Ayrs 67 B7
Mosedale Cumb 56 C5
Moseley W Midlands 35 G6
Moseley W Midlands 34 F5
Moseley Worcs 26 C5
Moss Arg/Bute 78 G2
Moss H'land 79 E9
Moss S Yorks 45 A9
Moss Wrex 42 G6
Moss Bank Mersey 43 C8
Moss Edge Lancs 49 E4
Moss End Brackn'l 18 D5
Moss of Barmuckity Moray 88 B2
Moss Pit Staffs 34 C5
Moss-side H'land 87 F11
Moss Side Lancs 49 F3
Mossat Aberds 82 B6
Mossbank Shetl'd 96 F6
Mossbay Cumb 56 D1
Mossblown S Ayrs 67 D7
Mossbrow Gtr Man 43 D10
Mossburnford Scot Borders 62 B2
Mossdale Dumf/Gal 55 B9
Mossend N Lanarks 68 D6
Mosser Cumb 56 D3
Mossfield H'land 87 D9
Mossgiel E Ayrs 67 D7
Mosside Angus 77 B7
Mossley Ches 44 F2
Mossley Gtr Man 44 B3
Mossley Hill Mersey 43 D6
Mosstodloch Moray 88 C3
Mosston Angus 77 C8
Mossy Lea Lancs 43 A8
Mosterton Dorset 8 D3
Moston Gtr Man 44 B2
Moston Shrops 34 C1
Moston Green Ches 43 F10
Mostyn Flints 42 D4
Mostyn Quay Flints 42 D4
Motcombe Dorset 9 B7
Mothecombe Devon 5 G7
Motherby Cumb 56 D6
Motherwell N Lanarks 68 E6
Mottingham London 19 D11
Mottisfont Hants 10 B2
Mottistone I/Wight 10 F3
Mottram in Longdendale Gtr Man 44 C3
Mottram St Andrew Ches 44 E2
Mouilpied Guernsey 11
Mouldsworth Ches 43 E8
Moulin Perth/Kinr 76 B2
Moulsecoomb Brighton/Hove 12 F2
Moulsford Oxon 18 C2
Moulsoe M/Keynes 28 D6
Moulton Ches 43 F9
Moulton Lincs 37 C9
Moulton Northants 28 B4
Moulton N Yorks 58 F3
Moulton Suffolk 30 B3
Moulton V/Glam 14 D6
Moulton Chapel Lincs 37 D8
Moulton Eaugate Lincs 37 D9
Moulton St Mary Norfolk 39 E9
Moulton Seas End Lincs 37 C9
Mounie Castle Aberds 83 A9
Mount Cornw'l 3 D6
Mount Cornw'l 4 E2
Mount H'land 87 G12
Mount Bures Essex 30 E6
Mount Canisp H'land 87 D10
Mount Hawke Cornw'l 2 E6
Mount Pleasant Ches 44 G2
Mount Pleasant Derby 45 H7
Mount Pleasant Derby 35 D8
Mount Pleasant Flints 42 E5
Mount Pleasant Hants 10 E1
Mount Pleasant W Yorks 51 G8
Mount Sorrel Wilts 9 B9
Mount Tabor W Yorks 51 G6
Mountain W Yorks 51 F6
Mountain Ash = Aberpennar Rh Cyn Taff 14 B6
Mountain Cross Scot Borders 69 F10
Mountain Water Pembs 22 D4
Mountbenger Scot Borders 70 H2
Mountfield E Sussex 12 D6
Mountgerald H'land 87 E8
Mountjoy Cornw'l 3 C7
Mountnessing Essex 20 B3
Mounton Monmouths 15 B11
Mountsorrel Leics 36 D1
Mousehole Cornw'l 2 G3
Mousen Northum 71 G10
Mouswald Dumf/Gal 60 F6
Mow Cop Ches 44 G2
Mowhaugh Scot Borders 62 A4
Mowsley Leics 36 G2
Moxley W Midlands 34 F5
Moy H'land 80 E6
Moy H'land 87 H10
Moy Hall H'land 87 H10
Moy Ho. Moray 87 E13
Moy Lodge H'land 80 E6
Moyles Court Hants 9 D10
Moylgrove Pembs 22 B6
Muasdale Arg/Bute 65 D7
Much Birch Heref'd 26 E2
Much Cowarne Heref'd 26 D3
Much Dewchurch Heref'd 25 E11
Much Hadham Herts 29 G11
Much Hoole Lancs 49 G4
Much Marcle Heref'd 26 E3
Much Wenlock Shrops 34 E2
Muchalls Aberds 83 D11
Muchelney Som'set 8 B3
Muchlarnick Cornw'l 4 F3
Muchrachd H'land 86 H5
Muckernich H'land 87 F8
Mucking Thurr'k 20 C3
Muckleford Dorset 8 E5
Mucklestone Staffs 34 B3
Muckleton Shrops 34 C1
Muckletown Aberds 83 A7
Muckley Corner Staffs 35 E6
Muckton Lincs 47 D7
Mudale H'land 93 F8
Muddiford Devon 6 C4
Mudeford Dorset 9 E10
Mudford Som'set 8 C4
Mudgley Som'set 15 G10
Mugdock Stirl 68 C4
Mugeary H'land 85 E9
Mugginton Derby 35 A8
Muggleswick Durham 58 B1
Muie H'land 93 J9
Muir Aberds 82 E2
Muir of Fairburn H'land 86 F7
Muir of Fowlis Aberds 83 B7
Muir of Ord H'land 87 F8
Muir of Pert Angus 77 D7
Muirden Aberds 89 C7
Muirdrum Angus 77 D8
Muirhead Angus 76 D6
Muirhead Fife 76 G5
Muirhead N Lanarks 68 D5
Muirhead S Ayrs 66 C6
Muirhouselaw Scot Borders 70 H5
Muirhouses Falk 69 B9
Muirkirk E Ayrs 68 H5
Muirmill Stirl 68 B6
Muirshearlich H'land 80 E3
Muirskie Aberds 83 D10
Muirtack Aberds 89 E9
Muirton H'land 87 E10
Muirton Perth/Kinr 76 E4
Muirton Perth/Kinr 76 F2
Muirton Mains H'land 86 F7
Muirton of Ardblair Perth/Kinr 76 C4
Muirton of Ballochy Angus 77 A9
Muiryfold Aberds 89 C7
Muker N Yorks 57 G11
Mulbarton Norfolk 39 E7
Mulben Moray 88 C3
Mulindry Arg/Bute 64 C4
Mullardoch House H'land 86 H5
Mullion Cornw'l 2 H5
Mullion Cove Cornw'l 2 H5
Mumby Lincs 47 E9
Munderfield Row Heref'd 26 C3
Munderfield Stocks Heref'd 26 C3
Mundesley Norfolk 39 B9
Mundford Norfolk 38 F4
Mundham Norfolk 39 F9
Mundon Essex 20 A5
Mundurno Aberd C 83 B11
Munerigie H'land 80 C4
Muness Shetl'd 96 C8
Mungasdale H'land 86 B2
Mungrisdale Cumb 56 C5
Munlochy H'land 87 F9
Munsley Heref'd 26 D3
Munslow Shrops 33 G11
Murchington Devon 5 C7
Murcott Oxon 28 G2
Murkle H'land 94 D3
Murlaggan H'land 80 D2
Murlaggan H'land 80 E5
Murra Orkney 95 H3
Murrayfield C/Edinb 69 C11
Murrow Cambs 37 E9
Mursley Bucks 28 F5
Murthill Angus 77 B7
Murthly Perth/Kinr 76 D3
Murton Cumb 57 D9
Murton Durham 58 B4
Murton Northum 71 F8
Murton C/York 52 D2
Musbury Devon 8 E1
Muscoates N Yorks 52 A2
Musdale Arg/Bute 74 E2
Musselburgh E Loth 70 C2
Muston Leics 36 B4
Muston N Yorks 53 B6
Mustow Green Worcs 26 A5
Mutehill Dumf/Gal 55 E9
Mutford Suffolk 39 G10
Muthill Perth/Kinr 75 F11
Mutterton Devon 7 F9
Muxton Telford 34 D3
Mybster H'land 94 E3
Myddfai Carms 24 F4
Myddle Shrops 33 C10
Mydroilyn Ceredig'n 23 A9
Myerscough Lancs 49 F4
Mylor Bridge Cornw'l 3 F7
Mynachlog-ddu Pembs 22 C6
Myndtown Shrops 33 G9
Mynydd Bach Ceredig'n 32 H3
Mynydd-bach Monmouths 15 B10
Mynydd Bodafon Angl 40 B6
Mynydd-isa Flints 42 F5
Mynyddygarreg Carms 23 F9
Mynytho Gwyn 40 G5
Myrebird Aberds 83 D9
Myrelandhorn H'land 94 E4
Myreside Perth/Kinr 76 E5
Myrtle Hill Carms 24 E4
Mytchett Surrey 18 F5
Mytholm W Yorks 50 G5
Mytholmroyd W Yorks 50 G6
Myton-on-Swale N Yorks 51 C10
Mytton Shrops 33 D10

N

Na Gearrannan W Isles 90 C6
Naast H'land 91 J13
Naburn C/York 52 E1
Nackington Kent 21 F8
Nacton Suffolk 31 D9
Nafferton ER Yorks 53 D6
Nailbridge Glos 26 G3
Nailsbourne Som'set 7 D11
Nailsea N Som'set 15 D10
Nailstone Leics 35 E10
Nailsworth Glos 16 B5
Nairn H'land 87 F11
Nalderswood Surrey 19 G9
Nancegollan Cornw'l 2 F5
Nancledra Cornw'l 2 F3
Nanhoron Gwyn 40 G4
Nannau Gwyn 32 C3
Nannerch Flints 42 F4
Nanpantan Leics 35 D11
Nanpean Cornw'l 3 D8
Nanstallon Cornw'l 3 C9
Nant-ddu Powys 25 G7
Nant-glas Powys 24 B6
Nant Peris Gwyn 41 E8
Nant Uchaf Denbs 42 G3
Nant-y-Bai Carms 24 D4
Nant-y-cafn Neath P Talb 24 H5
Nant-y-derry Monmouths 25 H10
Nant-y-ffin Carms 23 C10
Nant-y-moel Bridg 14 B5
Nant-y-pandy Conwy 41 C8
Nanternis Ceredig'n 23 A8
Nantgaredig Carms 23 D9
Nantgarw Rh Cyn Taff 15 C7
Nantglyn Denbs 42 F3
Nantgwyn Powys 32 H5
Nantlle Gwyn 41 E7
Nantmawr Shrops 33 C8
Nantmel Powys 25 B7
Nantmor Gwyn 41 F8
Nantwich Ches 43 G9
Nantycaws Carms 23 E9
Nantyffyllon Bridg 14 B4
Nantyglo Bl Gwent 25 G8
Naphill Bucks 18 B5
Nappa N Yorks 50 D4
Napton on the Hill Warwick 27 B11
Narberth = Arberth Pembs 22 E6
Narborough Leics 35 F11
Narborough Norfolk 38 D3
Nasareth Gwyn 40 E6
Naseby Northants 36 H2
Nash Bucks 28 E4
Nash Heref'd 25 B10
Nash Newp 15 C9
Nash Shrops 26 A2
Nash Lee Bucks 28 H5
Nassington Northants 37 F6
Nasty Herts 29 F10
Nateby Cumb 57 F9
Nateby Lancs 49 E4
Natland Cumb 57 H7
Naughton Suffolk 31 D7
Naunton Glos 27 F8
Naunton Worcs 26 E5
Naunton Beauchamp Worcs 26 C6
Navenby Lincs 46 G3
Navestock Heath Essex 20 B2
Navestock Side Essex 20 B2
Navidale H'land 93 H13
Nawton N Yorks 52 A2
Nayland Suffolk 30 E6
Nazeing Essex 29 H11
Neacroft Hants 9 E10
Neal's Green Warwick 35 G9
Neap Shetl'd 96 H7
Near Sawrey Cumb 56 G5
Neasham D'lington 58 E4
Neath = Castell-Nedd Neath P Talb 14 B3
Neath Abbey Neath P Talb 14 B3
Neatishead Norfolk 39 C9
Nebo Angl 40 A6
Nebo Ceredig'n 24 B2
Nebo Conwy 41 E10
Nebo Gwyn 40 E6
Necton Norfolk 38 E4
Nedd H'land 92 F4
Nedderton Northum 63 E8
Nedging Tye Suffolk 31 D7
Needham Norfolk 39 G8
Needham Market Suffolk 31 C7
Needingworth Cambs 29 A10
Needwood Staffs 35 C7
Neen Savage Shrops 34 H2
Neen Sollars Shrops 26 A3
Neenton Shrops 34 G2
Nefyn Gwyn 40 F5
Neilston E Renf 68 E3
Neinthirion Powys 32 E5
Neithrop Oxon 27 D11
Nelly Andrews Green Powys 33 E8
Nelson Caerph 15 B7
Nelson Lancs 50 F4
Nelson Village Northum 63 F8
Nemphlar S Lanarks 69 F7
Nempnett Thrubwell Bath/NE Som'set 15 E11
Nene Terrace Lincs 37 E8
Nenthall Cumb 57 B9
Nenthead Cumb 57 B9
Nenthorn Scot Borders 70 G5
Nerabus Arg/Bute 64 C3
Nercwys Flints 42 F5
Nerston S Lanarks 68 E5
Nesbit Northum 71 G8
Ness Ches 42 E6
Nesscliffe Shrops 33 D9
Neston Ches 42 E5
Neston Wilts 16 E5
Nether Alderley Ches 44 E2
Nether Blainslie Scot Borders 70 F4
Nether Booth Derby 44 D5
Nether Broughton Leics 36 C2
Nether Burrow Lancs 50 B2
Nether Cerne Dorset 8 E5
Nether Compton Dorset 8 C4
Nether Crimond Aberds 89 F8
Nether Dalgliesh Scot Borders 61 C8
Nether Dallachy Moray 88 B3
Nether Exe Devon 7 F8
Nether Glasslaw Aberds 89 C8
Nether Handwick Angus 76 C6
Nether Haugh S Yorks 45 C8
Nether Heage Derby 45 G7
Nether Heyford Northants 28 C4
Nether Hindhope Scot Borders 62 B3
Nether Howecleuch S Lanarks 60 B6
Nether Kellet Lancs 49 C5
Nether Kinmundy Aberds 89 D10
Nether Langwith Notts 45 E9
Nether Leask Aberds 89 E10
Nether Lenshie Aberds 89 D6
Nether Monynut Scot Borders 70 D6
Nether Padley Derby 44 E6
Nether Park Aberds 89 C10
Nether Poppleton C/York 52 D1
Nether Silton N Yorks 58 G5
Nether Stowey Som'set 7 C10
Nether Urquhart Fife 76 G4
Nether Wallop Hants 17 H10
Nether Wasdale Cumb 56 F3
Nether Whitacre Warwick 35 F8
Nether Worton Oxon 27 E11
Netheravon Wilts 17 G8
Netherbrae Aberds 89 C7
Netherbrough Orkney 95 G4
Netherburn S Lanarks 69 F7
Netherbury Dorset 8 E3
Netherby Cumb 61 F9
Netherby N Yorks 51 E9
Nethercote Warwick 28 B2
Nethercott Devon 6 C3
Netherend Glos 16 A2
Netherfield E Sussex 12 E6
Netherhampton Wilts 9 B10
Netherlaw Dumf/Gal 55 E10
Netherley Aberds 83 D10
Netherley Mersey 43 D7
Nethermill Dumf/Gal 60 E6
Nethermuir Aberds 89 D9
Netherplace E Renf 68 E4
Netherseal Derby 35 D8
Netherthird E Ayrs 67 E8
Netherthong W Yorks 44 B5
Netherthorpe S Yorks 45 D9
Netherton Angus 77 B8
Netherton Devon 5 D9
Netherton Hants 17 F10
Netherton Mersey 42 B6
Netherton Northum 62 C5
Netherton Oxon 17 B11
Netherton Perth/Kinr 76 B4
Netherton Stirl 68 C4
Netherton W Midlands 34 G5
Netherton Worcs 26 D6
Netherton W Yorks 44 A5
Netherton W Yorks 51 H8
Nethertown Cumb 56 F1
Nethertown H'land 94 C5
Netherwitton Northum 63 D7
Netherwood E Ayrs 68 H5
Nethy Bridge H'land 82 A2
Netley Hants 10 D3
Netley Marsh Hants 10 C2
Netteswell Essex 29 G11
Nettlebed Oxon 18 C4
Nettlebridge Som'set 16 G3
Nettlecombe Dorset 8 E4
Nettleden Herts 29 G7
Nettleham Lincs 46 E4
Nettlestead Kent 20 F3
Nettlestead Green Kent 20 F3
Nettlestone I/Wight 10 E5
Nettlesworth Durham 58 B3
Nettleton Lincs 46 B5
Nettleton Wilts 16 D5
Neuadd Carms 24 F3
Nevendon Essex 20 B4
Nevern Pembs 22 B5
New Abbey Dumf/Gal 60 G5
New Aberdour Aberds 89 B8
New Addington London 19 E10
New Alresford Hants 10 A4
New Alyth Perth/Kinr 76 C5
New Arley Warwick 35 G8
New Ash Green Kent 20 E3
New Barn Kent 20 E3
New Barnetby N Lincs 46 A4
New Barton Northants 28 B5
New Bewick Northum 62 A6
New-bigging Angus 76 C5
New Bilton Warwick 35 H10
New Bolingbroke Lincs 47 G7
New Boultham Lincs 46 E3
New Bradwell M/Keynes 28 D5
New Brancepeth Durham 58 B3
New Bridge Wrex 33 A8
New Brighton Flints 42 F5
New Brighton Mersey 42 C6
New Brinsley Notts 45 G8
New Broughton Wrex 42 G6
New Buckenham Norfolk 39 F6
New Byth Aberds 89 C8
New Catton Norfolk 39 D8
New Cheriton Hants 10 B4
New Costessey Norfolk 39 D7
New Cowper Cumb 56 B3
New Cross Ceredig'n 32 H2
New Cross London 19 D10
New Cumnock E Ayrs 67 E9
New Deer Aberds 89 D8
New Delaval Northum 63 F8
New Duston Northants 28 B4
New Earswick C/York 52 D2
New Edlington S Yorks 45 C9
New Elgin Moray 88 B2
New Ellerby ER Yorks 53 F7
New Eltham London 19 D11
New End Worcs 27 C7
New Farnley W Yorks 51 F8
New Ferry Mersey 42 D6
New Fryston W Yorks 51 G10
New Galloway Dumf/Gal 55 B9
New Gilston Fife 77 G7
New Grimsby I/Scilly 2 C2
New Hainford Norfolk 39 D8
New Hartley Northum 63 F9
New Haw Surrey 19 E7
New Hedges Pembs 22 F6
New Herrington Tyne/Wear 58 A4
New Hinksey Oxon 18 A2
New Holkham Norfolk 38 B4
New Holland N Lincs 53 G6
New Houghton Derby 45 F8
New Houghton Norfolk 38 C3
New Houses N Yorks 50 B4
New Humberstone Leics C 36 E2
New Hutton Cumb 57 G7
New Hythe Kent 20 F4
New Inn Carms 23 C9
New Inn Monmouths 15 A10
New Inn Torf 15 B9
New Invention Shrops 33 H8
New Invention W Midlands 34 E5
New Kelso H'land 86 G2
New Kingston Notts 35 C11
New Lanark S Lanarks 69 F7
New Lane Lancs 43 A7
New Lane End Warrington 43 C9
New Leake Lincs 47 G8
New Leeds Aberds 89 C9
New Longton Lancs 49 G5
New Luce Dumf/Gal 54 C4
New Malden London 19 E9
New Marske Redcar/Clevel'd 59 D7
New Marton Shrops 33 B9
New Micklefield W Yorks 51 F10
New Mill Aberds 83 E9
New Mill Herts 28 G6
New Mill Wilts 17 E8
New Mill W Yorks 44 B5
New Mills Ches 43 D10
New Mills Cornw'l 3 D7
New Mills Derby 44 D3
New Mills Powys 33 E6
New Milton Hants 9 E11
New Moat Pembs 22 D5
New Ollerton Notts 45 F10
New Oscott W Midlands 35 F6
New Park N Yorks 51 D8
New Pitsligo Aberds 89 C8
New Polzeath Cornw'l 3 B8
New Quay = Ceinewydd Ceredig'n 23 A8
New Rackheath Norfolk 39 D8
New Radnor Powys 25 B9
New Rent Cumb 56 C6
New Ridley Northum 62 H6
New Road Side N Yorks 50 E5
New Romney Kent 13 D9
New Rossington S Yorks 45 C10
New Row Ceredig'n 24 A4
New Row Lancs 50 F2
New Row N Yorks 59 E7
New Sarum Wilts 9 A10
New Silksworth Tyne/Wear 58 A4
New Stevenston N Lanarks 68 E6
New Street Staffs 44 G4
New Street Lane Shrops 34 B2
New Swanage Dorset 9 F9
New Totley S Yorks 45 E7
New Town E Loth 70 C3
New Tredegar = Tredegar Newydd Caerph 15 A7
New Trows S Lanarks 69 G7
New Ulva Arg/Bute 72 E6
New Walsoken Cambs 37 E10
New Waltham NE Lincs 46 B6
New Whittington Derby 45 E7
New Wimpole Cambs 29 D10
New Winton E Loth 70 C3
New Yatt Oxon 27 G10
New York Lincs 46 G6
New York N Yorks 51 C7
Newall W Yorks 51 E7
Newark Orkney 95 D8
Newark Peterbro 37 E8
Newark-on-Trent Notts 45 G11
Newarthill N Lanarks 68 E6
Newbarns Cumb 49 B2
Newbattle Midloth 70 D2
Newbiggin Cumb 56 G2
Newbiggin Cumb 49 C2
Newbiggin Cumb 56 D6
Newbiggin Cumb 57 B7
Newbiggin Cumb 57 D8
Newbiggin Durham 57 D11
Newbiggin N Yorks 57 G11
Newbiggin N Yorks 57 H11
Newbiggin-by-the-Sea Northum 63 E9
Newbiggin-on-Lune Cumb 57 F9
Newbigging Angus 77 D7
Newbigging Angus 77 D7
Newbigging S Lanarks 69 F9
Newbold Derby 45 E7
Newbold Leics 35 D10
Newbold on Avon Warwick 35 H10
Newbold on Stour Warwick 27 D9
Newbold Pacey Warwick 27 C9
Newbold Verdon Leics 35 E10
Newborough Angl 40 D6
Newborough Peterbro 37 E8
Newborough Staffs 35 C7
Newbottle Northants 28 E2
Newbottle Tyne/Wear 58 A4
Newbourne Suffolk 31 D9
Newbridge Caerph 15 B8
Newbridge Ceredig'n 23 A10
Newbridge Cornw'l 2 F3
Newbridge Cornw'l 4 E4
Newbridge Dumf/Gal 60 F5
Newbridge C/Edinb 69 C10
Newbridge Hants 10 C1
Newbridge I/Wight 10 F3
Newbridge Pembs 22 C4
Newbridge Green Worcs 26 E5
Newbridge-on-Usk Monmouths 15 B9
Newbridge on Wye Powys 25 C7
Newbrough Northum 62 G4
Newbuildings Devon 7 F6
Newburgh Aberds 89 F9
Newburgh Aberds 89 C9
Newburgh Scot Borders 61 B9
Newburgh Fife 76 F5
Newburgh Lancs 43 A7
Newburn Tyne/Wear 63 G7
Newbury W Berks 17 E11
Newbury Park London 19 C11
Newby Cumb 57 D7
Newby Lancs 50 E4
Newby N Yorks 50 B3
Newby N Yorks 58 E6
Newby N Yorks 59 G11
Newby Bridge Cumb 56 H5
Newby East Cumb 61 H10
Newby West Cumb 56 A5
Newby Wiske N Yorks 58 H4
Newcastle Monmouths 25 G11
Newcastle Shrops 33 G8
Newcastle Emlyn = Castell Newydd Emlyn Carms 23 B8
Newcastle-under-Lyme Staffs 44 H2
Newcastle Upon Tyne Tyne/Wear 63 G8
Newcastleton Scot Borders 61 E10
Newchapel Pembs 23 C7
Newchapel Powys 32 G5
Newchapel Staffs 44 G2
Newchapel Surrey 12 B2
Newchurch Carms 23 D8
Newchurch I/Wight 10 F4
Newchurch Kent 13 C9
Newchurch Lancs 50 F4
Newchurch Monmouths 15 B10
Newchurch Powys 25 C9
Newchurch Staffs 35 C7
Newcott Devon 7 F11
Newcraighall C/Edinb 70 C2
Newdigate Surrey 19 G8
Newell Green Brackn'l 18 D5
Newenden Kent 13 D7
Newent Glos 26 F4
Newerne Glos 16 A3
Newfield Durham 58 C3
Newfield H'land 87 D10
Newford I/Scilly 2 C3
Newfound Hants 18 F2
Newgale Pembs 22 D3
Newgate Norfolk 39 A6
Newgate Street Herts 19 A10
Newhall Ches 43 H9
Newhall Derby 35 C8
Newhall House H'land 87 E9
Newhall Point H'land 87 E10
Newham Northum 71 H10
Newham Hall Northum 71 H10
Newhaven Derby 44 G5
Newhaven C/Edinb 69 C11
Newhaven E Sussex 12 F3
Newhey Gtr Man 44 A3
Newholm N Yorks 59 E9
Newhouse N Lanarks 68 D6
Newick E Sussex 12 D3
Newingreen Kent 13 C10
Newington Kent 20 E5
Newington Kent 21 H8
Newington Kent 21 E10
Newington Notts 45 C10
Newington Oxon 18 B3
Newington Shrops 33 G10
Newland Glos 26 H2
Newland Kingston/Hull 53 F6
Newland N Yorks 52 G2
Newland Worcs 26 D4
Newlandrig Midloth 70 D2
Newlands Scot Borders 61 D11
Newlands H'land 87 G10
Newlands Moray 88 C3
Newlands Northum 62 H6
Newland's Corner Surrey 19 G7
Newlands of Geise H'land 94 D2
Newlands of Tynet Moray 88 B3
Newlands Park Angl 40 B4
Newlandsmuir S Lanarks 68 E5
Newlot Orkney 95 G6
Newlyn Cornw'l 2 G3
Newmachar Aberds 83 B10
Newmains N Lanarks 69 E7
Newmarket Suffolk 30 B3
Newmarket W Isles 91 D9
Newmill Scot Borders 61 B10
Newmill Cornw'l 2 F3
Newmill Moray 88 C4
Newmill of Inshewan Angus 77 A7
Newmills Monmouths 26 H2
Newmills of Boyne Aberds 88 C5
Newmiln Perth/Kinr 76 D4
Newmilns E Ayrs 67 C8
Newnham Cambs 29 C11
Newnham Glos 26 G3
Newnham Hants 18 F4
Newnham Herts 29 E9
Newnham Kent 20 F6
Newnham Northants 28 C2
Newnham Bridge Worcs 26 B3
Newpark Fife 77 F7
Newport Devon 6 C4
Newport ER Yorks 52 F4
Newport Essex 30 E2
Newport H'land 94 H3
Newport I/Wight 10 F4
Newport Norfolk 39 D11
Newport Telford 34 D3
Newport = Casnewydd Newp 15 C9
Newport = Trefdraeth Pembs 22 C5
Newport-on-Tay Fife 77 E7
Newport Pagnell M/Keynes 28 D5
Newpound Common W Sussex 11 B9
Newquay Cornw'l 3 C7
Newsbank Ches 44 F2
Newseat Aberds 89 E7
Newseat Aberds 89 D10
Newsham Northum 63 F9
Newsham N Yorks 58 E2
Newsham N Yorks 51 A9
Newsholme ER Yorks 52 G3
Newsholme Lancs 50 D4
Newsome W Yorks 44 A5
Newstead Scot Borders 70 G4
Newstead Notts 45 G9
Newstead Northum 71 H10
Newthorpe N Yorks 51 F10
Newton Arg/Bute 73 D9
Newton Scot Borders 62 A2
Newton Bridg 14 D4
Newton Cambs 29 D11
Newton Cambs 37 D10
Newton Card 15 D8
Newton Ches 43 G8
Newton Ches 43 F7
Newton Ches 43 E8
Newton Cumb 49 B2
Newton Derby 45 G8
Newton Dorset 9 C6
Newton Dumf/Gal 61 D7
Newton Dumf/Gal 61 F8
Newton Gtr Man 44 C3
Newton Heref'd 25 E10
Newton Heref'd 26 C2
Newton H'land 87 E10
Newton H'land 92 F5
Newton H'land 94 F5
Newton H'land 87 G10
Newton Lancs 49 F4
Newton Lancs 50 D2
Newton Lancs 50 B1
Newton Lincs 36 B6
Newton Moray 88 B1
Newton Norfolk 38 D4
Newton Notts 36 A2
Newton Northants 36 G4
Newton Northum 62 G6
Newton Perth/Kinr 75 D11
Newton S Lanarks 68 D5
Newton S Lanarks 69 G8
Newton Staffs 34 C6
Newton Suffolk 30 D6
Newton Swan 14 C2
Newton S Yorks 45 B9
Newton Warwick 35 H11
Newton Wilts 9 B11
Newton W Loth 69 C9
Newton Abbot Devon 5 D9
Newton Arlosh Cumb 61 H7
Newton Aycliffe Durham 58 D3
Newton Bewley Hartlep'l 58 D5
Newton Blossomville M/Keynes 28 C6
Newton Bromswold Northants 28 B6
Newton Burgoland Leics 35 E9
Newton by Toft Lincs 46 D4
Newton Ferrers Devon 4 G6
Newton Flotman Norfolk 39 F8
Newton Hall Northum 62 G6
Newton Harcourt Leics 36 F2
Newton Heath Gtr Man 44 B2
Newton Ho. Aberds 83 A8
Newton Kyme N Yorks 51 E10
Newton-le-Willows Mersey 43 C8
Newton-le-Willows N Yorks 58 H3
Newton Longville Bucks 28 E5
Newton Mearns E Renf 68 E4
Newton Morrell N Yorks 58 F3
Newton Mulgrave N Yorks 59 E8
Newton of Ardtoe H'land 79 D9
Newton of Balcanquhal Perth/Kinr 76 F4
Newton of Falkland Fife 76 G5
Newton on Ayr S Ayrs 66 D6
Newton on Ouse N Yorks 51 D11
Newton-on-Rawcliffe N Yorks 59 G9
Newton-on-the-Moor Northum 63 C7
Newton on Trent Lincs 46 E2
Newton Park Arg/Bute 73 G10
Newton Poppleford Devon 7 H9
Newton Purcell Oxon 28 E3
Newton Regis Warwick 35 E8
Newton Reigny Cumb 57 C6
Newton St Cyres Devon 7 G7
Newton St Faith Norfolk 39 D8
Newton St Loe Bath/NE Som'set 16 E4
Newton St Petrock Devon 6 E3
Newton Solney Derby 35 C8
Newton Stacey Hants 17 G11
Newton Stewart Dumf/Gal 55 C7
Newton Tony Wilts 17 G9
Newton Tracey Devon 6 D4
Newton under Roseberry Redcar/Clevel'd 59 E6
Newton upon Derwent ER Yorks 52 E3
Newton Valence Hants 10 A6
Newtonairds Dumf/Gal 60 E4
Newtongrange Midloth 70 D2
Newtonhill Aberds 83 D11
Newtonhill H'land 87 G8
Newtonmill Angus 77 A9
Newtonmore H'land 81 D9
Newtown Arg/Bute 73 C9
Newtown Ches 43 E8
Newtown Cornw'l 2 G6
Newtown Cumb 56 B2
Newtown Cumb 61 G11
Newtown Derby 44 D3
Newtown Devon 7 D6
Newtown Glos 16 A3
Newtown Glos 26 E6
Newtown Hants 10 C1
Newtown Hants 10 B2
Newtown Hants 10 C5
Newtown Hants 17 E11
Newtown Hants 10 C4
Newtown Hants 10 D3
Newtown Heref'd 26 D3
Newtown H'land 80 C5
Newtown I/Man 48 E3
Newtown I/Wight 10 E3
Newtown Northum 62 C6
Newtown Northum 71 H9
Newtown Northum 71 G8
Newtown Poole 9 E9
Newtown Shrops 33 B10
Newtown Staffs 44 F3
Newtown Staffs 44 F4
Newtown Wilts 9 B8
Newtown = Y Drenewydd Powys 33 F7
Newtown Linford Leics 35 E11
Newtown St Boswells Scot Borders 70 G4
Newtown Unthank Leics 35 E10
Newtyle Angus 76 C5
Neyland Pembs 22 F4
Niarbyl I/Man 48 E2
Nibley S Gloucs 16 C3
Nibley Green Glos 16 B4
Nibon Shetl'd 96 F5
Nicholashayne Devon 7 E10
Nicholaston Swan 23 H10
Nidd N Yorks 51 C9
Nigg Aberd C 83 C11
Nigg H'land 87 D11
Nigg Ferry H'land 87 E10
Nightcott Som'set 7 D7
Nilig Denbs 42 G3
Nine Ashes Essex 20 A2
Nine Mile Burn Midloth 69 E10
Nine Wells Pembs 22 D2
Ninebanks Northum 57 A9
Ninfield E Sussex 12 E6
Ningwood I/Wight 10 F2
Nisbet Scot Borders 70 H5
Nisthouse Orkney 95 G4
Nisthouse Shetl'd 96 G7
Niton I/Wight 10 G4
Nitshill C/Glasg 68 D4
No Man's Heath Ches 43 H8
No Man's Heath Warwick 35 E8
Noak Hill London 20 B2
Noblethorpe S Yorks 44 B6
Nobottle Northants 28 B3
Nocton Lincs 46 F4
Noke Oxon 28 G2
Nolton Pembs 22 E3
Nolton Haven Pembs 22 E3
Nomansland Devon 7 E7
Nomansland Wilts 10 C1
Noneley Shrops 33 C10
Nonikiln H'land 87 D9
Nonington Kent 21 F9
Noonsbrough Shetl'd 96 H4
Norbreck Blackp'l 49 E3
Norbridge Heref'd 26 D4
Norbury Ches 43 H8
Norbury Derby 35 A7
Norbury Shrops 33 F9
Norbury Staffs 34 C3
Nordelph Norfolk 38 E1
Norden Gtr Man 44 A2
Norden Heath Dorset 9 F8
Nordley Shrops 34 F2
Norham Northum 71 F8
Norley Ches 43 E8
Norleywood Hants 10 E2
Norman Cross Cambs 37 F7
Normanby N Lincs 52 H4
Normanby N Yorks 52 A3
Normanby Redcar/Clevel'd 59 E6
Normanby-by-Spital Lincs 46 D4
Normanby by Stow Lincs 46 D2
Normanby le Wold Lincs 46 C5
Normandy Surrey 18 F6
Norman's Bay E Sussex 12 F5
Norman's Green Devon 7 F9
Normanstone Suffolk 39 F11
Normanton Derby C 35 B9
Normanton Leics 36 A4
Normanton Lincs 46 H3
Normanton Notts 45 G11
Normanton Rutl'd 36 E5
Normanton W Yorks 51 G9
Normanton le Heath Leics 35 D9
Normanton on Soar Notts 35 C11
Normanton-on-the-Wolds Notts 36 B2
Normanton on Trent Notts 45 F11
Normoss Lancs 49 F3
Norney Surrey 18 G6
Norrington Common Wilts 16 E5
Norris Green Mersey 43 C6
Norris Hill Leics 35 D9
North Anston S Yorks 45 D9
North Aston Oxon 27 F11
North Baddesley Hants 10 C2
North Ballachulish H'land 74 A3
North Barrow Som'set 8 B5
North Barsham Norfolk 38 B5
North Benfleet Essex 20 C4
North Bersted W Sussex 11 D8
North Berwick E Loth 70 B4
North Boarhunt Hants 10 C5
North Bovey Devon 5 C8
North Bradley Wilts 16 F5
North Brentor Devon 4 C5
North Brewham Som'set 16 H4
North Buckland Devon 6 B3
North Burlingham Norfolk 39 D9
North Cadbury Som'set 8 B5
North Cairn Dumf/Gal 54 B2
North Carlton Lincs 46 E3
North Carrine Arg/Bute 65 H7
North Cave ER Yorks 52 F4
North Cerney Glos 27 H7
North Charford Wilts 9 C10
North Charlton Northum 63 A7
North Cheriton Som'set 8 B5
North Cliff ER Yorks 53 E8
North Cliffe ER Yorks 52 F4
North Clifton Notts 46 E2
North Coates Lincs 47 B7
North Cockerington Lincs 47 C7
North Coker Som'set 8 C4
North Collafirth Shetl'd 96 E5
North Common E Sussex 12 D2
North Connel Arg/Bute 74 D2
North Cornelly Bridg 14 C4
North Cove Suffolk 39 G10
North Cowton N Yorks 58 F3
North Crawley M/Keynes 28 D6
North Cray London 19 D11
North Creake Norfolk 38 B4
North Curry Som'set 8 B2
North Dalton ER Yorks 52 D5
North Dawn Orkney 95 H5
North Deighton N Yorks 51 D9
North Duffield N Yorks 52 F2
North Elkington Lincs 46 C6
North Elmham Norfolk 38 C5
North Elmshall W Yorks 45 A8
North End Bucks 28 F5
North End ER Yorks 53 F8
North End Essex 30 G3
North End Hants 17 E11
North End Lincs 37 A8
North End N Som'set 15 E10
North End Portsm'th 10 D5
North End Som'set 8 B1
North End W Sussex 11 D10
North Erradale H'land 91 J12
North Fambridge Essex 20 B5
North Fearns H'land 85 E10
North Featherstone W Yorks 51 G10
North Ferriby ER Yorks 52 G5
North Frodingham ER Yorks 53 D7
North Gluss Shetl'd 96 F5
North Gorley Hants 9 C10
North Green Norfolk 39 G8
North Green Suffolk 31 B10
North Greetwell Lincs 46 E4
North Grimston N Yorks 52 C4
North Halley Orkney 95 H6
North Halling Medway 20 E4
North Hayling Hants 10 D6
North Hazelrigg Northum 71 G9
North Heasley Devon 7 C6
North Heath W Sussex 11 B9
North Hill Cambs 37 H10
North Hill Cornw'l 4 D3
North Hinksey Oxon 27 H11
North Holmwood Surrey 19 G8
North Howden ER Yorks 52 F3
North Huish Devon 5 F8
North Hykeham Lincs 46 F3
North Johnston Pembs 22 E4
North Kelsey Lincs 46 B4
North Kelsey Moor Lincs 46 B4
North Kessock H'land 87 G9
North Killingholme N Lincs 53 H7
North Kilvington N Yorks 58 H5
North Kilworth Leics 36 G2
North Kirkton Aberds 89 C11
North Kiscadale N Ayrs 66 D3
North Kyme Lincs 46 G5
North Lancing W Sussex 11 D10
North Lee Bucks 28 H5
North Leigh Oxon 27 G10
North Leverton with Habblesthorpe Notts 45 D11
North Littleton Worcs 27 D7
North Lopham Norfolk 38 G6
North Luffenham Rutl'd 36 E5
North Marden W Sussex 11 C7
North Marston Bucks 28 F4
North Middleton Midloth 70 E2
North Middleton Northum 62 A6
North Molton Devon 7 D6
North Moreton Oxon 18 C2
North Mundham W Sussex 11 D7
North Muskham Notts 45 G11
North Newbald ER Yorks 52 F5
North Newington Oxon 27 E11
North Newnton Wilts 17 F8
North Newton Som'set 8 A1
North Nibley Glos 16 B4
North Oakley Hants 18 F2
North Ockendon London 20 C2
North Ormesby Middlesbro' 58 D6
North Ormsby Lincs 46 C6
North Otterington N Yorks 58 H4
North Owersby Lincs 46 C4
North Perrott Som'set 8 D3
North Petherton Som'set 8 A1
North Petherwin Cornw'l 4 C3
North Pickenham Norfolk 38 E4
North Piddle Worcs 26 C6
North Poorton Dorset 8 E4
North Port Arg/Bute 74 E3
North Queensferry Fife 69 B10
North Radworthy Devon 7 C6
North Rauceby Lincs 46 H4
North Reston Lincs 47 D7
North Rigton N Yorks 51 E8
North Rode Ches 44 F2
North Roe Shetl'd 96 E5
North Runcton Norfolk 38 D2
North Sandwick Shetl'd 96 D7
North Scale Cumb 49 C1
North Scarle Lincs 46 F2
North Seaton Northum 63 E8
North Shian Arg/Bute 74 C2
North Shields Tyne/Wear 63 G9
North Shoebury Southend 20 C6
North Shore Blackp'l 49 F3
North Side Cumb 56 D2
North Side Peterbro 37 F8
North Skelton Redcar/Clevel'd 59 E7
North Somercotes Lincs 47 C8
North Stainley N Yorks 51 B8
North Stainmore Cumb 57 E10
North Stifford Thurr'k 20 C3
North Stoke Bath/NE Som'set 16 E4
North Stoke Oxon 18 C3
North Stoke W Sussex 11 C9
North Street Hants 10 A5
North Street Kent 21 F7
North Street Medway 20 D5
North Street W Berks 18 D3
North Sunderland Northum 71 G11
North Tamerton Cornw'l 6 G2
North Tawton Devon 6 F5
North Thoresby Lincs 46 C6
North Tidworth Wilts 17 G9
North Togston Northum 63 C8
North Tuddenham Norfolk 38 D6
North Walbottle Tyne/Wear 63 G7
North Walsham Norfolk 39 B8
North Waltham Hants 18 G2
North Warnborough Hants 18 F4
North Water Bridge Angus 83 G8
North Watten H'land 94 E4
North Weald Bassett Essex 19 A11
North Wheatley Notts 45 D11
North Whilborough Devon 5 E9
North Wick Bath/NE Som'set 16 E2
North Willingham Lincs 46 D5
North Wingfield Derby 45 F8
North Witham Lincs 36 C5
North Woolwich London 19 D11
North Wootton Dorset 8 C5
North Wootton Norfolk 38 C2
North Wootton Som'set 16 G2
North Wraxall Wilts 16 D5
North Wroughton Swindon 17 C8
Northacre Norfolk 38 F5
Northallerton N Yorks 58 G4
Northam Devon 6 D3
Northam S'thampton 10 C3
Northampton Northants 28 B4
Northaw Herts 19 A9
Northbeck Lincs 37 A6
Northborough Peterbro 37 E7
Northbourne Kent 21 F10
Northbridge Street E Sussex 12 D6
Northchapel W Sussex 11 B8
Northchurch Herts 28 H6
Northcott Devon 6 G2
Northdown Kent 21 D10
Northdyke Orkney 95 F3
Northend Bath/NE Som'set 16 E4
Northend Bucks 18 B4
Northend Warwick 27 C10
Northenden Gtr Man 44 C2
Northfield Aberd C 83 C11
Northfield Scot Borders 71 D8
Northfield ER Yorks 52 G6

Pilsbury Derby 44 F5
Pilsdon Dorset 8 E3
Pilsgate Peterbro 37 E6
Pilsley Derby 44 E6
Pilsley Derby 45 F8
Pilton Devon 6 C4
Pilton Northants 36 G6
Pilton Rutl'd 36 E5
Pilton Som'set 16 G2
Pilton Green Swan 23 H9
Pimperne Dorset 9 D8
Pinchbeck Lincs 37 C8
Pinchbeck Bars Lincs 37 C7
Pinchbeck West Lincs 37 C8
Pincheon Green S Yorks 52 H2
Pinehurst Swindon 17 C8
Pinfold Lancs 43 A6
Pinged Carms 23 F9
Pinhoe Devon 7 G8
Pinkneys Green Windsor 18 C5
Pinley W Midlands 35 H9
Pinmill Suffolk 31 E9
Pinminnoch S Ayrs 66 G4
Pinmore S Ayrs 66 G5
Pinmore Mains S Ayrs 66 G5
Pinner London 19 C8
Pinvin Worcs 26 D6
Pinwherry S Ayrs 66 H4
Pinxton Derby 45 G8
Pipe and Lyde Heref'd 26 D2
Pipe Gate Shrops 34 A3
Piperhill H'land 87 F11
Piper's Pool Cornw'l 4 C3
Pipewell Northants 36 G4
Pippacott Devon 6 C4
Pipton Powys 25 E8
Pirbright Surrey 18 F6
Pirnmill N Ayrs 66 B1
Pirton Herts 29 E8
Pirton Worcs 26 D5
Pisgah Ceredig'n 32 H2
Pisgah Stirl 75 G10
Pishill Oxon 18 C4
Pistyll Gwyn 40 F5
Pitagowan Perth/Kinr 81 G10
Pitblae Aberds 89 B9
Pitcairngreen Perth/Kinr 76 E3
Pitcalnie H'land 87 D11
Pitcaple Aberds 83 A9
Pitch Green Bucks 18 A4
Pitch Place Surrey 18 F6
Pitchcombe Glos 26 H5
Pitchcott Bucks 28 F4
Pitchford Shrops 33 E11
Pitcombe Som'set 8 A5
Pitcorthie Fife 77 G8
Pitcox E Loth 70 C5
Pitcur Perth/Kinr 76 D5
Pitfichie Aberds 83 B8
Pitforthie Aberds 83 F10
Pitgrudy H'land 87 B10
Pitkennedy Angus 77 B8
Pitkevy Fife 76 G5
Pitkierie Fife 77 G8
Pitlessie Fife 76 G6
Pitlochry Perth/Kinr 76 B2
Pitmachie Aberds 83 A8
Pitmain H'land 81 C9
Pitmedden Aberds 89 F8
Pitminster Som'set 7 E11
Pitmuies Angus 77 C8
Pitmunie Aberds 83 B8
Pitney Som'set 8 B3
Pitscottie Fife 77 F7
Pitsea Essex 20 C4
Pitsford Northants 28 B4
Pitsmoor S Yorks 45 D7
Pitstone Bucks 28 G6
Pitstone Green Bucks 28 G6
Pittendreich Moray 88 B1
Pittentrail H'land 93 J10
Pittenweem Fife 77 G8
Pittington Durham 58 B4
Pittodrie Aberds 83 A8
Pitton Wilts 9 A11
Pittswood Kent 20 G3
Pittulie Aberds 89 B9
Pity Me Durham 58 B3
Pityme Cornw'l 3 B8
Pityoulish H'land 81 B11
Pixey Green Suffolk 39 H8
Pixham Surrey 19 F8
Pixley Heref'd 26 E3
Place Newton N Yorks 52 B4
Plaidy Aberds 89 C7
Plains N Lanarks 68 D6
Plaish Shrops 33 F11
Plaistow W Sussex 11 A9
Plaitford Hants 10 C1
Plank Lane Gtr Man 43 C9
Plâs Carms 23 D9
Plas-canol Gwyn 32 D1
Plas Gogerddan Ceredig'n 32 G2
Plas Llwyngwern Powys 32 E3
Plas Nantyr Wrex 33 B7
Plas-yn-Cefn Denbs 42 E3
Plastow Green Hants 18 E2
Platt Kent 20 F3
Platt Bridge Gtr Man 43 B9
Platts Common S Yorks 45 B7
Plawsworth Durham 58 B3
Plaxtol Kent 20 F3
Play Hatch Oxon 18 D4
Playden E Sussex 13 D8
Playford Suffolk 31 D9
Playing Place Cornw'l 3 E7
Playley Green Glos 26 E4
Plealey Shrops 33 E10
Plean Stirl 69 B7
Pleasington Blackb'n 50 G2
Pleasley Derby 45 F9
Pleckgate Blackb'n 50 F2
Plenmeller Northum 62 G3
Pleshey Essex 30 G3
Plockton H'land 85 E13
Plocrapol W Isles 90 H6
Ploughfield Heref'd 25 D10
Plowden Shrops 33 G9
Ploxgreen Shrops 33 E9
Pluckley Kent 20 G6
Pluckley Thorne Kent 13 B8
Plumbland Cumb 56 C3
Plumley Ches 43 E10
Plumpton Cumb 57 C6
Plumpton E Sussex 12 E2
Plumpton Green E Sussex 12 E2
Plumpton Head Cumb 57 C7
Plumstead London 19 D11
Plumstead Norfolk 39 B7
Plumtree Notts 36 B2
Plungar Leics 36 B3
Plush Dorset 8 D6
Plwmp Ceredig'n 23 A8
Plymouth Plym'th 4 F5
Plympton Plym'th 4 F6
Plymstock Plym'th 4 F6
Plymtree Devon 7 F9
Pockley N Yorks 59 H7
Pocklington ER Yorks 52 E4
Pode Hole Lincs 37 C8
Podimore Som'set 8 B4
Podington Beds 28 B6
Podmore Staffs 34 B3
Point Clear Essex 31 G7
Pointon Lincs 37 B7
Pokesdown Bournem'th 9 E10
Pol a Charra W Isles 84 G2
Polbae Dumf/Gal 54 B5
Polbain H'land 92 H2
Polbathic Cornw'l 4 F4
Polbeth W Loth 69 D9
Polchar H'land 81 C10
Pole Elm Worcs 26 D5
Polebrook Northants 37 G6
Polegate E Sussex 12 F4
Poles H'land 87 B10
Polesworth Warwick 35 E8
Polgigga Cornw'l 2 G2
Polglass H'land 92 J3
Polgooth Cornw'l 3 D8
Poling W Sussex 11 D9
Polkerris Cornw'l 4 F1
Polla H'land 92 D6
Pollington ER Yorks 52 H2
Polloch H'land 79 E10
Pollok C/Glasg 68 D4
Pollokshields C/Glasg 68 D4
Polmassick Cornw'l 3 E8
Polmont Falk 69 C8
Polnessan E Ayrs 67 E7
Polnish H'land 79 C10
Polperro Cornw'l 4 F3
Polruan Cornw'l 4 F2
Polsham Som'set 15 G11
Polstead Suffolk 30 E6
Poltalloch Arg/Bute 73 D7
Poltimore Devon 7 G8
Polton Midloth 69 D11
Polwarth Scot Borders 70 E6
Polyphant Cornw'l 4 C3
Polzeath Cornw'l 3 B8
Ponders End London 19 B10
Pondersbridge Cambs 37 F8
Pondtail Hants 18 F5
Ponsanooth Cornw'l 3 F6
Ponsworthy Devon 5 D8
Pont Aber Carms 24 F4
Pont Aber-Geirw Gwyn 32 C3
Pont-ar-gothi Carms 23 D10
Pont ar Hydfer Powys 24 F5
Pont-ar-llechau Carms 24 F4
Pont Cwm Pydew Denbs 32 B6
Pont Cyfyng Conwy 41 E9
Pont Cysyllte Wrex 33 A8
Pont Dolydd Prysor Gwyn 41 G9
Pont-faen Powys 24 E6
Pont Fronwydd Gwyn 32 C4
Pont-gareg Pembs 22 B6
Pont-Henri Carms 23 F9
Pont-Llogel Powys 32 D6
Pont Pen-y-benglog Gwyn 41 D8
Pont Rhyd-goch Conwy 41 D8
Pont-Rhyd-sarn Gwyn 32 C4
Pont Rhyd-y-cyff Bridg 14 C4
Pont-rhyd-y-groes Ceredig'n 24 A4
Pont-rug Gwyn 41 D7
Pont Senni = Sennybridge Powys 24 F6
Pont-siân Ceredig'n 23 B9
Pont-y-gwaith Rh Cyn Taff 14 B6
Pont-y-pant Conwy 41 E9
Pont y Pennant Gwyn 32 C5
Pont-y-Pŵl = Pontypool Torf 15 A8
Pont yclun Rh Cyn Taff 14 C6
Pont yr Afon-Gam Gwyn 41 F9
Pont-yr-hafod Pembs 22 D4
Pontamman Carms 24 G3
Pontantwn Carms 23 E9
Pontardawe Neath P Talb 14 A3
Pontarddulais Swan 23 F10
Pontarsais Carms 23 D9
Pontblyddyn Flints 42 F5
Pontbren Araeth Carms 24 F3
Pontbren Llwyd Rh Cyn Taff 24 H6
Pontefract W Yorks 51 G10
Ponteland Northum 63 F7
Ponterwyd Ceredig'n 32 G3
Pontesbury Shrops 33 E9
Pontfadog Wrex 33 B8
Pontfaen Pembs 22 C5
Pontgarreg Ceredig'n 23 A8
Ponthir Torf 15 B9
Ponthirwaun Ceredig'n 23 B7
Pontllanfraith Caerph 15 B7
Pontlliw Swan 14 A2
Pontllyfni Gwyn 40 E6
Pontlottyn Caerph 25 H8
Pontneddfechan Powys 24 H6
Pontnewydd Torf 15 B8
Pontrhydfendigaid Ceredig'n 24 B4
Pontrhydyfen Neath P Talb 14 B3
Pontrilas Heref'd 25 F10
Pontrobert Powys 33 D7
Ponts Green E Sussex 12 E5
Pontshill Heref'd 26 F3
Pontsticill Merth Tyd 25 G7
Pontwgan Conwy 41 C9
Pontyates Carms 23 F9
Pontyberem Carms 23 E10
Pontycymer Bridg 14 B5
Pontyglasier Pembs 22 C6
Pontypool = Pont-y-Pŵl Torf 15 A8
Pontypridd Rh Cyn Taff 14 C6
Pontywaun Caerph 15 B8
Pooksgreen Hants 10 C2
Pool Cornw'l 2 E5
Pool W Yorks 51 E8
Pool o'Muckhart Clack 76 G3
Pool Quay Powys 33 D8
Poole Poole 9 E9
Poole Keynes Glos 16 B6
Poolend Staffs 44 G3
Poolewe H'land 91 J13
Pooley Bridge Cumb 56 D6
Poolfold Staffs 44 G2
Poolhill Glos 26 F4
Poolsbrook Derby 45 E8
Pootings Kent 19 G11
Pope Hill Pembs 22 E4
Popeswood Brackn'l 18 E5
Popham Hants 18 G2
Poplar London 19 C10
Popley Hants 18 F3
Porchester Notts 36 A1
Porchfield I/Wight 10 E3
Porin H'land 86 F6
Poringland Norfolk 39 E8
Porkellis Cornw'l 2 F5
Porlock Som'set 7 B7
Porlock Weir Som'set 7 B7
Port Ann Arg/Bute 73 E8
Port Appin Arg/Bute 74 C2
Port Askaig Arg/Bute 64 B5
Port Bannatyne Arg/Bute 73 G9
Port Carlisle Cumb 61 G8
Port Charlotte Arg/Bute 64 C3
Port Clarence Stockton 58 D5
Port Driseach Arg/Bute 73 F8
Port e Vullen I/Man 48 C4
Port Ellen Arg/Bute 64 D4
Port Elphinstone Aberds 83 B9
Port Erin I/Man 48 F1
Port Erroll Aberds 89 E10
Port Eynon Swan 23 H9
Port Gaverne Cornw'l 3 A9
Port Glasgow Inverc/ 68 C2
Port Henderson H'land 85 A12
Port Isaac Cornw'l 3 A8
Port Lamont Arg/Bute 73 F9
Port Lion Pembs 22 F4
Port Logan Dumf/Gal 54 E3
Port Mholair W Isles 91 D10
Port Mor H'land 78 D7
Port Mulgrave N Yorks 59 E8
Port Nan Giùran W Isles 91 D10
Port nan Long W Isles 84 A3
Port Nis W Isles 91 A10
Port of Menteith Stirl 75 G8
Port Quin Cornw'l 3 A8
Port Ramsay Arg/Bute 79 G11
Port St Mary I/Man 48 F2
Port Sunlight Mersey 42 D6
Port Talbot Neath P Talb 14 B3
Port Tennant Swan 14 B2
Port Wemyss Arg/Bute 64 C2
Port William Dumf/Gal 54 E6
Portachoillan Arg/Bute 72 H6
Portavadie Arg/Bute 73 G8
Portbury N Som'set 15 D11
Portchester Hants 10 D5
Portclair H'land 80 B6
Portencalzie Dumf/Gal 54 B3
Portencross N Ayrs 66 B4
Portesham Dorset 8 F5
Portessie Moray 88 B4
Portfield Gate Pembs 22 E4
Portgate Devon 4 C5
Portgordon Moray 88 B3
Portgower H'land 93 H13
Porth Cornw'l 3 C7
Porth Rh Cyn Taff 14 B6
Porth Navas Cornw'l 3 G6
Porth Tywyn = Burry Port Carms 23 F9
Porth-y-waen Shrops 33 C8
Porthaethwy = Menai Bridge Angl 41 C7
Porthallow Cornw'l 3 G6
Porthallow Cornw'l 4 F3
Porthcawl Bridg 14 D4
Porthcothan Cornw'l 3 B7
Porthcurno Cornw'l 2 G2
Porthgain Pembs 22 C3
Porthill Shrops 33 D10
Porthkerry V/Glam 14 E6
Porthleven Cornw'l 2 G5
Porthllechog Angl 40 A6
Porthmadog Gwyn 41 G7
Porthmeor Cornw'l 2 F3
Portholland Cornw'l 3 E8
Porthoustock Cornw'l 3 G7
Porthpean Cornw'l 3 D9
Porthtowan Cornw'l 2 E5
Porthyrhyd Carms 23 E10
Porthyrhyd Carms 24 E4
Portincaple Arg/Bute 73 D11
Portington ER Yorks 52 F3
Portinnisherrich Arg/Bute 73 B8
Portinscale Cumb 56 D4
Portishead N Som'set 15 D10
Portkil Arg/Bute 73 E11
Portknockie Moray 88 B4
Portlethen Aberds 83 D11
Portling Dumf/Gal 55 D11
Portloe Cornw'l 3 F8
Portmahomack H'land 87 C12
Portmeirion Gwyn 41 G7
Portmellon Cornw'l 3 E9
Portmore Hants 10 E2
Portnacroish Arg/Bute 74 C2
Portnahaven Arg/Bute 64 C2
Portnalong H'land 85 E8
Portnaluchaig H'land 79 C9
Portnancon H'land 92 C7
Portnellan Stirl 75 E7
Portobello C/Edinb 70 C2
Porton Wilts 17 H8
Portpatrick Dumf/Gal 54 D3
Portreath Cornw'l 2 E5
Portree H'land 85 D9
Portscatho Cornw'l 3 F7
Portsea Portsm'th 10 D5
Portskerra H'land 93 C11
Portskewett Monmouths 15 C11
Portslade Brighton/Hove 12 F1
Portslade-by-Sea Brighton/Hove 12 F1
Portsmouth Portsm'th 10 E5
Portsmouth W Yorks 50 G5
Portsonachan Arg/Bute 74 E3
Portsoy Aberds 88 B5
Portswood S'hampton 10 C3
Porttanachy Moray 88 B3
Portuairk H'land 78 E7
Portway Heref'd 25 E11
Portway Worcs 27 A7
Portwrinkle Cornw'l 4 F4
Poslingford Suffolk 30 D4
Postbridge Devon 5 D7
Postcombe Oxon 18 B4
Postling Kent 13 C10
Postwick Norfolk 39 E8
Potholm Dumf/Gal 61 E9
Potsgrove Beds 28 F6
Pott Row Norfolk 38 C3
Pott Shrigley Ches 44 E3
Potten End Herts 29 H7
Potter Brompton N Yorks 52 B5
Potter Heigham Norfolk 39 D10
Potter Street Essex 29 H11
Potterhanworth Lincs 46 F4
Potterhanworth Booths Lincs 46 F4
Potterne Wilts 16 F6
Potterne Wick Wilts 17 F7
Potternewton W Yorks 51 F9
Potters Bar Herts 19 A9
Potter's Cross Staffs 34 G4
Potterspury Northants 28 D4
Potterton Aberds 83 B11
Potterton W Yorks 51 F10
Potto N Yorks 58 F5
Potton Beds 29 D9
Poughill Cornw'l 6 F1
Poughill Devon 7 F7
Poulshot Wilts 16 F6
Poulton Glos 17 A8
Poulton Mersey 42 C6
Poulton-le-Fylde Lancs 49 F3
Pound Bank Worcs 26 A4
Pound Green E Sussex 12 D4
Pound Green I/Wight 10 F2
Pound Green Suffolk 30 C4
Pound Hill W Sussex 12 C1
Poundfield E Sussex 12 C4
Poundland S Ayrs 66 H4
Poundon Bucks 28 F3
Poundsgate Devon 5 D8
Poundstock Cornw'l 4 B3
Powburn Northum 62 B6
Powderham Devon 5 C10
Powerstock Dorset 8 E4
Powfoot Dumf/Gal 61 G7
Powick Worcs 26 C5
Powmill Perth/Kinr 76 H3
Poxwell Dorset 8 F6
Poyle Slough 19 D7
Poynings W Sussex 12 E1
Poyntington Dorset 8 C5
Poynton Ches 44 D3
Poynton Green Telford 34 D1
Poystreet Green Suffolk 30 C6
Praa Sands Cornw'l 2 G4
Pratt's Bottom London 19 E11
Praze Cornw'l 2 F4
Praze-an-Beeble Cornw'l 2 F5
Predannack Wollas Cornw'l 2 H5
Prees Shrops 34 B1
Prees Green Shrops 34 B1
Prees Heath Shrops 34 B1
Prees Higher Heath Shrops 34 B1
Prees Lower Heath Shrops 34 B1
Preesall Lancs 49 E3
Preesgweene Shrops 33 B8
Prenderguest Scot Borders 71 E8
Prendwick Northum 62 B6
Prengwyn Ceredig'n 23 B9
Prenteg Gwyn 41 F7
Prenton Mersey 42 D6
Prescot Mersey 43 C7
Prescott Shrops 33 C10
Pressen Northum 71 G7
Prestatyn Denbs 42 D3
Prestbury Ches 44 E3
Prestbury Glos 26 F6
Presteigne = Llanandras Powys 25 B10
Presthope Shrops 34 F1
Prestleigh Som'set 16 G3
Preston Scot Borders 70 E6
Preston Brighton/Hove 12 F2
Preston Devon 5 D9
Preston Dorset 8 F6
Preston E Loth 70 C4
Preston ER Yorks 53 F7
Preston Glos 17 A7
Preston Glos 26 E3
Preston Herts 29 F8
Preston Kent 21 E7
Preston Kent 21 E9
Preston Lancs 49 G5
Preston Northum 71 H10
Preston Rutl'd 36 E4
Preston Shrops 33 D11
Preston Suffolk 30 C6
Preston Wilts 17 D7
Preston Wilts 17 D9
Preston Bagot Warwick 27 B8
Preston Bissett Bucks 28 F3
Preston Bowyer Som'set 7 D10
Preston Brockhurst Shrops 33 C11
Preston Brook Halton 43 D8
Preston Candover Hants 18 G3
Preston Capes Northants 28 C2
Preston Crowmarsh Oxon 18 B3
Preston Gubbals Shrops 33 D10
Preston on Stour Warwick 27 D9
Preston on the Hill Halton 43 D8
Preston on Wye Heref'd 25 D10
Preston Plucknett Som'set 8 C4
Preston-under-Scar N Yorks 58 G1
Preston upon the Weald Moors Telford 34 D2
Preston Wynne Heref'd 26 D2
Prestonmill Dumf/Gal 60 H5
Prestonpans E Loth 70 C2
Prestwich Gtr Man 44 B2
Prestwick Northum 63 F7
Prestwick S Ayrs 67 D6
Prestwood Bucks 18 A5
Price Town Bridg 14 B5
Prickwillow Cambs 38 G1
Priddy Som'set 15 F11
Priest Hutton Lancs 49 B5
Priest Weston Shrops 33 F8
Priesthaugh Scot Borders 61 C10
Primethorpe Leics 35 F11
Primrose Green Norfolk 39 D6
Primrose Valley N Yorks 53 B7
Primrosehill Herts 19 A7
Princes Gate Pembs 22 E6
Princes Risborough Bucks 18 A5
Princethorpe Warwick 27 A11
Princetown Caerph 25 G8
Princetown Devon 5 D6
Prion Denbs 42 F3
Prior Muir Fife 77 F8
Prior Park Northum 71 E8
Priors Frome Heref'd 26 E2
Priors Hardwick Warwick 27 C11
Priors Marston Warwick 27 C11
Priorslee Telford 34 D3
Priory Wood Heref'd 25 D9
Priston Bath/NE Som'set 16 E3
Pristow Green Norfolk 39 G7
Prittlewell Southend 20 C5
Privett Hants 10 B5
Prixford Devon 6 C4
Probus Cornw'l 3 E7
Proncy H'land 87 B10
Prospect Cumb 56 B3
Prudhoe Northum 62 G6
Ptarmigan Lodge Stirl 74 G6
Pubil Perth/Kinr 75 C7
Puckeridge Herts 29 F10
Puckington Som'set 8 C2
Pucklechurch S Gloucs 16 D3
Pucknall Hants 10 B2
Puckrup Glos 26 E5
Puddinglake Ches 43 F10
Puddington Ches 42 E6
Puddington Devon 7 E7
Puddledock Norfolk 39 F6
Puddletown Dorset 9 E6
Pudleston Heref'd 26 C2
Pudsey W Yorks 51 F8
Pulborough W Sussex 11 C9
Puleston Telford 34 C3
Pulford Ches 43 G6
Pulham Dorset 8 D6
Pulham Market Norfolk 39 G7
Pulham St Mary Norfolk 39 G8
Pulloxhill Beds 29 E7
Pumpherston W Loth 69 D9
Pumsaint Carms 24 D3
Puncheston Pembs 22 D5
Puncknowle Dorset 8 F4
Punnett's Town E Sussex 12 D5
Purbrook Hants 10 D5
Purewell Dorset 9 E10
Purfleet Thurr'k 20 D2
Puriton Som'set 15 G9
Purleigh Essex 20 A5
Purley London 19 E10
Purley W Berks 18 D3
Purlogue Shrops 33 H8
Purls Bridge Cambs 37 G10
Purse Caundle Dorset 8 C5
Purslow Shrops 33 G9
Purston Jaglin W Yorks 51 H10
Purton Glos 16 A3
Purton Glos 16 A3
Purton Wilts 17 C7
Purton Stoke Wilts 17 B7
Pury End Northants 28 D4
Pusey Oxon 17 B10
Putley Heref'd 26 E3
Putney London 19 D9
Putsborough Devon 6 B3
Puttenham Herts 28 G5
Puttenham Surrey 18 G6
Puxton N Som'set 15 E10
Pwll Carms 23 F9
Pwll-glas Denbs 42 G4
Pwll-Meyric Monmouths 15 B11
Pwll-trap Carms 23 E7
Pwll-y-glaw Neath P Talb 14 B3
Pwllcrochan Pembs 22 F4
Pwllgloyw Powys 25 E7
Pwllheli Gwyn 40 G5
Pycombe W Sussex 12 E1
Pye Corner Newp 15 C9
Pye Green Staffs 34 D5
Pyewipe NE Lincs 46 A6
Pyle I/Wight 10 G3
Pyle = Y Pîl Bridg 14 C4
Pylle Som'set 16 H3
Pymoor Cambs 37 G10
Pyrford Surrey 19 F7
Pyrton Oxon 18 B3
Pytchley Northants 28 A5
Pyworthy Devon 6 F2

Q

Quabbs Shrops 33 G8
Quadring Lincs 37 B8
Quainton Bucks 28 G4
Quarley Hants 17 G9
Quarndon Derby 35 A9
Quarrier's Homes Inverc/ 68 D2
Quarrington Lincs 37 A6
Quarrington Hill Durham 58 C4
Quarry Bank W Midlands 34 G5
Quarryford E Loth 70 D4
Quarryhill H'land 87 C10
Quarrywood Moray 88 B1
Quarter S Lanarks 68 E6
Quatford Shrops 34 F3
Quatt Shrops 34 G3
Quebec Durham 58 B2
Quedgeley Glos 26 G5
Queen Adelaide Cambs 38 G1
Queen Camel Som'set 8 B4
Queen Charlton Bath/NE Som'set 16 E3
Queen Dart Devon 7 E7
Queen Oak Dorset 9 A6
Queen Street Kent 20 G3
Queen Street Wilts 17 C7
Queenborough Kent 20 D6
Queenhill Worcs 26 E5
Queen's Head Shrops 33 C9
Queen's Park Beds 29 D7
Queen's Park Northants 28 B4
Queensbury W Yorks 51 F7
Queensferry C/Edinb 69 C10
Queensferry Flints 42 F6
Queenstown Blackp'l 49 F3
Queenzieburn N Lanarks 68 C5
Quemerford Wilts 17 E7
Quendale Shetl'd 96 M5
Quendon Essex 30 E2
Queniborough Leics 36 D2
Quenington Glos 17 A8
Quernmore Lancs 49 D5
Quethiock Cornw'l 4 E4
Quholm Orkney 95 G3
Quicks Green W Berks 18 D2
Quidenham Norfolk 38 G6
Quidhampton Hants 18 F2
Quidhampton Wilts 9 A10
Quilquox Aberds 89 E9
Quina Brook Shrops 33 B11
Quindry Orkney 95 J5
Quinton Northants 28 C4
Quinton W Midlands 34 G5
Quintrell Downs Cornw'l 3 C7
Quixhill Staffs 35 A7
Quoditch Devon 6 G3
Quoig Perth/Kinr 75 E11
Quorndon Leics 36 D1
Quothquan S Lanarks 69 G8
Quoyloo Orkney 95 F3
Quoyness Orkney 95 H3
Quoys Shetl'd 96 B8
Quoys Shetl'd 96 G7

R

Raasay Ho. H'land 85 E10
Rabbit's Cross Kent 20 G4
Raby Mersey 42 E6
Rachan Mill Scot Borders 69 G10
Rachub Gwyn 41 D8
Rackenford Devon 7 E7
Rackham W Sussex 11 C9
Rackheath Norfolk 39 D8
Racks Dumf/Gal 60 F6
Rackwick Orkney 95 J3
Rackwick Orkney 95 D5
Radbourne Derby 35 B8
Radcliffe Gtr Man 43 B10
Radcliffe Northum 63 C8
Radcliffe on Trent Notts 36 B2
Radclive Bucks 28 E3
Radcot Oxon 17 B9
Raddery H'land 87 F10
Radernie Fife 77 G7
Radford Semele Warwick 27 B10
Radipole Dorset 8 F5
Radlett Herts 19 B8
Radley Oxon 18 B2
Radmanthwaite Notts 45 F9
Radmoor Shrops 34 C2
Radmore Green Ches 43 G8
Radnage Bucks 18 B4
Radstock Bath/NE Som'set 16 F3
Radstone Northants 28 D2
Radway Warwick 27 D10
Radway Green Ches 43 G10
Radwell Beds 29 C7
Radwell Herts 29 E9
Radwinter Essex 30 E3
Radyr Card 15 C7
Rafford Moray 87 F13
Ragdale Leics 36 D2
Raglan Monmouths 25 H11
Ragnall Notts 46 E2
Rahane Arg/Bute 73 E11
Rainford Mersey 43 B7
Rainford Junction Mersey 43 B7
Rainham London 20 C2
Rainham Medway 20 E5
Rainhill Mersey 43 C7
Rainhill Stoops Mersey 43 C8
Rainow Ches 44 E3
Rainton N Yorks 51 B9
Rainworth Notts 45 G9
Raisbeck Cumb 57 F8
Raise Cumb 57 B9
Rait Perth/Kinr 76 E5
Raithby Lincs 47 D7
Raithby Lincs 47 F7
Rake W Sussex 11 B7
Rakewood Gtr Man 44 A3
Ram Carms 23 B10
Ram Lane Kent 20 G6
Ramasaig H'land 84 D6
Rame Cornw'l 2 F6
Rame Cornw'l 4 G5
Rameldry Mill Bank Fife 76 G6
Ramnageo Shetl'd 96 C8
Rampisham Dorset 8 D4
Rampside Cumb 49 C2
Rampton Cambs 29 B11
Rampton Notts 45 E11
Ramsbottom Gtr Man 50 H3
Ramsbury Wilts 17 D9
Ramscraigs H'land 94 H3
Ramsdean Hants 10 B6
Ramsdell Hants 18 F2
Ramsden Oxon 27 G10
Ramsden Bellhouse Essex 20 B4
Ramsden Heath Essex 20 B4
Ramsey Cambs 37 G8
Ramsey Essex 31 E9
Ramsey I/Man 48 C4
Ramsey Forty Foot Cambs 37 G9
Ramsey Heights Cambs 37 G7
Ramsey Island Essex 30 H6
Ramsey Mereside Cambs 37 G8
Ramsey St Mary's Cambs 37 G8
Ramseycleuch Scot Borders 61 B8
Ramsgate Kent 21 E10
Ramsgill N Yorks 51 B7
Ramshorn Staffs 44 H4
Ramsnest Common Surrey 11 A8
Ranais W Isles 91 E9
Ranby Lincs 46 E6
Ranby Notts 45 D10
Rand Lincs 46 E5
Randwick Glos 26 H5
Ranfurly Renf 68 D2
Rangag H'land 94 F3
Rangemore Staffs 35 C7
Rangeworthy S Gloucs 16 C3
Rankinston E Ayrs 67 E7
Ranmoor S Yorks 45 D7
Ranmore Common Surrey 19 F8
Rannerdale Cumb 56 E3
Rannoch School Perth/Kinr 75 B8
Rannoch Station Perth/Kinr 75 B7
Ranochan H'land 79 C11
Ranskill Notts 45 D10
Ranton Staffs 34 C4
Ranworth Norfolk 39 D9
Raploch Stirl 69 A6
Rapness Orkney 95 D6
Rascal Moor ER Yorks 52 F4
Rascarrel Dumf/Gal 55 E10
Rashiereive Aberds 89 F9
Raskelf N Yorks 51 B10
Rassau Bl Gwent 25 G8
Rastrick W Yorks 51 G7
Ratagan H'land 85 G14
Ratby Leics 35 E11
Ratcliffe Culey Leics 35 F9
Ratcliffe on Soar Leics 35 C10
Ratcliffe on the Wreake Leics 36 D2
Rathen Aberds 89 B10
Rathillet Fife 76 E6
Rathmell N Yorks 50 D4
Ratho C/Edinb 69 C10
Ratho Station C/Edinb 69 C10
Rathven Moray 88 B4
Ratley Warwick 27 D10
Ratlinghope Shrops 33 F10
Rattar H'land 94 C4
Ratten Row Lancs 49 E4
Rattery Devon 5 E8
Rattlesden Suffolk 30 C6
Rattray Perth/Kinr 76 C4
Raughton Head Cumb 56 B5
Raunds Northants 28 A6
Ravenfield S Yorks 45 C8
Ravenglass Cumb 56 G2
Ravenhead Mersey 43 C8
Raveningham Norfolk 39 F9
Ravenscar N Yorks 59 F10
Ravenscraig Inverc/ 73 F11
Ravensdale I/Man 48 C3
Ravensden Beds 29 C7
Ravenseat N Yorks 57 F10
Ravenshead Notts 45 G9
Ravensmoor Ches 43 G9
Ravensthorpe Northants 28 A3
Ravensthorpe W Yorks 51 G8
Ravenstone Leics 35 D10
Ravenstone M/Keynes 28 C5
Ravenstonedale Cumb 57 F9
Ravenstown Cumb 49 B3
Ravenstruther S Lanarks 69 F8
Ravensworth N Yorks 58 F2
Raw N Yorks 59 F10
Rawcliffe ER Yorks 52 G2
Rawcliffe C/York 52 D1
Rawcliffe Bridge ER Yorks 52 G2
Rawdon W Yorks 51 F8
Rawmarsh S Yorks 45 C8
Rawreth Essex 20 B4
Rawridge Devon 7 F11
Rawtenstall Lancs 50 G4
Raxton Aberds 89 E8
Raydon Suffolk 31 E7
Raylees Northum 62 D5
Rayleigh Essex 20 B5
Rayne Essex 30 F4
Rayners Lane London 19 C8
Raynes Park London 19 E9
Reach Cambs 30 B2
Read Lancs 50 F3
Reading Reading 18 D4
Reading Street Kent 13 C8
Reagill Cumb 57 E8
Rearquhar H'land 87 B10
Rearsby Leics 36 D2
Reaster H'land 94 D4
Reawick Shetl'd 96 J5
Reay H'land 93 C12
Rechullin H'land 85 C13
Reculver Kent 21 E9
Red Dial Cumb 56 B4
Red Hill Worcs 26 C5
Red Houses Jersey 11
Red Lodge Suffolk 30 A3
Red Rail Heref'd 26 F2
Red Rock Gtr Man 43 B8
Red Roses Carms 23 E7
Red Row Northum 63 D8
Red Street Staffs 44 G2
Red Wharf Bay Angl 41 B7
Redberth Pembs 22 F5
Redbourn Herts 29 G8
Redbourne N Lincs 46 C3
Redbrook Glos 26 G2
Redbrook Wrex 33 A11
Redburn H'land 87 E8
Redburn H'land 87 G12
Redburn Northum 62 G3
Redcar Redcar/Clevel'd 59 D7
Redcastle Angus 77 B9
Redcastle H'land 87 G8
Redcliff Bay N Som'set 15 D10
Redding Falk 69 C8
Reddingmuirhead Falk 69 C8
Reddish Gtr Man 44 C2
Redditch Worcs 27 B7
Rede Suffolk 30 C5
Redenhall Norfolk 39 G8
Redesdale Camp Northum 62 D4
Redesmouth Northum 62 E4
Redford Aberds 83 F9
Redford Angus 77 C8
Redford Durham 58 C1
Redfordgreen Scot Borders 61 B9
Redgorton Perth/Kinr 76 E3
Redgrave Suffolk 38 H6
Redhill Aberds 89 E6
Redhill Aberds 83 C9
Redhill N Som'set 15 E11
Redhill Surrey 19 F9
Redhouse Arg/Bute 73 G7
Redhouses Arg/Bute 64 B4
Redisham Suffolk 39 G10
Redland Bristol 16 D2
Redland Orkney 95 F4
Redlingfield Suffolk 31 A8
Redlynch Som'set 8 A6
Redlynch Wilts 9 B11
Redmarley D'Abitot Glos 26 E4
Redmarshall Stockton 58 D4
Redmile Leics 36 B3
Redmire N Yorks 58 G1
Redmoor Cornw'l 4 E1
Rednal Shrops 33 C9
Redpath Scot Borders 70 G4
Redpoint H'land 85 B12
Redruth Cornw'l 2 E5
Redvales Gtr Man 44 B2
Redwick Newp 15 C10
Redwick S Gloucs 15 C11
Redworth D'lington 58 D3
Reed Herts 29 E10
Reedham Norfolk 39 E10
Reedness ER Yorks 52 G3
Reeds Beck Lincs 46 F6
Reepham Lincs 46 E4
Reepham Norfolk 39 C6
Reeth N Yorks 58 G1
Regaby I/Man 48 C4
Regoul H'land 87 F11
Reiff H'land 92 H2
Reigate Surrey 19 F9
Reighton N Yorks 53 B7
Reighton Gap N Yorks 53 B7
Reinigeadal W Isles 90 G7
Reiss H'land 94 E5
Rejerrah Cornw'l 3 D6
Releath Cornw'l 2 F5
Relubbus Cornw'l 2 F4
Relugas Moray 87 G12
Remenham Wokingham 18 C4
Remenham Hill Wokingham 18 C4
Remony Perth/Kinr 75 C10
Rempstone Notts 36 C1
Rendcomb Glos 27 H7
Rendham Suffolk 31 B10
Rendlesham Suffolk 31 C10
Renfrew Renf 68 D4
Renhold Beds 29 C7
Renishaw Derby 45 E8
Rennington Northum 63 B8
Renton W Dunb 68 C2
Renwick Cumb 57 B7
Repps Norfolk 39 D10
Repton Derby 35 C9
Reraig H'land 85 F13
Rescobie Angus 77 B8
Resipole H'land 79 E10
Resolis H'land 87 E9
Resolven Neath P Talb 14 A4
Reston Scot Borders 71 D7
Reswallie Angus 77 B8
Retew Cornw'l 3 D8
Retford Notts 45 D11
Rettendon Essex 20 B4
Rettendon Place Essex 20 B4
Revesby Lincs 46 F6
Revesby Bridge Lincs 47 F7
Rew Street I/Wight 10 E3
Rewe Devon 7 G8
Reydon Suffolk 39 H10
Reydon Smear Suffolk 39 H10
Reymerston Norfolk 38 E6
Reynalton Pembs 22 F5
Reynoldston Swan 23 G9
Rezare Cornw'l 4 D4
Rhaeadr Gwy = Rhayader Powys 24 B6
Rhandirmwyn Carms 24 D4
Rhayader = Rhaeadr Gwy Powys 24 B6
Rhedyn Gwyn 40 G4
Rhemore H'land 79 F8
Rhencullen I/Man 48 C3
Rhes-y-cae Flints 42 E4
Rhewl Denbs 42 F4
Rhewl Denbs 42 H4
Rhian H'land 93 H8
Rhicarn H'land 92 G3
Rhiconich H'land 92 D5
Rhicullen H'land 87 D9
Rhidorroch Ho. H'land 86 B4
Rhifail H'land 93 E10
Rhigos Rh Cyn Taff 24 H6
Rhilochan H'land 93 J10
Rhiroy H'land 86 C4
Rhisga = Risca Caerph 15 B8
Rhiw Gwyn 40 H4
Rhiwabon = Ruabon Wrex 33 A9
Rhiwbina Card 15 C7
Rhiwbryfdir Gwyn 41 F8
Rhiwderin Newp 15 C8
Rhiwlas Gwyn 41 D7
Rhiwlas Gwyn 32 B5
Rhiwlas Powys 33 B7
Rhodes Gtr Man 44 B2
Rhodes Minnis Kent 21 G8
Rhodesia Notts 45 E9
Rhodiad Pembs 22 D2
Rhondda Rh Cyn Taff 14 B5
Rhonehouse or Kelton Hill Dumf/Gal 55 D10
Rhoose = Y Rhws V/Glam 14 E6
Rhôs Carms 23 C8
Rhôs Neath P Talb 14 A3
Rhos-fawr Gwyn 40 G5
Rhos-hill Pembs 22 B6
Rhos-on-Sea Conwy 41 B10
Rhos-y-brithdir Powys 33 C7
Rhos-y-garth Ceredig'n 24 A3
Rhos-y-gwaliau Gwyn 32 B5
Rhos-y-llan Gwyn 40 G4
Rhos-y-Madoc Wrex 33 A9
Rhos-y-meirch Powys 25 B9
Rhosaman Carms 24 G4
Rhosbeirio Angl 40 A5
Rhoscefnhir Angl 41 C7
Rhoscolyn Angl 40 C4
Rhoscrowther Pembs 22 F4
Rhosesmor Flints 42 F5
Rhosgadfan Gwyn 41 E7
Rhosgoch Angl 40 B6
Rhosgoch Powys 25 D8
Rhoshirwaun Gwyn 40 H3
Rhoslan Gwyn 40 F6
Rhoslefain Gwyn 32 E1
Rhosllanerchrugog Wrex 42 H5
Rhosmaen Carms 24 F3
Rhosmeirch Angl 40 C6
Rhosneigr Angl 40 C5
Rhosnesni Wrex 42 G6
Rhosrobin Wrex 42 G6
Rhossili Swan 23 H9
Rhosson Pembs 22 D2
Rhostryfan Gwyn 40 E6
Rhostyllen Wrex 42 H6
Rhosybol Angl 40 B6
Rhu Arg/Bute 73 G7
Rhu Arg/Bute 73 E11
Rhuallt Denbs 42 E3
Rhuddall Heath Ches 43 F8
Rhuddlan Ceredig'n 23 B9
Rhuddlan Denbs 42 E3
Rhue H'land 86 B3
Rhulen Powys 25 D8
Rhunahaorine Arg/Bute 65 D8
Rhuthun = Ruthin Denbs 42 G4
Rhyd Gwyn 41 F8
Rhyd Powys 32 E5
Rhyd-Ddu Gwyn 41 E7
Rhyd-moel-ddu Powys 33 H6
Rhyd-Rosser Ceredig'n 24 B2
Rhyd-uchaf Gwyn 32 B5
Rhyd-wen Gwyn 32 D3
Rhyd-y-clafdy Gwyn 40 G5
Rhyd-y-foel Conwy 42 E2
Rhyd-y-fro Neath P Talb 24 H4
Rhyd-y-gwin Swan 14 A2
Rhyd-y-meirch Monmouths 25 H10
Rhyd-y-meudwy Denbs 42 G4
Rhyd-y-pandy Swan 14 A2
Rhyd-y-sarn Gwyn 41 F8
Rhyd-yr-onen Gwyn 32 E2
Rhydaman = Ammanford Carms 24 G3
Rhydargaeau Carms 23 D9
Rhydcymerau Carms 23 C10
Rhydd Worcs 26 D5
Rhydding Neath P Talb 14 B3
Rhydfudr Ceredig'n 24 B2
Rhydlewis Ceredig'n 23 B8
Rhydlios Gwyn 40 G3
Rhydlydan Conwy 41 E10
Rhydness Powys 25 D8
Rhydowen Ceredig'n 23 B9
Rhydspence Heref'd 25 D9
Rhydtalog Flints 42 G5
Rhydwyn Angl 40 B5
Rhydycroesau Shrops 33 B8
Rhydyfelin Ceredig'n 32 H1
Rhydyfelin Rh Cyn Taff 14 C6
Rhydymain Gwyn 32 C4
Rhydymwyn Flints 42 F5
Rhyl = Y Rhyl Denbs 42 D3
Rhymney = Rhymni Caerph 25 H8
Rhymni = Rhymney Caerph 25 H8
Rhynd Fife 77 E7
Rhynd Perth/Kinr 76 E4
Rhynie Aberds 82 A6
Rhynie H'land 87 D11
Ribbesford Worcs 26 A4
Ribblehead N Yorks 50 B3
Ribbleton Lancs 50 F1
Ribchester Lancs 50 F2
Ribigill H'land 93 D8
Riby Lincs 46 B5
Riby Cross Roads Lincs 46 B5
Riccall N Yorks 52 F2
Riccarton E Ayrs 67 C7
Richards Castle Heref'd 25 B11
Richings Park Bucks 19 D7
Richmond London 19 D8
Richmond N Yorks 58 F2
Rickarton Aberds 83 E10
Rickinghall Suffolk 38 H6
Rickleton Tyne/Wear 58 A3
Rickling Essex 29 E11
Rickmansworth Herts 19 B7
Riddings Cumb 61 F10
Riddings Derby 45 G8
Riddlecombe Devon 6 E5
Riddlesden W Yorks 51 E6
Riddrie C/Glasg 68 D5
Ridge Dorset 9 F8
Ridge Hants 10 C2
Ridge Wilts 9 A8
Ridge Green Surrey 19 G10
Ridge Lane Warwick 35 F8
Ridgebourne Powys 25 B7
Ridgehill N Som'set 15 E11
Ridgeway Cross Heref'd 26 D4
Ridgewell Essex 30 D4
Ridgewood E Sussex 12 D3
Ridgmont Beds 28 E6
Riding Mill Northum 62 G6
Ridleywood Wrex 43 G7
Ridlington Norfolk 39 B9
Ridlington Rutl'd 36 E4
Ridsdale Northum 62 E5
Riechip Perth/Kinr 76 C3
Riemore Perth/Kinr 76 C3
Rienachait H'land 92 F3
Rievaulx N Yorks 59 H6
Rift House Hartlep'l 58 C5
Rigg Dumf/Gal 61 G8
Riggend N Lanarks 68 C6
Rigsby Lincs 47 E8
Rigside S Lanarks 69 G7
Riley Green Lancs 50 G2
Rileyhill Staffs 35 D7
Rilla Mill Cornw'l 4 D3
Rillington N Yorks 52 B4
Rimington Lancs 50 E4
Rimpton Som'set 8 B5
Rimswell ER Yorks 53 G9
Rinaston Pembs 22 D4
Ringasta Shetl'd 96 M5
Ringford Dumf/Gal 55 D9
Ringinglow S Yorks 44 D6
Ringland Norfolk 39 D7
Ringles Cross E Sussex 12 D3
Ringmer E Sussex 12 E3
Ringmore Devon 5 G7
Ringorm Moray 88 D2
Ring's End Cambs 37 E9
Ringsfield Suffolk 39 G10
Ringsfield Corner Suffolk 39 G10
Ringshall Herts 28 G6
Ringshall Suffolk 31 C7
Ringshall Stocks Suffolk 31 C7
Ringstead Norfolk 38 A3
Ringstead Northants 36 H5
Ringwood Hants 9 D10
Ringwould Kent 21 G10
Rinmore Aberds 82 B6

Rinnigill Orkney 95 J4
Rinsey Cornw'l 2 G4
Riof W Isles 90 D6
Ripe E Sussex 12 E4
Ripley Derby 45 G7
Ripley Hants 9 E10
Ripley N Yorks 51 C8
Ripley Surrey 19 F7
Riplingham ER Yorks 52 F5
Ripon N Yorks 51 B9
Rippingale Lincs 37 C6
Ripple Kent 21 G10
Ripple Worcs 26 E5
Ripponden W Yorks 50 H6
Rireavach H'land 86 B3
Risabus Arg/Bute 64 D4
Risbury Heref'd 26 C2
Risby Suffolk 30 B4
Risca = Rhisga Caerph 15 B8
Rise ER Yorks 53 E7
Riseden E Sussex 12 C5
Risegate Lincs 37 C8
Riseholme Lincs 46 E3
Riseley Beds 29 B7
Riseley Wokingham 18 E4
Rishangles Suffolk 31 B8
Rishton Lancs 50 F3
Rishworth W Yorks 50 H6
Rising Bridge Lancs 50 G3
Risley Derby 35 B10
Risley Warrington 43 C9
Risplith N Yorks 51 C8
Rispond H'land 92 C7
Rivar Wilts 17 E10
Rivenhall End Essex 30 G5
River Bank Cambs 30 B2
Riverhead Kent 20 F2
Rivington Lancs 43 A9
Roa Island Cumb 49 C2
Roachill Devon 7 D7
Road Green Norfolk 39 F8
Roade Northants 28 C4
Roadhead Cumb 61 F11
Roadmeetings S Lanarks 69 F7
Roadside H'land 94 D3
Roadside of Catterline Aberds 83 F10
Roadside of Kinneff Aberds 83 F10
Roadwater Som'set 7 C9
Roag H'land 85 D7
Roath Card 15 D7
Roberton Scot Borders 61 B10
Roberton S Lanarks 69 H8
Robertsbridge E Sussex 12 D6
Roberttown W Yorks 51 G7
Robeston Cross Pembs 22 F3
Robeston Wathen Pembs 22 E5
Robin Hood W Yorks 51 G9
Robin Hood's Bay N Yorks 59 F10
Roborough Devon 6 E4
Roborough Devon 4 E6
Roby Mersey 43 C7
Roby Mill Lancs 43 B8
Rocester Staffs 35 B7
Roch Pembs 22 D3
Roch Gate Pembs 22 D3
Rochdale Gtr Man 44 A2
Roche Cornw'l 3 C8
Rochester Medway 20 E4
Rochester Northum 62 D4
Rochford Essex 20 B5
Rock Cornw'l 3 B8
Rock Northum 63 A8
Rock Worcs 26 A4
Rock W Sussex 11 C10
Rock Ferry Mersey 42 D6
Rockbeare Devon 7 G9
Rockbourne Hants 9 C10
Rockcliffe Cumb 61 G9
Rockcliffe Dumf/Gal 55 D11
Rockfield H'land 87 C12
Rockfield Monmouths 25 G11
Rockford Hants 9 D10
Rockhampton S Gloucs 16 B3
Rockingham Northants 36 F4
Rockland All Saints Norfolk 38 F5
Rockland St Mary Norfolk 39 E9
Rockland St Peter Norfolk 38 F5
Rockley Wilts 17 D8
Rockwell End Bucks 18 C4
Rockwell Green Som'set 7 D10
Rodborough Glos 16 A5
Rodbourne Swindon 17 C8
Rodbourne Wilts 16 C6
Rodbourne Cheney Swindon 17 C8
Rodd Heref'd 25 B10
Roddam Northum 62 A6
Rodden Dorset 8 F5
Rode Som'set 16 F5
Rode Heath Ches 44 G2
Rodeheath Ches 44 F2
Roden Telford 34 D1
Rodhuish Som'set 7 C9
Rodington Telford 34 D1
Rodley Glos 26 G4
Rodley W Yorks 51 F8
Rodmarton Glos 16 B6
Rodmell E Sussex 12 F3
Rodmersham Kent 20 E6
Rodney Stoke Som'set 15 F10
Rodsley Derby 35 A8
Rodway Som'set 15 H8
Rodwell Dorset 8 G5
Roe Green Herts 29 E10
Roecliffe N Yorks 51 C9
Roehampton London 19 D9
Roesound Shetl'd 96 G5
Roffey W Sussex 11 A10
Rogart H'land 93 J10
Rogart Station H'land 93 J10
Rogate W Sussex 11 B7
Rogerstone Newp 15 C8
Roghadal W Isles 90 J5
Rogiet Monmouths 15 C10
Rogue's Alley Cambs 37 E9
Roke Oxon 18 B3
Roker Tyne/Wear 63 H10
Rollesby Norfolk 39 D10
Rolleston Leics 36 E3
Rolleston Notts 45 G11
Rolleston-on-Dove Staffs 35 C8
Rolston ER Yorks 53 E8
Rolvenden Kent 13 C7
Rolvenden Layne Kent 13 C7
Romaldkirk Durham 57 D11
Romanby N Yorks 58 G4
Romannobridge Scot Borders 69 F10
Romansleigh Devon 7 D6
Romford London 20 C2
Romiley Gtr Man 44 C3
Romsey Hants 10 B2
Romsey Town Cambs 29 C11
Romsley Shrops 34 G3
Romsley Worcs 34 H5
Ronague I/Man 48 E2
Rookhope Durham 57 B11
Rookley I/Wight 10 F4
Rooks Bridge Som'set 15 F9
Roos ER Yorks 53 F8
Roosebeck Cumb 49 C2
Rootham's Green Beds 29 C8
Rootpark S Lanarks 69 E8
Ropley Hants 10 A5
Ropley Dean Hants 10 A5
Ropsley Lincs 36 B5
Rora Aberds 89 C10
Rorandle Aberds 83 B8
Rorrington Shrops 33 E9
Roscroggan Cornw'l 2 E5
Rose Cornw'l 3 D6
Rose Ash Devon 7 D6
Rose Green W Sussex 11 E8
Rose Grove Lancs 50 F4
Rose Hill E Sussex 12 E3
Rose Hill Lancs 50 F4
Rose Hill Suffolk 31 D8
Roseacre Kent 20 F4
Roseacre Lancs 49 F4
Rosebank S Lanarks 69 F7
Rosebrough Northum 71 H10
Rosebush Pembs 22 D5
Rosecare Cornw'l 4 B2
Rosedale Abbey N Yorks 59 G8
Roseden Northum 62 A6
Rosefield H'land 87 F11
Rosehall H'land 92 J7
Rosehaugh Mains H'land 87 F9
Rosehearty Aberds 89 B9
Rosehill Shrops 34 B2
Roseisle Moray 88 B1
Roselands E Sussex 12 F5
Rosemarket Pembs 22 F4
Rosemarkie H'land 87 F10
Rosemary Lane Devon 7 E10
Rosemount Perth/Kinr 76 C4
Rosenannon Cornw'l 3 C8
Rosewell Midloth 69 D11
Roseworth Stockton 58 D5
Roseworthy Cornw'l 2 F5
Rosgill Cumb 57 E7
Roshven H'land 79 D10
Roskhill H'land 85 D7
Roskill House H'land 87 F9
Rosley Cumb 56 B5
Roslin Midloth 69 D11
Rosliston Derby 35 D8
Rosneath Arg/Bute 73 E11
Ross Dumf/Gal 55 E9
Ross Northum 71 G10
Ross Perth/Kinr 75 E10
Ross-on-Wye Heref'd 26 F3
Rossett Wrex 42 G6
Rossett Green N Yorks 51 D9
Rossie Ochill Perth/Kinr 76 F3
Rossie Priory Perth/Kinr 76 D5
Rossington S Yorks 45 C10
Rosskeen H'land 87 E9
Rossland Renf 68 C3
Roster H'land 94 G4
Rostherne Ches 43 D10
Rosthwaite Cumb 56 E4
Roston Derby 35 A7
Rosyth Fife 69 B10
Rothbury Northum 62 C6
Rotherby Leics 36 D2
Rotherfield E Sussex 12 D4
Rotherfield Greys Oxon 18 C4
Rotherfield Peppard Oxon 18 C4
Rotherham S Yorks 45 C8
Rothersthorpe Northants 28 C4
Rotherwick Hants 18 F4
Rothes Moray 88 D2
Rothesay Arg/Bute 73 G9
Rothiebrisbane Aberds 89 E7
Rothienorman Aberds 89 E7
Rothiesholm Orkney 95 F7
Rothley Leics 36 D1
Rothley Northum 62 E6
Rothley Shield East Northum 62 D6
Rothmaise Aberds 89 E6
Rothwell Lincs 46 C5
Rothwell Northants 36 G4
Rothwell W Yorks 51 G9
Rothwell Haigh W Yorks 51 G9
Rotsea ER Yorks 53 D6
Rottal Angus 82 G5
Rotten End Suffolk 31 B10
Rottingdean Brighton/Hove 12 F2
Rottington Cumb 56 E1
Roud I/Wight 10 F4
Rough Close Staffs 34 B5
Rough Common Kent 21 F8
Rougham Norfolk 38 C4
Rougham Suffolk 30 B6
Rougham Green Suffolk 30 B6
Roughburn H'land 80 E5
Roughlee Lancs 50 E4
Roughley W Midlands 35 F7
Roughsike Cumb 61 F11
Roughton Lincs 46 F6
Roughton Norfolk 39 B8
Roughton Shrops 34 F3
Roughton Moor Lincs 46 F6
Roundhay W Yorks 51 F9
Roundstonefoot Dumf/Gal 61 C7
Roundstreet Common W Sussex 11 B9
Roundway Wilts 17 E7
Rous Lench Worcs 27 C7
Rousdon Devon 8 E1
Routenburn N Ayrs 73 G10
Routh ER Yorks 53 E6
Row Cornw'l 4 D1
Row Cumb 56 H6
Row Heath Essex 31 G8
Rowanburn Dumf/Gal 61 F10
Rowardennan Stirl 74 H6
Rowde Wilts 16 E6
Rowen Conwy 41 C9
Rowfoot Northum 62 G2
Rowhedge Essex 31 F7
Rowhook W Sussex 11 A10
Rowington Warwick 27 B9
Rowland Derby 44 E6
Rowland's Castle Hants 10 C6
Rowlands Gill Tyne/Wear 63 H7
Rowledge Surrey 18 G5
Rowley ER Yorks 52 F5
Rowley Shrops 33 E9
Rowley Hill W Yorks 44 A5
Rowley Regis W Midlands 34 G5
Rowlstone Heref'd 25 F10
Rowly Surrey 19 G7
Rowney Green Worcs 27 A7
Rownhams Hants 10 C2
Rowrah Cumb 56 E2
Rowsham Bucks 28 G5
Rowsley Derby 44 F6
Rowstock Oxon 17 C11
Rowston Lincs 46 G4
Rowton Ches 43 F7
Rowton Shrops 33 D9
Rowton Telford 34 D2
Roxburgh Scot Borders 70 G6
Roxby N Lincs 52 H5
Roxby N Yorks 59 E8
Roxton Beds 29 C8
Roxwell Essex 30 H3
Royal Leamington Spa Warwick 27 B10
Royal Oak D'lington 58 D3
Royal Oak Lancs 43 B7
Royal Tunbridge Wells Kent 12 C4
Roybridge H'land 80 E4
Roydhouse W Yorks 44 A6
Roydon Essex 29 H11
Roydon Norfolk 38 C3
Roydon Norfolk 39 G6
Roydon Hamlet Essex 29 H11
Royston Herts 29 D10
Royston S Yorks 45 A7
Royton Gtr Man 44 B3
Rozel Jersey 11
Ruabon = Rhiwabon Wrex 33 A9
Ruaig Arg/Bute 78 G3
Ruan Lanihorne Cornw'l 3 E7
Ruan Minor Cornw'l 2 H6
Ruarach H'land 80 A1
Ruardean Glos 26 G3
Ruardean Woodside Glos 26 G3
Rubery Worcs 34 H5
Ruckcroft Cumb 57 B7
Ruckhall Common Heref'd 25 E11
Ruckinge Kent 13 C9
Ruckland Lincs 47 E7
Ruckley Shrops 33 E11
Rudbaxton Pembs 22 D4
Rudby N Yorks 58 F5
Ruddington Notts 36 B1
Rudford Glos 26 F4
Rudge Shrops 34 F4
Rudge Som'set 16 F5
Rudgeway S Gloucs 16 C3
Rudgwick W Sussex 11 A9
Rudhall Heref'd 26 F3
Rudheath Ches 43 E9
Rudley Green Essex 20 A5
Rudry Caerph 15 C7
Rudston ER Yorks 53 C6
Rudyard Staffs 44 G3
Rufford Lancs 49 H4
Rufforth C/York 51 D11
Rugby Warwick 35 H11
Rugeley Staffs 34 D6
Ruglen S Ayrs 66 F5
Ruilick H'land 87 G8
Ruishton Som'set 8 B1
Ruisigearraidh W Isles 90 J4
Ruislip London 19 C7
Ruislip Common London 19 C7
Rumbling Bridge Perth/Kinr 76 H3
Rumburgh Suffolk 39 G9
Rumford Cornw'l 3 B7
Rumney Card 15 D8
Runcorn Halton 43 D8
Runcton W Sussex 11 D7
Runcton Holme Norfolk 38 E2
Rundlestone Devon 5 D6
Runfold Surrey 18 G5
Runhall Norfolk 39 E6
Runham Norfolk 39 E11
Runham Norfolk 39 D10
Runnington Som'set 7 D10
Runsell Green Essex 30 H4
Runswick Bay N Yorks 59 E9
Runwell Essex 20 B4
Ruscombe Wokingham 18 D4
Rush Green London 20 C2
Rush-head Aberds 89 D8
Rushall Heref'd 26 E3
Rushall Norfolk 39 G7
Rushall Wilts 17 F8
Rushall W Midlands 34 E6
Rushbrooke Suffolk 30 B5
Rushbury Shrops 33 F11
Rushden Herts 29 E10
Rushden Northants 28 B6
Rushenden Kent 20 D6
Rushford Norfolk 38 G5
Rushlake Green E Sussex 12 E5
Rushmere Suffolk 39 G10
Rushmere St Andrew Suffolk 31 D9
Rushmoor Surrey 18 G5
Rushmoor Wilts 9 C8
Rushock Worcs 26 A5
Rusholme Gtr Man 44 C2
Rushton Ches 43 F8
Rushton Northants 36 G4
Rushton Shrops 34 E2
Rushton Spencer Staffs 44 F3
Rushwick Worcs 26 C5
Rushyford Durham 58 D3
Ruskie Stirl 75 G9
Ruskington Lincs 46 G4
Rusland Cumb 56 H5
Rusper W Sussex 19 H9
Ruspidge Glos 26 G3
Russell's Water Oxon 18 C4
Russel's Green Suffolk 31 A9
Rusthall Kent 12 C4
Rustington W Sussex 11 D9
Ruston N Yorks 52 A5
Ruston Parva ER Yorks 53 C6
Ruswarp N Yorks 59 F9
Rutherford Scot Borders 70 G5
Rutherglen S Lanarks 68 D5
Ruthernbridge Cornw'l 3 C9
Ruthin = Rhuthun Denbs 42 G4
Ruthrieston Aberd C 83 C11
Ruthven Aberds 88 D5
Ruthven Angus 76 C5
Ruthven H'land 87 H11
Ruthven H'land 81 D9
Ruthven House Angus 76 C6
Ruthvoes Cornw'l 3 C8
Ruthwell Dumf/Gal 60 G6
Ruyton-XI-Towns Shrops 33 C9
Ryal Northum 62 F6
Ryal Fold Blackb'n 50 G2
Ryall Dorset 8 E3
Ryarsh Kent 20 F3
Rydal Cumb 56 F5
Ryde I/Wight 10 E4
Rye E Sussex 13 D8
Rye Foreign E Sussex 13 D7
Rye Harbour E Sussex 13 E8
Rye Park Herts 29 G10
Rye Street Worcs 26 E4
Ryecroft Gate Staffs 44 F3
Ryehill ER Yorks 53 G8
Ryhall Rutl'd 36 D6
Ryhill W Yorks 45 A7
Ryhope Tyne/Wear 58 A5
Rylstone N Yorks 50 D5
Ryme Intrinseca Dorset 8 C4
Ryther N Yorks 52 F1
Ryton Glos 26 E4
Ryton N Yorks 52 B3
Ryton Shrops 34 E3
Ryton Tyne/Wear 63 G7
Ryton-on-Dunsmore Warwick 27 A10

S

Sabden Lancs 50 F3
Sacombe Herts 29 G10
Sacriston Durham 58 B3
Sadberge D'lington 58 E4
Saddell Arg/Bute 65 E8
Saddington Leics 36 F2
Saddle Bow Norfolk 38 D2
Saddlescombe W Sussex 12 E1
Sadgill Cumb 57 F6
Saffron Walden Essex 30 E2
Sageston Pembs 22 F5
Saham Hills Norfolk 38 E5
Saham Toney Norfolk 38 E5
Saighdinis W Isles 84 B3
Saighton Ches 43 F7
St Abb's Scot Borders 71 D8
St Abb's Haven Scot Borders 71 D8
St Agnes Cornw'l 2 D6
St Agnes I/Scilly 2 D2
St Albans Herts 29 H8
St Allen Cornw'l 3 D7
St Andrews Fife 77 F8
St Andrew's Major V/Glam 15 D7
St Anne Alderney 11
St Annes Lancs 49 G3
St Ann's Dumf/Gal 60 D6
St Ann's Chapel Cornw'l 4 D5
St Ann's Chapel Devon 5 G7
St Anthony Cornw'l 3 G6
St Anthony's Hill E Sussex 12 F5
St Arvans Monmouths 15 B11
St Asaph = Llanelwy Denbs 42 E3
St Athan V/Glam 14 E6
St Aubin Jersey 11
St Austell Cornw'l 3 D9
St Bees Cumb 56 E1
St Blazey Cornw'l 4 F1
St Boswells Scot Borders 70 G4
St Brelade Jersey 11
St Breock Cornw'l 3 B8
St Breward Cornw'l 4 D1
St Briavels Glos 16 A2
St Bride's Pembs 22 E3
St Brides Major V/Glam 14 D4
St Bride's Netherwent Monmouths 15 C10
St Brides super Ely V/Glam 14 D6
St Brides Wentlooge Newp 15 C8
St Budeaux Plym'th 4 F5
St Buryan Cornw'l 2 G3
St Catherine Bath/NE Som'set 16 D4
St Catherine's Arg/Bute 73 C10
St Clears = Sanclêr Carms 23 E7
St Cleer Cornw'l 4 E3
St Clement Cornw'l 3 E7
St Clements Jersey 11
St Clether Cornw'l 4 C3
St Colmac Arg/Bute 73 G9
St Columb Major Cornw'l 3 C8
St Columb Minor Cornw'l 3 C7
St Columb Road Cornw'l 3 D8
St Combs Aberds 89 B10
St Cross South Elmham Suffolk 39 G8
St Cyrus Aberds 77 A10
St David's Perth/Kinr 76 E2
St David's = Tyddewi Pembs 22 D2
St Day Cornw'l 2 E6
St Dennis Cornw'l 3 D8
St Devereux Heref'd 25 E11
St Dogmaels Pembs 22 B6
St Dogwells Pembs 22 D4
St Dominick Cornw'l 4 E5
St Donat's V/Glam 14 E5
St Edith's Wilts 16 E6
St Endellion Cornw'l 3 B8
St Enoder Cornw'l 3 D7
St Erme Cornw'l 3 D7
St Erney Cornw'l 4 F4
St Erth Cornw'l 2 F4
St Ervan Cornw'l 3 B7
St Eval Cornw'l 3 C7
St Ewe Cornw'l 3 E8
St Fagans Card 15 D7
St Fergus Aberds 89 C10
St Fillans Perth/Kinr 75 E9
St Florence Pembs 22 F5
St Genny's Cornw'l 4 B2
St George Conwy 42 E2
St George's V/Glam 14 D6
St Germans Cornw'l 4 F4
St Giles Lincs 46 E3
St Giles in the Wood Devon 6 E4
St Giles on the Heath Devon 6 G2
St Harmon Powys 24 A6
St Helen Auckland Durham 58 D2
St Helena Warwick 35 E8
St Helen's E Sussex 13 E7
St Helens I/Wight 10 F5
St Helens Mersey 43 C8
St Helier London 19 E9
St Helier Jersey 11
St Hilary Cornw'l 2 F4
St Hilary V/Glam 14 D6
Saint Hill W Sussex 12 C2
St Illtyd Bl Gwent 15 A8
St Ippollitts Herts 29 F8
St Ishmael's Pembs 22 F3
St Issey Cornw'l 3 B8
St Ive Cornw'l 4 E4
St Ives Cambs 29 A10
St Ives Cornw'l 2 E4
St Ives Dorset 9 D10
St James South Elmham Suffolk 39 G9
St Jidgey Cornw'l 3 C8
St John Cornw'l 4 F5
St John's I/Man 48 D2
St John's Jersey 11
St John's Surrey 18 F6
St John's Worcs 26 C5
St John's Chapel Durham 57 C10
St John's Fen End Norfolk 37 D11
St John's Highway Norfolk 37 D11
St John's Town of Dalry Dumf/Gal 55 A9
St Judes I/Man 48 C3
St Just Cornw'l 2 F2
St Just in Roseland Cornw'l 3 F7
St Katherine's Aberds 89 E7
St Keverne Cornw'l 3 G6
St Kew Cornw'l 3 B9
St Kew Highway Cornw'l 3 B9
St Keyne Cornw'l 4 E3
St Lawrence Cornw'l 3 C9
St Lawrence Essex 20 A6
St Lawrence I/Wight 10 G4
St Leonard's Bucks 28 H6
St Leonards Dorset 9 D10
St Leonards E Sussex 13 F6
Saint Leonards S Lanarks 68 E5
St Levan Cornw'l 2 G2
St Lythans V/Glam 15 D7
St Mabyn Cornw'l 3 B9
St Madoes Perth/Kinr 76 E4
St Margaret South Elmham Suffolk 39 G9
St Margaret's Heref'd 25 E10
St Margarets Herts 29 G10
St Margaret's at Cliffe Kent 21 G10
St Margaret's Hope Orkney 95 J5
St Mark's I/Man 48 E2
St Martin Cornw'l 4 F3
St Martins Cornw'l 2 G6
St Martin's Jersey 11
St Martins Perth/Kinr 76 D4
St Martin's Shrops 33 B9
St Mary Bourne Hants 17 F11
St Mary Church V/Glam 14 D6
St Mary Cray London 19 E11
St Mary Hill V/Glam 14 D5
St Mary Hoo Medway 20 D5
St Mary in the Marsh Kent 13 D9
St Mary's Jersey 11
St Mary's Orkney 95 H5
St Mary's Bay Kent 13 D9
St Maughans Monmouths 25 G11
St Mawes Cornw'l 3 F7
St Mawgan Cornw'l 3 C7
St Mellion Cornw'l 4 E4
St Mellons Card 15 C8
St Merryn Cornw'l 3 B7
St Mewan Cornw'l 3 D8
St Michael Caerhays Cornw'l 3 E8
St Michael Penkevil Cornw'l 3 E7
St Michael South Elmham Suffolk 39 G9
St Michael's Kent 13 C7
St Michaels Worcs 26 B2
St Michael's on Wyre Lancs 49 E4
St Minver Cornw'l 3 B8
St Monans Fife 77 G8
St Neot Cornw'l 4 E2
St Neots Cambs 29 B8
St Newlyn East Cornw'l 3 D7
St Nicholas Pembs 22 C3
St Nicholas V/Glam 14 D6
St Nicholas at Wade Kent 21 E9
St Ninians Stirl 68 A6
St Osyth Essex 31 G8
St Osyth Heath Essex 31 G8
St Ouens Jersey 11
St Owens Cross Heref'd 26 F2
St Paul's Cray London 19 E11
St Paul's Walden Herts 29 F8
St Peter Port Guernsey 11
St Peter's Jersey 11
St Peter's Kent 21 E10
St Petrox Pembs 22 G4
St Pinnock Cornw'l 4 E3
St Quivox S Ayrs 67 D6
St Ruan Cornw'l 2 H6
St Sampson Guernsey 11
St Stephen Cornw'l 3 D8
St Stephen's Cornw'l 4 C4
St Stephens Cornw'l 4 F5
St Stephens Herts 29 H8
St Teath Cornw'l 4 C1
St Thomas Devon 7 G8
St Tudy Cornw'l 4 D1
St Twynnells Pembs 22 G4
St Veep Cornw'l 4 F2
St Vigeans Angus 77 C9
St Wenn Cornw'l 3 C8
St Weonards Heref'd 25 F11
Saintbury Glos 27 E8
Salcombe Devon 5 H8
Salcombe Regis Devon 7 H10
Salcott Essex 30 G6
Sale Gtr Man 43 C10
Sale Green Worcs 26 C6
Saleby Lincs 47 E8
Salehurst E Sussex 12 D6
Salem Ceredig'n 32 G2
Salem Carms 24 F3
Salen Arg/Bute 79 G8
Salen H'land 79 E9
Salesbury Lancs 50 F2
Salford Beds 28 E6
Salford Gtr Man 44 C2
Salford Oxon 27 F9
Salford Priors Warwick 27 C7
Salfords Surrey 19 G9
Salhouse Norfolk 39 D9
Saline Fife 69 A9
Salisbury Wilts 9 B10
Sallachan H'land 74 A2
Sallachy H'land 86 H2
Sallachy H'land 93 J8
Salle Norfolk 39 C7
Salmonby Lincs 47 E7
Salmond's Muir Angus 77 D8
Salperton Glos 27 F7
Salph End Beds 29 C7
Salsburgh N Lanarks 69 D7
Salt Staffs 34 C5
Salt End ER Yorks 53 G7
Saltaire W Yorks 51 F7
Saltash Cornw'l 4 F5
Saltburn H'land 87 E10
Saltburn-by-the-Sea Redcar/Clevel'd 59 D7
Saltby Leics 36 C4
Saltcoats Cumb 56 G2
Saltcoats N Ayrs 66 B5
Saltdean Brighton/Hove 12 F2
Salter Lancs 50 C2
Salterforth Lancs 50 E4
Salterswall Ches 43 F9
Saltfleet Lincs 47 C8
Saltfleetby All Saints Lincs 47 C8
Saltfleetby St Clements Lincs 47 C8
Saltfleetby St Peter Lincs 47 D8
Saltford Bath/NE Som'set 16 E3
Salthouse Norfolk 39 A6
Saltmarshe ER Yorks 52 G3
Saltney Flints 43 F6
Salton N Yorks 52 B3
Saltwick Northum 63 F7
Saltwood Kent 21 H8
Salum Arg/Bute 78 G3
Salvington W Sussex 11 D10
Salwarpe Worcs 26 B5
Salway Ash Dorset 8 E3
Sambourne Warwick 27 B7
Sambrook Telford 34 C3
Samhla W Isles 84 B2
Samlesbury Lancs 50 F1
Samlesbury Bottoms Lancs 50 G2
Sampford Arundel Som'set 7 E10
Sampford Brett Som'set 7 B9
Sampford Courtenay Devon 6 F5
Sampford Peverell Devon 7 E9
Sampford Spiney Devon 4 D6
Sampool Bridge Cumb 56 H6
Samuelston E Loth 70 C3
Sanachan H'land 85 D13
Sanaigmore Arg/Bute 64 A3
Sanclêr = St Clears Carms 23 E7
Sancreed Cornw'l 2 G3
Sancton ER Yorks 52 F5
Sand H'land 86 B2
Sand Shetl'd 96 J5
Sand Hole ER Yorks 52 F4
Sand Hutton N Yorks 52 D2
Sandaig H'land 85 H12
Sandal Magna W Yorks 51 H9
Sandale Cumb 56 B4
Sandbach Ches 43 F10
Sandbank Arg/Bute 73 E10
Sandbanks Poole 9 F9
Sandend Aberds 88 B5
Sanderstead London 19 E10
Sandfields Glos 26 F6
Sandford Cumb 57 E9
Sandford Devon 7 F7
Sandford Dorset 9 F8
Sandford I/Wight 10 F4
Sandford N Som'set 15 F10
Sandford Shrops 34 B1
Sandford S Lanarks 68 F6
Sandford on Thames Oxon 18 A2
Sandford Orcas Dorset 8 B5
Sandford St Martin Oxon 27 F11
Sandfordhill Aberds 89 D11
Sandgate Kent 21 H8
Sandgreen Dumf/Gal 55 D8
Sandhaven Aberds 89 B9
Sandhead Dumf/Gal 54 E3
Sandhills Surrey 18 H6
Sandhoe Northum 62 G5
Sandholme ER Yorks 52 F4
Sandholme Lincs 37 B9
Sandhurst Brackn'l 18 E5
Sandhurst Glos 26 F5
Sandhurst Kent 13 D6
Sandhurst Cross Kent 13 D6
Sandhutton N Yorks 51 A9
Sandiacre Derby 35 B10
Sandilands Lincs 47 D9
Sandilands S Lanarks 69 G7
Sandiway Ches 43 E9
Sandleheath Hants 9 C10
Sandling Kent 20 F4
Sandlow Green Ches 43 F10
Sandness Shetl'd 96 H3
Sandon Essex 20 A4
Sandon Herts 29 E10
Sandon Staffs 34 B5
Sandown I/Wight 10 F4
Sandplace Cornw'l 4 F3
Sandridge Herts 29 G8
Sandridge Wilts 16 E6
Sandringham Norfolk 38 C2
Sandsend N Yorks 59 E9
Sandside Ho. H'land 93 C12
Sandsound Shetl'd 96 J5
Sandtoft N Lincs 45 B11
Sandway Kent 20 F5
Sandwell W Midlands 34 G6
Sandwich Kent 21 F10
Sandwick Cumb 56 E6
Sandwick Orkney 95 K5
Sandwick Shetl'd 96 L6
Sandwith Cumb 56 E1
Sandy Beds 29 D8
Sandy Carms 23 F9
Sandy Bank Lincs 46 G6
Sandy Haven Pembs 22 F3
Sandy Lane Wilts 16 E6
Sandy Lane Wrex 33 A9
Sandycroft Flints 42 F6
Sandyford Dumf/Gal 61 D8
Sandyford Stoke 44 G2
Sandygate I/Man 48 C3
Sandyhills Dumf/Gal 55 D11
Sandylands Lancs 49 C4
Sandypark Devon 5 C8
Sandysike Cumb 61 G9
Sangobeg H'land 92 C7
Sangomore H'land 92 C7
Sanna H'land 78 E7
Sanndabhaig W Isles 91 D9
Sanndabhaig W Isles 84 D3
Sannox N Ayrs 66 B3
Sanquhar Dumf/Gal 60 C3
Santon N Lincs 46 A3
Santon Bridge Cumb 56 F3
Santon Downham Suffolk 38 G4
Sapcote Leics 35 F10
Sapey Common Heref'd 26 B4
Sapiston Suffolk 38 H5
Sapley Cambs 29 A9
Sapperton Glos 16 A6
Sapperton Lincs 36 B6
Saracen's Head Lincs 37 C9
Sarclet H'land 94 F5
Sardis Carms 23 F10
Sarn Bridg 14 C5
Sarn Powys 33 F8
Sarn Bach Gwyn 40 H5
Sarn Meyllteyrn Gwyn 40 G4
Sarnau Ceredig'n 23 A8
Sarnau Carms 23 E8
Sarnau Gwyn 32 B5
Sarnau Powys 25 E7
Sarnau Powys 33 D8
Sarnesfield Heref'd 25 C10
Saron Carms 23 C8
Saron Carms 24 G3
Saron Denbs 42 F3
Saron Gwyn 40 E6
Saron Gwyn 41 D7
Sarratt Herts 19 B7
Sarre Kent 21 E9
Sarsden Oxon 27 F9
Sarsgrum H'land 92 C6
Satley Durham 58 B2
Satron N Yorks 57 G11
Satterleigh Devon 6 D5
Satterthwaite Cumb 56 G5
Satwell Oxon 18 C4
Sauchen Aberds 83 B8
Saucher Perth/Kinr 76 D4
Sauchie Clack 69 A7
Sauchieburn Aberds 83 G8
Saughall Ches 42 E6
Saughtree Scot Borders 61 D11
Saul Glos 26 H4
Saundby Notts 45 D11
Saundersfoot Pembs 22 F6
Saunderton Bucks 18 A4
Saunton Devon 6 C3
Sausthorpe Lincs 47 F7
Saval H'land 93 J8
Savary H'land 79 G9
Savile Park W Yorks 51 G6
Sawbridge Warwick 28 B2
Sawbridgeworth Herts 29 G11
Sawdon N Yorks 59 H10
Sawley Derby 35 B10
Sawley Lancs 50 E3
Sawley N Yorks 51 C8
Sawston Cambs 29 D11
Sawtry Cambs 37 G7
Saxby Leics 36 D4
Saxby Lincs 46 D4
Saxby All Saints N Lincs 52 H5
Saxelbye Leics 36 C3
Saxham Street Suffolk 31 B7
Saxilby Lincs 46 E2
Saxlingham Norfolk 38 B6
Saxlingham Green Norfolk 39 F8
Saxlingham Nethergate Norfolk 39 F8
Saxlingham Thorpe Norfolk 39 F8
Saxmundham Suffolk 31 B10
Saxon Street Cambs 30 C3
Saxondale Notts 36 B2
Saxtead Suffolk 31 B9
Saxtead Green Suffolk 31 B9
Saxthorpe Norfolk 39 B7
Saxton N Yorks 51 F10
Sayers Common W Sussex 12 E1
Scackleton N Yorks 52 B2
Scadabhagh W Isles 90 H6
Scaftworth Notts 45 C10
Scagglethorpe N Yorks 52 B4
Scaitcliffe Lancs 50 G3
Scalasaig Arg/Bute 72 D2
Scalby ER Yorks 52 G4
Scalby N Yorks 59 G11
Scaldwell Northants 28 A4
Scale Houses Cumb 57 B7
Scaleby Cumb 61 G10
Scaleby Hill Cumb 61 G10
Scales Cumb 49 B2
Scales Cumb 56 D5
Scales Lancs 49 F4
Scalford Leics 36 C3
Scaling N Yorks 59 E8
Scaling Dam Redcar/Clevel'd 59 E8
Scallastle Arg/Bute 79 H9
Scalloway Shetl'd 96 K6
Scalpay W Isles 90 H7
Scalpay Ho. H'land 85 F11
Scalpsie Arg/Bute 73 H9
Scamadale H'land 79 B10
Scamblesby Lincs 46 E6
Scamodale H'land 79 D11
Scampston N Yorks 52 B4
Scampton Lincs 46 E3
Scapa Orkney 95 H5
Scapegoat Hill W Yorks 51 H6
Scar Orkney 95 D7
Scarborough N Yorks 59 H11
Scarcliffe Derby 45 F8
Scarcroft W Yorks 51 E9
Scarcroft Hill W Yorks 51 E9
Scardroy H'land 86 F5
Scarff Shetl'd 96 E4
Scarfskerry H'land 94 C4
Scargill Durham 58 E1
Scarinish Arg/Bute 78 G3
Scarisbrick Lancs 43 A6
Scarning Norfolk 38 D5
Scarrington Notts 36 A3
Scartho NE Lincs 46 B6
Scarwell Orkney 95 F3
Scatness Shetl'd 96 M5
Scatraig H'land 87 H10
Scawby N Lincs 46 B3
Scawsby S Yorks 45 B9
Scawton N Yorks 51 A11
Scayne's Hill W Sussex 12 D2
Scethrog Powys 25 F8
Scholar Green Ches 44 G2
Scholes W Yorks 44 B5
Scholes W Yorks 51 G7
Scholes W Yorks 51 F9
School Green Ches 43 F9
Scleddau Pembs 22 C4
Sco Ruston Norfolk 39 C8
Scofton Notts 45 D10
Scole Norfolk 39 H7
Scolpaig W Isles 84 A2
Scone Perth/Kinr 76 E4
Sconser H'land 85 E10
Scoonie Fife 76 G6
Scoor Arg/Bute 78 K7
Scopwick Lincs 46 G4
Scoraig H'land 86 B3
Scorborough ER Yorks 52 E6
Scorrier Cornw'l 2 E6
Scorton Lancs 49 E5
Scorton N Yorks 58 F3
Scotbheinn W Isles 84 C3
Scotby Cumb 61 H10
Scotch Corner N Yorks 58 F3
Scotforth Lancs 49 D4
Scothern Lincs 46 E4
Scotland Gate Northum 63 E8
Scotlandwell Perth/Kinr 76 G4
Scotsburn H'land 87 D10
Scotscalder Station H'land 94 E2
Scotscraig Fife 77 E7
Scots'Gap Northum 62 E6
Scotston Aberds 83 F9
Scotston Perth/Kinr 76 C2
Scotstoun C/Glasg 68 D4
Scotstown H'land 79 E11
Scotswood Tyne/Wear 63 G7
Scottas H'land 85 H12
Scotter Lincs 46 B2
Scotterthorpe Lincs 46 B2
Scottlethorpe Lincs 37 C6
Scotton Lincs 46 C2
Scotton N Yorks 58 G2
Scotton N Yorks 51 D9
Scottow Norfolk 39 C8
Scoughall E Loth 70 B5
Scoulag Arg/Bute 73 H10
Scoulton Norfolk 38 E5
Scourie H'land 92 E4
Scourie More H'land 92 E4
Scousburgh Shetl'd 96 M5
Scrabster H'land 94 C2
Scrafield Lincs 47 F7
Scrainwood Northum 62 C5
Scrane End Lincs 37 A9
Scraptoft Leics 36 E2
Scratby Norfolk 39 D11
Scrayingham N Yorks 52 C3
Scredington Lincs 37 A6
Scremby Lincs 47 F8
Scremerston Northum 71 F9
Screveton Notts 36 A3
Scrivelsby Lincs 46 F6
Scriven N Yorks 51 D9
Scrooby Notts 45 C10
Scropton Derby 35 B7
Scrub Hill Lincs 46 G6
Scruton N Yorks 58 G3
Sculcoates Kingston/Hull 53 F6
Sculthorpe Norfolk 38 B4
Scunthorpe N Lincs 46 A2
Scurlage Swan 23 H9
Sea Palling Norfolk 39 C10
Seaborough Dorset 8 D3
Seacombe Mersey 42 C6
Seacroft Lincs 47 F9
Seacroft W Yorks 51 F9
Seadyke Lincs 37 B9
Seafield S Ayrs 66 D6
Seafield W Loth 69 D9
Seaford E Sussex 12 G3
Seaforth Mersey 42 C6
Seagrave Leics 36 D2
Seaham Durham 58 B5
Seahouses Northum 71 G11
Seal Kent 20 F2
Sealand Flints 42 F6
Seale Surrey 18 G5
Seamer N Yorks 58 E5
Seamer N Yorks 52 A6
Seamill N Ayrs 66 B5
Searby Lincs 46 B4
Seasalter Kent 21 E7
Seascale Cumb 56 F2
Seathorne Lincs 47 F9
Seathwaite Cumb 56 G4
Seathwaite Cumb 56 E4
Seatoller Cumb 56 E4
Seaton Cornw'l 4 F4
Seaton Cumb 56 C2
Seaton Devon 8 F1
Seaton Durham 58 A4
Seaton ER Yorks 53 E7
Seaton Northum 63 F9
Seaton Rutl'd 36 F5
Seaton Burn Tyne/Wear 63 F8
Seaton Carew Hartlep'l 58 D6
Seaton Delaval Northum 63 F9
Seaton Ross ER Yorks 52 E3
Seaton Sluice Northum 63 F9
Seatown Aberds 88 B5
Seatown Dorset 8 E3
Seave Green N Yorks 59 F6
Seaview I/Wight 10 E5
Seaville Cumb 56 A3
Seavington St Mary Som'set 8 C3
Seavington St Michael Som'set 8 C3
Sebergham Cumb 56 B5
Seckington Warwick 35 E8
Second Coast H'land 86 B2
Sedbergh Cumb 57 G8
Sedbury Glos 15 B11
Sedbusk N Yorks 57 G10
Sedgeberrow Worcs 27 E7
Sedgebrook Lincs 36 B4
Sedgefield Durham 58 D4
Sedgeford Norfolk 38 B3
Sedgehill Wilts 9 B7
Sedgley W Midlands 34 F5
Sedgwick Cumb 57 H7
Sedlescombe E Sussex 13 E6
Sedlescombe Street E Sussex 13 E6
Seend Wilts 16 E6
Seend Cleeve Wilts 16 E6
Seer Green Bucks 18 B6
Seething Norfolk 39 F9
Sefton Mersey 42 B6
Seghill Northum 63 F8
Seifton Shrops 33 G10
Seighford Staffs 34 C4
Seilebost W Isles 90 H5
Seion Gwyn 41 D7
Seisdon Staffs 34 F4
Seisiadar W Isles 91 D10
Selattyn Shrops 33 B8
Selborne Hants 10 A6
Selby N Yorks 52 F2
Selham W Sussex 11 B8
Selhurst London 19 E10
Selkirk Scot Borders 70 H3
Sellack Heref'd 26 F2
Sellafield Station Cumb 56 F2
Sellafirth Shetl'd 96 D7
Sellibister Orkney 95 D8
Sellindge Kent 13 C9
Sellindge Lees Kent 13 C10
Selling Kent 21 F7
Sells Green Wilts 16 E6
Selly Oak W Midlands 34 G6
Selmeston E Sussex 12 F4
Selsdon London 19 E10
Selsey W Sussex 11 E7
Selsfield Common W Sussex 12 C2
Selsted Kent 21 G9
Selston Notts 45 G8
Selworthy Som'set 7 B8
Semblister Shetl'd 96 H5
Semer Suffolk 30 D6
Semington Wilts 16 E5
Semley Wilts 9 B7
Send Surrey 19 F7
Send Marsh Surrey 19 F7
Senghenydd Caerph 15 B7
Sennen Cornw'l 2 G2
Sennen Cove Cornw'l 2 G2
Sennybridge = Pont Senni Powys 24 F6
Serlby Notts 45 D10
Sessay N Yorks 51 B10
Setchey Norfolk 38 D2
Setley Hants 10 D2
Setter Shetl'd 96 H5
Setter Shetl'd 96 E6
Setter Shetl'd 96 J7
Settiscarth Orkney 95 G4
Settle N Yorks 50 C4
Settrington N Yorks 52 B4
Seven Kings London 19 C11
Seven Sisters Neath P Talb 24 H5
Sevenhampton Glos 27 F7
Sevenoaks Kent 20 F2
Sevenoaks Weald Kent 20 F2
Severn Beach S Gloucs 15 C11
Severn Stoke Worcs 26 D5
Severnhampton Swindon 17 B9
Sevington Kent 13 B9
Sewards End Essex 30 E2
Sewardstone Essex 19 B10
Sewardstonebury Essex 19 B10
Sewerby ER Yorks 53 C7
Seworgan Cornw'l 2 F6
Sewstern Leics 36 C4
Sezincote Glos 27 E8
Sgarasta Mhor W Isles 90 H5
Sgiogarstaigh W Isles 91 A10
Shabbington Bucks 28 H3
Shackerstone Leics 35 E9
Shackleford Surrey 18 G6
Shade W Yorks 50 G5
Shadforth Durham 58 B4
Shadingfield Suffolk 39 G10
Shadoxhurst Kent 13 C8
Shadsworth Blackb'n 50 G3
Shadwell Norfolk 38 G5
Shadwell W Yorks 51 F9
Shaftesbury Dorset 9 B7
Shafton S Yorks 45 A7
Shalbourne Wilts 17 E10
Shalcombe I/Wight 10 F2
Shalden Hants 18 G3
Shaldon Devon 5 D10
Shalfleet I/Wight 10 F3
Shalford Essex 30 F4
Shalford Surrey 19 G7
Shalford Green Essex 30 F4
Shallowford Devon 6 B6
Shalmsford Street Kent 21 F7
Shalstone Bucks 28 E3
Shamley Green Surrey 19 G7
Shandon Arg/Bute 73 E11
Shandwick H'land 87 D11
Shangton Leics 36 F3
Shankhouse Northum 63 F8
Shanklin I/Wight 10 F4
Shanquhar Aberds 88 E5
Shanzie Perth/Kinr 76 B5
Shap Cumb 57 E7
Shapwick Dorset 9 D
Shapwick Som'set 15 H1
Shardlow Derby 35 B1

Shareshill *Staffs* 34 E5
Sharlston *W Yorks* 51 H9
Sharlston Common *W Yorks* 51 H9
Sharnbrook *Beds* 28 C6
Sharnford *Leics* 35 F10
Sharoe Green *Lancs* 49 F5
Sharow *N Yorks* 51 B9
Sharp Street *Norfolk* 39 C9
Sharpenhoe *Beds* 29 E7
Sharperton *Northum* 62 C5
Sharpness *Glos* 16 A3
Sharpthorne *W Sussex* 12 C2
Sharrington *Norfolk* 38 B6
Shatterford *Worcs* 34 G3
Shaugh Prior *Devon* 4 E6
Shavington *Ches* 43 G10
Shaw *Gtr Man* 44 B3
Shaw *W Berks* 17 E11
Shaw *Wilts* 16 E5
Shaw Green *Lancs* 49 H5
Shaw Mills *N Yorks* 51 C8
Shawbury *Shrops* 34 C1
Shawdon Hall *Northum* 62 B6
Shawell *Leics* 35 G11
Shawford *Hants* 10 B3
Shawforth *Lancs* 50 G4
Shawhead *Dumf/Gal* 60 F4
Shawhill *Dumf/Gal* 61 G8
Shawton *S Lanarks* 68 F5
Shawtonhill *S Lanarks* 68 F5
Shear Cross *Wilts* 16 G5
Shearington *Dumf/Gal* 60 G6
Shearsby *Leics* 36 F2
Shebbear *Devon* 6 F3
Shebdon *Staffs* 34 C3
Shebster *H'land* 93 C13
Sheddens *E Renf* 68 E4
Shedfield *Hants* 10 C4
Sheen *Staffs* 44 F5
Sheepscar *W Yorks* 51 F9
Sheepscombe *Glos* 26 G5
Sheepstor *Devon* 5 E6
Sheepwash *Devon* 6 F3
Sheepway *N Som'set* 15 D10
Sheepy Magna *Leics* 35 E9
Sheepy Parva *Leics* 35 E9
Sheering *Essex* 30 G2
Sheerness *Kent* 20 D6
Sheet *Hants* 11 B6
Sheffield *S Yorks* 45 D7
Sheffield Bottom *W Berks* 18 E3
Sheffield Green *E Sussex* 12 D3
Shefford *Beds* 29 E8
Shefford Woodlands *W Berks* 17 D10
Sheigra *H'land* 92 C4
Sheinton *Shrops* 34 E2
Shelderton *Shrops* 33 H10
Sheldon *Derby* 44 F5
Sheldon *Devon* 7 F10
Sheldon *W Midlands* 35 G7
Sheldwich *Kent* 21 F7
Shelf *W Yorks* 51 G7
Shelfanger *Norfolk* 39 G7
Shelfield *Warwick* 27 B8
Shelfield *W Midlands* 34 E6
Shelford *Notts* 36 A2
Shellacres *Northum* 71 F7
Shelley *Essex* 20 A2
Shelley *Suffolk* 31 E7
Shelley *W Yorks* 44 A6
Shellingford *Oxon* 17 B10
Shellow Bowells *Essex* 30 H3
Shelsley Beauchamp *Worcs* 26 B4
Shelsley Walsh *Worcs* 26 B4
Shelthorpe *Leics* 35 D11
Shelton *Beds* 29 B7
Shelton *Norfolk* 39 F8
Shelton *Notts* 36 A3
Shelton *Shrops* 33 D10
Shelton Green *Norfolk* 39 F8
Shelve *Shrops* 33 F9
Shelwick *Heref'd* 26 D2
Shenfield *Essex* 20 B3
Shenington *Oxon* 27 D10
Shenley *Herts* 19 A8
Shenley Brook End *M/Keynes* 28 E5
Shenley Church End *M/Keynes* 28 E5
Shenleybury *Herts* 19 A8
Shenmore *Heref'd* 25 E10
Shennanton *Dumf/Gal* 54 C6
Shenstone *Staffs* 35 E7
Shenstone *Worcs* 26 A5
Shenton *Leics* 35 E9
Shenval *H'land* 80 A6
Shenval *Moray* 82 A4
Shepeau Stow *Lincs* 37 D9
Shephall *Herts* 29 F9
Shepherd's Green *Oxon* 18 C4
Shepherd's Port *Norfolk* 38 B2
Shepherdswell *Kent* 21 G9
Shepley *W Yorks* 44 B5
Shepperdine *S Gloucs* 16 B3
Shepperton *Surrey* 19 E7
Shepreth *Cambs* 29 D10
Shepshed *Leics* 35 D10
Shepton Beauchamp *Som'set* 8 C3
Shepton Mallet *Som'set* 16 G3
Shepton Montague *Som'set* 8 A5
Shepway *Kent* 20 F4
Sheraton *Durham* 58 C5
Sherborne *Dorset* 8 C5
Sherborne *Glos* 27 G8
Sherborne St John *Hants* 18 F3
Sherbourne *Warwick* 27 B9
Sherburn *Durham* 58 B4
Sherburn *N Yorks* 52 B5
Sherburn Hill *Durham* 58 B4
Sherburn in Elmet *N Yorks* 51 F10
Shere *Surrey* 19 G7
Shereford *Norfolk* 38 C4
Sherfield English *Hants* 10 B1
Sherfield on Loddon *Hants* 18 F3
Sherford *Devon* 5 G8
Sheriff Hutton *N Yorks* 52 C2
Sheriffhales *Shrops* 34 D3
Sheringham *Norfolk* 39 A7
Sherington *M/Keynes* 28 D5
Shernal Green *Worcs* 26 B6
Shernborne *Norfolk* 38 B3
Sherrington *Wilts* 16 H6
Sherston *Wilts* 16 C5
Sherwood Green *Devon* 6 D4
Shettleston *C/Glasg* 68 D5
Shevington *Gtr Man* 43 B8
Shevington Moor *Gtr Man* 43 A8
Shevington Vale *Gtr Man* 43 B8
Sheviock *Cornw'l* 4 F4
Shide *I/Wight* 10 F3
Shiel Bridge *H'land* 80 B1
Shieldaig *H'land* 85 C13
Shieldaig *H'land* 85 A13
Shieldhill *Dumf/Gal* 60 E6
Shieldhill *Falk* 69 C7
Shieldhill *S Lanarks* 69 F9
Shielfoot *H'land* 79 E9
Shielhill *Angus* 77 B7
Shielhill *Invercl* 73 F11
Shifford *Oxon* 17 A10
Shifnal *Shrops* 34 E3
Shilbottle *Northum* 63 C7
Shildon *Durham* 58 D3
Shillingford *Devon* 7 D8
Shillingford *Oxon* 18 B2
Shillingford St George *Devon* 5 C10
Shillingstone *Dorset* 9 C7
Shillington *Beds* 29 E8
Shillmoor *Northum* 62 C4
Shilton *Oxon* 27 H9
Shilton *Warwick* 35 G10
Shilvington *Northum* 63 E7
Shimpling *Norfolk* 39 G7
Shimpling *Suffolk* 30 C5
Shimpling Street *Suffolk* 30 C5
Shincliffe *Durham* 58 B3
Shiney Row *Tyne/Wear* 58 A4
Shinfield *Wokingham* 18 E4
Shingham *Norfolk* 38 E3
Shingle Street *Suffolk* 31 D10
Shinner's Bridge *Devon* 5 E8
Shinness *H'land* 93 H8
Shipbourne *Kent* 20 F2
Shipdham *Norfolk* 38 E5
Shipham *Som'set* 15 F10
Shiphay *Torbay* 5 E9
Shiplake *Oxon* 18 D4
Shipley *Derby* 35 A10
Shipley *Northum* 63 B7
Shipley *Shrops* 34 F4
Shipley *W Sussex* 11 B10
Shipley *W Yorks* 51 F7
Shipley Shiels *Northum* 62 D3
Shipmeadow *Suffolk* 39 G9
Shippea Hill Station *Cambs* 38 G2
Shippon *Oxon* 17 B11
Shipston-on-Stour *Warwick* 27 D9
Shipton *Glos* 27 G7
Shipton *N Yorks* 52 D1
Shipton *Shrops* 34 F1
Shipton Bellinger *Hants* 17 G9
Shipton Gorge *Dorset* 8 E3
Shipton Green *W Sussex* 11 D7
Shipton Moyne *Glos* 16 C5
Shipton on Cherwell *Oxon* 27 G11
Shipton Solers *Glos* 27 G7
Shipton-under-Wychwood *Oxon* 27 G9
Shiptonthorpe *ER Yorks* 52 E4
Shirburn *Oxon* 18 B3
Shirdley Hill *Lancs* 42 A6
Shirebrook *Derby* 45 F9
Shiregreen *S Yorks* 45 C7
Shirehampton *Bristol* 15 D11
Shiremoor *Tyne/Wear* 63 F9
Shirenewton *Monmouths* 15 B10
Shireoaks *Notts* 45 D9
Shirkoak *Kent* 13 C8
Shirl Heath *Heref'd* 25 C11
Shirland *Derby* 45 G7
Shirley *Derby* 35 A8
Shirley *London* 19 E10
Shirley *S'thampton* 10 C3
Shirley *W Midlands* 35 H7
Shirrell Heath *Hants* 10 C4
Shirwell *Devon* 6 C4
Shirwell Cross *Devon* 6 C4
Shiskine *N Ayrs* 66 D2
Shobdon *Heref'd* 25 B11
Shobnall *Staffs* 35 C8
Shobrooke *Devon* 7 F7
Shoby *Leics* 36 D2
Shocklach *Ches* 43 H7
Shoeburyness *Southend* 20 C6
Sholden *Kent* 21 F10
Sholing *S'thampton* 10 C3
Shoot Hill *Shrops* 33 D10
Shop *Cornw'l* 6 E1
Shop *Cornw'l* 3 B7
Shop Corner *Suffolk* 31 E9
Shore Mill *H'land* 87 E10
Shoreditch *London* 19 C10
Shoreham *Kent* 20 E2
Shoreham-By-Sea *W Sussex* 11 D11
Shoresdean *Northum* 71 F8
Shoreswood *Northum* 71 F8
Shoreton *H'land* 87 E9
Shorncote *Glos* 17 B7
Shorne *Kent* 20 D3
Short Heath *W Midlands* 34 E5
Shortacombe *Devon* 4 C6
Shortgate *E Sussex* 12 E3
Shortlanesend *Cornw'l* 3 E7
Shortlees *E Ayrs* 67 C7
Shortstown *Beds* 29 D7
Shorwell *I/Wight* 10 F3
Shoscombe *Bath/NE Som'set* 16 F4
Shotatton *Shrops* 33 C9
Shotesham *Norfolk* 39 F8
Shotgate *Essex* 20 B4
Shotley *Suffolk* 31 E9
Shotley Bridge *Durham* 58 A1
Shotley Gate *Suffolk* 31 E9
Shotleyfield *Northum* 58 A1
Shottenden *Kent* 21 F7
Shottermill *Surrey* 11 A7
Shottery *Warwick* 27 C8
Shotteswell *Warwick* 27 D11
Shottisham *Suffolk* 31 D10
Shottle *Derby* 45 H7
Shottlegate *Derby* 45 H7
Shotton *Durham* 58 C5
Shotton *Flints* 42 F6
Shotton *Northum* 71 G7
Shotton Colliery *Durham* 58 B4
Shotts *N Lanarks* 69 D7
Shotwick *Ches* 42 E6
Shouldham *Norfolk* 38 E2
Shouldham Thorpe *Norfolk* 38 E2
Shoulton *Worcs* 26 C5
Shover's Green *E Sussex* 12 C5
Shrawardine *Shrops* 33 D10
Shrawley *Worcs* 26 B5
Shrewley Common *Warwick* 27 B9
Shrewsbury *Shrops* 33 D10
Shrewton *Wilts* 17 G7
Shripney *W Sussex* 11 D8
Shrivenham *Oxon* 17 C9
Shropham *Norfolk* 38 F5
Shrub End *Essex* 30 F6
Shucknall *Heref'd* 26 D2
Shudy Camps *Cambs* 30 D3
Shulishadermor *H'land* 85 D9
Shurdington *Glos* 26 G6
Shurlock Row *Windsor* 18 D5
Shurrery *H'land* 93 D13
Shurrery Lodge *H'land* 93 D13
Shurton *Som'set* 7 B11
Shustoke *Warwick* 35 F8
Shute *Devon* 8 E1
Shute *Devon* 7 F7
Shutford *Oxon* 27 D10
Shuthonger *Glos* 26 E5
Shutlanger *Northants* 28 C4
Shuttington *Warwick* 35 E8
Shuttlewood *Derby* 45 E8
Siabost bho Dheas *W Isles* 90 C7
Siabost bho Thuath *W Isles* 90 C7
Siadar *W Isles* 91 B8
Siadar Iarach *W Isles* 91 B8
Siadar Uarach *W Isles* 91 B8
Sibbaldbie *Dumf/Gal* 61 E7
Sibbertoft *Northants* 36 G2
Sibdon Carwood *Shrops* 33 G10
Sibford Ferris *Oxon* 27 E10
Sibford Gower *Oxon* 27 E10
Sible Hedingham *Essex* 30 E4
Sibsey *Lincs* 47 G7
Sibson *Cambs* 37 F6
Sibson *Leics* 35 E9
Sibthorpe *Notts* 45 H11
Sibton *Suffolk* 31 B10
Sibton Green *Suffolk* 31 A10
Sicklesmere *Suffolk* 30 B5
Sicklinghall *N Yorks* 51 E9
Sid *Devon* 7 H10
Sidbury *Devon* 7 G10
Sidbury *Shrops* 34 G2
Sidcot *N Som'set* 15 F10
Sidcup *London* 19 D11
Siddick *Cumb* 56 C2
Siddington *Ches* 44 E2
Siddington *Glos* 17 B7
Sidemoor *Worcs* 26 A6
Sidestrand *Norfolk* 39 B8
Sidford *Devon* 7 G10
Sidlesham *W Sussex* 11 E7
Sidley *E Sussex* 12 F6
Sidlow *Surrey* 19 G9
Sidmouth *Devon* 7 H10
Sigford *Devon* 5 D8
Sigglesthorne *ER Yorks* 53 E7
Sighthill *C/Edinb* 69 C10
Sigingstone *V/Glam* 14 D5
Signet *Oxon* 27 G9
Silchester *Hants* 18 E3
Sildinis *W Isles* 91 F7
Sileby *Leics* 36 D1
Silecroft *Cumb* 49 A1
Silfield *Norfolk* 39 F7
Silian *Ceredig'n* 23 A10
Silk Willoughby *Lincs* 37 A6
Silkstone *S Yorks* 44 B6
Silkstone Common *S Yorks* 44 B6
Silloth *Cumb* 56 A3
Sills *Northum* 62 C4
Sillyearn *Moray* 88 C5
Siloh *Carms* 24 E4
Silpho *N Yorks* 59 G10
Silsden *W Yorks* 50 E6
Silsoe *Beds* 29 E7
Silver End *Essex* 30 G5
Silverburn *Midloth* 69 D11
Silverdale *Lancs* 49 B4
Silverdale *Staffs* 44 H2
Silvergate *Norfolk* 39 C7
Silverhill *E Sussex* 13 E6
Silverley's Green *Suffolk* 39 H8
Silverstone *Northants* 28 D3
Silverton *Devon* 7 F8
Silvington *Shrops* 34 H2
Silwick *Shetl'd* 96 J4
Simmondley *Derby* 44 C4
Simonburn *Northum* 62 F4
Simonsbath *Som'set* 7 C6
Simonstone *Lancs* 50 F3
Simprim *Scot Borders* 71 F7
Simpson *M/Keynes* 28 E5
Simpson Cross *Pembs* 22 E3
Sinclair's Hill *Scot Borders* 71 E7
Sinclairston *E Ayrs* 67 E7
Sinderby *N Yorks* 51 A9
Sinderhope *Northum* 57 A10
Sindlesham *Wokingham* 18 E4
Singdean *Scot Borders* 61 C11
Singleborough *Bucks* 28 E4
Singleton *Lancs* 49 F3
Singleton *W Sussex* 11 C7
Singlewell *Kent* 20 D3
Sinkhurst Green *Kent* 13 B7
Sinnahard *Aberds* 82 B6
Sinnington *N Yorks* 59 H8
Sinton Green *Worcs* 26 B5
Sipson *London* 19 D7
Sirhowy *Bl Gwent* 25 G8
Sisland *Norfolk* 39 F9
Sissinghurst *Kent* 13 C6
Sisterpath *Scot Borders* 70 F6
Siston *S Gloucs* 16 D3
Sithney *Cornw'l* 2 G5
Sittingbourne *Kent* 20 E5
Six Ashes *Staffs* 34 G3
Six Hills *Leics* 36 C2
Six Mile Bottom *Cambs* 30 C2
Sixhills *Lincs* 46 D5
Sixpenny Handley *Dorset* 9 C8
Sizewell *Suffolk* 31 B11
Skail *H'land* 93 E10
Skaill *Orkney* 95 G3
Skaill *Orkney* 95 E5
Skaill *Orkney* 95 H6
Skares *E Ayrs* 67 E8
Skateraw *E Loth* 70 C6
Skaw *Shetl'd* 96 G7
Skeabost *H'land* 85 D9
Skeabrae *Orkney* 95 F3
Skeeby *N Yorks* 58 F3
Skeffington *Leics* 36 E3
Skeffling *ER Yorks* 53 H9
Skegby *Notts* 45 F8
Skegness *Lincs* 47 F9
Skelberry *Shetl'd* 96 M5
Skelbo *H'land* 87 B10
Skelbrooke *S Yorks* 45 A9
Skeldyke *Lincs* 37 B9
Skellingthorpe *Lincs* 46 E3
Skellister *Shetl'd* 96 H6
Skellow *S Yorks* 45 A9
Skelmanthorpe *W Yorks* 44 A6
Skelmersdale *Lancs* 43 B7
Skelmonae *Aberds* 89 E8
Skelmorlie *N Ayrs* 73 G10
Skelmuir *Aberds* 89 D9
Skelpick *H'land* 93 D10
Skelton *Cumb* 56 C6
Skelton *ER Yorks* 52 G3
Skelton *N Yorks* 58 F1
Skelton *Redcar/Clevel'd* 59 E7
Skelton *C/York* 52 D1
Skelton-on-Ure *N Yorks* 51 C9
Skelwick *Orkney* 95 D5
Skelwith Bridge *Cumb* 56 F5
Skendleby *Lincs* 47 F8
Skene Ho. *Aberds* 83 C9
Skenfrith *Monmouths* 25 F11
Skerne *ER Yorks* 52 D6
Skeroblingarry *Arg/Bute* 65 F8
Skerray *H'land* 93 C9
Skerton *Lancs* 49 C4
Sketchley *Leics* 35 F10
Sketty *Swan* 14 B2
Skewen *Neath P Talb* 14 B3
Skewsby *N Yorks* 52 B2
Skeyton *Norfolk* 39 C8
Skiag Bridge *H'land* 92 G5
Skibo Castle *H'land* 87 C10
Skidbrooke *Lincs* 47 C8
Skidbrooke North End *Lincs* 47 C8
Skidby *ER Yorks* 52 F6
Skilgate *Som'set* 7 D8
Skillington *Lincs* 36 C4
Skinburness *Cumb* 61 H7
Skinflats *Falk* 69 B8
Skinidin *H'land* 84 D7
Skinnet *H'land* 93 C8
Skinningrove *Redcar/Clevel'd* 59 D8
Skipness *Arg/Bute* 73 H7
Skippool *Lancs* 49 E3
Skipsea *ER Yorks* 53 D7
Skipsea Brough *ER Yorks* 53 D7
Skipton *N Yorks* 50 D5
Skipton-on-Swale *N Yorks* 51 B9
Skipwith *N Yorks* 52 F2
Skirbeck *Lincs* 37 A9
Skirbeck Quarter *Lincs* 37 A9
Skirlaugh *ER Yorks* 53 F7
Skirling *Scot Borders* 69 G9
Skirmett *Bucks* 18 C4
Skirpenbeck *ER Yorks* 52 D3
Skirwith *Cumb* 57 C8
Skirza *H'land* 94 D5
Skulamus *H'land* 85 F11
Skullomie *H'land* 93 C9
Skyborry Green *Shrops* 25 A9
Skye of Curr *H'land* 82 A1
Skyreholme *N Yorks* 51 C6
Slackhall *Derby* 44 D4
Slackhead *Moray* 88 B4
Slad *Glos* 26 H5
Slade *Devon* 6 B4
Slade *Pembs* 22 E4
Slade Green *London* 20 D2
Slaggyford *Northum* 57 A8
Slaidburn *Lancs* 50 D3
Slaithwaite *W Yorks* 44 A4
Slaley *Northum* 62 H5
Slamannan *Falk* 69 C7
Slapton *Bucks* 28 F6
Slapton *Devon* 5 G9
Slapton *Northants* 28 D3
Slatepit Dale *Derby* 45 F7
Slattocks *Gtr Man* 44 B2
Slaugham *W Sussex* 12 D1
Slaughterford *Wilts* 16 D5
Slawston *Leics* 36 F3
Sleaford *Hants* 18 H5
Sleaford *Lincs* 46 H4
Sleagill *Cumb* 57 E7
Sleapford *Telford* 34 D2
Sledge Green *Worcs* 26 E5
Sledmere *ER Yorks* 52 C5
Sleightholme *Durham* 57 E11
Sleights *N Yorks* 59 F9
Slepe *Dorset* 9 E8
Slickly *H'land* 94 D4
Sliddery *N Ayrs* 66 D2
Sligachan Hotel *H'land* 85 F9
Slimbridge *Glos* 16 A4
Slindon *Staffs* 34 B4
Slindon *W Sussex* 11 D8
Slinfold *W Sussex* 11 A10
Sling *Gwyn* 41 D8
Slingsby *N Yorks* 52 B2
Slioch *Aberds* 88 E5
Slip End *Beds* 29 G7
Slip End *Herts* 29 E9
Slipton *Northants* 36 H5
Slitting Mill *Staffs* 34 D6
Slochd *H'land* 81 A10
Slockavullin *Arg/Bute* 73 D7
Sloley *Norfolk* 39 C8
Sloothby *Lincs* 47 E8
Slough *Slough* 18 D6
Slough Green *W Sussex* 12 D1
Sluggan *H'land* 81 A10
Slumbay *H'land* 85 E13
Slyfield *Surrey* 18 F6
Slyne *Lancs* 49 C4
Smailholm *Scot Borders* 70 G5
Small Dole *W Sussex* 11 C11
Small Hythe *Kent* 13 C7
Smallbridge *Gtr Man* 50 H5
Smallburgh *Norfolk* 39 C9
Smallburn *Aberds* 89 D10
Smallburn *E Ayrs* 68 H5
Smalley *Derby* 35 A10
Smallfield *Surrey* 12 B2
Smallridge *Devon* 8 D2
Smannell *Hants* 17 G10
Smardale *Cumb* 57 F9
Smarden *Kent* 13 B7
Smarden Bell *Kent* 13 B7
Smeatharpe *Devon* 7 E10
Smeeth *Kent* 13 C9
Smeeton Westerby *Leics* 36 F2
Smercleit *W Isles* 84 G2
Smerral *H'land* 94 G3
Smethwick *W Midlands* 34 G6
Smirisary *H'land* 79 D9
Smisby *Derby* 35 D9
Smith Green *Lancs* 49 D4
Smithfield *Cumb* 61 G10
Smithincott *Devon* 7 E9
Smith's Green *Essex* 30 F2
Smithstown *H'land* 85 A12
Smithton *H'land* 87 G10
Smithy Green *Ches* 43 E10
Smockington *Leics* 35 G10
Smoogro *Orkney* 95 H4
Smyth's Green *Essex* 30 G6
Snaigow House *Perth/Kinr* 76 C3
Snailbeach *Shrops* 33 E9
Snailwell *Cambs* 30 B3
Snainton *N Yorks* 52 A5
Snaith *ER Yorks* 52 G2
Snape *N Yorks* 51 A8
Snape *Suffolk* 31 C10
Snape Green *Lancs* 43 A6
Snarestone *Leics* 35 E9
Snarford *Lincs* 46 D4
Snargate *Kent* 13 D8
Snave *Kent* 13 D9
Snead *Powys* 33 F9
Sneath Common *Norfolk* 39 G7
Sneaton *N Yorks* 59 F9
Sneatonthorpe *N Yorks* 59 F10
Snelland *Lincs* 46 D4
Snelston *Derby* 35 A7
Snettisham *Norfolk* 38 B2
Snig's End *Glos* 26 F4
Sniseabhal *W Isles* 84 E2
Snitter *Northum* 62 C6
Snitterby *Lincs* 46 C3
Snitterfield *Warwick* 27 C9
Snitton *Shrops* 34 H1
Snodhill *Heref'd* 25 D10
Snodland *Kent* 20 E3
Snowden Hill *S Yorks* 44 B6
Snowdown *Kent* 21 F9
Snowshill *Glos* 27 E7
Snydale *W Yorks* 51 H10
Soar *Angl* 40 C5
Soar *Carms* 24 F3
Soar *Devon* 5 H8
Soar-y-Mynydd *Ceredig'n* 24 C4
Soberton *Hants* 10 C5
Soberton Heath *Hants* 10 C5
Sockbridge *Cumb* 57 D7
Sockburn *D'lington* 58 F4
Soham *Cambs* 30 A2
Soham Cotes *Cambs* 38 H1
Solas *W Isles* 84 A3
Soldon Cross *Devon* 6 E2
Soldridge *Hants* 10 A5
Sole Street *Kent* 20 E3
Sole Street *Kent* 21 G7
Solihull *W Midlands* 35 H7
Sollers Dilwyn *Heref'd* 25 C11
Sollers Hope *Heref'd* 26 E3
Sollom *Lancs* 49 H4
Solva *Pembs* 22 D2
Somerby *Leics* 36 D3
Somerby *Lincs* 46 B4
Somercotes *Derby* 45 G8
Somerford *Dorset* 9 E10
Somerford Keynes *Glos* 17 B7
Somerley *W Sussex* 11 E7
Somerleyton *Suffolk* 39 F10
Somersal Herbert *Derby* 35 B7
Somersby *Lincs* 47 E7
Somersham *Cambs* 37 H9
Somersham *Suffolk* 31 D7
Somerton *Oxon* 27 F11
Somerton *Som'set* 8 B3
Sompting *W Sussex* 11 D10
Sonning *Wokingham* 18 D4
Sonning Common *Oxon* 18 C4
Sonning Eye *Oxon* 18 D4
Sontley *Wrex* 42 H6
Sopley *Hants* 9 E10
Sopwell *Herts* 29 H8
Sopworth *Wilts* 16 C5
Sorbie *Dumf/Gal* 55 E7
Sordale *H'land* 94 D3
Sorisdale *Arg/Bute* 78 E5
Sorn *E Ayrs* 68 H4
Sornhill *E Ayrs* 67 C8
Sortat *H'land* 94 D4
Sotby *Lincs* 46 E6
Sots Hole *Lincs* 46 F5
Sotterley *Suffolk* 39 G10
Soudley *Shrops* 34 C3
Soughton *Flints* 42 F5
Soulbury *Bucks* 28 F5
Soulby *Cumb* 57 E9
Souldern *Oxon* 28 E2
Souldrop *Beds* 28 B6
Sound *Ches* 43 H9
Sound *Shetl'd* 96 H5
Sound *Shetl'd* 96 J6
Sound Heath *Ches* 43 H9
Soundwell *S Gloucs* 16 D3
Sourhope *Scot Borders* 62 A4
Sourin *Orkney* 95 E5
Sourton *Devon* 6 G4
Soutergate *Cumb* 49 A2
South Acre *Norfolk* 38 D4
South Allington *Devon* 5 H8
South Alloa *Falk* 69 A7
South Ambersham *W Sussex* 11 B8
South Anston *S Yorks* 45 D9
South Ascot *Windsor* 18 E6
South Ballachulish *H'land* 74 B3
South Balloch *S Ayrs* 66 G6
South Bank *Redcar/Clevel'd* 59 D6
South Barrow *Som'set* 8 B5
South Beach *Gwyn* 40 G5
South Benfleet *Essex* 20 C4
South Bersted *W Sussex* 11 D8
South Brent *Devon* 5 E7
South Brewham *Som'set* 16 H4
South Broomhill *Northum* 63 D8
South Burlingham *Norfolk* 39 E9
South Cadbury *Som'set* 8 B5
South Cairn *Dumf/Gal* 54 C2
South Carlton *Lincs* 46 E3
South Cave *ER Yorks* 52 F5
South Cerney *Glos* 17 B7
South Chard *Som'set* 8 D2
South Charlton *Northum* 63 A7
South Cheriton *Som'set* 8 B5
South Cliffe *ER Yorks* 52 F4
South Clifton *Notts* 46 E2
South Cockerington *Lincs* 47 D7
South Cornelly *Bridg* 14 C4
South Cove *Suffolk* 39 G10
South Creagan *Arg/Bute* 74 C2
South Creake *Norfolk* 38 B4
South Croxton *Leics* 36 D2
South Croydon *London* 19 E10
South Dalton *ER Yorks* 52 E5
South Darenth *Kent* 20 E2
South Duffield *N Yorks* 52 F2
South Elkington *Lincs* 46 D6
South Elmsall *W Yorks* 45 A8
South End *Bucks* 28 F5
South End *Cumb* 49 C2
South End *N Lincs* 53 G7
South Erradale *H'land* 85 A12
South Fambridge *Essex* 20 B5
South Fawley *W Berks* 17 C10
South Ferriby *N Lincs* 52 G5
South Garth *Shetl'd* 96 D7
South Garvan *H'land* 80 F1
South Glendale *W Isles* 84 G2
South Godstone *Surrey* 19 G10
South Gorley *Hants* 9 C10
South Green *Essex* 20 B3
South Green *Kent* 20 E5
South-haa *Shetl'd* 96 E5
South Ham *Hants* 18 F3
South Hanningfield *Essex* 20 B4
South Harting *W Sussex* 11 C6
South Hatfield *Herts* 29 H9
South Hayling *Hants* 10 E6
South Hazelrigg *Northum* 71 G9
South Heath *Bucks* 18 A6
South Heighton *E Sussex* 12 F3
South Hetton *Durham* 58 B4
South Hiendley *W Yorks* 45 A7
South Hill *Cornw'l* 4 D4
South Hinksey *Oxon* 18 A2
South Hole *Devon* 6 D1
South Holme *N Yorks* 52 B2
South Holmwood *Surrey* 19 G8
South Hornchurch *London* 20 C2
South Hykeham *Lincs* 46 F3
South Hylton *Tyne/Wear* 63 H9
South Kelsey *Lincs* 46 C4
South Kessock *H'land* 87 G9
South Killingholme *N Lincs* 53 H7
South Kilvington *N Yorks* 51 A10
South Kilworth *Leics* 36 G2
South Kirkby *W Yorks* 45 A8
South Kirkton *Aberds* 83 C9
South Kiscadale *N Ayrs* 66 D3
South Kyme *Lincs* 46 H5
South Lancing *W Sussex* 11 D10
South Leigh *Oxon* 27 H10
South Leverton *Notts* 45 D11
South Littleton *Worcs* 27 D7
South Lopham *Norfolk* 38 G6
South Luffenham *Rutl'd* 36 E5
South Malling *E Sussex* 12 E3
South Marston *Swindon* 17 C8
South Middleton *Northum* 62 A5
South Milford *N Yorks* 51 F10
South Millbrex *Aberds* 89 D8
South Milton *Devon* 5 G8
South Mimms *Herts* 19 A9
South Molton *Devon* 6 D6
South Moreton *Oxon* 18 C2
South Mundham *W Sussex* 11 D7
South Muskham *Notts* 45 G11
South Newbald *ER Yorks* 52 F5
South Newington *Oxon* 27 E11
South Newton *Wilts* 9 A9
South Normanton *Derby* 45 G8
South Norwood *London* 19 E10
South Nutfield *Surrey* 19 G10
South Ockendon *Thurr'k* 20 C2
South Ormsby *Lincs* 47 E7
South Otterington *N Yorks* 58 H4
South Owersby *Lincs* 46 C4
South Oxhey *Herts* 19 B8
South Perrott *Dorset* 8 D3
South Petherton *Som'set* 8 C3
South Petherwin *Cornw'l* 4 C4
South Pickenham *Norfolk* 38 E4
South Pool *Devon* 5 G8
South Port *Arg/Bute* 74 E3
South Radworthy *Devon* 7 C6
South Rauceby *Lincs* 46 H4
South Raynham *Norfolk* 38 C4
South Reston *Lincs* 47 D8
South Runcton *Norfolk* 38 E2
South Scarle *Notts* 46 F2
South Shian *Arg/Bute* 74 C2
South Shields *Tyne/Wear* 63 G9
South Shore *Blackp'l* 49 F3
South Somercotes *Lincs* 47 C8
South Stainley *N Yorks* 51 C9
South Stainmore *Cumb* 57 E10
South Stifford *Thurr'k* 20 D3
South Stoke *Oxon* 18 C2
South Stoke *W Sussex* 11 D9
South Street *E Sussex* 12 E2
South Street *London* 19 F11
South Street *Kent* 21 E8
South Street *Kent* 21 F7
South Tawton *Devon* 6 G5
South Thoresby *Lincs* 47 E8
South Tidworth *Wilts* 17 G9
South Town *Hants* 18 H3
South View *Hants* 18 F3
South Walsham *Norfolk* 39 D9
South Warnborough *Hants* 18 G4
South Weald *Essex* 20 B2
South Weston *Oxon* 18 B4
South Wheatley *Cornw'l* 4 B3
South Wheatley *Notts* 45 D11
South Whiteness *Shetl'd* 96 J5
South Widcombe *Bath/NE Som'set* 16 F2
South Wigston *Leics* 36 F1
South Willingham *Lincs* 46 D5
South Wingfield *Derby* 45 G7
South Witham *Lincs* 36 D5
South Wonston *Hants* 17 H11
South Woodham Ferrers *Essex* 20 B5
South Wootton *Norfolk* 38 C2
South Wraxall *Wilts* 16 E5
South Zeal *Devon* 6 G5
Southall *London* 19 C8
Southam *Glos* 26 F6
Southam *Warwick* 27 B11
Southampton *S'thampton* 10 C3
Southborough *Kent* 12 B4
Southbourne *Bournem'th* 9 E10
Southbourne *W Sussex* 11 D6
Southburgh *Norfolk* 38 E5
Southburn *ER Yorks* 52 D5
Southchurch *Southend* 20 C6
Southcott *Wilts* 17 F8
Southcourt *Bucks* 28 G5
Southdean *Scot Borders* 62 C2
Southdene *Mersey* 43 C7
Southease *E Sussex* 12 F3
Southend *Arg/Bute* 65 H7
Southend *W Berks* 18 D2
Southend *Wilts* 17 D8
Southend-on-Sea *Southend* 20 C5
Southernden *Kent* 20 G5
Southerndown *V/Glam* 14 D4
Southerness *Dumf/Gal* 60 H5
Southery *Norfolk* 38 F2
Southfield *Northum* 63 F8
Southfleet *Kent* 20 D3
Southgate *Ceredig'n* 32 H1
Southgate *London* 19 B9
Southgate *Norfolk* 39 C7
Southgate *Swan* 23 H10
Southill *Beds* 29 D8
Southleigh *Devon* 7 G11
Southminster *Essex* 20 B6
Southmoor *Oxon* 17 B10
Southoe *Cambs* 29 B8
Southolt *Suffolk* 31 B8
Southorpe *Peterbro* 37 E6
Southowram *W Yorks* 51 G7
Southport *Mersey* 49 H3
Southpunds *Shetl'd* 96 L6
Southrepps *Norfolk* 39 B8
Southrey *Lincs* 46 F5
Southrop *Glos* 17 A8
Southrope *Hants* 18 G3
Southsea *Portsm'th* 10 E5
Southstoke *Bath/NE Som'set* 16 E4
Southtown *Norfolk* 39 E11
Southtown *Orkney* 95 J5
Southwaite *Cumb* 56 B6
Southwark *London* 19 D10
Southwater *W Sussex* 11 B10
Southwater Street *W Sussex* 11 B10
Southway *Som'set* 15 G11
Southwell *Dorset* 8 G5
Southwell *Notts* 45 G10
Southwick *Hants* 10 D5
Southwick *Northants* 36 F6
Southwick *Tyne/Wear* 63 H9
Southwick *Wilts* 16 F5
Southwick *W Sussex* 11 D11
Southwold *Suffolk* 39 H11
Southwood *Norfolk* 39 E9
Southwood *Som'set* 8 A4
Soval Lodge *W Isles* 91 E8
Sowber Gate *N Yorks* 58 H4
Sowerby *N Yorks* 51 A10
Sowerby *W Yorks* 50 G6
Sowerby Bridge *W Yorks* 51 G6
Sowerby Row *Cumb* 56 C5
Sowood *W Yorks* 51 H6
Sowton *Devon* 7 G8
Soyal *H'land* 87 B8
Spa Common *Norfolk* 39 B8
Spacey Houses *N Yorks* 51 D9
Spadeadam Farm *Cumb* 61 F11
Spalding *Lincs* 37 C8
Spaldington *ER Yorks* 52 F3
Spaldwick *Cambs* 29 A8
Spalford *Notts* 46 F2
Spanby *Lincs* 37 B6
Sparham *Norfolk* 39 D6
Spark Bridge *Cumb* 49 A3
Sparkford *Som'set* 8 B5
Sparkhill *W Midlands* 35 G6
Sparkwell *Devon* 5 F6
Sparrow Green *Norfolk* 38 D5
Sparrowpit *Derby* 44 D4
Sparsholt *Hants* 10 A3
Sparsholt *Oxon* 17 C10
Spartylea *Northum* 57 B10
Spaunton *N Yorks* 59 H8
Spaxton *Som'set* 7 C11
Spean Bridge *H'land* 80 E4
Spear Hill *W Sussex* 11 C10
Speen *Bucks* 18 B5
Speen *W Berks* 17 E11
Speeton *N Yorks* 53 B7
Speke *Mersey* 43 D7
Speldhurst *Kent* 12 B4
Spellbrook *Herts* 29 G11
Spelsbury *Oxon* 27 F10
Spelter *Bridg* 14 B4
Spencers Wood *Wokingham* 18 E4
Spennithorne *N Yorks* 58 H2
Spennymoor *Durham* 58 C3
Spetchley *Worcs* 26 C5
Spetisbury *Dorset* 9 D8
Spexhall *Suffolk* 39 G9
Spey Bay *Moray* 88 B3
Speybridge *H'land* 82 A2
Speyview *Moray* 88 D2
Spilsby *Lincs* 47 F8
Spindlestone *Northum* 71 G10
Spinkhill *Derby* 45 E8
Spinningdale *H'land* 87 C9
Spirthill *Wilts* 16 D6
Spital Hill *S Yorks* 45 C10
Spital in the Street *Lincs* 46 D3
Spithurst *E Sussex* 12 E3
Spittal *Dumf/Gal* 54 D6
Spittal *E Loth* 70 C3
Spittal *H'land* 94 E3
Spittal *Northum* 71 E9
Spittal *Pembs* 22 D4
Spittal *Stirl* 68 B4
Spittal of Glenmuick *Aberds* 82 E5
Spittal of Glenshee *Perth/Kinr* 82 F3
Spittalfield *Perth/Kinr* 76 C4
Spixworth *Norfolk* 39 D8
Splayne's Green *E Sussex* 12 D3
Spofforth *N Yorks* 51 D9
Spon End *W Midlands* 35 H9
Spon Green *Flints* 42 F5
Spondon *Derby C* 35 B10
Spooner Row *Norfolk* 39 F6
Sporle *Norfolk* 38 D4
Spott *E Loth* 70 C5
Spratton *Northants* 28 A4
Spreakley *Surrey* 18 G5
Spreyton *Devon* 6 G5
Spridlington *Lincs* 46 D4
Spring Vale *S Yorks* 44 B6
Spring Valley *I/Man* 48 E3
Springburn *C/Glasg* 68 D5
Springfield *Dumf/Gal* 61 G9
Springfield *Essex* 30 H4
Springfield *Fife* 76 F6
Springfield *Moray* 87 F13
Springfield *W Midlands* 35 G6
Springhill *Staffs* 34 E5
Springholm *Dumf/Gal* 55 C11
Springkell *Dumf/Gal* 61 F8
Springside *N Ayrs* 67 C6
Springthorpe *Lincs* 46 D2
Springwell *Tyne/Wear* 63 H8
Sproatley *ER Yorks* 53 F7
Sproston Green *Ches* 43 F10
Sprotbrough *S Yorks* 45 B9
Sproughton *Suffolk* 31 D8
Sprouston *Scot Borders* 70 G6
Sprowston *Norfolk* 39 D8
Sproxton *Leics* 36 C4
Sproxton *N Yorks* 52 A2
Spurstow *Ches* 43 G8
Spynie *Moray* 88 B2
Squires Gate *Blackp'l* 49 F3
Srannda *W Isles* 90 J5
Sronphadruig Lodge *Perth/Kinr* 81 F9
Stableford *Shrops* 34 F3
Stableford *Staffs* 34 B4
Stacey Bank *S Yorks* 44 C6
Stackhouse *N Yorks* 50 C4
Stackpole *Pembs* 22 G4
Staddiscombe *Devon* 4 F6
Staddlethorpe *ER Yorks* 52 G4
Stadhampton *Oxon* 18 B3
Stadhlaigearraidh *W Isles* 84 E2
Staffield *Cumb* 57 B7
Staffin *H'land* 85 B9
Stafford *Staffs* 34 C5
Stagsden *Beds* 28 D6
Stainburn *Cumb* 56 D2
Stainburn *N Yorks* 51 E8
Stainby *Lincs* 36 C5
Staincross *S Yorks* 45 A7
Staindrop *Durham* 58 D2
Staines *Surrey* 19 D7
Stainfield *Lincs* 37 C6
Stainfield *Lincs* 46 E5
Stainforth *N Yorks* 50 C4
Stainforth *S Yorks* 45 A10
Staining *Lancs* 49 F3
Stainland *W Yorks* 51 H6
Stainsacre *N Yorks* 59 F10
Stainsby *Derby* 45 F8
Stainton *Cumb* 57 H7
Stainton *Cumb* 57 D6
Stainton *Durham* 58 E1
Stainton *Middlesbro'* 58 E5
Stainton *N Yorks* 58 G2
Stainton *S Yorks* 45 C9
Stainton by Langworth *Lincs* 46 E4
Stainton le Vale *Lincs* 46 C5
Stainton with Adgarley *Cumb* 49 B2
Staintondale *N Yorks* 59 G10
Stair *Cumb* 56 D4
Stair *E Ayrs* 67 D7
Stairhaven *Dumf/Gal* 54 D5
Staithes *N Yorks* 59 E8
Stake Pool *Lancs* 49 E4
Stakeford *Northum* 63 E8
Stalbridge *Dorset* 8 C6
Stalbridge Weston *Dorset* 8 C6
Stalham *Norfolk* 39 C9
Stalham Green *Norfolk* 39 C9
Stalisfield Green *Kent* 20 F6
Stalling Busk *N Yorks* 57 H11
Stallingborough *NE Lincs* 46 A5
Stalmine *Lancs* 49 E3
Stalybridge *Gtr Man* 44 C3
Stambourne *Essex* 30 E4
Stambourne Green *Essex* 30 E4
Stamford *Lincs* 36 E6
Stamford Bridge *Ches* 43 F7
Stamford Bridge *ER Yorks* 52 D3
Stamfordham *Northum* 62 F6
Stanah *Cumb* 56 E5
Stanborough *Herts* 29 G9
Stanbridge *Beds* 28 F6
Stanbridge *Dorset* 9 D9
Stanbrook *Worcs* 26 D5
Stanbury *W Yorks* 50 F6
Stand *Gtr Man* 43 B10
Stand *N Lanarks* 68 D6
Standburn *Falk* 69 C8
Standeford *Staffs* 34 E5
Standen *Kent* 13 B7
Standford *Hants* 11 A7
Standingstone *Cumb* 56 C2
Standish *Gtr Man* 43 A8
Standlake *Oxon* 17 A10
Standon *Hants* 10 B3
Standon *Herts* 29 F10
Standon *Staffs* 34 B4
Stane *N Lanarks* 69 E7
Stanfield *Norfolk* 38 C5
Stanford *Beds* 29 D8
Stanford *Kent* 13 C10
Stanford Bishop *Heref'd* 26 C3
Stanford Bridge *Worcs* 26 B4
Stanford Dingley *W Berks* 18 D2
Stanford in the Vale *Oxon* 17 B10
Stanford le Hope *Thurr'k* 20 C3
Stanford on Avon *Northants* 36 H1
Stanford on Soar *Notts* 35 C11
Stanford on Teme *Worcs* 26 B4
Stanford Rivers *Essex* 20 A2
Stanfree *Derby* 45 E8
Stanghow *Redcar/Clevel'd* 59 E7
Stanground *Peterbro* 37 F8
Stanhoe *Norfolk* 38 B4
Stanhope *Scot Borders* 69 H10
Stanhope *Durham* 57 C11
Stanion *Northants* 36 G5
Stanley *Derby* 35 A10
Stanley *Durham* 58 A2
Stanley *Lancs* 43 B7
Stanley *Perth/Kinr* 76 D4
Stanley *Staffs* 44 G3
Stanley *W Yorks* 51 G9
Stanley Common *Derby* 35 A10
Stanley Gate *Lancs* 43 B7
Stanley Hill *Heref'd* 26 D3
Stanlow *Ches* 43 E7
Stanmer *Brighton/Hove* 12 F2
Stanmore *London* 19 B8
Stanmore *Hants* 10 B3
Stanmore *W Berks* 17 D11
Stannergate *Dundee C* 77 D7
Stanningley *W Yorks* 51 F8
Stannington *Northum* 63 F8
Stannington *S Yorks* 45 D7
Stansbatch *Heref'd* 25 B10
Stansfield *Suffolk* 30 C4
Stanstead *Suffolk* 30 D5
Stanstead Abbotts *Herts* 29 G10
Stansted *Kent* 20 E3
Stansted Airport *Essex* 30 F2
Stansted Mountfitchet *Essex* 30 F2
Stanton *Glos* 27 E7
Stanton *Monmouths* 25 F10
Stanton *Northum* 63 E7
Stanton *Staffs* 44 H5
Stanton *Suffolk* 30 A6
Stanton by Bridge *Derby* 35 C9
Stanton-by-Dale *Derby* 35 B10
Stanton Drew *Bath/NE Som'set* 16 E2
Stanton Fitzwarren *Swindon* 17 B8
Stanton Harcourt *Oxon* 27 H11
Stanton Hill *Notts* 45 F8
Stanton in Peak *Derby* 44 F6
Stanton Lacy *Shrops* 33 H10
Stanton Long *Shrops* 34 F1
Stanton-on-the-Wolds *Notts* 36 B2
Stanton Prior *Bath/NE Som'set* 16 E3
Stanton St Bernard *Wilts* 17 E7
Stanton St John *Oxon* 28 H2
Stanton St Quintin *Wilts* 16 D6
Stanton Street *Suffolk* 30 B6
Stanton under Bardon *Leics* 35 D10
Stanton upon Hine Heath *Shrops* 34 C1
Stanton Wick *Bath/NE Som'set* 16 E3
Stanwardine in the Fields *Shrops* 33 C10
Stanwardine in the Wood *Shrops* 33 C10
Stanway *Essex* 30 F6
Stanway *Glos* 27 E7
Stanway Green *Suffolk* 31 A9
Stanwell *Surrey* 19 D7
Stanwell Moor *Surrey* 19 D7
Stanwick *Northants* 28 A6
Stanwick-St-John *N Yorks* 58 E2
Stanwix *Cumb* 61 H10
Stanydale *Shetl'd* 96 H4
Staoinebrig *W Isles* 84 E2
Stape *N Yorks* 59 G8
Stapehill *Dorset* 9 D9
Stapeley *Ches* 43 H9
Stapenhill *Staffs* 35 C8
Staple *Kent* 21 F9
Staple *Som'set* 7 B10
Staple Cross *E Sussex* 13 D6
Staple Fitzpaine *Som'set* 8 C1
Staplefield *W Sussex* 12 D1
Stapleford *Cambs* 29 C11
Stapleford *Herts* 29 G10
Stapleford *Leics* 36 D4
Stapleford *Lincs* 46 G2
Stapleford *Notts* 35 B10
Stapleford *Wilts* 17 H7
Stapleford Abbotts *Essex* 20 B2
Stapleford Tawney *Essex* 20 B2
Staplegrove *Som'set* 7 D11
Staplehay *Som'set* 7 D11
Staplehurst *Kent* 13 B6
Staplers *I/Wight* 10 F4
Stapleton *Bristol* 16 D3
Stapleton *Cumb* 61 F11
Stapleton *Heref'd* 25 B10
Stapleton *Leics* 35 F10
Stapleton *N Yorks* 58 E3
Stapleton *Shrops* 33 E10
Stapleton *Som'set* 8 B3
Stapley *Som'set* 7 E10
Staploe *Beds* 29 B8
Staplow *Heref'd* 26 D3
Star *Fife* 76 G6
Star *Pembs* 23 C7
Star *Som'set* 15 F10
Stara *Orkney* 95 F3
Starbeck *N Yorks* 51 D9
Starbotton *N Yorks* 50 B5
Starcross *Devon* 5 C10
Stareton *Warwick* 27 A10
Starkholmes *Derby* 45 G7

T

Wheatley Hill *Durham* 58 C4
Wheaton Aston *Staffs* 34 D4
Wheddon Cross *Som'set* 7 C8
Wheedlemont *Aberds* 82 A6
Wheelerstreet *Surrey* 18 G6
Wheelock *Ches* 43 G10
Wheelock Heath *Ches* 43 G10
Wheelton *Lancs* 50 G2
Wheen *Angus* 82 F5
Wheldrake *C/York* 52 E2
Whelford *Glos* 17 B8
Whelpley Hill *Bucks* 18 A6
Whempstead *Herts* 29 F10
Whenby *N Yorks* 52 C2
Whepstead *Suffolk* 30 C5
Wherstead *Suffolk* 31 D8
Wherwell *Hants* 17 G10
Wheston *Derby* 44 E5
Whetsted *Kent* 20 G3
Whetstone *Leics* 36 F1
Whicham *Cumb* 49 A1
Whichford *Warwick* 27 E10
Whickham *Tyne/Wear* 63 G8
Whiddon *Devon* 6 G5
Whigstreet *Angus* 77 C7
Whilton *Northants* 28 B3
Whim Farm *Scot Borders* 69 E11
Whimble *Devon* 6 G2
Whimple *Devon* 7 G9
Whimpwell Green *Norfolk* 39 C9
Whinburgh *Norfolk* 38 E6
Whinnieliggate *Dumf/Gal* 55 D10
Whinnyfold *Aberds* 89 E10
Whippingham *I/Wight* 10 E4
Whipsnade *Beds* 29 G7
Whipton *Devon* 7 G8
Whirlow *S Yorks* 45 D7
Whisby *Lincs* 46 F3
Whissendine *Rutl'd* 36 D4
Whissonsett *Norfolk* 38 C5
Whistlefield *Arg/Bute* 73 D10
Whistlefield *Arg/Bute* 73 D11
Whistley Green *Wokingham* 18 D4
Whiston *Mersey* 43 C7
Whiston *Northants* 28 B5
Whiston *Staffs* 34 D4
Whiston *Staffs* 44 H4
Whiston *S Yorks* 45 D8
Whitbeck *Cumb* 49 A1
Whitbourne *Heref'd* 26 C4
Whitburn *Tyne/Wear* 63 G10
Whitburn *W Loth* 69 D8
Whitburn Colliery *Tyne/Wear* 63 G10
Whitby *Ches* 43 E6
Whitby *N Yorks* 59 E9
Whitbyheath *Ches* 43 E6
Whitchurch *Bath/NE Som'set* 16 E3
Whitchurch *Bucks* 28 F4
Whitchurch *Card* 15 C7
Whitchurch *Devon* 4 D5
Whitchurch *Hants* 17 G11
Whitchurch *Heref'd* 26 G2
Whitchurch *Oxon* 18 D3
Whitchurch *Pembs* 22 D2
Whitchurch *Shrops* 33 A11
Whitchurch Canonicorum *Dorset* 8 E2
Whitchurch Hill *Oxon* 18 D3
Whitcombe *Dorset* 8 F6
Whitcott Keysett *Shrops* 33 G8
White Coppice *Lancs* 50 H2
White Lackington *Dorset* 8 E6
White Ladies Aston *Worcs* 26 C6
White Lund *Lancs* 49 C4
White Mill *Carms* 23 D9
White Ness *Shetl'd* 96 J5
White Notley *Essex* 30 G4
White Pit *Lincs* 47 E7
White Post *Notts* 45 F11
White Rocks *Heref'd* 25 F11
White Roding *Essex* 30 G2
White Waltham *Windsor* 18 D5
Whiteacre Heath *Warwick* 35 F8
Whitebridge *H'land* 81 B6
Whitebrook *Monmouths* 26 H2
Whiteburn *Scot Borders* 70 F4
Whitecairn *Dumf/Gal* 54 D6
Whitecairns *Aberds* 83 B11
Whitecastle *S Lanarks* 69 F9
Whitechapel *Lancs* 50 E1
Whitecleat *Orkney* 95 H6
Whitecraig *E Loth* 70 C2
Whitecroft *Glos* 26 H3
Whitecross *Cornw'l* 3 B8
Whitecross *Falk* 69 C8
Whitecross *Staffs* 34 C4
Whiteface *H'land* 87 C10
Whitefarland *N Ayrs* 66 B11
Whitefaulds *S Ayrs* 66 F5
Whitefield *Gtr Man* 44 B2
Whitefield *Perth/Kinr* 76 D4
Whiteford *Aberds* 83 A9
Whitegate *Ches* 43 F9
Whitehall *Blackb'n* 50 G2
Whitehall *W Sussex* 11 B10
Whitehall Village *Orkney* 95 F7
Whitehill *Hants* 11 A6
Whitehills *Aberds* 89 B6
Whitehills *S Lanarks* 68 E5
Whitehough *Derby* 44 D4
Whitehouse *Aberds* 83 B8
Whitehouse *Arg/Bute* 73 G7
Whiteinch *C/Glasg* 68 D4
Whitekirk *E Loth* 70 B4
Whitelaw *S Lanarks* 68 F5
Whiteleas *Tyne/Wear* 63 G9
Whiteley Bank *I/Wight* 10 F4
Whiteley Green *Ches* 44 E3
Whiteley Village *Surrey* 19 E7
Whitemans Green *W Sussex* 12 D2
Whitemire *Moray* 87 F12
Whitemoor *Cornw'l* 3 D8
Whitemore *Staffs* 44 F2
Whitenap *Hants* 10 B2
Whiteoak Green *Oxon* 27 G10
Whiteparish *Wilts* 9 B11
Whiterashes *Aberds* 89 F8
Whiterow *H'land* 94 F5
Whiteshill *Glos* 26 H5
Whiteside *Northum* 62 G3
Whiteside *W Loth* 69 D8
Whitesmith *E Sussex* 12 E4
Whitestaunton *Som'set* 8 C1
Whitestone *Devon* 7 G7
Whitestone *Devon* 6 B3
Whitestone *Warwick* 35 G8
Whitestones *Aberds* 89 C8
Whitestreet Green *Suffolk* 30 E6
Whitewall Corner *N Yorks* 52 B3
Whiteway *Glos* 16 A6
Whiteway *Glos* 26 G6
Whitewell *Aberds* 89 B8
Whitewell *Lancs* 50 E2
Whitewell Bottom *Lancs* 50 G4
Whiteworks *Devon* 4 D1
Whitfield *Kent* 21 G10
Whitfield *Northants* 28 E3
Whitfield *Northum* 62 H3
Whitfield *S Gloucs* 16 B3
Whitford *Devon* 8 E1
Whitford *Flints* 42 E4
Whitgift *ER Yorks* 52 G4
Whitgreave *Staffs* 34 C4
Whithorn *Dumf/Gal* 54 E6
Whiting Bay *N Ayrs* 66 D3
Whitington *Norfolk* 38 F3
Whitkirk *W Yorks* 51 F9
Whitland *Carms* 22 E6
Whitletts *S Ayrs* 67 D6
Whitley *N Yorks* 52 G1
Whitley *Wilts* 16 E5
Whitley Bay *Tyne/Wear* 63 F9
Whitley Chapel *Northum* 62 H5
Whitley Lower *W Yorks* 51 H8
Whitley Row *Kent* 19 F11
Whitlock's End *W Midlands* 35 H7

Whitminster *Glos* 26 H4
Whitmore *Staffs* 34 A4
Whitnage *Devon* 7 E9
Whitnash *Warwick* 27 B10
Whitney *Cumb* 56 C4
Whitrigg *Cumb* 61 H8
Whitsbury *Hants* 9 C10
Whitsome *Scot Borders* 71 E7
Whitson *Newp* 15 C9
Whitstable *Kent* 21 E8
Whitstone *Cornw'l* 6 G1
Whittingham *Northum* 62 B6
Whittingslow *Shrops* 33 G10
Whittington *Glos* 27 F7
Whittington *Lancs* 50 B2
Whittington *Shrops* 33 B9
Whittington *Staffs* 34 G4
Whittington *Staffs* 35 C7
Whittington *Worcs* 26 C5
Whittle-le-Woods *Lancs* 50 G1
Whittlebury *Northants* 28 D3
Whittlesey *Cambs* 37 F8
Whittlesford *Cambs* 29 D11
Whitton *Scot Borders* 62 B3
Whitton *N Lincs* 52 G5
Whitton *Northum* 62 C6
Whitton *Powys* 25 B9
Whitton *Shrops* 26 A2
Whitton *Stockton* 58 D4
Whitton *Suffolk* 31 D8
Whittonditch *Wilts* 17 D9
Whittonstall *Northum* 62 H6
Whitway *Hants* 17 F11
Whitwell *Derby* 45 E9
Whitwell *Herts* 29 F8
Whitwell *I/Wight* 10 G4
Whitwell *N Yorks* 58 F3
Whitwell *Rutl'd* 36 E5
Whitwell-on-the-Hill *N Yorks* 52 C3
Whitwell Street *Norfolk* 39 C7
Whitwick *Leics* 35 D10
Whitwood *W Yorks* 51 G10
Whitworth *Lancs* 50 H4
Whixall *Shrops* 33 B11
Whixley *N Yorks* 51 D10
Whoberley *W Midlands* 35 H9
Whorlton *Durham* 58 E2
Whorlton *N Yorks* 58 F5
Whygate *Northum* 62 F3
Whyle *Heref'd* 26 B2
Whyteleafe *Surrey* 19 F10
Wibdon *Glos* 16 B2
Wibsey *W Yorks* 51 F7
Wibtoft *Leics* 35 G10
Wichenford *Worcs* 26 B4
Wichling *Kent* 20 F6
Wick *Bournem'th* 9 E10
Wick *Devon* 7 F10
Wick *H'land* 94 E5
Wick *S Gloucs* 16 D4
Wick *Shetl'd* 96 K6
Wick *V/Glam* 14 D5
Wick *Wilts* 9 B10
Wick *Worcs* 26 D6
Wick *W Sussex* 11 D9
Wick Hill *Wokingham* 18 E4
Wick St Lawrence *N Som'set* 15 E9
Wicken *Cambs* 30 A2
Wicken *Northants* 28 E4
Wicken Bonhunt *Essex* 29 E11
Wickenby *Lincs* 46 D4
Wickersley *S Yorks* 45 D8
Wickford *Essex* 20 B4
Wickham *Hants* 10 C4
Wickham *W Berks* 17 D10
Wickham Bishops *Essex* 30 G5
Wickham Market *Suffolk* 31 C10
Wickham St Paul *Essex* 30 E5
Wickham Skeith *Suffolk* 31 B7
Wickham Street *Suffolk* 30 C4
Wickham Street *Suffolk* 31 B7
Wickhambreaux *Kent* 21 F9
Wickhambrook *Suffolk* 30 C4
Wickhamford *Worcs* 27 D7
Wickhampton *Norfolk* 39 E10
Wicklewood *Norfolk* 39 E6
Wickmere *Norfolk* 39 B7
Wickstreet *E Sussex* 12 E4
Wickwar *S Gloucs* 16 C4
Widdington *Essex* 30 E2
Widdrington *Northum* 63 D8
Widdrington Station *Northum* 63 D8
Wide Open *Tyne/Wear* 63 F8
Widecombe in the Moor *Devon* 5 D8
Widegates *Cornw'l* 4 F3
Widemouth Bay *Cornw'l* 6 G1
Widewall *Orkney* 95 J5
Widford *Essex* 30 H3
Widford *Herts* 29 G11
Widham *Wilts* 17 C7
Widmer End *Bucks* 18 B5
Widmerpool *Notts* 36 C2
Widnes *Halton* 43 D8
Wigan *Gtr Man* 43 B8
Wiggaton *Devon* 7 G10
Wiggenhall St Germans *Norfolk* 38 D1
Wiggenhall St Mary Magdalen *Norfolk* 38 D1
Wiggenhall St Mary the Virgin *Norfolk* 38 D1
Wigginton *Herts* 28 G6
Wigginton *Oxon* 27 E10
Wigginton *Staffs* 35 E8
Wigginton *C/York* 52 D1
Wigglesworth *N Yorks* 50 D4
Wiggonby *Cumb* 56 A4
Wiggonholt *W Sussex* 11 C9
Wighill *N Yorks* 51 E10
Wighton *Norfolk* 38 B5
Wigley *Hants* 10 C2
Wigmore *Heref'd* 25 B11
Wigmore *Medway* 20 E4
Wigsley *Notts* 46 E2
Wigsthorpe *Northants* 36 G6
Wigston *Leics* 36 F2
Wigthorpe *Notts* 45 D9
Wigtoft *Lincs* 37 B8
Wigton *Cumb* 56 B4
Wigtown *Dumf/Gal* 55 D7
Wigtwizzle *S Yorks* 44 C6
Wike *W Yorks* 51 E9
Wike Well End *S Yorks* 45 A10
Wilbarston *Northants* 36 G4
Wilberfoss *ER Yorks* 52 D3
Wilberlee *W Yorks* 44 A4
Wilburton *Cambs* 29 A11
Wilby *Norfolk* 38 F6
Wilby *Northants* 28 B5
Wilby *Suffolk* 31 B9
Wilcot *Wilts* 17 E8
Wilcott *Shrops* 33 D9
Wilcrick *Newp* 15 C10
Wilday Green *Derby* 45 E7
Wildboarclough *Ches* 44 F3
Wilden *Beds* 29 C7
Wildhern *Hants* 17 F10
Wildhill *Herts* 29 H9
Wildmoor *Worcs* 34 H5
Wildsworth *Lincs* 46 C2
Wilford *Notts* 36 B1
Wilkesley *Ches* 34 A2
Wilkhaven *H'land* 87 C12
Wilkieston *W Loth* 69 D10
Willand *Devon* 7 E9
Willaston *Ches* 42 E6
Willaston *Ches* 43 G9
Willen *M/Keynes* 28 D5
Willenhall *W Midlands* 35 H9
Willenhall *W Midlands* 34 F5
Willerby *ER Yorks* 52 F6
Willerby *N Yorks* 52 B6
Willersey *Glos* 27 E8
Willersley *Heref'd* 25 D10
Willesborough *Kent* 13 B9
Willesborough Lees *Kent* 13 B9

Willesden *London* 19 C9
Willett *Som'set* 7 C10
Willey *Shrops* 34 F2
Willey *Warwick* 35 G10
Willey Green *Surrey* 18 G6
Williamscott *Oxon* 27 D11
Willian *Herts* 29 E9
Willingale *Essex* 30 H2
Willingdon *E Sussex* 12 F4
Willingham *Cambs* 29 A11
Willingham by Stow *Lincs* 46 D2
Willington *Beds* 29 D8
Willington *Derby* 35 C8
Willington *Durham* 58 C2
Willington *Tyne/Wear* 63 G9
Willington Corner *Ches* 43 F8
Willisham Tye *Suffolk* 31 C7
Willitoft *ER Yorks* 52 F3
Williton *Som'set* 7 B9
Willoughbridge *Staffs* 34 A3
Willoughby *Lincs* 47 E8
Willoughby *Warwick* 28 B2
Willoughby-on-the-Wolds *Notts* 36 C2
Willoughby Waterleys *Leics* 36 F1
Willoughton *Lincs* 46 C3
Willows Green *Essex* 30 G3
Willsbridge *S Gloucs* 16 D3
Willsworthy *Devon* 4 D6
Wilmcote *Warwick* 27 C8
Wilmington *Devon* 7 G11
Wilmington *E Sussex* 12 F4
Wilmington *Kent* 20 D2
Wilminstone *Devon* 4 D5
Wilmslow *Ches* 44 D2
Wilnecote *Staffs* 35 E8
Wilpshire *Lancs* 50 F2
Wilsden *W Yorks* 51 F6
Wilsford *Lincs* 36 A6
Wilsford *Wilts* 17 F8
Wilsford *Wilts* 17 H8
Wilsill *N Yorks* 51 C7
Wilsley Pound *Kent* 13 C6
Wilsom *Hants* 18 H4
Wilsontown *S Lanarks* 69 E8
Wilstead *Beds* 29 D7
Wilsthorpe *Lincs* 37 D6
Wilstone *Herts* 28 G6
Wilton *Cumb* 56 E2
Wilton *Heref'd* 26 F2
Wilton *N Yorks* 59 H8
Wilton *Redcar/Clevel'd* 59 E6
Wilton *Wilts* 9 A9
Wilton *Wilts* 17 F9
Wimbish *Essex* 30 E2
Wimbish Green *Essex* 30 E3
Wimblebury *Staffs* 34 D6
Wimbledon *London* 19 D9
Wimblington *Cambs* 37 F10
Wimborne Minster *Dorset* 9 E9
Wimborne St Giles *Dorset* 9 C9
Wimbotsham *Norfolk* 38 E2
Wimpson *S'thampton* 10 C2
Wimpstone *Warwick* 27 D9
Wincanton *Som'set* 8 B6
Wincham *Ches* 43 E9
Winchburgh *W Loth* 69 C9
Winchcombe *Glos* 27 F7
Winchelsea *E Sussex* 13 E8
Winchelsea Beach *E Sussex* 13 E8
Winchester *Hants* 10 B3
Winchet Hill *Kent* 12 B6
Winchfield *Hants* 18 F4
Winchmore Hill *Bucks* 18 B6
Winchmore Hill *London* 19 B10
Wincle *Ches* 44 F3
Wincobank *S Yorks* 45 C7
Windermere *Cumb* 56 G6
Winderton *Warwick* 27 D10
Windhill *H'land* 87 G8
Windhouse *Shetl'd* 96 D6
Windlehurst *Gtr Man* 44 D3
Windlesham *Surrey* 18 E6
Windley *Derby* 35 A9
Windmill Hill *E Sussex* 12 E5
Windmill Hill *Som'set* 8 C2
Windrush *Glos* 27 G8
Windsor *N Lincs* 45 A11
Windsor *Windsor* 18 D6
Windsoredge *Glos* 16 A5
Windygates *Fife* 76 G6
Windyknowe *W Loth* 69 D8
Windywalls *Scot Borders* 70 G6
Wineham *W Sussex* 11 B11
Winestead *ER Yorks* 53 G8
Winewall *Lancs* 50 E5
Winfarthing *Norfolk* 39 G7
Winford *I/Wight* 10 F4
Winford *N Som'set* 15 E11
Winforth Newburgh *Dorset* 9 F7
Wing *Bucks* 28 F5
Wing *Rutl'd* 36 E4
Wingate *Durham* 58 C4
Wingates *Gtr Man* 43 B9
Wingates *Northum* 63 D7
Wingerworth *Derby* 45 F7
Wingfield *Beds* 29 F7
Wingfield *Suffolk* 39 H8
Wingfield *Wilts* 16 F5
Wingham *Kent* 21 F9
Wingmore *Kent* 21 G8
Wingrave *Bucks* 28 G5
Winkburn *Notts* 45 G11
Winkfield *Brack'll* 18 D6
Winkfield Row *Brack'll* 18 D5
Winkhill *Staffs* 44 G4
Winklebury *Hants* 18 F3
Winkleigh *Devon* 6 F5
Winksley *N Yorks* 51 B8
Winkton *Dorset* 9 E10
Winlaton *Tyne/Wear* 63 G7
Winless *H'land* 94 E5
Winmarleigh *Lancs* 49 E4
Winnal *Heref'd* 25 E11
Winnall *Hants* 10 B3
Winnersh *Wokingham* 18 D4
Winscales *Cumb* 56 D2
Winscombe *N Som'set* 15 F10
Winsford *Ches* 43 F9
Winsford *Som'set* 7 C8
Winsham *Som'set* 8 D2
Winshill *Staffs* 35 C8
Winskill *Cumb* 57 C7
Winslade *Hants* 18 G3
Winsley *Wilts* 16 E5
Winslow *Bucks* 28 F4
Winson *Glos* 27 H7
Winson Green *W Midlands* 34 G6
Winsor *Hants* 10 C2
Winster *Cumb* 56 G6
Winster *Derby* 44 F6
Winston *Durham* 58 E2
Winston *Suffolk* 31 B8
Winston Green *Suffolk* 31 B8
Winstone *Glos* 26 H6
Winswell *Devon* 6 E3
Winter Gardens *Essex* 20 C4
Winterborne Bassett *Wilts* 17 D7
Winterborne Clenston *Dorset* 9 D7
Winterborne Herringston *Dorset* 8 F5
Winterborne Houghton *Dorset* 9 D7
Winterborne Kingston *Dorset* 9 E7
Winterborne Monkton *Dorset* 8 F5
Winterborne Stickland *Dorset* 9 D7
Winterborne Whitechurch *Dorset* 9 D7
Winterborne Zelston *Dorset* 9 E7
Winterbourne *S Gloucs* 16 C3
Winterbourne *W Berks* 17 D11
Winterbourne Abbas *Dorset* 8 E5
Winterbourne Dauntsey *Wilts* 9 A10

Winterbourne Down *S Gloucs* 16 D3
Winterbourne Earls *Wilts* 9 A10
Winterbourne Gunner *Wilts* 17 H8
Winterbourne Steepleton *Dorset* 8 F5
Winterbourne Stoke *Wilts* 17 G7
Winteringham *N Yorks* 52 G5
Winterley *Ches* 43 G10
Wintersett *W Yorks* 51 H9
Wintershill *Hants* 10 C4
Winterton *N Lincs* 52 H5
Winterton-on-Sea *Norfolk* 39 D10
Winthorpe *Lincs* 47 F9
Winthorpe *Notts* 46 G2
Winton *Bournem'th* 9 E9
Winton *Cumb* 57 E9
Winton *N Yorks* 58 G5
Wintringham *N Yorks* 52 B5
Winwick *Cambs* 37 G7
Winwick *Northants* 28 A3
Winwick *Warrington* 43 C9
Wirksworth *Derby* 44 G6
Wirswall *Ches* 33 A11
Wisbech *Cambs* 37 E10
Wisbech St Mary *Cambs* 37 E10
Wisborough Green *W Sussex* 11 B9
Wiseton *Notts* 45 D11
Wishaw *N Lanarks* 68 E6
Wishaw *Warwick* 35 F7
Wisley *Surrey* 19 F7
Wispington *Lincs* 46 E6
Wissenden *Kent* 13 B8
Wissett *Suffolk* 39 H9
Wistanstow *Shrops* 33 G10
Wistanswick *Shrops* 34 C2
Wistaston *Ches* 43 G9
Wistaston Green *Ches* 43 G9
Wiston *Pembs* 22 E5
Wiston *S Lanarks* 69 G8
Wiston *W Sussex* 11 C10
Wistow *Cambs* 37 G8
Wistow *N Yorks* 52 F1
Wistow *Leics* 36 F2
Wiswell *Lancs* 50 F3
Witcham *Cambs* 37 G10
Witchampton *Dorset* 9 D8
Witchford *Cambs* 37 H11
Witham *Essex* 30 G5
Witham Friary *Som'set* 16 G4
Witham on the Hill *Lincs* 37 D6
Withcall *Lincs* 46 D6
Withdean *Brighton/Hove* 12 F2
Witherenden Hill *E Sussex* 12 D5
Witheridge *Devon* 7 E7
Witherley *Leics* 35 F9
Withern *Lincs* 47 D8
Withernsea *ER Yorks* 53 G9
Withernwick *ER Yorks* 53 E7
Withersdale Street *Suffolk* 39 G8
Withersfield *Suffolk* 30 D3
Witherslack *Cumb* 49 A4
Withiel *Cornw'l* 3 C8
Withiel Florey *Som'set* 7 C8
Withington *Glos* 27 G7
Withington *Gtr Man* 44 C2
Withington *Heref'd* 26 D2
Withington *Shrops* 34 D1
Withington *Staffs* 34 B6
Withington Green *Ches* 44 E2
Withleigh *Devon* 7 E8
Withnell *Lancs* 50 G2
Withybrook *Warwick* 35 G10
Withycombe *Som'set* 7 B9
Withycombe Raleigh *Devon* 5 C11
Withyham *E Sussex* 12 C3
Withypool *Som'set* 7 C7
Witley *Surrey* 18 H6
Witnesham *Suffolk* 31 C8
Witney *Oxon* 27 G10
Wittering *Peterbro* 37 E6
Wittersham *Kent* 13 D7
Witton *Angus* 83 E7
Witton *Worcs* 26 B5
Witton Bridge *Norfolk* 39 B9
Witton Gilbert *Durham* 58 B3
Witton-le-Wear *Durham* 58 C2
Witton Park *Durham* 58 C2
Wiveliscombe *Som'set* 7 D9
Wivelrod *Hants* 18 H3
Wivelsfield *E Sussex* 12 D2
Wivelsfield Green *E Sussex* 12 D2
Wivenhoe *Essex* 31 F7
Wivenhoe Cross *Essex* 31 F7
Wiveton *Norfolk* 38 A6
Wix *Essex* 31 F8
Wixford *Warwick* 27 C7
Wixhill *Shrops* 34 C1
Wixoe *Suffolk* 30 D4
Woburn *Beds* 28 E6
Woburn Sands *M/Keynes* 28 E6
Wokefield Park *W Berks* 18 E3
Woking *Surrey* 19 F7
Wokingham *Wokingham* 18 E5
Wolborough *Devon* 5 D9
Wold Newton *ER Yorks* 52 B6
Wold Newton *NE Lincs* 46 C6
Woldingham *Surrey* 19 F10
Wolfclyde *S Lanarks* 69 G9
Wolferton *Norfolk* 38 C2
Wolfhill *Perth/Kinr* 76 D4
Wolf's Castle *Pembs* 22 D4
Wollaston *Northants* 28 B6
Wollaston *Shrops* 33 D9
Wollaton *Nott'ham* 35 B11
Wollerton *Shrops* 34 B2
Wollescote *W Midlands* 34 G5
Wolsingham *Durham* 58 C1
Wolstanton *Staffs* 44 H2
Wolston *Warwick* 35 H10
Wolvercote *Oxon* 27 H11
Wolverhampton *W Midlands* 34 F5
Wolverley *Shrops* 33 B10
Wolverley *Worcs* 34 H4
Wolverton *Hants* 18 F2
Wolverton *M/Keynes* 28 D5
Wolverton *Warwick* 27 B9
Wolverton Common *Hants* 18 F2
Wolvesnewton *Monmouths* 15 B10
Wolvey *Warwick* 35 G10
Wolviston *Stockton* 58 D5
Wombleton *N Yorks* 59 H7
Wombourne *Staffs* 34 F5
Wombwell *S Yorks* 45 B7
Womenswold *Kent* 21 F9
Womersley *N Yorks* 51 H11
Wonastow *Monmouths* 25 G11
Wonersh *Surrey* 19 G7
Wonson *Devon* 5 C7
Wonston *Hants* 17 H11
Wooburn *Bucks* 18 C6
Wooburn Green *Bucks* 18 C6
Wood Dalling *Norfolk* 39 C6
Wood End *Herts* 29 F10
Wood End *Warwick* 27 A8
Wood End *Warwick* 35 H8
Wood Enderby *Lincs* 46 F6
Wood Field *Surrey* 19 F8
Wood Green *London* 19 B10
Wood Hayes *W Midlands* 34 E5
Wood Lanes *Ches* 44 D3
Wood Norton *Norfolk* 38 C6
Wood Street *Norfolk* 39 C9
Wood Street *Surrey* 18 F6
Wood Walton *Cambs* 37 G8
Woodacott *Devon* 6 F2
Woodale *N Yorks* 50 B6
Woodbank *Arg/Bute* 65 G7
Woodbastwick *Norfolk* 39 D9
Woodbeck *Notts* 45 E11
Woodborough *Notts* 45 H10
Woodborough *Wilts* 17 F8
Woodbridge *Dorset* 8 C6
Woodbridge *Suffolk* 31 D9
Woodbury *Devon* 5 C11
Woodbury Salterton *Devon* 5 C11
Woodchester *Glos* 16 A5

Woodchurch *Kent* 13 C8
Woodchurch *Mersey* 42 D5
Woodcombe *Som'set* 7 B8
Woodcote *Oxon* 18 C3
Woodcott *Hants* 17 F11
Woodcroft *Glos* 15 B11
Woodcutts *Dorset* 9 C8
Wooddings *Cambs* 30 C3
Wooddon *Oxon* 27 G11
Woodend *Cumb* 56 G3
Woodend *Northants* 28 D3
Woodend *W Sussex* 11 D7
Woodend Green *Northants* 28 D3
Woodfalls *Wilts* 9 B10
Woodfield *Oxon* 28 F2
Woodfield *S Ayrs* 66 D6
Woodford *Corn'wl* 6 E1
Woodford *Devon* 5 F8
Woodford *Glos* 16 B3
Woodford *London* 19 B11
Woodford *Gtr Man* 44 D2
Woodford *Northants* 36 H5
Woodford Bridge *London* 19 B11
Woodford Halse *Northants* 28 C2
Woodgate *Norfolk* 38 D6
Woodgate *W Midlands* 34 G5
Woodgate *Worcs* 26 B6
Woodgate *W Sussex* 11 D8
Woodgreen *Hants* 9 C10
Woodhall *Herts* 29 G9
Woodhall *Invercl* 68 C2
Woodhall *N Yorks* 57 G11
Woodhall Spa *Lincs* 46 F5
Woodham *Surrey* 19 E7
Woodham Ferrers *Essex* 20 A4
Woodham Mortimer *Essex* 20 A5
Woodham Walter *Essex* 30 H5
Woodhaven *Fife* 77 E7
Woodhead *Aberds* 89 D7
Woodhey *Gtr Man* 50 H4
Woodhill *Shrops* 34 G3
Woodhorn *Northum* 63 E8
Woodhouse *Leics* 35 D11
Woodhouse *S Yorks* 45 D8
Woodhouse *W Yorks* 52 F1
Woodhouse *W Yorks* 51 F8
Woodhouse Eaves *Leics* 35 D11
Woodhouse Park *Gtr Man* 44 D2
Woodhouselee *Midloth* 69 D11
Woodhouselees *Dumf/Gal* 61 F9
Woodhurst *Cambs* 37 H9
Woodingdean *Brighton/Hove* 12 F2
Woodland *Devon* 5 E8
Woodland *Durham* 58 D1
Woodlands *Aberds* 83 D9
Woodlands *Dorset* 9 D9
Woodlands *Hants* 10 C2
Woodlands *H'land* 87 F8
Woodlands *N Yorks* 51 D9
Woodlands *S Yorks* 45 B9
Woodlands Park *Windsor* 18 D5
Woodlands St Mary *W Berks* 17 D10
Woodleigh *Devon* 5 G8
Woodlesford *W Yorks* 51 G9
Woodley *Gtr Man* 44 C3
Woodley *Wokingham* 18 D4
Woodmancote *Glos* 16 B4
Woodmancote *Glos* 26 H6
Woodmancote *Glos* 27 F7
Woodmancote *W Sussex* 11 D6
Woodmancott *Hants* 18 G2
Woodmansey *ER Yorks* 53 F6
Woodmansterne *Surrey* 19 F9
Woodminton *Wilts* 9 B9
Woodnesborough *Kent* 21 F10
Woodnewton *Northants* 36 F6
Woodplumpton *Lancs* 49 F5
Woodrising *Norfolk* 38 E5
Wood's Green *E Sussex* 12 C5
Woodseaves *Shrops* 34 B2
Woodseaves *Staffs* 34 C3
Woodsend *Wilts* 17 D9
Woodsetts *S Yorks* 45 D9
Woodsford *Dorset* 9 E6
Woodside *Aberd C* 83 C11
Woodside *Aberds* 89 D10
Woodside *Brack'll* 18 D6
Woodside *Fife* 77 G7
Woodside *Hants* 10 E2
Woodside *Herts* 29 H9
Woodside *Perth/Kinr* 76 D5
Woodside of Arbeadie *Aberds* 83 D9
Woodstock *Oxon* 27 G11
Woodstock *Pembs* 22 D5
Woodthorpe *Derby* 45 E8
Woodthorpe *Leics* 35 D11
Woodthorpe *Lincs* 47 D8
Woodthorpe *C/York* 52 E1
Woodton *Norfolk* 39 F8
Woodtown *Devon* 6 D3
Woodtown *Devon* 6 D3
Woodvale *Mersey* 42 A6
Woodville *Derby* 35 D9
Woodyates *Dorset* 9 C9
Woofferton *Shrops* 26 B2
Wookey *Som'set* 15 G11
Wookey Hole *Som'set* 15 G11
Wool *Dorset* 9 F7
Woolacombe *Devon* 6 B3
Woolage Green *Kent* 21 G9
Woolavington *Som'set* 15 G9
Woolbeding *W Sussex* 11 B7
Wooldale *W Yorks* 44 B5
Wooler *Northum* 71 H8
Woolfardisworthy *Devon* 7 F7
Woolfardisworthy *Devon* 6 D2
Woolfords Cottages *S Lanarks* 69 E9
Woolhampton *W Berks* 18 E2
Woolhope *Heref'd* 26 E3
Woolland *Dorset* 9 D6
Woollaton *Devon* 6 E3
Woolley *Bath/NE Som'set* 16 E4
Woolley *Cambs* 37 H7
Woolley *Cornw'l* 6 E1
Woolley *Derby* 45 F7
Woolley *W Yorks* 45 A7
Woolmer Green *Herts* 29 G9
Woolmere Green *Worcs* 26 B6
Woolpit *Suffolk* 30 B6
Woolscott *Warwick* 27 B11
Woolsington *Tyne/Wear* 63 G7
Woolstanwood *Ches* 43 G9
Woolstaston *Shrops* 33 F10
Woolsthorpe *Lincs* 36 C4
Woolsthorpe *Lincs* 36 C5
Woolston *Devon* 5 G8
Woolston *S'hampton* 10 C3
Woolston *Shrops* 33 C9
Woolston *Shrops* 33 G10
Woolston *Warrington* 43 D9
Woolston Green *Devon* 5 E8
Woolstone *M/Keynes* 28 E5
Woolstone *Glos* 26 E6
Woolstone *Oxon* 17 C9
Woolton *Mersey* 43 D7
Woolton Hill *Hants* 17 E11
Woolverstone *Suffolk* 31 E8
Woolverton *Som'set* 16 F4
Woolwich *London* 19 D11
Woolwich Ferry *London* 19 D11
Woonton *Heref'd* 25 C10
Wooperton *Northum* 62 A6
Woore *Shrops* 34 A3
Wootten Green *Suffolk* 31 A9
Wootton *Beds* 29 D7
Wootton *Hants* 9 E11
Wootton *Heref'd* 25 C10
Wootton *Kent* 21 G9
Wootton *N Lincs* 52 H6
Wootton *Northants* 28 C4
Wootton *Oxon* 27 G11
Wootton *Oxon* 27 H11
Wootton *Shrops* 33 C9

Wootton *Shrops* 33 C9
Wootton *Staffs* 34 C4
Wootton *Staffs* 44 H5
Wootton Bassett *Wilts* 17 C7
Wootton Bridge *I/Wight* 10 E4
Wootton Common *I/Wight* 10 E4
Wootton Courtenay *Som'set* 7 B8
Wootton Fitzpaine *Dorset* 8 E2
Wootton Green *Suffolk* 31 A9
Wootton Rivers *Wilts* 17 E8
Wootton St Lawrence *Hants* 18 F2
Wootton Wawen *Warwick* 27 B8
Worcester *Worcs* 26 C5
Worcester Park *London* 19 E9
Wordsley *W Midlands* 34 G4
Worfield *Shrops* 34 F3
Work *Orkney* 95 G5
Workington *Cumb* 56 D1
Worksop *Notts* 45 E9
Worlaby *N Lincs* 46 A4
World's End *W Berks* 17 D11
Worle *N Som'set* 15 E9
Worleston *Ches* 43 G9
Worlingham *Suffolk* 39 G10
Worlington *Suffolk* 30 A3
Worlingworth *Suffolk* 31 B9
Wormald Green *N Yorks* 51 C9
Wormbridge *Heref'd* 25 E11
Wormegay *Norfolk* 38 D2
Wormelow Tump *Heref'd* 25 E11
Wormhill *Derby* 44 E5
Wormingford *Essex* 30 E6
Worminghall *Bucks* 28 H3
Wormington *Glos* 27 E7
Worminster *Som'set* 16 G2
Wormit *Fife* 76 E6
Wormleighton *Warwick* 27 C11
Wormley *Herts* 29 H10
Wormley *Surrey* 18 H6
Wormley West End *Herts* 29 H10
Wormshill *Kent* 20 F5
Wormsley *Heref'd* 25 D11
Worplesdon *Surrey* 18 F6
Worrall *S Yorks* 45 C7
Worsbrough *S Yorks* 45 B7
Worsbrough Common *S Yorks* 45 B7
Worsley *Gtr Man* 43 B10
Worstead *Norfolk* 39 C9
Worsthorne *Lancs* 50 F4
Worston *Lancs* 50 E3
Worswell *Devon* 4 G6
Worth *Kent* 21 F10
Worth *W Sussex* 12 C2
Worth Matravers *Dorset* 9 G8
Wortham *Suffolk* 39 H6
Worthen *Shrops* 33 E9
Worthenbury *Wrex* 33 A10
Worthing *Norfolk* 38 D5
Worthing *W Sussex* 11 D10
Worthington *Leics* 35 C10
Worting *Hants* 18 F3
Wortley *S Yorks* 45 C7
Wortley *W Yorks* 51 F8
Worton *N Yorks* 57 G11
Worton *Wilts* 16 F6
Wortwell *Norfolk* 39 G8
Wotherton *Shrops* 33 E8
Wotter *Devon* 4 E6
Wotton *Surrey* 19 G8
Wotton-under-Edge *Glos* 16 B4
Wotton Underwood *Bucks* 28 G3
Woughton on the Green *M/Keynes* 28 E5
Wouldham *Kent* 20 E4
Wrabness *Essex* 31 E8
Wrafton *Devon* 6 C3
Wragby *Lincs* 46 E5
Wragby *W Yorks* 51 H10
Wragholme *Lincs* 47 C7
Wramplingham *Norfolk* 39 E7
Wrangbrook *W Yorks* 45 A8
Wrangham *Aberds* 89 E6
Wrangle *Lincs* 47 G8
Wrangle Bank *Lincs* 47 G8
Wrangle Lowgate *Lincs* 47 G8
Wrangway *Som'set* 7 E10
Wrantage *Som'set* 8 B2
Wrawby *N Lincs* 46 B4
Wraxall *Dorset* 8 E4
Wraxall *N Som'set* 15 D10
Wraxall *Som'set* 16 H3
Wray *Lancs* 50 C2
Wraysbury *Windsor* 19 D7
Wrayton *Lancs* 50 B2
Wrea Green *Lancs* 49 F3
Wreay *Cumb* 56 C6
Wreay *Cumb* 56 B6
Wrecclesham *Surrey* 18 G5
Wrecsam = Wrexham *Wrex* 42 G6
Wrekenton *Tyne/Wear* 63 H8
Wrelton *N Yorks* 59 H8
Wrenbury *Ches* 43 H9
Wrench Green *N Yorks* 59 H10
Wreningham *Norfolk* 39 F7
Wrentham *Suffolk* 39 G10
Wrenthorpe *W Yorks* 51 G9
Wrentnall *Shrops* 33 E10
Wressle *ER Yorks* 52 F3
Wressle *N Lincs* 46 B3
Wrestlingworth *Beds* 29 D9
Wretham *Norfolk* 38 G5
Wretton *Norfolk* 38 F2
Wrexham = Wrecsam *Wrex* 42 G6
Wrexham Industrial Estate *Wrex* 42 H6
Wribbenhall *Worcs* 34 H3
Wrightington Bar *Lancs* 43 A8
Wrinehill *Staffs* 43 H10
Wrington *N Som'set* 15 E10
Writhlington *Bath/NE Som'set* 16 F4
Writtle *Essex* 30 H3
Wrockwardine *Telford* 34 D2
Wroot *N Lincs* 45 B11
Wrotham *Kent* 20 F3
Wrotham Heath *Kent* 20 F3
Wroughton *Swindon* 17 C8
Wroxall *I/Wight* 10 G4
Wroxall *Warwick* 27 A9
Wroxeter *Shrops* 34 E1
Wroxham *Norfolk* 39 D9
Wroxton *Oxon* 27 D11
Wyaston *Derby* 35 A7
Wyberton *Lincs* 37 A9
Wyboston *Beds* 29 C8
Wybunbury *Ches* 43 H10
Wych Cross *E Sussex* 12 C3
Wychbold *Worcs* 26 B6
Wyck *Hants* 18 H4
Wyck Rissington *Glos* 27 F8
Wycoller *Lancs* 50 F5
Wycomb *Leics* 36 C3
Wycombe Marsh *Bucks* 18 B5
Wyddial *Herts* 29 E10
Wye *Kent* 21 G7
Wyesham *Monmouths* 26 G2
Wyfordby *Leics* 36 D3
Wyke *Dorset* 9 B6
Wyke *Shrops* 34 E2
Wyke *Surrey* 18 F6
Wyke *W Yorks* 51 G7
Wyke Regis *Dorset* 8 G5
Wykeham *N Yorks* 52 A5
Wykeham *N Yorks* 59 H9
Wyken *W Midlands* 35 G9
Wyken *Shrops* 34 F3
Wykey *Shrops* 33 C9
Wykin *Leics* 35 F10
Wylam *Northum* 63 G7
Wylde Green *W Midlands* 35 F7
Wyllie *Caerph* 15 B7
Wylye *Wilts* 17 H7
Wymering *Portsm'th* 10 D5
Wymeswold *Leics* 36 C2
Wymington *Beds* 28 B6
Wymondham *Leics* 36 D4
Wymondham *Norfolk* 39 E7
Wyndham *Bridg end* 14 B5
Wynford Eagle *Dorset* 8 E4
Wyng *Orkney* 95 J4
Wynyard Village *Stockton* 58 D5

Wyre Piddle *Worcs* 26 D6
Wysall *Notts* 36 C2
Wythall *Worcs* 35 H6
Wytham *Oxon* 27 H11
Wythburn *Cumb* 56 E5
Wythenshawe *Gtr Man* 44 D2
Wythop Mill *Cumb* 56 D3
Wyton *Cambs* 29 A9
Wyverstone *Suffolk* 31 B7
Wyverstone Street *Suffolk* 31 B7
Wyville *Lincs* 36 C4
Wyvis Lodge *H'land* 86 D7

Y

Y Bala = Bala *Gwyn* 32 B5
Y Barri = Barry *V/Glam* 15 E7
Y Bont-Faen = Cowbridge *V/Glam* 14 D5
Y Drenewydd = Newtown *Powys* 33 F7
Y Felinheli *Gwyn* 41 D7
Y Fenni = Abergavenny *Monmouths* 25 G9
Y Fflint = Flint *Flints* 42 E5
Y Ffôr *Gwyn* 40 G5
Y-Ffrith *Denbs* 42 D3
Y Gelli Gandryll = Hay-on-Wye *Powys* 25 D9
Y Mwmbwls = The Mumbles *Swan* 14 C2
Y Pîl = Pyle *Bridg end* 14 C4
Y Rhws = Rhoose *V/Glam* 14 E6
Y Rhyl = Rhyl *Denbs* 42 D3
Y Trallwng = Welshpool *Powys* 33 E8
Y Waun = Chirk *Wrex* 33 B8
Yaddlethorpe *N Lincs* 46 B2
Yafford *I/Wight* 10 F3
Yafforth *N Yorks* 58 G4
Yalding *Kent* 20 F3
Yanworth *Glos* 27 G7
Yapham *ER Yorks* 52 D3
Yapton *W Sussex* 11 D8
Yarburgh *Lincs* 47 C7
Yarcombe *Devon* 7 F11
Yard *Som'set* 7 C9
Yardley *W Midlands* 35 G7
Yardley Gobion *Northants* 28 D4
Yardley Hastings *Northants* 28 C5
Yardro *Powys* 25 C9
Yarkhill *Heref'd* 26 D3
Yarlet *Staffs* 34 C5
Yarlington *Som'set* 8 B5
Yarlside *Cumb* 49 C2
Yarm *Stockton* 58 E5
Yarmouth *I/Wight* 10 F2
Yarnbrook *Wilts* 16 F5
Yarnfield *Staffs* 34 B4
Yarnscombe *Devon* 6 D4
Yarnton *Oxon* 27 G11
Yarpole *Heref'd* 25 B11
Yarrow *Scot Borders* 70 H2
Yarrow Feus *Scot Borders* 70 H2
Yarsop *Heref'd* 25 D11
Yarwell *Northants* 37 F6
Yate *S Gloucs* 16 C4
Yateley *Hants* 18 E5
Yatesbury *Wilts* 17 D7
Yattendon *W Berks* 18 D2
Yatton *Heref'd* 25 B11
Yatton *N Som'set* 15 E10
Yatton Keynell *Wilts* 16 D5
Yaverland *I/Wight* 10 F5
Yaxham *Norfolk* 38 D6
Yaxley *Cambs* 37 F7
Yaxley *Suffolk* 31 A8
Yazor *Heref'd* 25 D11
Yeading *London* 19 C8
Yeadon *W Yorks* 51 E8
Yealand Conyers *Lancs* 49 B5
Yealand Redmayne *Lancs* 49 B5
Yealmpton *Devon* 4 F6
Yearby *Redcar/Clevel'd* 59 D7
Yearsley *N Yorks* 52 B1
Yeaton *Shrops* 33 D10
Yeaveley *Derby* 35 A7
Yedingham *N Yorks* 52 B5
Yeldon *Beds* 29 B7
Yelford *Oxon* 17 A10
Yelland *Devon* 6 C3
Yelling *Cambs* 29 B9
Yelvertoft *Northants* 36 H1
Yelverton *Devon* 4 E6
Yelverton *Norfolk* 39 E8
Yenston *Som'set* 8 B6
Yeo Mill *Devon* 7 D7
Yeoford *Devon* 7 G6
Yeolmbridge *Cornw'l* 4 C4
Yeovil *Som'set* 8 C4
Yeovil Marsh *Som'set* 8 C4
Yeovilton *Som'set* 8 B4
Yerbeston *Pembs* 22 F5
Yesnaby *Orkney* 95 G3
Yetlington *Northum* 62 C6
Yetminster *Dorset* 8 C4
Yettington *Devon* 7 H9
Yetts o'Muckhart *Clack* 76 G3
Yieldshields *S Lanarks* 69 E7
Yiewsley *London* 19 C7
Ynys-meudwy *Neath P Talb* 14 H4
Ynysboeth *Rhn Cyn Taff* 14 B6
Ynysddu *Caerph* 15 B7
Ynysgyfflog *Gwyn* 32 D2
Ynyshir *Rhn Cyn Taff* 14 B6
Ynyslas *Ceredig'n* 32 F2
Ynystawe *Swan* 14 A2
Ynysybwl *Rhn Cyn Taff* 14 B6
Yockenthwaite *N Yorks* 50 B5
Yockleton *Shrops* 33 D9
Yokefleet *ER Yorks* 52 G4
Yoker *C/Glasg* 68 D4
Yonder Bognie *Aberds* 88 D5
York *C/York* 52 D1
York Town *Surrey* 18 E5
Yorkletts *Kent* 21 E7
Yorkley *Glos* 26 H3
Yorton *Shrops* 33 C11
Youlgreave *Derby* 44 F6
Youlstone *Devon* 6 E1
Youlthorpe *ER Yorks* 52 D3
Youlton *N Yorks* 51 C10
Young's End *Essex* 30 G4
Young Wood *Lincs* 46 E5
Yoxall *Staffs* 35 D7
Yoxford *Suffolk* 31 B10
Yr Hôb = Hope *Flints* 42 G6
Yr Wyddgrug = Mold *Flints* 42 F5
Ysbyty-Cynfyn *Ceredig'n* 32 H3
Ysbyty Ifan *Conwy* 41 F10
Ysbyty Ystwyth *Ceredig'n* 32 H3
Ysceifiog *Flints* 42 E4
Yspitty *Carms* 23 G10
Ystalyfera *Neath P Talb* 14 H4
Ystrad *Rhn Cyn Taff* 14 B5
Ystrad Aeron *Ceredig'n* 23 A10
Ystrad-mynach *Caerph* 15 B7
Ystradfellte *Powys* 24 H6
Ystradffin *Carms* 24 D4
Ystradgynlais *Powys* 24 H4
Ystradmeurig *Ceredig'n* 32 H3
Ystradowen *Carms* 24 H3
Ystradowen *V/Glam* 14 D6
Ystumtuen *Ceredig'n* 32 H3
Ythanbank *Aberds* 89 E9
Ythanwells *Aberds* 89 E6
Ythsie *Aberds* 89 E8

Z

Zeal Monachorum *Devon* 6 F6
Zeals *Wilts* 9 A6
Zelah *Cornw'l* 3 D7
Zennor *Cornw'l* 2 F3